QUICKBOOKS ONLINE 2026 MASTERY GUIDE

A STEP-BY-STEP HANDBOOK FOR SMALL BUSINESS ACCOUNTING, BOOKKEEPING, PAYROLL, INVENTORY, REPORTS & AUTOMATIONS

KENNETH RADNOR

TABLE OF CONTENTS

“GOOD ACCOUNTING ISN’T ABOUT NUMBERS—IT’S ABOUT CLARITY, CONTROL, AND CONFIDENT DECISIONS.”

“AUTOMATION DOESN’T REPLACE GOOD ACCOUNTING—IT MAKES IT SMARTER, FASTER, AND MORE RELIABLE.”

LET GET STARTED

INTRODUCTION

QuickBooks Online 2026 is a cloud-based accounting platform designed to help individuals and businesses manage their financial activities in an organized, secure, and efficient way. Because it operates entirely online, users can perform essential bookkeeping tasks—such as tracking income and expenses, managing sales and purchases, storing receipts, and generating financial reports—from any internet-connected device without relying on traditional desktop software.

At its foundation, QuickBooks Online streamlines the recording of daily financial transactions. It organizes business data, keeps accurate books, and reduces the need for manual work through built-in automation. Features like automatic bank transaction categorization, sales tax calculations, reconciliation assistance, and AI-enhanced reporting help minimize errors and support informed financial decision-making.

One of the platform's strengths is continuous improvement. Since it is cloud-based, updates roll out automatically. The 2026 version includes enhanced automation tools, smoother navigation, expanded reporting options, and improvements to workflow efficiency. These upgrades make day-to-day accounting tasks easier for both new and experienced users. QuickBooks Online also supports real-time collaboration, allowing multiple users—including business owners, staff, and accountants—to access the same data from different locations.

The system is organized around key areas of financial management. Users can create invoices, manage customer records, and track revenue under **Sales and Income**. The **Expenses and Vendors** section supports entering bills, paying vendors, attaching receipts, and monitoring spending. **Banking** tools allow users to connect financial accounts, review transactions, and reconcile balances. **Reporting** provides essential financial statements such as Profit and Loss, Balance Sheet, and Cash Flow reports. Depending on the subscription plan, features like **Inventory**, **Projects**, and **Payroll** offer deeper management capabilities.

This introduction lays the groundwork for the chapters that follow. The remainder of the book will explore each feature of QuickBooks Online 2026 in detail, demonstrating how to use the platform effectively in real-world financial situations.

PART I: GETTING STARTED

CHAPTER ONE

GETTING STARTED WITH QUICKBOOKS ONLINE

To get started with QuickBooks Online, sign up for an account, set up your company profile with basic information, and then connect your bank and credit card accounts. Once your accounts are connected, you can import existing data, set up sales tax, and start customizing and sending invoices. The platform also offers features like payroll, project management, and reporting that can be set up as needed.

MANAGING YOUR BILLING AND SUBSCRIPTION

This section explains how to manage your QuickBooks Online billing and subscription settings. You'll learn how to update payment information, switch plans, change billing frequency, review payment history, and manage additional services like Payroll.

Accessing Your Billing & Subscription Settings

1. Click the **Gear icon**.
2. Select **Account and Settings.**

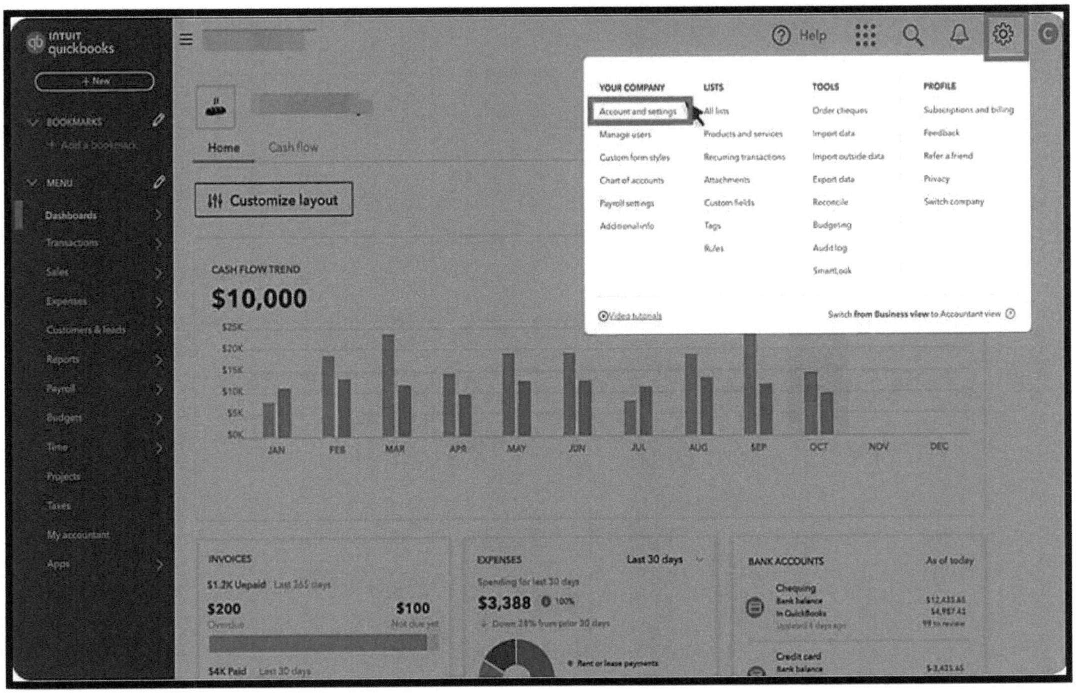

3. You'll land on the **Company** tab, where you can update company and contact details.

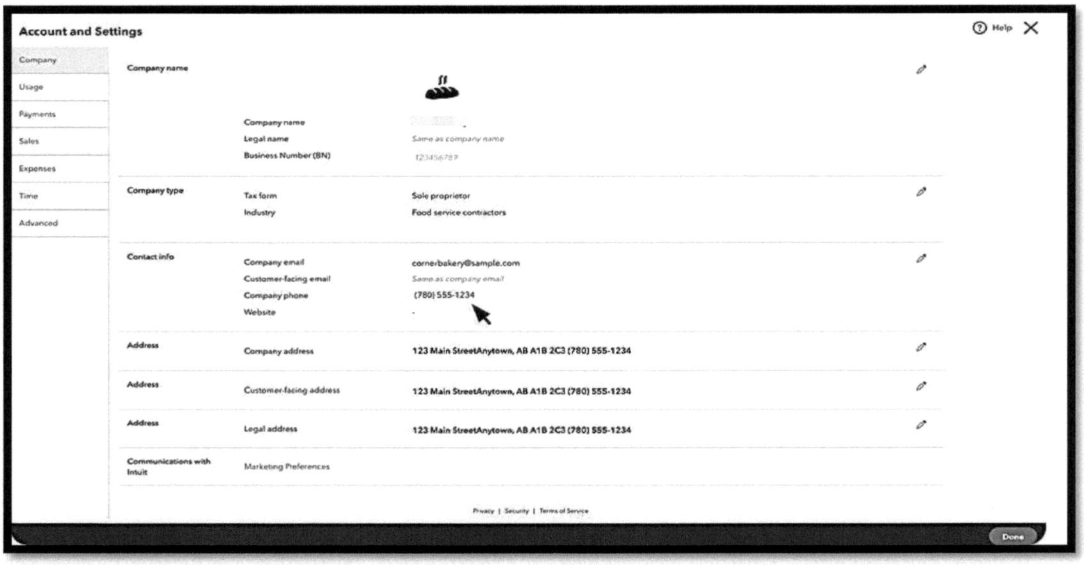

If you manage multiple companies, make sure you are working inside the correct one before making any changes.

Editing Billing & Subscription Information

Once inside **Account and Settings**, open the **Billing & Subscription** tab. This is where you can adjust all your subscription-related options.

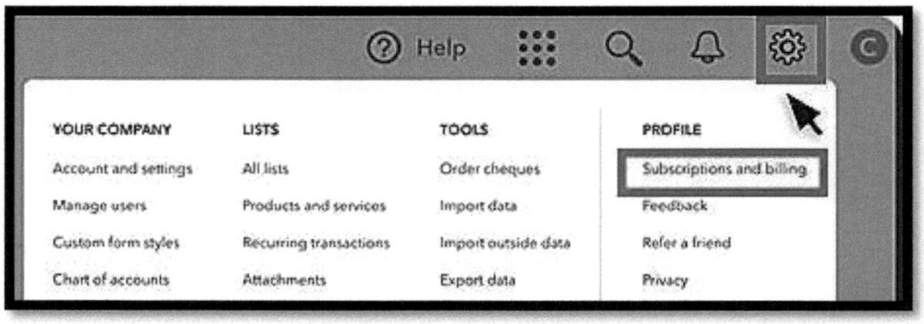

Update Payment Method

- ❖ Click **Edit** next to your payment information.

❖ Enter the new card or billing details.

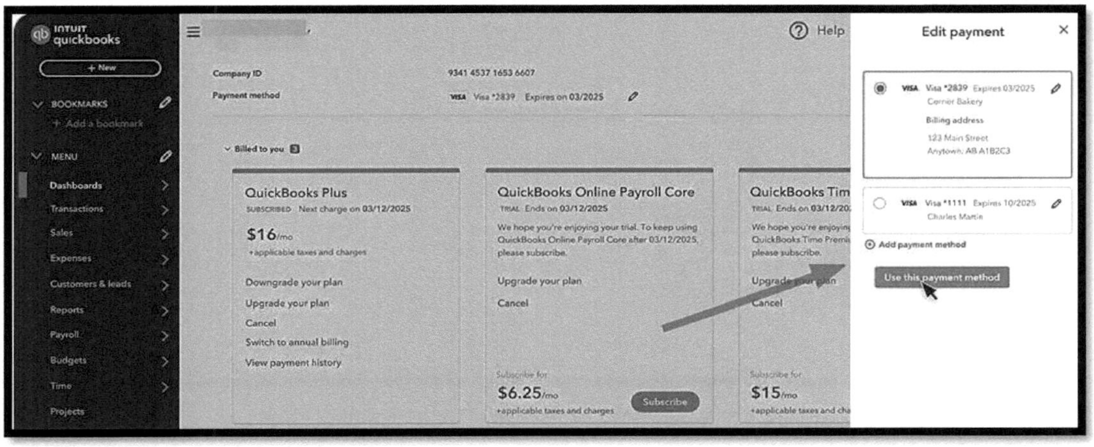

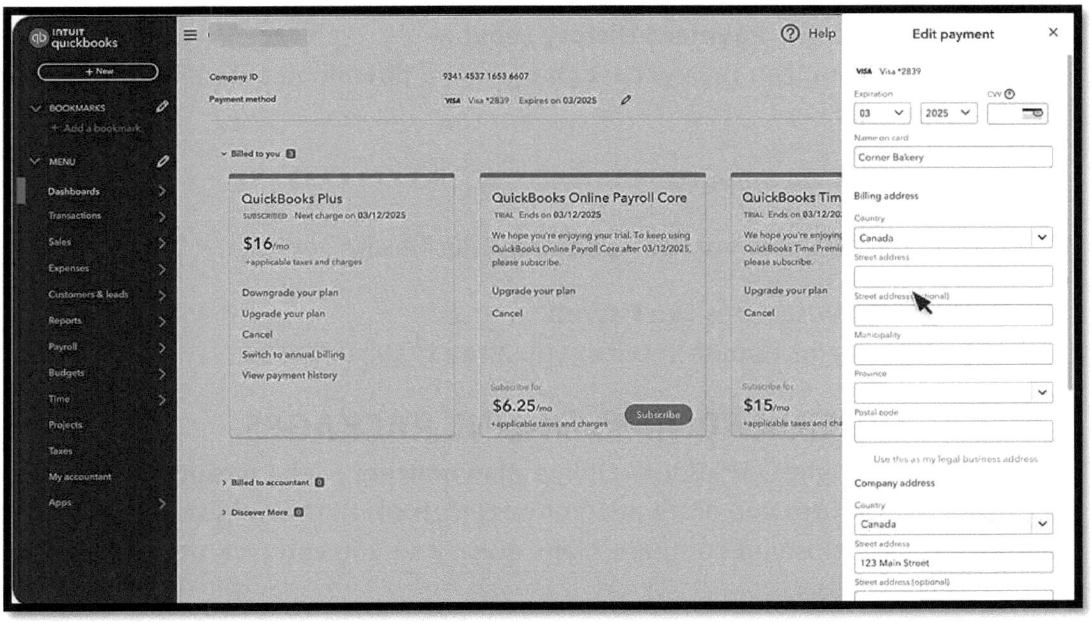

❖ Save your changes.

Change Billing Frequency

❖ Choose whether you want to be billed **monthly** or **annually**, depending on available options.

Upgrade, Downgrade, or Cancel Your Plan

❖ Select **Upgrade** to view available plans and switch to a higher-level subscription.
❖ You can also **downgrade** or **cancel** your existing plan from this same section.

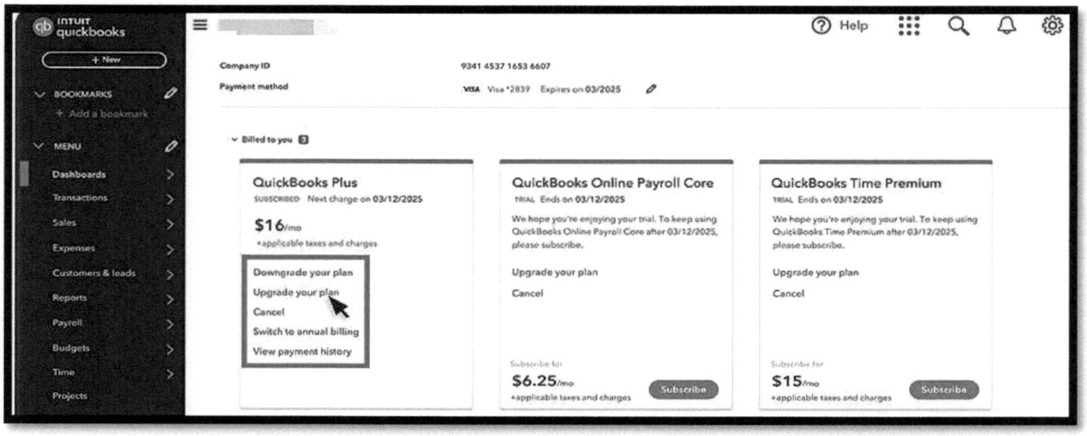

Viewing Payment History

❖ Scroll to the **Payment History** section.
❖ Here, you can review past charges and download a detailed history report if needed.

Managing Add-On Services

This tab also lets you manage additional QuickBooks services:

❖ Add new services like **Payroll**
❖ Manage or update services you already subscribe to

COMPARE QUICKBOOKS ONLINE PACKAGES

Choosing the right QuickBooks Online plan matters — the wrong package can mean paying for features you don't need or missing tools that would save time and money. This section helps you compare plans quickly so you can pick the one that fits your business.

Why compare plans?

Each QuickBooks Online plan targets different business needs: from simple income/expense tracking for sole proprietors to project, inventory, and team-management tools for growing companies. Comparing plans helps you match features to real tasks — invoicing, payroll, inventory, job costing, multi-user access, reporting, and integrations — rather than buying on name alone.

What to look for

When evaluating packages, pay attention to:

- **Core bookkeeping features:** invoicing, expense tracking, bank reconciliation
- **User seats & permissions:** how many users and what role controls are available
- **Payroll & contractors:** included or add-on, and tax filing support
- **Inventory & project tracking:** FIFO costing, job profitability, time tracking
- **Reporting & budgets:** built-in reports, custom report builder, forecasting tools
- **Integrations & add-ons:** POS, e-commerce, CRM, expense apps
- **Billing options & support:** monthly vs annual pricing, dedicated support, migration help

Quick decision guide

- **Solo/freelancer:** Choose the plan that covers invoicing, expense capture, and bank connections.
- **Growing small business:** Prioritize multi-user access, project/job tracking, and inventory.
- **Larger SMB or scaling teams:** Look for advanced reporting, automation, and dedicated support.

Next steps

Below you'll find a detailed comparison table showing features, monthly pricing, and user limits to make the decision straightforward. Take your time reviewing it — and if you want personalized guidance, the Quick Focus Team is available to help you choose or migrate.

I reviewed and compared all five QuickBooks Online subscription tiers — **Solopreneur, Simple Start, Essentials, Plus, and Advanced** — with monthly prices ranging from **$20 to $275**. Below is a clear breakdown of what each plan offers, what you get for the price, and which type of business each one is best suited for.

1. QuickBooks Online Solopreneur

Best for: freelancers, sole proprietors, and one-person businesses

This plan covers the essentials for self-employed users, such as tracking income, expenses, and basic tax preparation needs.

2. QuickBooks Online Simple Start

Best for: small businesses that need fundamental bookkeeping tools

Simple Start adds features like invoicing, basic reporting, and sales tax tracking, making it ideal for newer businesses with straightforward accounting needs.

3. QuickBooks Online Essentials

Best for: service-based businesses that track billable hours and manage unpaid bills

Essentials introduces time tracking, accounts payable, and multi-user access — useful for companies that bill clients for time and expenses.

4. QuickBooks Online Plus

Best for: growing businesses managing inventory, projects, or job costs

Plus includes inventory tracking, project profitability, budgeting, and more advanced reporting, making it a strong choice for retail, contracting, and scaling operations.

5. QuickBooks Online Advanced

Best for: established businesses with complex workflows and larger teams

Advanced provides the highest level of customization, deeper automation, enhanced reporting, and more user seats — designed for companies that require robust performance and advanced controls.

QuickBooks Online Comparison Chart

Pricing, Features & Capabilities Across All Plans

The chart below provides a simplified, side-by-side view of major features included in each subscription level. Later sections of your book can expand on each plan with deeper comparisons.

Feature	Solopreneur	Simple Start	Essentials	Plus	Advanced
Fit Small Business Rating	Not rated	3.73 ★	3.81 ★	4.61 ★	4.69 ★
Monthly Pricing	$20	$38	$75	$115	$275

Users Included	1	1	3	5	25
Chart of Accounts	Fixed	Up to 250	Up to 250	Up to 250	Unlimited
Sales Channel Connections	0	1	3	All	All
Connect Bank Accounts	✓	✓	✓	✓	✓
Send Invoices	✓	✓	✓	✓	✓
Manage Expenses	✓	✓	✓	✓	✓
Accept Payments	✓	✓	✓	✓	✓
Create Estimates	✓	✓	✓	✓	✓
Track Mileage	✓	✓	✓	✓	✓
Capture Receipts	✓	✓	✓	✓	✓
Print Balance Sheet	✓	✓	✓	✓	✓
File 1099s	✗	✓	✓	✓	✓
Double-Entry Accounting	✗	✓	✓	✓	✓
Print Checks	✗	✓	✓	✓	✓
Run Payroll	✗	✓	✓	✓	✓
Contractor Payments	✗	✓	✓	✓	✓
Track Sales Tax	✗	✓	✓	✓	✓
Modern View Reports	✗	✓	✓	✓	✓
Manage Bills	✗	✓	✓	✓	✓
Time Tracking & Add to Invoices	✗	✗	✓	✓	✓
Track Delayed Charges	✗	✗	✓	✓	✓
Recurring Transactions	✗	✗	✓	✓	✓
Multicurrency	✗	✗	✓	✓	✓
Track Expenses by Customer	✗	✗	✓	✓	✓
Budgeting	✗	✗	✗	✓	✓
Inventory & COGS Tracking	✗	✗	✗	✓	✓

Project, Class & Location Tracking	✕	✕	✕	✓	✓
Batch Invoicing	✕	✕	✕	✕	✓
Fixed Asset Accounting	✕	✕	✕	✕	✓
Enhanced Custom Fields	✕	✕	✕	✕	✓
Automated Workflows	✕	✕	✕	✕	✓
Revenue Recognition	✕	✕	✕	✓	✓
Data Restoration	✕	✕	✕	✕	✓
Batch Data Entry/Edit	✕	✕	✕	✕	✓
Excel Data Sync	✕	✕	✕	✕	✓
24/7 Support & Training	✕	✕	✕	✕	✓

How Much Does QuickBooks Online Cost—Across Different Countries?

Determining the cost of QuickBooks Online is not as straightforward as it seems. Pricing varies widely based on **your country**, the **subscription level**, and the **features** you need. Every QuickBooks Online edition—whether for the U.S., Canada, the U.K., Australia, India, or other regions—has its own pricing structure. These differences reflect each country's tax laws, reporting requirements, and business standards.

Why Every Country Has Its Own QuickBooks Online Version

Intuit creates localized versions of QuickBooks Online so that businesses can operate accurately within their country's financial system. This ensures:

- ❖ **Local currency support**

- ❖ **Compliance with regional tax rules** (e.g., VAT, GST, Sales Tax, Payroll Tax)
- ❖ **Country-specific financial reports**
- ❖ **Easier filing of mandatory returns**

Because tax regulations differ significantly around the world, using the QuickBooks Online edition designed for your region helps you stay compliant without manual workarounds.

How Currency and Reporting Work

Most countries require businesses to file financial statements and tax returns in **local currency**. QuickBooks Online supports this in two key ways:

1. **Reporting Currency:** You can set a home currency that aligns with your country's requirements.
2. **Multicurrency Transactions:** If your business deals with foreign suppliers or international customers, QuickBooks Online allows you to record those transactions in their original currencies while still reporting in your home currency.

This ensures accuracy in exchange-rate tracking, financial reports, and tax filings.

Pricing Depends on Your Country and Subscription Tier

Each country generally offers a tiered pricing structure—ranging from basic freelancer packages to advanced business-grade plans with multiple users and automation features.

As you move up the tiers, you get more functionality, such as:

- ❖ Time tracking, Inventory management, Project costing, Multicurrency, Advanced reporting, Automations and workflow tools, and More users

Important Tip: Always Check for Discounts

QuickBooks frequently offers **promotional rates**, especially for new subscribers. These deals may include:

- ❖ 30–50% off for the first three months
- ❖ Discounts when paying annually
- ❖ Bundled savings with payroll or payments
- ❖ Occasional regional promotions

Before subscribing, check the **Intuit website for your country** to get the best available deal.

QuickBooks Online Payroll Subscriptions

QuickBooks Online offers optional payroll add-ons, and it's important to understand that **payroll pricing is separate from your regular QuickBooks Online subscription**. These payroll plans vary significantly by country and by feature level. For example, payroll can cost as little as **£4 per month in the United Kingdom** for a basic plan, while more advanced options—such as the **Elite Payroll plan in the United States**—can cost up to **$130 per month**.

Adding Payroll to Your QuickBooks Online Plan

Once you choose your QuickBooks Online subscription (Simple Start, Essentials, Plus, or Advanced), you can add a payroll package that suits your business needs. These payroll add-ons typically cover features such as:

- Employee and contractor payments, Automated tax calculations, Tax form filings (e.g., W-2s, 1099s, P60s, etc.), Direct deposit, Time tracking and scheduling, HR tools and compliance support, and Benefits administration (country dependent)

The level of automation, compliance support, and reporting increases as you move up to higher-tier payroll plans.

Affordability and Value

Considering the range of features, QuickBooks Online Payroll is generally priced competitively compared to other payroll software. It streamlines payroll processing, reduces administrative errors, and helps ensure compliance with local employment and tax regulations—all of which make it a cost-effective investment for many businesses.

Special Offers and Pricing Notes

The monthly fee for both QuickBooks Online and QuickBooks Payroll may vary depending on promotions. Intuit frequently runs **special discounts for new users**, which can significantly reduce your initial subscription cost for the first few months. After the promotional period ends, the regular ongoing rate applies.

WHAT YOU'LL NOTICE WHEN YOU LOG IN

Just like previous major QuickBooks updates, Intuit has introduced new names, reorganized menus, and refreshed the overall layout. During the August webinar, several key changes stood out:

1. Navigation Updates

❖ **Modules are now called "Apps."**

The familiar left-side navigation menu is now located inside the **App Drawer**, which you can open to access all your tools.

❖ **New App Carousel:**

A convenient carousel appears at the top of the screen, giving you instant access to essential apps so you don't always need to open the drawer.

❖ **"Apps" is now "My Integrations."**

What used to be the Apps section has been renamed **My Integrations**, accessible via an icon on the top menu bar.

Think of this redesign as *rearranging your office*, not moving to a completely new one. The tools are still there—just in slightly different places.

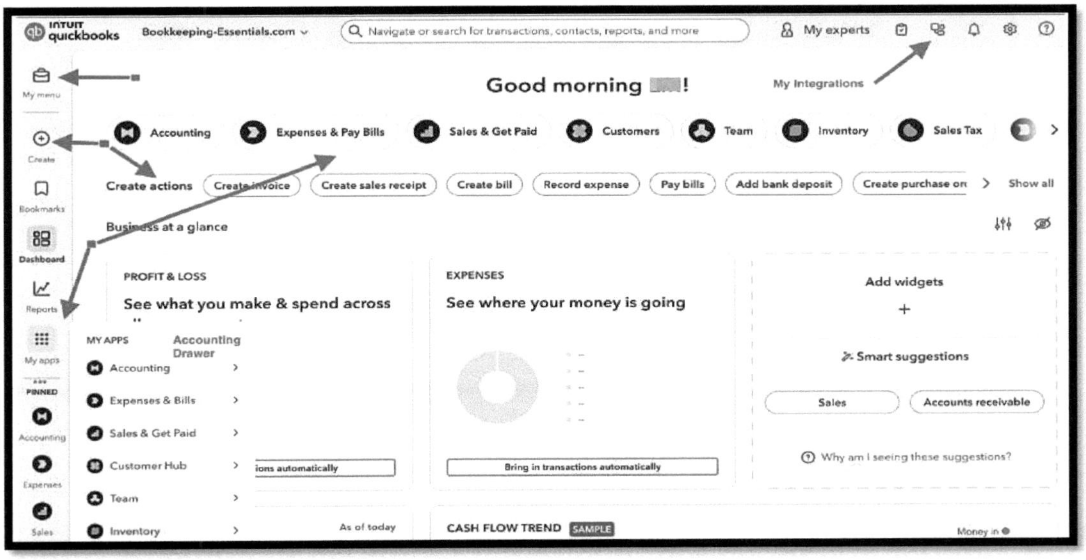

2. Updated Terminology

❖ The familiar **"New"** button is now labeled **"Create."**

It still lives in the same location and functions exactly the same—it just has a more intuitive name.

3. More Flexible Customization

QuickBooks Online now gives you greater control over your workspace:

❖ **Bookmarks and pinned items** can be personalized for faster access.

- **Dashboard widgets** are more customizable—you can add, remove, resize, and reorder them as you like.
- The **Business at a Glance** section now includes more funnel-style widgets designed to help you stay on top of your core workflows and daily tasks.

A Helpful Mindset

As with previous updates, the 2026 visual redesign is best viewed as a light reorganization rather than a full system change. Everything you need is still there—just presented in a cleaner, more modern layout.

EXPLORING THE NEW QUICKBOOKS ONLINE INTERFACE

The New interface has undergone a significant redesign. Regular users may notice a different layout, but the improved navigation is cleaner and easier to use.

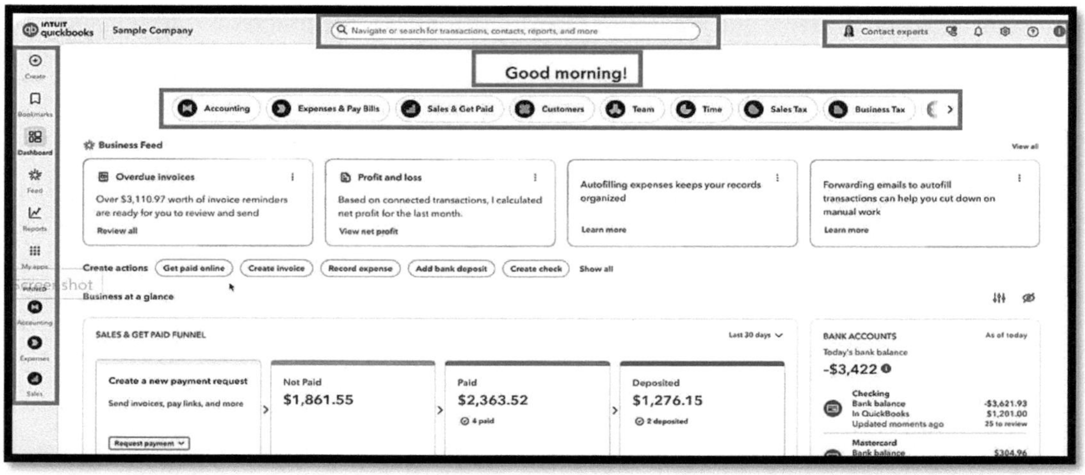

Top-Left Area

- Your **company name**
- The **QuickBooks logo**, which returns you to the homepage

Left Navigation Menu

A slim, streamlined sidebar providing quick access to major functions.

At the top is the **Create (+) button**, previously known as the *New* button, used for creating customers, vendors, invoices, bills, and other transactions.

Top-Center Area

A new **Smart Search bar**, a personalized greeting, and an **app carousel** that offers shortcuts to key modules like Accounting, Expenses, and Payroll.

Top-Right Area

Links to: Contact experts, Integrations, Notifications, Settings, Help, and Your Intuit account

The New Homepage Layout

The redesigned dashboard gives you a clear snapshot of your business:

1. Business Feed Highlights

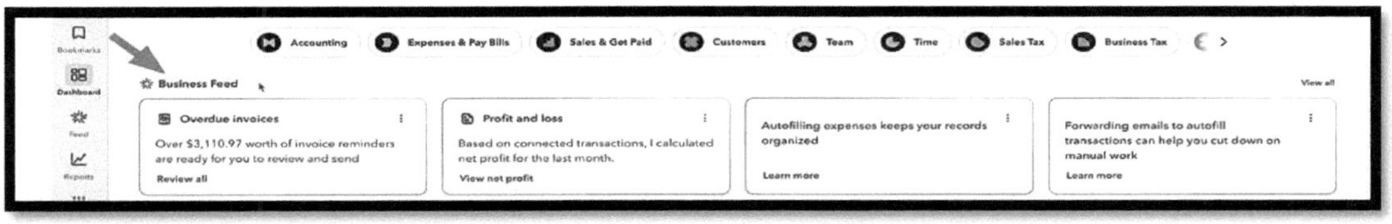

This section summarizes work completed by **Intuit Assist**, the new AI assistant. It surfaces insights and tasks that need your attention.

2. Create Actions

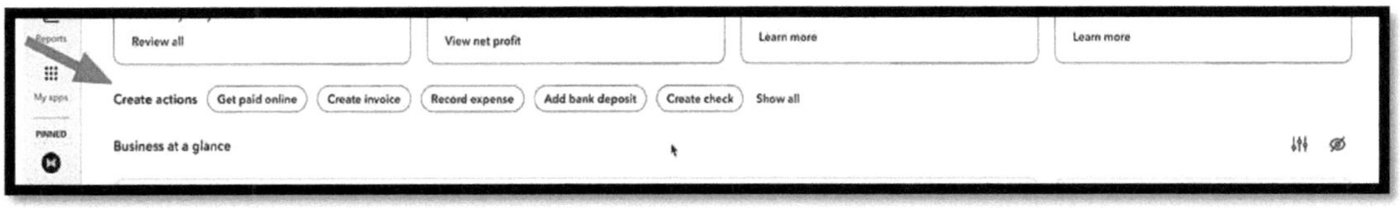

Customizable shortcuts for your most common tasks (e.g., creating invoices or capturing expenses).

3. Business Overview

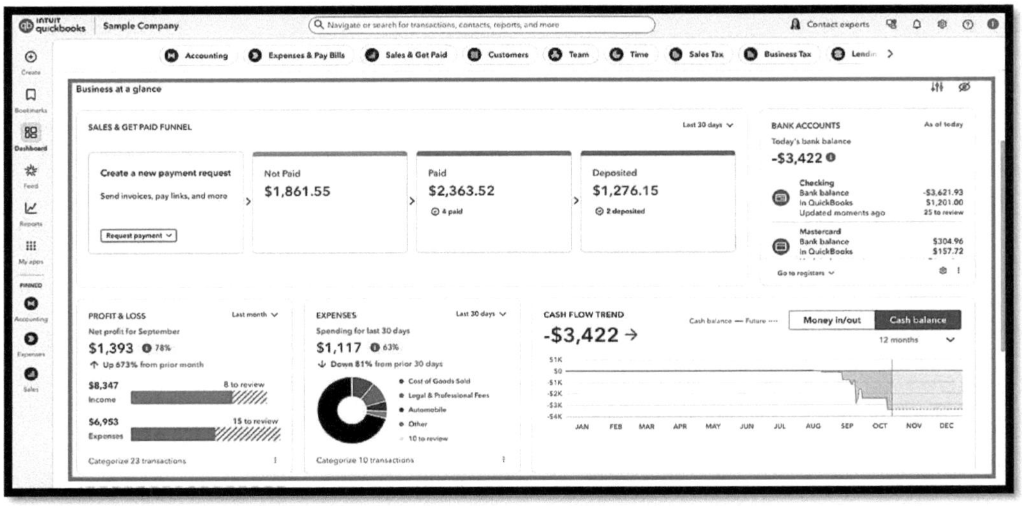

A set of financial widgets displaying: Sales funnel, Bank balances, Profit and loss, Expenses, and Cash flow

You can rearrange or remove widgets using the **Customize** option to build a dashboard that suits your workflow. A **Privacy** toggle lets you hide sensitive information whenever needed.

Customize option

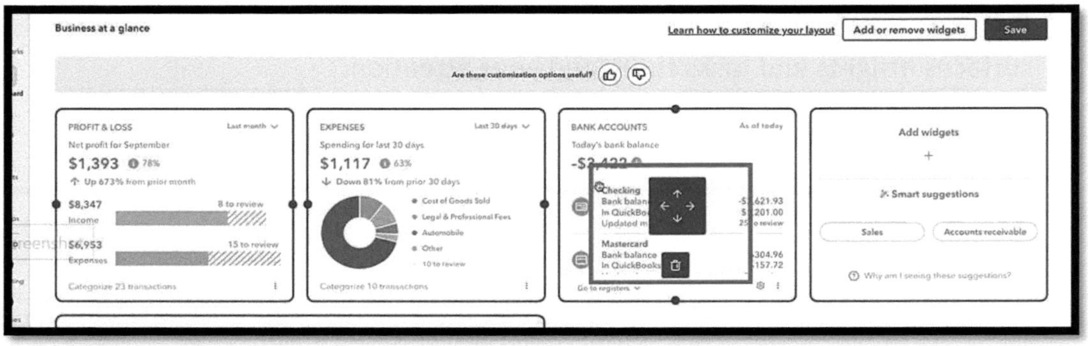

Customizing your widgets

Click Add or Remove widgets to customize your dashboard

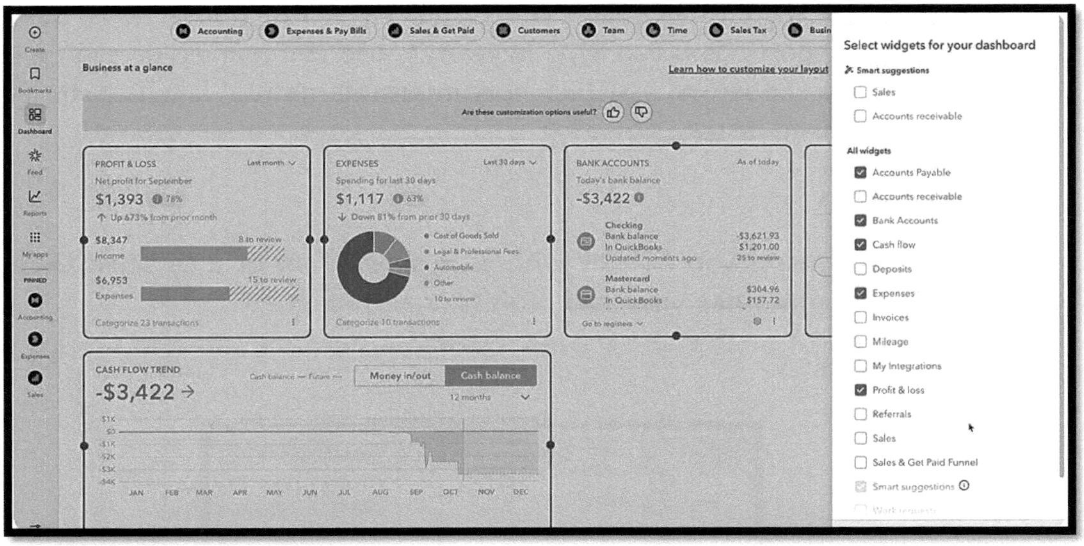

Select widgets to display on dashboard

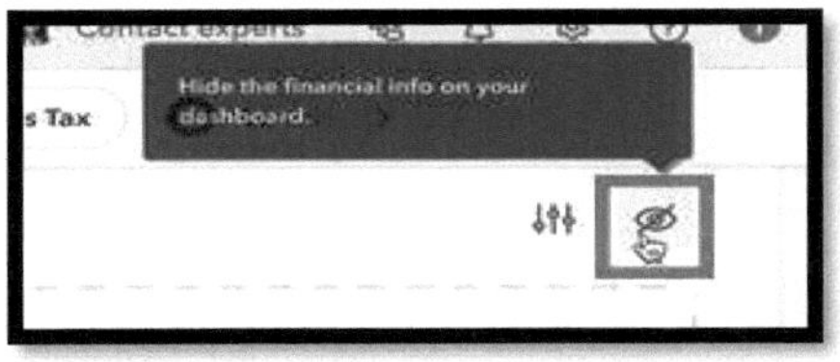

Privacy button

How the New QuickBooks Online Works

The redesigned QuickBooks Online interface introduces a more intuitive layout and smarter tools. Let's walk through the main features starting with the buttons at the top of the screen.

Top Navigation Tools

Smart Search Bar

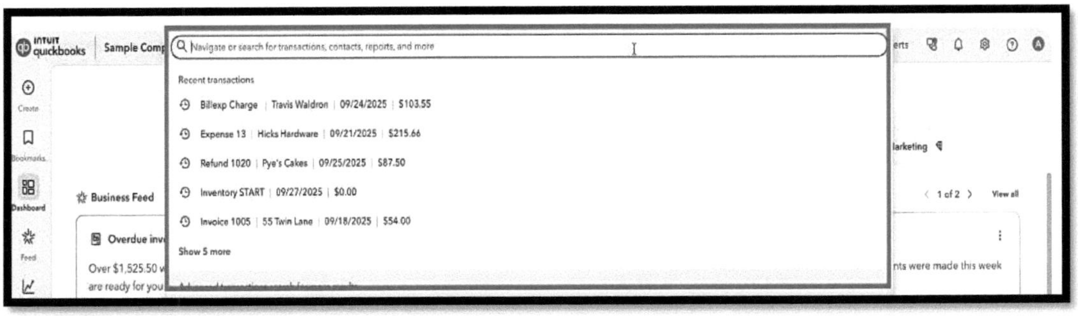

The new smart search bar allows you to quickly locate transactions, customers, vendors, and reports. You can type keywords, use commands, or even enter full questions—QuickBooks' AI assistant now interprets natural language to help you find what you need faster.

Contact Experts

This option connects you directly with your accountant or a certified QuickBooks ProAdvisor—useful when you need professional guidance.

My Integrations

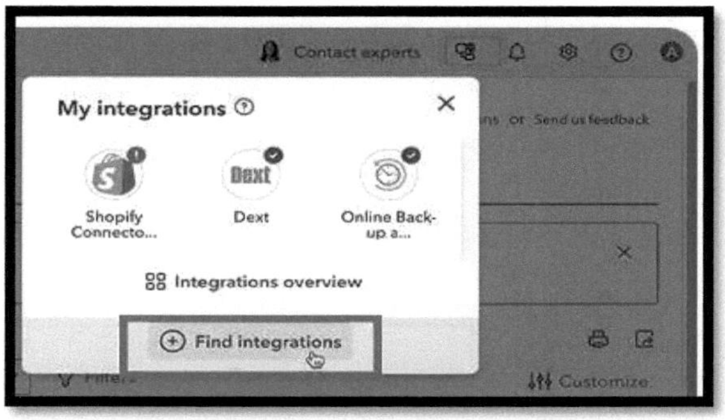

This section shows all third-party applications linked to your QuickBooks account. You can browse for more apps by selecting **Find Integrations**.

Notifications

The bell icon displays alerts related to your account, updates, or tasks that need attention.

Help Menu

Opens an assistance panel where you can ask questions to the AI assistant or search through QuickBooks' help articles and FAQs.

Settings Menu (Gear Icon)

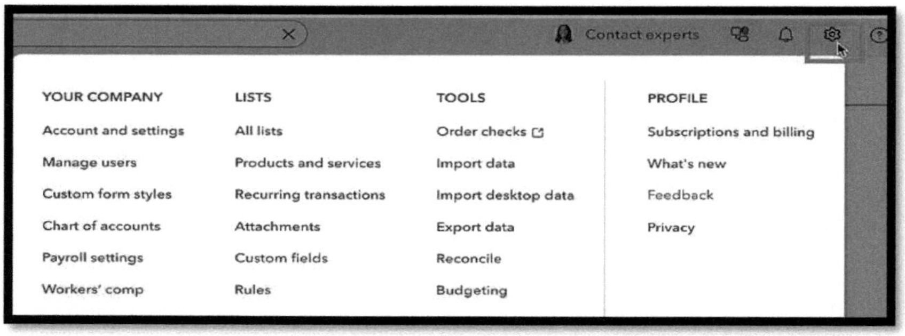

The gear icon is where you configure your company's setup and core accounting settings.

Account and Settings

Here you set up your company information, including: Logo, Business name, Address and contact details, Website, Industry, EIN/SSN, and Business structure and tax details

- ❖ **Usage Limits:** Shows your plan's restrictions on features such as billable users, chart of accounts size, and class/location tracking.

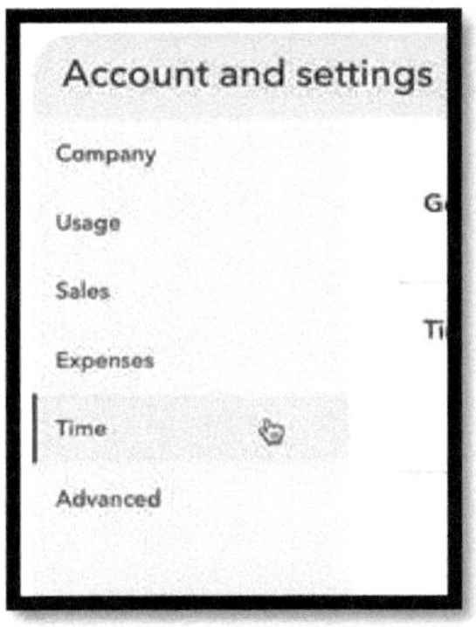

- ❖ **Sales, Expenses, and Time Settings:** Customize how your forms appear, set default terms, and configure expense tracking options.
- ❖ **Advanced Settings:** Choose between cash or accrual accounting, enable multicurrency, and adjust automation preferences.

Manage Users

Add, remove, or edit users and assign different levels of access depending on their role (admin, standard user, accountant, etc.).

Chart of Accounts

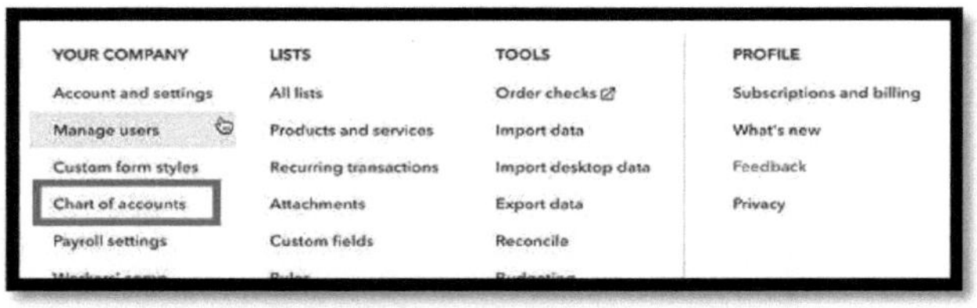

This is the backbone of your accounting system. It lists every asset, liability, equity, income, and expense account in your business. Proper setup is crucial. If you're unsure how to structure your accounts, consult an accountant before making changes.

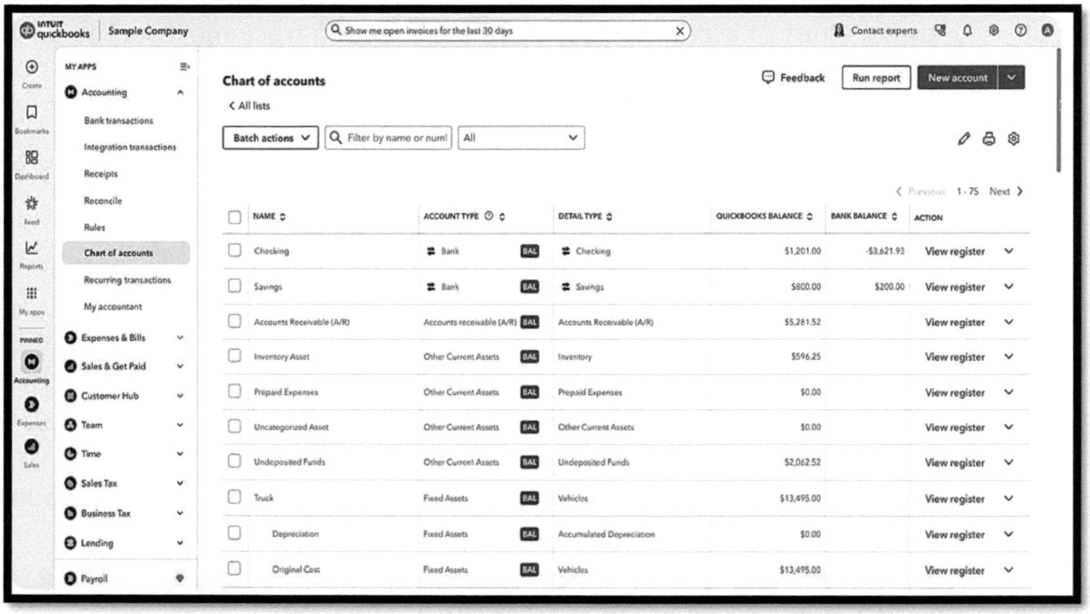

Additional Tools in Settings: Keyboard Shortcuts

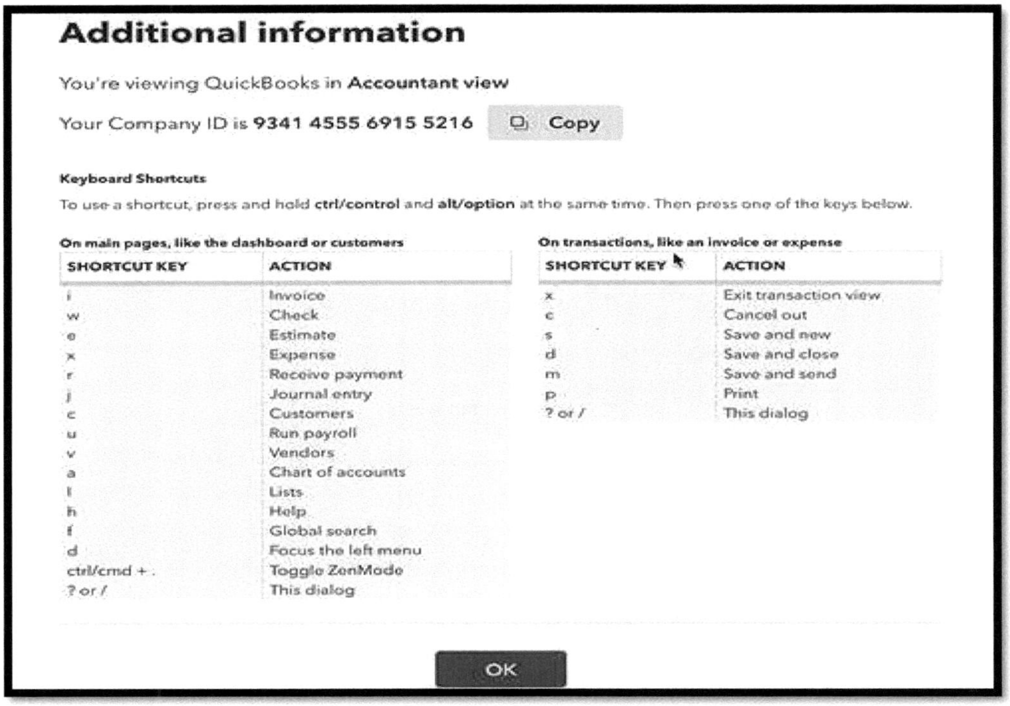

Additional information

You're viewing QuickBooks in **Accountant view**

Your Company ID is **9341 4555 6915 5216** Copy

Keyboard Shortcuts

To use a shortcut, press and hold **ctrl/control** and **alt/option** at the same time. Then press one of the keys below.

On main pages, like the dashboard or customers

SHORTCUT KEY	ACTION
i	Invoice
w	Check
e	Estimate
x	Expense
r	Receive payment
j	Journal entry
c	Customers
u	Run payroll
v	Vendors
a	Chart of accounts
l	Lists
h	Help
f	Global search
d	Focus the left menu
ctrl/cmd + .	Toggle ZenMode
? or /	This dialog

On transactions, like an invoice or expense

SHORTCUT KEY	ACTION
x	Exit transaction view
c	Cancel out
s	Save and new
d	Save and close
m	Save and send
p	Print
? or /	This dialog

OK

QuickBooks offers a set of keyboard commands to speed up navigation. Print the list and keep it handy—great for power users.

Products and Services List

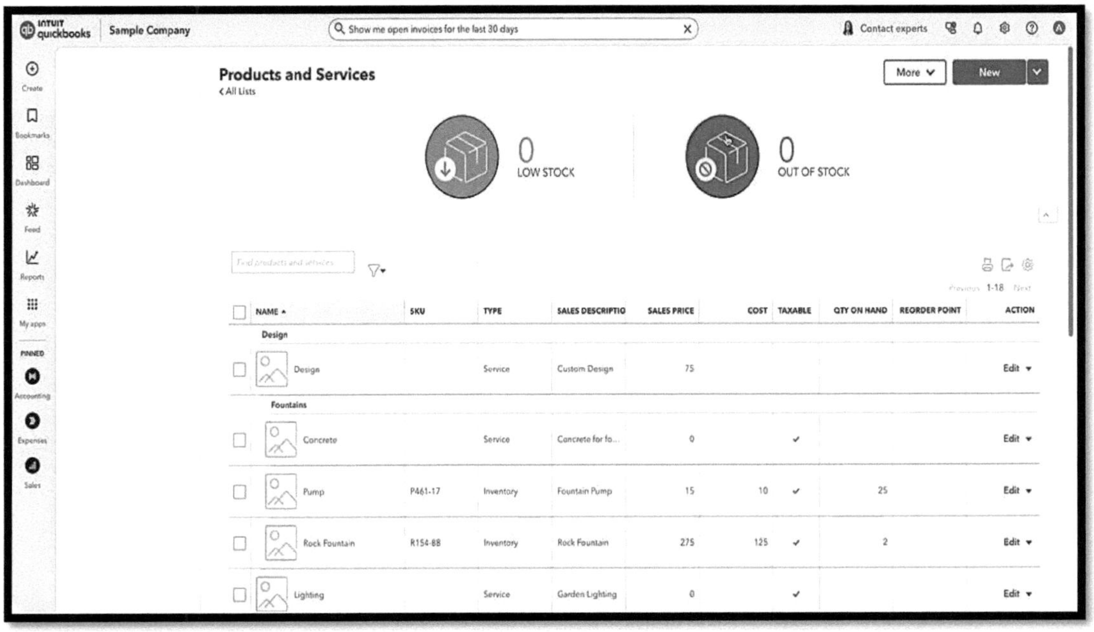

Create or edit the items you sell. This makes invoicing faster and ensures accurate tracking of inventory, income, or service activity.

Recurring Transactions

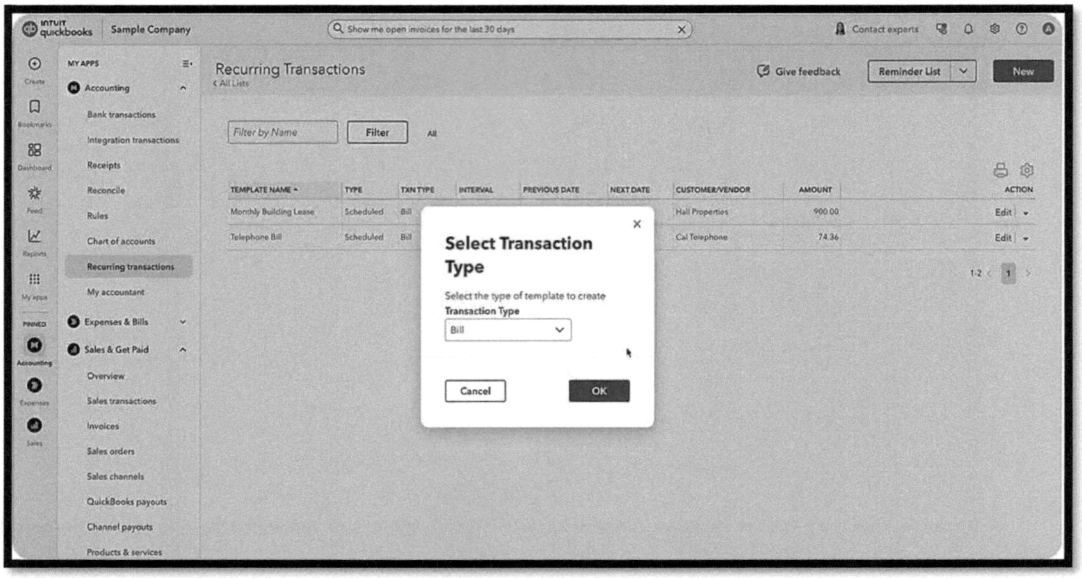

Use templates and automation rules to create repeating invoices or automatically categorize bank transactions. These tools save time and improve consistency.

Check Ordering, Importing/Exporting Data & Bank Reconciliation

Under the **Tools** section you can:

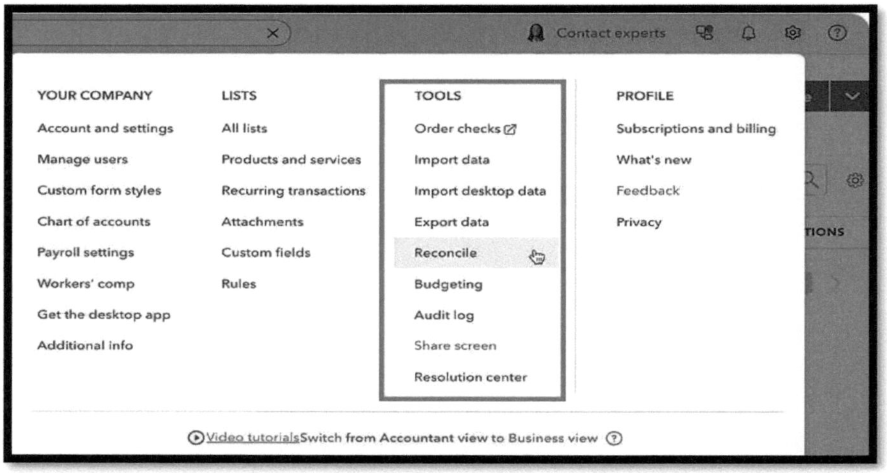

- Order checks
- Import or export lists and data

❖ Reconcile your bank accounts
❖ Set up budgets
❖ View the audit log to see who made changes
❖ Share your screen with support
❖ Access the resolution center for billing or account issues

Left Navigation Menu

At the top of the navigation bar is the **Create (+) button**, which allows you to quickly create: Customer invoices, Vendor bills, Estimates, Expenses, Time entries, Journal entries, And more

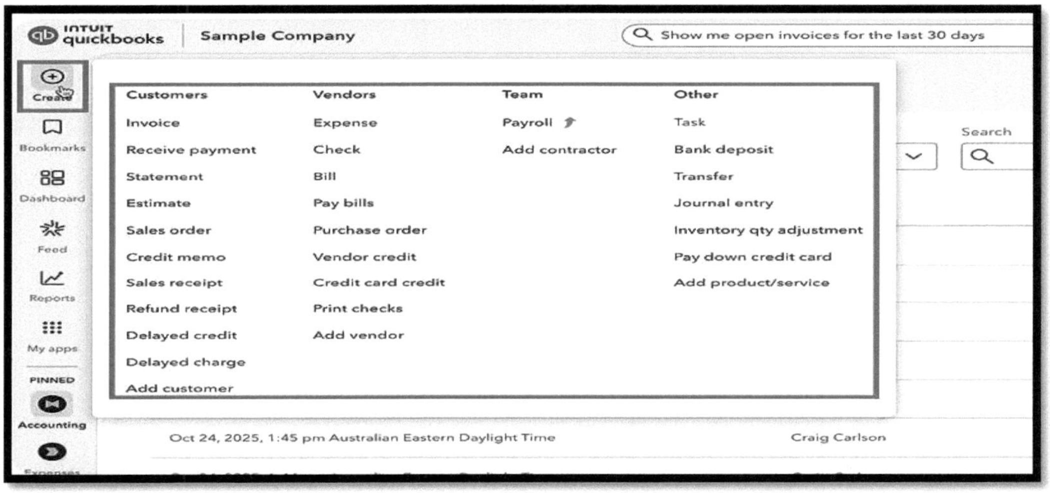

Creating a Sales Invoice

To create an invoice:

1. Select **Create → Invoice**.
2. Choose an existing customer or add a new one.
3. Select the product or service sold.
4. Enter the quantity and rate.
5. Add any discounts or sales tax.
6. Click **Review and Send**.

QuickBooks generates a clean PDF of the invoice and prepares an email you can customize before sending. This is the standard process when recording a sale to a customer.

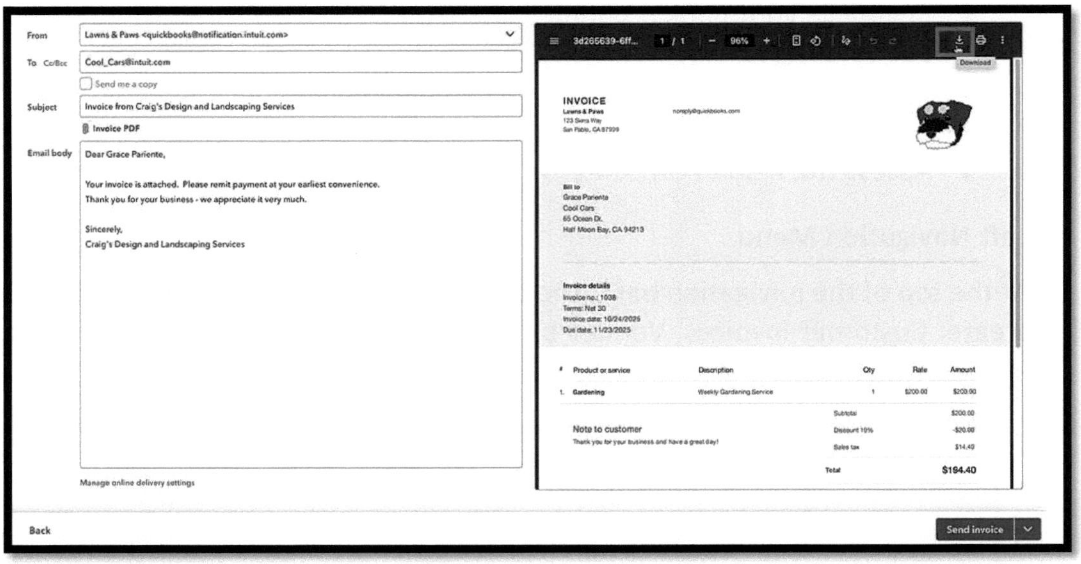

Vendor Transactions

Recording Purchases

You can record purchases in two ways:

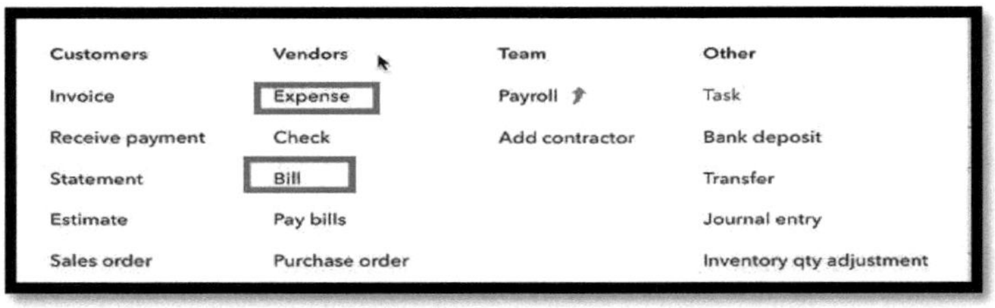

❖ **Expense:** Use this when the money has already left your bank account. AI can autofill details from uploaded receipts.

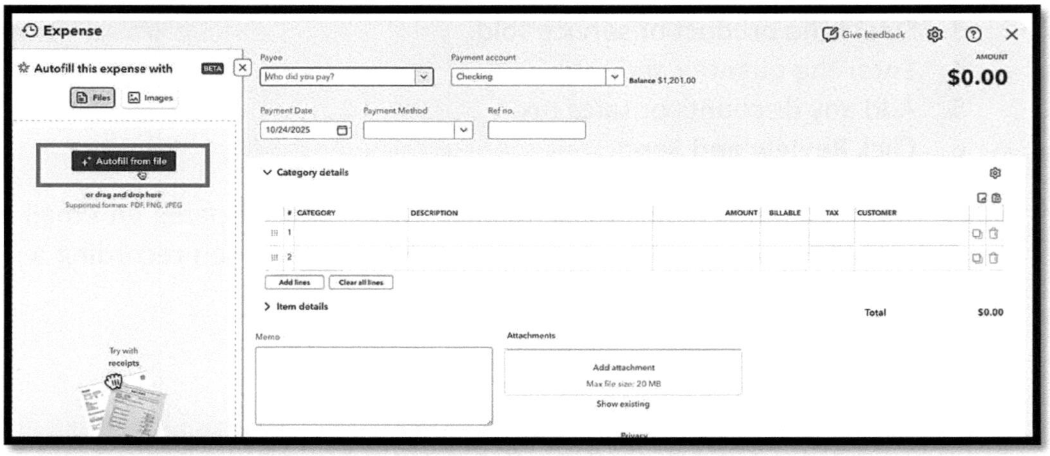

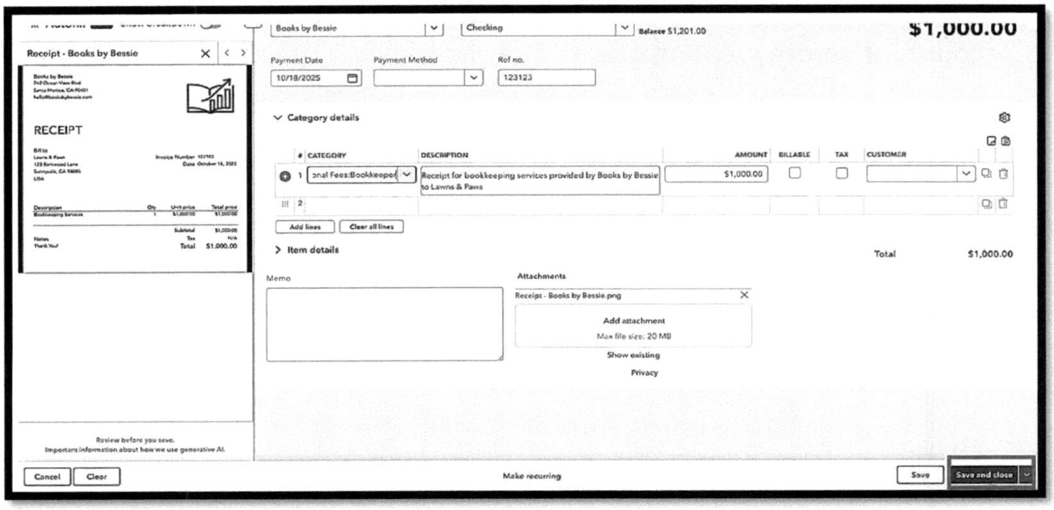

❖ **Bill:** Use this when you owe money and will pay later. Enter payment terms or due dates. This increases your Accounts Payable balance until paid.

Paying Bills

Click **Save** or **Schedule Payment** after entering bill details.

Other Important Forms

Journal Entries

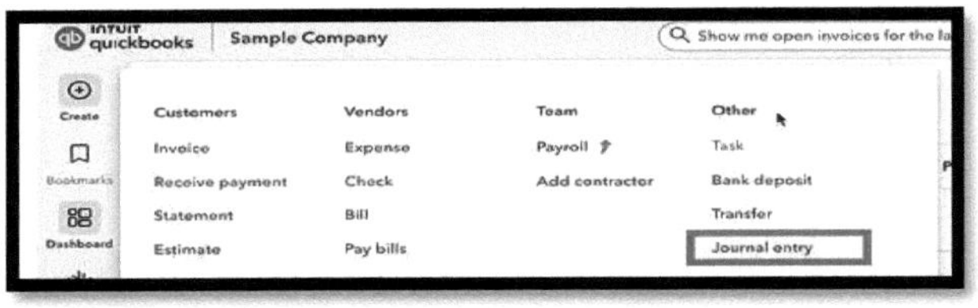

`

Use these only when necessary. They bypass the normal workflows, so consult an accountant before creating one.

Bookmarks & Dashboard

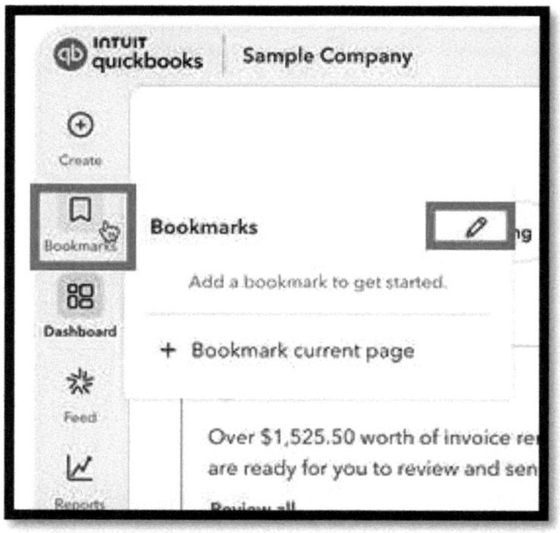

You can bookmark your most frequently visited pages.

The **Dashboard** brings you back to your homepage,

Business Feed

The **Business Feed**—powered by AI—shows tasks, alerts, and personalized insights.

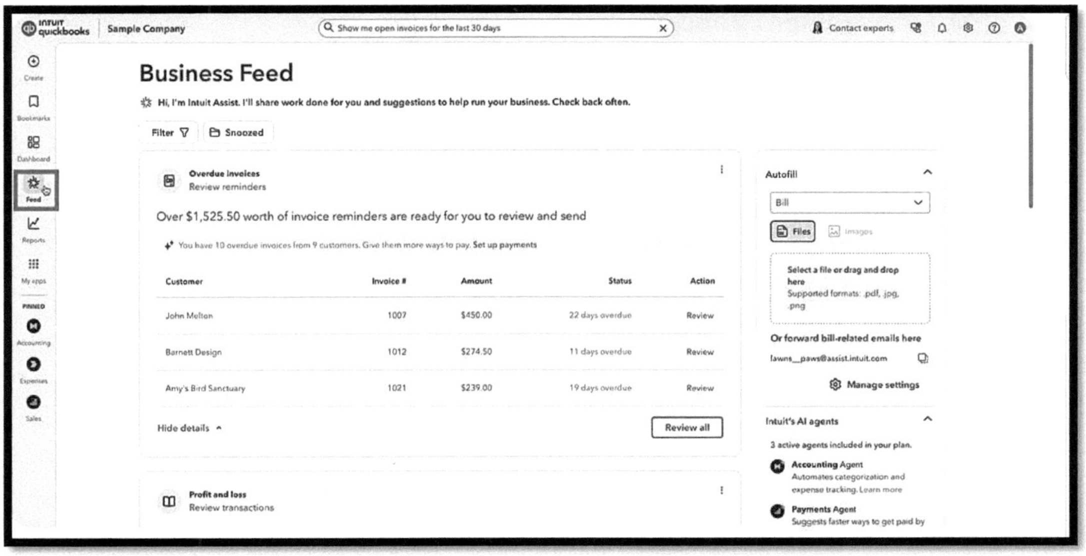

Reports

Reports now have their own menu category.

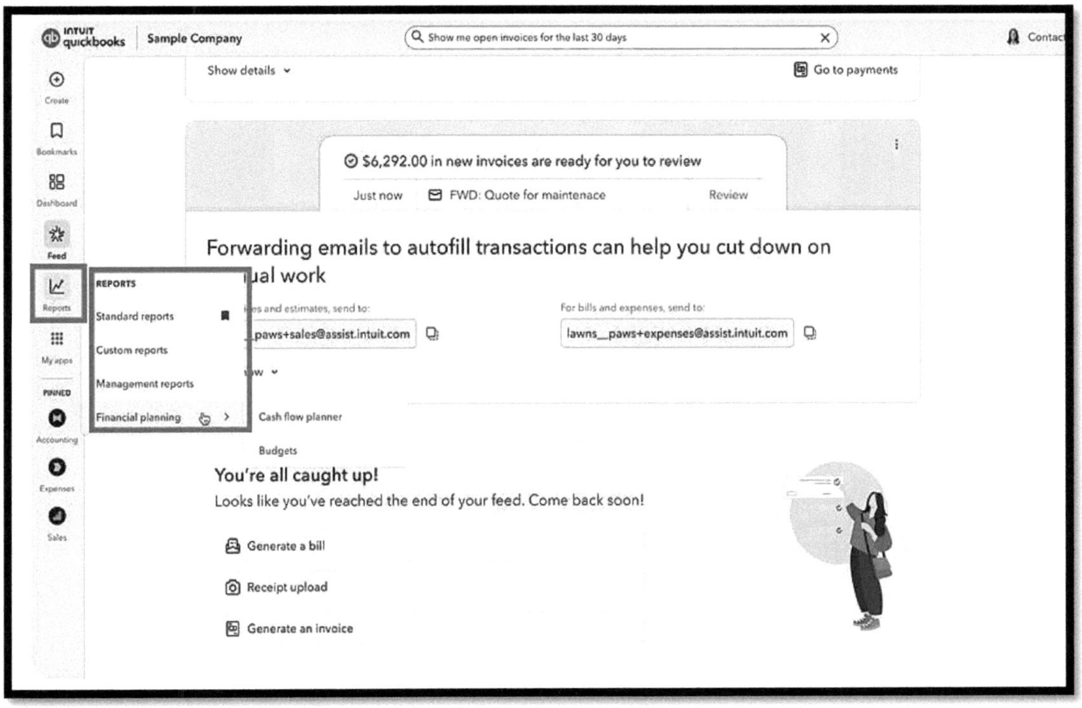

You can access:

- ❖ **Standard Reports**
- ❖ **Custom Reports**

- ❖ **Management Reports**
- ❖ **Financial Planning Reports**

Key examples include:

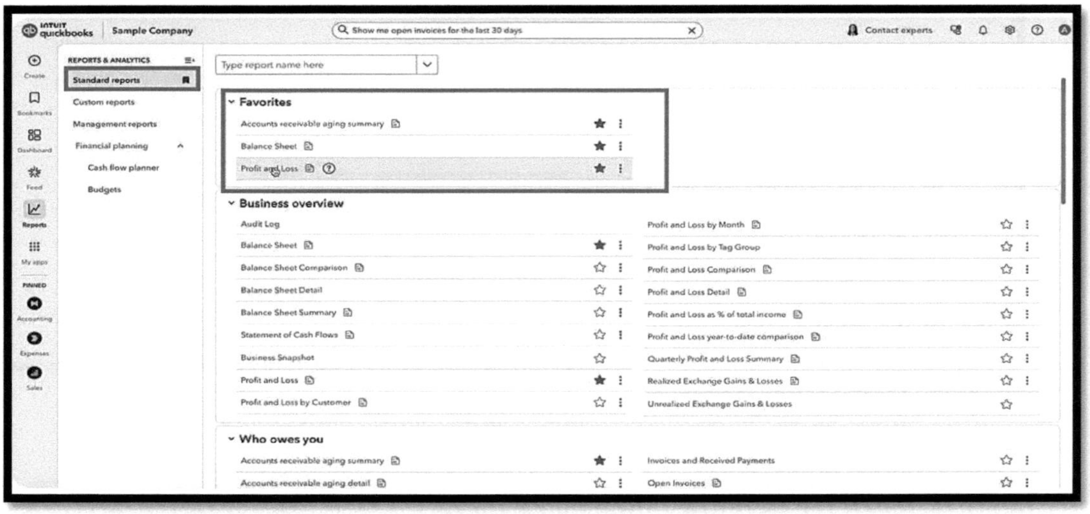

- ❖ **Balance Sheet:** Snapshot of assets, liabilities, and equity.
- ❖ **Profit & Loss Statement:** Summary of income and expenses.
- ❖ **Cash Flow Statement:** Details of cash movement in and out of your business.

You can "favorite" reports for quick access.

My Apps

This section houses all your connected and pinned apps. Customize it as needed.

Accounting

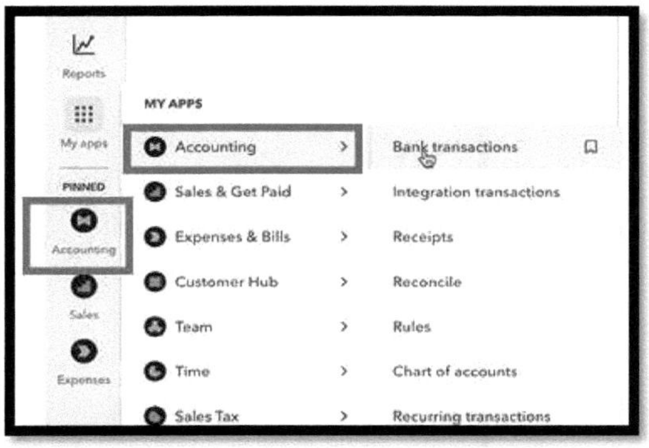

This is where you manage bank feeds:

- ❖ Connect new accounts
- ❖ Review downloaded transactions
- ❖ Match QuickBooks transactions with bank activity
- ❖ Categorize uncategorized items
- ❖ Create bank rules for recurring transactions
- ❖ Perform bank reconciliations

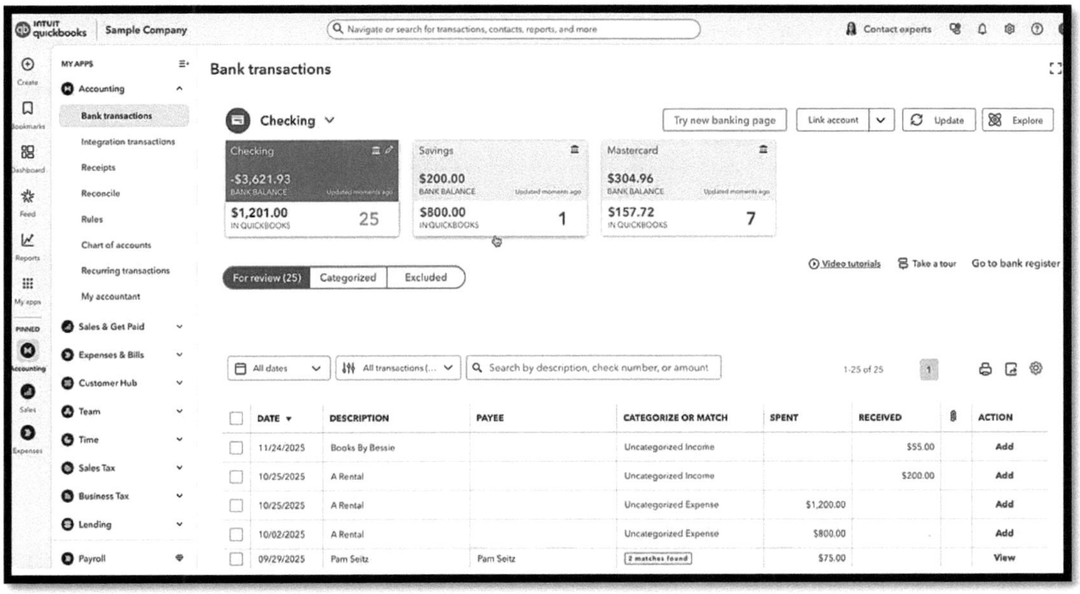

`

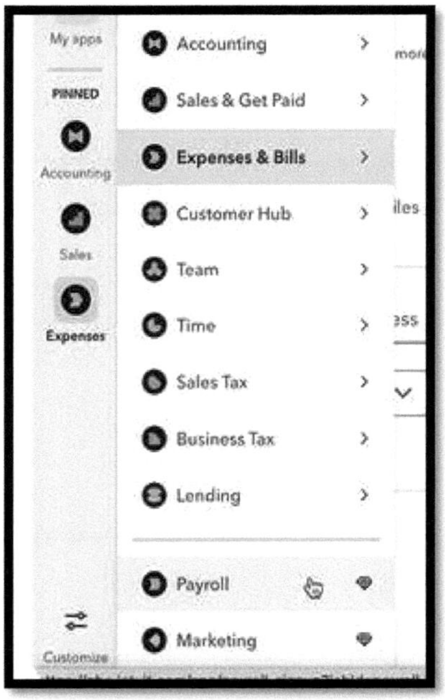

Sales & Get Paid

From the **Sales Overview**, you can:

- ❖ Manage estimates, invoices, and payments
- ❖ Identify overdue invoices (highlighted in orange)
- ❖ Send automated or AI-enhanced reminders

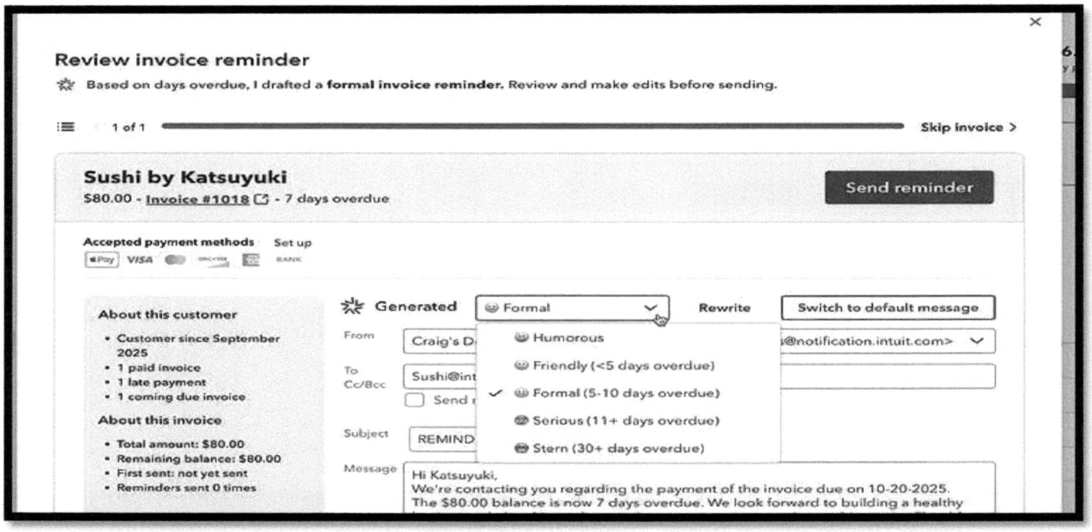

Expenses & Bills

Track, record, and manage expenses here:

`

- View overdue bills
- Schedule payments
- Add and manage vendors
- Track mileage

Customer Hub & Team

- **Customer Hub:** Track customer details and leads
- **Team:** Add employees or contractors

Taxes, Loans, Payroll, and Marketing

- **Taxes:** Manage sales tax and business tax setup
- **Loan & Banking:** Find financing through QuickBooks Marketplace
- **Payroll:** Run payroll and issue direct deposits to employees and contractors
- **Marketing:** Manage campaigns from within QuickBooks

HOW TO CONVERT QUICKBOOKS DESKTOP TO QUICKBOOKS ONLINE

This section walks you step-by-step through converting your QuickBooks Desktop company file to QuickBooks Online. Moving to the cloud gives you anytime, anywhere access to your financial data—but a smooth transition depends on preparing your Desktop file properly. Below, you'll learn how to clean up your data, update your software, check file-size limits, back up your company file, and finally export it to QuickBooks Online.

Step 1: Prepare Your QuickBooks Desktop File for Export

Before initiating the migration, you must ensure your Desktop company file is accurate, updated, and within QuickBooks Online's import limits.

Step 1a: Clean Up and Update Your Books

Make sure your Desktop data is complete and up to date. This helps prevent errors during conversion.

- Reconcile every bank and credit card account
- Review and correct account balances
- Process all outstanding payroll
- Update or adjust inventory
- Close out any lingering transactions

The cleaner your file, the smoother your migration.

Step 1b: Update QuickBooks Desktop

QuickBooks Online only converts data from the latest version of QuickBooks Desktop.

To update:

1. Go to **Help** in the top menu.
2. Select **Update QuickBooks Desktop**.
3. Click **Update Now**, then install the available updates.

This prevents compatibility issues and ensures the export tools function properly.

Step 1c: Check File Size Requirements

QuickBooks Online can only import company files under a certain size:

- **Pro/Premier:** up to **750,000 targets**
- **Enterprise:** up to **1,200,000 targets**

To check your file size:

1. Press **F2** or **Ctrl + 1** in QuickBooks Desktop.

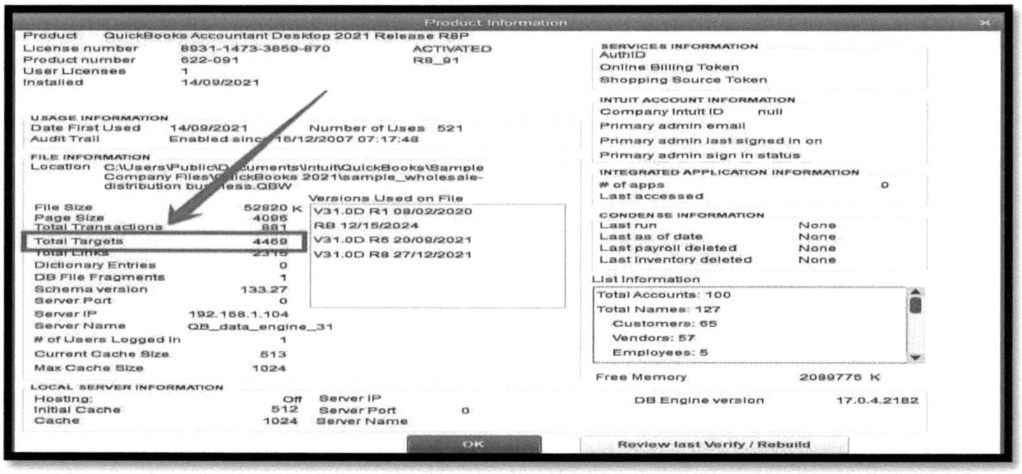

2. In the **Product Information** window, review the **Total Targets** count.

If your file exceeds the limit, you must reduce its size before converting.

Shrinking the File (Condensing Data)

You can reduce file size using the Condense Data tool:

1. Go to **File > Utilities > Condense Data**.
2. Choose whether to keep all transactions or remove selected details.

Important: Condensing a file is permanent.

Before condensing, always:

- Reconcile all accounts
- Print essential reports
- Create a full backup

If condensing doesn't bring the target count low enough, you may need to export only certain data (lists, balances, etc.).

Step 1d: Back Up Your Company File

Before converting, create a local backup for safety and future reference.

To back up:

1. Select **File > Back Up Company > Create Local Backup**.
2. Save the backup to a secure folder on your computer.

QuickBooks recommends that your working company file be stored on a **local drive**, not a network drive, for the conversion process.

If you normally work off a server or shared drive, restore your backup to your local machine and use that version for the migration.

Step 2: Start the Migration Process

Once your QuickBooks Desktop file is ready, go to the **Company** menu and select **Export Your Company File to QuickBooks Online**.

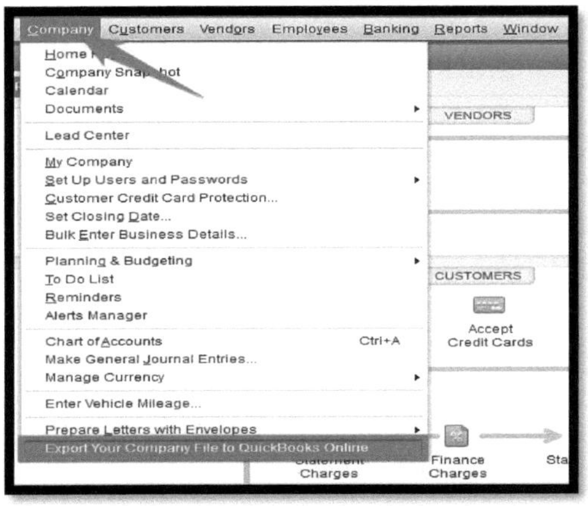

QuickBooks Desktop will open a new window to begin the migration. Click **Get Started** to continue.

Step 3: Choose the Data You Want to Transfer

QuickBooks will ask what information you want to move to QuickBooks Online. You'll see two options:

- **Bring all your company data** – Transfers everything, including customers, vendors, settings, lists, and all transactions.
- **Choose what to bring over** – Ideal for large files or selective migration (e.g., lists, balances).

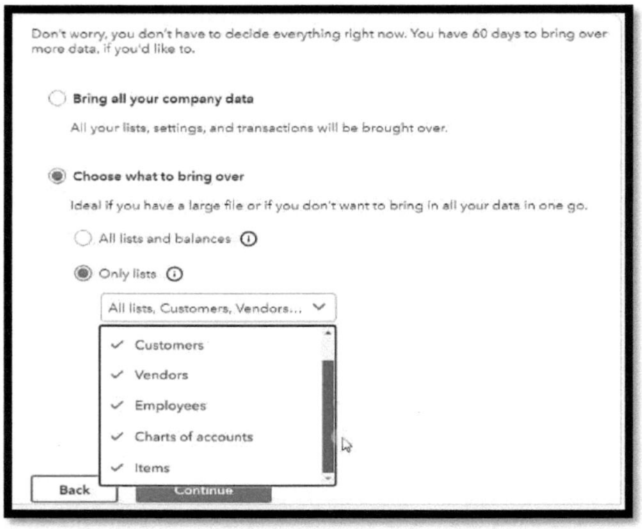

You'll also be asked whether you want to include **inventory**. If you choose Yes, QuickBooks Online will recalculate your inventory using the **FIFO method** from your selected start date.

Important: Switching to FIFO may require filing **IRS Form 3115**. Consult a tax professional before migrating inventory.

Step 4: Sign In or Create Your QuickBooks Online Account

After selecting your data, sign in to the QuickBooks Online company that will receive the migrated file.

You must complete the migration **within 60 days** of starting your QuickBooks Online subscription. If this window has passed, you can cancel your subscription and create a new company under the same email address.

If you already have an account, click **Yes, sign me in**, then select **Continue**.

If you need a new account, click **No, I need to create one** to start a **30-day free trial**.

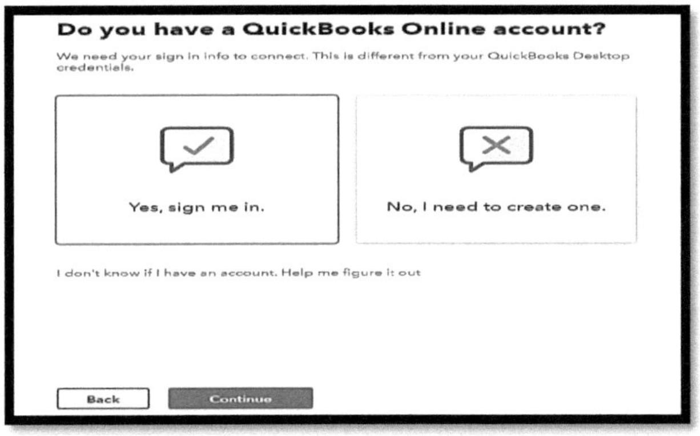

Step 5: Select the Destination Company

Once logged in, QuickBooks will display the list of your Online companies. Select the company where you want the data transferred, then click **Continue**.

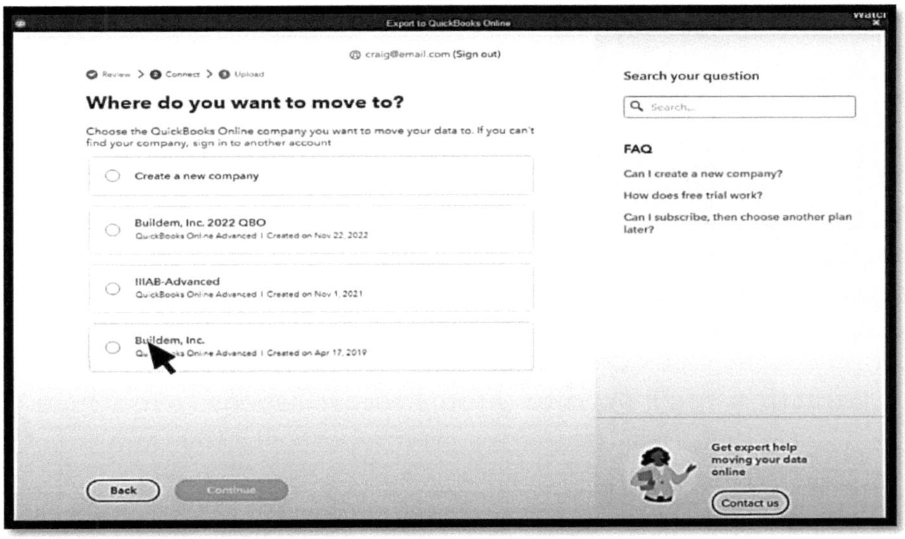

If you migrate into an existing company, the migration will **overwrite all existing data**. If you're creating a new company, you'll be asked to confirm your company name. You can adjust company settings now or after the migration.

Step 6: Export Your Data

Review your selection, then click **Upload** to begin the transfer. The upload typically takes a few minutes, though larger files may take longer.

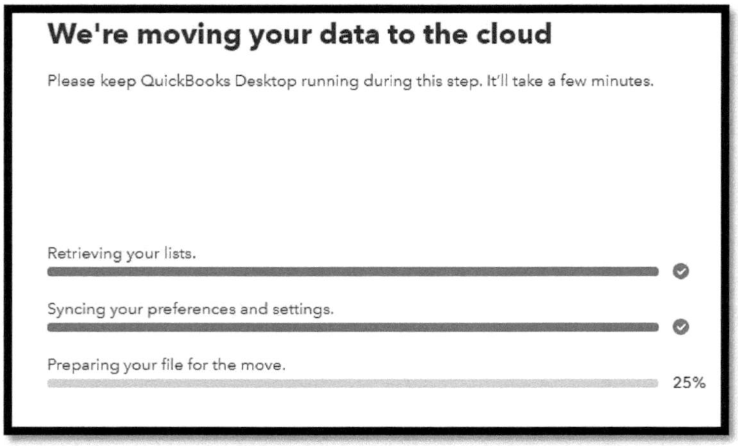

Step 7: Check for Email Confirmation

QuickBooks will email you once the migration is complete. Large files may take several hours.

After receiving the confirmation email, click **Complete your setup** to log in and review your data in QuickBooks Online.

To ensure accuracy, compare reports from QuickBooks Desktop with the same reports in QuickBooks Online. This helps verify that everything transferred correctly.

What's Not Imported When You Convert QuickBooks Desktop to Online

While QuickBooks Online imports most of your data, certain items **do not transfer** automatically. Here's what to expect:

- **Bank and credit card reconciliations:** Your past reconciliation reports will not transfer. You'll need to resume reconciliations from where you left off in QuickBooks Desktop. Access prior reports directly from your Desktop files if needed.
- **Recurring credit card transactions:** Existing recurring charges in the Merchant Center must be canceled. Recreate them in QuickBooks Online using recurring sales receipts.
- **Audit trail:** Historical audit data cannot be transferred. You will, however, benefit from an improved audit trail going forward in QuickBooks Online.
- **Inventory from QuickBooks for Mac:** Inventory cannot be migrated from a Mac. If you have a Windows version, use that computer for the transfer.
- **Reports:** Some Desktop reports do not exist in Online. QuickBooks Online provides a variety of reports to replace many Desktop versions, so you'll need to adjust to the new format.

Tip: If you prefer keeping your Desktop features while accessing your files remotely, consider a **hosted QuickBooks Desktop** solution.

Considerations for a Smooth Transition

To ensure a successful migration:

- Condense your data file if it exceeds QuickBooks' target limits.
- Move the company file to a **local drive** and switch to **single-user mode** before exporting.
- Address payroll data carefully—existing records may need to be removed or a new company file set up without payroll.
- Manually re-enter any items that don't transfer automatically, such as **custom templates** and certain reports.

Common migration issues include:

- Files that exceed the **target limit** (Step 1c).
- Company files stored on **network drives** or in **multi-user mode**, which can cause export errors.
- Payroll conflicts: QuickBooks Online cannot overwrite existing employee records linked to payroll items. Manual re-entry may be required to ensure proper reporting.

For complex migrations, QuickBooks offers additional support:

- **Migration Toolkit:** Guides you through the process.
- **Free Assisted Migration Service:** A QuickBooks representative can perform the migration at no charge.
    - Call **800-459-5183**, Monday–Friday, 8 a.m.–8 p.m. ET.

Following these steps and precautions will make your transition from QuickBooks Desktop to Online smoother and less error-prone.

Features Not Supported by QuickBooks Online

While QuickBooks Online covers most accounting needs, some features from Desktop are **not available**, including:

- Barcode scanning for inventory management
- Inventory assemblies
- Certain customized forms
- QuickBooks Statement Writer
- Processing multiple vendor ship-to addresses
- Using the average cost inventory method

Tip: Many unsupported features can still be accessed through **third-party app integrations**.

If you prefer the familiar Desktop interface, you can install the **QuickBooks Online Desktop App**, which provides all Online features while offering a Desktop-like interface and extended login periods (up to six months). QuickBooks provides a download link after completing your migration.

When to Move from QuickBooks Desktop to QuickBooks Online

QuickBooks Online is an excellent choice for small businesses, and existing Desktop users may consider switching if they:

1. **Manage books independently or collaborate with remote accountants**

    - QuickBooks Online is cloud-based, making it easier to share files and collaborate.

      Desktop requires creating an **Accountant's Copy** to share with your bookkeeper, which is less convenient.

2. **Need mobile access for expenses and invoices**

    - The QuickBooks Online mobile app allows you to track income, expenses, and send invoices on the go.
    - Desktop's mobile app is limited to receipt capture and mileage tracking.

3. **Require extensive integration with third-party apps**

    - QuickBooks Online supports over **750 third-party apps**, compared to about 200 for Desktop.
    - This is ideal for businesses using tools for CRM, e-commerce, and industry-specific needs.

4. **Anticipate business growth and need scalability**

    - QuickBooks Online offers four subscription plans, allowing you to upgrade as your business grows and add users or features as needed.

HOW TO SWITCH BETWEEN COMPANIES IN QUICKBOOKS ONLINE

Many users manage multiple companies or clients in QuickBooks Online. Fortunately, the platform allows you to **seamlessly switch between company files**—perfect for accountants, bookkeepers, or business owners overseeing several entities.

Note: Each company requires its own active QuickBooks Online subscription.

Step 1: Log in to QuickBooks Online

Start by logging into your QuickBooks Online account with your credentials. You'll land on the dashboard of your **primary company**.

Step 2: Access the Company Switcher

Click the **gear icon** in the top-right corner of the screen. Under **Profile**, select **Switch company**.

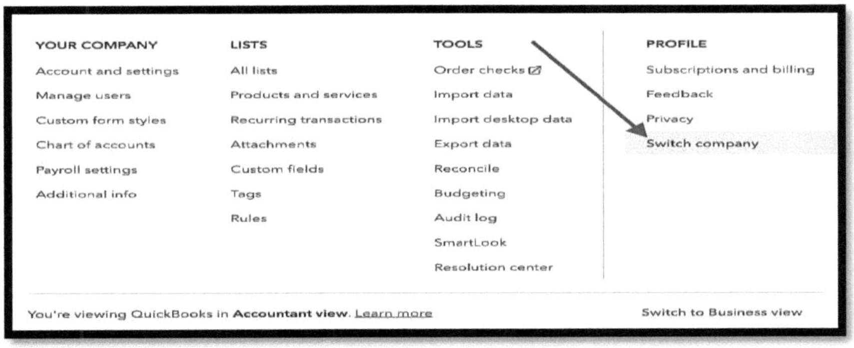

Step 3: Select the Company

QuickBooks Online will display a list of all companies you can access, including those you own or that have been shared with you. Click the **company name** you want to switch to.

Step 4: Confirm Your Selection

Double-check that you've selected the correct company. Confirm your choice to proceed—QuickBooks will switch you to the selected company's data.

Step 5: Start Working in the New Company

Once confirmed, QuickBooks Online transitions to the new company. You can now manage its financial data just as you would your primary company.

This process makes it quick and easy to **move between multiple QuickBooks Online accounts** without logging out or losing your workflow.

TOP QUICKBOOKS ONLINE FEATURES YOU NEED TO KNOW

QuickBooks Online 2026 has evolved with powerful tools and AI enhancements designed to make managing your business faster, smarter, and more efficient. Here are the top features that could solve problems you didn't even know you had:

1. AI Agents Handle Daily Tasks

QuickBooks Online now includes **three specialized AI agents** to streamline bookkeeping and business management:

- **Accounting Agent:** Keeps your books accurate and flags items that need attention.
- **Payments Agent:** Speeds up bill processing and ensures timely payments.
- **Finance Agent:** Summarizes financial data, helping you stay on track with your goals.

These agents do the heavy lifting but **don't make decisions for you**—you review and approve all actions. Accountants can expect an enhanced AI client-service experience in a beta release soon.

2. Inventory Tracking for Any Plan

Even **Simple Start and Essentials subscribers** can now access inventory management for **$40/month** as an add-on. Features include:

- Inventory tracking and management
- Sales and purchase orders
- Shipping management
- Consolidated inventory dashboard

No need to upgrade your plan to manage stock effectively—setup is guided and intuitive.

3. Turn Invoices Into Automatic Payments

Recurring invoices can now be converted into **recurring payments**, improving cash flow and eliminating manual reconciliation.

Setup process:

1. Create a recurring payment from a recurring invoice in the Sales tab.
2. Send the payment request to your customer.
3. Customers securely submit payment through QuickBooks' portal.
4. Payments are processed automatically on schedule.

This ensures **predictable cash flow** while keeping customer payment information secure.

4. Calculate True Employee Costs

For **Plus and Advanced users**, the built-in **employee cost rate calculator** integrates with QuickBooks Online Payroll to factor in:

- Pay rates and benefits
- Tax obligations and insurance
- Overhead expenses
- FICA contributions

Employee costs automatically apply to project time entries, providing **real-time profitability insights**. You can also update multiple employees' cost rates simultaneously.

5. Reverse Direct Deposits Easily

QuickBooks Online Payroll allows you to **reverse direct deposits within five days**:

1. Go to Reports in Payroll.
2. Select the direct deposit to reverse.
3. Click **Reverse** and complete the request.

This solves errors like duplicates, miscalculations, or terminated employees efficiently—no external bank calls needed.

6. Switch from QuickBooks Desktop to Online with Ease

Migrating from Desktop to Online has never been simpler:

- **Preserve payroll data:** Import Desktop accounting data without affecting QuickBooks Online Payroll.
- **Handle larger datasets:** Migrate up to 1.2 million line items (up from 750,000).
- **Pre-migration checklist:** Step-by-step guide to prepare your files.
- **AI-powered time estimates:** Get realistic expectations for migration duration.

These improvements reduce migration headaches, preserve historical data, and make the transition smoother for established businesses.

7. Access Professional Cleanup Services for Firms

QuickBooks Live Expert Cleanup helps accounting firms manage client workload during peak periods:

- QuickBooks-certified bookkeepers complete cleanup within 30 days
- Books prepared for tax readiness

- Year-end financial reports included
- Optional review call with the client

Pricing:

- Prior tax year: $800 flat rate
- Current tax year: $150/month

Ideal for firms that need to maintain client relationships without overextending internal resources.

8. Accept Payments Anywhere with Your iPhone

With **Tap to Pay on iPhone**, your phone becomes a complete payment processing device—no extra hardware required. Available via the **QuickBooks GoPayment app** or **QuickBooks mobile app**, this feature offers:

- No separate card readers or cables needed
- 2.5% processing fee
- Lower costs than manually keyed-in payments
- Team members can process payments safely without accessing sensitive info

Simply tap your customer's card or phone to complete a transaction. This feature is rolling out in phases for iPhone users; Android support hasn't been announced yet.

9. Give Customers Their Own Financial Dashboard

QuickBooks Customer Hub, powered by Mailchimp, strengthens customer relationships for $15/month (first month free). Key benefits:

- Collect and display reviews and testimonials
- Facilitate referrals with easy-to-use tools
- Allow customers to request repeat services

This is perfect for service-based businesses that rely on customer satisfaction and referrals. Access Customer Hub via the **Customers & Leads** tab.

10. Replace Confusing Tags with Custom Fields

QuickBooks Online now uses **custom fields** instead of tags, offering greater flexibility for tracking business-specific data. Existing tags remain, but new users will use custom fields. Benefits include:

- Track sales reps on invoices
- Monitor project codes across transactions

- Categorize expenses by department or location
- Generate reports based on custom criteria

QuickBooks also expanded custom field limits:

- Simple Start: 1 field
- Essentials & Plus: 4 fields (up from 3)
- Advanced: 12 fields

Custom fields appear directly on forms, making data entry intuitive for your team.

SWITCH BETWEEN BUSINESS AND ACCOUNTANT VIEW IN QUICKBOOKS ONLINE

QuickBooks Online lets you **choose the interface that best suits your accounting style**. Whether you prefer a simplified layout or a detailed accounting view, you can switch between **Business** and **Accountant** views at any time—your data remains intact.

Why Two Views?

1. **Business View**

   - Ideal for beginners or those who prefer simplicity.
   - Uses everyday language.
   - Focuses on common tasks like sales, invoicing, and expenses.

2. **Accountant View**

   - Designed for experienced accountants or users needing full QuickBooks functionality.
   - Uses traditional accounting terminology.
   - Offers a more detailed interface with advanced features.

Key Differences

Feature	Business View	Accountant View
Dashboard	Cash flow chart visible	No cash flow chart
Language	Simplified menus	Standard accounting terms
Functionality	Same as Accountant view	Full features accessible

How to Switch Views

1. Click **Settings** ⚙ in the top-right corner.
2. Select **Switch to Business View** or **Switch to Accountant View**.

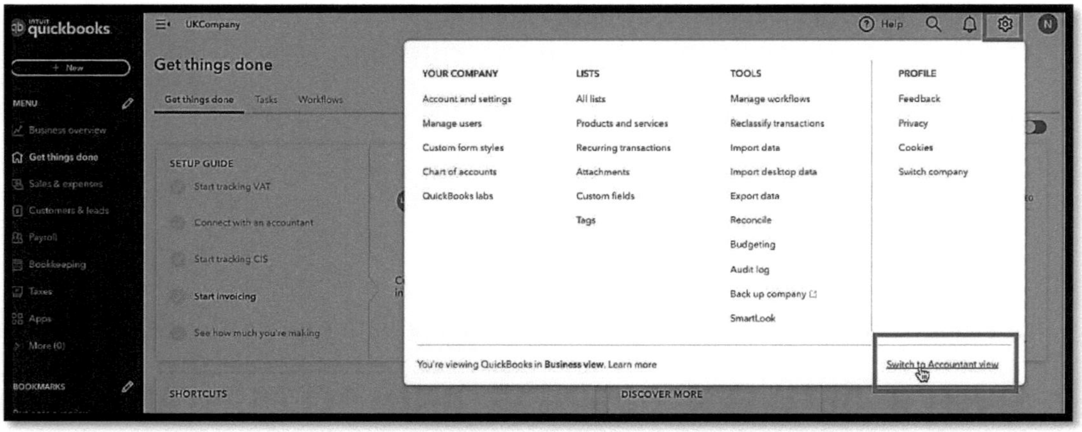

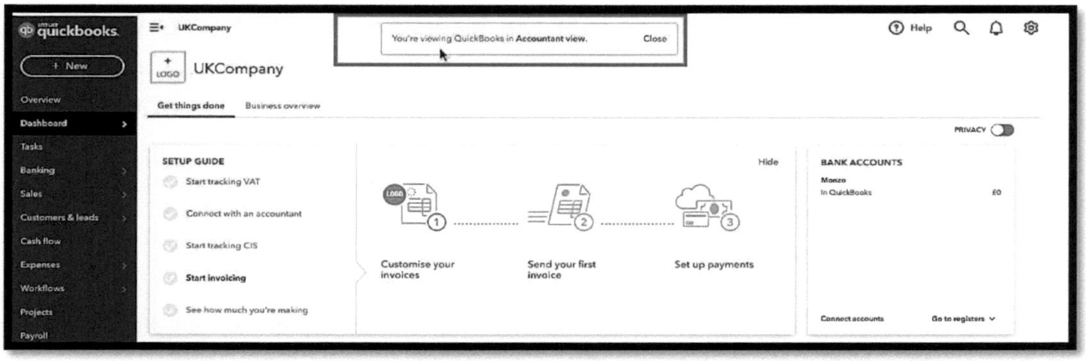

QuickBooks determines your default view based on your initial setup, but you can switch at any time.

Manage Bookmarks

Bookmarks let you **pin frequently used pages** for quick access, saving time in your daily tasks.

To customize bookmarks:

1. Next to **Bookmarks**, click **Edit** ✎.
2. Check the pages you want to display.
3. To reorder bookmarks, click **Reorder** ⠿ and drag items into your preferred order.
4. To remove a bookmark, uncheck the pages you no longer need.
5. Click **Save** to apply your changes.

This setup ensures your QuickBooks Online workspace is **tailored to your workflow**, whether you prefer simplicity or full accounting control.

QUICKBOOKS CHART OF ACCOUNTS: EVERYTHING YOU NEED TO KNOW

Managing your business finances in QuickBooks Online starts with a solid understanding of the **Chart of Accounts (COA)**. Think of the COA as the backbone of your accounting system—it organizes all financial transactions into meaningful categories, ensuring accurate reporting and insights. Whether you're a small business owner or an experienced accountant, a well-structured COA keeps your financial data organized and actionable.

What is the Chart of Accounts in QuickBooks?

The **Chart of Accounts** is a complete list of all accounts your business uses to track transactions. It includes:

- **Assets** – what your business owns
- **Liabilities** – what your business owes
- **Income** – money coming in
- **Expenses** – money going out
- **Equity** – owner's stake in the business

Each account acts as a category for transactions, helping you monitor cash flow, profits, and financial health. In essence, the COA provides a **financial map of your business.**

How to Access the Chart of Accounts in QuickBooks Online

1. Click the **Settings** ⚙ icon in the top-right corner.

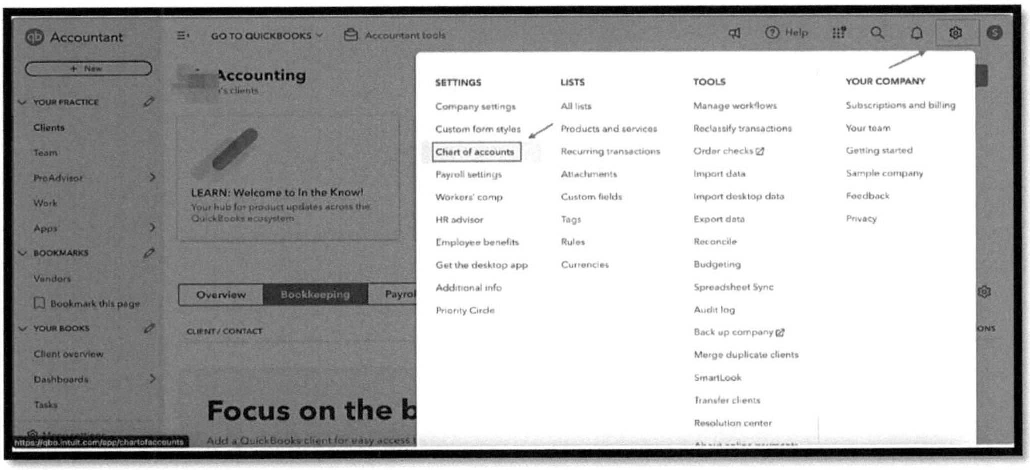

2. Select **Chart of Accounts** from the drop-down menu.

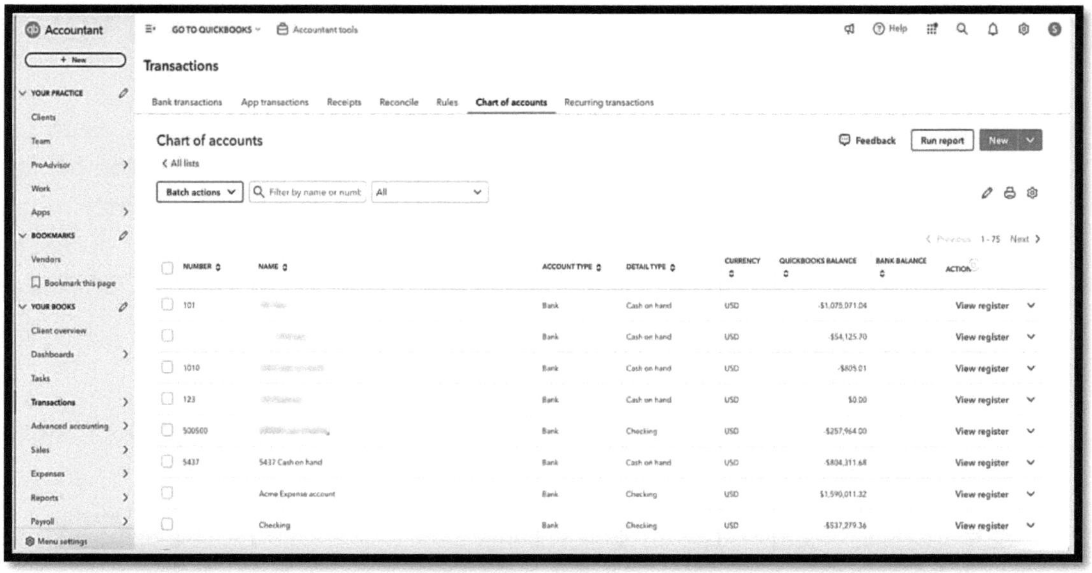

Here, you'll see a list of all accounts in your company file. Ensure your COA covers all workflows so transactions are recorded correctly for accurate reporting.

QuickBooks Online comes with default accounts such as **Sales**, **Services**, and **Billable Expense Income**, but you can customize or add new accounts to fit your business needs.

How to Add a New Account in QuickBooks Online

1. On the **Chart of Accounts** page, click **New**.

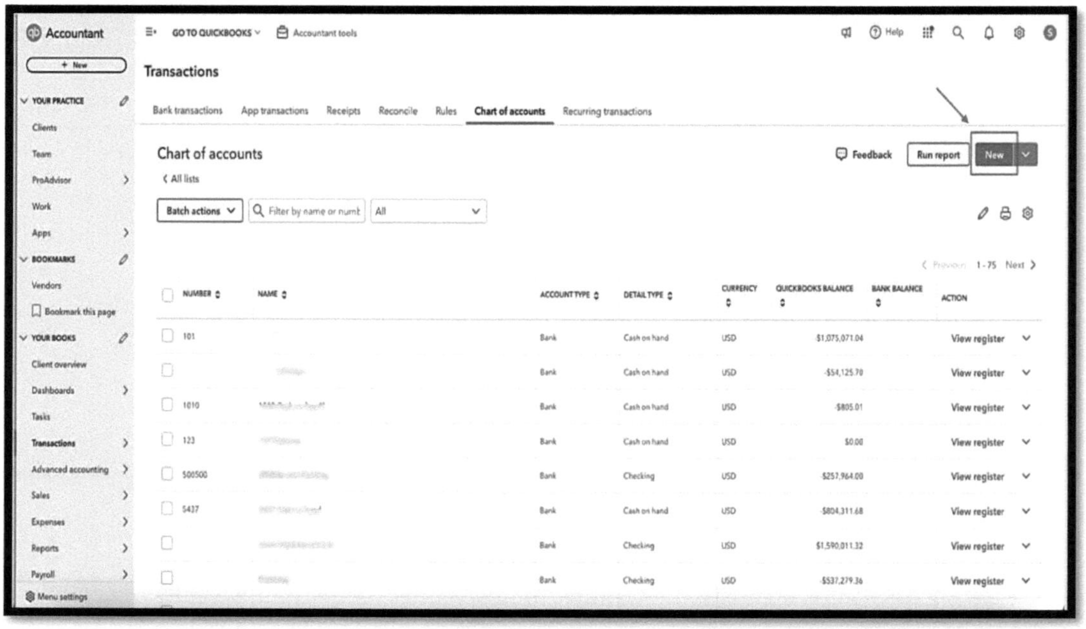

2. A form will appear—fill in the required fields:

Field	Purpose	Example (Construction Business)
Account Name	The name you want to assign to the account. Should be descriptive.	"Construction Income"
Account Number	Unique numeric identifier for organization and reporting.	"4000"
Account Type	Broad category for financial reporting.	"Income" or "Expense"
Detail Type	More specific classification within the account type.	"Service/Fee Income" or "Discounts/Refunds Given"

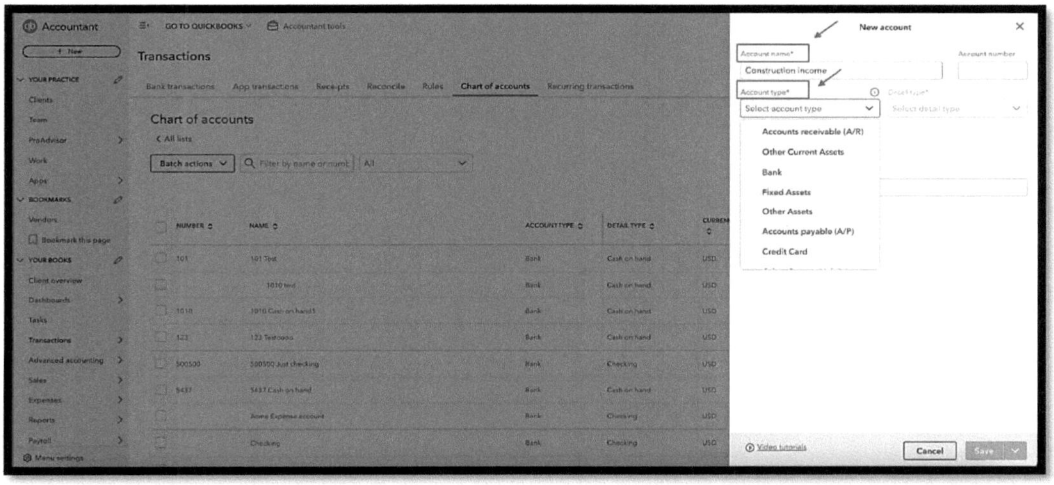

3. Click **Save** to add the account.

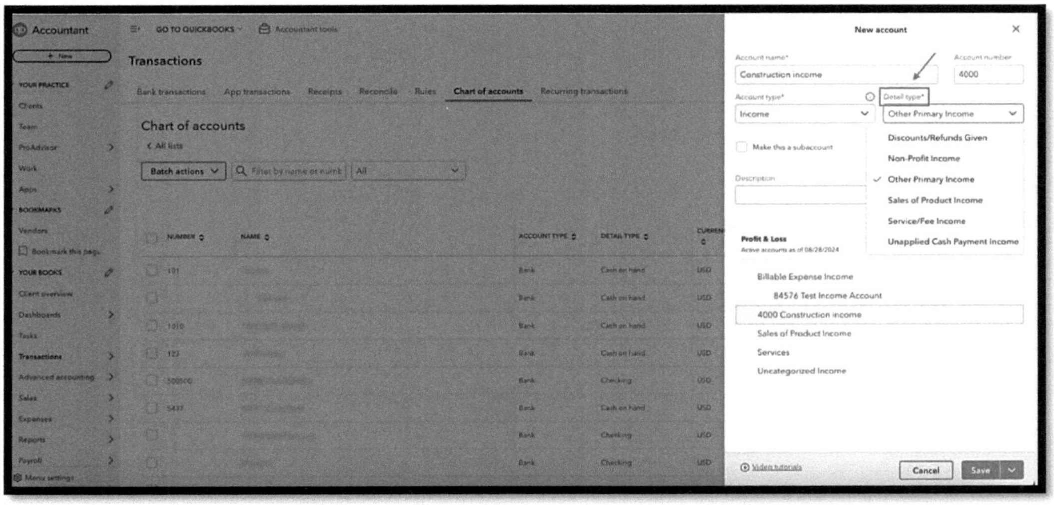

Now your new account is searchable. Typing the account name (e.g., "Construction") in the search bar will display it in your COA list.

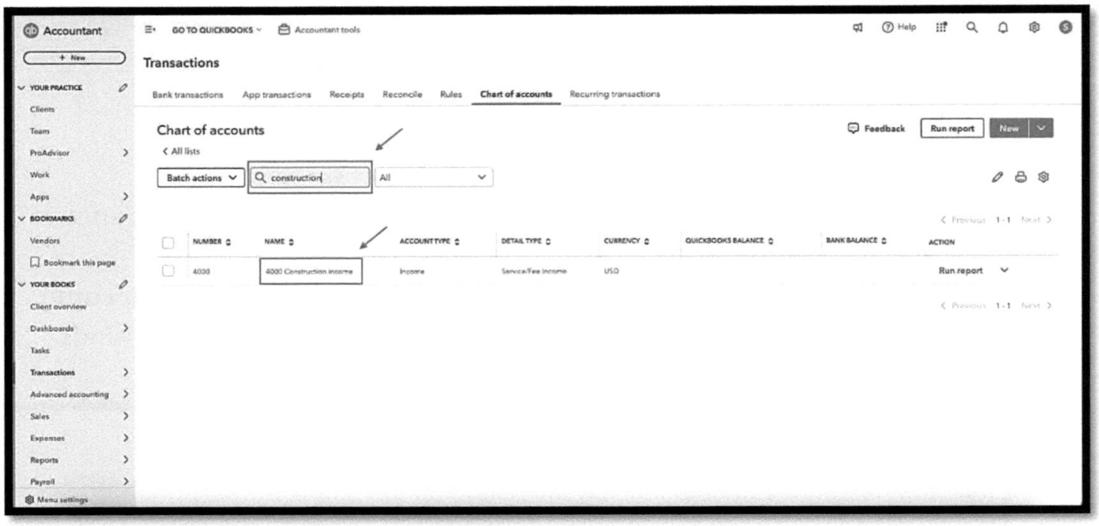

Tips for a Well-Organized COA

- Keep account names clear and consistent.
- Use account numbers for easier organization and reporting.
- Review and clean up old or unused accounts periodically.
- Align account types and detail types with your business operations for accurate financial insights.

How to Deactivate and Reactivate Accounts in the QuickBooks Online Chart of Accounts

Keeping your Chart of Accounts clean and organized is essential for accurate financial reporting. As your business grows or changes, some accounts may no longer be needed. Instead of deleting them, QuickBooks Online allows you to **deactivate (make inactive)** these accounts so they no longer appear in your active list—but their historical data remains intact.

Below is a clear guide on **how to deactivate and reactivate** accounts in QuickBooks Online.

How to Deactivate a Chart of Accounts Entry in QuickBooks Online

Follow these steps to remove an account from your active list:

Step 1: Open the Chart of Accounts

1. Go to **Transactions** in the left navigation menu.

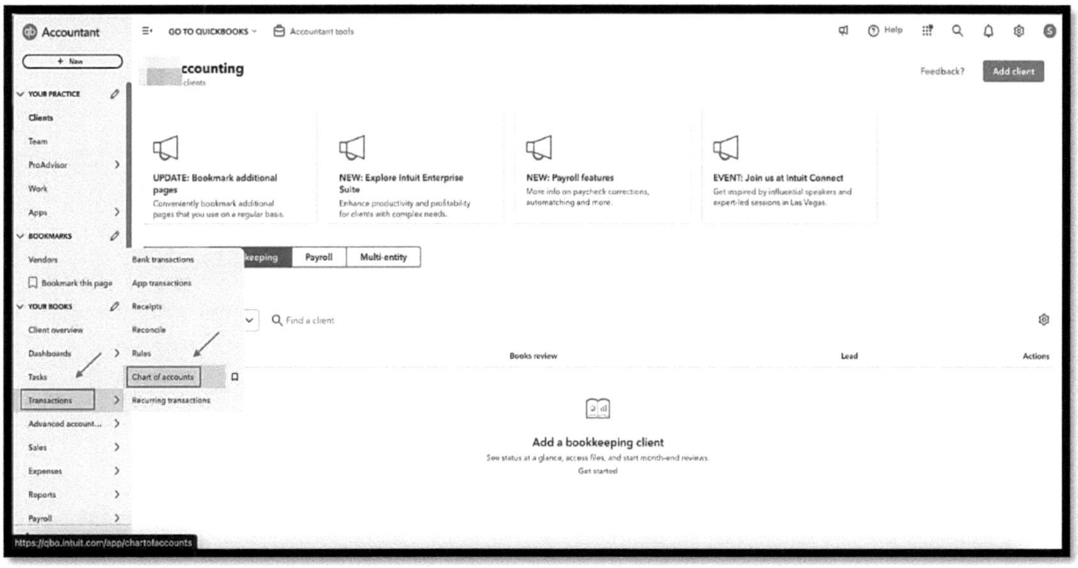

2. Select **Chart of Accounts.**

You will now see the full list of all your accounts.

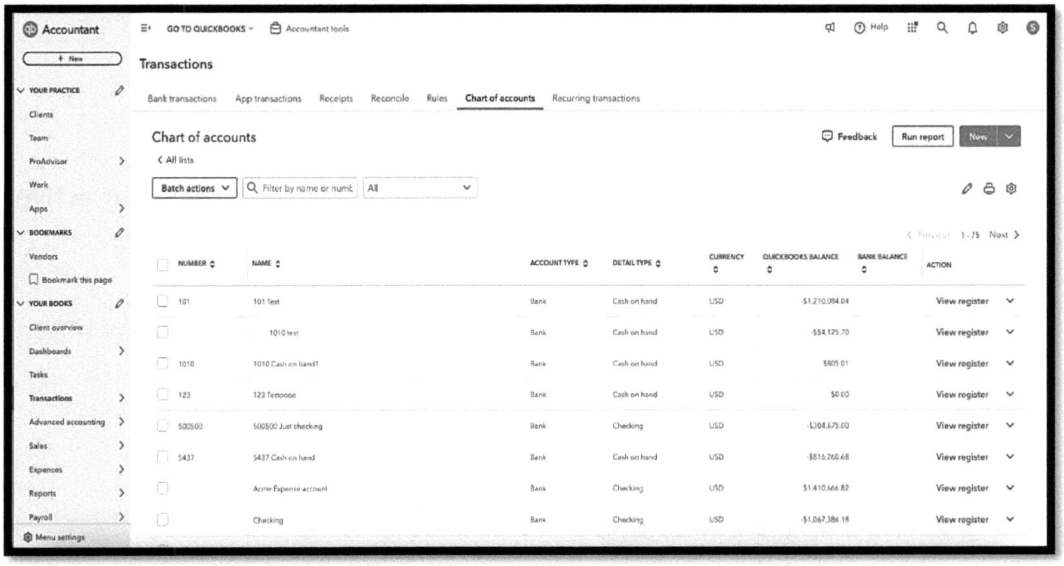

Step 2: Make the Account Inactive

1. Find the account you want to deactivate.
2. Select **Batch actions** at the top of the list.
3. Click **Make inactive.**

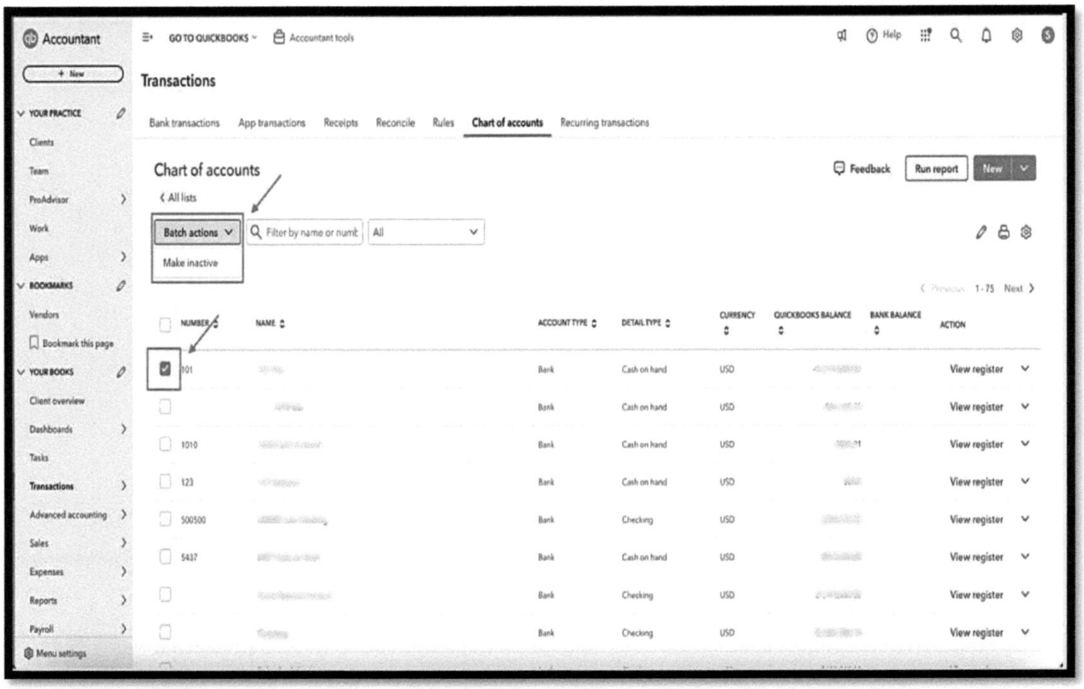

QuickBooks will display a confirmation message:

"Are you sure you want to make this account inactive?"

Click **Yes, make inactive** to confirm.

Your account is now successfully deactivated and removed from your active list.

How to Reactivate an Account in QuickBooks Online

If you need to use an inactive account again, you can restore it at any time.

Step 1: Open the Chart of Accounts

- Again, go to **Transactions** → **Chart of Accounts**.

Step 2: Show Inactive Accounts

1. Click the small **Gear icon** above the Action column.
2. Check the box for **Include inactive**.

All inactive accounts will now be visible, typically marked with *(deleted)* next to the name.

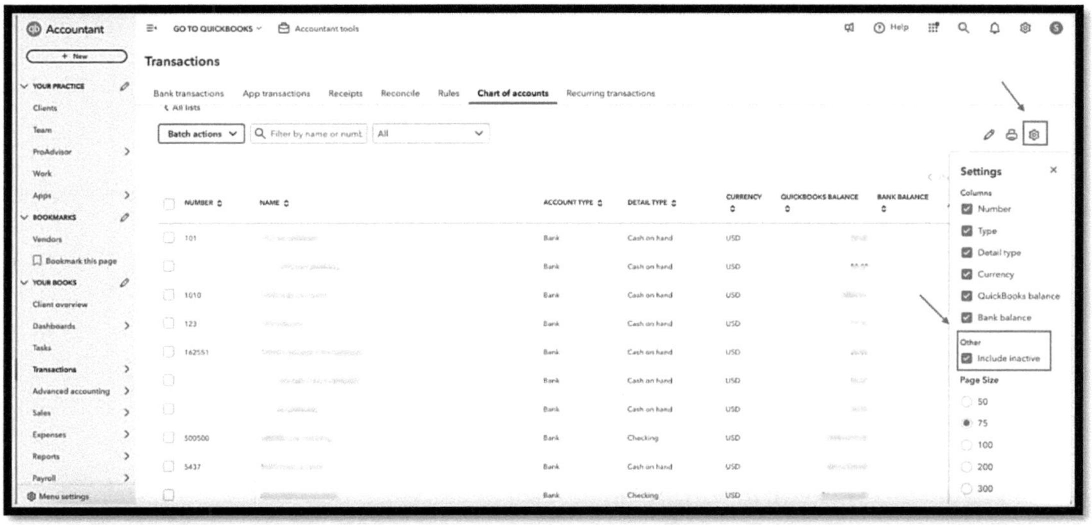

Step 3: Make the Account Active Again

1. Search for the account by typing its name in the search bar.

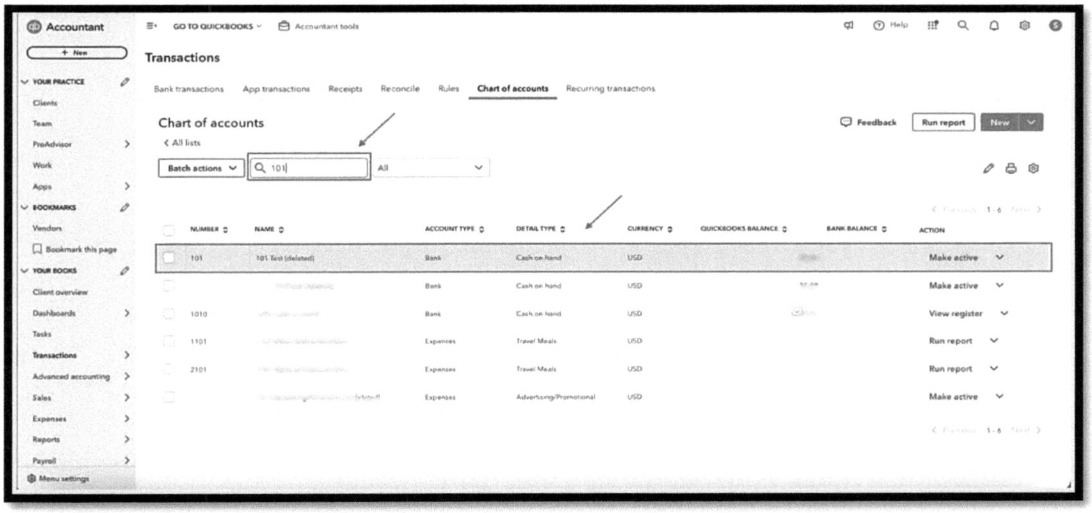

2. Click **Make active** in the Action column.

Your account is now restored and ready for use.

How to Import and Export the Chart of Accounts in QuickBooks Online

QuickBooks Online allows you to quickly build or modify your Chart of Accounts (COA) by importing a spreadsheet—saving time and reducing manual data entry. This is especially helpful when setting up a new company, migrating from another accounting system, or moving from QuickBooks Desktop to Online.

Below is a complete step-by-step guide on how to **import**, **review**, **fix**, and **export** your Chart of Accounts in QuickBooks Online.

Importing a Chart of Accounts in QuickBooks Online

Tip: Importing is easiest during your initial company setup. If you only need a few accounts, creating them manually may be faster.

Step 1: Prepare Your Spreadsheet

You can use **Excel**, **Google Sheets**, or a **CSV file**. Before importing:

Your spreadsheet should include these columns:

- **Account Number** (optional)
- **Account Name**
- **Type**
- **Detail Type**

Subaccount formatting:

Use this format in the Account Name column:

Main Account: Subaccount

Example: Utilities: Gas

This ensures QuickBooks creates the subaccount correctly.

Once formatted, save as:

- .xlsx
- .csv
- Google Sheet (connecting your Google account during upload)

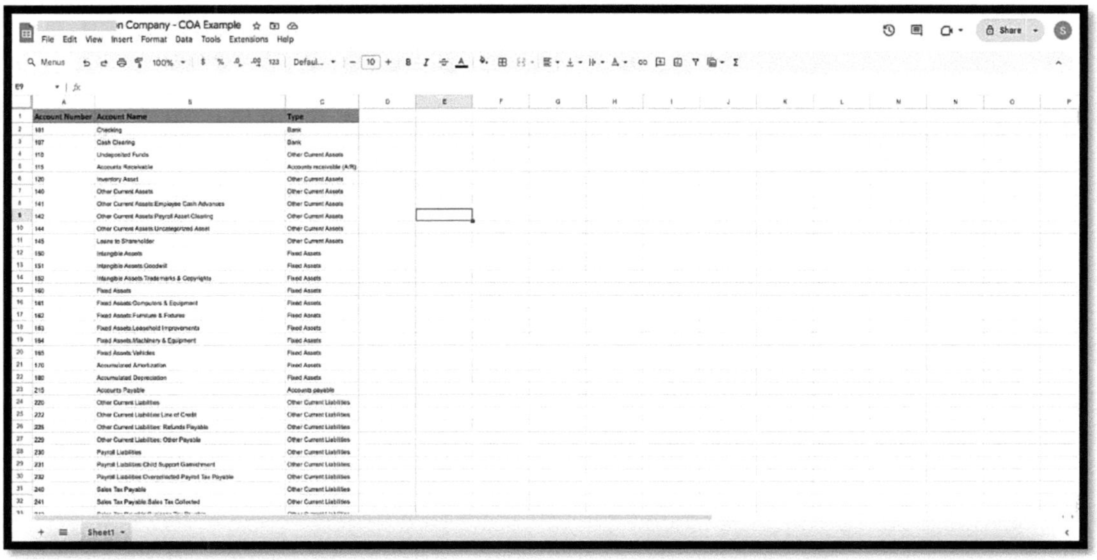

Account Number	Account Name	Type
101	Checking	Bank
107	Cash Clearing	Bank
110	Undeposited Funds	Other Current Assets
115	Accounts Receivable	Accounts receivable (A/R)
120	Inventory Asset	Other Current Assets
140	Other Current Assets	Other Current Assets
141	Other Current Assets:Employee Cash Advances	Other Current Assets
142	Other Current Assets:Payroll Asset Clearing	Other Current Assets
144	Other Current Assets:Uncategorized Asset	Other Current Assets
145	Loans to Shareholder	Other Current Assets
150	Intangible Assets	Fixed Assets
151	Intangible Assets:Goodwill	Fixed Assets
152	Intangible Assets:Trademarks & Copyrights	Fixed Assets
160	Fixed Assets	Fixed Assets
161	Fixed Assets:Computers & Equipment	Fixed Assets
162	Fixed Assets:Furniture & Fixtures	Fixed Assets
163	Fixed Assets:Leasehold Improvements	Fixed Assets
164	Fixed Assets:Machinery & Equipment	Fixed Assets
165	Fixed Assets:Vehicles	Fixed Assets
170	Accumulated Amortization	Fixed Assets
180	Accumulated Depreciation	Fixed Assets
215	Accounts Payable	Accounts payable
220	Other Current Liabilities	Other Current Liabilities
222	Other Current Liabilities:Line of Credit	Other Current Liabilities
225	Other Current Liabilities: Refunds Payable	Other Current Liabilities
229	Other Current Liabilities: Other Payable	Other Current Liabilities
230	Payroll Liabilities	Other Current Liabilities
231	Payroll Liabilities:Child Support Garnishment	Other Current Liabilities
232	Payroll Liabilities:Overcollected Payroll Tax Payable	Other Current Liabilities
240	Sales Tax Payable	Other Current Liabilities
241	Sales Tax Payable:Sales Tax Collected	Other Current Liabilities

Step 2: Upload Your File

1. Log in to QuickBooks Online.
2. Go to **Settings ⚙ → Import Data**.
3. Choose **Chart of Accounts**, then select **Import**.

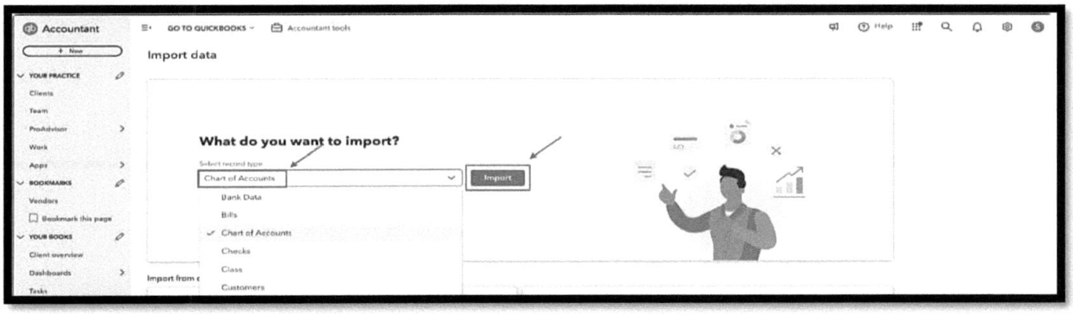

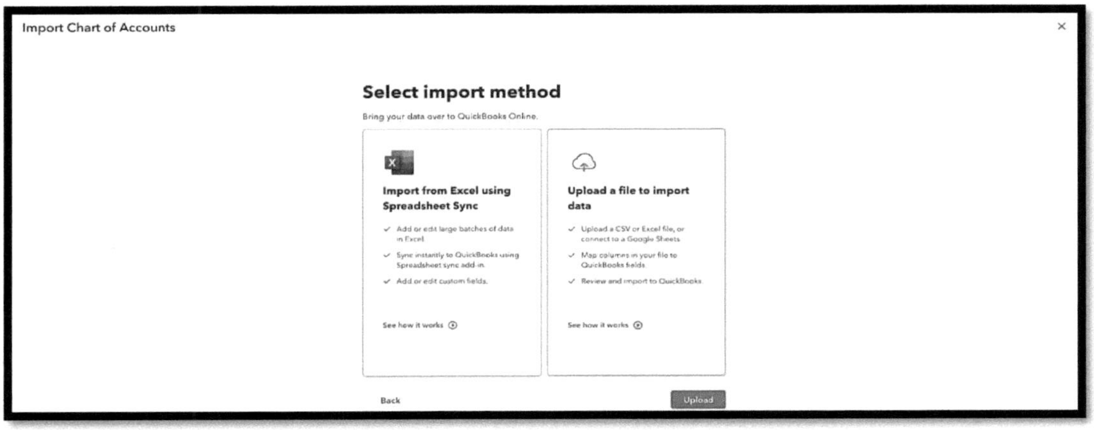

You now have **two upload options**:

Option 1: Import Using Spreadsheet Sync (Excel Add-In)

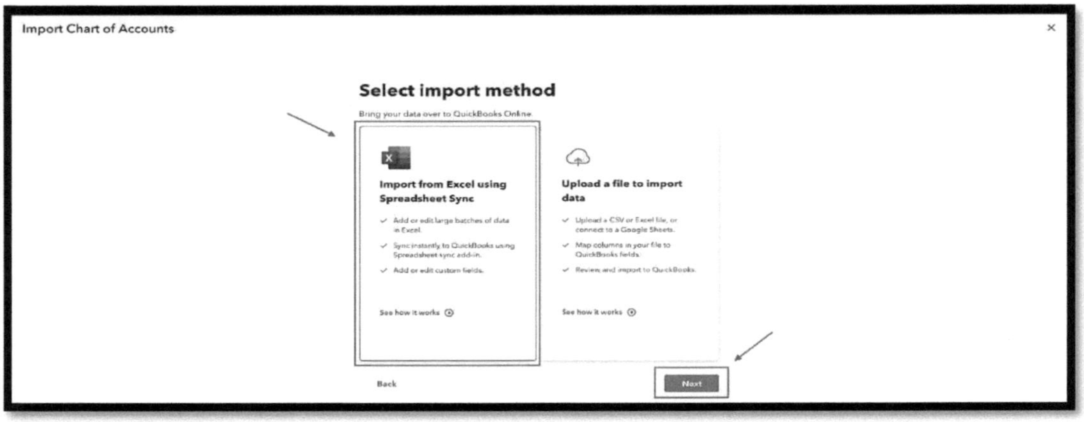

Choose **Import from Excel using Spreadsheet Sync → Next.**

Spreadsheet Sync allows two-way data flow between QuickBooks and Excel.

Follow the prompts:

1. Let your browser open Excel.
2. Approve the add-in by selecting **Trust this add-in**.
3. Sign in with your Intuit account.
4. Follow the on-screen GIF/tutorial.

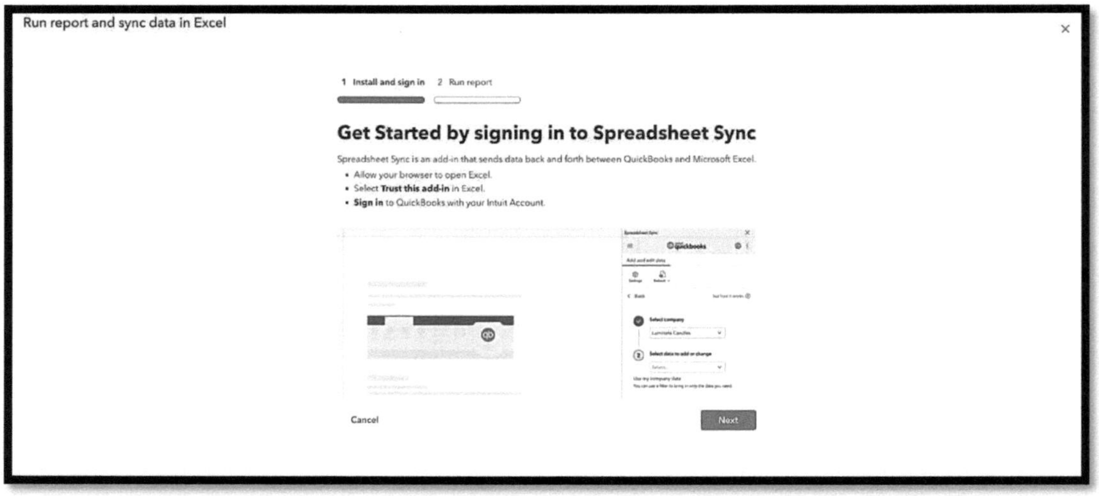

After setup, you can:

❖ Run QuickBooks reports in Excel

- ❖ Filter & modify data
- ❖ Refresh reports anytime

Click **Let's go!** when ready.

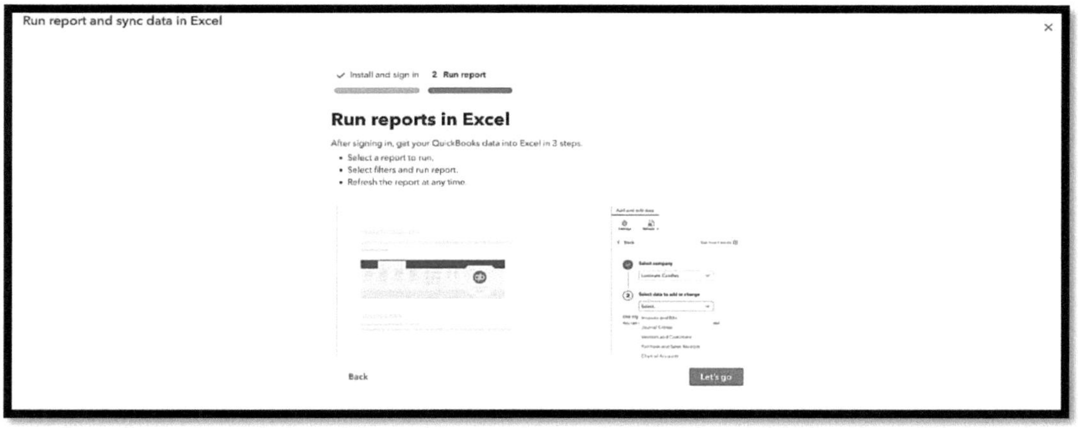

Option 2: Upload a File Directly

Select **Upload a file to import data → Upload**.

You may:

- ❖ Browse your computer for your .csv or .xlsx
- ❖ Or connect Google Sheets (requires signing in to your Gmail)

Choose your file and continue.

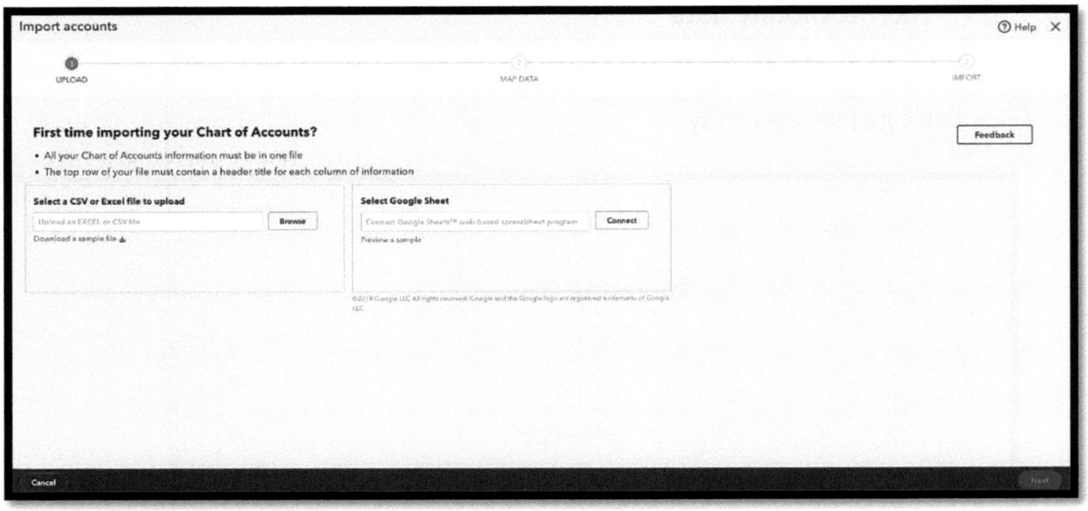

Step 3: Map Your Fields

QuickBooks will load your spreadsheet and ask you to match your column names with its fields.

Use the **Your Field ▼** dropdowns to map:

- ❖ Account Name
- ❖ Account Number
- ❖ Type
- ❖ Detail Type

If your spreadsheet does not include a matching column (e.g., you're not using account numbers), choose **No Match**.

Click **Next** to continue.

Step 4: Review and Import

Before importing, QuickBooks shows you a preview of all accounts.

Check the following:

- ❖ Account Type and Detail Type are correct
- ❖ All required fields are filled
- ❖ Red-highlighted fields indicate errors—hover to see the issue

You may **deselect** any account you don't want to import.

If everything looks correct, click **Import**.

Step 5: Enter Opening Balances

After your accounts are imported:

- ❖ Enter opening balances using a **journal entry**, or
- ❖ Let QuickBooks pull balances automatically when you connect your bank accounts

Step 6: Connect Bank and Credit Card Accounts

To download transactions automatically:

1. Go to **Transactions → Bank transactions**
2. Connect your bank or credit card
3. QuickBooks will begin importing your activity

This helps categorize transactions into the newly created COA accounts.

How to Run and Export a Chart of Accounts Report

If you need a copy of your Chart of Accounts—for a client, an audit, or internal review—QuickBooks lets you export it quickly.

Step 1: Open the Chart of Accounts

- ❖ Log in to QuickBooks Online
- ❖ Go to **Transactions → Chart of Accounts**

Step 2: Run the Chart of Accounts Report

Click **Run report** in the upper-right corner.

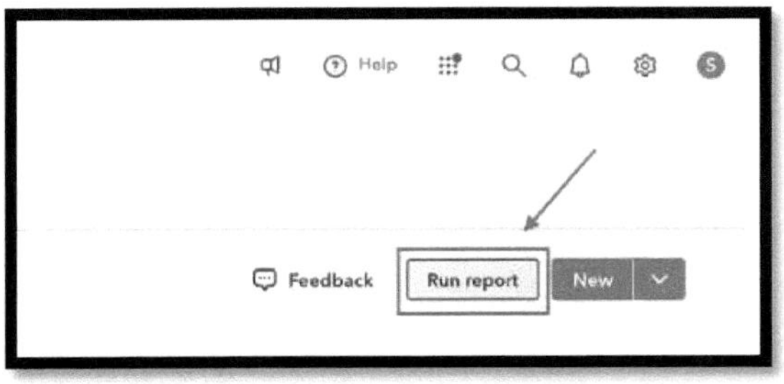

This generates a full report of all active accounts.

Step 3: Export the Report

Select the **Export icon** and choose one of two formats:

PDF

- ❖ Preview the report
- ❖ Adjust orientation (portrait/landscape)
- ❖ Email the PDF directly if needed

XLSX (Excel)

- ❖ File downloads automatically
- ❖ Ideal for editing or sharing

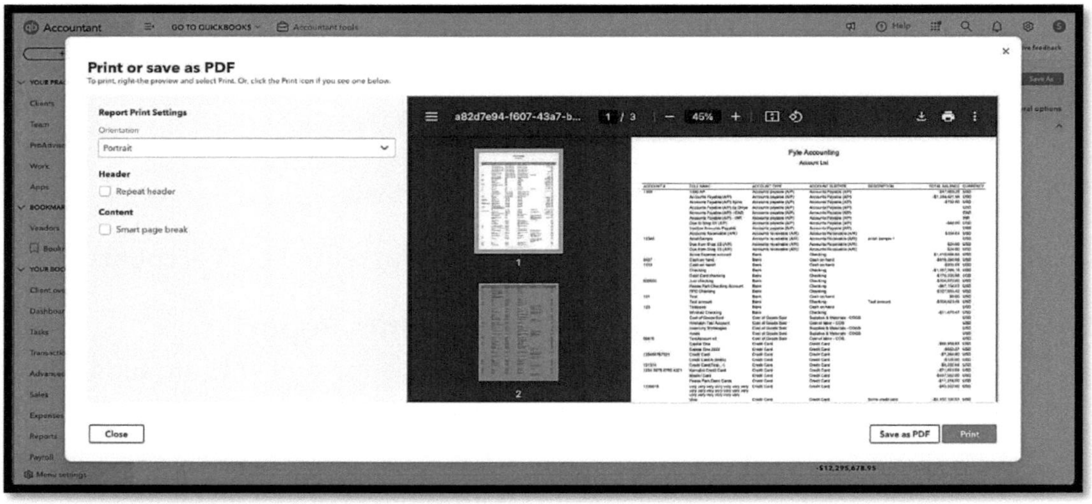

If you frequently export COA data, you may want to explore automated solutions to streamline the process.

How to Delete a Chart of Accounts in QuickBooks Online

In QuickBooks Online (QBO), you *delete* an account by marking it **inactive**. Although the **Action** column offers various options, the correct way to remove an account is through the **View register** dropdown.

Follow the steps below:

Steps to Delete (Make Inactive) an Account in QBO

1. **Log in** to your QuickBooks Online account.
2. Go to the **Transactions** menu on the left sidebar and select **Chart of Accounts.**
3. Locate the account you want to remove and click the **checkbox** beside it.
4. In the **Action** column, click the **View register** dropdown and select **Make inactive.**

Once completed, the account will be hidden from your active Chart of Accounts but can be restored at any time if needed.

How to Merge Accounts in QuickBooks Online

Merging accounts helps streamline your books by combining duplicate or similar accounts into one. This process improves accuracy and simplifies your financial organization.

Steps to Merge Accounts in QBO

1. Go to the **Gear** icon.
2. Select **All Lists**.

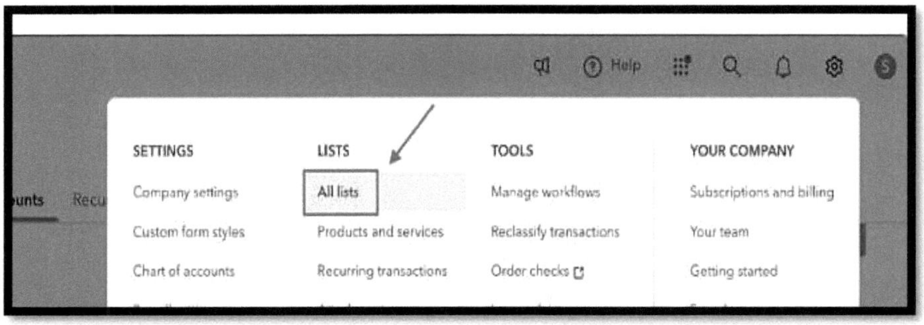

3. Click **Chart of Accounts.**

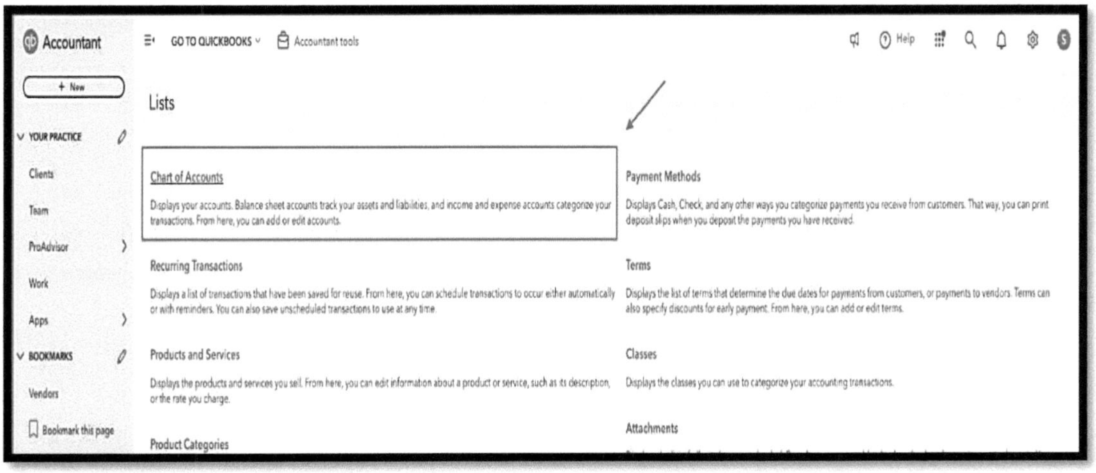

4. Identify the account **you want to keep**.
5. Open the account you want to merge and **rename it exactly** to match the name of the account you want to keep.
6. Click **Save**.
7. When prompted, confirm by selecting **Yes, merge accounts**.
8. Click **Save** again to complete the process.

Important Notes

❖ Merging accounts is **permanent** and cannot be undone.
❖ Accounts connected to **online banking** cannot be merged or deleted.
❖ Save reconciliation reports **before merging** accounts that have reconciliation history.
❖ Parent accounts cannot be merged if they contain sub-accounts.
❖ Sub-accounts can only be merged if both belong to the **same parent account**.
❖ If one account is a sub-account and the other is not, update the **Account Type** to match exactly before merging.

How to Print Your Chart of Accounts in QuickBooks Online

Printing your Chart of Accounts is easy and useful for audits, reviews, or documentation.

Steps to Print the Chart of Accounts

1. Go to the **Transactions** menu and select **Chart of Accounts**.
2. Click the **Print** icon located above the **Action** column.

3. In the Print window, confirm your print settings and choose the number of copies.
4. Click **Print**.

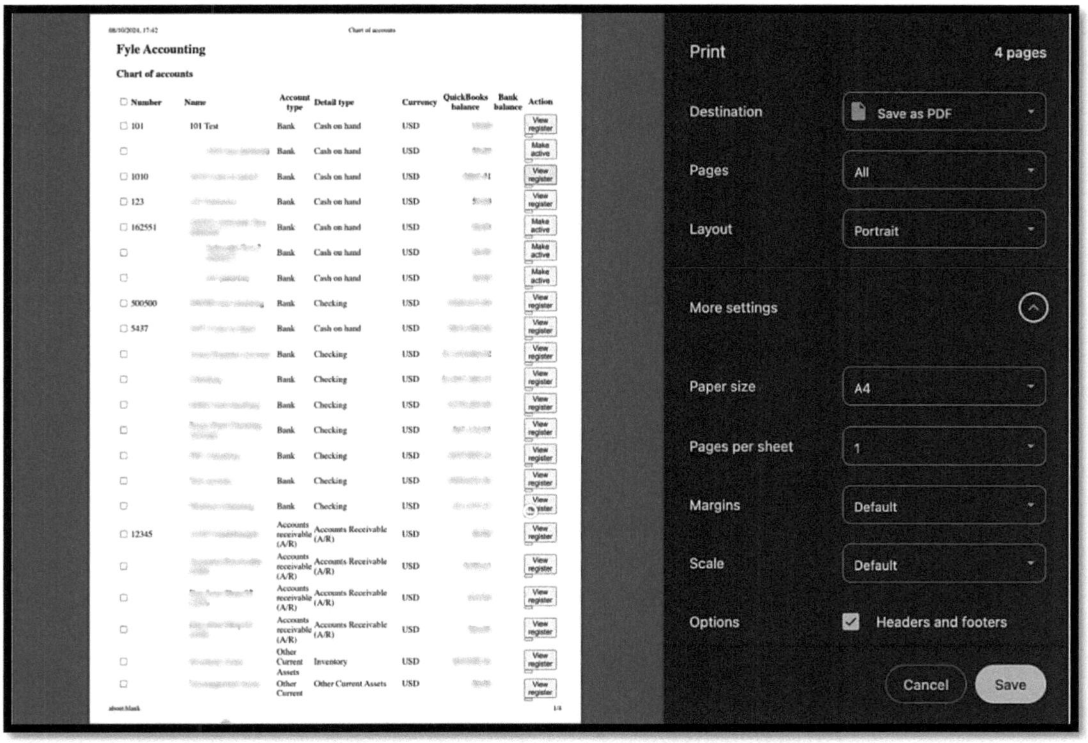

WORKING WITH ATTACHMENTS IN QUICKBOOKS ONLINE

QuickBooks Online (QBO) allows you to add attachments to customer and vendor profiles, as well as their associated transactions. This feature helps keep records organized and makes it easier for accountants to manage financial documentation during audits or at fiscal year-end.

Transactions That Support Attachments

Note: QuickBooks Online does **not** support adding PDF attachments to statements sent to customers.

You can attach documents to the following transactions and profiles:

- Bills, Checks, Credit Card transactions, Credit Memos, Customers, Delayed Charges, Estimates, Expenses, Invoices, Receive Payments, Refund Receipts, Sales Receipts, Vendors, and Vendor Credits

Additional Notes:

- When opening attachments from a web-based email (Gmail, Yahoo, Outlook, etc.), ensure Adobe Acrobat (latest version) is the default PDF viewer.
- You **cannot** attach files directly to list items such as Accounts or Employee Names.

- ❖ Attachment file names must **not** contain special characters.

Supported Attachment File Types

For security and compatibility, QuickBooks Online supports the following file formats:

- ❖ PDF, JPEG, PNG, DOC, XLSX, CSV, TIFF, GIF, and XML

How to Attach a Document

Attach to a Vendor Profile

1. Select **Vendors**.
2. Choose a vendor and open the **Vendor Details** tab.
3. Select **Attachments**.
4. Browse for the file you want to upload and select **Open**.

Attach to a Customer Profile

1. Go to **Customer Hub** and select **Customers**.
2. Choose a customer and open the **Customer Details** tab.
3. Select **Attachments**.
4. Browse for the file and click **Open**.

Attach to a Transaction

1. Open the transaction you wish to edit.
2. Select **Attachments**.
3. Browse for the document and select **Open**.
4. Click **Save and close**.

View, Edit, or Delete Attachments

You can also upload files directly to the **Attachments** list without linking them to a specific profile or transaction. From this list, you can edit, download, remove, or use attachments to create new transactions.

Manage Attachments

1. Select **Settings** ⚙.
2. Choose **Attachments**.
3. In the Attachments list, choose one of the following actions:
   - ❖ **Upload Attachment** – Select **Attachments**, choose a file, then select **Open**.
   - ❖ **Download** – Select a file from the list and click **Download**.

- ❖ **Edit** – Select the **Download ▼** dropdown next to a file and choose **Edit**. You may update the File Name or add Notes.
- ❖ **Delete** – Select **Download ▼ > Delete**, then confirm by selecting **Yes**.
- ❖ **Create Invoice** – Select **Download ▼ > Create invoice** to generate a new invoice with the attachment included.
- ❖ **Create Expense** – Select **Download ▼ > Create expense** to open a new expense with the file attached.

Move Your Files from QuickBooks Desktop to QuickBooks Online

Migrating from QuickBooks Desktop to QuickBooks Online is a straightforward process, especially when it comes to bringing your attachments along. QuickBooks ensures that your files and documents stay connected to the transactions they belong to.

1. Start the Migration

Begin by launching the built-in **migration tool** within QuickBooks Desktop. This tool prepares your company file and guides you through the transfer process.

2. Choose to Include Attachments

During migration setup, you'll be asked whether you want to include your attachments. Select this option if you want supporting documents—such as receipts, bills, and invoices—to transfer with your data.

3. Let QuickBooks Handle the Transfer

Once initiated, QuickBooks automatically moves your attachments and maps them to the correct transactions in QuickBooks Online. No extra steps are required on your part.

CHAPTER TWO

MANAGING USERS, MULTICURRENCY, AND CUSTOM FIELD

QuickBooks Online (QBO) handles user management, multicurrency, and custom fields through specific settings available in its Plus or Advanced subscription tiers.

ADD AND MANAGE USERS IN QUICKBOOKS ONLINE

QuickBooks Online allows you to add users to help with company operations and bookkeeping. Each user can be assigned a specific role with customized permissions, and you can also give your accountant secure access to your company's books.

Note: Only users with administrative permissions can manage user profiles.

Adding a New User

Your subscription determines how many users you can add. Some roles, like **View-only** or **Track time only**, do **not** count toward your user limit.

Steps:

1. Go to **Settings ⚙ → Manage users**.
2. Select **Add user**, then enter the user's **name** and **email address**.
   - ❖ Allowed characters:
     - ❖ **Name:** letters, numbers, and periods
     - ❖ **Email:** letters, numbers, periods, and "@"
3. Open the **Roles ▼** dropdown and choose the user's role.
4. Review the permissions for the role by expanding each section.
5. Adjust **Account management** settings if applicable.
6. Select **Send invitation**.

The invited user will receive an email to accept the invitation and create access.

Managing User Roles and Permissions

You can update a user's role or permissions at any time. **Note:** "Track time only" roles cannot be edited; they must be deleted and re-added.

Steps to Edit a User:

1. Go to **Settings ⚙ → Manage users**.
2. Find the user and select **Edit** in the *Action* column.

3. Change the **Role** or adjust account permissions as needed.
4. Select **Save changes**.

Ask the user to sign out and sign back in to apply updates.

Deleting a User

Deleting a user is permanent, but their activity remains in the **Audit Log**.

Steps to Delete a Standard User:

1. Go to **Settings ⚙ → Manage users**.
2. Click the **ellipsis (...)** next to the user and select **Delete**.
3. Confirm by selecting **Delete user**.

Steps to Delete an Accountant User:

1. Go to **Settings ⚙ → Manage users → Accountants** tab.
2. Find the accountant, select **Delete** in the *Action* column.
3. Confirm by selecting **Delete** again.

GUIDE TO CUSTOM FIELDS IN QUICKBOOKS ONLINE

Custom fields in QuickBooks Online (QBO) help you track additional information and tailor your accounting processes to your business needs. They enhance organization, reporting, and form clarity.

What Are Custom Fields?

Custom fields let you add personalized information to transactions. Examples include:

- Purchase order numbers
- Sales representative names
- Project or job identifiers

These fields can appear on:

- Invoices
- Sales receipts
- Estimates
- Credit memos
- Refund receipts
- Purchase orders

Creating and Managing Custom Fields

Creating a Custom Field

1. Click the **Gear icon ⚙ → Custom Fields** under the **Lists** section.
2. Click **Add Field**.
3. Name the field (e.g., "Customer PO" or "Sales Rep").
4. Choose where the field will appear (invoices, sales receipts, estimates, etc.).
5. Decide if it should appear on printed forms.
6. Click **Save**.

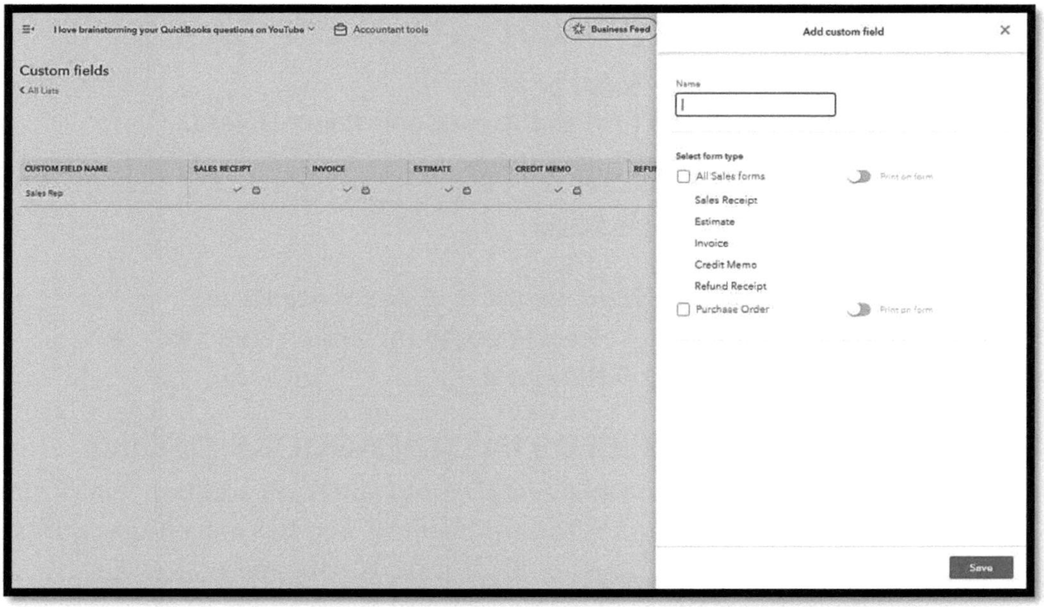

Renaming or Inactivating a Field

- **Rename:** Click **Edit** under ACTIONS, change the name, and save.
- **Make inactive:** Click the dropdown next to Edit → **Make Inactive** (inactive fields stay in historical transactions but won't appear on new ones).
- **Reactivate:** Toggle **Include Inactive**, locate the field, and click **Make Active**.

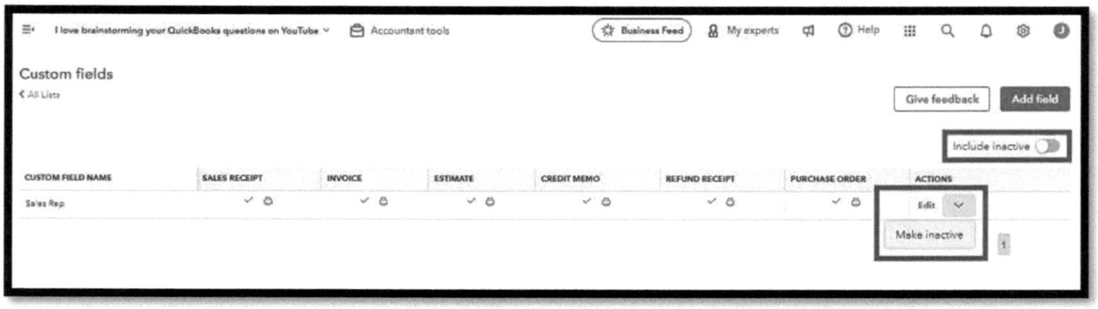

Using Custom Fields on Forms

Custom fields improve clarity on both digital and printed forms.

Form Type	Location
Sales Receipts, Credit Memos, Refund Receipts	Middle section; below BILL TO on print
Invoices & Estimates	Middle section; below Bill to box; on PDF, appear right of details
Purchase Orders	Below mailing address; on print, appear right of details

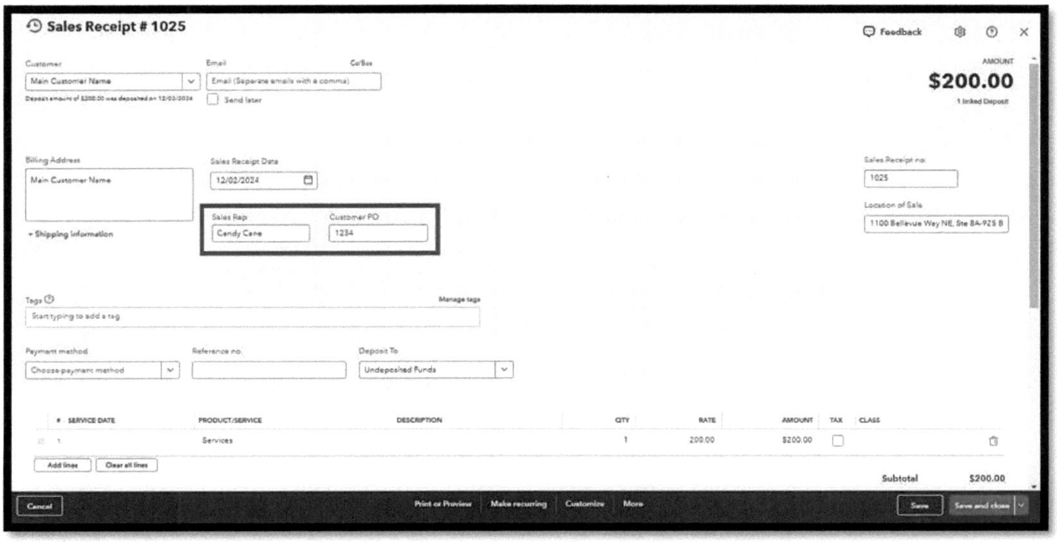

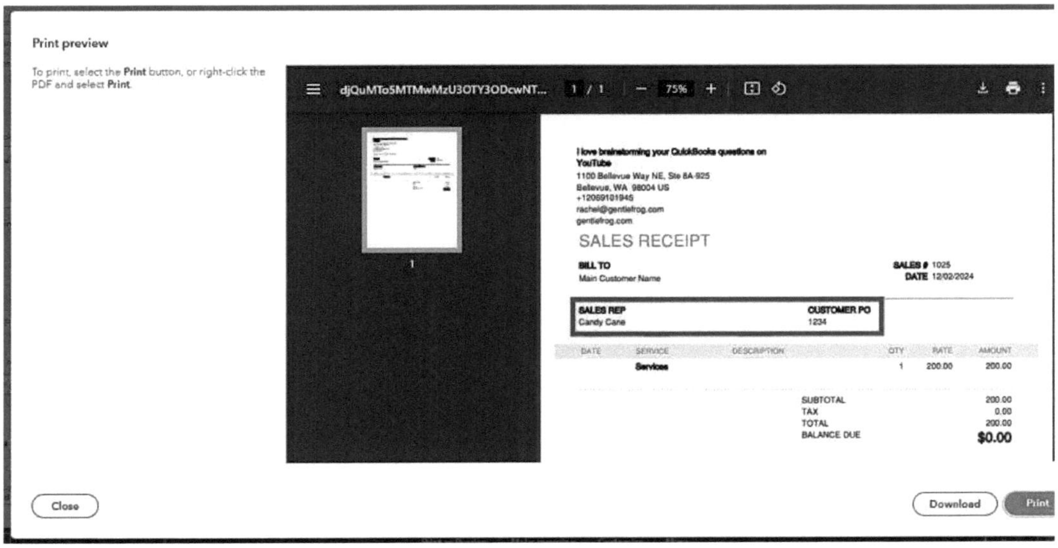

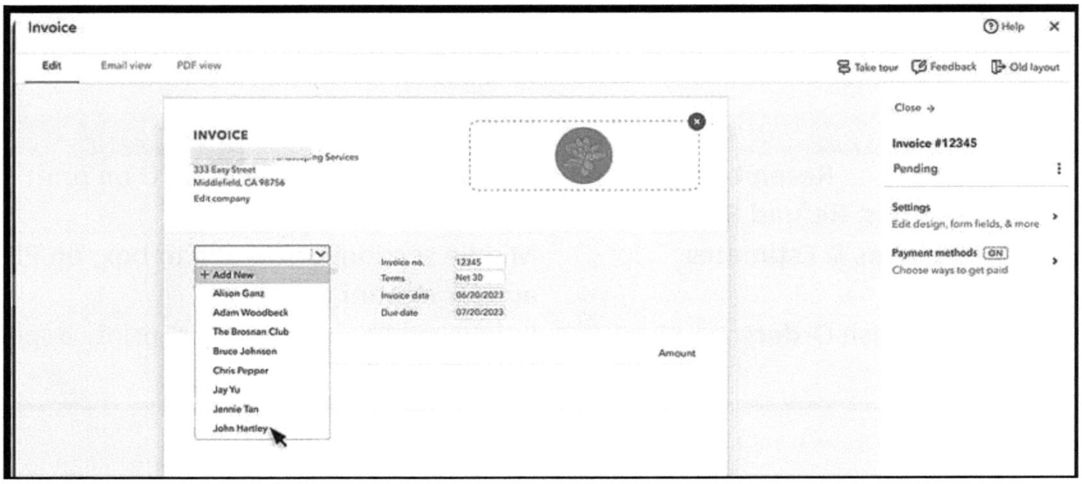

Searching Transactions Using Custom Fields

1. Click the **magnifying glass** (search) in the upper-right corner.
2. Click **Advanced transaction search**.

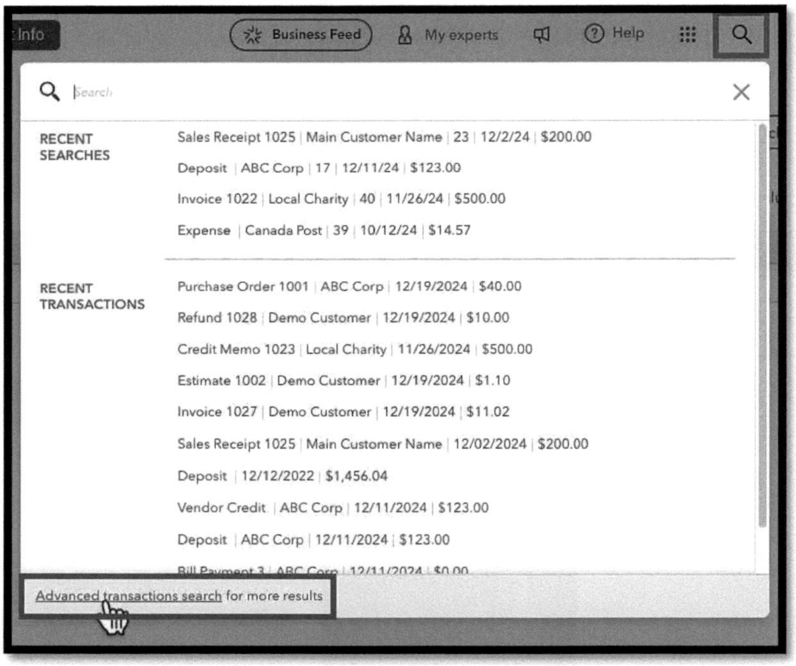

3. Click **More Filters**.
4. Scroll to the bottom to see your **custom fields**.
5. Enter your search term and hit **Enter**.

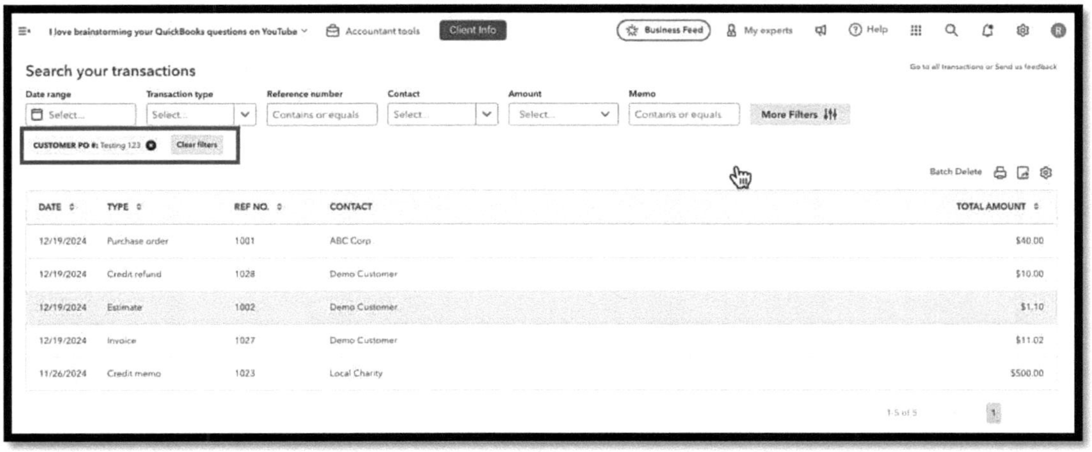

This allows you to quickly locate transactions tied to specific projects, clients, or internal references.

Using Custom Fields in Reports

Custom fields can make reports more insightful:

Grouping by Custom Field

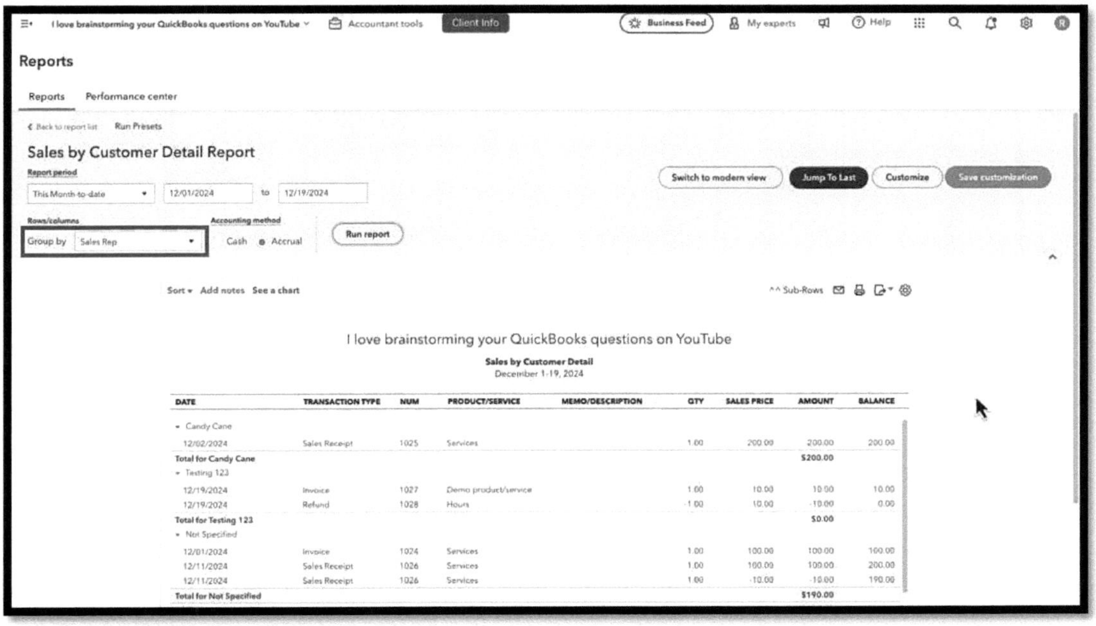

- ❖ Open a report (e.g., **Sales by Customer Detail**) → **Group by** → select your custom field.

Sorting by Custom Field

`

❖ Customize the report → **Columns** → select the custom field → **Sort** by the field.

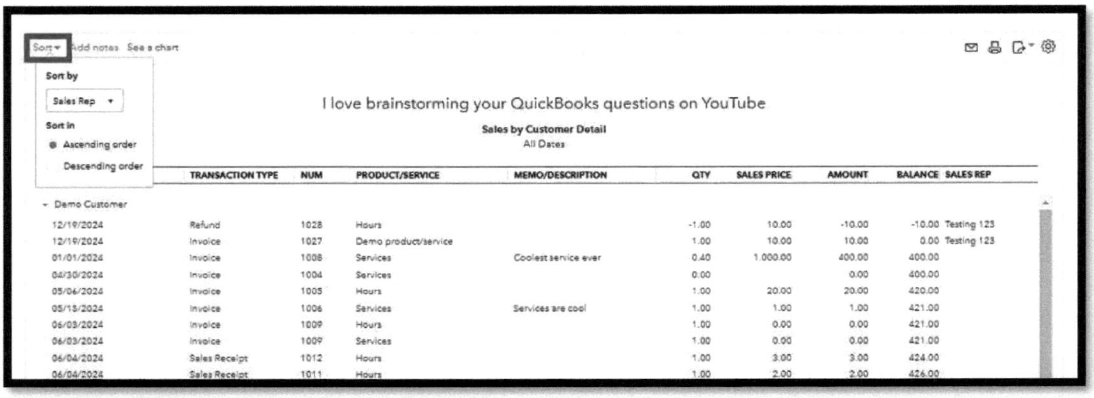

Saving Customized Reports

❖ Once configured, click **Save Customization** for future use.

Using custom fields in reports helps you gain granular insights for better business decisions.

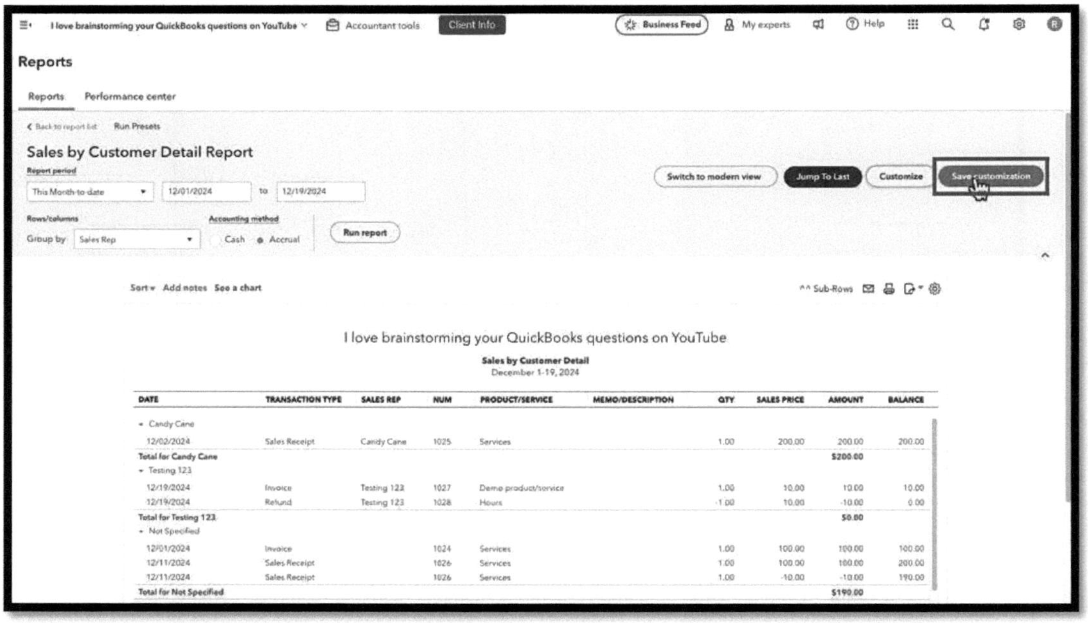

Best Practices for Custom Fields

1. **Plan Ahead:**

❖ Know your QBO plan's custom field limits:

    - Simple Start: 1
    - Essentials: 4
    - Plus: 4
    - Advanced: 12
  - Define the purpose of each field before creating it.

2. **Use Consistent Naming:**
   - Clear, descriptive names help your team understand each field's function.
3. **Limit Field Usage:**
   - Only activate essential fields to avoid clutter.
4. **Review and Update Regularly:**
   - Deactivate unused fields and rename outdated ones.
5. **Leverage Reporting:**
   - Explore how custom fields can enhance insights and support decision-making.

SETTING UP AND USING MULTICURRENCY IN QUICKBOOKS ONLINE

QuickBooks Online's multicurrency feature allows businesses to manage transactions, record expenses, and generate reports in multiple currencies. This is especially useful for companies working with international clients, suppliers, or operations in different countries.

With multicurrency enabled, QuickBooks automatically converts amounts based on prevailing exchange rates, streamlining international financial management.

Turning on Multicurrency

1. Click the **Gear icon ⚙ → Account and Settings**.
2. Go to **Advanced → Currency → Edit**.
3. Select your **Home Currency** from the dropdown.
4. Click **Save**.

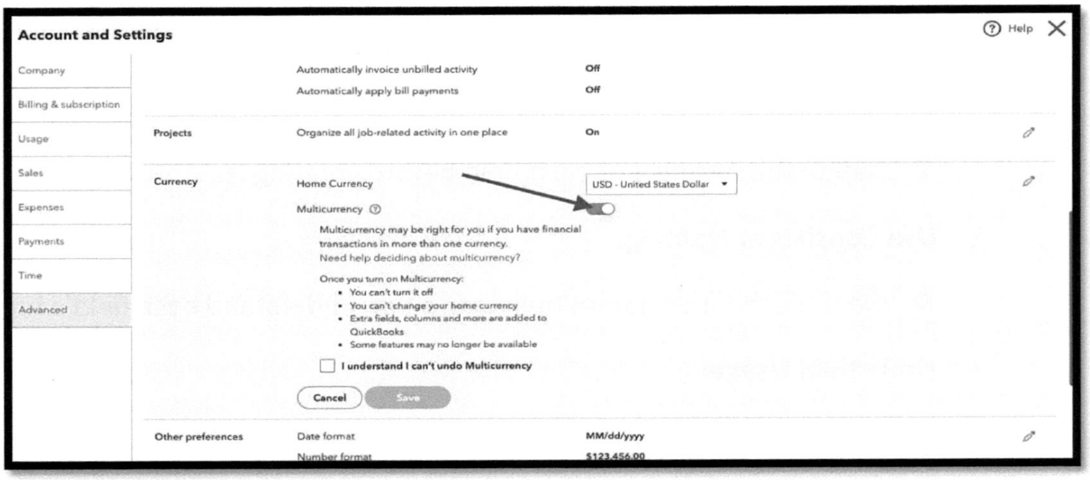

Important: Once multicurrency is turned on, it **cannot be turned off**.

After enabling, you'll see a **Manage Currencies** link to add, edit, or remove currencies for your business.

Adding a New Currency

1. Click the **Gear icon ⚙ → Currencies** (visible only after multicurrency is enabled).
2. Click **Add currency**.
3. Select the desired currency from the dropdown and save.

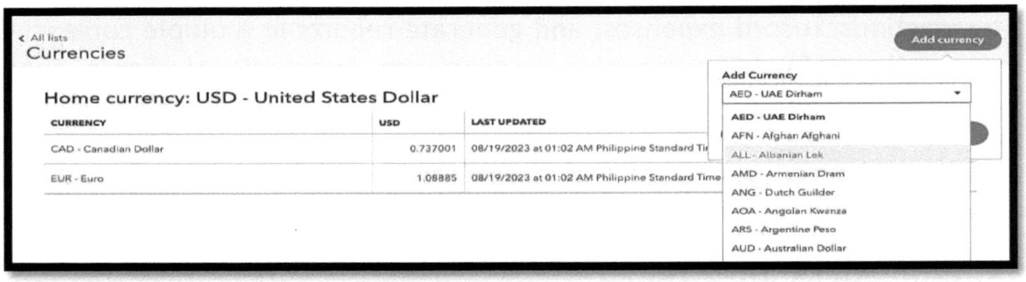

Using Multicurrency in QuickBooks

Transactions

- When creating invoices, bills, or expenses, select the appropriate currency for each transaction.
- QuickBooks automatically converts the amount to your home currency using the current exchange rate.
- Exchange rates are updated automatically, but you can manually adjust them if needed.

- ❖ For historical transactions, use the exchange rate at the transaction date.

Bank Accounts

- ❖ Create separate bank accounts for each currency to simplify record-keeping and reconciliation.
- ❖ When reconciling, ensure each transaction has the correct currency assigned. QuickBooks handles the conversion automatically.

Payments

- ❖ Deposit payments in foreign currencies and let QuickBooks calculate conversions to your home currency.

Advanced Multicurrency Tips

1. **Currency Gains and Losses:**

    - ❖ Fluctuating exchange rates can result in gains or losses. QuickBooks calculates these automatically, but understanding them is important for accurate financial analysis.

2. **Multicurrency Invoicing:**

    - ❖ For clients in different currencies, use QuickBooks' multicurrency invoicing to streamline conversions and recordkeeping.

3. **Currency Accounts:**

    - ❖ Maintain separate accounts for each currency to keep transactions organized and simplify reporting.

Assigning and Changing a Customer's Currency in QuickBooks Online

QuickBooks Online allows you to assign a specific currency to each customer, ensuring transactions are recorded in the correct foreign currency.

Assign a Foreign Currency to a New Customer

1. Go to **New Customer**.
2. In the **Customer Information** window, select the customer's currency from the **Currency** dropdown. This is the currency they will use to pay you.
3. Complete the required details and click **Save**.

Change the Currency for an Existing Customer

Once a customer has recorded transactions, QuickBooks does **not** allow changing their currency directly. To record future transactions in a new currency:

1. Make the existing customer **inactive**. Their previous transactions remain in QuickBooks.
2. Add the customer again using the **New Customer** steps above, and select the correct currency.

All **new transactions** for this customer will now be recorded in the assigned currency.

This approach ensures historical data remains accurate while allowing future transactions in the correct currency.

Add an Account with a Foreign Currency

By default, accounts use your home currency. To create a foreign currency account:

1. Go to **Settings ⚙ → Chart of Accounts**.
2. Click **New**.
3. Select the **Account Type** and **Detail Type**.
4. Enter the **Account Name** and optional **Description**.
5. Choose the **Currency** from the dropdown.
6. Enter the **Starting Date** and **Opening Balance**.
7. Click **Save**.

Note: Once a transaction is posted, the account's currency cannot be changed.

Add Transactions in a Foreign Currency

1. Go to **Accounting → Bank Transactions**.
2. Under **For Review**, open the transaction and click **Add**.
3. Enter the foreign amount or the bank-provided exchange rate.

QuickBooks Online calculates the home currency equivalent automatically.

Tip: You can split transactions across accounts or taxes, but not across multiple currencies.

Exchange Rates

QuickBooks uses exchange rates to convert foreign currency transactions into your home currency:

- Exchange rates are updated automatically every 4 hours from IHS Markit.
- You can manually enter custom exchange rates if needed.
- For historical transactions, use the rate applicable at the transaction date.

Example:

- ❖ Foreign currency: 1 CAD
- ❖ Home currency: USD
- ❖ Exchange rate: 1 CAD = 0.79 USD

Depositing Payments to a Bank with a Different Currency

1. Deposit the invoice payment to a bank account with the same currency.
2. Go to **+ New → Transfer**.
3. Select:
   - ❖ **Transfer Funds From:** Source account
   - ❖ **Transfer Funds To:** Destination account
   - ❖ **Currency:** Currency of the destination account
   - ❖ **Transfer Amount:** Payment value in the selected currency
4. Enter the **date** and click **Save and Close**.

Pay Employees in a Different Currency

1. Create a supplier profile for your employee:
   - ❖ Go to **Expenses → Suppliers → New Supplier**
   - ❖ Enter the employee's details
   - ❖ Select the **Currency**
   - ❖ Optionally, add the currency to their display name and click **Save**
2. Pay the employee:
   - ❖ Go to **+ New → Expense**
   - ❖ Select the employee supplier
   - ❖ Choose the payroll account under **Category**
   - ❖ Enter the payment details and click **Save** or **Save and Close**

Change a Customer or Supplier's Currency

QuickBooks does **not** allow changing currency for existing profiles with transactions. To use a new currency:

1. Make the existing customer or supplier **inactive**:
   - ❖ Customers: **Sales → Customers → Action → Make inactive**
   - ❖ Suppliers: **Expenses → Suppliers → Action → Make inactive**
2. Create a new customer or supplier with the updated currency:
   - ❖ Go to **Sales → Customers → New Customer** (or **Expenses → Suppliers → New Supplier**)
   - ❖ Fill in the original details
   - ❖ Select the new **Currency**
   - ❖ Optionally, add the currency to the display name and click **Save.**

PART II: CORE DAY-TO-DAY OPERATIONS

CHAPTER THREE

BILL FLAWLESSLY, COLLECT EFFORTLESSLY

Billing in QuickBooks Online involves managing your subscription with Intuit or managing the bills and invoices you create for your customers and vendors.

HOW TO ADD CUSTOMERS IN QUICKBOOKS ONLINE

Adding customers in QuickBooks Online makes invoicing easier and helps you track who owes you money. Here's a clear, streamlined guide to adding customers—individually or in bulk—plus how to pull customer details into invoices and manage them through the Customer List and the QuickBooks Business Network.

Accessing Your Customer List

1. Navigate to **Customers & Leads** on the left menu.
2. Select **Customers** to open your full customer list.

This page shows each customer's profile, open balance, total outstanding invoices, and other key details.

Adding a New Customer Manually

1. Select **New Customer**.

2. Fill out the contact information fields.

Key Fields Explained

- **Display Name:** A unique name you assign to track the customer's transactions. This appears on invoices, sales receipts, and other forms.
- **Notes & Attachments:** Add additional information or upload supporting documents.
- **Payment Details:** Enter preferred payment methods, billing address, or other payment preferences.
- **Terms:**
  Set custom payment terms (e.g., Net 15, Net 30).
  - If left empty, QuickBooks applies your default company terms.
  - You can still adjust terms on individual invoices.
- **Preferred Language & Delivery Options:** Choose how the customer prefers to receive communications.
- **Additional Info:** Record customer type and indicate whether they are **exempt from sales tax**.

Using the QuickBooks Business Network for Faster Setup

If your customer is another business using QuickBooks, the QuickBooks Business Network can automatically fill and update their contact details.

How It Works

1. In the **Company Name** field, type their business name.
2. If they appear in the dropdown, they're part of the network.
3. Select their name and click **Save and Send** to send a connection request.

Benefits

- Their email, phone number, and address remain up-to-date automatically.
- You'll see their real contact details only *after* they accept your request.

❖ Any changes they make to their QuickBooks account sync automatically—unless you manually edit the field.

If you overwrite any field yourself, that field will stop syncing with their updates.

Adding Customers in Bulk (Importing from a Spreadsheet)

If you have many customers to add, QuickBooks lets you import them all at once.

How to Import

1. Go to your customer list and select **Import Customers**.

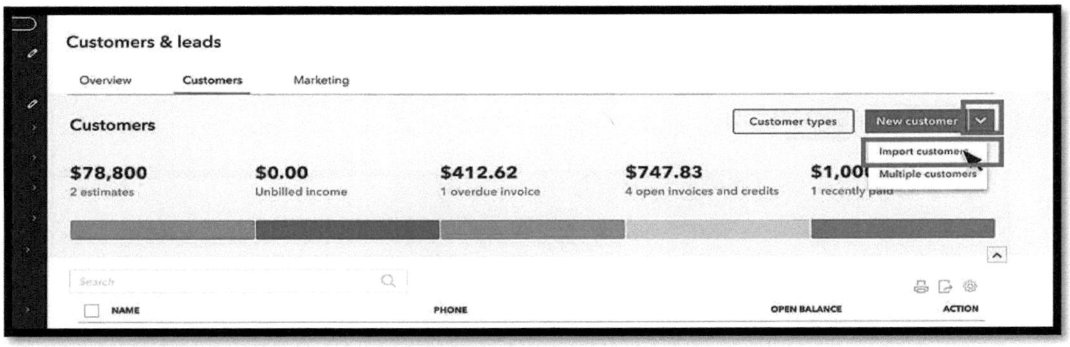

2. Upload your spreadsheet and click **Next**.

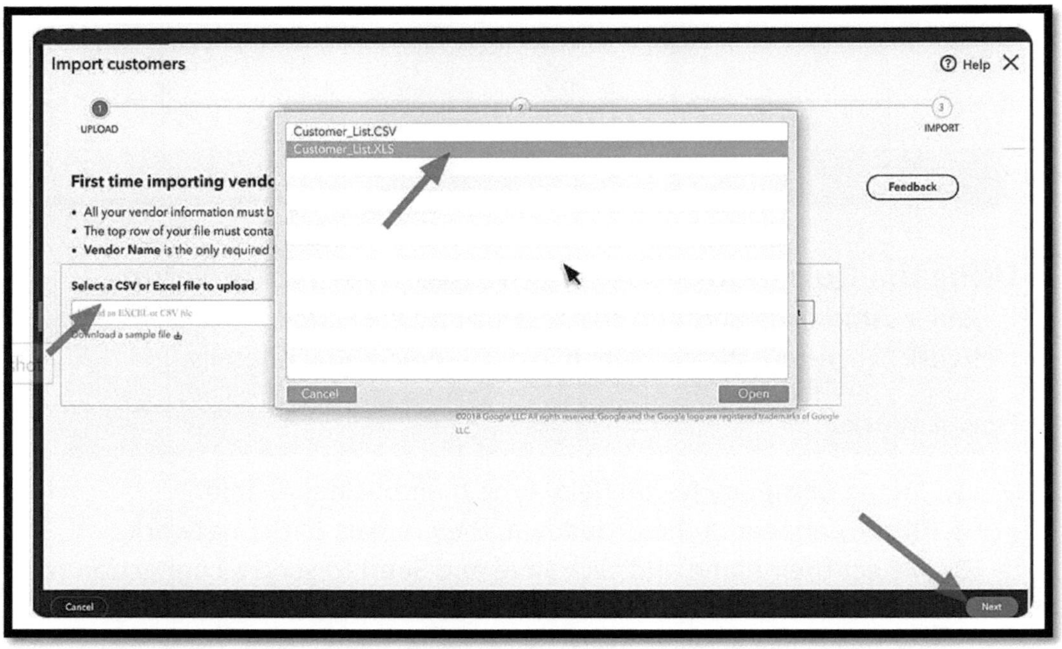

3. Map your spreadsheet columns to QuickBooks fields (e.g., Name → Display Name).
4. Select **Next**, review the preview, then click **Import**.

All imported customers will now appear in your list.

Managing Your Customer List

You can customize and filter your customer list using the gear icon.

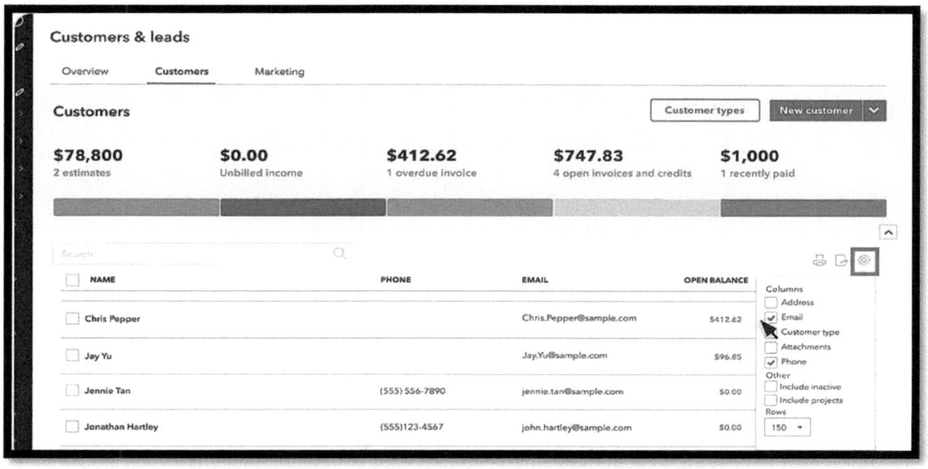

You can:

- ❖ Show or hide specific columns
- ❖ Filter customers by transaction types or payment status
- ❖ Select a customer to view all past transactions
- ❖ Choose **Edit** to update their profile

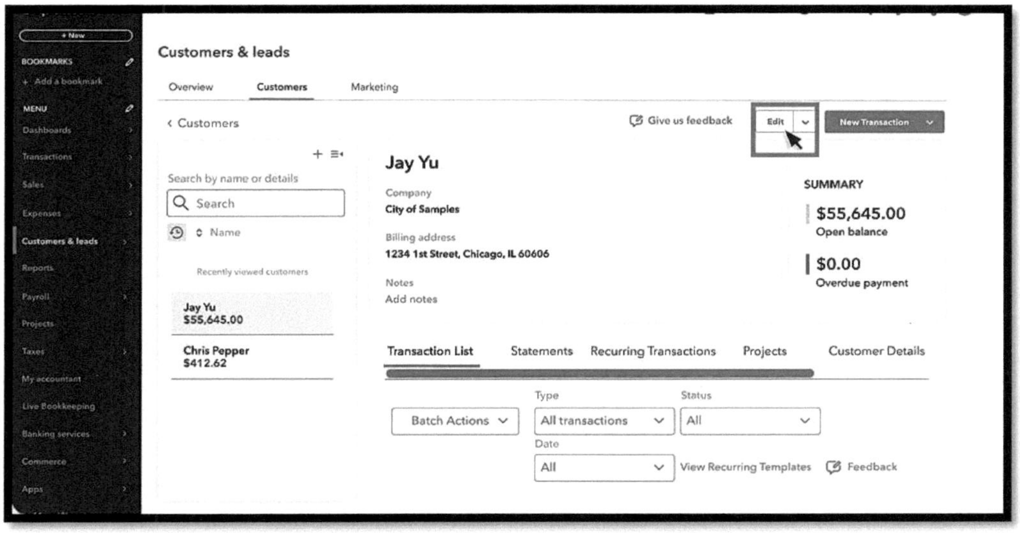

Using Customer Info on Transactions

When you create a new transaction—such as an invoice or sales receipt:

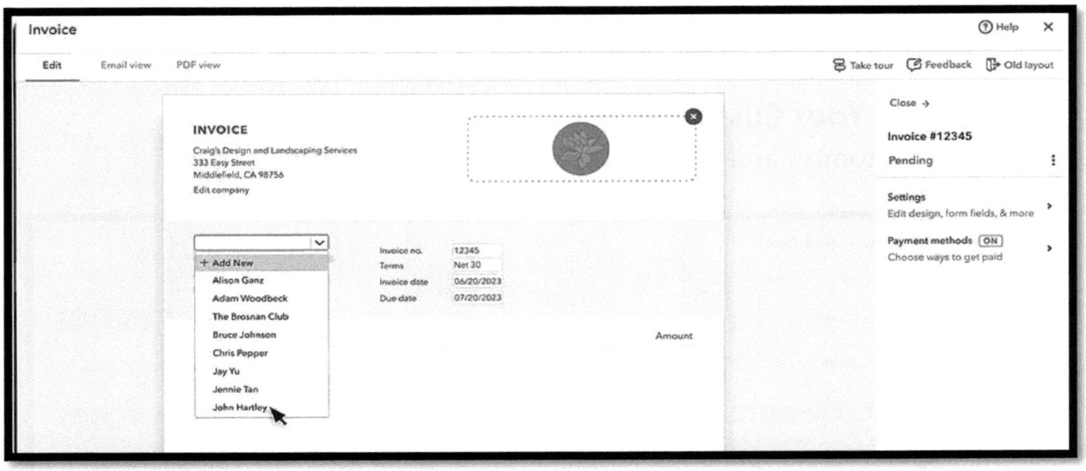

1. Select the customer.
2. QuickBooks automatically fills in their saved contact information, terms, tax settings, and delivery preferences.

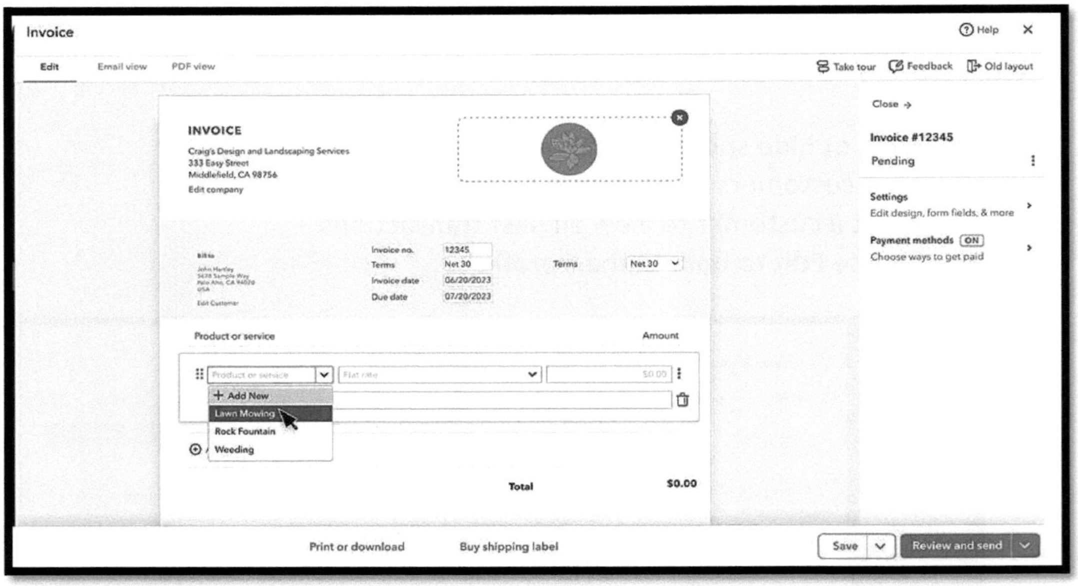

Customer Notifications

- Customers receive an email when you send an invoice.
- Customers connected through the Business Network also get an **in-app QuickBooks notification** showing a pending bill or invoice to review.

QUICKBOOKS ONLINE: HOW TO SET UP SALES TAX

Setting up sales tax correctly in QuickBooks Online is essential for staying compliant and ensuring your invoices calculate the right tax every time. Here's a streamlined, step-by-step guide:

1. Go to the Taxes Center

From your QuickBooks Online dashboard, look at the left-hand navigation menu and select **Taxes**.

This opens the main hub where all your sales tax settings and agencies are managed.

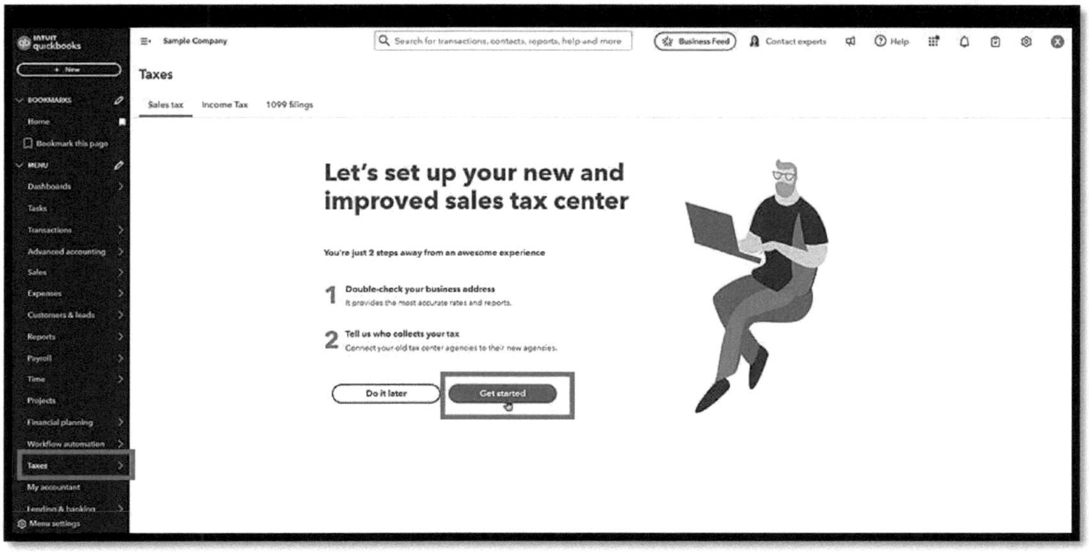

2. Enter or Confirm Your Business Address

Your business address determines which tax rates apply to your company. Make sure the address is:

- Accurate

❖ Complete
❖ Up to date

Because QuickBooks uses this information to automatically assign the correct tax rules based on your location.

3. Select Your Tax Agencies

QuickBooks will display a list of **state and local tax agencies** relevant to your region.

❖ Choose the appropriate agency (or agencies) that your business is required to remit sales tax to.
❖ Double-check that QuickBooks displays the correct **current tax rates** for each agency.

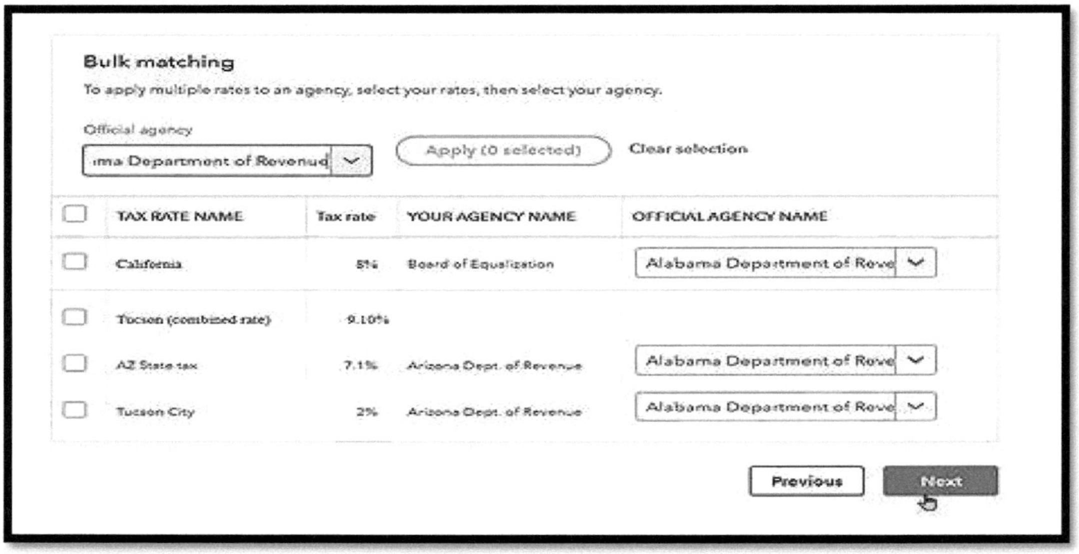

This ensures that your invoices calculate sales tax correctly.

4. Save Your Sales Tax Settings

Once your address and agencies are confirmed:

❖ Click **Save**

This activates the tax settings and applies them to your account moving forward.

4. Apply Sales Tax to Invoices

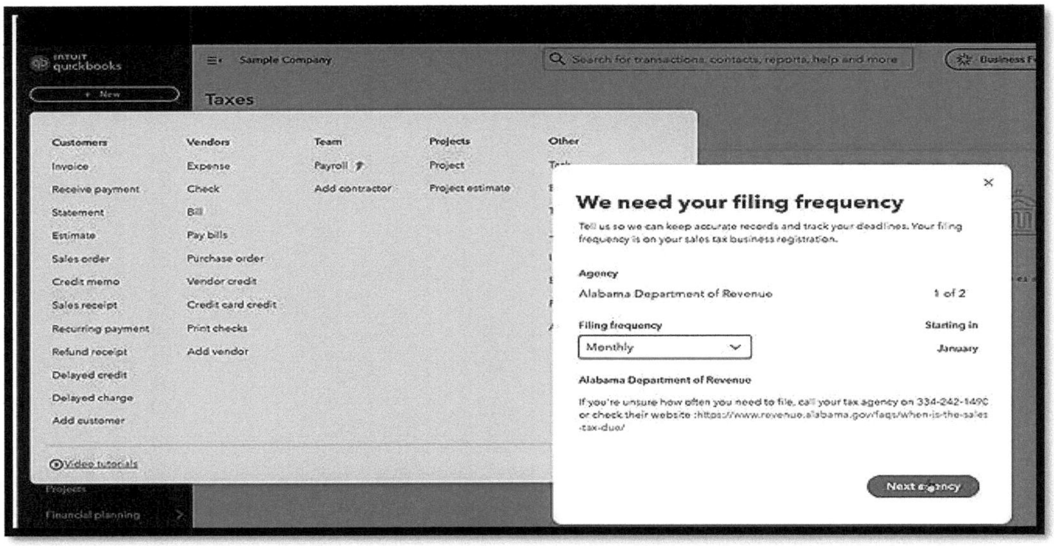

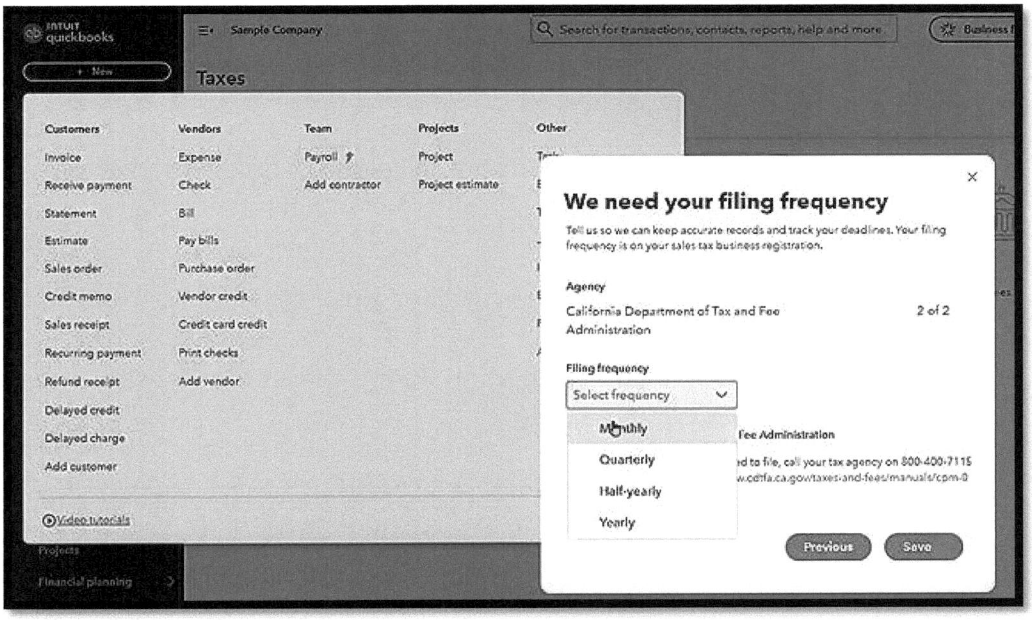

Now that your sales tax is set up:

- ❖ Open or create a new invoice

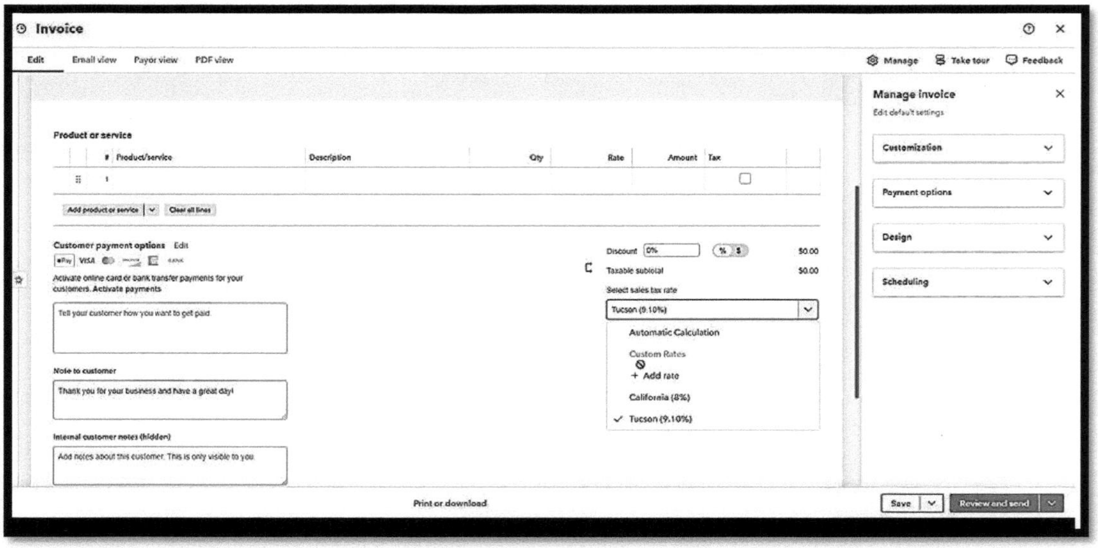

- ❖ Use the **Sales Tax** dropdown to apply the correct tax rate
- ❖ QuickBooks will automatically calculate tax based on the agency and rate you selected

This ensures consistent and compliant tax calculations on every sale.

Final Tips

- ❖ Review your tax setup whenever your **business address**, **local laws**, or **tax rates** change.
- ❖ Keeping your sales tax information updated ensures you stay compliant and avoid filing errors.

With these steps completed, your sales tax workflow in QuickBooks Online is ready to support accurate, efficient, and stress-free bookkeeping.

IMPLEMENTING AUTOMATED SALES TAX FEATURES IN QUICKBOOKS ONLINE

Once you've set up the basics of your QuickBooks Online account and understand your sales tax responsibilities, the next step is to activate QuickBooks' automated sales tax system. This feature takes the guesswork out of calculating tax, helps you stay compliant, and streamlines everyday bookkeeping.

Below is a clear, step-by-step guide to getting everything configured properly.

1. Enable Sales Tax Tracking

Before QuickBooks can calculate tax for you, you must turn on sales tax tracking.

Access Sales Tax Settings

- From your QuickBooks Online dashboard, select **Taxes** in the left-hand menu.
- Choose **Sales Tax**. This opens the central hub for all sales tax setup and management.

Enable Sales Tax

- Follow the prompts to turn on automatic sales tax.
- QuickBooks will ask for details such as your business's **physical location**, which determines the correct jurisdiction-based rates.

2. Set Up Tax Agencies and Rates

After enabling tax tracking, you'll need to define the agencies you remit tax to and the tax rates for each area where you have a tax obligation.

Add Tax Agencies

- Add each state, county, city, or special tax district where you collect and remit sales tax.
- Provide the agency name and choose your filing frequency (e.g., monthly, quarterly, annually).

Define Tax Rates

- Assign the correct tax rate for each agency.
- QuickBooks allows you to set layered rates—state, county, city, and special district—ensuring accuracy for combined tax jurisdictions.

3. Assign Tax Categories to Products and Services

Accurate sales tax calculation depends on correctly identifying which items are taxable.

Review Available Tax Categories

- QuickBooks provides a list of common tax categories matched to standard tax rules—services, goods, food items, digital products, labor, and more.

Assign Categories to Each Item

- Go to your Products and Services list.
- Assign each item to the appropriate category based on its taxability.

This step ensures QuickBooks applies the correct tax rate automatically when the item appears on an invoice or sales receipt.

4. Manage Sales Tax Exemptions

Some customers or products qualify for exemptions, and QuickBooks lets you handle these easily.

Identify Exempt Transactions

- ❖ Exemptions may apply to nonprofits, resellers, or specific goods such as groceries or medical items.
- ❖ Know the exemption rules for each jurisdiction you collect tax in.

Set Up Exemptions in QuickBooks

- ❖ Mark a customer as tax-exempt by updating their customer profile.
- ❖ Alternatively, mark individual transactions as exempt during invoice creation. QuickBooks will remove tax from these sales and track them separately for reporting.

Integrating Sales Tax Automation Solutions with QuickBooks Online

Integrating an automated sales tax solution with QuickBooks Online can dramatically improve accuracy, efficiency, and compliance in your tax processes. These tools expand QuickBooks' built-in capabilities, ensuring your sales tax is handled with expert-level precision.

1. Enhanced Accuracy

Automated sales tax solutions are designed to keep up with constantly changing tax rules across thousands of jurisdictions. When connected to QuickBooks Online, they ensure every transaction is calculated using the most accurate, up-to-date data.

Key Benefits

- ❖ **Real-time Tax Updates:** Rates and tax laws change frequently. These tools automatically update in real time, so your sales tax calculations always reflect the latest regulations.
- ❖ **Address Validation:** Many tax engines verify customer addresses to pinpoint the exact tax jurisdiction. This is crucial when tax rates vary by city, county, or even neighborhood.

2. Streamlined Compliance

Sales tax compliance can be complicated, especially for businesses selling across multiple states. Automated solutions simplify compliance by handling the most tedious aspects for you.

Compliance Features

- **Nexus Detection:** These tools can track where you've established sales tax nexus—based on sales volume, transaction count, or physical presence—helping you understand where you must collect tax.
- **Automated Filing & Remittance:** Some solutions can prepare, file, and even remit your sales tax returns directly to tax agencies, reducing errors and ensuring on-time submissions.

3. Time Savings and Operational Efficiency

Automating tax tasks frees you and your team to focus on more valuable activities.

Efficiency Boosts

- **Automatic Tax Calculations:** No more manual tax entries or second-guessing. Each transaction is taxed accurately based on product type and customer location.
- **Multi-Channel Integration:** These solutions sync with QuickBooks Online and major e-commerce platforms, POS systems, and marketplaces—giving you one centralized view of all your sales tax data.

4. Better Decision-Making Support

Automation tools don't just calculate tax—they also deliver insights you can use to guide business strategy.

Helpful Features

- **Reporting & Analytics:** Access detailed reports showing where you're collecting the most tax, which items generate the highest tax amounts, and trends across jurisdictions.
- **Audit Support:** If you're ever audited, having well-organized digital tax records and system-generated reports makes the process much easier and faster.

Choosing the Right Sales Tax Automation Tool

When selecting a solution, consider how seamlessly it integrates with QuickBooks Online, how intuitive the interface is, and how much manual work it eliminates. The goal is full automation with minimal data re-entry.

Managing and Reporting Sales Tax in QuickBooks Online

Next, let's look at how QuickBooks Online helps you maintain accurate sales tax records, adjust tax rates, and manage sales across multiple jurisdictions.

Adding and Editing Sales Tax Rates

QuickBooks Online makes it simple to update your tax rates whenever laws or operational needs change.

Adding a New Sales Tax Rate

1. Go to the **Taxes** tab in your QuickBooks Online dashboard.
2. Select **Add Tax** to create a new tax rate or agency.
3. Enter the details, including the agency name, rate percentage, and applicable jurisdiction.
4. Review your information and click **Save**.

Your new tax rate will now be available for use in invoices, sales receipts, and other taxable transactions.

Editing Sales Tax Rates in QuickBooks Online

When tax rates change, updating them in QuickBooks Online is simple:

- Go to the **Taxes** section and locate the tax rate you want to modify.
- Select the rate, adjust the percentage or agency information, and save your changes.
- All future transactions will automatically reflect the updated rate.

Managing Multiple Sales Tax Jurisdictions

If your business operates in several states, counties, or cities, QuickBooks Online helps you stay compliant across all jurisdictions.

Setting Up New Jurisdictions

- For every new location where you have sales tax obligations, create the appropriate **tax agency** and **tax rates**.
- This ensures QuickBooks calculates taxes correctly for each region based on current rules.

Automatic Tax Application

- As you record sales, QuickBooks Online detects the customer's location and the tax category of your product or service.

- It automatically applies the correct rate, eliminating manual work and reducing errors.

Using Automated Sales Tax Calculations

QuickBooks Online's automated system boosts accuracy and efficiency.

Categorize Products and Services

- Make sure each item is assigned to the correct **tax category**.
- This step ensures QuickBooks knows when to tax—or not tax—specific products and services.

Processing Sales

- During checkout or invoicing, QuickBooks instantly calculates the appropriate sales tax using location and item tax rules.
- This keeps your tax collection precise on every transaction.

Generating Accurate Sales Tax Reports

Reliable sales tax reporting is essential for reconciliation and filing.

Access Key Reports

- From the **Taxes** section, generate reports that show:
  - Total tax collected
  - Sales by jurisdiction
  - Liability summaries for specific periods

Prepare for Filing

- Use these reports to reconcile collected amounts with your liability.
- Detailed breakdowns make it easier to file accurately with each tax agency.

Maintaining Sales Tax Compliance

Consistency is the key to staying compliant. Here are practical steps and habits to follow:

1. Update Tax Rates Regularly

Tax rules change frequently at state and local levels.

- **Set a routine review cycle**, such as monthly or quarterly.
- **Use alerts or notifications** from QuickBooks or tax services to stay notified of tax rate updates.

2. Review Your Sales Tax Settings

Changes in your business can affect your sales tax responsibilities.

- **Monitor nexus status:** If your sales grow or expand into new states, you may develop tax obligations in new jurisdictions. Update QuickBooks accordingly.
- **Audit item taxability:** Ensure product and service categories are still accurate based on current tax laws.

3. Prepare for Sales Tax Audits

Being organized is your best defense.

- Keep all invoices, receipts, and tax payments recorded in QuickBooks.
- Regularly review **Sales Tax Liability** reports to confirm compliance.
- Store supporting documents in QuickBooks so everything is in one place if an auditor requests information.

Using QuickBooks Online Data to Stay Compliant

QuickBooks Online gives you powerful tools to manage compliance proactively.

- **Run sales tax reports regularly** to monitor liabilities and detect discrepancies early.
- **Analyze transaction data** to confirm correct tax application and identify unusual patterns.
- **Use insights** to better plan future tax payments, avoid penalties, and maintain compliance across all tax jurisdictions.

HOW TO ADD PRODUCTS & SERVICES IN QUICKBOOKS ONLINE

QuickBooks includes a few default product and service items, but creating your own ensures accurate reporting and saves time when recording sales. Setting up your products and services before you begin invoicing helps streamline bookkeeping and improves the quality of your financial data. Here's how to do it.

Navigating to Products & Services

1. From the left-hand menu, select **Sales**.
2. Then choose **Products and Services**.

- ❖ If you're adding items for the first time, select **Create items**.

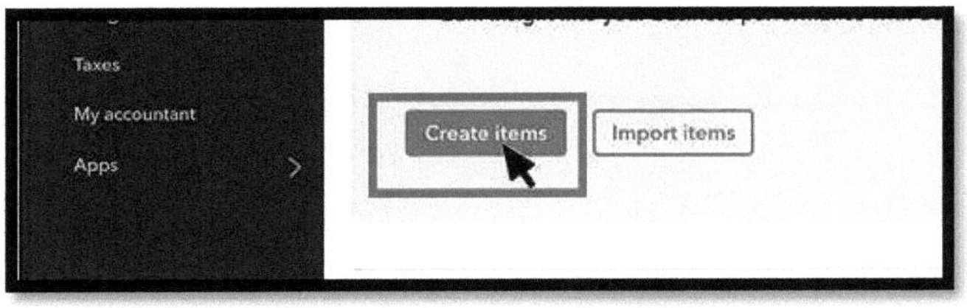

- ❖ If you already have items set up, click **New**.

Choosing the Type of Item

From the dropdown menu, choose the appropriate item type:

- ❖ **Non-stock Item:** Physical goods you sell but do *not* track inventory counts for.
- ❖ **Stock Item:** Physical goods you sell *and* track as inventory within QuickBooks.
- ❖ **Service:** Any service your business provides.

In this section, the example used is a bakery adding **Catering Services**, but the steps are the same for all item types.

Entering Product or Service Details

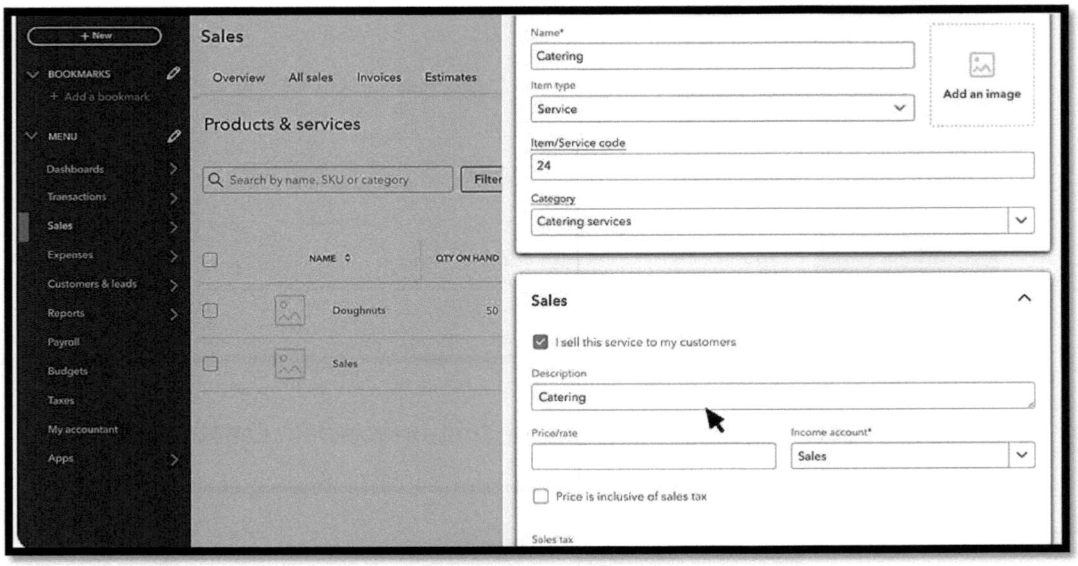

After selecting the type, fill in the item details:

1. Item or Service Code (Optional)

Use this if your business tracks internal codes or SKUs.

2. Category

Group related products and services—helpful for organization and reporting.

3. Upload Image (Optional)

You can add a photo for easier recognition when selecting items later.

4. Description

Enter a clear description of the item or service.

This will appear on customer invoices, receipts, and sales forms.

5. Price or Rate

Set a default price to speed up future invoicing.

(Example: **£50 per person** for catering.)

You can leave this blank and enter the price manually during each sale, but setting a default saves time.

6. Income Account

Choose the account where sales of this item will be recorded on your **Profit and Loss** statement.

You *don't* need separate accounts for every item—only for groups you want to track. (Example: Selecting **Catering Services Income**.)

7. VAT / Sales Tax Settings

If VAT or sales tax is enabled, choose whether this item is **taxable** or **non-taxable**.

8. Purchasing Information (Optional)

If you need to track purchase costs—for items you buy before selling—check the box to enable purchasing fields:

- Purchase description
- Cost
- Expense account
- Preferred supplier

Save Your Item

When finished, select **Save and Close**.

Your new product or service is now ready to use when creating invoices, sales receipts, or estimates.

Adding Multiple Items at Once (Batch Import)

If you have many products or services, QuickBooks allows bulk importing from a spreadsheet.

Steps to Import Items

1. Go to **Products and Services**.
2. Select **Batch Import**.

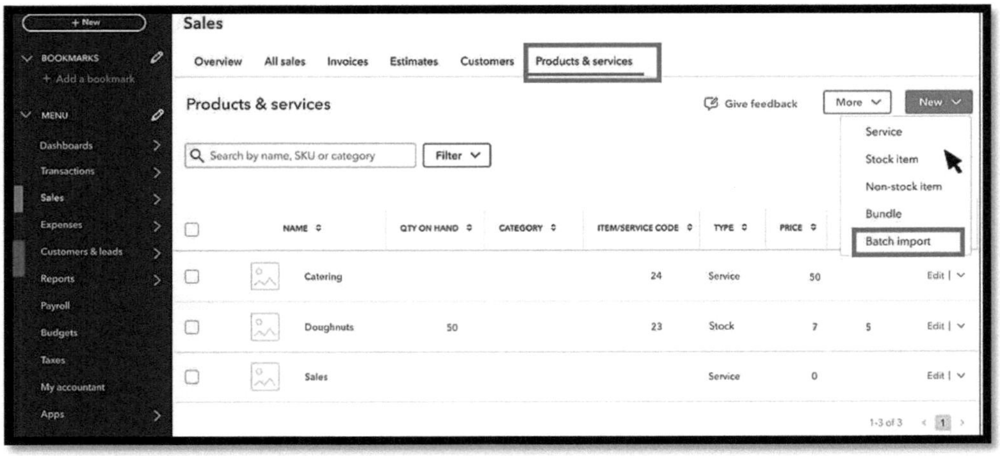

3. Choose **Import CSV/Excel**.
4. Click **Browse** and upload your spreadsheet.
5. Select **Next**.
6. Map your spreadsheet columns to QuickBooks fields.
7. Select **Next** again to preview.
8. If everything looks correct, click **Save**.

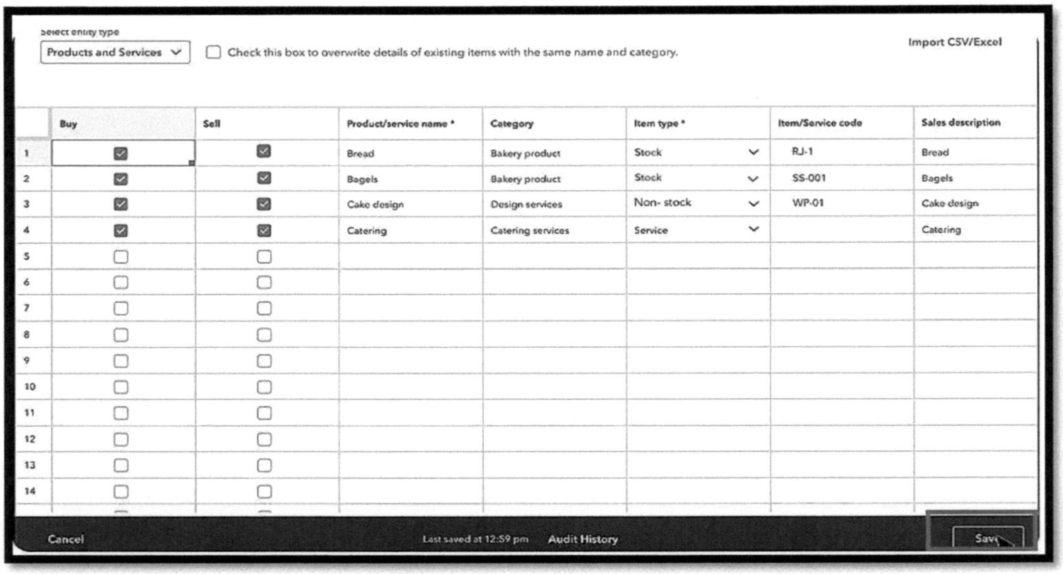

Your items will be added automatically.

HOW TO CATEGORIZE TRANSACTIONS IN QUICKBOOKS ONLINE

Once you connect your bank or credit card to QuickBooks Online, new transactions flow in automatically every day. These downloaded items aren't yet part of your books—you must review, categorize, and post them. Here's a step-by-step guide to doing exactly that.

Accessing Your Downloaded Transactions

1. On the Banking page, you'll see a **card** for each connected bank account and credit card.

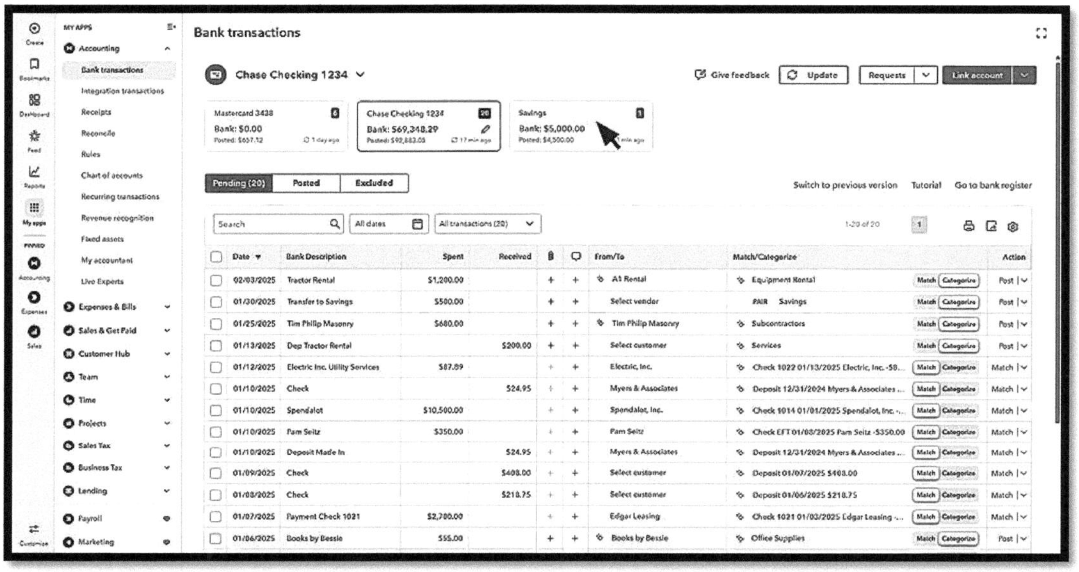

2. Select a card to view all transactions imported from that account.

Important:

These downloaded items *are not yet recorded* in QuickBooks. You must categorize and post them before they affect your reports.

Categorizing Each Transaction

1. Choose the Customer or Vendor

- ❖ Select who the transaction is associated with.
- ❖ This helps improve reporting accuracy and makes later reconciliation easier.

2. Pick the Correct Category

- ❖ Choose the account (expense, income, asset, etc.) that best explains what the money was spent on or received for.
- ❖ The **"From"** field is optional but helpful for reporting on who you paid or who paid you.

3. Adjust the Transaction Type (if needed)

❖ Click the transaction to open details.

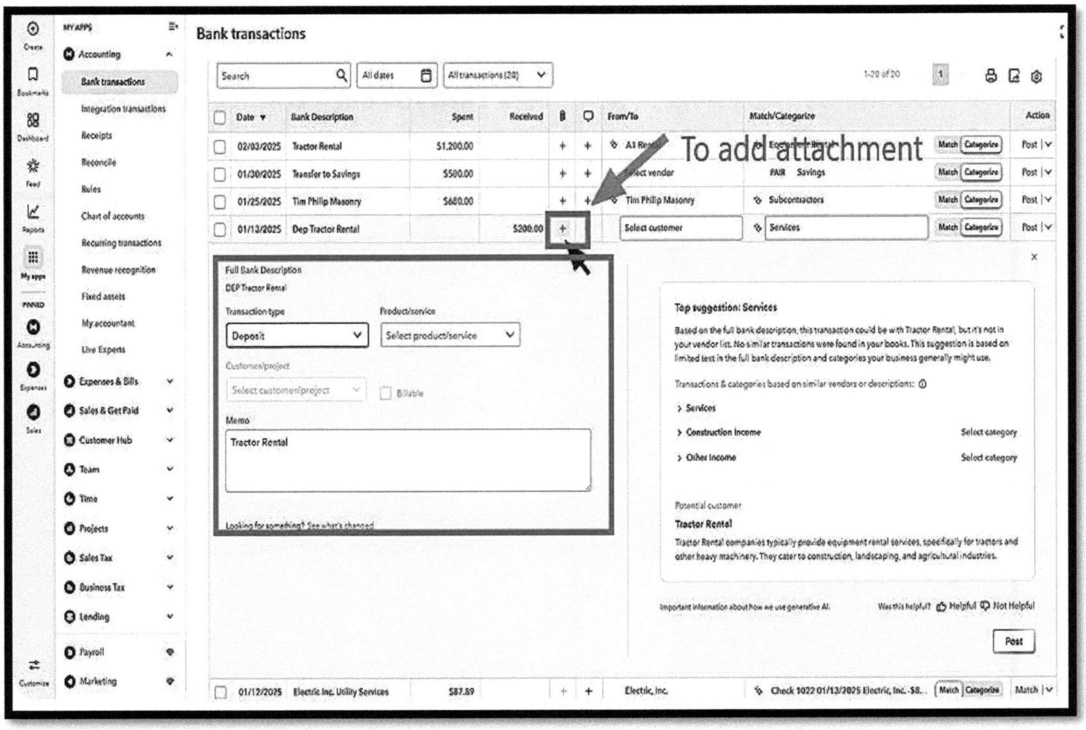

❖ Use the dropdown to change the type (expense, transfer, income, etc.).

If the transaction is income, you can also specify the **product or service** that was sold.

4. Add Notes or Attachments

❖ Use the memo field for context.

❖ Upload a receipt or document using **Add attachment** for audit-ready documentation.

Using QuickBooks' Smart Category Suggestions

QuickBooks' AI helps speed up categorizing by analyzing:

❖ Vendor name

❖ Bank description

❖ Amount

❖ Your past 24 months of activity

❖ Previously used categories

Each transaction shows category suggestions QuickBooks thinks are correct.

Accepting a Suggestion

If one of the suggested categories looks right, simply select it and click **Post**.

Choosing a Category Manually

If the suggestions don't apply, choose the correct category from the list.

Splitting a Transaction

Some expenses or deposits need to be divided:

- ❖ Select **Split**

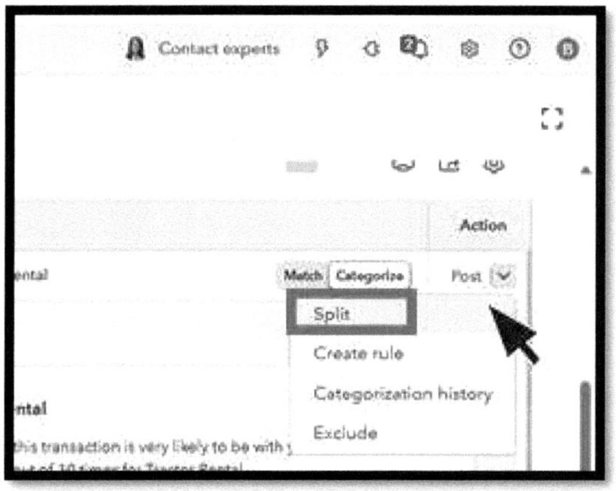

- ❖ Assign amounts to multiple categories
- ❖ Ensure the split totals match the full transaction amount

Matching Transactions Already Entered

Sometimes QuickBooks detects that a downloaded bank transaction corresponds to something you already recorded manually—like:

- ❖ An invoice payment
- ❖ A bill payment
- ❖ A bank deposit

In these cases, you'll see **Match** instead of Categorize.

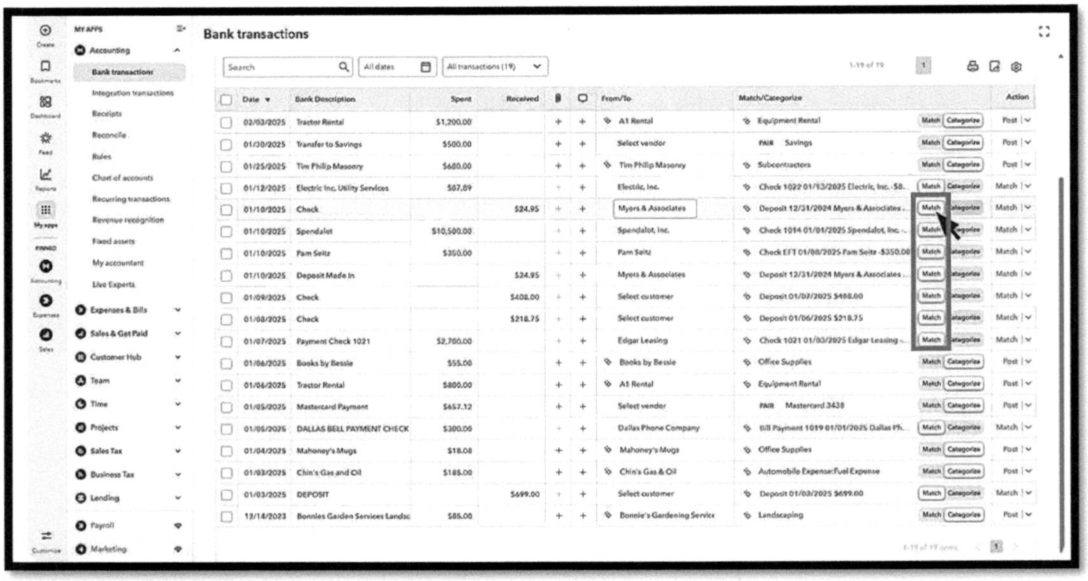

To Match:

`

1. Select the suggested match.
2. Review the matching details.
3. If correct, click **Match** to prevent duplicates.

If the Match Is Wrong

You have two options:

- **Categorize** → add it as a new transaction
- **Find other matches** → search for the correct manual entry

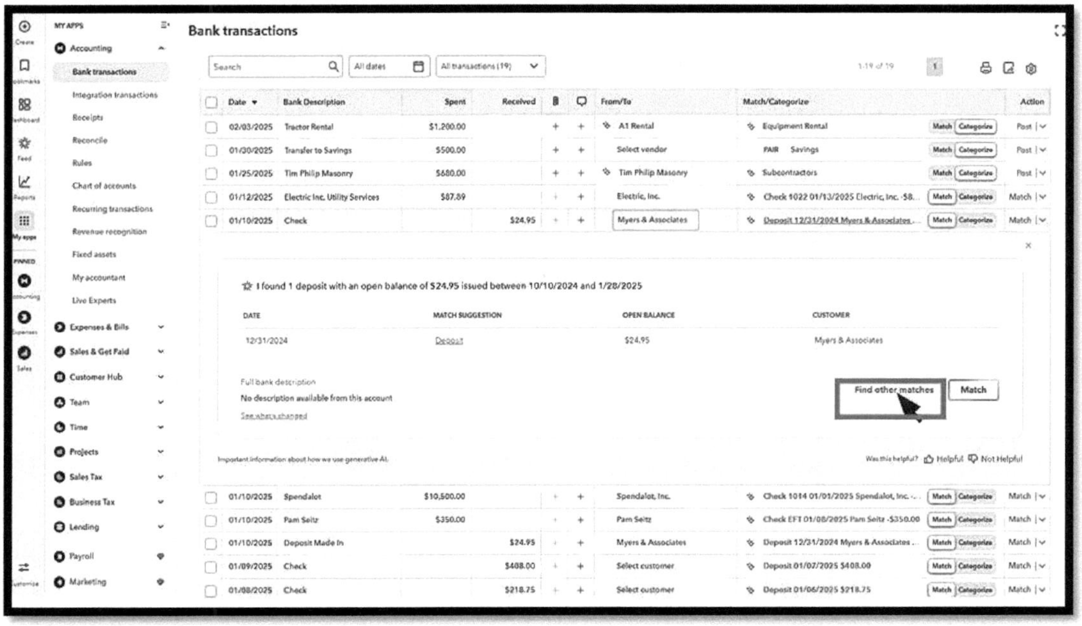

Final Step: Post the Transaction

Once everything is accurate—customer/vendor, category, notes, and any attachments—click **Post**.

This officially moves the transaction from your bank feed into your QuickBooks books.

CREATING ESTIMATES AND CONVERTING THEM TO INVOICES IN QUICKBOOKS ONLINE

An **estimate** lets you give a customer a clear proposal or cost outline for work you plan to complete. In QuickBooks Online, you can easily create, customize, send, track, and later convert that estimate into an invoice. Here's a streamlined walkthrough of the entire process.

1. Creating an Estimate

1. Go to **New → Estimate**.

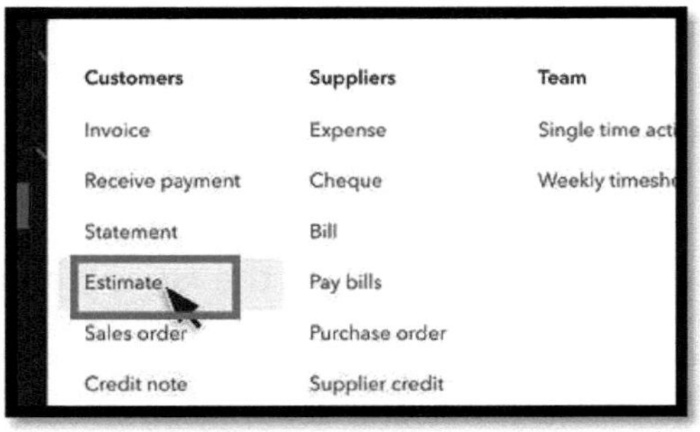

2. If necessary, update your **company information** and **logo**.
3. Select your **customer**.

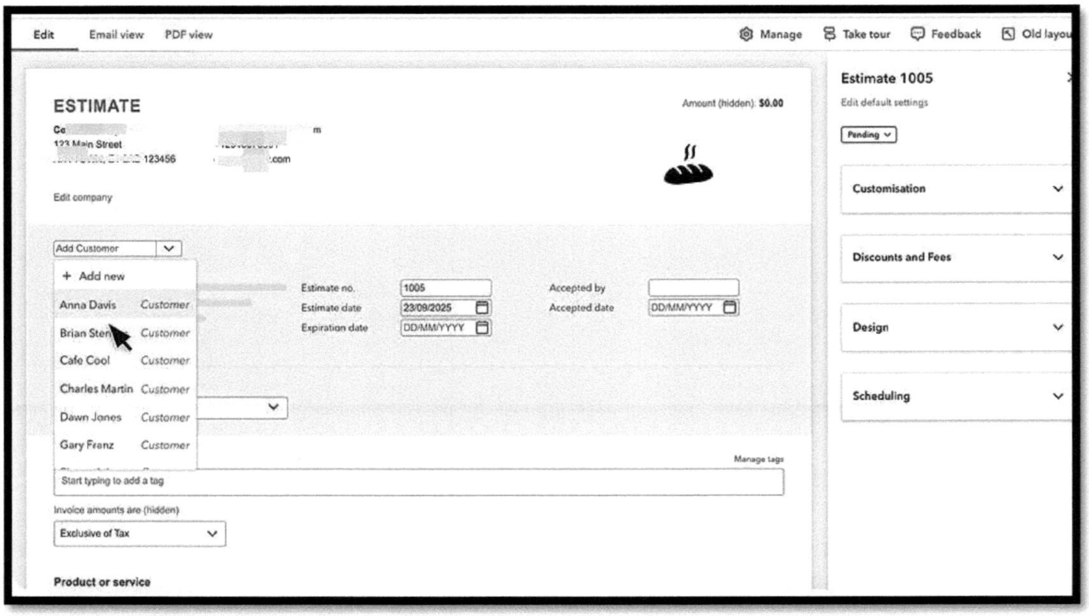

- ❖ If the customer isn't listed, add them directly from this screen.
- ❖ Their address and email will auto-populate if you've saved them previously.

4. Under **Manage**, choose which fields you want to show or hide on the estimate.

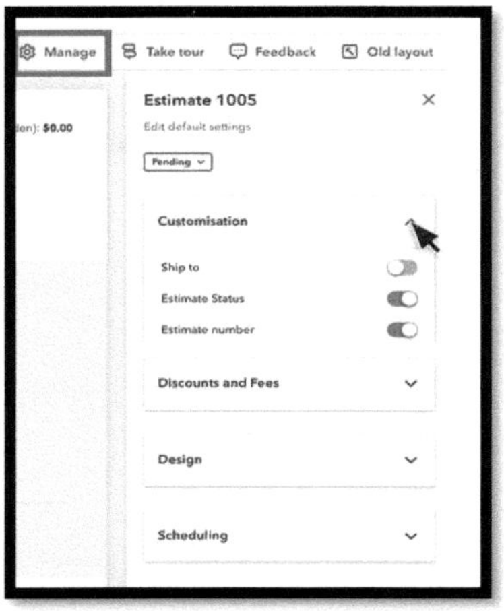

5. Under **Discounts and Fees**, turn on any extra options your estimate might need.

2. Customizing the Design

- Go to **Design** to change the estimate's **color scheme**, **fonts**, and overall layout to match your branding.

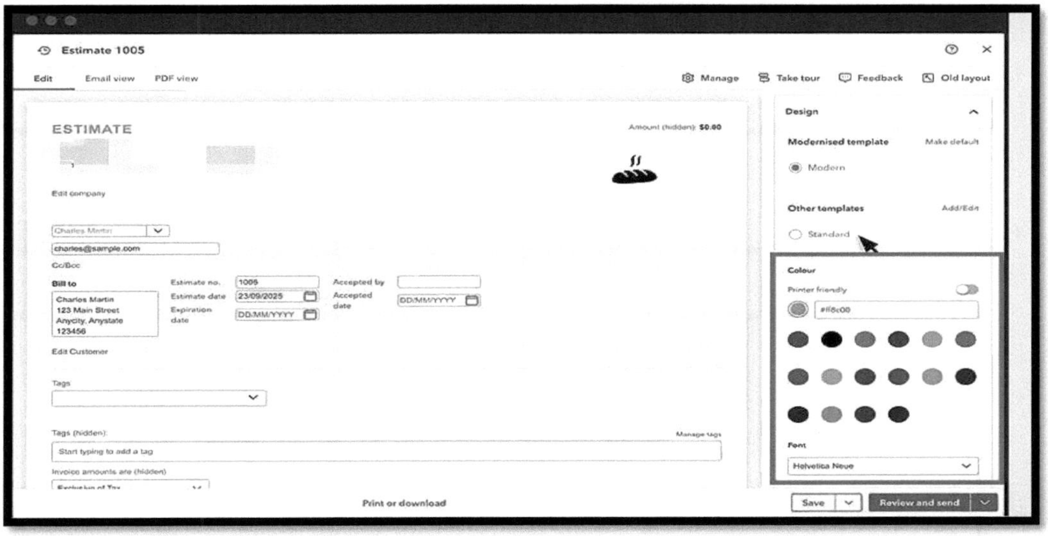

- If you've created templates in the older estimate format, you can select them here—just note that some features may not be compatible with older templates.

3. Adding Products, Services, and Details

1. Select **Product/Service** and enter the items included in the proposal.

2. Adjust **quantity**, **rate**, or **descriptions** as needed.
3. Need a new product or service? Add it from this screen.

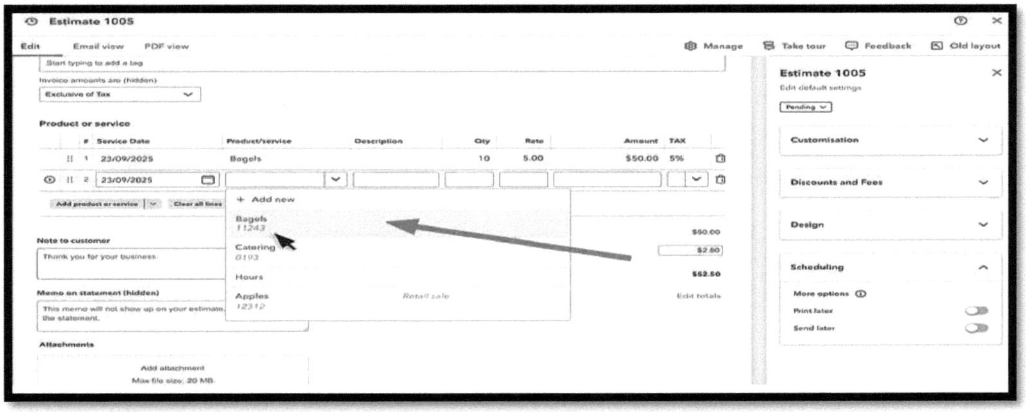

4. Include **notes** or **attach photos/documents** that help explain the project.

4. Sending the Estimate

When the estimate looks complete:

- ❖ Select **Review and Send**.
- ❖ You'll see a preview of the email your customer will receive, including a link where they can **view and approve** the estimate online.

❖ Click **Send Estimate**.

5. Tracking Estimate Status

In **Sales → Estimates**, you can track each estimate's progress. QuickBooks shows whether a customer has:

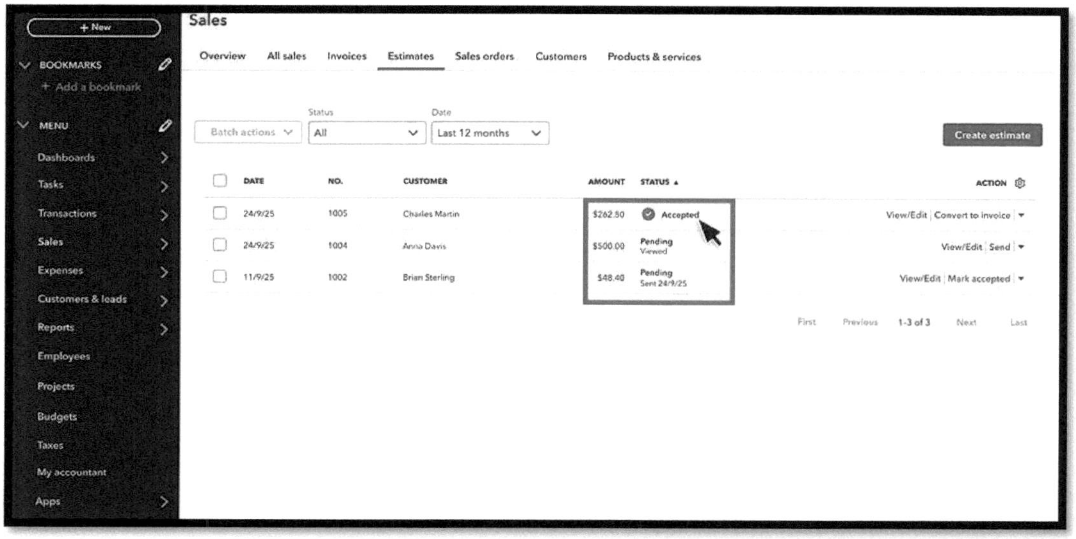

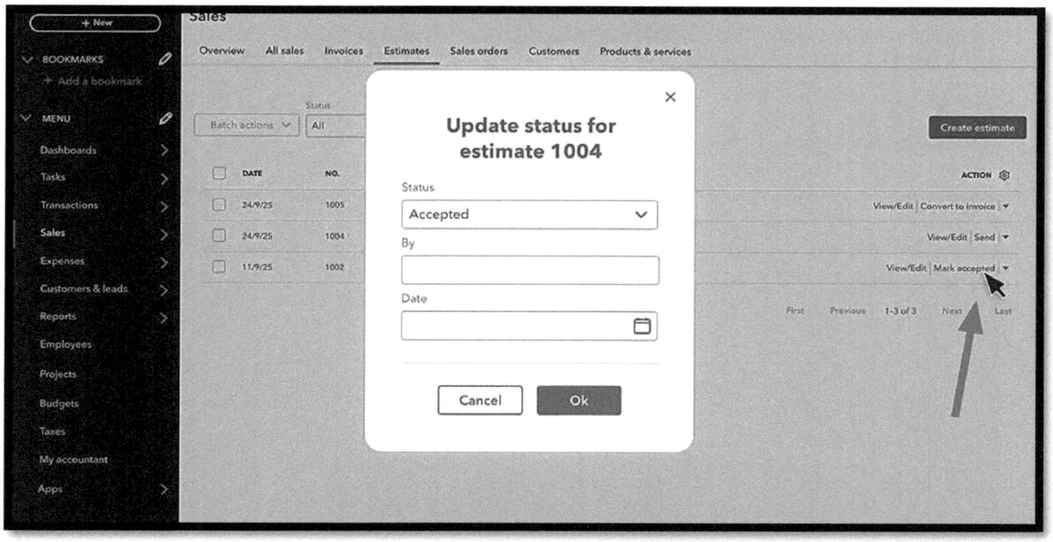

❖ Viewed
❖ Accepted
❖ Declined

If the customer verbally agrees, you can manually mark the estimate as **Accepted**.

6. Converting an Estimate to an Invoice

When you're ready to bill:

1. Open the estimate.
2. Select **Convert to Invoice**.
3. Choose whether to invoice for:

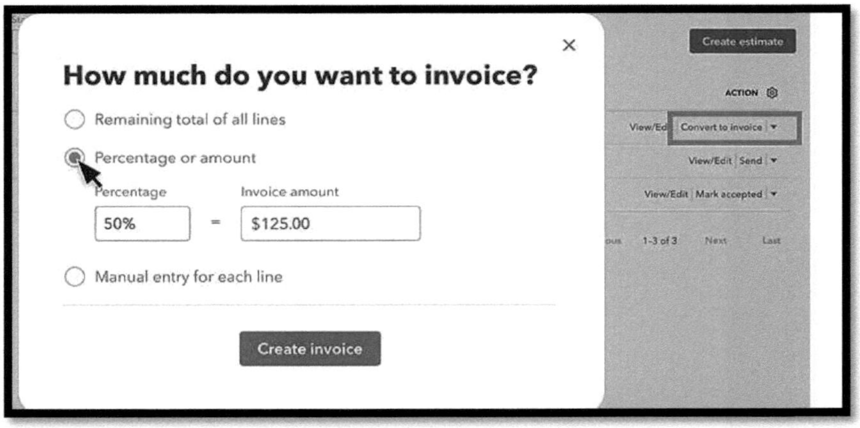

- ❖ **The full amount**, or
- ❖ **A partial amount** (progress invoicing).

QuickBooks automatically pulls all items, quantities, and details from the estimate into the invoice. You can still update any quantities, rates, or add additional products/services before sending.

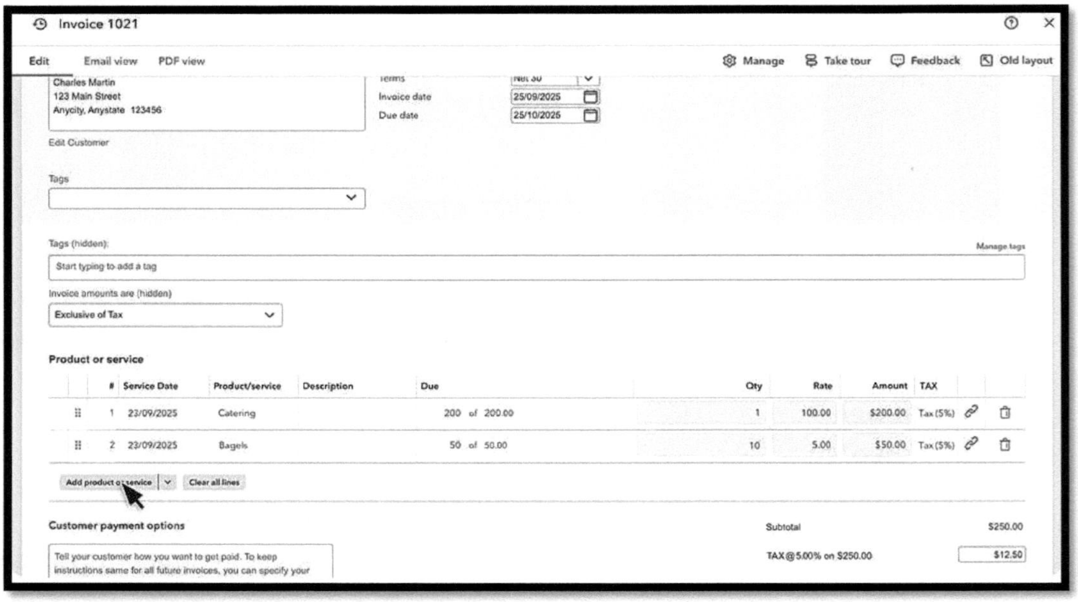

HOW TO WRITE OFF BAD DEBT IN QUICKBOOKS ONLINE

When a customer stops responding and you can no longer collect what they owe, it's time to write off the balance as bad debt. Below is a clear, step-by-step guide on how to properly record and track bad debts in QuickBooks Online.

Step 1: Identify the Bad Debt

If you already know which customer's balance needs to be written off, move on to Step 2.
Otherwise:

1. Go to **Reports** in the left-side menu.
2. Run the **Accounts Receivable Aging Detail** report.

Review the list of overdue accounts.

As the accountant for Gadget Garage, I reviewed our overdue accounts and found outstanding balances from **Brian**, **Emily**, and **Rachel**. After reaching out to all three customers, only Emily failed to respond. Following a discussion with the business owner, we determined that Emily's balance was uncollectible and should be written off as **bad debt**.

A/R Aging Detail Report
Gadget Garage
As of July 30, 2025

Date	Transaction Type	Num	Customer Full Name	Location Full Name	Due Date	Amount	Open Balance
61 - 90 days past due (1)							
04/22/2025	Invoice	1011	Brian Matthews	-	05/22/2025	6,749.90	6,749.90
Total for 61 - 90 days past due						**$6,749.90**	**$6,749.90**
31 - 60 days past due (1)							
05/26/2025	Invoice	1010	Emily Patel	HQ	06/25/2025	600.00	600.00
Total for 31 - 60 days past due						**$600.00**	**$600.00**
1 - 30 days past due (1)							
06/20/2025	Invoice	1009	Rachel Nguyen	Knoxville	07/20/2025	500.00	500.00
Total for 1 - 30 days past due						**$500.00**	**$500.00**
CURRENT (3)							
07/17/2025	Invoice	1007	Jason Cole	-	08/16/2025	129.99	129.99
07/21/2025	Invoice	1008	Michael Rogers	-	08/20/2025	1,999.99	1,999.99
07/24/2025	Invoice	1012	Greg Wallace	HQ	08/23/2025	300.00	300.00
Total for CURRENT						**$2,429.98**	**$2,429.98**
TOTAL						**$10,279.88**	**$10,279.88**

Wednesday, July 30, 2025 04:13 PM GMT+08:00

Step 2: Create a Bad Debt Expense Account

You need a dedicated expense account to track uncollectible customer balances.

1. Select the **gear icon (⚙)**.
2. Choose **Chart of accounts**.
3. Click **New**.
4. Set **Account Type** to *Expenses*.

5. Set **Detail Type** to *Bad Debts*.
6. Name it **Bad Debt** (or a similar, clear label).

Note: Bad debt is sometimes called *Uncollectible Accounts Expense* or *Doubtful Accounts Expense*, but "Bad Debt" is the most straightforward term.

Step 3: Create a Bad Debt Item

This item allows QuickBooks to apply the write-off correctly when you issue a credit memo.

1. Select the **gear icon (⚙)**.
2. Click **Products and services**.
3. Choose **New**, then select **Service**.
4. Name the item **Bad Debt**.
5. **Uncheck** "I sell this item to my customers."
6. Under **Purchasing information**, select the **Bad Debt** expense account created in Step 2.
7. Save and close.

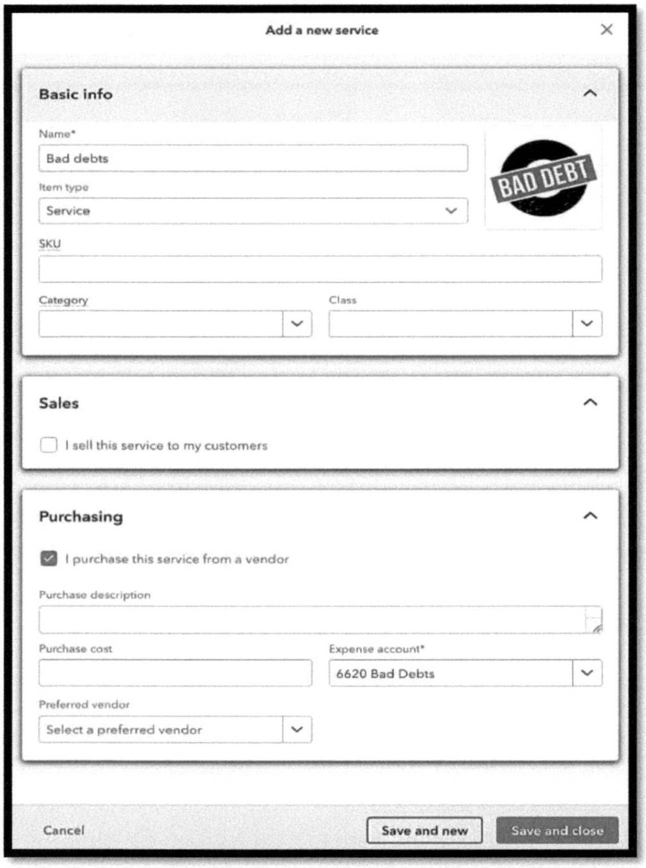

This ensures the write-off posts to the proper expense account.

Step 4: Create a Credit Memo for the Bad Debt

This step clears the invoice and records the loss.

1. Select **+ New**.
2. Choose **Credit Memo** under the *Customers* section.
3. Select the customer (e.g., *Emily Patel*).
4. Choose the **Bad Debt** item.
5. Enter the amount to be written off (e.g., *$600*).
6. Click **Save and send** or **Save and close**.

A/R Aging Detail Report
Gadget Garage
As of July 30, 2025

Date	Transaction Type	Num	Customer Full Name	Location Full Name	Due Date	Amount	Open Balance
61 - 90 days past due (1)							
04/22/2025	Invoice	1011	Brian Matthews	-	05/22/2025	6,749.90	6,749.90
Total for 61 - 90 days past due						$6,749.90	$6,749.90
31 - 60 days past due (1)							
05/26/2025	Invoice	1010	Emily Patel	HQ	06/25/2025	600.00	600.00
Total for 31 - 60 days past due						$600.00	$600.00
1 - 30 days past due (1)							
06/20/2025	Invoice	1009	Rachel Nguyen	Knoxville	07/20/2025	500.00	500.00
Total for 1 - 30 days past due						$500.00	$500.00
CURRENT (3)							
07/17/2025	Invoice	1007	Jason Cole	-	08/16/2025	129.99	129.99
07/21/2025	Invoice	1008	Michael Rogers	-	08/20/2025	1,999.99	1,999.99
07/24/2025	Invoice	1012	Greg Wallace	HQ	08/23/2025	300.00	300.00
Total for CURRENT						$2,429.98	$2,429.98
TOTAL						$10,279.88	$10,279.88

Wednesday, July 30, 2025 04:13 PM GMT+08:00

QuickBooks will automatically apply the credit memo to the unpaid invoice, reducing the customer's balance to zero.

Step 5: Review How the Credit Memo Was Applied

After saving:

- ❖ The credit memo will display a **PAID** status.

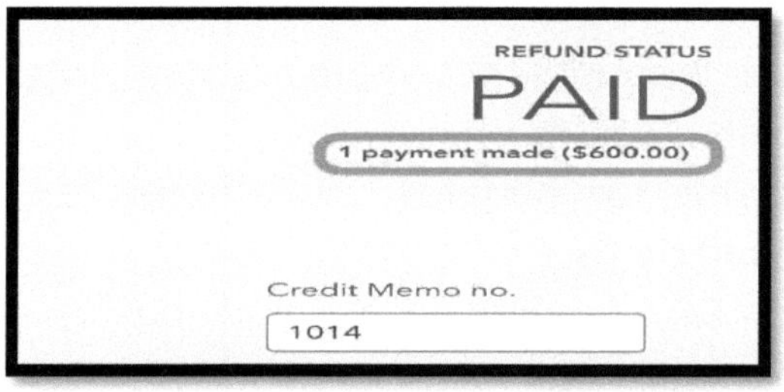

- ❖ Select the green hyperlink beneath this status to view the payment record.

Here, you can confirm that the credit memo fully cleared the outstanding invoice.

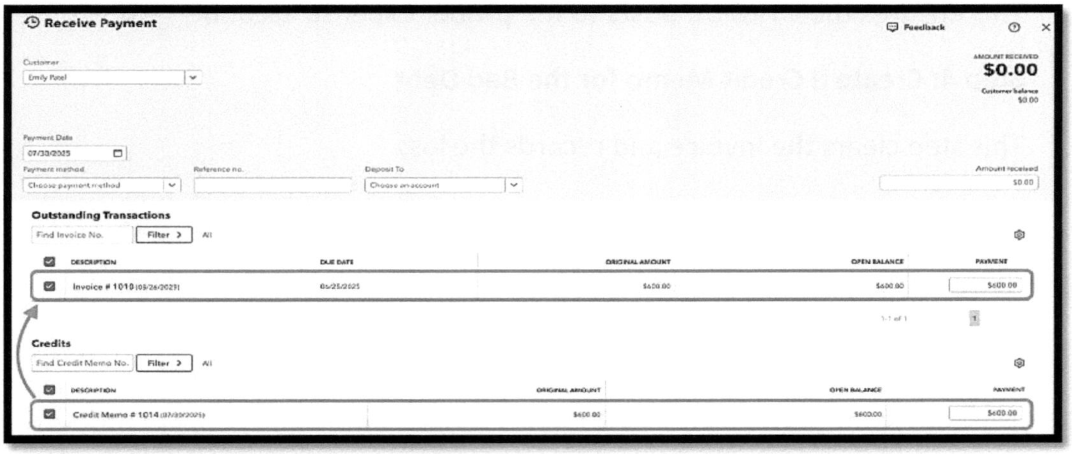

Step 6: Run a Bad Debt Report

To see all your write-offs:

1. Go to **Chart of accounts**.
2. Find the **Bad Debt** expense account.
3. Select the dropdown ($_v$) and choose **Run report**.

Your P&L statement will also reflect these write-offs under **Expenses**.

Why Write Off Bad Debt?

Writing off uncollectible invoices matters because:

- It keeps your **accounts receivable accurate** by removing amounts you won't collect.
- It may provide **tax benefits**, since many tax rules allow deductions for legitimate bad debts.
- It maintains **GAAP-compliance** if your business follows accrual accounting standards.

What if a Customer Pays After You Wrote Off the Debt?

It's uncommon, but it happens. Before taking action, consult your accountant. Typical approach:

1. **Void** the credit memo (never delete it—voiding preserves the audit trail).
   - ❖ This restores the original invoice.
2. Record the payment through **Receive Payment**, just as you would for any customer payment.

Your accountant may have a preferred method, so verify before making changes.

CHAPTER FOUR

MANAGING EXPENSES, MANAGING BILLS, AND SETTLING OUTSTANDING BALANCES

In QuickBooks Online (QBO), managing expenses, bills, and outstanding balances involves a streamlined process using specific transaction forms to ensure accurate financial tracking and timely payments.

HOW TO ENTER BILLS, PAY VENDORS, AND AVOID ERRORS IN QUICKBOOKS ONLINE

In this section, you'll learn how to **enter bills**, **pay vendors**, **print checks**, **apply vendor credits**, and handle old or incorrect bills—along with several common mistakes to avoid.

Why Entering Bills Matters (and Why Your Reports May Be Misleading)

One of the biggest mistakes QuickBooks Online users make is skipping bills altogether and recording expenses directly from the bank feed. It feels faster—but it causes inaccurate financials.

Here's why:

When you only record expenses after they clear the bank, **your profit and loss (P&L) reflects the wrong month**.

Example:

- Your phone bill is dated **August 25** for **$90**
- You pay it on **September 2**
- If you categorize it from the bank feed, QuickBooks will show the expense in **September**
- But the bill rightfully belongs to **August**

This makes:

- **August look more profitable than it actually was**
- **September look more expensive than it should be**

Entering bills fixes this by posting the expense to the correct date.

When the payment later clears, QuickBooks simply reduces accounts payable—no double-counting.

In short:

- ❖ Entering bills = accurate financial statements
- ❖ Entering bills = better cash-flow planning
- ❖ Entering bills = no unpleasant surprises

Bills vs. Expenses (A Common Point of Confusion)

Many users mix these up. Here's the difference:

Expense

You pay immediately—cash, debit, credit card, etc.

The cost is recorded as soon as the payment is made.

Example:
You swipe your card at a restaurant → that's an **expense**.

Accounts Payable (A/P)

You receive a bill **now**, but pay **later**.

The bill might be due in 15, 30, or 60 days, depending on your vendor.

Example:
Vendor sends a bill today → you pay next month → that's **accounts payable**.

Why does a bill say "invoice" on it?

From the vendor's point of view, they send you an **invoice**.

From your point of view in QuickBooks, you enter it as a **bill**.

Same document—two perspectives.

How to Enter Bills in QuickBooks Online

1. Uploading a Bill from Your Computer

1. Save the bill or vendor invoice to your computer.
2. In QuickBooks, click **Add New → Bill**
   - ❖ (In some layouts, select the **AI icon** on the left.)

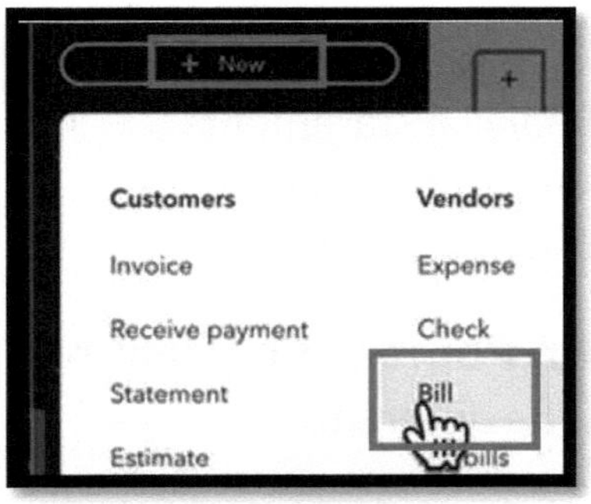

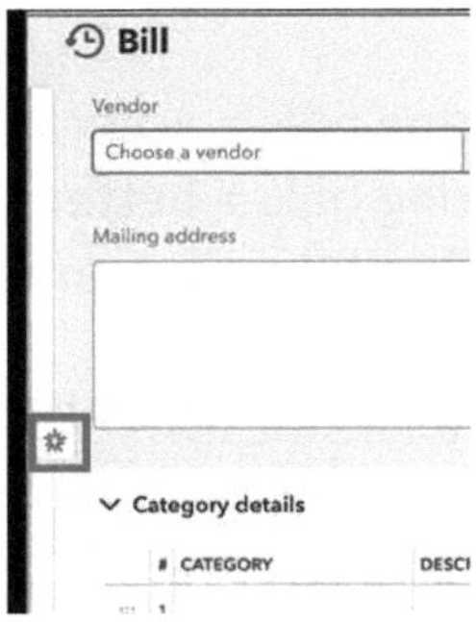

3. Upload or drag-and-drop the file.

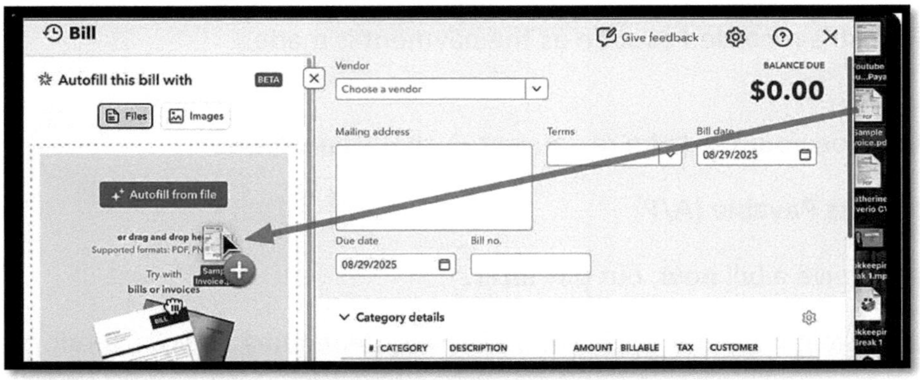

4. QuickBooks automatically extracts data (vendor name, amount, date, etc.).
5. Review the fields and fill in anything missing—especially:
   - Vendor
   - Category (expense account)
   - Description
   - Amount
6. If the vendor isn't listed, add them directly inside the form.
7. If you uploaded the wrong file, click **Clear** to reset the screen.
8. If everything looks good, click **Save and Close**.

QuickBooks will now:

- Record the bill under Accounts Payable
- Add it to your unpaid bills list
- Ensure your expense shows in the correct period

How to Manually Add Bills and Vendors in QuickBooks Online

Before you can manually enter bills in QuickBooks Online, you must have your vendors set up in the system. There are two ways to do this: **import vendors in bulk** or **create them manually**.

Option 1: Import Vendors in Bulk

1. Go to **Expenses** on the left menu.
2. Select **Vendors.**
3. Click the **green arrow** beside the "New Vendor" button and choose **Import Vendors.**

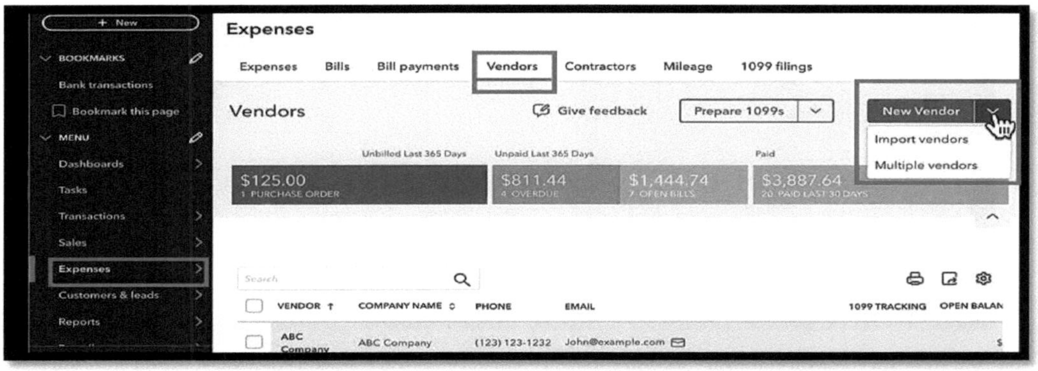

If you have a Google Sheet or CSV file, you can paste the link directly into QuickBooks to pull the data in.

Important:

Before importing, open the **Sample File** QuickBooks provides.

- Delete the sample data
- Keep the column headers
- Copy/paste your vendor information **column by column**
- Make sure the formatting exactly matches QuickBooks' required structure

This ensures your import uploads cleanly without errors.

Option 2: Create a Vendor Manually ("On the Fly")

When entering a new bill, you can quickly add a vendor directly from the bill form.

Steps to Create a New Vendor Manually

1. Click **+ New** → **Bill.**
2. In the **Vendor** dropdown, select **Add a vendor.**

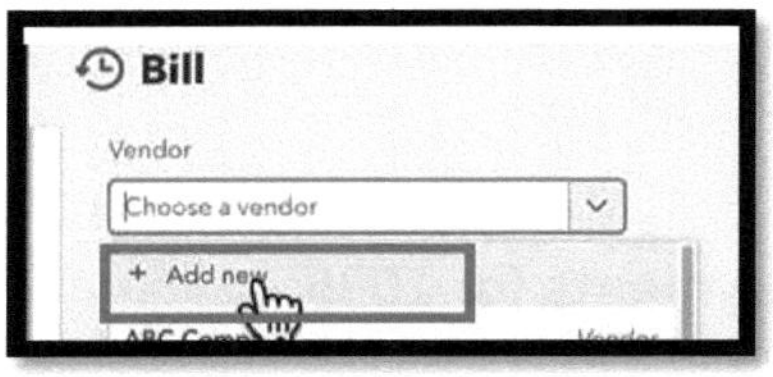

3. A vendor setup window appears—fill it out carefully.

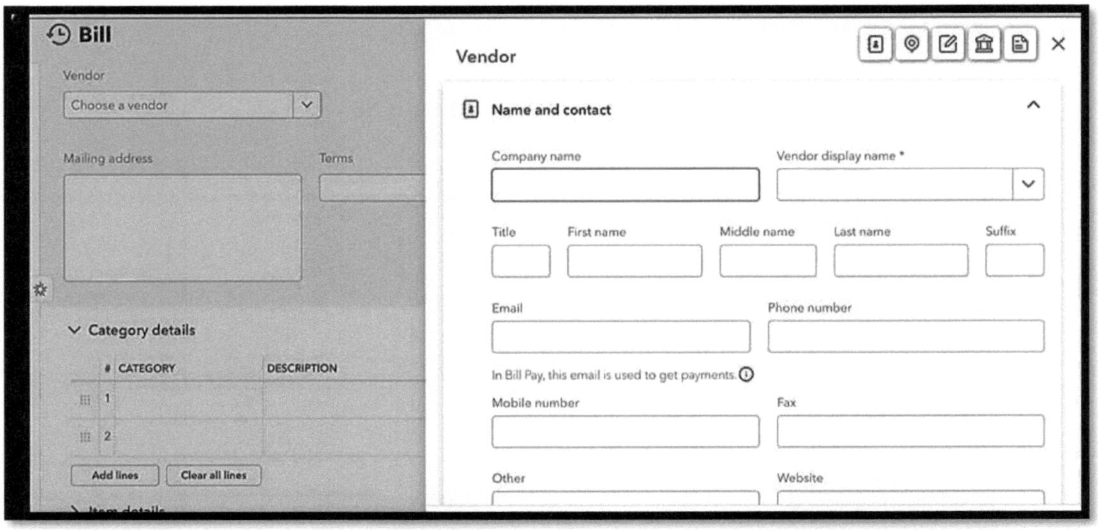

Example Vendor Setup (with details explained)

- **Vendor name:** xxxxx xxxxx
- **Email:** xxxxt@ch.com
- **Phone:** 525-987-2222
- **Website:** Optional
- **Mailing address:**
- 12345 Park Lane
- Suite 200
- Denver, CO 80202

Why these fields matter

- **Email & phone:** Essential for communication and sending purchase orders or remittances.
- **Mailing address:** Required for mailing checks and issuing year-end 1099 forms.
- **Notes:** A great place to store reminders or vendor-specific instructions.
- **Attachments:** Upload the vendor's **W-9** here so it's always accessible at tax time.
- **Account number / Business ID:** Helps with ACH payments and vendor identification.

1099 Tracking

Check the box **Track payments for 1099**—even if you're unsure.

You can always exclude a vendor later, but you can't retroactively retrieve missing data.

Critical Warning: Never Enter an Opening Balance

Leave the **Opening Balance** field set to **$0.00**.

Entering an amount here causes QuickBooks to automatically create a journal entry that:

- Increases the vendor's payable balance
- Credits **Opening Balance Equity** (a temporary account that should always be empty)

This creates messy, inaccurate financials and can lead to major cleanup work later.

Save the Vendor

Click **Save**, and the vendor will appear in your vendor list.

From now on, whenever you select this vendor on a bill, QuickBooks will automatically fill in all these details.

Before Saving the Bill: Check the Date

QuickBooks defaults to **today's date**, but this isn't always correct.

You must enter the **bill date printed on the vendor bill**, not:

- Today's date
- The date you received it
- The date you are entering it

Correct bill dates ensure

- accurate expense timing
- accurate accounts payable aging
- accurate month-end financial reports

Understanding Bill Numbers & Duplicate Detection

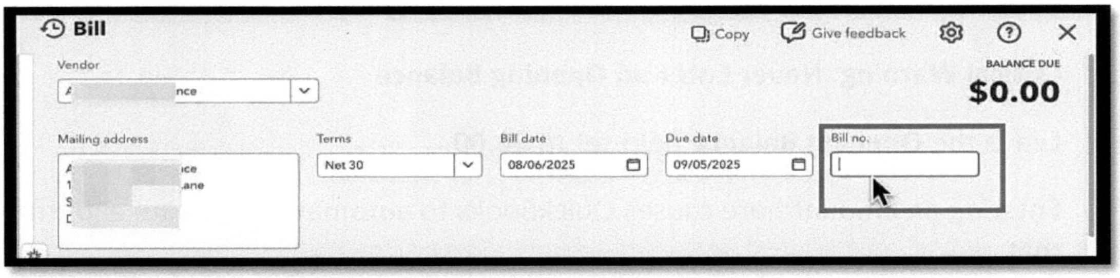

A key detail to pay attention to when entering bills in QuickBooks Online (QBO) is the **bill number**. Most vendors include a bill or invoice number, and entering it correctly is important. Here's why:

If a vendor sends you the same bill twice—and this happens more often than you'd expect—QBO can alert you to potential duplicates *as long as the bill number is entered*. When you try to enter a duplicate, QBO will display a warning such as:

"This might be a duplicate bill. You've already received this. Is this a duplicate?"

To make sure this protection is enabled, check your settings:

1. Click the **Gear** icon.
2. Select **Account and Settings**.
3. Go to **Advanced**.
4. Scroll to **Other Preferences**.
5. Make sure **"Warn me if I enter a bill number that's already been used for that vendor"** is turned on.

Click the pencil icon to edit, turn the feature on, then save your changes.

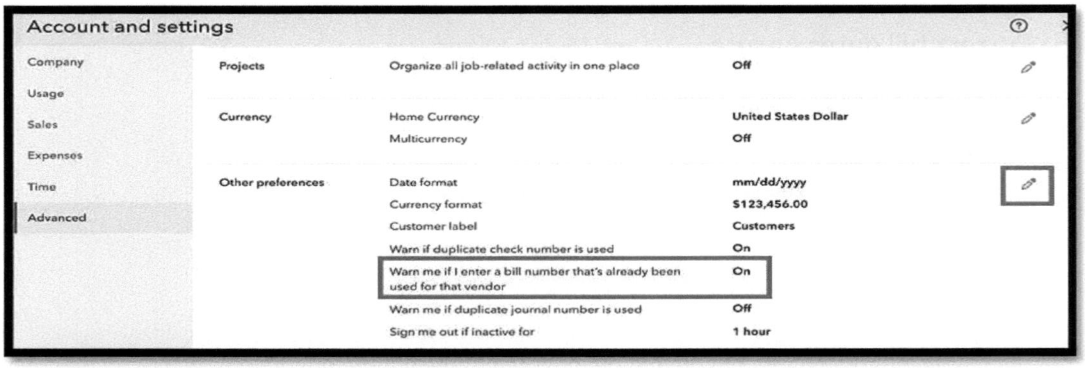

Now, back to entering a bill.

If a bill doesn't have a number, you can leave the field blank or create a simple reference like the vendor name plus the month and year. But whenever possible, enter the actual bill number.

Category Details

Under the **Category** section, choose the appropriate expense category.

For example, if you're renting equipment from *Aerotech Maintenance*, you might enter:

- **Description:** Machine rental
- **Amount:** $250
- **Category:** Equipment rental (or your relevant expense account)

You'll also see a **Billable** checkbox. This is used when you plan to pass the expense on to a customer. For example, if the equipment rental is for a specific client project, checking *Billable* allows you to later include this cost on that customer's invoice.

There's also a **Taxable** option, which you would select only if the expense should be taxed. We'll leave it unchecked for this example.

If the bill includes multiple unrelated expenses, you can add additional category lines. For instance, you could add "Equipment repairs" as a second category if needed.

Item Details

The **Item Details** section is different—it's specifically for inventory or products you purchase to resell.

For example, if you're buying oil filters to sell to your customers:

❖ **Product/Service:** Oil Filters
❖ **Quantity:** 3
❖ **Rate:** $10
❖ **Total:** $30

This goes under *Item Details* because it's inventory.

Equipment rental, on the other hand, is **not** inventory since you're not reselling the equipment.

If you enter a billable inventory item, you can also link it to the customer here.

And if you add something by accident? Just click the **trash can** icon to delete the line.

Saving the Bill

You'll see three saving options:

❖ **Save and Close** – saves and exits the bill.
❖ **Save and New** – saves the bill and opens a fresh form, useful when entering multiple bills.
❖ **Save** – saves the bill but keeps you on the same page.

For this example, we'll just click **Save**.

When you click **Save** on a bill in QuickBooks Online (QBO), you'll notice a **More** option with several useful features. Let's go through them:

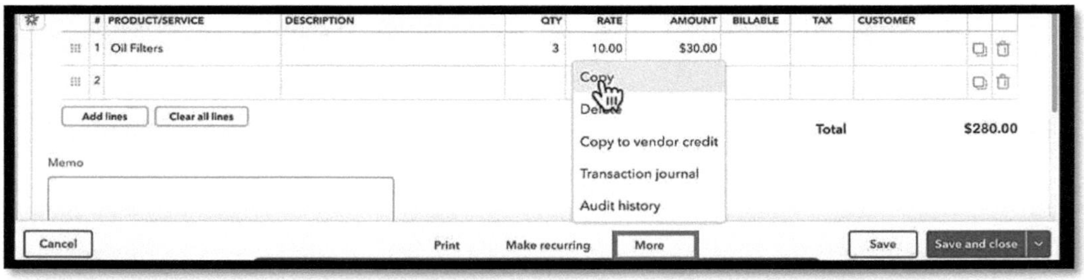

❖ **Copy:** This is great if you have similar bills from the same vendor. Instead of re-entering all the information, you can copy an existing bill and update details like the **bill date** or **bill number**. Most other information can stay the same, saving you time.
❖ **Delete vs. Void:** While you can delete a bill, it's generally better to **void** it. Voiding achieves the same effect but keeps a record in the system, so you can still see that the transaction existed and was voided. Deleting, on the other hand, removes it completely with no historical record.

- ❖ **Transaction Journal:** QuickBooks automatically creates journal entries for every bill, handling the debits and credits for you. For example:
  - ❖ **Accounts Payable** is credited $280, reflecting the amount you owe.
  - ❖ **Inventory Asset** increases by $30 for the oil filters you purchased.
  - ❖ **Machine Rental** is recorded as an expense, debited $250.

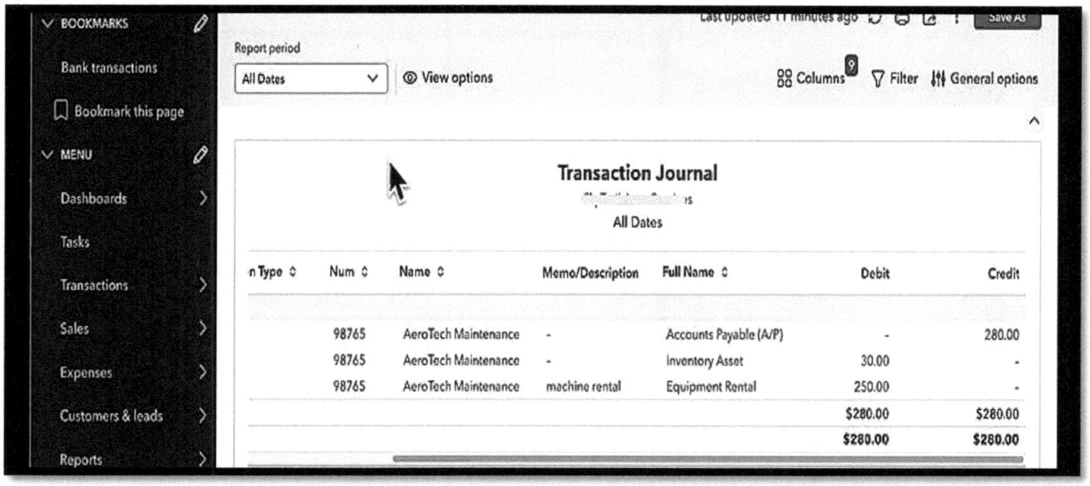

This keeps your books balanced while reducing human error.

Reviewing Past Entries and Audit History

Click the **clock icon** on a new bill to see your previous entries.

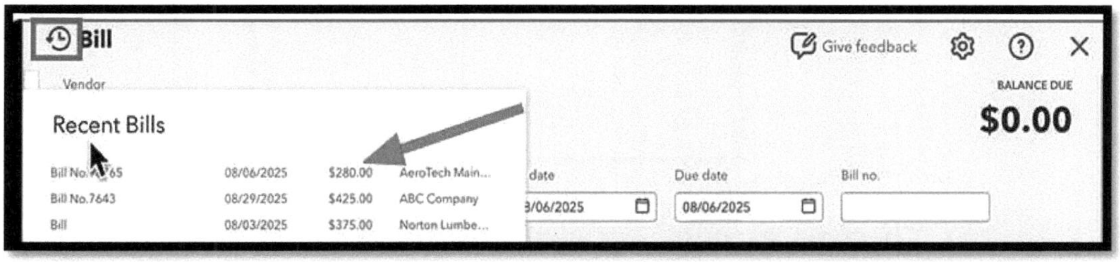

Under **More**, you'll find **Audit History**, which is incredibly useful for:

- ❖ Tracking exactly who entered, edited, or deleted a bill.
- ❖ Seeing the creation date, amount, and all details.
- ❖ Monitoring login and logout times for team members.

For example, in QuickBooks' sample company, you can see which staff member created a bill, and if it was deleted, the system records who deleted it and when. This feature is especially helpful if multiple people access QuickBooks or if a client wants to review the books.

How to Pay Bills in QuickBooks Online

When you're ready to pay bills in QuickBooks Online (QBO):

1. **Navigate to Pay Bills:**

   ❖ Click **+ New**, go to **Vendors**, and select **Pay Bills**.

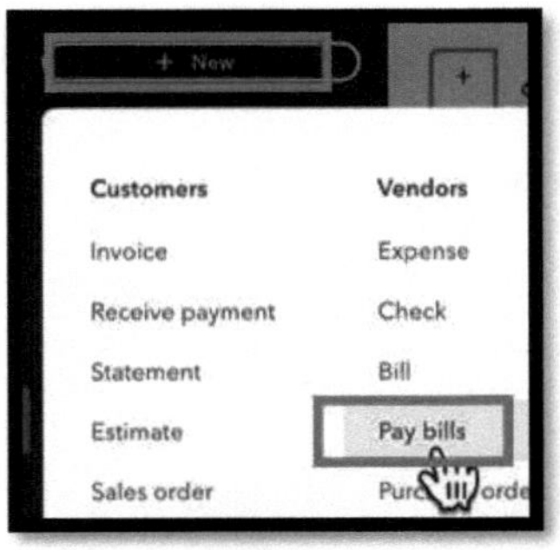

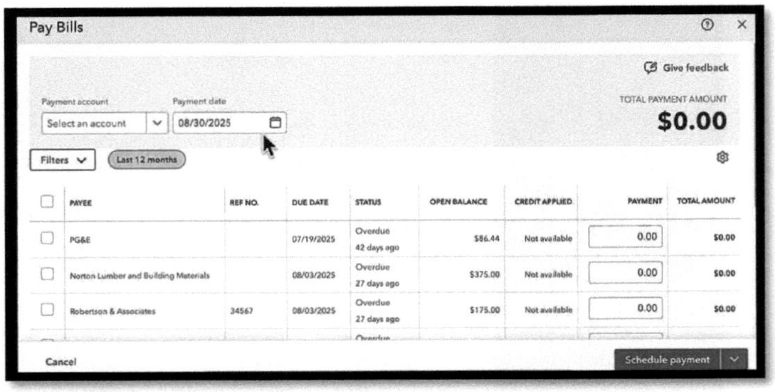

   ❖ This opens a list of all the bills you've entered in QuickBooks.

2. **Select the Correct Payment Account:**

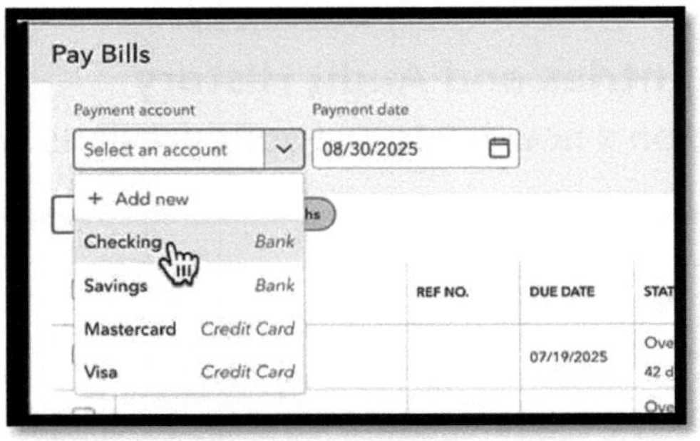

   ❖ **Checking Account:** For electronic payments or debit cards, select your checking account. Do **not** select credit card for debit payments—credit cards are liabilities.

   ❖ **Credit Card:** If paying with a credit card, choose the correct credit card account.

3. **Review Payment Details:**

   ❖ **Account Balance:** Your current balance in the selected account.

   ❖ **Payment Date:** Defaults to today, but you can change it if needed.

   ❖ **Starting Check Number:** Enter your check number, or use "71" for electronic payments.

- ❖ **Print Later Option:** If printing checks later, select this option. You won't need a check number now; you'll assign it during printing.

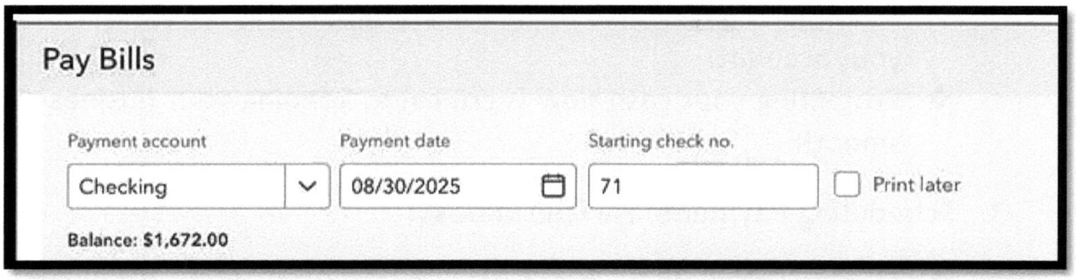

4. **Enter Payee Reference Number:**

- ❖ Typically, this is the **bill number**. Entering it helps track payments and prevents duplicate payments.

5. **Verify Bill Details:**

- ❖ Check the **due date**, **balance**, any **credits applied**, and the **payment amount**.
- ❖ By default, QuickBooks will select the full bill amount for payment.

How to Handle Partial Payments and Bill Payments in QuickBooks Online

1. **Partial Payments:**

- ❖ If you don't want to pay a vendor, in full, you can enter a **partial payment**.

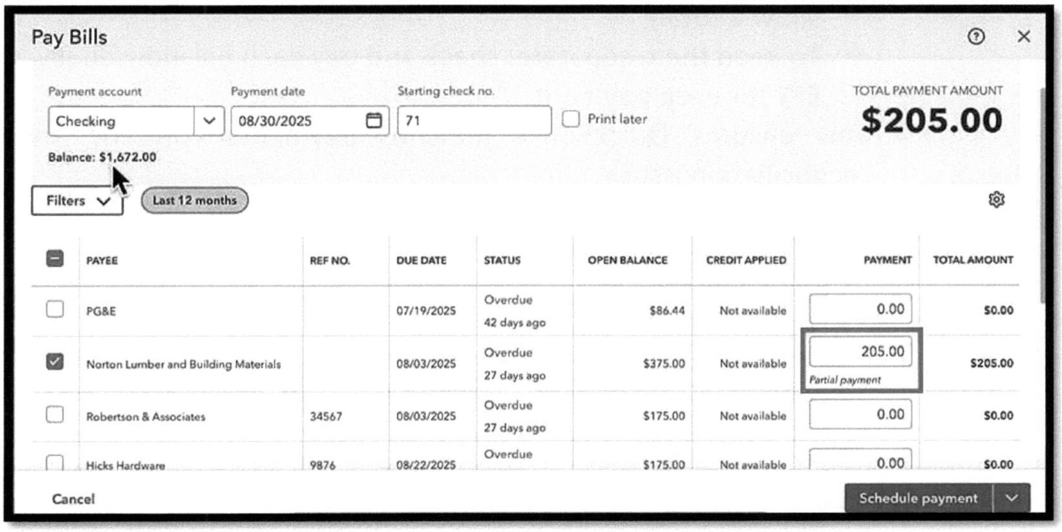

- ❖ The remaining balance stays in QuickBooks, so you can pay it later.

2. **Check Totals and Cash Flow:**

   - Always review the **total payment amount** before confirming. For example, if paying $25 toward a larger balance, ensure it won't overdraw your account.
   - Protecting your cash flow is critical to keeping your business operations smooth.

3. **Scheduling Payments via QuickBooks:**

   - Clicking **Schedule Payment** uses QuickBooks' **electronic payment service** to pay the vendor automatically.
   - This moves money from your bank account to the vendor without printing checks or manual transfers.
   - **Note:** QuickBooks charges a fee for this convenience. Evaluate if it's cost-effective compared to manual payments, especially if you handle many bills monthly.

4. **Paying with a Debit Card or Manual Methods:**

   - If using a debit card, type **EFT** as the payment reference and save.
   - You can pay multiple bills in one transaction, but if you want to keep them separate, record each bill individually to avoid confusion in the bank feed.

5. **Handling Multiple Bills:**

   - For example, if you have two bills:
     - To combine payments: check both and pay once (QuickBooks will show a total).
     - To keep them separate: check and pay each bill individually, entering **EFT** for each payment.
   - This ensures QuickBooks matches payments correctly and avoids reconciliation issues.

Printing Checks in QuickBooks Online

1. **Select Bills to Print:**

   - Choose the bills you want to pay, e.g., John and Associates, Dav Telephone, Mic Hardware, and ABC Company.
   - Check the **total payment amount** to ensure it's within budget.

2. **Print Later Option:**

   - Select **Print Later** and hit **Save and Close**.

- ❖ When ready, go to **+ New → Vendor → Print Checks**.
- ❖ Choose the correct **payment account** and enter the starting check number carefully. QuickBooks assigns sequential numbers to subsequent checks.

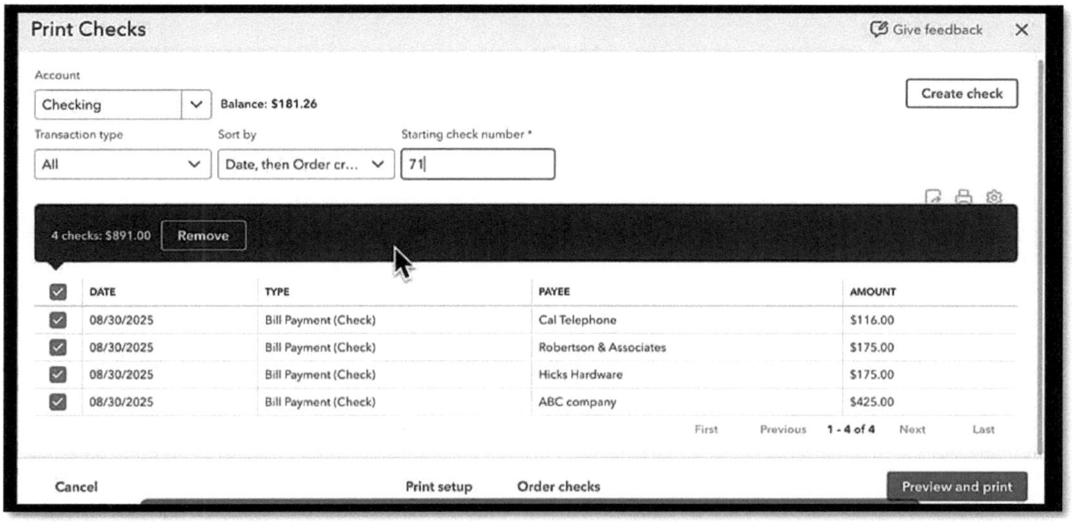

- ❖ Preview, print, and review.
- ❖ After printing, QuickBooks will ask if the checks printed correctly. If there was a printer issue, select **Some checks need reprinting** and enter the correct starting number.

Note: Printing checks is only the first step; you still need to stuff envelopes, add postage, and mail them.

Handling Vendor Credits

1. **When to Use Vendor Credits:**

- If a vendor, agrees you don't need to pay part of a bill, don't just reduce the bill. Instead, use a **vendor credit**.

2. **Creating a Vendor Credit:**

- Go to **+ New → Vendor → Vendor Credit**.
- Select the vendor, category or line item, and enter the **amount** (positive number).

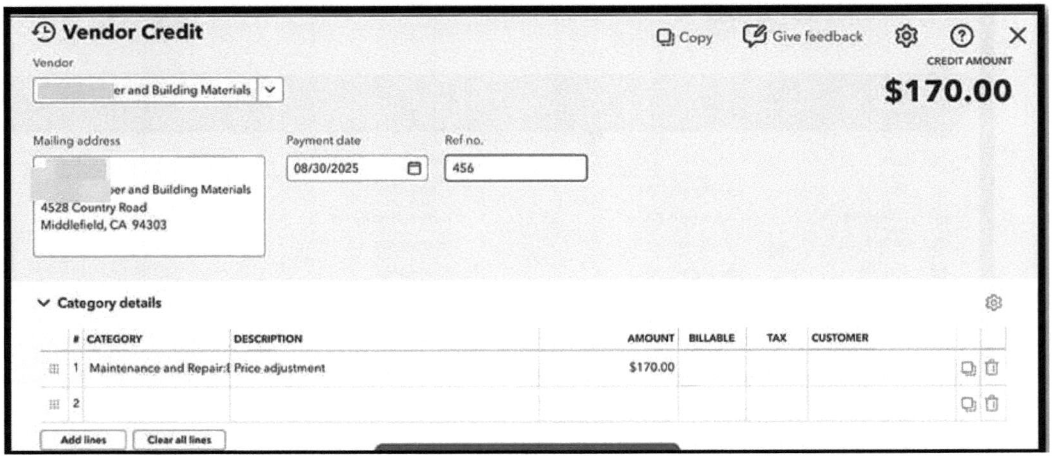

- Add notes (e.g., refund, price adjustment) and a reference number if available.
- Click **Save and Close**.

3. **Applying the Credit:**

- Go back to the original bill, click **Mark as Paid**, and select the vendor credit.

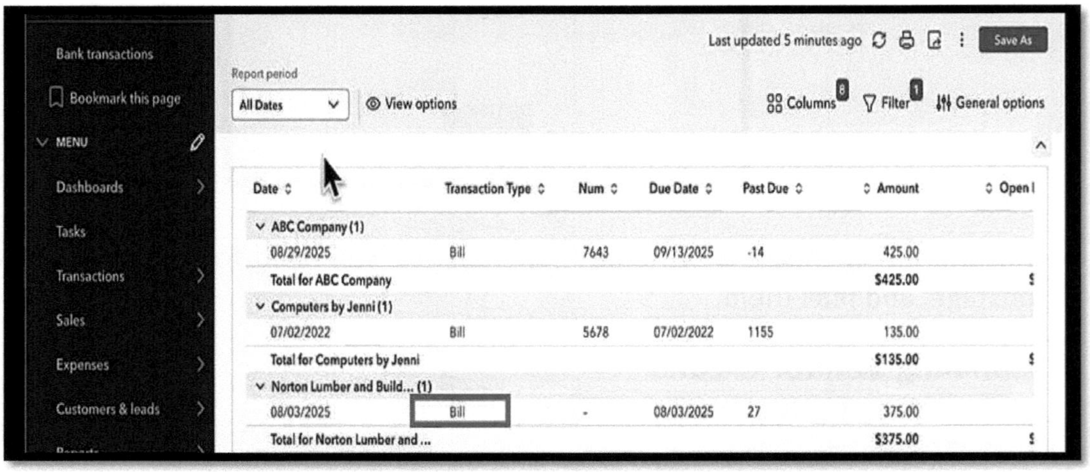

- ❖ The bill balance updates to zero, and it will no longer appear in **unpaid bills reports**.

Writing Off Old Bills

- ❖ **Do Not Delete Old Bills:** Deleting alters historical financial statements.

Option 1 – Apply a Vendor Credit:

- ❖ Use the same process as above to zero out the bill.

Option 2 – Use a Journal Entry (Advanced):

- ❖ Go to **+ New → Other → Journal Entry**.
- ❖ Enter the **current date**, debit **Accounts Payable** for the bill amount, and credit the **original expense account** (e.g., computer repair).
- ❖ Save and close, but note: the bill still appears in unpaid reports until the credit is applied.

Final Step:

- ❖ Go to the original bill, click **Mark as Paid**, ensure the journal entry is applied, and save.
- ❖ Refresh the unpaid bills report; the bill should now be cleared and correctly recorded in the **Accounts Payable register**.

CHAPTER FIVE

BANK ACCOUNT, DEPOSIT AND TRANSFERS IN QUICKBOOKS ONLINE

In QuickBooks Online (QBO), you can manage bank accounts by connecting them for automatic downloads or recording transactions manually. Deposits and transfers are handled via specific functions in the + New menu or the Banking section.

HOW TO CONNECT YOUR BANK & CREDIT CARD ACCOUNTS TO QUICKBOOKS ONLINE

Connecting your bank and credit card accounts to **QuickBooks Online (QBO)** is the quickest and most accurate way to bring your financial transactions into your books. In this section, we'll walk through how to link your accounts and choose how far back QuickBooks should import your transaction history.

Step 1: Go to the Transactions Menu

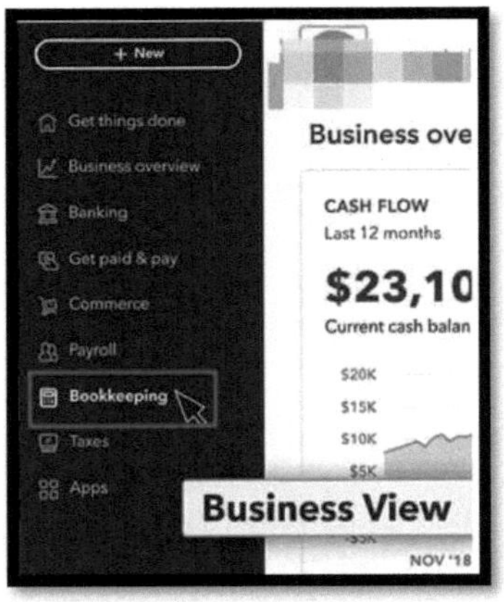

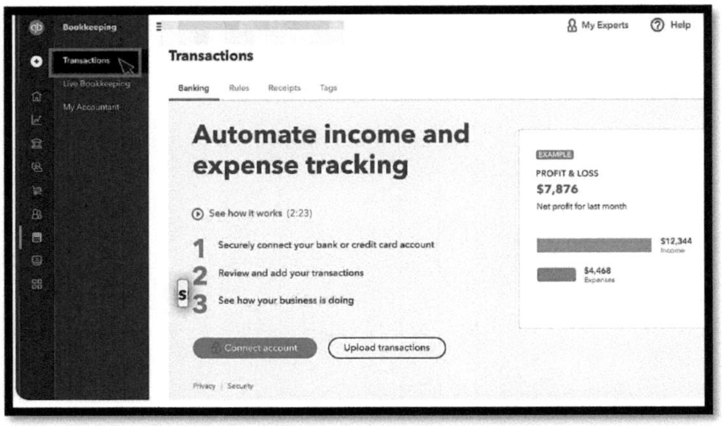

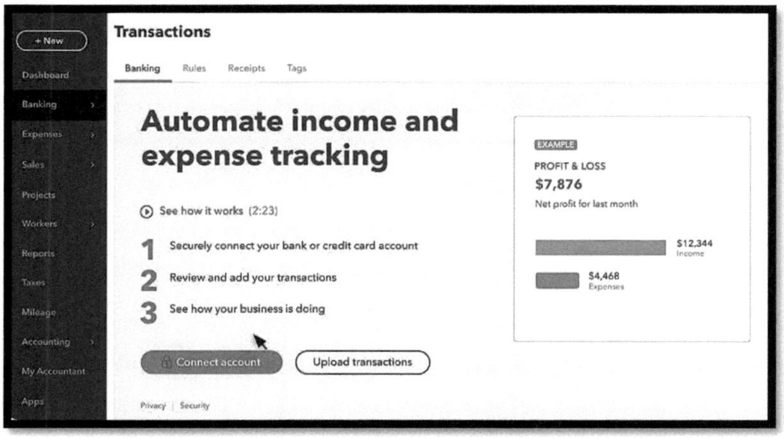

Start by selecting the **Transactions** menu in QBO.

There are two ways to bring in your bank and credit card data:

Option 1: Manually Upload Transactions

You can download your transaction history directly from your bank and upload it to QuickBooks.

- Download a file (usually CSV, QBO, OFX, or QFX) from your bank's website.
- Upload the file into QuickBooks so the system adds those transactions to the selected account.

This is useful if:

- Your bank doesn't support automatic connections, or
- You only need to import a specific set of past transactions.

Note:
If you choose manual uploads, you'll need to download and upload a new file each time you want updated transactions.

Option 2: Connect Your Bank or Credit Card Automatically

This is the recommended method because QuickBooks will continuously download new transactions for you.

To connect:

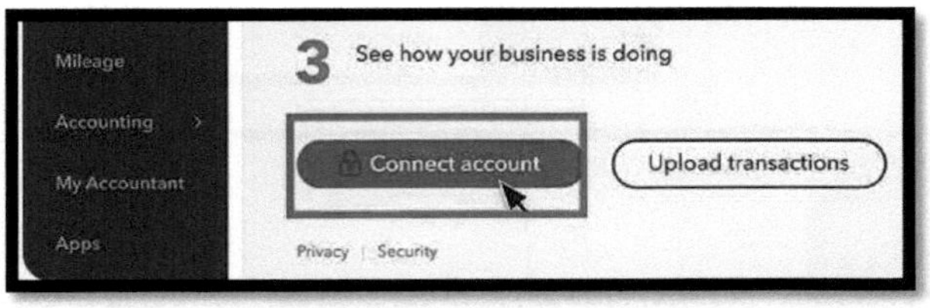

1. Select your bank or credit card from the list of popular institutions, or type its name into the search bar.
2. Enter the same username and password you use for your bank's online portal.
3. Complete any extra security steps required by your bank (such as verification codes or multi-factor authentication).

Once logged in, QuickBooks will detect all accounts associated with that financial institution.

Step 2: Choose Which Accounts to Connect

QuickBooks will display all available accounts, including business and personal ones.

- **Select only the accounts you use for business.**
- Leave personal accounts unselected to keep them separate from your business records.

Next, QuickBooks will ask you to link each online account with an existing account in your Chart of Accounts.

- ❖ If the account already exists in your Chart of Accounts, choose it from the dropdown menu.

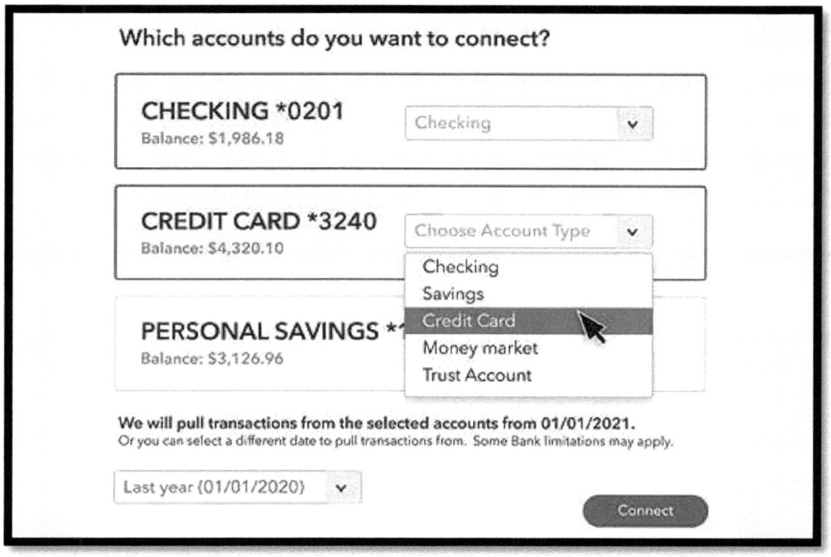

- ❖ If it does not exist, you can have QuickBooks create the appropriate account for you.

Step 3: Select Your Transaction Start Date

Now decide how far back QuickBooks should pull transactions.

- ❖ The default option is the beginning of the **previous year**.
- ❖ Many businesses prefer importing from the start of the **current year**.
- ❖ If you need a different date range, select **Custom** and enter your desired start date.

Once ready, click **Connect**.

Step 4: Review Your Imported Transactions

After QuickBooks finishes the connection:

- ❖ All transactions that cleared your bank or credit card from the chosen date up to today will appear in your banking dashboard.
- ❖ New transactions will automatically show up whenever they clear your financial institution.

The final step is to **categorize** these transactions so they post to the correct accounts.

You're now set up to automatically download and manage your business transactions in QuickBooks Online.

UNDERSTANDING THE BANK FEED PROCESS AND MATCHING TRANSACTIONS IN QUICKBOOKS ONLINE

Once your transactions have been imported into QuickBooks Online (QBO), they appear in the **For Review** tab. From here, your job is to review, match, and categorize each transaction so it posts correctly to your books. This is a critical step in keeping your financial statements accurate and preventing duplication.

Matching Transactions

Matching occurs when QuickBooks Online recognizes that a bank feed transaction corresponds to an existing transaction already recorded in your books—such as an invoice payment, bill payment, expense, or transfer. Matching ensures accuracy and prevents duplicate entries.

How to Match Transactions in QuickBooks Online

1. Go to the Banking Tab

- Navigate to **Banking** (or **Transactions > Banking**) and open the **For Review** tab.

2. Review the Imported Transaction

- QBO will display the bank feed transaction, including the **date, amount, and payee** (if available).

- ❖ If QBO finds a likely match, it will display a **Match** suggestion.

3. Confirm or Find a Match

- ❖ **If QBO suggests a match:**

  Review it carefully to confirm that the amount, date, and payee align with your records.

- ❖ **If no match appears automatically:**
  Select **Find Match** to search manually.

From here, you can:

- ❖ Filter by **amount**, **date range**, or **customer/vendor** name.
- ❖ Select the correct invoice, bill, or payment.

Once you find the correct match:

- ❖ Check the box next to the transaction.
- ❖ Click **Save**.

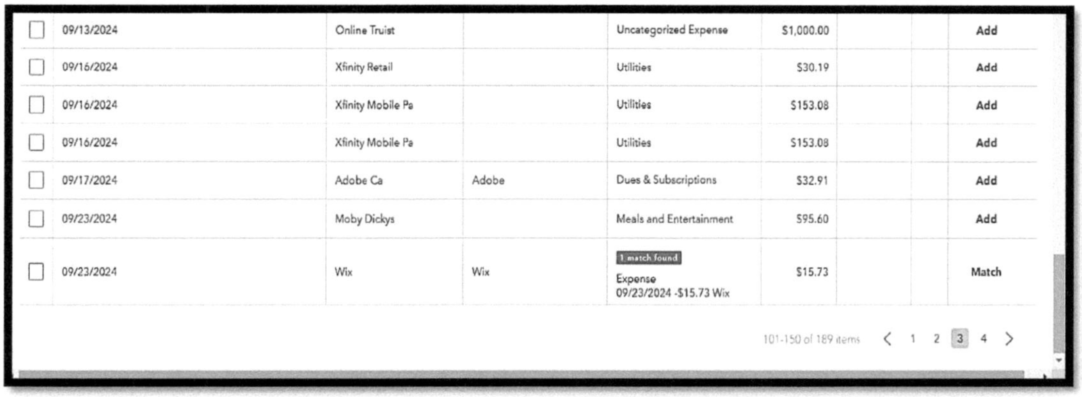

☐	09/13/2024	Online Truist		Uncategorized Expense	$1,000.00			Add
☐	09/16/2024	Xfinity Retail		Utilities	$30.19			Add
☐	09/16/2024	Xfinity Mobile Pa		Utilities	$153.08			Add
☐	09/16/2024	Xfinity Mobile Pa		Utilities	$153.08			Add
☐	09/17/2024	Adobe Ca	Adobe	Dues & Subscriptions	$32.91			Add
☐	09/23/2024	Moby Dickys		Meals and Entertainment	$95.60			Add
☐	09/23/2024	Wix	Wix	1 match found Expense 09/23/2024 -$15.73 Wix	$15.73			Match

101-150 of 189 items < 1 2 3 4 >

4. If No Match Exists — Use Categorize

If the transaction has no corresponding invoice, bill, or entry in QBO, you'll categorize it instead. This is common for:

- ❖ Miscellaneous expenses
- ❖ Bank fees
- ❖ Deposits that were never recorded
- ❖ One-off transactions

CATEGORIZING TRANSACTIONS

If QuickBooks Online cannot locate a match, you must **manually assign the correct category** based on your chart of accounts.

How to Categorize Transactions

1. Go to the For Review Tab

Locate the unmatched transaction in the **Banking > For Review** tab.

2. Select the Transaction

Click on it to view details such as amount, description, and any bank memo text.

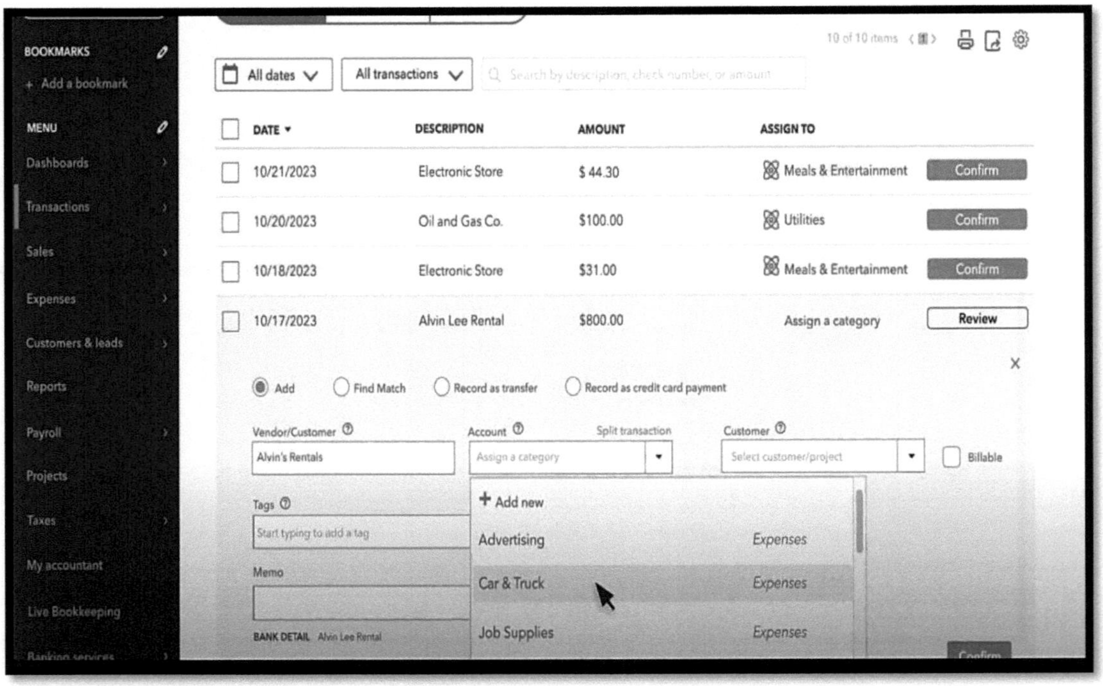

3. Choose the Correct Category

Use the **Category** field to choose the appropriate account. Examples include:

- **Expenses:** Office supplies, utilities, subscriptions
- **Income:** Sales, service revenue, customer payments
- **Owner's Equity or Draw:** Personal withdrawals, owner contributions
- **Bank Charges:** Monthly bank fees, overdraft fees

You can also: Add descriptions, Attach receipts, and Add a vendor or customer name for better reporting

4. Optional: Add a Vendor or Customer

Assigning a vendor or customer helps with:

- Expense tracking
- Profitability reporting
- Job costing (if used)

5. Optional: Create Bank Rules

To set this up, open the **Banking** page, click the **gear icon** in the upper-right corner, and select **Bank Rules**. From there, create a new rule and define the conditions that QuickBooks should look for, such as the **transaction description**, **amount range**, or **specific payee**.

Once the rule is active, QBO will automatically recognize and categorize matching transactions, saving you time and reducing errors.

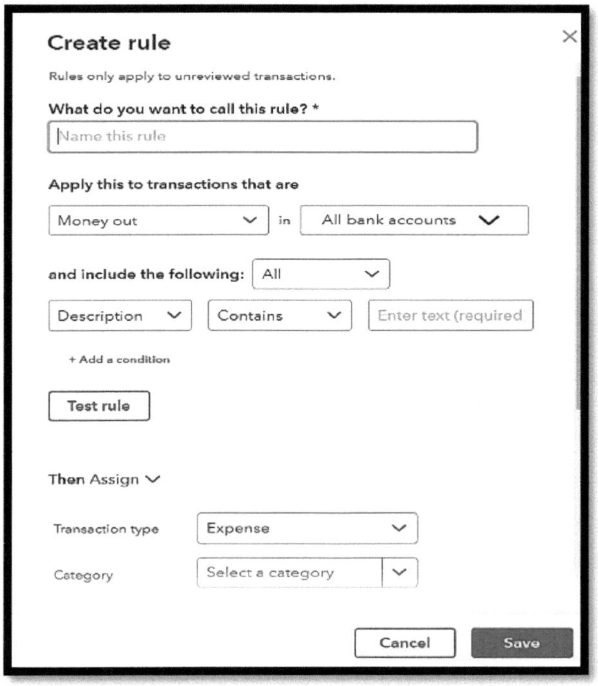

6. Save the Transaction

Once everything is correct, click **Add** to record the transaction in your books.

Step 5: Maintain Consistency

Regularly reviewing and processing your bank feed transactions ensures:

- Your books stay accurate
- Reconciliation is quick and stress-free
- Reports remain reliable
- Tax preparation becomes much easier

Set aside time—daily, weekly, or at least monthly—to review, match, and categorize new transactions. Consistency is the key to clean books.

HOW TO MANUALLY ENTER BANK TRANSACTIONS IN QUICKBOOKS ONLINE

If you need to catch up on older transactions in QuickBooks Online—or you're dealing with entries that refuse to sync—you can enter those bank transactions manually. In this walkthrough, you'll learn when to use this method, how to enter transactions directly in the check register, and how to edit them afterward.

Keep in mind: **manual entry should not be your primary method** for recording routine bank activity, since QuickBooks normally handles this automatically through connected accounts.

Step 1: Open the Chart of Accounts

From the left navigation menu, go to **Transactions > Chart of Accounts**.

If you access this section often, click the **bookmark (ribbon) icon** next to it. QuickBooks will save it under **Bookmarks**, giving you one-click access going forward.

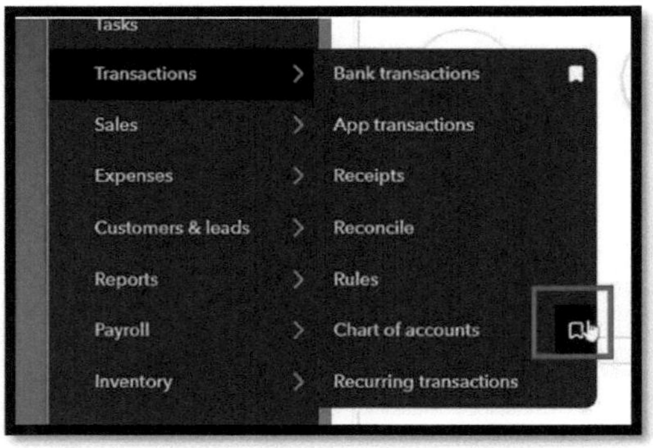

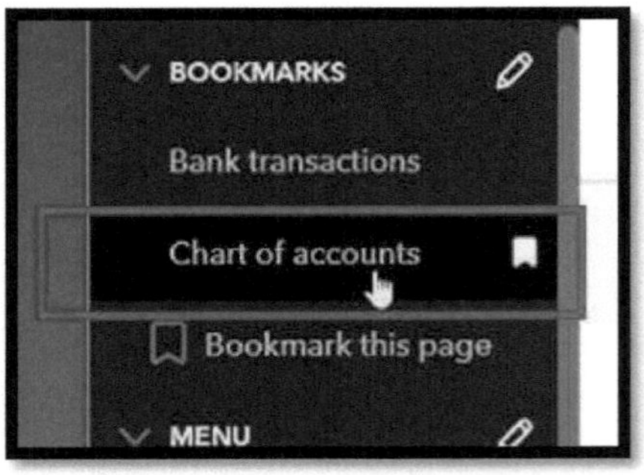

Step 2: Open the Check Register

Find the bank account you want to update, hover over it, and click **View Register**.

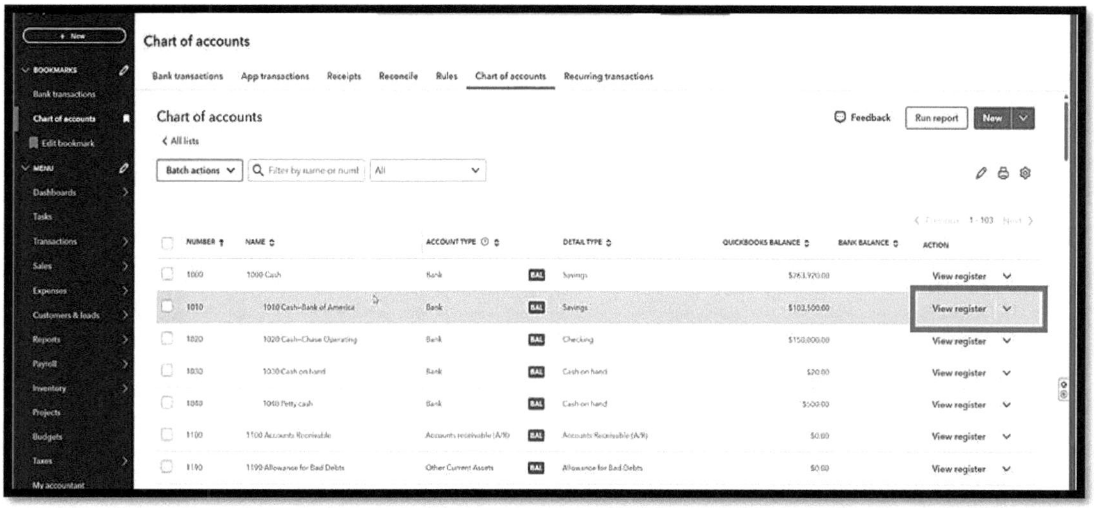

The register is your central hub for reviewing and modifying account activity. You typically don't need to use it for everyday bookkeeping, because QuickBooks automatically posts to the register when you enter invoices, bills, receive payments, or record sales receipts.

Step 3: Add a New Transaction

Inside the register, click **Add Check** (or the appropriate option) and choose the transaction type you want to enter.

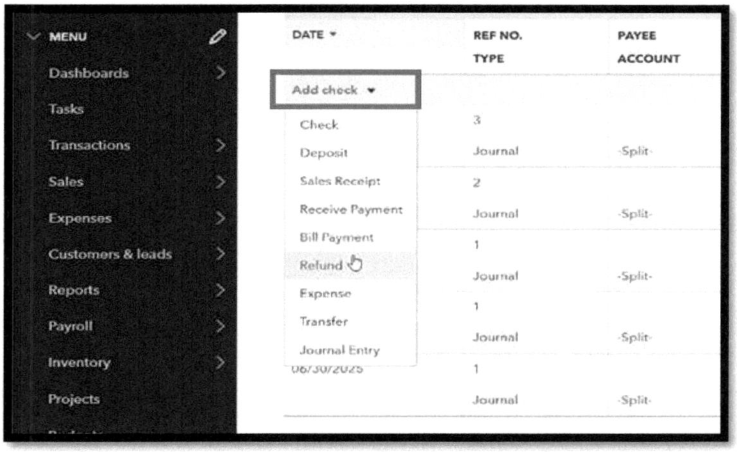

To keep your records accurate, it's best to complete **all fields**, but the essential fields you must fill in are:

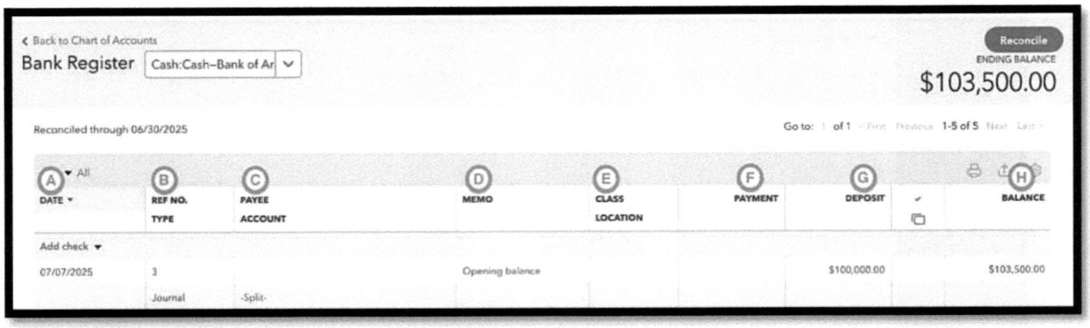

a. Date: Enter the actual date the transaction occurred—*not* the date you're entering it into QuickBooks.

b. Ref No. / Type: Record the transaction's reference number (e.g., a check number). The transaction type is automatically assigned based on what you selected when creating the entry.

c. Payee / Account:

For **payments**, select the appropriate vendor or employee.

For **deposits**, select the customer. If you're linking the transaction to an account, begin typing the account name and QuickBooks will display matching options.

d. Memo: Add a brief description that explains the purpose of the transaction, such as *"July rent payment."* This helps provide clarity during future reviews or audits.

e. Class / Location: Assign the transaction to specific classes or locations if your business tracks these. If the fields are missing, enable **Track Classes** and/or **Track Locations** in your Advanced Settings.

f. Payment: Enter the transaction amount if it is a **payment**. Leave it blank for deposits.

g. Deposit: Enter the **deposit** amount. Leave it blank for payments.

h. Balance: This field displays the running balance for the account after each transaction is recorded.

These minimum fields allow the transaction to save properly.

Step 4: Understand Other Transaction Types

QuickBooks has multiple transaction forms—like expense, bill, check, invoice, or sales receipt screens—which automatically feed information into the register.

Whenever possible, use those proper input screens instead of entering items directly into the register. Manual register entry is best reserved for catch-up work or unsynced transactions.

Step 5: Edit an Existing Transaction

To change a transaction already in the register, click on it and select **Edit**.

QuickBooks opens the standard transaction window, so the layout will feel familiar. Once you make your changes, click **Save and Close**.

HOW TO RECONCILE CREDIT CARDS IN QUICKBOOKS ONLINE

Reconciling your credit card accounts in QuickBooks Online (QBO) is a vital skill for bookkeepers, accountants, and business owners who manage their own finances. The reconciliation process ensures that the transactions recorded in QBO match your actual credit card statement, helping you maintain clean, accurate, and up-to-date financial records.

What Is Credit Card Reconciliation in QuickBooks?

Credit card reconciliation is the process of comparing the transactions recorded in your QuickBooks credit card register with those listed on your credit card statement. The purpose is to:

- Confirm that all transactions are recorded correctly
- Identify discrepancies or missing entries
- Ensure the ending balance in QBO matches your statement balance

This process is essential for reliable reporting, tax preparation, and financial accuracy.

How to Reconcile a Credit Card in QuickBooks Online

Reconciling card expenses in QBO is straightforward. Follow the steps below:

Step 1: Open the Reconcile Tool

1. Log in to QuickBooks Online.
2. From the left menu, select **Transactions** → **Reconcile**.

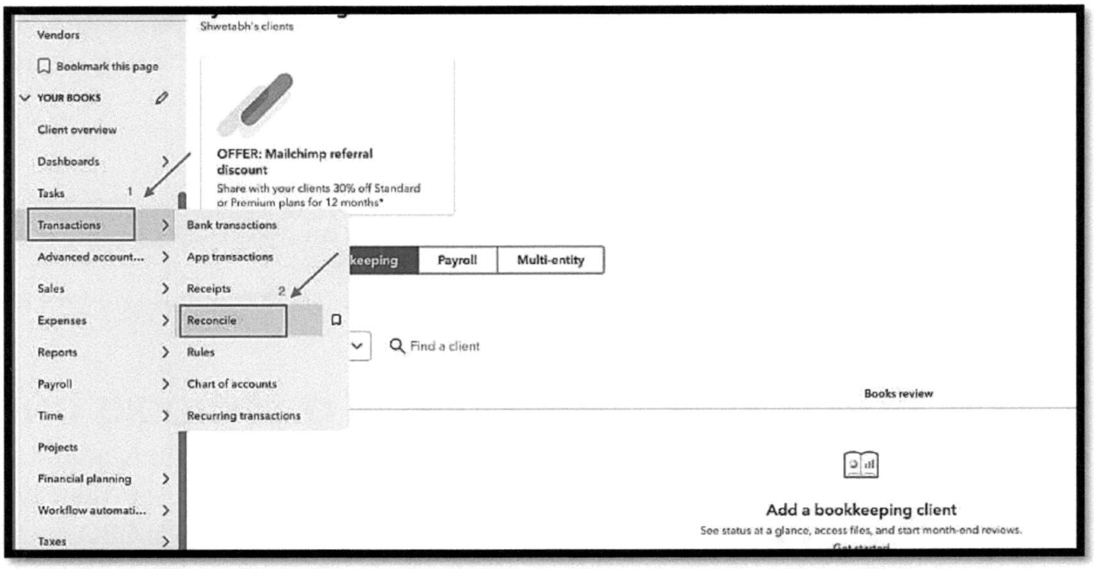

Note on Navigation: QuickBooks offers two interface views—**Business View** and **Accountant View**.

If your navigation menu looks different:

- ❖ Click the **Gear icon** (top-right).
- ❖ Check whether the bottom of the pop-up says **Switch to Accountant View**.

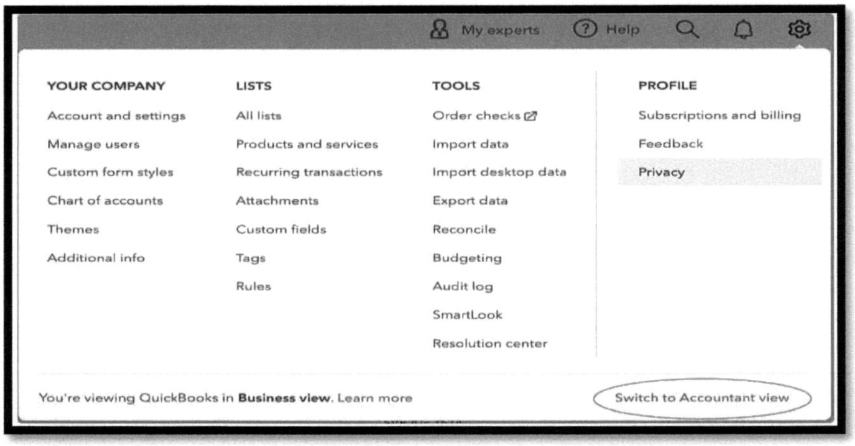

- ❖ If so, click it.

This will give you the layout used in most professional tutorials.

Once you click **Reconcile**, the reconciliation setup screen will appear.

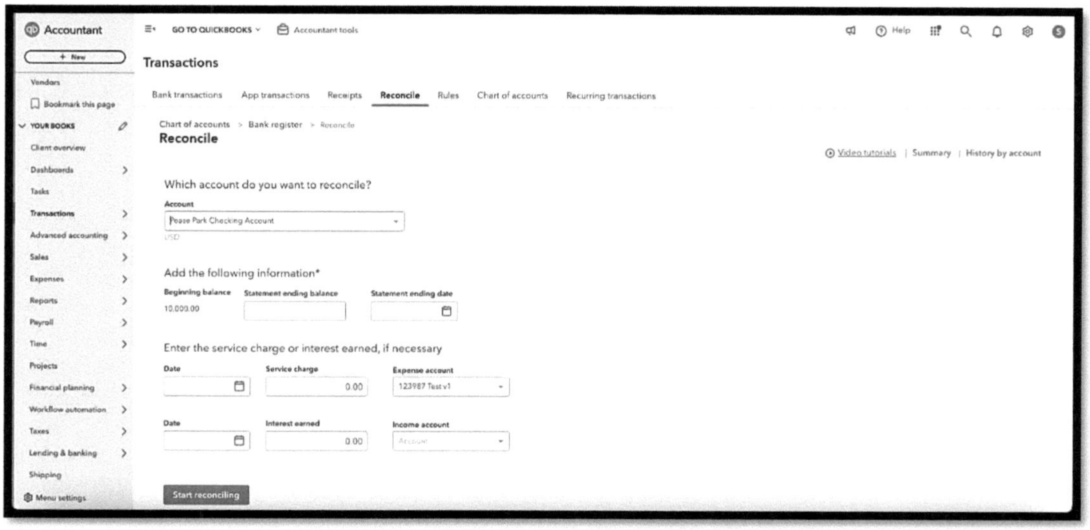

Step 2: Enter Your Statement Details

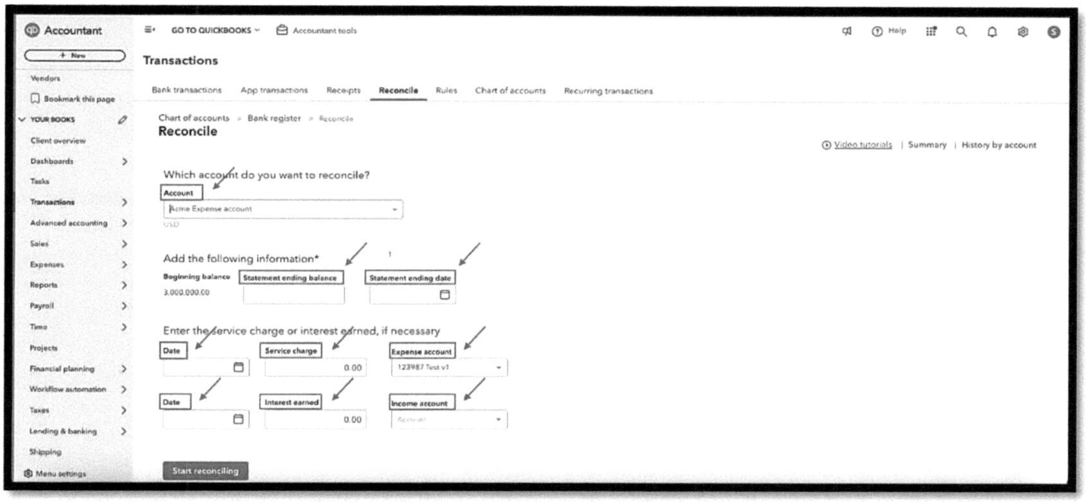

Before starting the reconciliation, fill in the required fields:

- ❖ **Account:** Select the credit card account you want to reconcile.
- ❖ **Beginning Balance:** QBO automatically fills this based on your last reconciliation.
- ❖ **Statement Ending Balance:** Enter the ending balance shown on your credit card statement.
- ❖ **Statement Ending Date:** Enter the end date from your statement.

You can also add:

- ❖ **Service charges** (date, amount, and expense account)

❖ **Interest earned** (date, amount, and income account)

These entries are optional but should be included if they appear on your statement.

Once everything is complete, click **Start reconciling**.

Important:
Ensure that the *opening balance* in QBO matches the opening balance on your statement before you begin.

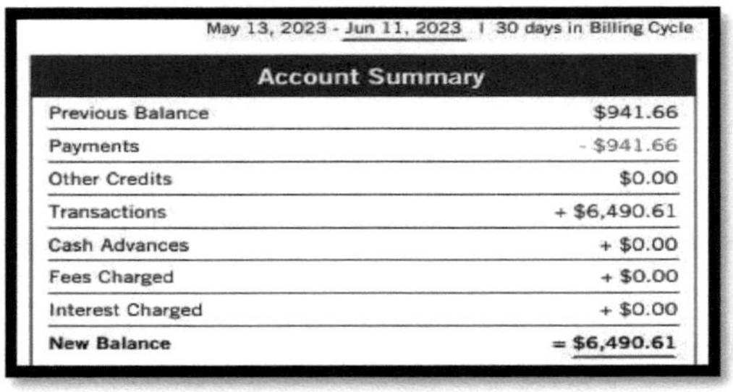
May 13, 2023 - Jun 11, 2023 | 30 days in Billing Cycle

Account Summary	
Previous Balance	$941.66
Payments	- $941.66
Other Credits	$0.00
Transactions	+ $6,490.61
Cash Advances	+ $0.00
Fees Charged	+ $0.00
Interest Charged	+ $0.00
New Balance	**= $6,490.61**

Step 3: Match and Reconcile Transactions

After clicking **Start reconciling**, you'll see a list of transactions that have not yet been cleared.

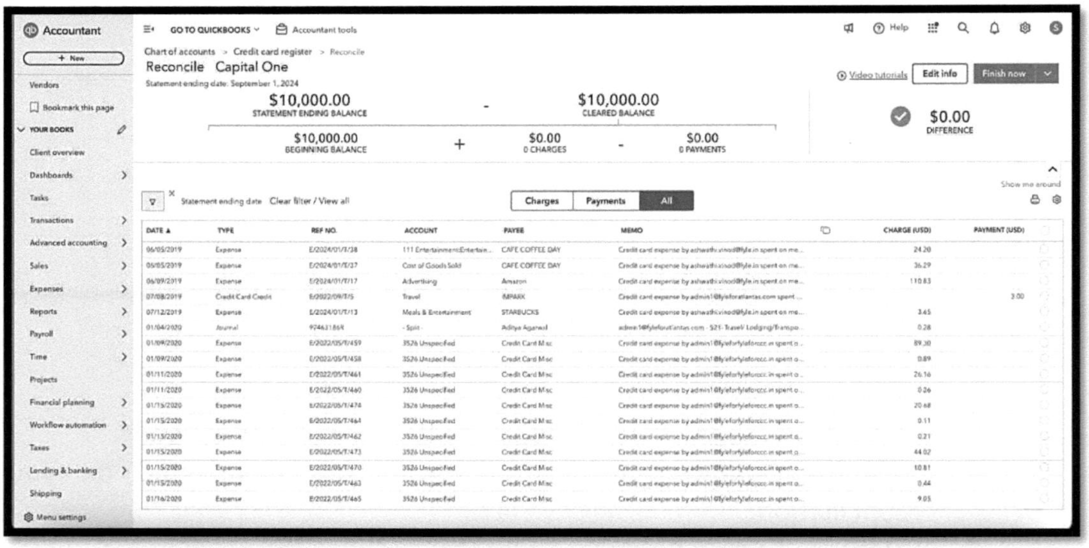

Follow these steps:

1. Compare each transaction in QBO with the transactions listed on your credit card statement.
2. When a transaction matches, check it off.

3. Continue until the **Difference** at the top of the screen shows **$0.00**.

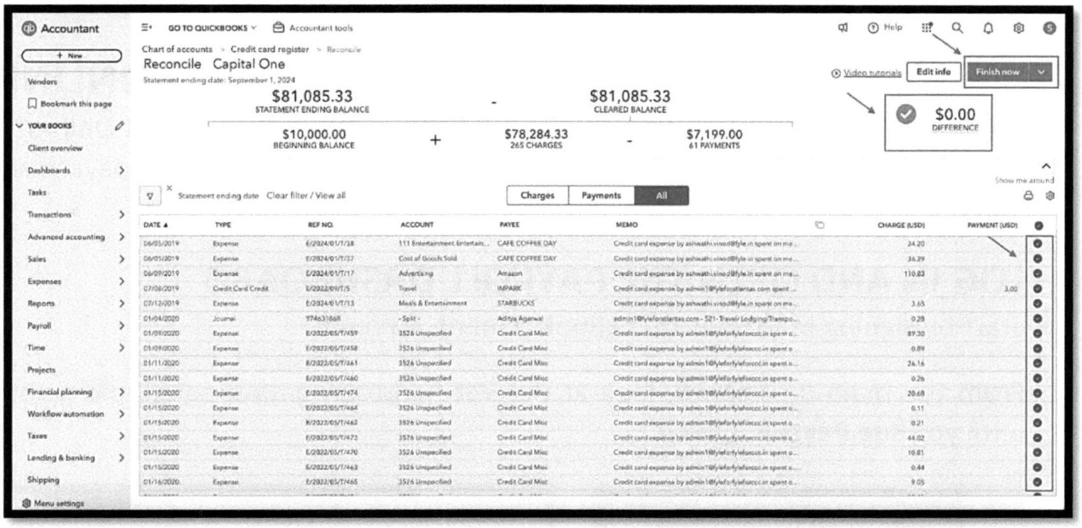

You have three options at this point:

- ❖ **Finish now** – Select this once the difference is zero and all transactions are matched.
- ❖ **Save for later** – Use this if you need more time; QBO will save your progress.
- ❖ **Close without saving** – Exit the reconciliation without keeping your changes.

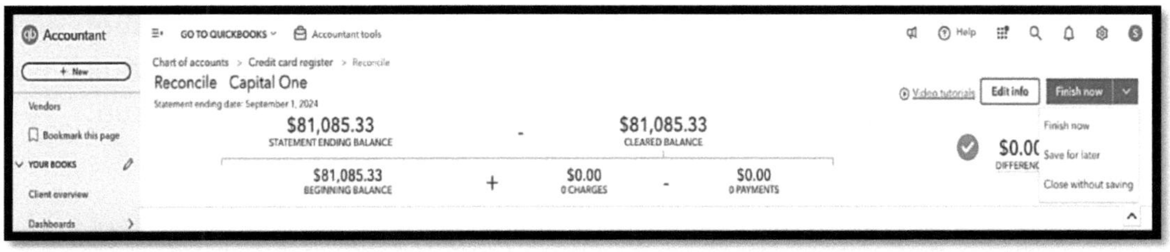

After clicking **Finish now**, QuickBooks will confirm that the reconciliation is complete and display the final summary screen.

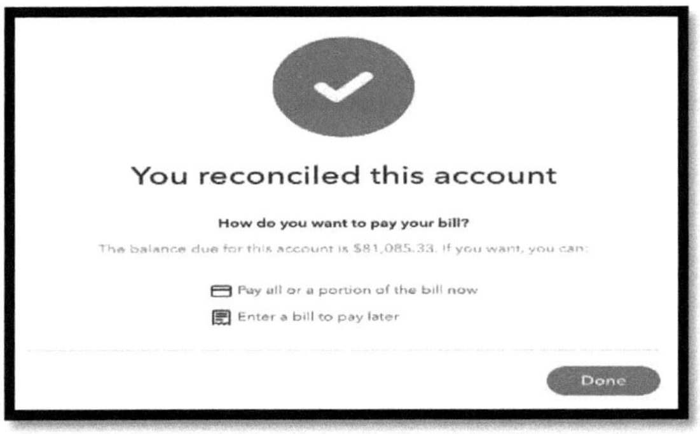

CHAPTER SIX

HOW TO DO PAYROLL IN QUICKBOOKS ONLINE

Are you trying to learn how to set up and run payroll in QuickBooks Online? You're in the right place. In this walkthrough, you'll see how to set up your payroll account, add employees, and run and review payroll right inside QuickBooks.

LOG IN AND OPEN THE PAYROLL DASHBOARD

Start by signing in to your QuickBooks Online account.

From the main dashboard, look at the left-hand navigation panel and scroll down until you see **Payroll**. Click it.

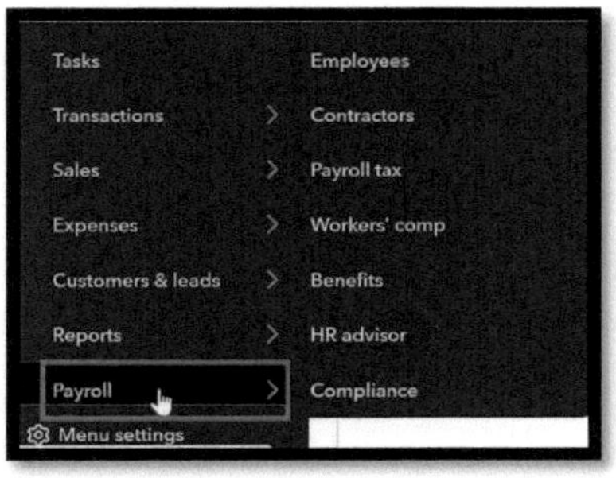

Once you land on the Payroll dashboard, you'll see a welcome screen with a **Get Started** button. Selecting this launches QuickBooks' setup wizard, which walks you through each required step until payroll is fully set up and ready to run.

If You Don't Already Have a Payroll Plan

Even if you haven't purchased a QuickBooks Payroll subscription yet, the dashboard will look the same. However, clicking **Get Started** will first prompt you to choose the features you need so QuickBooks can recommend the right plan.

You'll see a screen similar to the example (the narrator used a plan that already included payroll, so this step didn't appear during their signup).

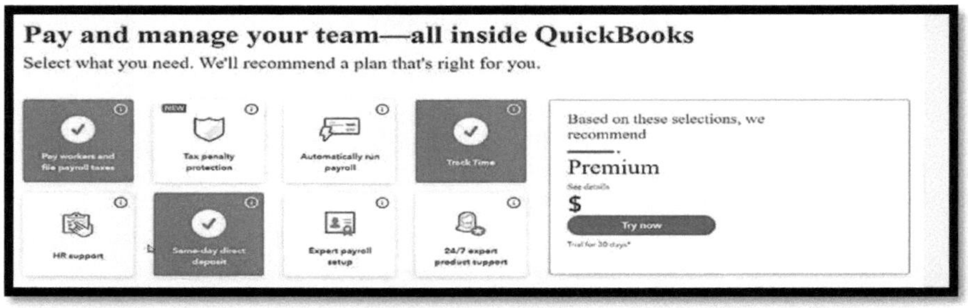

On this selection screen:

- ❖ Choose the features your business needs.
- ❖ **Tip:** At minimum, select **Pay Workers** and **File Taxes**.

  These include full-service payroll processing and automated tax filings.

- ❖ You can also add optional tools like automated pay runs or 24/7 support.
- ❖ If you don't have a separate time-tracking system, select **Track Time** so you can use QuickBooks Time for clock-ins/outs and employee hours.

On the right side, QuickBooks automatically updates the recommended plan based on the features you've chosen. In a real setup session, this area will show the monthly price, per-employee fees, and any available promotions.

The call-to-action button may say **Try Now**, **Sign Up**, or **Sign Up and Save**, depending on the current offer. Click the button to proceed with the purchase, or scroll down to compare alternative payroll plans if you want to review more options.

CONTINUING THE PAYROLL SETUP IN QUICKBOOKS ONLINE

Now let's return to the Payroll dashboard to begin the setup process.

Step 1: Click the **Get Started**

Click the **Get Started** button to launch the setup wizard.

Step 2: Indicate Whether You've Paid Employees This Year

The next screen asks whether you've paid any employees during the current calendar year.
Notice the year displayed—QuickBooks automatically updates this based on when you sign up (for example, it shows **2025** now, but it will show **2026** if you begin next year).

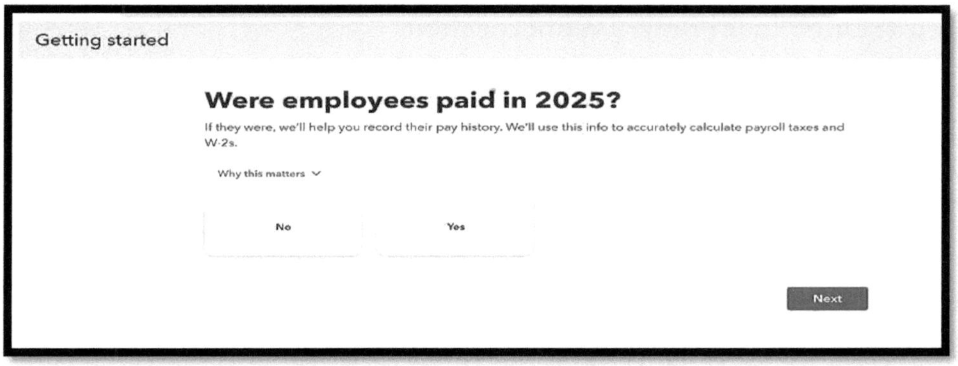

If you **have** already paid employees this year, select **Yes**.

Later in the setup, QuickBooks will ask you to enter each employee's year-to-date payroll details so it can create accurate records, tax forms, and reports.

If you choose **Yes**, make sure you have the following ready:

- Prior payroll registers
- Year-to-date totals for each employee
- Pay dates and pay periods
- Data from your previous payroll provider, if applicable

For this demonstration, I will selects **No** to keep things simple, but choose **Yes** if it applies to your business.

Once you've made your selection, click **Next**.

Step 3: Choose Your First Payroll Date

QuickBooks will now ask when you plan to run your **first payroll with QuickBooks**. Click the calendar icon and select the appropriate date—e.g., **August 1**.

After choosing your date, click **Next**.

Step 4: Enter Your Primary Work Location

Next, QuickBooks needs your company's primary work location for tax and compliance purposes.

In the example, the company is fictional, and the address fields auto-filled because the information was already entered during the initial QuickBooks Online setup.

All that remained was to enter the official **business name**, then click **Next**.

Step 5: Confirm Payroll Contact Information

The next screen asks for the name, phone number, and email address of your **payroll contact**—the person responsible for handling payroll tasks for the business.

In this example, QuickBooks again auto-populated the details because they were entered earlier during account setup. All that's needed is to review the information for accuracy and click **Next**.

ADD YOUR EMPLOYEES TO QUICKBOOKS ONLINE

Now it's time to begin entering your employees into the system. Before you start, make sure you have each employee's essential information on hand—such as hire dates, pay rates, tax IDs, deductions, and other wage-related details. Having everything ready ensures a smooth setup.

When you're prepared, click **Add Employee**.

Enter Employee Personal Information

You'll be taken through several screens to complete the employee's profile. The first screen requests personal information.

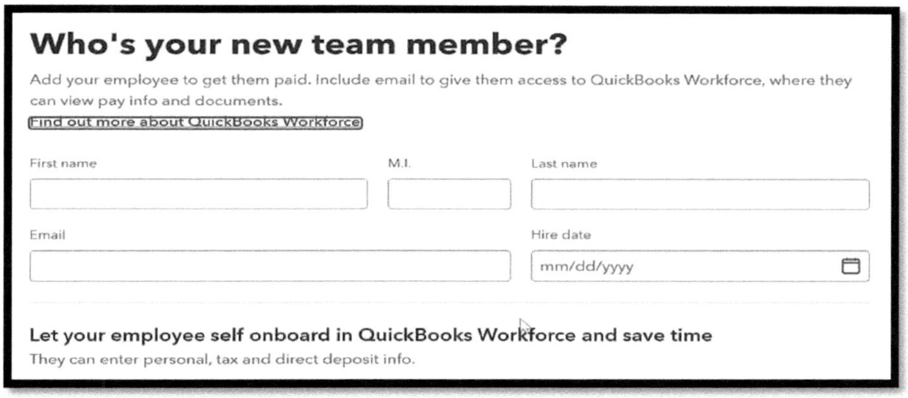

For example, we'll enter:

- **Name**
- **Hire date**
- **Email:** Optional, but highly recommended

Why add an email?

Because QuickBooks uses it to send employees access to **QuickBooks Workforce**, where they can view pay stubs, W-2s, and other payroll documents.

If you're hiring a new employee, you also have the option to let them **self-onboard**. This feature allows employees to enter their tax details, direct deposit info, and personal information themselves. It's a major time-saver and reduces data entry errors.

To activate this, toggle the **Self-Onboarding** option.

For this demo, we are not using self-onboarding—so we simply click **Add Employee** to continue.

Complete the Employee Profile

You'll now see the employee's full profile page, which includes sections for:

- Tax withholdings
- Base pay
- Payment method
- Deductions
- Time off
- Additional pay types

Red circles appear next to any sections that still need information. Hovering your mouse over them will show exactly what's missing.

To fill in the required fields, click **Edit** on the right side of each data block.

For example, under **Personal Information**, required fields include:

- Address
- City
- ZIP code
- Date of birth
- Social Security Number

Once those are entered, click **Save**. You'll see the red indicator disappear, confirming the section is now complete.

What If You Don't Finish the Setup?

If you need to stop midway because you don't have all the information, that's completely fine.

Simply exit the page. QuickBooks will save your progress automatically. When you return to the **Payroll Dashboard**, instead of the initial welcome screen, you'll now see your setup organized into clear sections—each with its own checklist.

Each setup area includes:

- ❖ A list of tasks
- ❖ **Green check marks** for completed steps
- ❖ **Start** buttons to pick up exactly where you left off

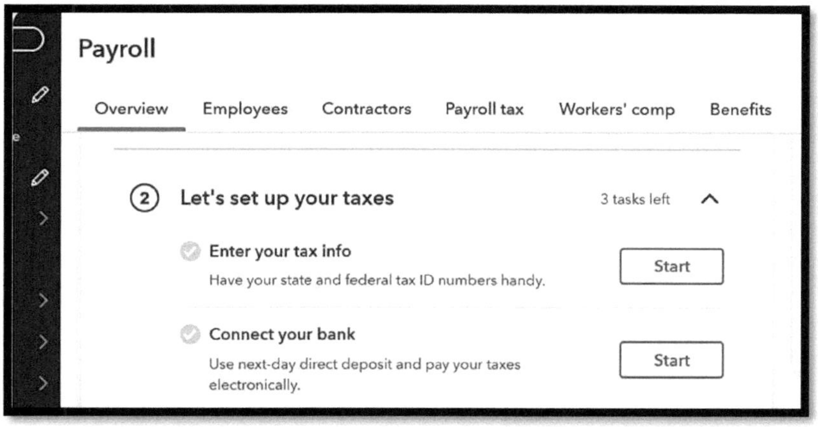

This structured checklist allows you to finish payroll setup at your own pace.

If you never exit the setup wizard, QuickBooks will guide you through the entire process seamlessly without needing to manually open each task.

Back on the employee setup page, click **Finish Up** under the "Add Your Employee" task.
Here you'll see:

- ❖ Buttons to **Add another employee**
- ❖ An option to **Import employee data** if you want to upload multiple employees at once
- ❖ A list of employees with indicators showing what information is still missing

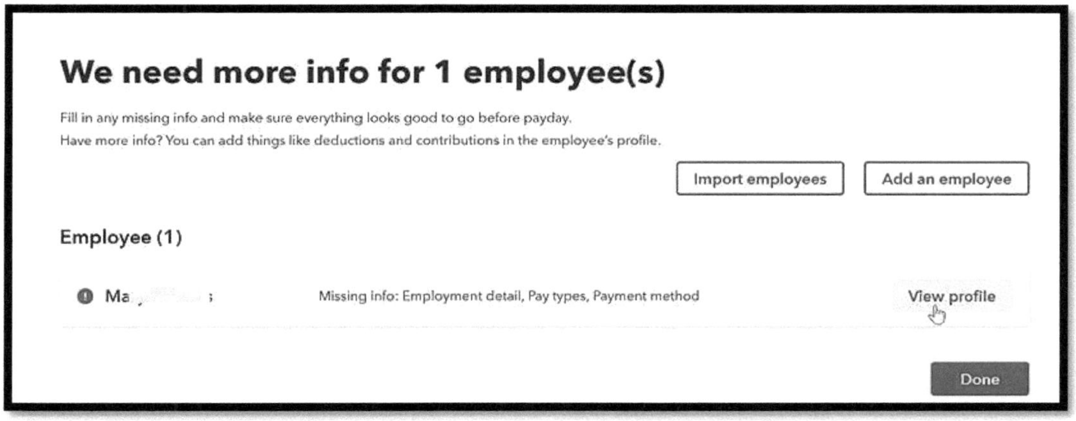

Let's click **View Profile** to continue updating the details.

Enter Employment Details

Click **Edit** to complete the employment information. To keep things simple, we'll start with the required fields—specifically, **the pay schedule**, which tells QuickBooks how often how the employee should be paid.

1. Click the dropdown arrow.
2. Select **Add a pay schedule**.

A new window appears showing:

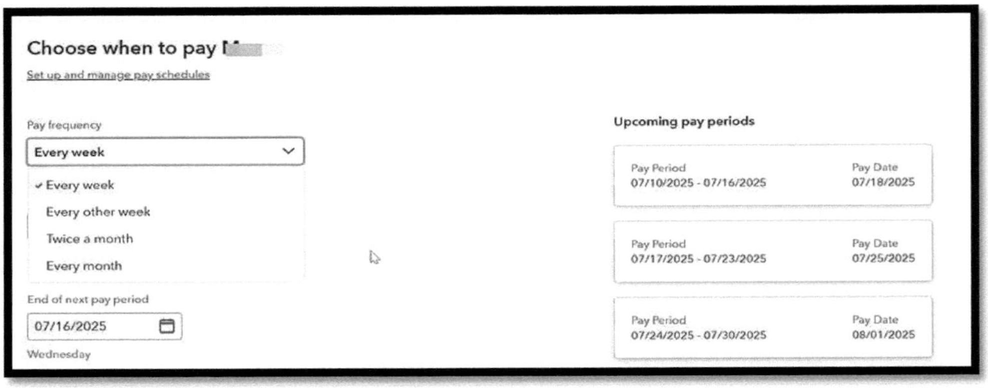

- **Pay frequency** (weekly, bi-weekly, semi-monthly, or monthly)
- A preview of upcoming **pay periods**, based on your selection

For this example, choose **Every other week**.

Next, enter:

- The **next pay date**
- The **end date** of the next pay period

After selecting these, review the upcoming pay dates on the right to make sure everything looks correct.

You can also:

- **Name the pay schedule**
- Check the box to **apply this schedule to all future employees**

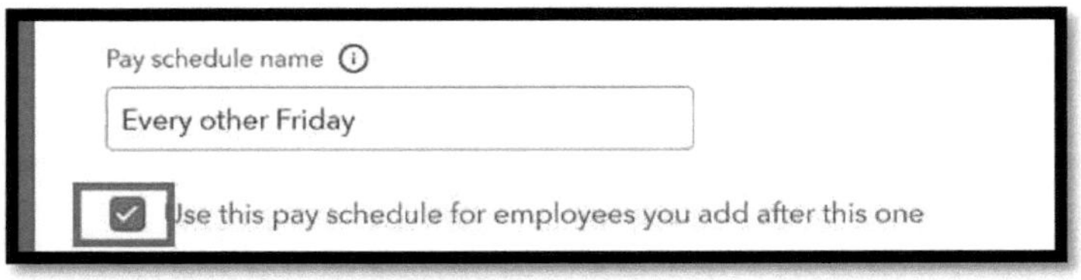

Once everything looks good, click **Save**. QuickBooks brings you back to the main Employment Details page.

Additional Employment Information

Continue filling in the required fields:

- **Employee ID** (since she is the first employee, we'll use "1")
- **Workers' compensation** details (if your state requires it)
  - You can also add your policy directly to QuickBooks
  - Or click **Need Workers' Comp Insurance** to explore coverage options

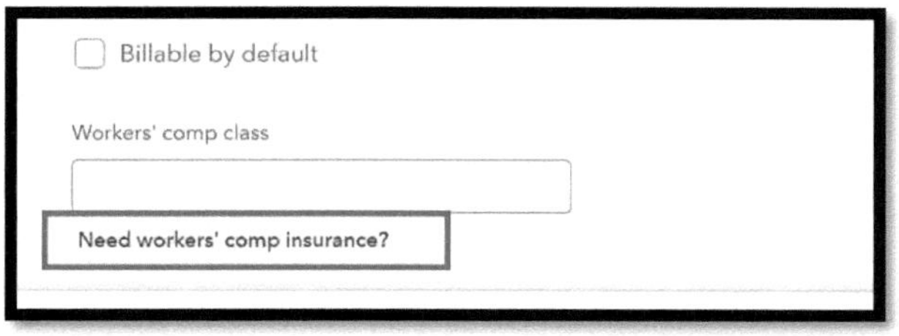

You'll also see a field for **billable rates**—the amount you charge clients for work performed by this employee.

Important: This is *not* the employee's pay rate. It's used to help QuickBooks calculate client invoices and job costing reports. For this demo, we'll leave it blank and click **Save**.

Enter Tax Withholding Information

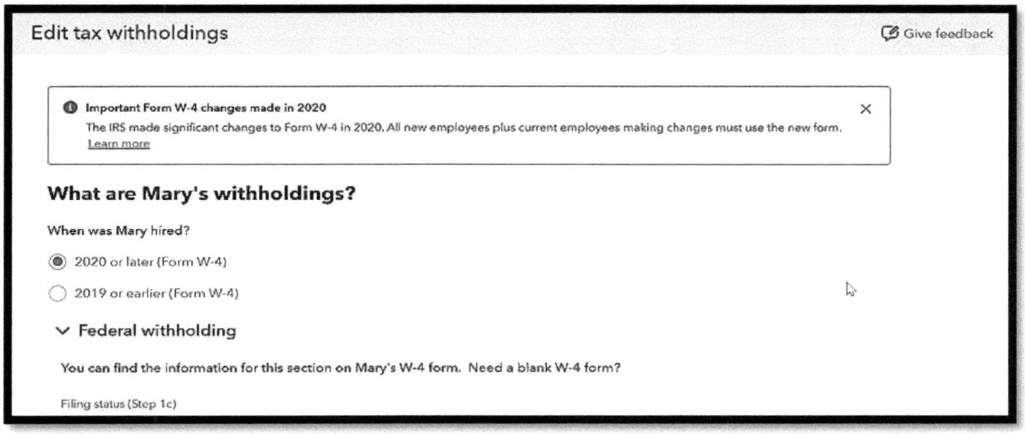

Next, scroll down to the **Tax Withholdings** section.

You'll need the employee's **W-4 form** to complete:

- Filing status

- Dependent information
- Additional withholding amounts
- Any exemptions

QuickBooks also provides a link to a blank W-4 if needed.

Because the W-4 changed in 2020, QuickBooks will ask whether the employee was hired before or after that year.

For example:

- If the employee was hired **before 2020**, QuickBooks uses the older form (fewer fields).
- If hired **2020 or later**, you'll use the newer format.

For this walkthrough, select **2020** and enter:

- **Single filing status**
- No exemptions

Click **Save** to continue.

Scroll down to review the remaining items that need to be completed before payroll can run.

SET UP THE EMPLOYEE'S PAYMENT METHOD

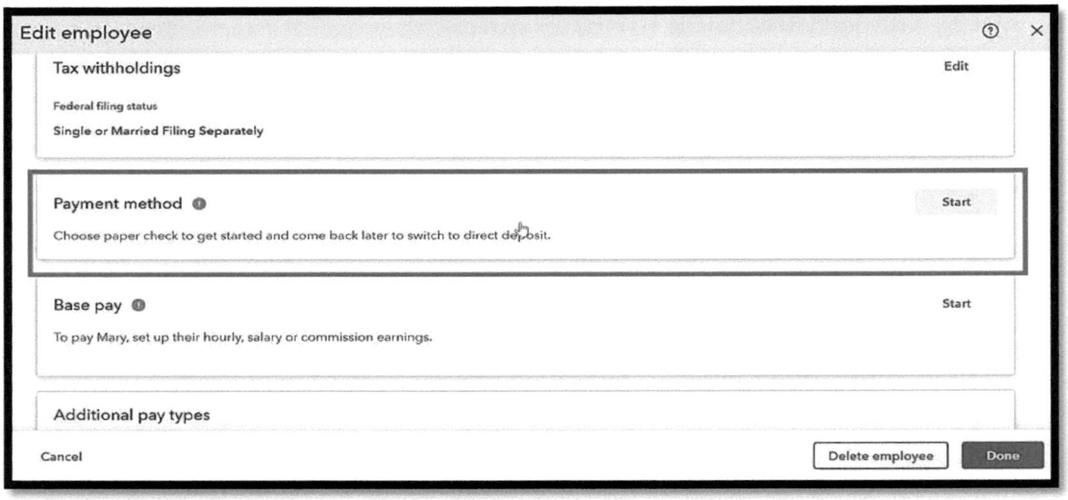

Next, QuickBooks asks how you want to pay the employee. Click **Start** under *Payment Method.*

You'll see two options:

1. **Direct Deposit**

    - ❖ Requires the employee's **bank account number**, **routing number**, and confirmation of whether it's a checking or savings account.
    - ❖ The employee must provide a **voided check** and a **signed direct deposit authorization form**.
    - ❖ If you don't already have the form, QuickBooks provides one when you select this option.

2. **Paper Check**

    - ❖ You'll manually print checks yourself.
    - ❖ Make sure you're using **MICR-compatible ink and check stock** so banks can process the checks without issues.

For this demonstration, we'll choose **Paper Check** to keep things simple. Click **Save** to continue.

Set Up the Employee's Base Pay

Click **Start** next to *Base Pay*.

A window appears where you'll enter compensation details:

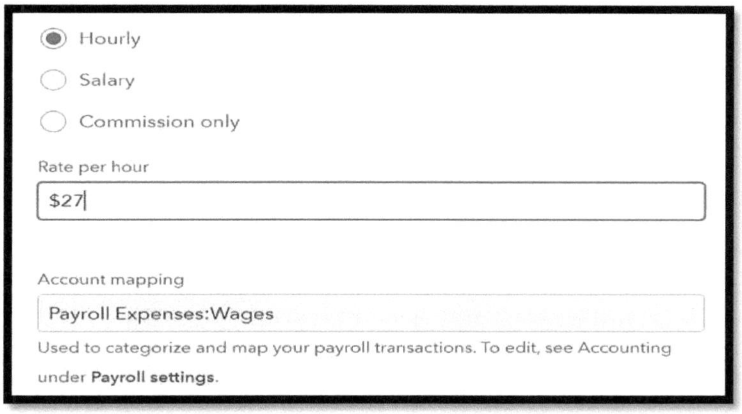

- ❖ **Compensation type:** Choose *Hourly*.
- ❖ **Hourly rate:** Enter **$27 per hour**.
- ❖ **Default hours per day:** Enter **8**.
- ❖ **Days worked per week:** Enter **5**.

The *Account Mapping* field is already filled in based on how your Chart of Accounts was set up earlier. If you don't use QuickBooks for accounting, you won't need to adjust this field.

Click **Save**, then close the confirmation window.

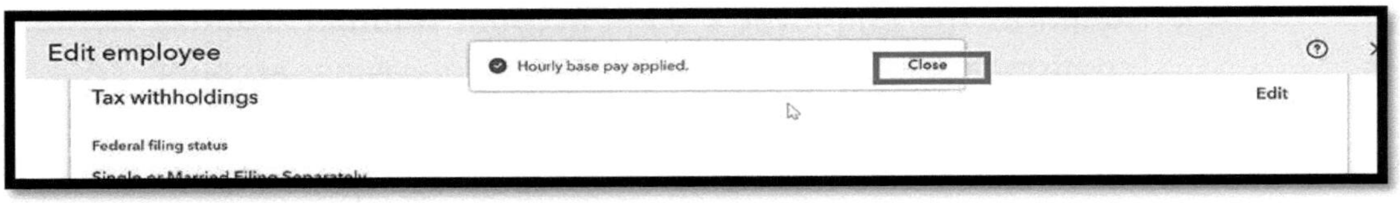

Add Additional Pay Types (Optional)

QuickBooks also allows you to set up extra earnings, such as:

- Overtime
- Holiday pay
- Bonuses
- Double-time
- Tips
- Commissions

Click the dropdown arrow to view available options.

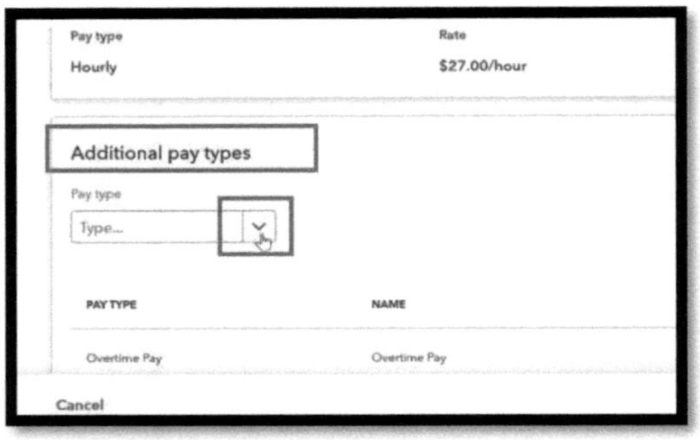

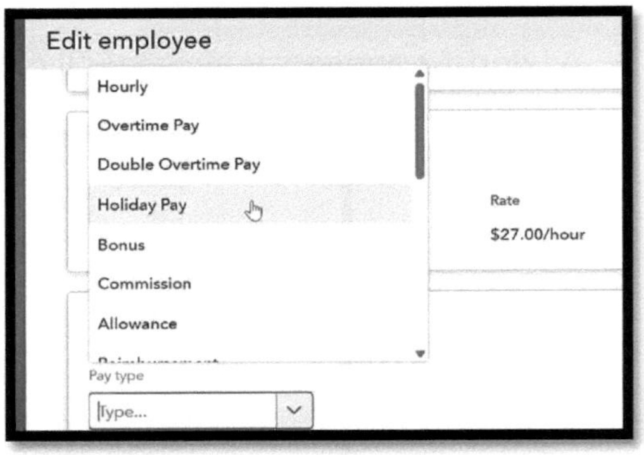

For example, if employee qualifies for **Overtime Pay**, select that item. You can adjust the account mapping if needed—though we'll keep the default settings for this walkthrough.

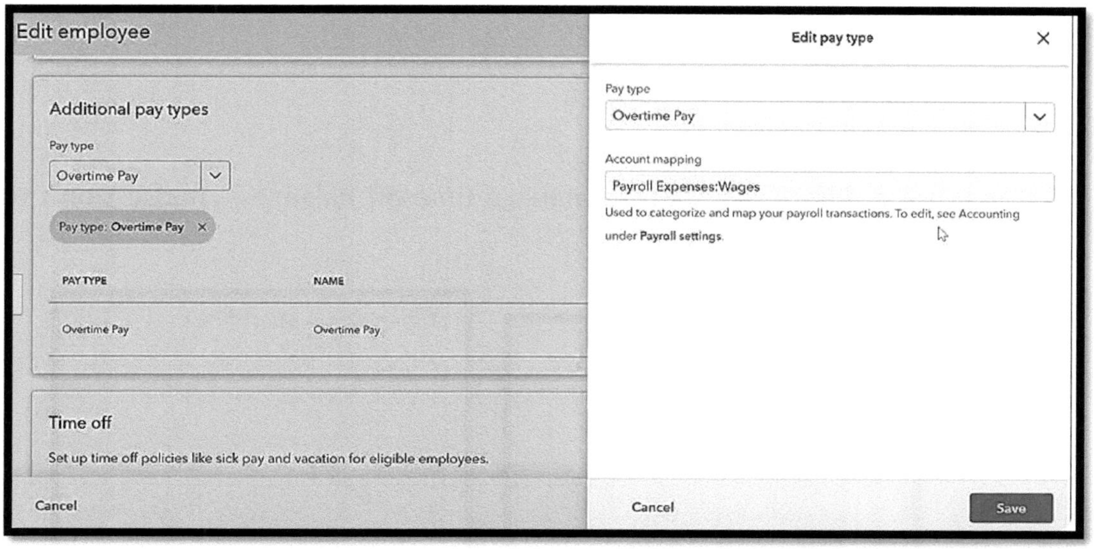

Click **Cancel** to return to the main pay-type list, or continue adding other applicable pay types.

ADDITIONAL PAY TYPES

Aside from overtime, QuickBooks allows you to add other earnings such as **commissions, bonuses, allowances, reimbursements**, and even **tips**, which are especially useful for retail and restaurant businesses.

If you're processing payroll for a church, QuickBooks also supports **clergy housing allowances**.

For this example, we'll only activate overtime for the employee, but you can add as many pay types as needed. Click **Add** to include them when applicable.

Time Off Policies

Next is the **Time Off** section. You'll notice there's no red indicator next to it, meaning QuickBooks does not require this information to run payroll. However, it's still a good idea to complete this section so your employee profile is thorough—and to ensure any paid or unpaid leave is tracked properly.

Click **Start** under *Time Off*.

Here, you can set up policies for:

- Vacation pay
- Paid Time Off (PTO)
- Sick leave
- Unpaid time off

If you use a different system to manage time-off balances, choose **Don't track in QuickBooks**.

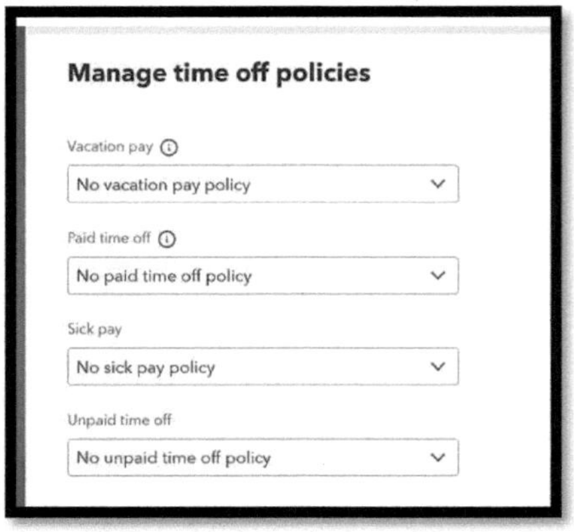

But if you want QuickBooks to manage accruals, choose **Add a policy** and configure it:

- Enter the **policy name** (e.g., "Unlimited Vacation").
- Set the **accrual frequency**:
  - Unlimited
  - Beginning of the year
  - Every pay period
  - Per hours worked
  - Employee anniversary date
- If not unlimited, enter **hours per year** and any **accrual caps**.

Click **Save** when finished.

For this demonstration, we won't add a policy, so we'll simply exit this section.

Deductions and Contributions

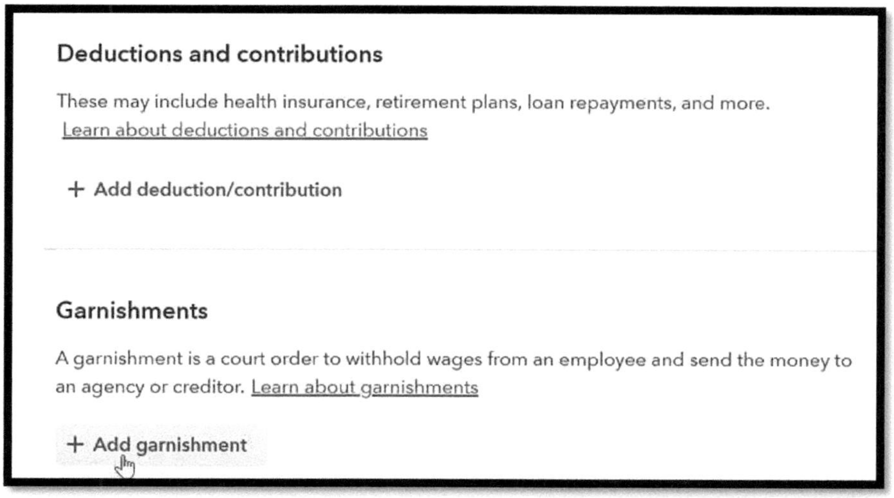

Click **Start** to set up deductions and contributions—this includes:

- Health insurance
- Retirement plans
- Flexible Spending Accounts (FSA)
- Health Savings Accounts (HSA)
- Other voluntary deductions

If the employee has a **garnishment**, scroll down and select **Add garnishment**.

Choose the type:

- Federal tax levy
- Child or spousal support
- Other garnishments

For this employee, we'll add **child support**:

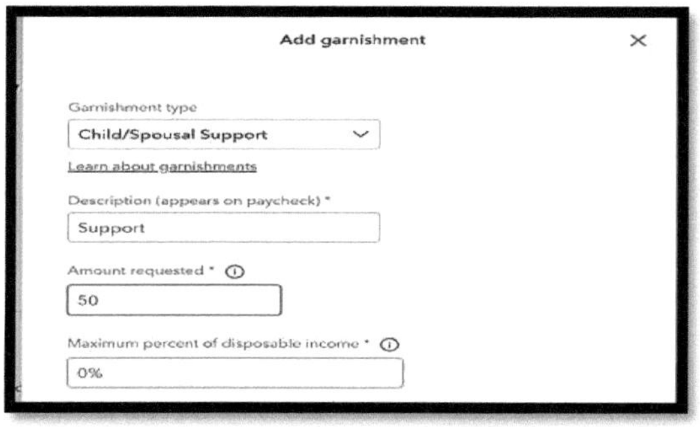

- ❖ Description on paycheck: *Support*
- ❖ Amount: **$50**
- ❖ Maximum percentage of disposable income: **25%**

Click **Save** and then **Done**.

Emergency Contact

Next, go to **Emergency Contact**. Here you can record:

- ❖ Name
- ❖ Relationship
- ❖ Phone number
- ❖ Email address

This section isn't required for payroll, but it's good practice to fill it out for HR completeness.
For this example, we'll leave it blank and click **Cancel**.

Reviewing the Employee Profile

At this point, the Employee profile is complete. All required sections no longer have red indicators. Click **Done** in the bottom-right corner.

You will return to the employee list, where you can add additional employees if needed.

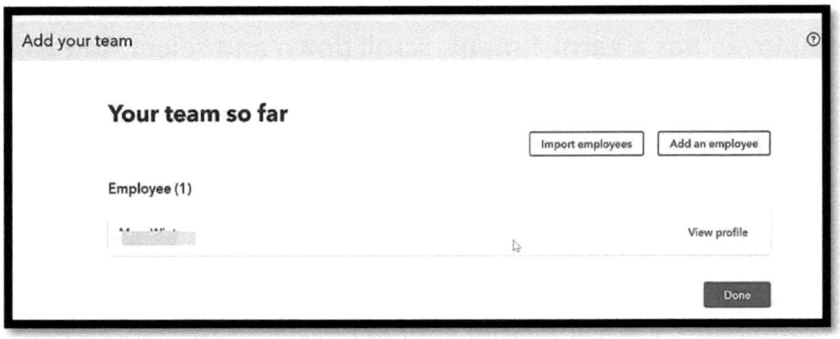

Click Done

Click **Continue Setup**.

Finishing Payroll Setup

On the payroll dashboard, you'll see the remaining tasks needed before you can run payroll:

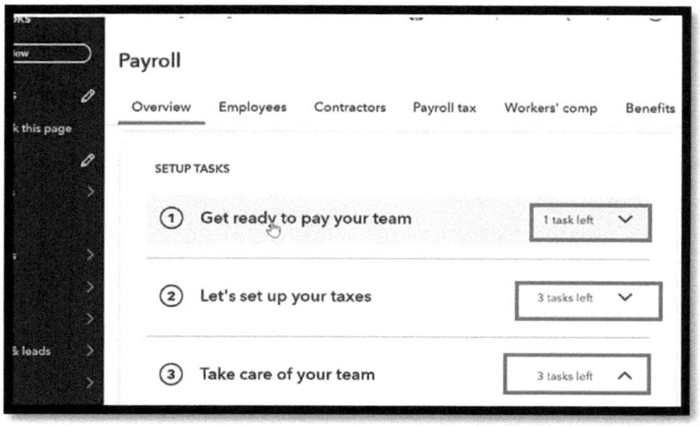

1. **Add the company's bank account** (for paying employees and tax deposits)
2. **Enter company tax information**

There is also a section where QuickBooks can connect you with:

- Retirement plan providers
- Health benefits providers
- Workers' compensation insurance partners

You can explore those as needed, but we'll skip them in this walkthrough.

ADDING COMPANY BANK AND TAX DETAILS

Company Bank Account Setup

There are still a few tasks left, including adding the company's bank details and completing tax setup.

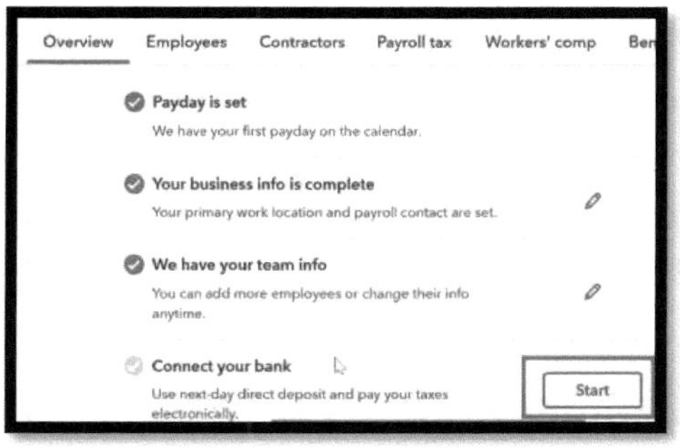

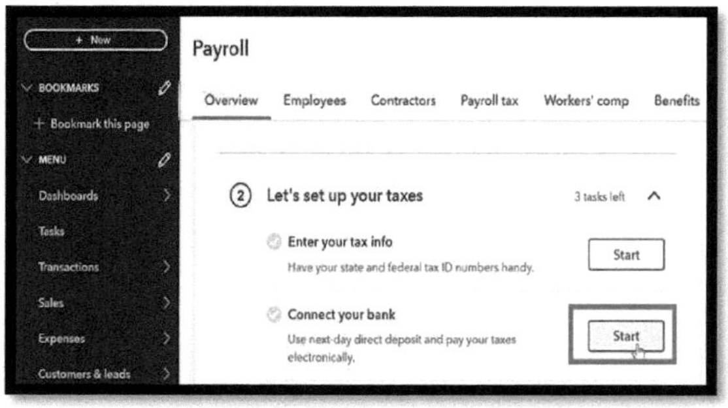

Under **Get Ready to Pay Your Team or under Let's set up your taxes**, select "Start" on **Connect Your Bank**.

Bank setup is required if you plan to:

- ❖ Pay employees through direct deposit
- ❖ Remit payroll taxes electronically

Click **Start**, and QuickBooks will ask for details like your business type, website, principal officer, and bank account information.

Since I selected paper check earlier, direct deposit isn't required for this demo, so I'll exit this screen.

Company Tax Information

Next, click the task for **Company Tax Setup**.

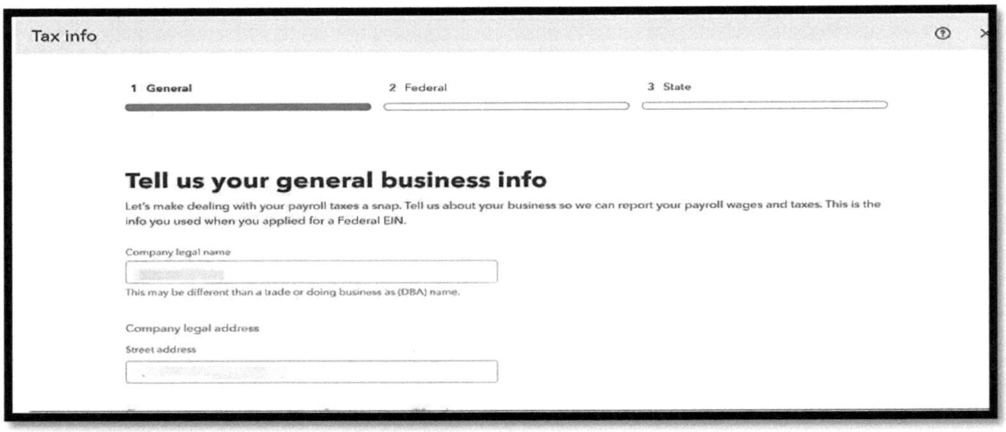

Review your general business information. If your legal business name differs from the trade name, enter the correct legal name and address as they appear on your tax documents.

Click **Next**, then enter your **Employer Identification Number (EIN)**.

Select your payroll tax form—most businesses use **Form 941**, but agricultural businesses may need **Form 943**.

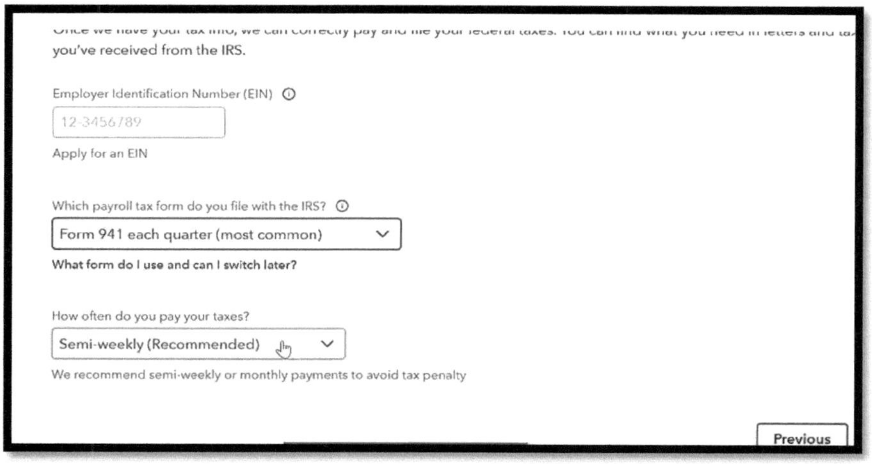

Indicate your tax deposit schedule:

- Semiweekly
- Monthly
- Quarterly
- Not sure

If you're unsure, consult your accountant or payroll expert to avoid penalties. I'll select **Semiweekly** for this example.

Click **Next**.

QuickBooks will then determine whether you need to enter state unemployment details based on your business address.

For example, with Tennessee selected, the system asks for your state unemployment account number and rate. I'll leave these fields blank for the demo and click **Done**. If the system warns that something is missing, select **No Thanks** to continue.

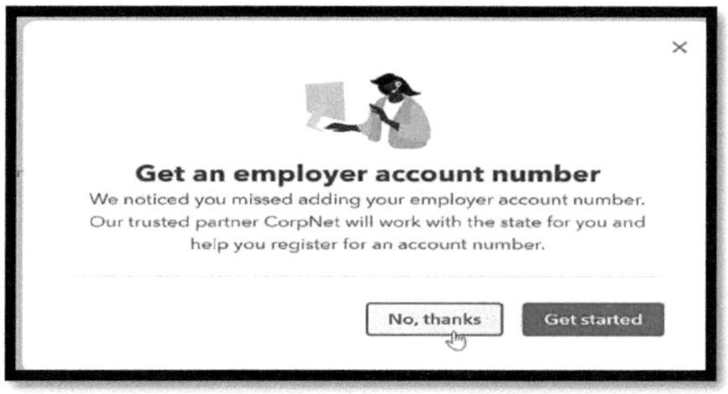

SETTING UP YOUR TAX PREFERENCES

The final step is setting up your tax preferences. This section determines whether QuickBooks will automatically file and pay your payroll taxes. Normally, enabling this feature requires completing the **Connect Your Bank** setup—which I skipped. However, there's a workaround, and I'll show you how to adjust your tax preferences without linking a bank.

To do this, you'll need to access the payroll settings. Go to the **Gear icon** in the upper-right corner, then select **Payroll Settings**.

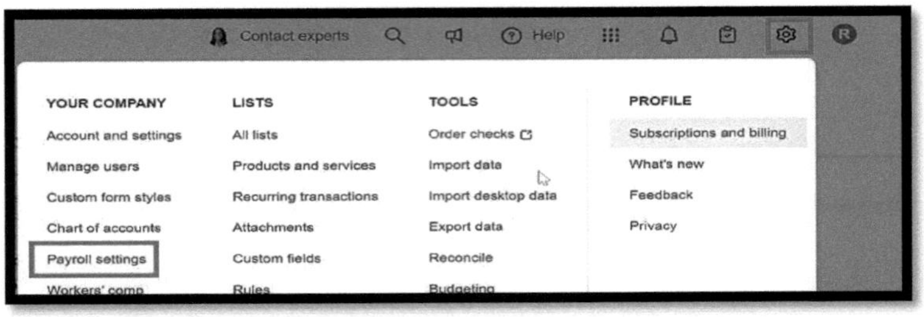

Under the **Taxes and Forms** section, click the **pencil icon** to edit your tax preferences.

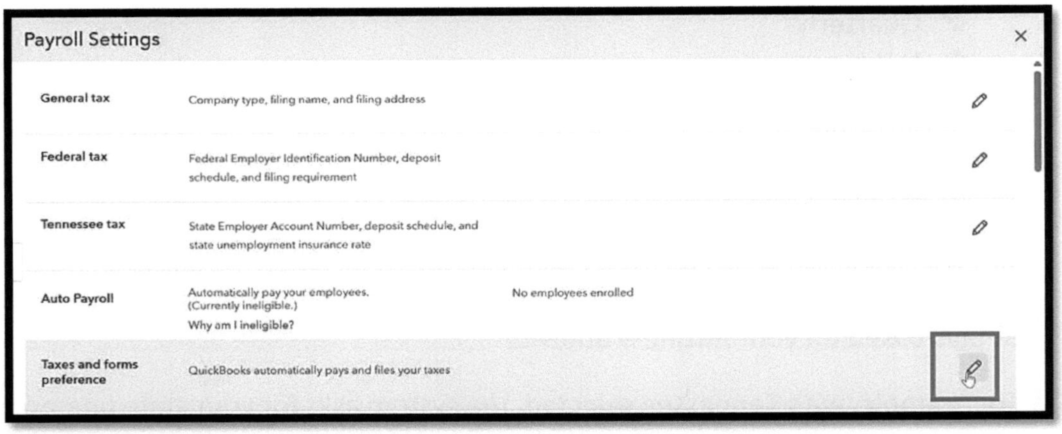

You'll see that QuickBooks has **automatic tax filing and payments** turned on by default. I recommend keeping this option enabled because it's free and ensures your taxes are filed on time. However, for this demonstration, I'll turn it off by selecting **"I'll pay and file my taxes myself."**

With this option, QuickBooks still prepares your tax forms and payments, but you must manually approve them before they are submitted. Note that this manual option comes with an additional service fee, which is why the automatic option is generally better.

After selecting the manual option, click **Next**.

QuickBooks will show you the services available if you choose automatic tax filing. Since I'm not enabling that feature right now, I'll select **"Do it myself."**

Next, QuickBooks displays reminders about upcoming tax deadlines. Review these carefully, then click **Confirm**.

You'll then see a brief survey asking why you chose the manual option. I'll select **"I prefer handling it this way,"** and click **Done.**

Finally, click **Done** again on the main window.

Your setup is now complete.

RUN PAYROLL

It's finally time to run payroll, and QuickBooks Online gives you two ways to begin. From the **Payroll Dashboard**, you can click **"Pay my Team"** or **"Run Payroll."**

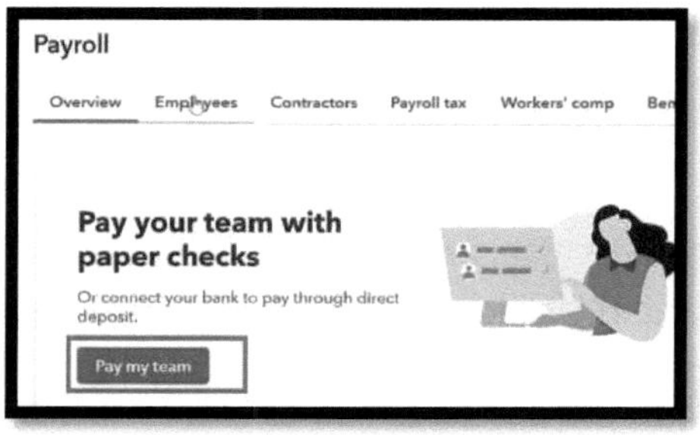

You can also access it by selecting the **Employees** tab at the top and clicking **"Run Payroll"** on the right side.

Let's use that option.

On the payroll screen, first verify that the **pay period** and **pay date** are correct. These fields are located in the upper-left corner. If you adjust the pay period, QuickBooks automatically updates the pay date.

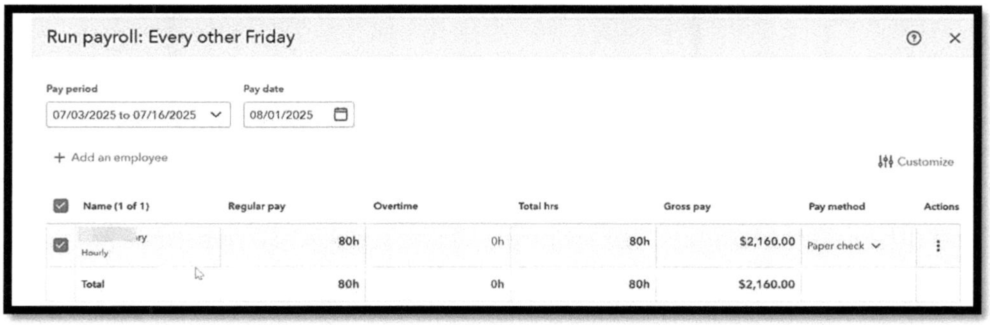

Below that, you'll see a spreadsheet-style pay grid listing all employees scheduled to be paid. In this example, the only have one employee, whom we added earlier.

You can rearrange the grid by dragging and dropping columns—for instance, moving *Total Hours* or *Gross Pay* to another position. You can also customize the grid by showing or hiding fields like the **Memo** column.

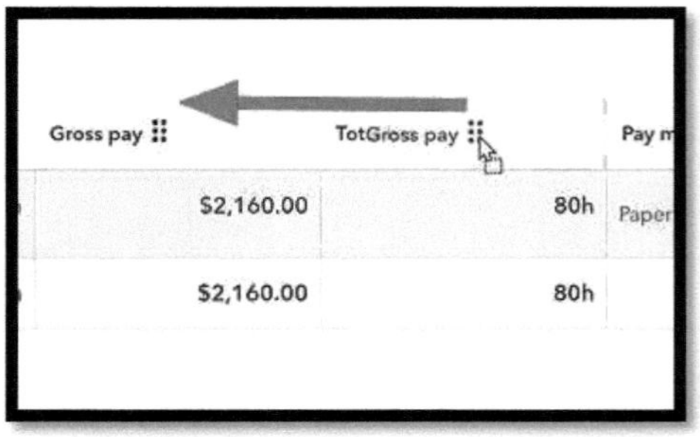

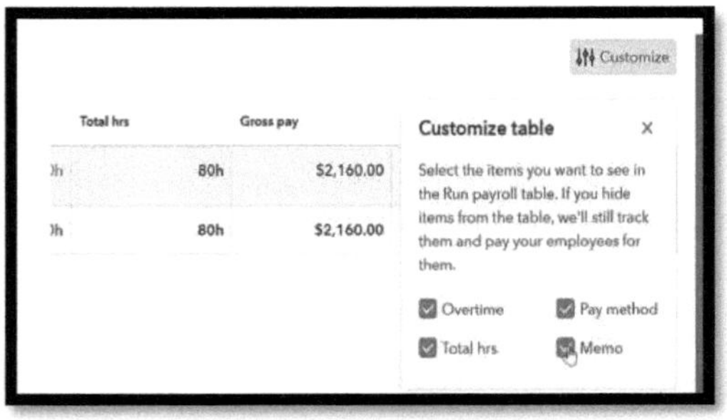

If you enabled direct deposit, you can switch an employee's payment method between **Direct Deposit** and **Paper Check** using the dropdown arrow—without having to open the employee's profile. QuickBooks lets you make this change right here in the payroll run.

Next is the **Regular Pay** column. Since we set the Employee schedule as 8 hours a day, 5 days per week, the system automatically calculates **80 hours** for this biweekly period and computes her regular pay accordingly.

Because we assigned **Overtime Pay** as an additional pay type during setup, QuickBooks includes an overtime column as well. If her actual hours differ from the preset schedule—or if she worked overtime—you can update these amounts manually.

To do this, click the **three dots** under **Actions**, then choose **Edit Paycheck**.

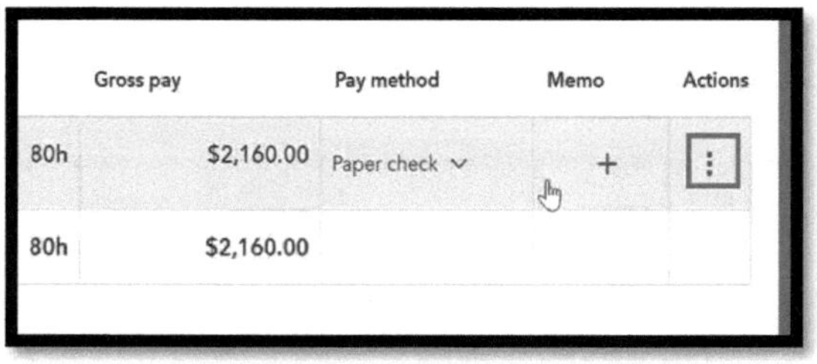

A detailed pay window appears where you can adjust regular hours, overtime hours, and other editable fields. For example, if she worked 10 overtime hours, QuickBooks will automatically apply the correct overtime rate and calculate the pay.

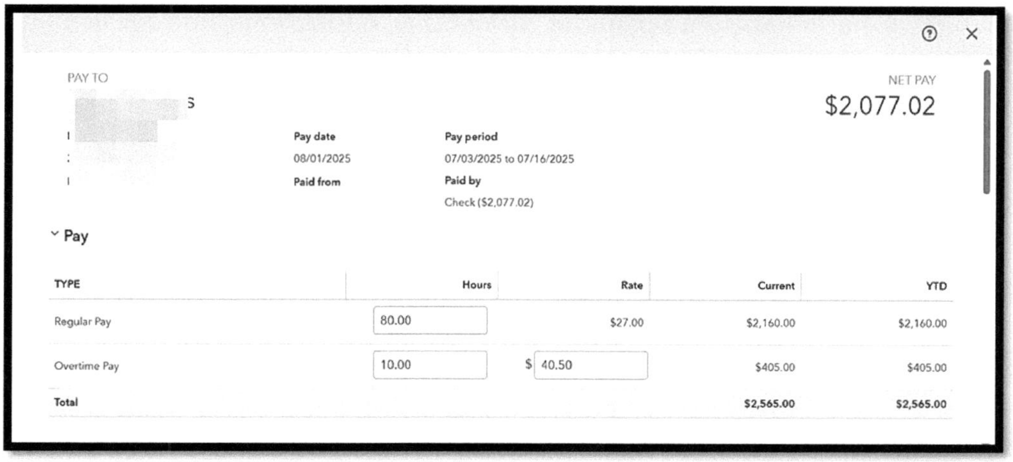

Scrolling down shows taxes, deductions, and other earnings. Only items with editable fields can be modified.

Since Employee has a child support garnishment set up, you'll also see that $50 deduction listed under **Support**.

If needed, you can review the employee tax amounts as well.

When you're finished, click **Save** to return to the main pay grid.

Review the details once again, then select **Preview Payroll**.

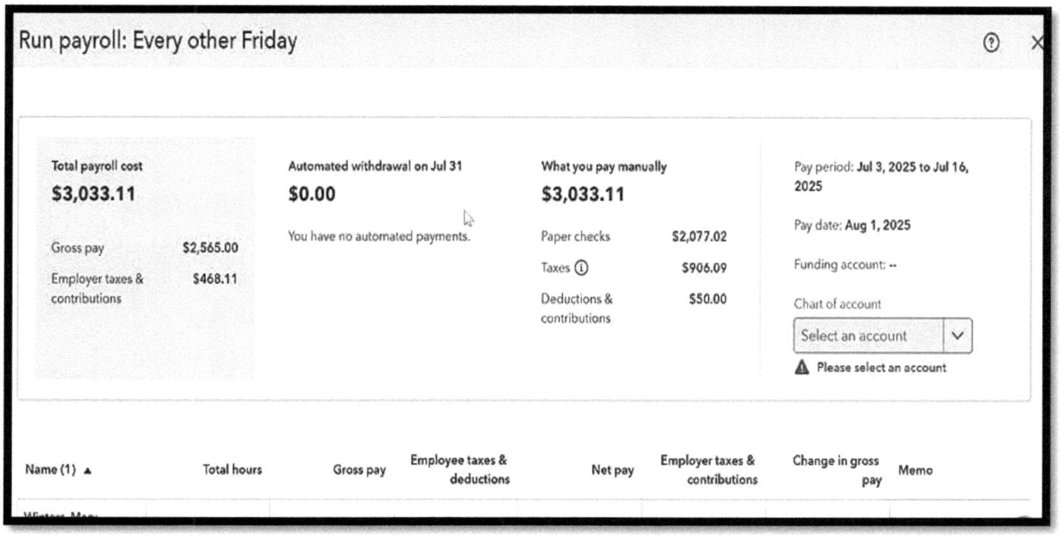

This screen displays a full payroll summary, including:

- **Total payroll cost**
- A breakdown of **gross pay**, **employer taxes**, and **contributions**

- What needs to be paid out for net pay, deductions, and tax liabilities

You'll also see a summary grid showing each employee's hours, taxes, deductions, and net pay.

Since this is the first payroll run and the accounting module is enabled, QuickBooks asks you to select a **Chart of Accounts** entry for payroll. You can choose an existing account or create a new one.

It's best practice to use a dedicated payroll account for clearer tracking, but for now, I'll use an existing one.

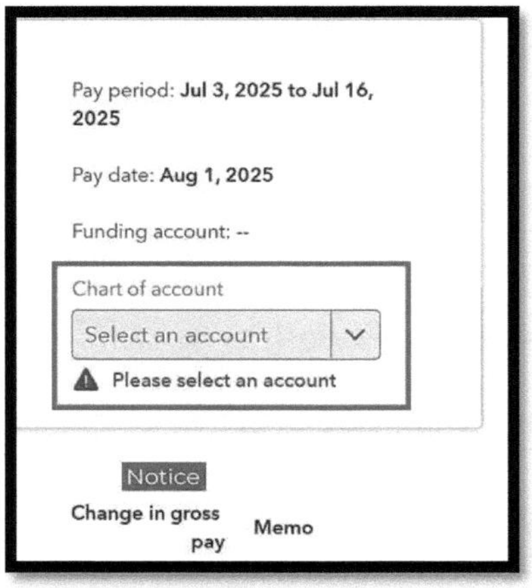

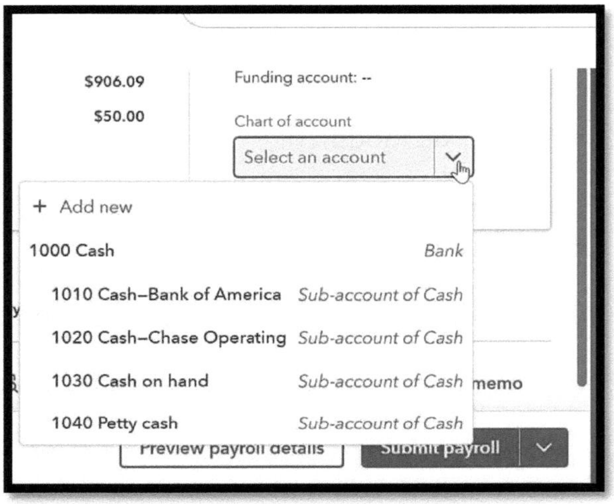

This is your final opportunity to review. You can use the on-screen summary or click **Preview Payroll Details** at the bottom-right for a more detailed report, which you can print or save as a PDF.

Once you've confirmed everything, click **Submit Payroll**.

Since this is a test, I won't submit it. But normally, QuickBooks will move on to either the **paper check printing** step or the **direct deposit** processing.

You'll also see a **Print Pay Stubs** option. If your employees have email addresses on file, they can access their pay stubs anytime through the **QuickBooks Workforce portal**.

And that's it—your payroll is complete.

The next time you're ready to pay your employees, simply return to the Payroll Dashboard to start the process.

MANAGING CONTRACTOR PAYMENTS AND 1099S THE EASY WAY WITH QUICKBOOKS ONLINE

The rise of self-employment during and after the COVID-19 pandemic created millions of new entrepreneurs—many of whom had to quickly learn how to manage finances, taxes, and contractor payments. Nearly five years later, most industries have embraced freelancers and gig workers for their flexibility and specialized skills. But with that flexibility comes responsibility: business owners must follow IRS rules to avoid penalties and maintain compliance.

QuickBooks Online (QBO) simplifies contractor onboarding, payments, and annual 1099 reporting, but everything must be set up correctly from the start.

Employee or Independent Contractor? The IRS Cares About the Difference

Before you hire and onboard a contractor, confirm whether they truly qualify as an independent contractor rather than an employee. Misclassification can trigger IRS penalties, back taxes, and increased audit scrutiny.

General rule:

- **Independent contractors** control *how* they perform the work.
- **Employees** are subject to the company's control over *what* they do and *how* they do it.

If you're unsure, consult a tax professional. The IRS has made worker classification a major compliance priority.

Setting Up Contractors in QuickBooks Online

Once confirmed as an independent contractor, you can begin creating their records in QBO. Follow these steps:

1. Collect Form W-9

- Every contractor must provide a completed **IRS Form W-9**, which includes their legal name, address, and Taxpayer Identification Number (TIN).
- You'll use this information when preparing the contractor's **Form 1099-NEC** at year-end.
- Since contractors are self-employed, you do **not** withhold payroll taxes. They handle their own quarterly estimated taxes and file Form 1040 annually.

2. Set Them Up as a Vendor

- In QBO, go to **Expenses → Vendors → New Vendor**.

- Enter the contractor's information from their W-9.
- **Important:** Check the box for **"Track payments for 1099"** so QBO will monitor payments for year-end reporting.

3. Track Contractor Payments

- The contractor's vendor profile will display a **Transaction List**, allowing you to review each payment.
- For any contractor paid **over $600** in a calendar year, you must file **Form 1099-NEC**.
- Note: You typically **do not** send 1099s to corporations or LLCs taxed as C-Corp or S-Corp.

How to Pay Independent Contractors in QuickBooks Online

When a contractor submits an invoice, open their vendor profile and select **New Transaction**. You can pay them using:

1. Bank Transfer (ACH)

- Efficient, secure, and integrated with QBO.
- Reduces manual paperwork and speeds up payment processing.

2. Check

- Traditional method for those who prefer physical payments.
- Be sure to record the payment in QBO so it counts toward 1099 reporting.

3. Credit Card

- Convenient for managing cash flow and earning rewards.
- QuickBooks allows credit card payments to be recorded directly to the contractor's vendor account.

As you record payments, QBO automatically tracks them for 1099 purposes, significantly reducing year-end workload.

Why 1099 Compliance Matters More Than Ever

The IRS is paying closer attention to contractor payments as the gig economy expands. With millions of individuals earning income outside traditional employment, ensuring accurate worker classification and proper 1099 filing is essential.

Non-compliance can lead to:

- IRS penalties
- Back taxes
- Possible audits
- Delays in business funding or licensing

QuickBooks Online provides built-in tools to help ensure compliance, making it easier to track payments and file correct 1099-NEC forms.

PART III: INVENTORY, PROJECTS, AND TRACKING

CHAPTER SEVEN

MONITORING INVENTORY AND MANAGING PURCHASE ORDERS

Monitoring inventory and managing purchase orders in QuickBooks Online are essential parts of keeping your business organized, efficient, and profitable. QuickBooks Online helps you track stock levels in real time, monitor product availability, and automatically update quantities as you buy and sell items. With built-in tools for creating and sending purchase orders, you can manage vendor relationships, prevent stockouts, and maintain accurate records of incoming inventory. Together, these features streamline your operations, improve purchasing decisions, and ensure your financial data stays accurate and up to date.

MANAGING INVENTORY AND PURCHASE ORDER IN QUICKBOOKS ONLINE

QuickBooks Online makes it easy to track your inventory, create purchase orders, receive stock, and adjust quantities when needed. Here's a clear breakdown of how to manage your stock from start to finish.

Preparing to Track Inventory

Before you begin, ensure your inventory products are already set up in QuickBooks. Next, confirm that purchase orders are turned on:

1. Go to **Settings → Account and Settings**.
2. Select the **Expenses** tab.
3. Under **Purchase Orders**, choose **Edit** and enable **Use Purchase Orders**.
4. (Optional) Add custom fields, allow custom transaction numbers, or set a default message.
5. Select **Save**, then **Done**.

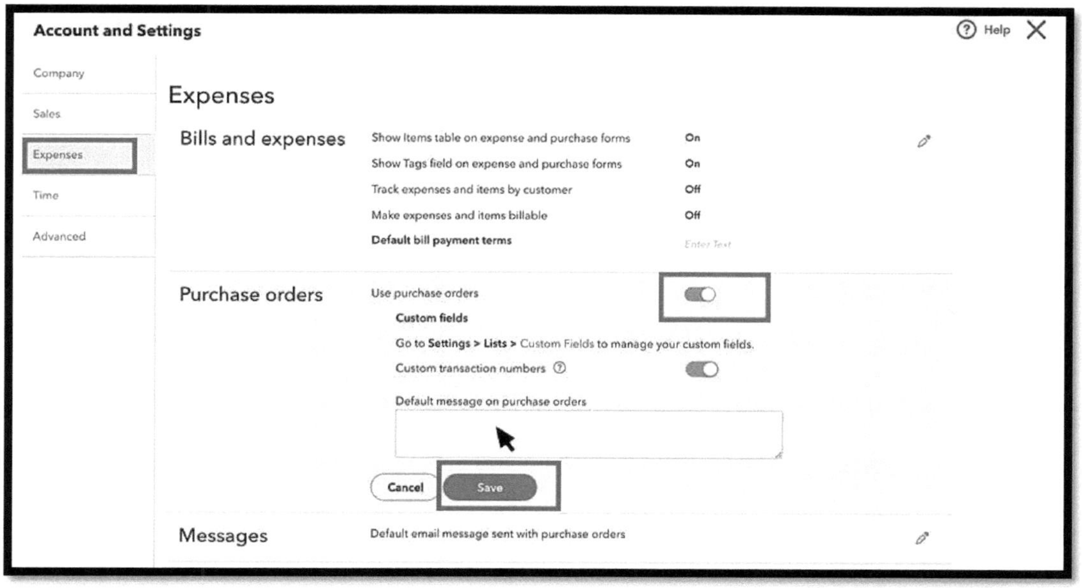

Reordering Inventory

To see what items need restocking:

1. Go to **Sales → Products and Services**.

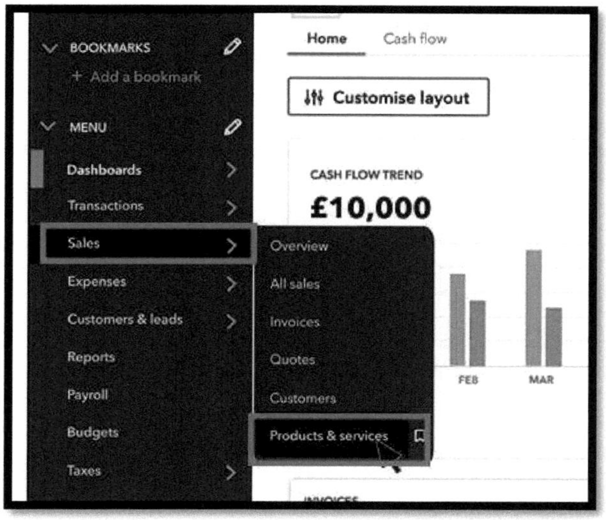

2. Review items marked **Low Stock** or **Out of Stock**.
3. Select the product(s), then choose **Batch actions → Reorder** to create a purchase order.

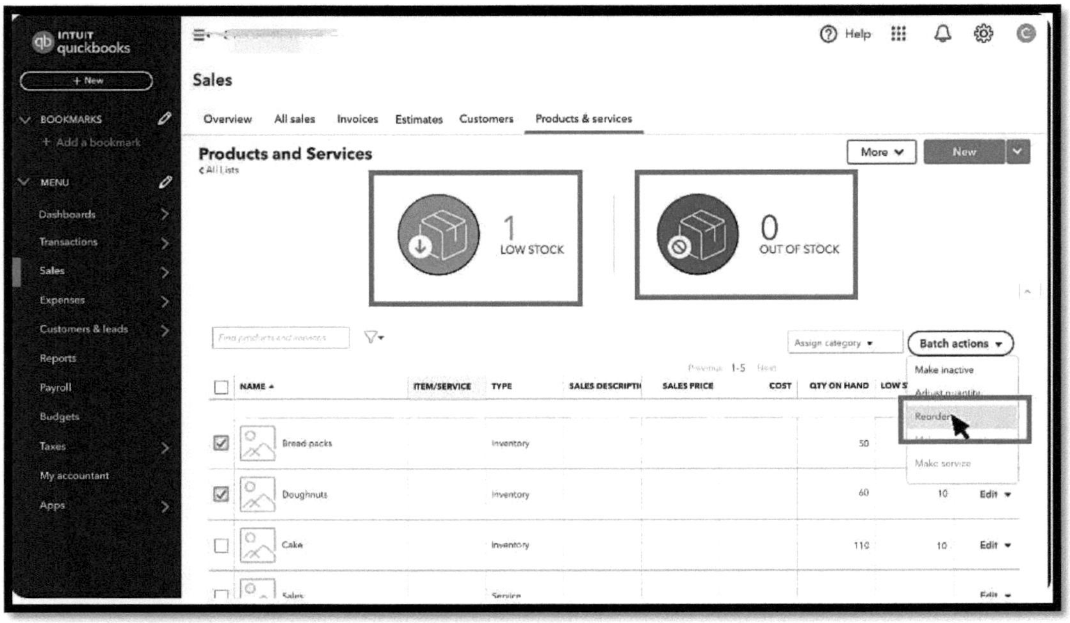

In the purchase order:

- ❖ Choose your **supplier** (QuickBooks selects your preferred supplier automatically if one is set).
- ❖ Add or adjust item details — quantity, rate, amount.
- ❖ Hover over the item quantity to view *current stock on hand* and your *reorder point*.

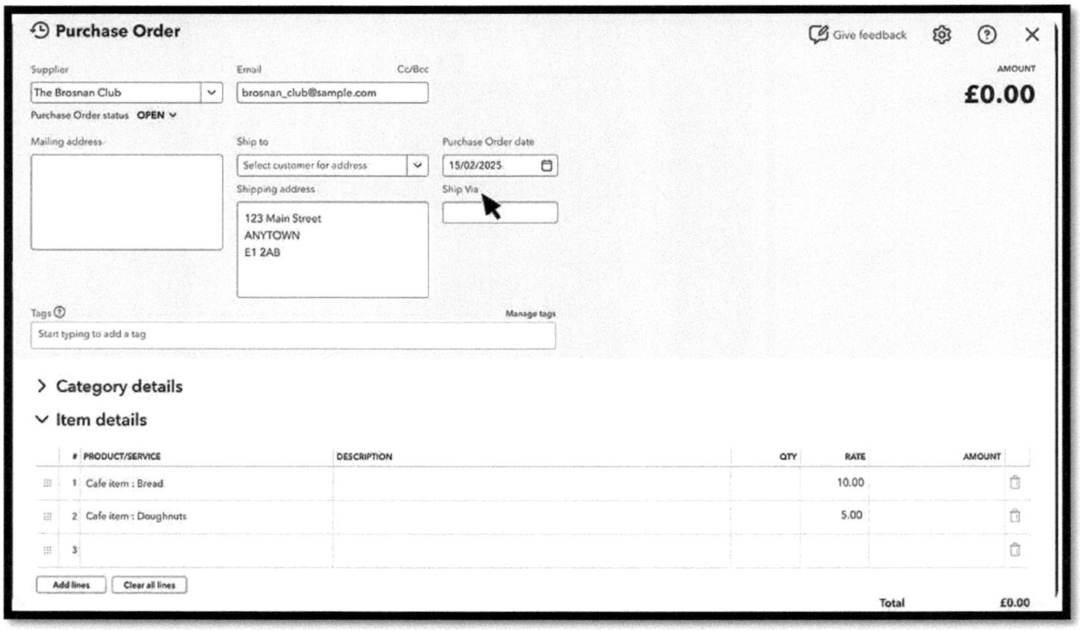

- ❖ Add more items, attachments, memos, or supplier messages if needed.
- ❖ Save and send the purchase order to your supplier.

You'll receive a customizable email preview before sending.

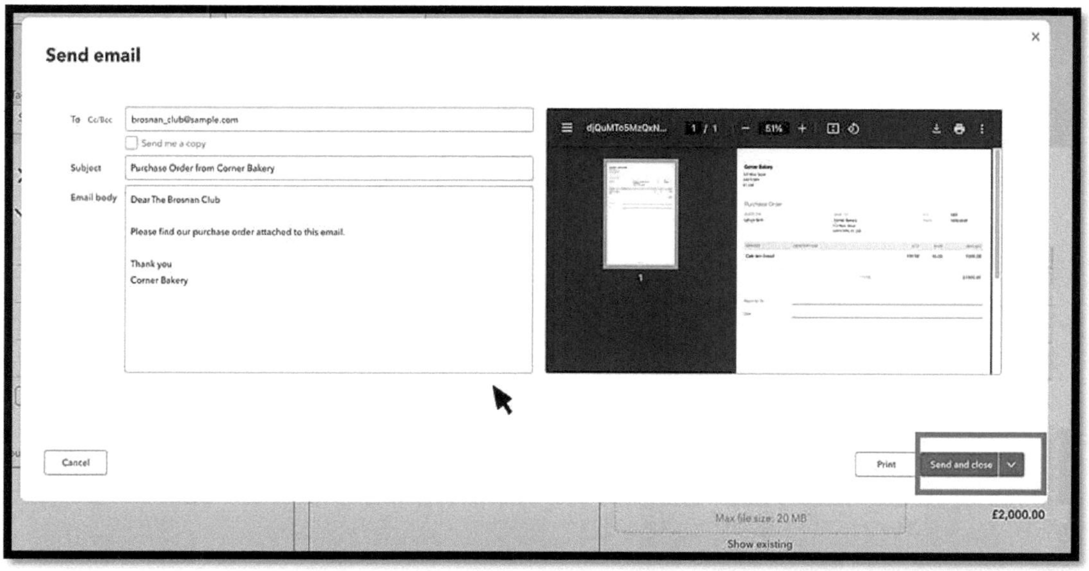

Note: A purchase order does *not* change your inventory levels—it only places an order.

Receiving and Recording Inventory

When your stock arrives, you must record how you paid for it. That's what actually updates your inventory counts.

Choose one of three transaction types:

- ❖ **Expense**: if you already paid (other than by check)
- ❖ **Check**: if you paid by check
- ❖ **Bill**: if you received an invoice and will pay later

To record:

1. Go to **+ New** → choose **Expense**, **Check**, or **Bill**.
2. Select the supplier. If you have an open purchase order, you'll see it on the right.

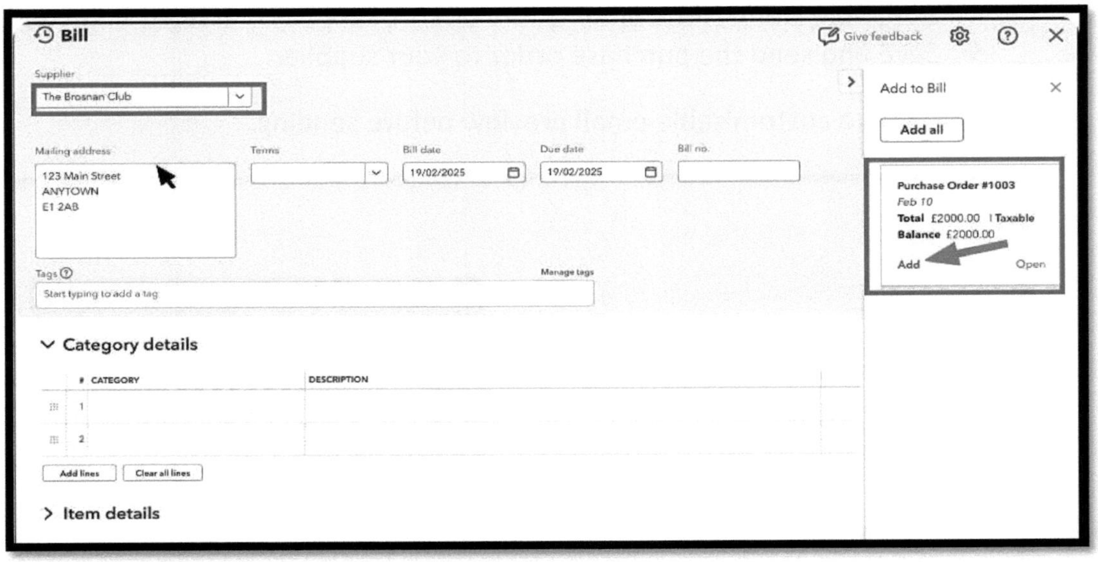

3. Select **Add** to pull the PO details into the transaction.
4. Adjust quantities or prices if they differ from the purchase order.
5. Save.

QuickBooks will now update your stock levels under **Products and Services**.

Adjusting Inventory Quantities

If your physical count doesn't match what QuickBooks shows:

1. Go to **Products and Services**.
2. For the item, open the **Edit** dropdown and select **Adjust Quantity**.
3. Enter the actual quantity you have.
4. Choose an **Adjustment Account**, such as:
   - *Inventory Shrinkage* (default)

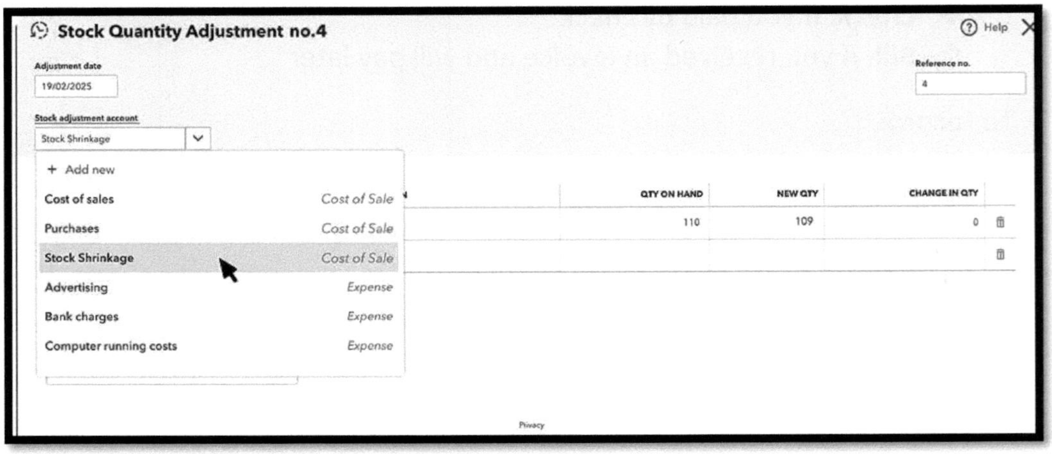

- ❖ A custom expense or cost-of-sales account (e.g., theft, spoilage, donations)

  Since this affects your financial statements, consult your accountant if unsure.

5. Save your changes.

You're Now Ready to Manage Inventory Efficiently

With purchase orders, accurate item setup, proper receiving methods, and adjustment tools, QuickBooks Online gives you complete control over your inventory—from ordering stock to keeping your counts accurate.

CHAPTER EIGHT

CLASSES, LOCATIONS AND PROJECTS TRACKING

You can track classes, locations, and projects in QuickBooks Online by first enabling these features in **Account and settings** under the **Advanced** section. Classes track segments like departments or products, locations track profitability by business location, and Projects track specific jobs or client work. For detailed financial reports, assign the corresponding class, location, or project to your transactions, which can be done at the transaction level or on each line item, depending on your needs and QuickBooks version.

HOW TO USE CLASS AND LOCATION TRACKING IN QUICKBOOKS ONLINE TO IMPROVE YOUR DATA ANALYSIS

QuickBooks Online (QBO) includes two powerful—but often overlooked—tools for organizing financial data: **Class Tracking** and **Location Tracking.** These features add extra layers of categorization beyond your standard Chart of Accounts, helping you analyze performance more accurately across departments, locations, or business segments.

What Are Class and Location Tracking? Why Use Them?

In every accounting system, transactions are categorized through the **Chart of Accounts**—for example, sales, office expenses, travel, supplies, or equipment. While these accounts give you basic structure, many businesses need deeper visibility.

This is where **Class** and **Location** tracking come in:

- They allow you to group transactions by **division**, **department**, **project**, **storefront**, or **region**.
- They layer on top of your existing accounts, giving you more meaningful reporting.
- They help companies with multiple locations or business units compare performance and understand which segments are profitable.

Examples:

- A retail business tracking each store separately
- A nonprofit dividing transactions by program
- A contractor separating residential vs. commercial work

How to Turn On Class and Location Tracking in QBO

Note: These features are available only in **QuickBooks Online Plus**.

1. Select the **Gear icon** (top right).
2. Choose **Account and Settings**.
3. Go to the **Advanced** tab.
4. Scroll to **Categories**.
5. Turn on **Class Tracking** and/or **Location Tracking**.

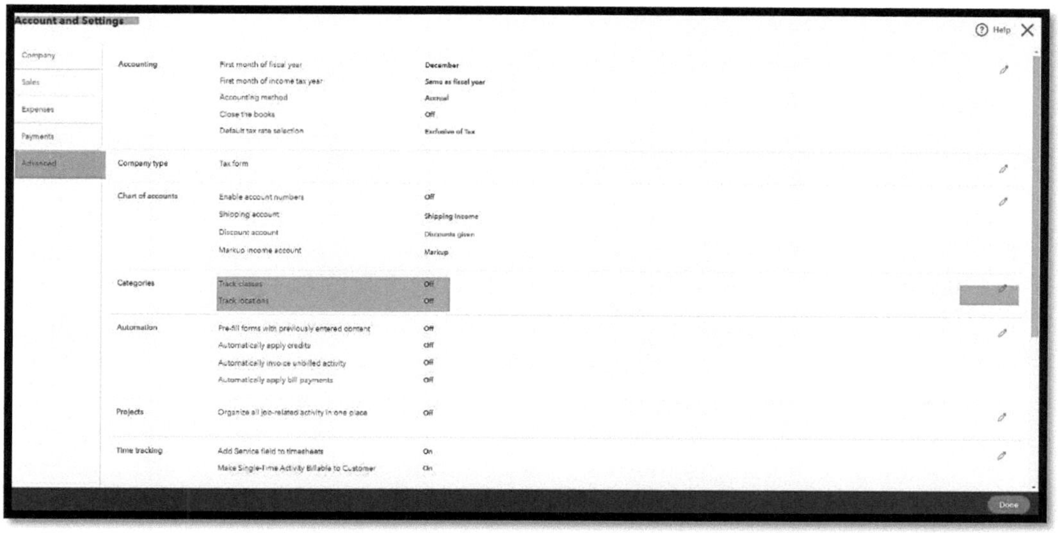

6. Save your changes.

Once activated, new **Class** and **Location** fields will appear on all major transactions, including invoices, bills, expenses, checks, and journal entries.

Setting Up Classes and Locations

After enabling tracking:

- Select the **Gear icon** again.
- Choose **All Lists**.
- Select **Classes** or **Locations**.
- Create each class or location you want to track.

Many businesses also create an "Admin," "General," or "Corporate" class/location for company-wide transactions that don't belong to a specific segment.

Creating Classes

To create a new class, go to the **Classes** screen and click **New**. A small window will appear where you can enter the class name. For example, you might create a class called **Contract Client Repairs** to track repairs for contract clients separately from walk-in customers. Once entered, click **Save**.

Creating Locations

Adding a new location is similar. Click **New** on the Locations screen, then name your location. You can optionally assign a parent location by selecting **Is a sub-location**. For example, creating a location called **HQ** allows you to track all transactions occurring in your main office. Click **Save** when done.

Editing and Inactivating Classes and Locations

You can update or mark a class or location as inactive if it's no longer relevant. Go to the **Class** or **Locations** screen, click the dropdown arrow in the **Action** column, and choose **Edit** or **Make Inactive**. While you cannot permanently delete these entries, inactive items can be reactivated anytime and remain visible in historical reports.

Assigning Classes and Locations to Transactions

When creating transactions—such as invoices, expenses, bills, or checks—you will see fields for both **Class** and **Location**. For invoices, you can enable the global setting **One per row in transaction** to assign a specific class to each product or service line.

For instance, in a sample invoice, the **Location** could be set to **HQ** and the **Class** to **Contract Client Repairs**. These fields are internal and will not appear on customer-facing documents. This setup allows precise tracking of your operations across different divisions, offices, or service types.

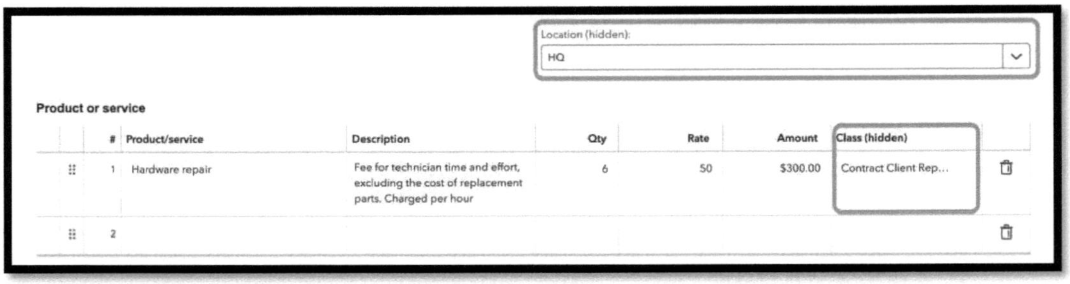

Key Differences Between Class Tracking and Location Tracking

Although similar, they serve different purposes:

1. **Balance Sheet vs. Profit & Loss**
   - **Class Tracking** applies only to **Profit & Loss** accounts (income and expenses).
   - **Location Tracking** applies to **both** Profit & Loss **and** Balance Sheet accounts (assets, liabilities, equity).
2. **How They Apply to Transactions**
   - **Locations** apply to the entire transaction — one location per transaction.
   - **Classes** can be assigned **per line item** or for the **entire** transaction.

This makes class tracking more flexible.

Example:
If a single supplier bill contains items for multiple departments:

- You can assign **each line** to a different **class**.
- But you can only assign **one location** to the whole bill.

This does **not** affect account categorization—you can still split items across different accounts; the difference is in how you tag them with classes or locations.

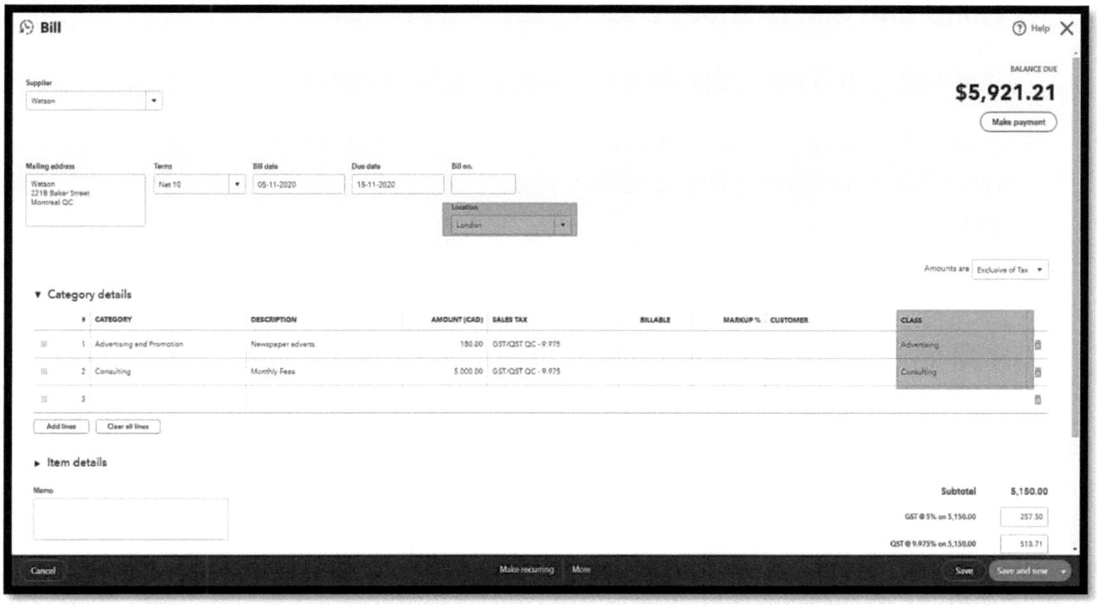

Examples of Locations and Classes in QuickBooks Online

Businesses can use **Location Tracking** and **Class Tracking** in QuickBooks Online (QBO) to organize financial data more effectively. These tools help categorize transactions for clearer reporting, deeper analysis, and better managerial decision-making. Below are practical examples of how different organizations might use them.

1. Businesses with Separate Divisions (e.g., Products vs. Services)

Companies offering both **products and services**, or operating **retail and wholesale** divisions, can use Locations to separate divisions.

Classes can then categorize individual items or service types within those divisions.

2. Property Management Companies

Assign each **property** its own Location and each **rental unit** a Class.

Since supplier bills often cover multiple units, classes make it easy to allocate expenses line-by-line to the correct unit.

3. Businesses with Multiple Offices or Geographic Locations

If your company operates in different **cities, states, or countries**, Location Tracking is ideal.

You can also use **Classes** to break down details within each location—for example, tracking revenue by product line or service type for each branch.

4. Nonprofits and Charities Tracking Separate Funds

Nonprofits often need detailed reporting on fund usage.

Each fund can be set up as a **Location**, ensuring every transaction is assigned to the correct funding source for accurate reporting on both the **profit & loss** and **balance sheet**.

5. Businesses with Multiple Service or Product Lines

Use Classes or Locations to track profitability across service or product categories—for example:

- A **web developer** offering design, hosting, and consulting
- A **photographer** offering portraits, weddings, and corporate packages
- A **retailer** selling both shoes and clothing

This helps determine which lines are most profitable.

6. Businesses Tracking Sales Reps

QBO does not include a built-in "sales rep" field.

If classes aren't being used for other purposes, you can assign each **salesperson** a Class.
This provides full **profit and loss insight**, not just sales totals.

How to Run Reports Using Classes and Locations

Setting up reports for class or location tracking in QBO is straightforward:

Profit and Loss by Class or Location

- ❖ Go to **Reports → Business Overview**.
- ❖ Select **Profit and Loss by Class** or **Profit and Loss by Location**.
- ❖ Customize and save the report using **Save Customization**.
- ❖ Use **Report Filters** to show only specific classes or locations.

Balance Sheet by Location

You cannot generate a balance sheet by class, but you *can* generate one by location:

1. Open the **Balance Sheet** report.
2. Under **Display Columns By**, choose **Location**.

   This provides insight into how assets, liabilities, and equity are distributed across locations.

Why Class and Location Tracking Matters

Using Class and Location Tracking:

- ❖ Gives clearer insight into which divisions, services, or locations are profitable
- ❖ Helps evaluate spending and ROI for specific areas
- ❖ Allows for more granular financial transparency
- ❖ Helps identify exactly where assets and liabilities are allocated

These features make QBO a powerful tool for analyzing performance and improving business decision-making.

HOW TO SET UP PROJECTS IN QUICKBOOKS ONLINE

QuickBooks Online (QBO) lets you **group invoices, expenses, and time entries** under a single project or client. This makes it easier to **track profitability** for each job. The feature is especially useful for **freelancers, contractors, and service-based businesses** with multiple clients.

Note: Projects are available only on **QBO Plus and Advanced plans**. Users on lower-tier plans must upgrade to access this feature.

1. Enable the Projects Feature

If you don't see **Projects** in the left-hand menu:

1. Click the **gear icon (Settings) → Account and Settings**.
2. Select **Advanced**, scroll down to **Projects**, and click the **pencil icon**.

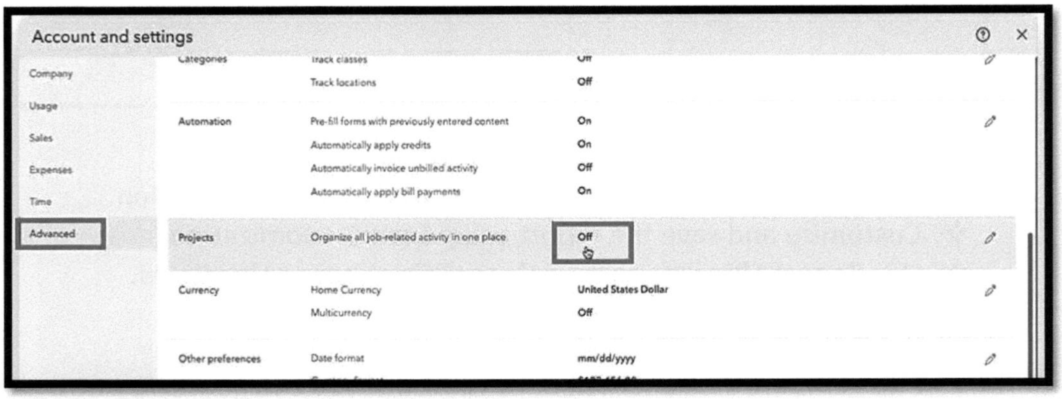

3. Toggle **Projects** on and click **Save**, then **Done**.
4. You'll now see **Projects** under **Time** in the left-hand menu.

2. Create a New Project

1. Click **Projects → New Project**.

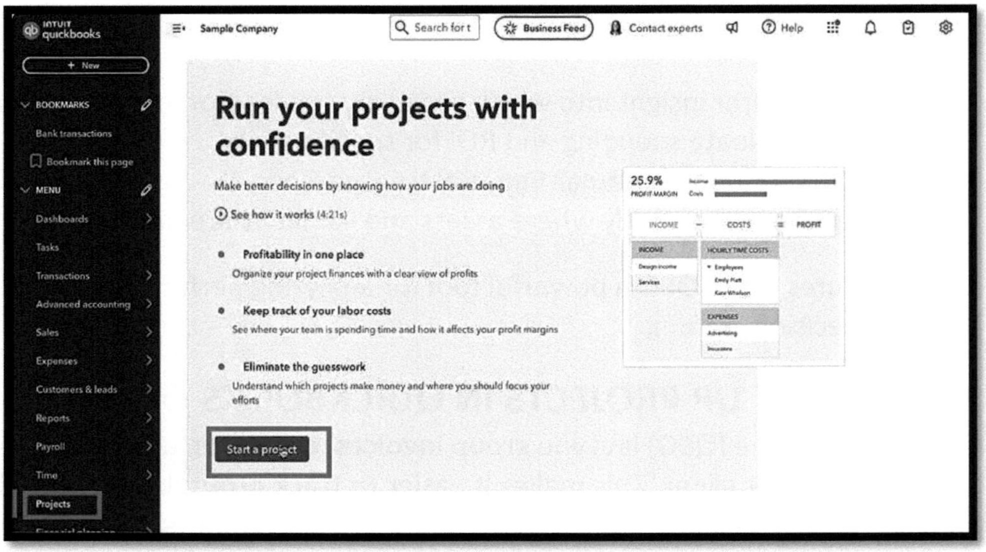

2. Optional: Use the **Project Management Agent** to upload PDFs, contracts, or estimates. This tool auto-fills project details to save time.
3. For manual setup:

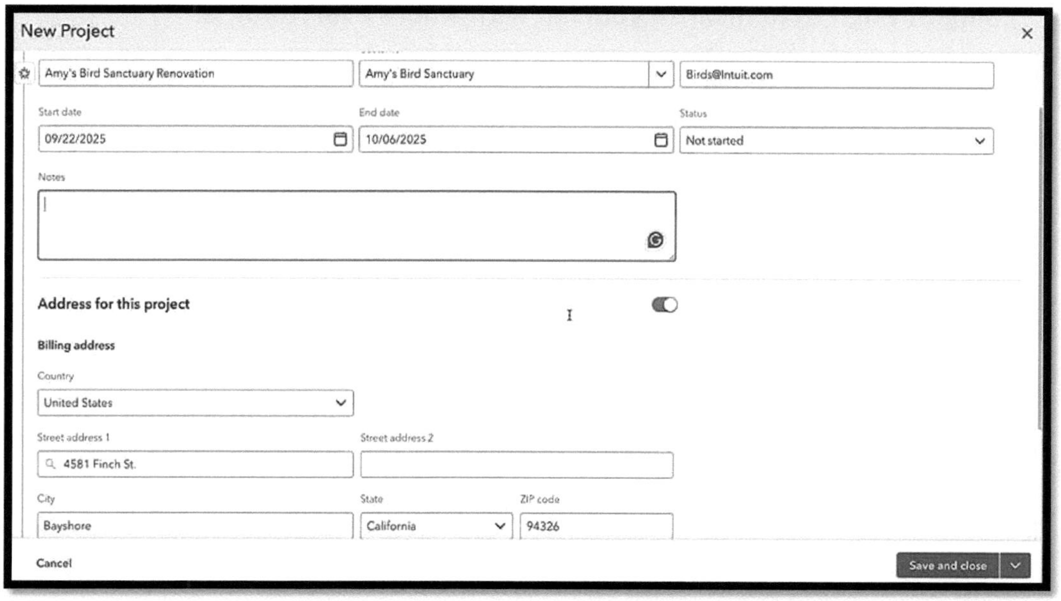

- ❖ **Project Name:** Be descriptive (e.g., *Amy's Bird Sanctuary Renovation*).
- ❖ **Customer:** Select an existing client or add a new one.
- ❖ **Email:** Auto-fills from the client record; editable if needed.
- ❖ **Start & End Dates:** Use the calendar tool to select dates.
- ❖ **Status:** Choose *Not Started, In Progress, Completed,* or *Canceled*.
- ❖ **Notes:** Add internal notes for the team.
- ❖ **Address & Shipping Address:** Auto-fills from customer info; editable if necessary.
- ❖ **Custom Fields:** Add optional details like PO numbers, sales agent names, or other identifiers via **Manage Custom Fields**.

4. Click **Save and Close** to finish setting up the project.

3. Key Benefits

- ❖ **Consolidates financial activity** under one project for easy profitability tracking.
- ❖ **Organizes invoices, expenses, and time entries** in one location.
- ❖ Reduces **manual data entry** with the Project Management Agent.
- ❖ Ideal for businesses managing **multiple clients, jobs, or service lines** efficiently.

Navigating the Projects Dashboard in QuickBooks Online

Once you've set up a project, the **Projects Dashboard** gives you a complete overview of all related financial activity.

Tip: QuickBooks provides a short walkthrough at the top of the dashboard. It's worth going through to familiarize yourself with where everything is.

1. Dashboard Overview

The main dashboard displays key project metrics:

- **Open estimates and invoices**
- **Overdue invoices**
- **Estimates vs. actual costs**
- **Profit margins** and overall financial health

As you add invoices, payments, receipts, and expenses, these numbers update automatically.

2. Adding Items to a Project

To add transactions:

1. Click the **Add to Project** dropdown (top right).
2. Select the type of entry: **Invoice, Estimate, Expense, Payment**, etc.

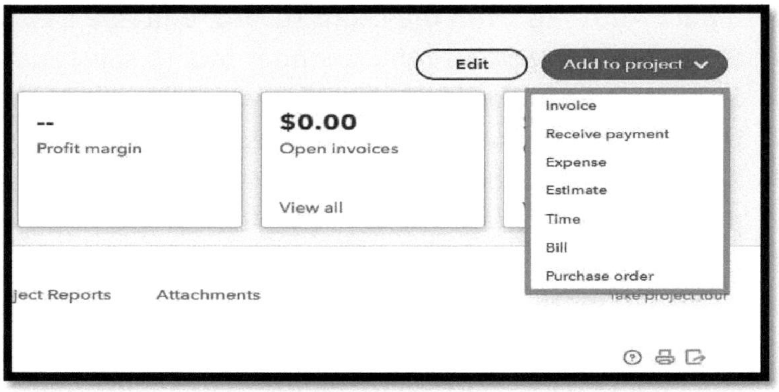

3. Fill out the form, then **Save and Close** or **Save and Send**.

This ensures all project-related transactions are grouped under that specific project for easy tracking.

3. Project Tabs Explained

- **Overview:** Displays all financial activity, including open invoices, overdue payments, profit margins, and payroll expenses if tracked.

- **Transactions:** Lists all project-related entries such as invoices, expenses, and payments.
- **Time Activity:** Shows tracked hours if QuickBooks Time is enabled.
- **Project Reports:** Provides critical insights such as:
  - Estimates vs. actual costs
  - Unbilled time and expenses
  - Work in progress by project
- **Project Details:** Lets you update project information like addresses, emails, dates, and other notes.
- **Change Log:** Tracks any modifications to estimates, ensuring you can monitor scope changes or client-requested adjustments.
- **Attachments:** Upload and store PDFs, emails, contracts, or any other documents related to the project.

4. Benefits

Using the Projects Dashboard, you can:

- **Monitor profitability** of each project in real time.
- **Track costs and revenue** efficiently in one place.
- **Keep all project-related documents** and transactions organized.
- **Generate detailed reports** for better decision-making and project management.

Adding an Estimate to a Project

1. Click **Add to Project** and select **Estimate**.
2. The **Customer/Project** field will automatically populate with your project.
3. Complete the estimate as usual and click **Save** or **Review and Send**.

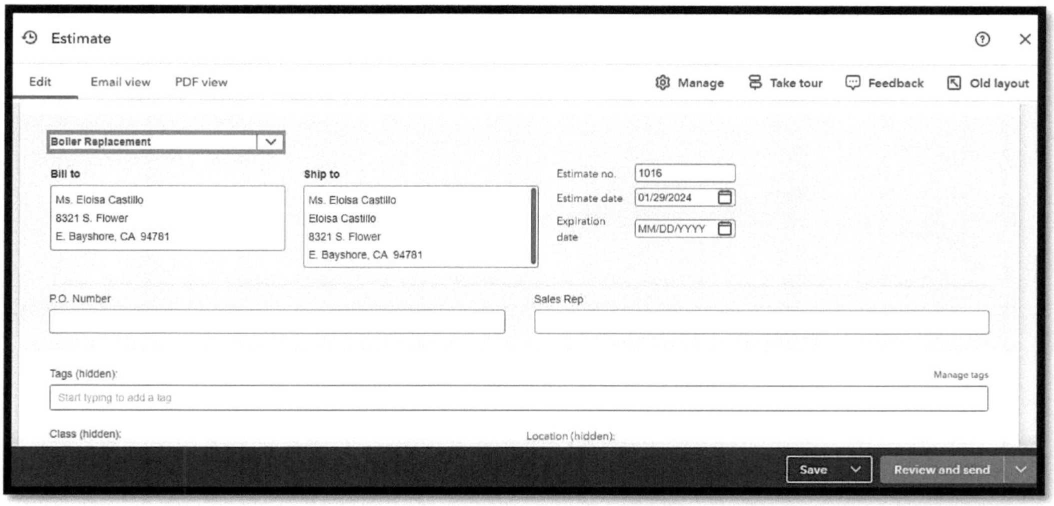

The estimate will now appear under the **Transactions** tab in the project dashboard.

Assigning Expenses or Bills

1. Click **Add to Project** and select **Bill** or **Expense**.
2. QuickBooks automatically populates the **Customer/Project** field.
3. Record the expense or bill, then click **Save** or **Save and Schedule Payment**.

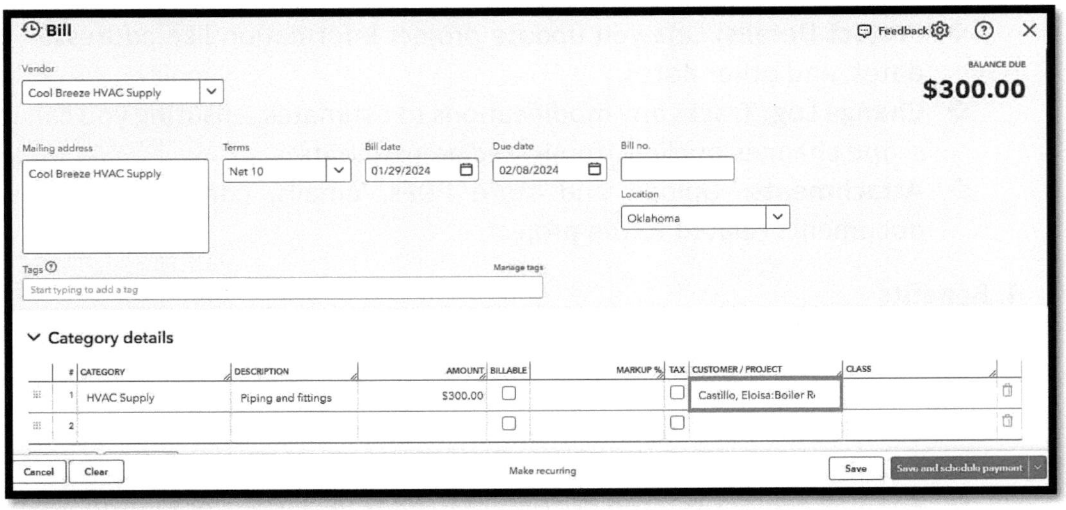

Recording Hourly Costs

1. Select **Time** from **Add to Project**.
2. Enter hours worked manually or use the built-in timer. Ensure the **Customer/Project** field is pre-populated.
3. Click **Save** or **Save and New**.

QuickBooks calculates total labor costs based on the employee's hourly rate. For billable hours, you can invoice clients directly for time tracked.

Tip: If you haven't set an employee's hourly rate, click **Employee Hourly Rate** on the Projects screen to add or edit rates.

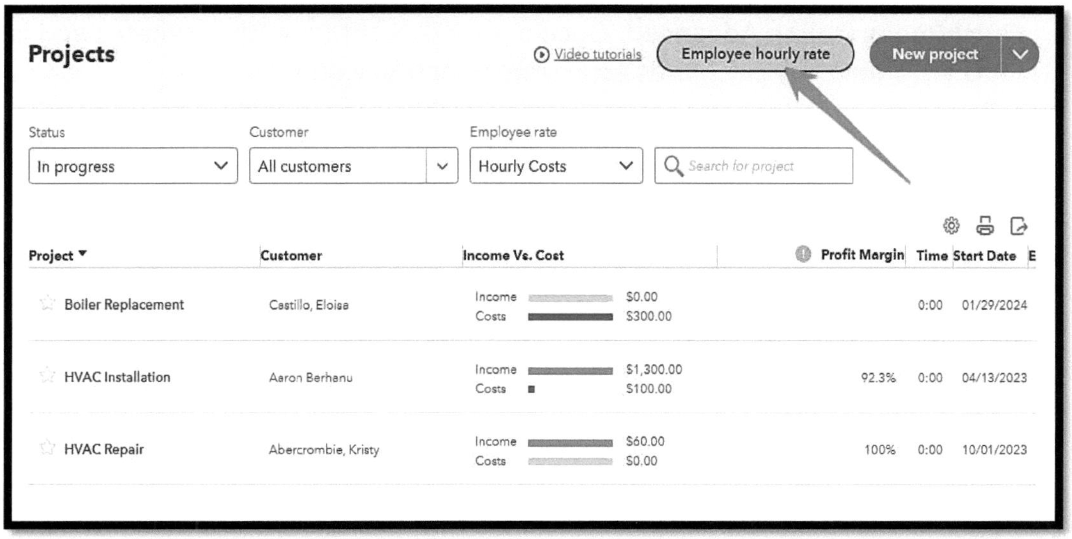

Linking an Invoice to a Project

1. Click **Add to Project → Invoice**.
2. Create the invoice as usual. To include a previously created estimate, click **Add** on the right-hand side of the invoice form.
3. Click **Save** or **Review and Send**.

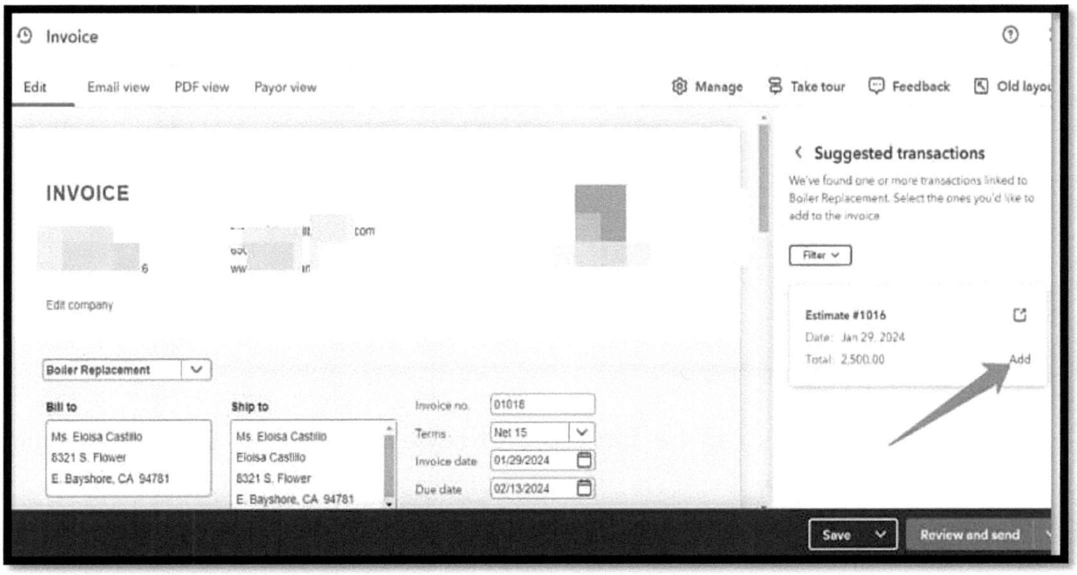

The project dashboard will now show all related transactions, including estimates, expenses, time entries, and invoices, along with profitability insights such as total income, expenses, and profit.

Tracking Estimates vs Actuals

To compare estimates against actual income and expenses, you must use **QuickBooks Online Advanced**. Once a project is set up with estimates and invoices, QBO automatically calculates estimated vs actual values.

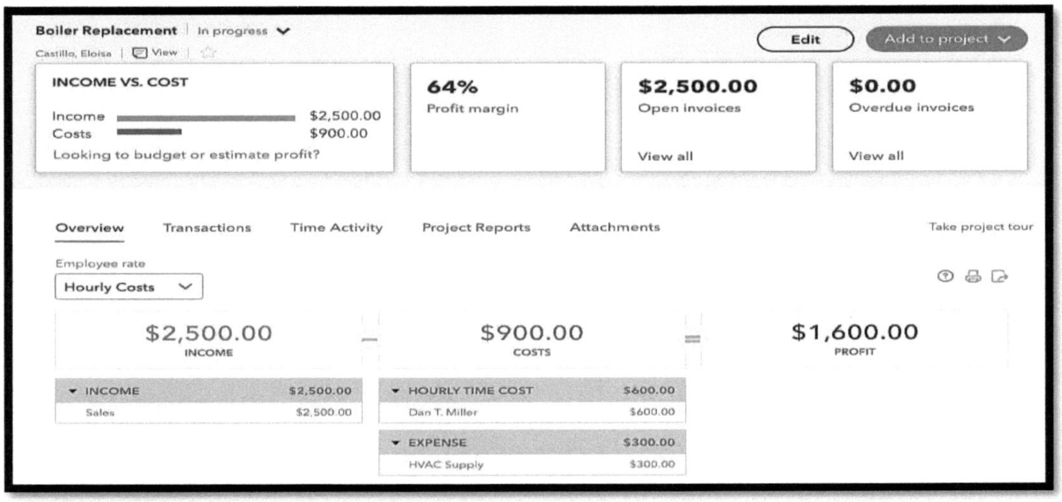

Updating Project Status

1. Click the **status arrow** next to the project.
2. Choose the appropriate status: **Not Started, In Progress, Completed,** or **Canceled**.

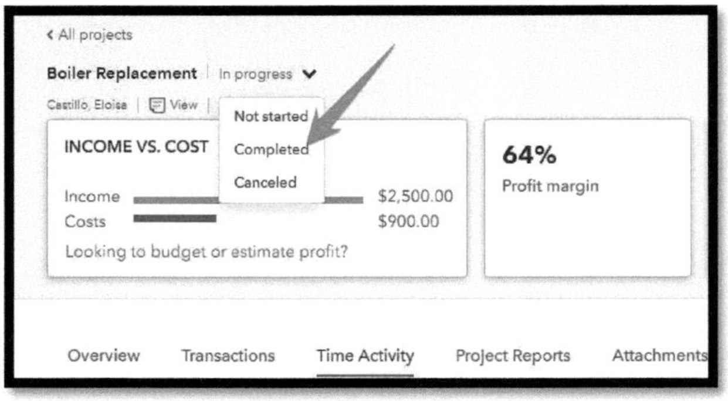

Completed projects can be filtered and reviewed in your **Projects list** using the "Completed" status.

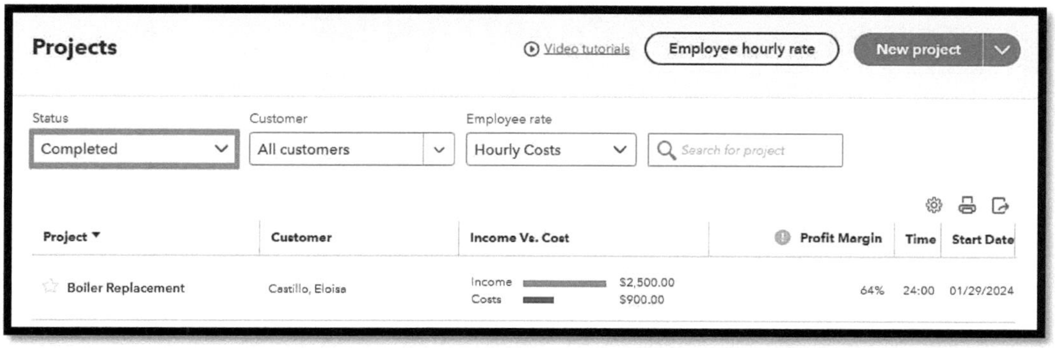

Running Project Profitability Reports

From the **Project Reports** tab in the project dashboard, you can generate:

- **Project Profitability Report:** Detailed income, expenses, and net profit.
- **Time Cost by Employees or Vendors:** Breakdown of labor costs per team member or vendor.
- **Unbilled Time and Expenses:** Hours worked and expenses recorded but not yet invoiced.

For a summary across multiple projects, go to **Reports → Project Profitability Summary**.

Advanced Plan Features:

- Estimates vs Actuals by Project
- Estimates and Progress Invoicing Summary
- Work-in-Progress by Project

CHAPTER NINE

BUDGETS IN QUICKBOOKS ONLINE

A budget in QuickBooks Online helps you plan, control, and track your business finances with clarity. By outlining your expected income and expenses for the year, you can compare actual performance against your goals, identify trends early, and make informed decisions. QuickBooks Online makes budgeting simple by using your existing financial data, allowing you to build accurate, organized budgets that keep your business on track.

HOW TO CREATE A BUDGET IN QUICKBOOKS ONLINE

Creating a budget in QuickBooks Online is one of the most effective ways to understand your financial performance, plan ahead, and prevent unexpected cash-flow issues. Whether your books are perfectly organized or still a little messy, QuickBooks gives you the tools to build a clear, reliable budget.

Why create a budget in QuickBooks Online?

A budget gives you more than numbers—it gives you control of your business. It helps you:

- **Gain clarity:** Understand exactly where your money is coming from and where it's going.
- **Plan effectively:** Make smarter financial decisions using real data and trends.
- **Monitor performance:** Compare your actual results against your expectations.
- **Reduce stress:** Stay prepared and avoid financial surprises.

Before You Begin: Prepare Your QuickBooks File

A budget is only as accurate as the data behind it. Make sure to:

- **Clean up your books:** Resolve uncategorized, duplicated, or unreconciled transactions.
- **Organize your Chart of Accounts:** Ensure income and expense categories are accurate and meaningful.
- **Review past data:** Use the previous 12 months to inform your estimates.
- **Consider future plans:** Think about expected changes—new hires, equipment purchases, price changes, or seasonal shifts.

Step 1: Open the Budgeting Tool

1. Log in to QuickBooks Online.
2. Click the **Gear icon (⚙)** in the upper-right corner.
3. Under **Tools**, select **Budgeting**.
4. Click **Create Budget** to get started.

Step 2: Configure Your Budget Settings

After selecting **Create Budget**, you'll see several setup options:

1. Budget Type

Choose **Profit and Loss**, which is the standard for most small businesses.

2. Period

Select your fiscal year—e.g., **FY 2025 (Jan–Dec 2025)**.

3. Budget Format

- **Consolidated:** A single, overall budget.
- **Subdivided:** Break your budget down by **class, customer, or location** for deeper insight.

4. Pre-fill Data

Choose whether to start with actual numbers or a blank template:

- Selecting something like **"Actuals 2025 (YTD)"** automatically fills your budget using current-year performance.

Choosing Between Custom and Import

At the bottom, you'll see two setup paths:

- **Custom Budget (Recommended)**

Build your budget directly in QuickBooks by entering estimated income and expenses. Best for most small business owners.

- **Import Budget**

Use this if your budget is already prepared in Excel or another program. Helpful for accountants or advanced users.

Tip: If this is your first time, use **Custom Budget**—it's simple, intuitive, and easy to revise later.

Click **Next** to continue.

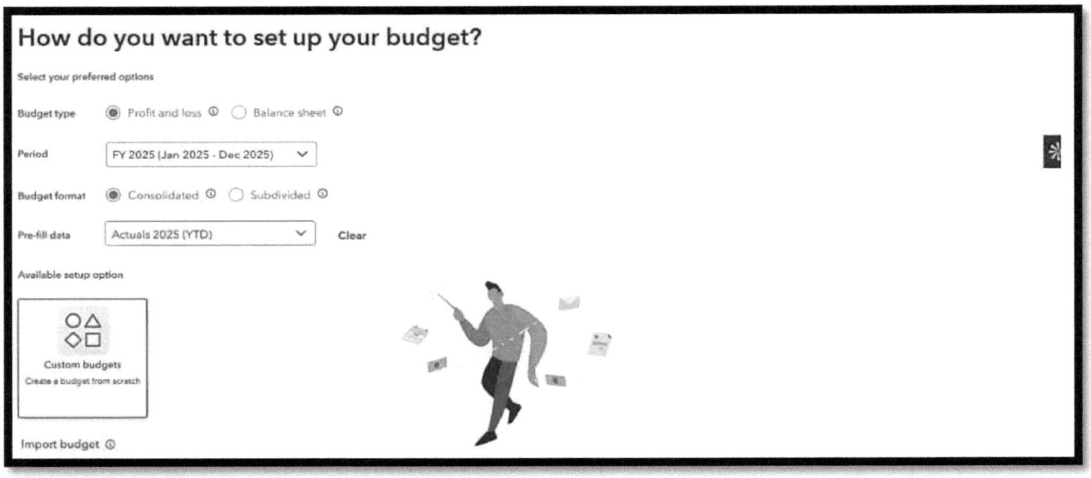

Step 3: Enter Your Income and Expenses

You'll now see a spreadsheet-style budgeting screen.

Understanding the Layout

- ❖ **Account Rows (Left):** Pulled from your Chart of Accounts—Sales, Services, Rent, Utilities, etc.
- ❖ **Monthly Columns (Top):** Enter estimated amounts for each month in your fiscal year.
- ❖ **Reference Data:** If you pre-filled with actuals, you'll see year-to-date numbers to guide your projections.
- ❖ **Frequency Options:** Switch between **Monthly, Quarterly,** or **Yearly** views depending on how detailed you want your budget to be.

From here, simply fill in your expected income and expenses month by month, making adjustments as needed to match your business goals.

How to Fill Out Your Budget in QuickBooks Online

1. Estimate Your Income

Begin with your revenue accounts. Use realistic, data-driven projections:

- ❖ Review your past income, especially if you pre-filled the budget with actual data.
- ❖ Adjust for seasonal trends if your business has busy or slow months.
- ❖ Increase projected revenue if you expect growth, new products, or expanded services.

Example:
If your average monthly service income is $5,000 and you anticipate 10% growth, enter approximately $5,500 per month—or increase it gradually throughout the year.

2. Estimate Your Expenses

Next, outline all business costs you expect for the year:

- **Fixed expenses** (consistent every month): rent, insurance, subscriptions.
- **Variable expenses** (change with workload or sales): supplies, payroll, marketing.
- **Occasional expenses:** annual fees, one-time purchases, or seasonal costs.
  - You can enter these in the specific month they occur or spread them evenly over the year.

Tip: Use your Profit & Loss report or the "Actuals" column to ground your estimates in real data.

Tools Available in the Budgeting Screen

QuickBooks provides features to help you work efficiently:

- **Batch Actions:** Apply edits or copy values to multiple rows at once.
- **Search Bar:** Quickly locate specific accounts.
- **Export/Print:** Save or share your budget outside QuickBooks.
- **Save Options:** Choose *Save* or *Save and Close* at any time.

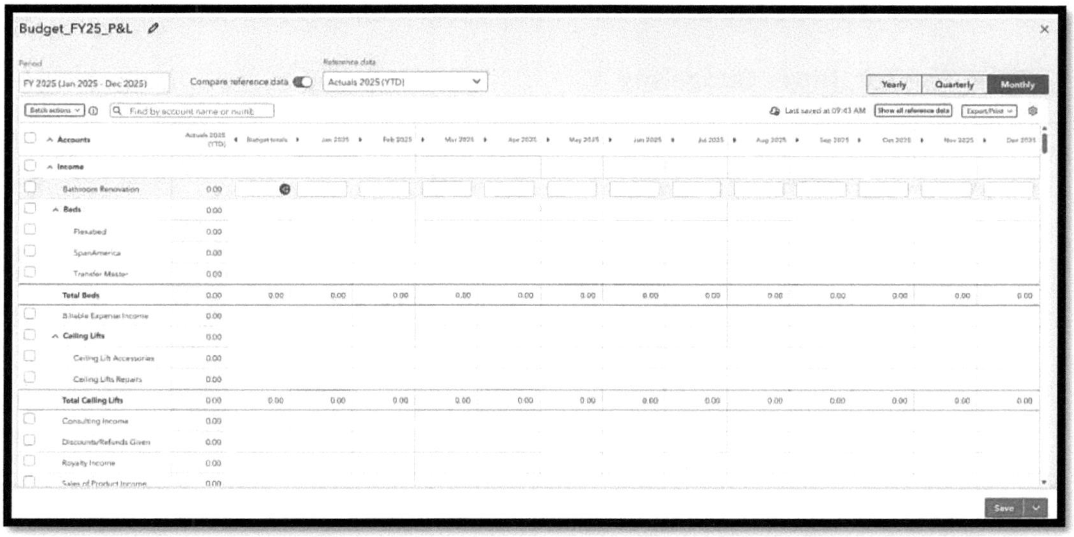

Step 4: Review and Fine-Tune Your Budget

Before finalizing your budget, take a moment to validate your numbers:

- **Are income and expense projections realistic?** Adjust anything that looks extreme.
- **Does projected income cover projected costs?** A budget should support profitability or help you prepare for shortfalls.
- **Are any categories missing?** Ensure taxes, insurance, payroll, and software fees are included.

How to Edit Your Budget Later

You can revisit and change your budget anytime:

1. Click the **Gear icon (⚙)**
2. Select **Budgeting**
3. Open the budget you want to update

Pro Tip:

It's safer to *slightly overestimate expenses and underestimate income*. This leaves room for unexpected costs or slower months.

Step 5: Keep Your Budget Updated

Your budget should evolve as your business changes:

- **Review monthly** to compare actual results to your plan.
- **Adjust projections** when income or expenses shift.
- **Update directly** in the Budgeting tool whenever needed.

Final Tips for Better Budgeting

- Start with accurate, organized financial data.
- Avoid overly optimistic revenue forecasts.
- Break your budget down monthly for better visibility and control.
- Review regularly—don't set it and forget it.

A thoughtful, well-maintained budget helps you plan smarter, stay in control, and navigate your financial year with confidence.

EXPERT TIPS FOR EFFECTIVE BUDGETING IN QUICKBOOKS ONLINE

To get the most out of your budgeting tools in QuickBooks Online, keep these practical best practices in mind:

1. Review and Adjust Regularly

Budgets shouldn't stay static. Compare your budget to actual results each month to spot major variances. If market conditions or operations shift, revise your budget accordingly.
Flexible budgeting helps prevent cash-flow issues—one of the leading causes of small-business failure.

2. Use Realistic Projections

Base your numbers on historical data, current trends, and known upcoming changes. Avoid overly optimistic income estimates or underestimated expenses, as they can lead to misguided decisions.

QuickBooks' built-in reports and past performance data make it easy to set achievable targets.

3. Categorize Transactions Consistently

Accurate budget reports rely on clean, consistent categorization. Create clear rules for expenses and income, and apply them uniformly.

Regular reconciliation ensures that your budget-vs-actual comparisons remain accurate and meaningful.

4. Align Your Budget With Business Goals

Your budget should reflect the direction of your business. If you plan to invest in marketing, expansion, or equipment, ensure those priorities are clearly represented in your financial plan.

This shifts your budget from a simple tracking tool to a strategic guide.

5. Get Comfortable With Your Numbers

QuickBooks Online is designed to make financial data approachable. View your numbers as insights that help you make better decisions—not something to fear.

The more familiar you are with your financial reports, the more confidently you can steer your business toward long-term stability and growth.

PART IV: REPORTING AND DATA MANAGEMENT

CHAPTER TEN

OVERVIEW OF QUICKBOOKS ONLINE REPORTS

QuickBooks Online (QBO) is built to support ongoing financial reporting—whether weekly, monthly, or quarterly. The platform provides an easy-to-use reporting center where you can access, customize, and export reports. While exporting reports still requires manual work, QBO also allows you to automate reporting through dashboards, scheduled reports, and custom-built report templates.

This section breaks down the reports available in each QBO subscription plan so you can understand exactly what you get at every level.

QUICKBOOKS ONLINE REPORTS BY SUBSCRIPTION PLAN

QBO offers **five plans**—four standard subscription levels plus **Solopreneur**, a basic plan marketed separately for sole proprietors.

Each plan includes a different set of features and reporting tools. Because financial reporting is essential to all users, even the lowest-tier plan includes several core reports.

Reports in the Solopreneur Plan

The **Solopreneur** plan includes essential reports designed for individuals running small, simple operations. These reports are basic, less customizable, and primarily focused on sales and tax compliance.

Included Reports: Profit and Loss, Profit and Loss by Customer, Profit and Loss by Month, Sales Tax Liability, Taxable Sales Detail, Taxable Sales Summary, Sales by Customer Summary, and Sales by Product/Service Summary.

Important: This plan does *not* include a Balance Sheet report.

Reports in the Simple Start Plan

The **Simple Start** plan includes everything in Solopreneur plus essential financial statements, activity logs, and customer-focused reports.

Additional Reports Available in Simple Start: Audit Log, Balance Sheet, Balance Sheet Detail, Balance Sheet Comparison, Profit and Loss Comparison, P&L % of Total

Income, Year-to-Date P&L Comparison, Quarterly Profit and Loss Summary, Statement of Cash Flows, Customer Contact List, Deposit Detail, Estimates by Customer, Products and Services List, A/R Summary, Collections Report, Customer Balance Summary, Invoice List, Invoice & Received Payments, Open Invoices, Statement List, and Check Detail

Simple Start also provides **Customized Reports** and **Management Reports**, which bundle multiple reports into presentation-ready packages.

Reports in the Essentials Plan

The **Essentials** plan builds on Simple Start by adding deeper financial insights, accounts payable reports, and enhanced sales tracking.

Additional Reports Available in Essentials: Balance Sheet Summary, Business Snapshot, Profit and Loss Detail, Realized & Unrealized Exchange Gains/Losses, Income by Customer Summary, Payment Method List, Sales by Customer Detail / Customer Type Detail, Sales by Product/Service Detail, Transaction List by Customer, Unbilled Charges, A/R Aging Detail, Customer Balance Detail, A/P Aging Summary and Detail, Bill Payments List, Unpaid Bills, Vendor Balance Summary & Detail, and Expenses by Vendor Summary.

Essentials also unlocks:

Auto-Sent Reports (schedule reports to be emailed automatically)

Grouped Reports (run multiple custom reports at once)

Reports in the Plus Plan

The **Plus** plan includes everything from lower tiers and adds advanced budgeting, class/location tracking, time tracking, and inventory-related reports.

Additional Reports Available in Plus: Budget Overview, Budget vs. Actuals, Custom Summary Report, Profit and Loss by Class / Location, Total Deposits and Payments, Inventory Valuation Detail / Summary, Physical Inventory Worksheet, Sales by Class (Detail & Summary), Sales by Location (Detail & Summary), Time Activities by Customer Detail, Unbilled Time, Uninvoiced Charges, Terms List, 1099 Contractor Summary & Detail, and Bills and Applied Payments.

These extra reports make Plus the most flexible general-use plan for small and growing businesses.

Reports in the Advanced Plan

The **Advanced** plan includes *all* reports available in every lower plan.

While it does not add new report types, it provides powerful tools for reporting:

Advanced Plan Reporting Features

- **Custom Report Builder** with deeper filters and more data sources
- **Enhanced layouts** and visual customization
- **Over 100+ built-in reports**

Even with these, you may still want more personalized reporting—especially if you need nontraditional date ranges or recurring comparison views (e.g., "this quarter vs. same quarter last year"). The Advanced tools make this easier but still require setup.

HOW TO ACCESS AND USE REPORTS IN QUICKBOOKS ONLINE

Navigating QuickBooks Online's reporting tools is simple once you know where to look. Every report—from your Profit and Loss to your Accounts Aging—lives inside the **Reports Center**, which you can access from the menu on the left side of your dashboard.

If you're using the **Business View**, follow the path **Business overview > Reports**. If you're in **Accountant View**, simply click **Reports** and you're in.

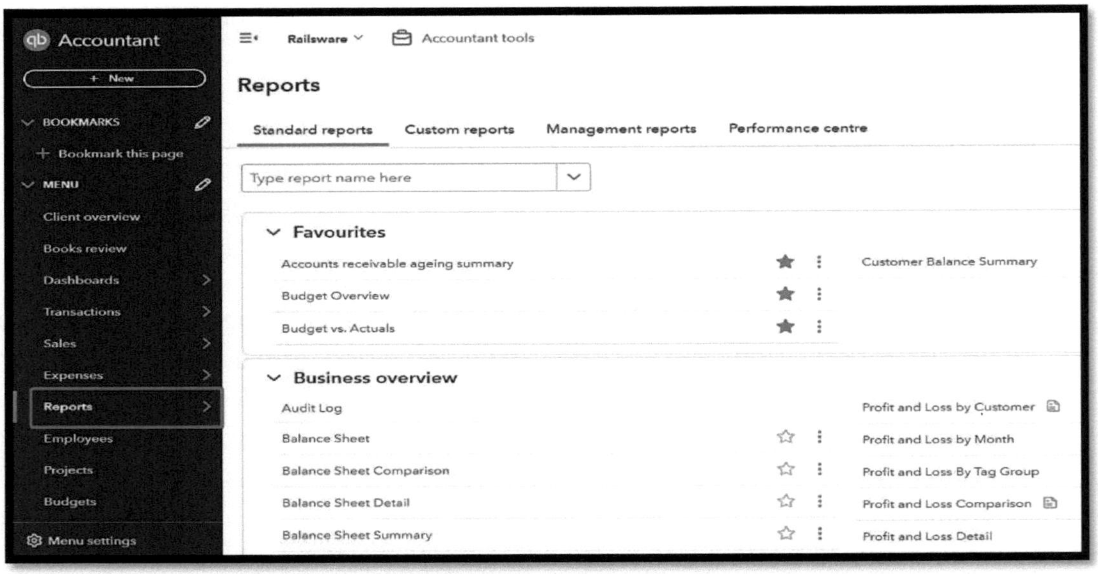

Understanding the Reports Center

Depending on your subscription plan, your Reports Center includes between two and four main sections. Each offers a different level of insight and flexibility:

1. Standard Reports

This is where QuickBooks stores all pre-built reports—everything from financial statements to sales summaries.

2. Custom Reports ***(available from the Simple Start plan)***

Any standard report you customize and save for later appears here.

3. Management Reports ***(also Simple Start and above)***

These let you package multiple reports into a polished, presentation-ready format—great for meetings or client updates.

4. Performance Center

This space features charts and visual summaries that help you track business performance at a glance.

How Standard Reports Are Organized

QuickBooks makes it easy to find what you need by grouping reports into categories based on purpose. For example:

- **Favorites** – reports you've starred for quick access
- **Business Overview** – Balance Sheet, Audit Log, and other core business snapshots
- **Who Owes You** – aging reports, customer balances, open invoices
- **Projects** *(Plus plan or higher)* – project profitability
- **Sales and Customers** – sales summaries and customer lists
- **What You Owe** – unpaid bills, accounts payable aging
- **Expenses and Suppliers** – vendor lists, check details
- **Sales Tax** – liability reports and tax summaries
- **Employees** – time activities and employee contact lists
- **For My Accountant** – general ledger, P&L comparisons
- **Payroll** – employee time activity reports

The exact reports available depend on your QuickBooks Online plan.

Classic vs. Modern View: What's Changing?

QuickBooks is gradually transitioning reports to a cleaner, more intuitive **Modern view**. Reports that already use this format are marked with a small paper icon.

The Modern view offers smoother navigation, automatic updates as you adjust filters, and an overall cleaner layout.

How to Customize Reports in QuickBooks Online

Customizing a report helps you see your data exactly the way you need it. Start by selecting any report from its category.

In both views, you can update basics like:

- Reporting period
- Column display
- Accounting method (cash or accrual)

Customization in Classic View

Click **Customize** to open a detailed menu with advanced options such as filters, formatting, and data organization. After adjusting the settings, click **Run report** to update your results.

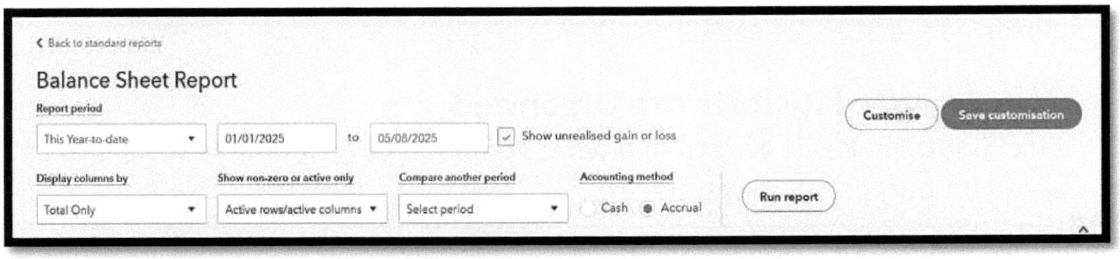

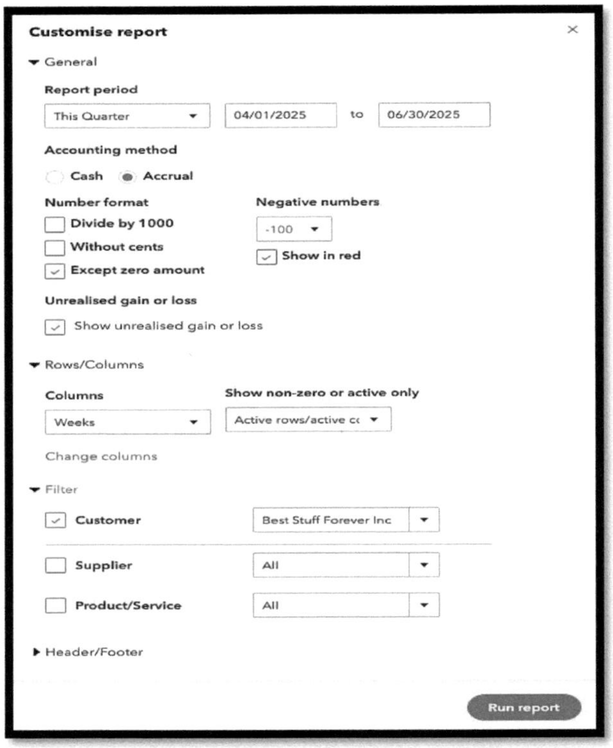

Customization in Modern View

Here, customization tools appear on the right side of the screen. Adjustments update immediately—no need to re-run the report.

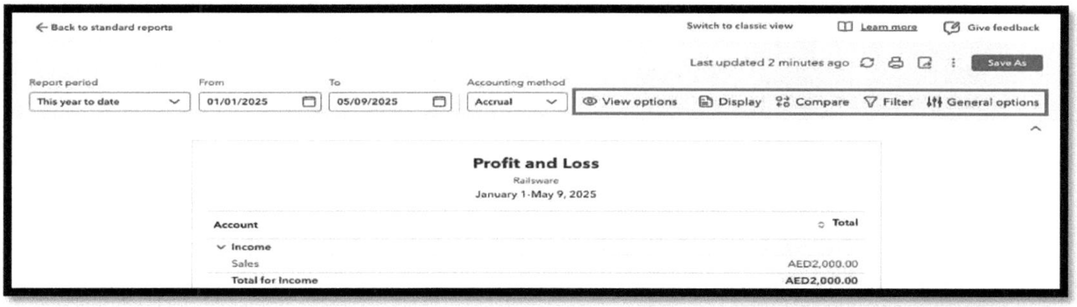

How to Create Custom Reports

If you find yourself making the same adjustments every time you open a report, you can save it as a custom version for future use.

In the **Classic view**, click **Save customization** after you make your changes. Name your report and, if you're on the Essentials plan or higher, assign it to a group.

In the **Modern view**, the equivalent button is **Save As**.

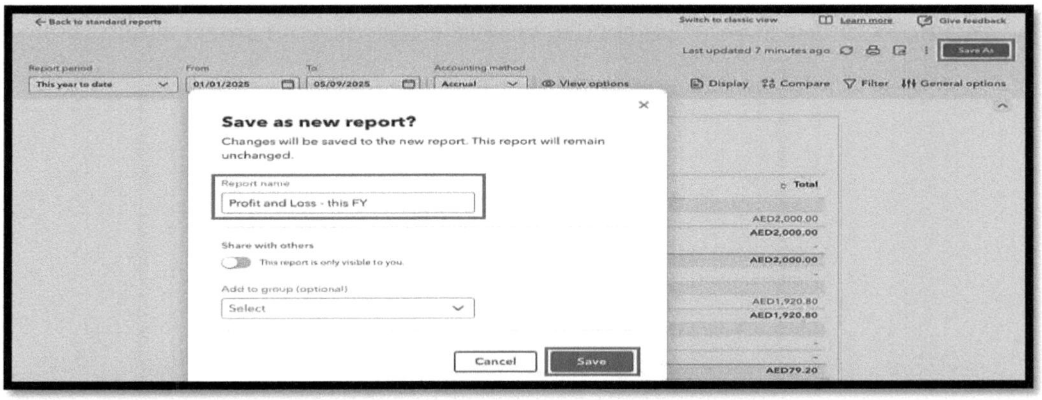

Either way, QuickBooks saves your custom report in the same place.

Where to Find Your Custom Reports

All saved custom reports appear under **Reports > Custom Reports.**

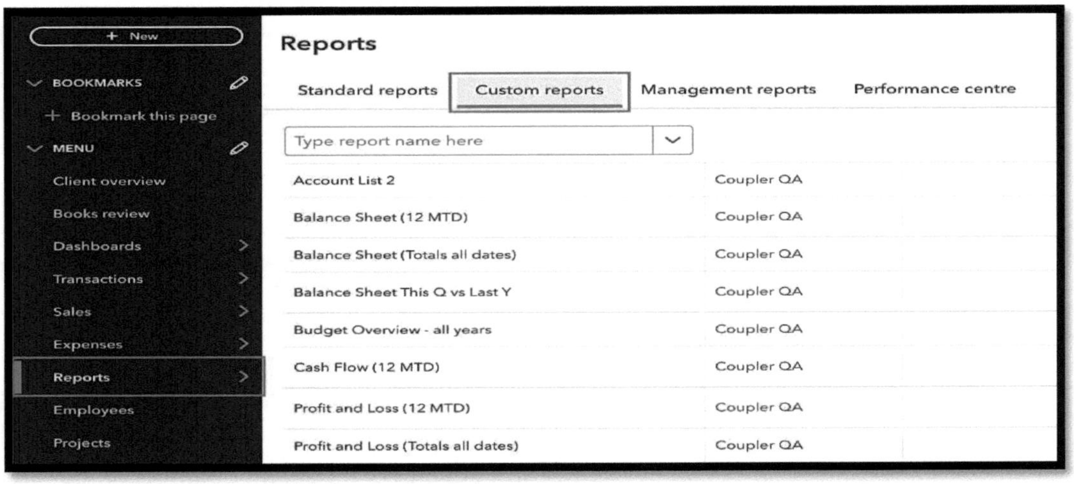

This is where you'll find every customized report created by users on your company's QuickBooks account.

How to Share Custom Reports in QuickBooks Online

Sharing custom reports in QuickBooks Online is a powerful way to keep your team aligned and your stakeholders informed. Whether you're collaborating internally or distributing insights externally, QuickBooks provides several flexible methods to manage report access.

Sharing Reports Internally

If you're working in the **Classic view**, QuickBooks lets you choose who can access a custom report the moment you save it. After clicking **Save customization**, you'll see a sharing option that allows you to select the teammates who should have access. QuickBooks then makes the report available to them automatically.

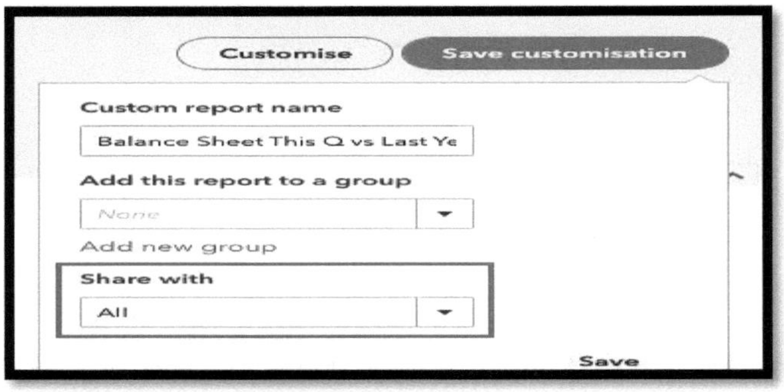

The **Modern view** simplifies this even further. When you select **Save As**, you can immediately toggle on **Share with others**. With one click, your report becomes visible to the users in your company file who have the appropriate permissions—no additional steps required.

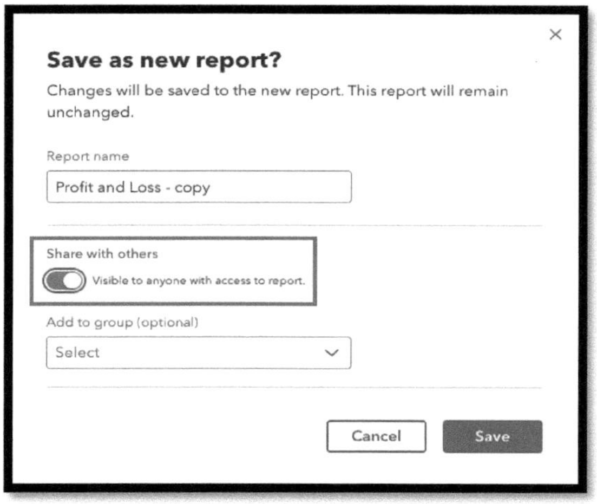

Sharing Reports Externally

QuickBooks doesn't directly support external sharing through in-app links, but exporting your reports serves as the most efficient alternative. From the Custom Reports list, you can open the menu next to any report and export it as either a **PDF** or **Excel file**. Once exported, the file can be emailed, uploaded to shared drives, or delivered to clients however you prefer.

If your stakeholders need data that updates regularly—daily, weekly, or monthly—you can also schedule exports to platforms like **Google Sheets** or **Microsoft Excel**. This makes it easy to maintain a live spreadsheet that updates itself without repeated manual downloads.

Automating Report Delivery

Users subscribed to the **Essentials, Plus, or Advanced** plans can take advantage of QuickBooks' **Auto Send Reports** feature. This tool allows you to schedule email delivery of specific custom reports at regular intervals.

After opening any custom report, simply click **Edit**, enable **Set email schedule**, and choose where and how often the report should be sent. You can personalize the email message, select recipients, and decide whether to send the report as an Excel file or in HTML format.

Even **standard reports** can be automated—just save them as custom reports first, and then schedule them the same way.

Scheduling Quarterly Reports

Although QuickBooks does not include a dedicated "Quarterly" frequency, scheduling quarterly reports is still straightforward. In the recurrence settings, select:

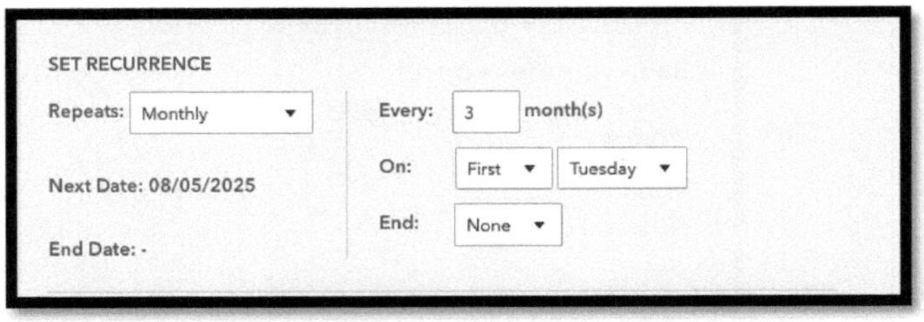

Repeats: Monthly

Every: 3 months

QuickBooks will then deliver the report every quarter automatically.

When Automations Feel Limiting

While QuickBooks' scheduled report options are useful, they may not meet the needs of users who rely heavily on spreadsheets. Many accountants prefer working in Excel or Google Sheets for deeper analysis, custom formatting, and integration with other tools. Although QuickBooks can email Excel attachments, these files still have to be downloaded manually—which may feel inefficient for teams that prefer fully cloud-based workflows.

TYPES OF QUICKBOOKS ONLINE REPORTS

QuickBooks Online offers an extensive library of reports, each designed to give you insight into a specific part of your business. Whether you're tracking payroll, analyzing vendor activity, reviewing budgets, or preparing accountant-ready statements, QuickBooks organizes everything in one central hub. Below is an easy-to-understand guide to the most commonly used report categories and how to access, customize, and export them efficiently.

Standard Payroll Reports in QuickBooks Online

Payroll reporting is located at the bottom of the Reports page, where QuickBooks provides a collection of 19 payroll-specific reports. Users on the Simple Start plan and above can access nearly all of these reports. However, certain advanced payroll reports—such as Payroll Summary by Employee, Recent/Edited Time Activities, and Time Activities by Employee Detail—are available only to those on the Plus or Advanced plans.

Quarterly Payroll Reports

Creating quarterly payroll reports is straightforward. Open any payroll report and adjust the reporting period to a quarterly range such as *Last Year* or *Last Quarter*. Reports in the Modern view update immediately, while those in the Classic view require clicking **Run report** to refresh the data.

If you want to reuse the same custom report repeatedly, save it by clicking **Save Customization** (Classic view) or **Save As** (Modern view). From there, your quarterly report will appear in the **Custom Reports** tab and automatically pull updated data for the saved period.

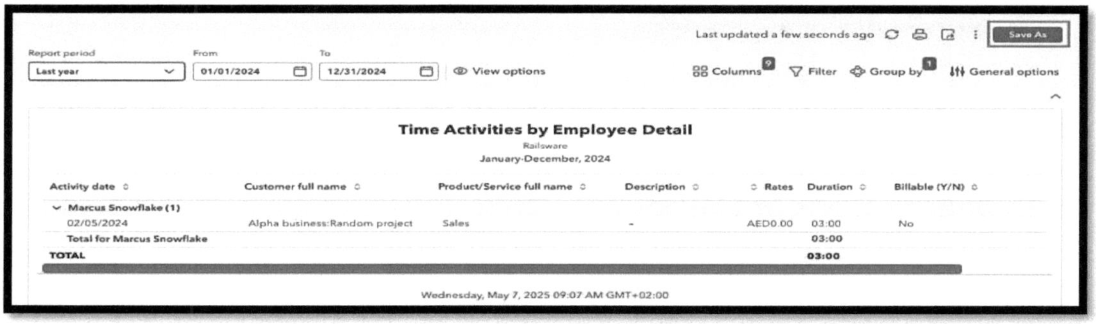

You can also email it directly using QuickBooks' scheduling tool, which allows recurring quarterly deliveries.

Exporting Employee Reports

Employee-related reports—like Employee Directory and Employee Details—are available on all plans except Solopreneur. Exporting them is simple. Open the report and choose to download it as a PDF or Excel file, depending on your needs. This is ideal for HR documentation, compliance reporting, or onboarding materials.

Exporting Productivity Reports

While QuickBooks doesn't have a dedicated "productivity report," the **Time Activities by Employee Detail** report comes closest. It provides a detailed breakdown of how employees spend their time, making it useful for monitoring productivity, project costing, and billable hours.

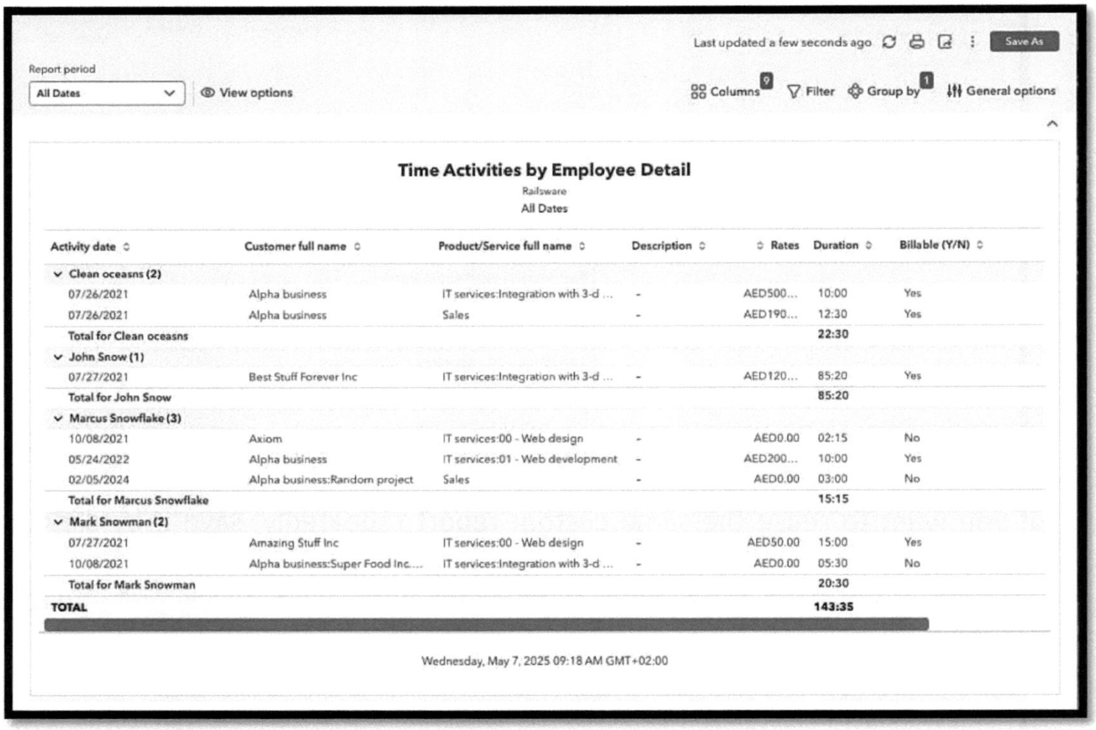

Time Activities by Employee Detail
Railsware
All Dates

Activity date	Customer full name	Product/Service full name	Description	Rates	Duration	Billable (Y/N)
Clean oceasns (2)						
07/26/2021	Alpha business	IT services:Integration with 3-d ...	-	AED500...	10:00	Yes
07/26/2021	Alpha business	Sales	-	AED190...	12:30	Yes
Total for Clean oceasns					**22:30**	
John Snow (1)						
07/27/2021	Best Stuff Forever Inc	IT services:Integration with 3-d ...	-	AED120...	85:20	Yes
Total for John Snow					**85:20**	
Marcus Snowflake (3)						
10/08/2021	Axiom	IT services:00 - Web design	-	AED0.00	02:15	No
05/24/2022	Alpha business	IT services:01 - Web development	-	AED200...	10:00	Yes
02/05/2024	Alpha business:Random project	Sales	-	AED0.00	03:00	No
Total for Marcus Snowflake					**15:15**	
Mark Snowman (2)						
07/27/2021	Amazing Stuff Inc	IT services:00 - Web design	-	AED50.00	15:00	Yes
10/08/2021	Alpha business:Super Food Inc....	IT services:Integration with 3-d ...	-	AED0.00	05:30	No
Total for Mark Snowman					**20:30**	
TOTAL					**143:35**	

Wednesday, May 7, 2025 09:18 AM GMT+02:00

This report is restricted to Plus and Advanced plans. Like any other, it can be customized, saved as a template, or scheduled to be emailed automatically.

Budget Reports in QuickBooks Online

If budgeting is part of your workflow, QuickBooks offers two essential reports: **Budget Overview** and **Budget vs. Actuals**. These appear under the Business Overview category but are only available on the Plus and Advanced plans.

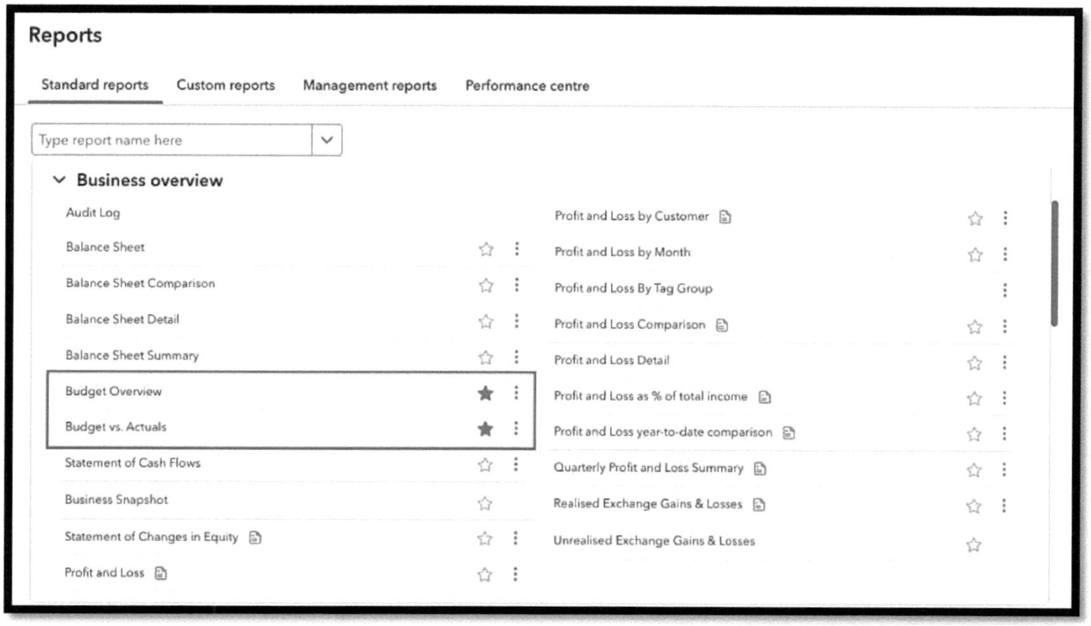

One small trick: the option to save these reports isn't immediately visible because they contain many columns. Scroll all the way to the right and the save icon will appear.

Accountant Reports in QuickBooks Online

The *For My Accountant* section contains a long list of accountant-focused reports. Most are available across all plans, but a few advanced ones—such as Recurring Template List, Transaction Detail by Account, Recent Automatic Transactions, and Transaction List with Splits—require the Essentials plan or above.

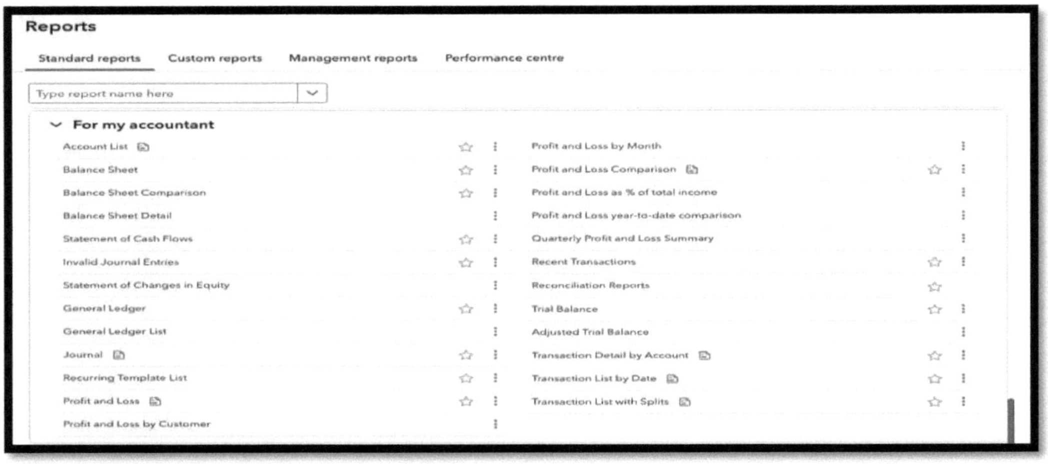

Plus and Advanced users gain access to additional comparison-based reports, such as Profit and Loss Comparison, Balance Sheet Comparison, as well as Class and Location Lists.

All these reports can be exported as Excel or PDF files, making them ideal for audits, tax preparation, and financial reviews.

Automating Accountant Reports

If you regularly export accountant reports, QuickBooks allows you to automate the process by scheduling emails. You can choose a report, set a recurring interval, and send it automatically to any designated email address.

Though PDF and Excel exports are supported, many accountants prefer exporting directly into spreadsheet-based tools like Google Sheets. This allows for deeper analysis, custom formulas, or integration into dashboards and visualization tools.

Vendor Reports in QuickBooks Online

Vendor reports are located under two categories: **What You Owe** and **Expenses and Suppliers.**

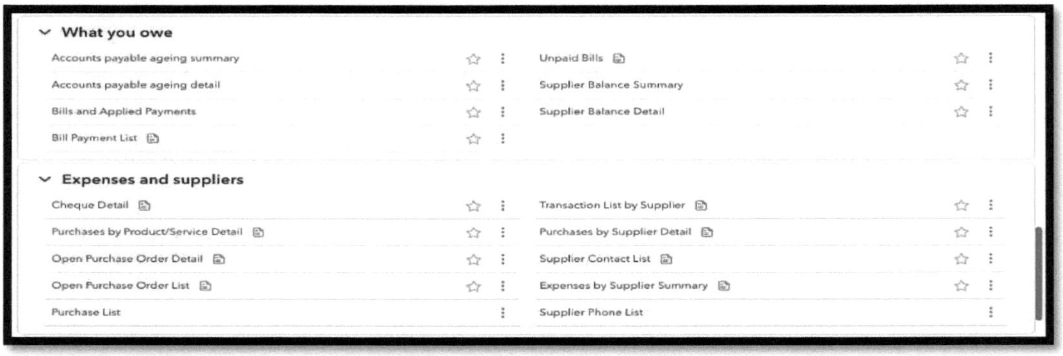

The availability depends on your plan:

- Simple Start users have access to only a few core reports, such as Check Detail, Supplier Contact List, and Transaction List by Supplier.
- Essentials expands this offering to include Vendor Balance Detail and Vendor Summary.
- Plus and Advanced plans include an even broader suite of vendor reports, ideal for businesses managing multiple suppliers or high purchasing volume.

Expense Reports in QuickBooks Online

Expense reporting is tightly connected to vendor reporting. Simple Start and Essentials users see only a limited selection of expense-related reports. Meanwhile, Plus and Advanced users enjoy full access, including sophisticated reports such as:

- Open Purchase Order List
- Purchases by Class Detail
- Purchases by Vendor Detail
- Purchases by Product/Service
- Purchases by Location

These reports offer clearer visibility into purchasing trends and cost allocation, helping you make smarter budgeting and procurement decisions.

Reconciliation Reports

Reconciliation reports are easy to locate in QuickBooks Online. Simply open the **Reports** menu and navigate to the **For my accountant** section. You'll notice this report immediately—it's the only one that doesn't offer a three-dots menu for customization.

You can also access reconciliation details through **Transactions > Reconcile**. These reports are available across all plans except Solopreneur.

Sales Reports in QuickBooks Online

QuickBooks Online offers up to **10 detailed sales reports**, but your access depends on your subscription level.

Solopreneur and Simple Start users can only view broad summaries such as **Sales by Customer Summary** and **Sales by Product/Service Summary**. Essentials subscribers gain access to more detail, including breakdowns by customer type and product/service.

Plus and Advanced members receive the full suite, which includes powerful class-based and location-based sales reports. All sales reports can be found under **Sales and customers** on the Reports page.

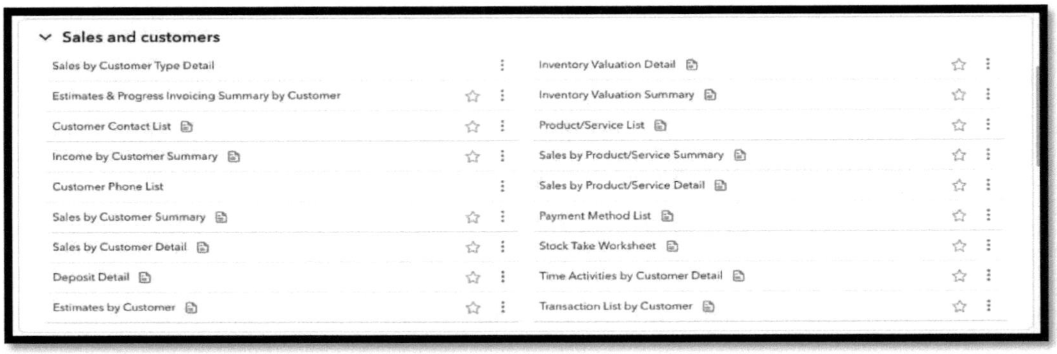

MRR Reporting Limitations in QuickBooks Online

QuickBooks Online does **not** support Monthly Recurring Revenue (MRR) or Annual Recurring Revenue (ARR) reporting. While you can export monthly revenue and manually calculate a rough average in a spreadsheet, the platform doesn't distinguish between new, renewed, or churned subscriptions—making any "MRR" you derive inaccurate.

For true subscription metrics, a dedicated analytics tool integrated with your product is a far more reliable solution.

Inventory Reports

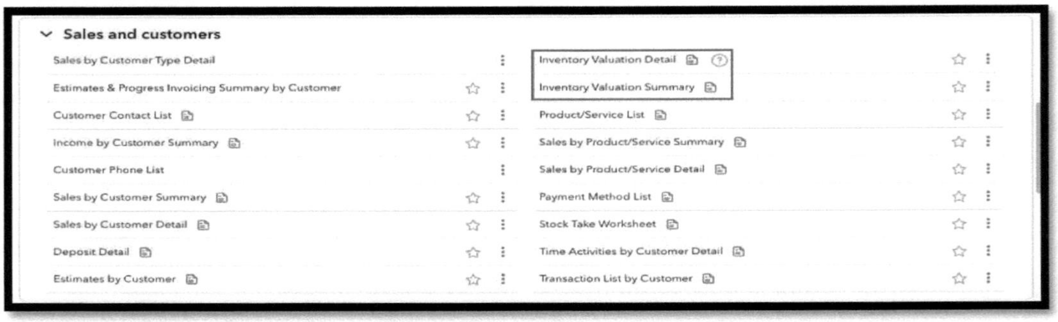

Inventory reporting is available only to **Plus and Advanced** users. The two inventory reports—**Inventory Valuation Summary** and **Inventory Valuation Detail**—live under the **Sales and customers** category. These reports allow you to understand the value of your stock across locations, transactions, and time periods.

Job Costing Reports

If you need job-related cost insights, QuickBooks Online hides them under the **Projects** tab rather than the standard Reports section. After selecting a project, open **Project Reports** and choose **Time cost by employee or supplier**.

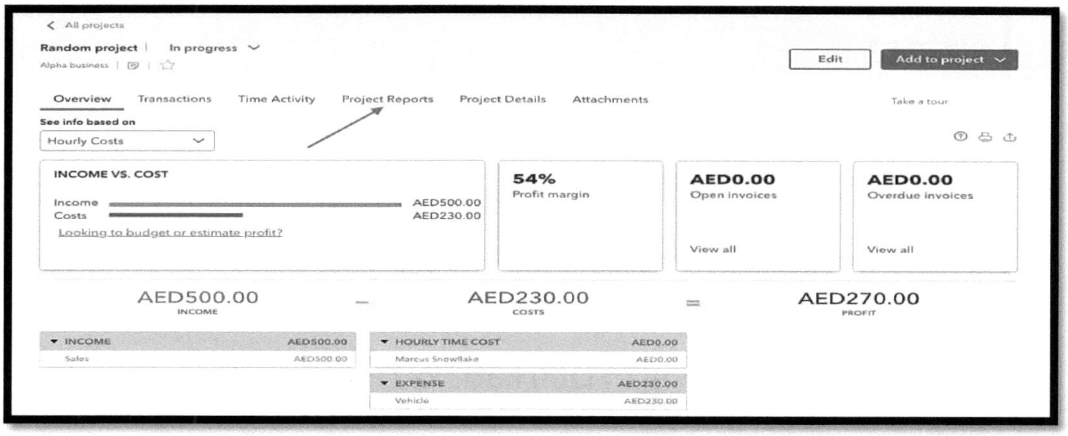

This area also houses reports like **Project Profitability** and **Unbilled Time and Expenses**, but you must have Projects enabled in your account to view them.

Class-Based Reporting

QuickBooks Online provides several reports that separate financial data by class, but only for Plus and Advanced users. These include Profit & Loss by Class, Sales by Class (Detail and Summary), and Purchases by Class. A dedicated **Class List** report is also available, giving you a structured view of how your classes are organized.

Graph and Visual Reports

If you prefer visual insights, the **Business Snapshot** report is your go-to option. Located under **Business Overview**, it offers charts and summarized metrics that help you quickly understand performance trends across your business.

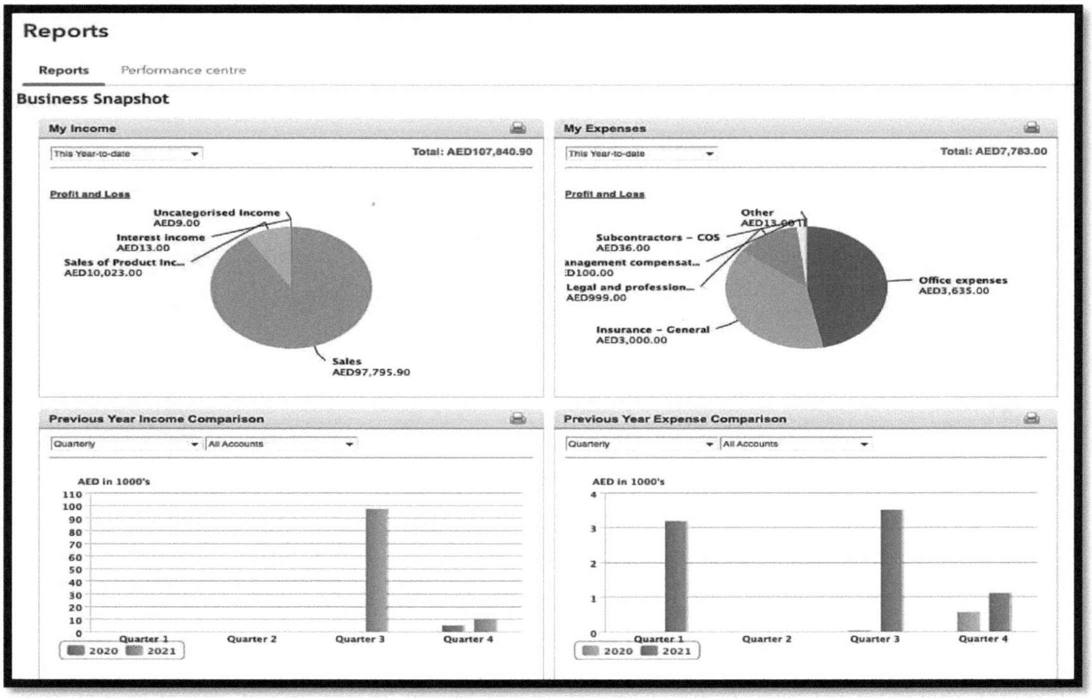

Management Reporting in QuickBooks Online

Management reports elevate your financial presentations by turning ordinary reports into polished, professional PDF packages. These can include a customized cover page, executive summary, and themed layouts.

When you first open **Management reports**, you'll see two starter templates—**Basic Company Financials** and **Expanded Company Financials**. You can modify these or create your own.

Creating a New Management Report

Start by choosing the report you want to feature. If it requires adjustments, save it as a **custom report** so it appears on the Custom Reports tab.

Then open **Management reports**, select **+ Management report**, and begin building your package. You can set a title, reporting period, cover details, and then add the financial reports or charts you want included.

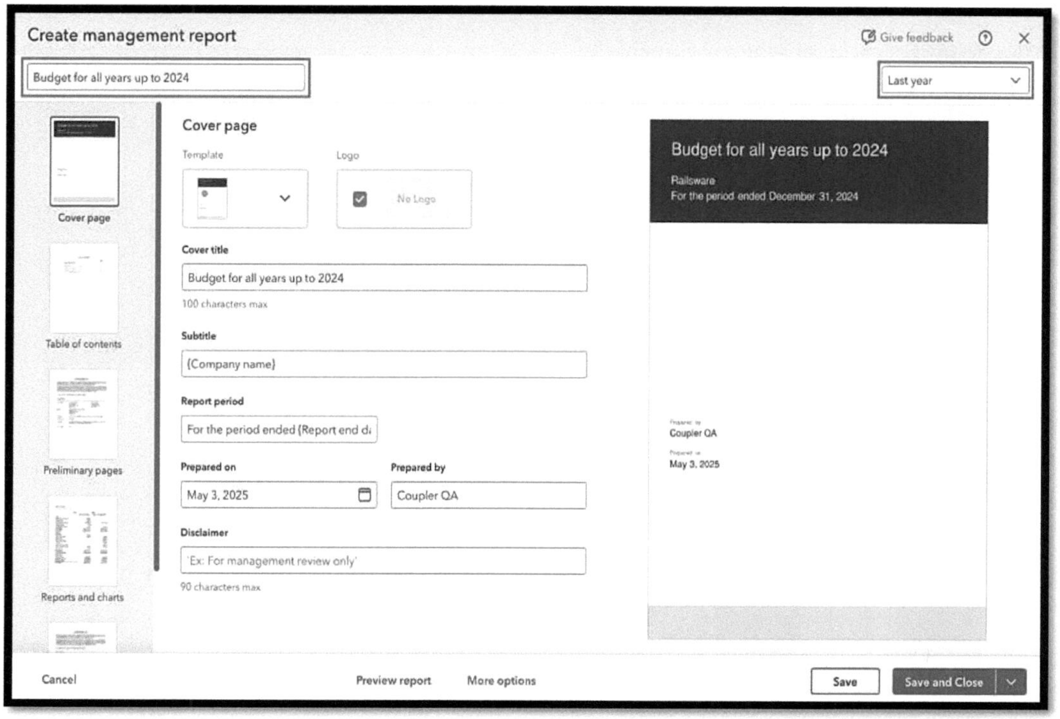

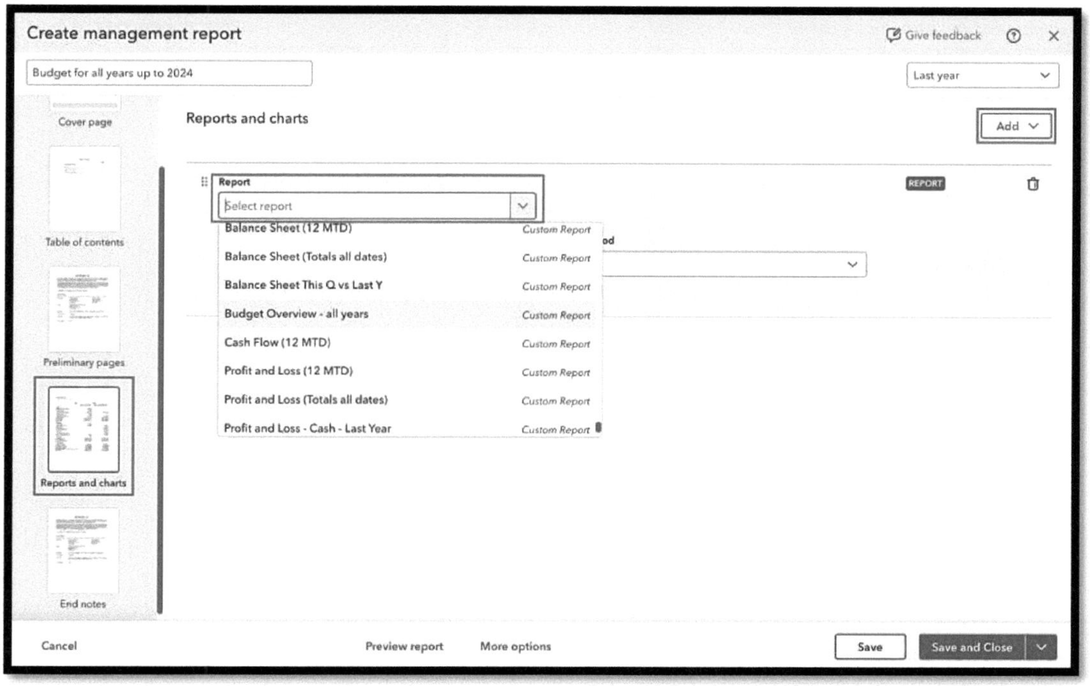

Once finished, save it and preview the final version. It can be downloaded as a PDF or printed instantly.

×

Print or save as PDF

To print, right-the preview and select Print. Or, click the Print icon if you see one below.

5f2f71b9-ba9d-40fb-908f-6060c0cf1397 1 / 6 — 98% +

Management Report

Railsware

For the period ended December 31, 2025

1

2

Save as PDF Print

CHAPTER ELEVEN

GENERATING CUSTOM REPORTS AND CHARTS

QuickBooks Online allows businesses to transform raw financial data into meaningful insights through custom reports and charts. By tailoring reports to your specific needs, you can track performance, monitor cash flow, analyze expenses, and make data-driven decisions.

CUSTOM REPORT BUILDER IN QUICKBOOKS ONLINE ADVANCED

Customizable reports are essential for monitoring a company's financial health and making informed business decisions. QuickBooks Online Advanced offers a powerful **Custom Report Builder**, enabling users to create reports tailored to their specific needs. This feature allows you to filter, group, and visualize data in ways that provide meaningful insights for business leaders, accountants, and stakeholders.

What is the Custom Report Builder?

Available exclusively in **QuickBooks Online Advanced**, the Custom Report Builder is an enhanced reporting tool that lets you:

- ❖ Add, remove, or rearrange columns
- ❖ Adjust fonts, colors, and formatting
- ❖ Filter data based on specific criteria
- ❖ Select fields to include and group data for deeper insights

How to Use the Custom Report Builder

1. **Navigate to Reports**: Go to the **Reports** tab in QuickBooks Online Advanced.
2. **Create a New Report**: Click **+ Create New Report**.

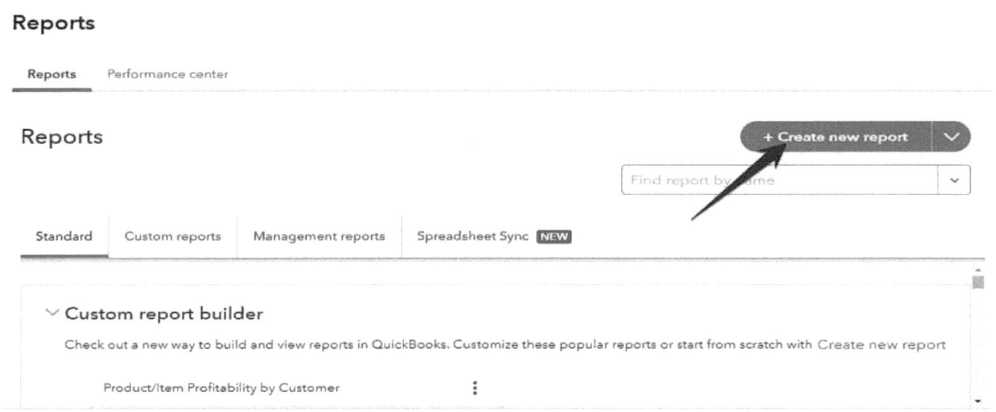

3. **Select a Report Type**: Choose from blank templates, invoices, expenses, sales, bills, and more.
4. **Customize Your Report**:
   - ❖ Set the reporting period
   - ❖ Choose **table** or **chart view**
   - ❖ Apply filters (e.g., specific customers, categories, or date ranges)
5. **Schedule or Export Reports**: Reports can be scheduled to email automatically or exported for offline use.

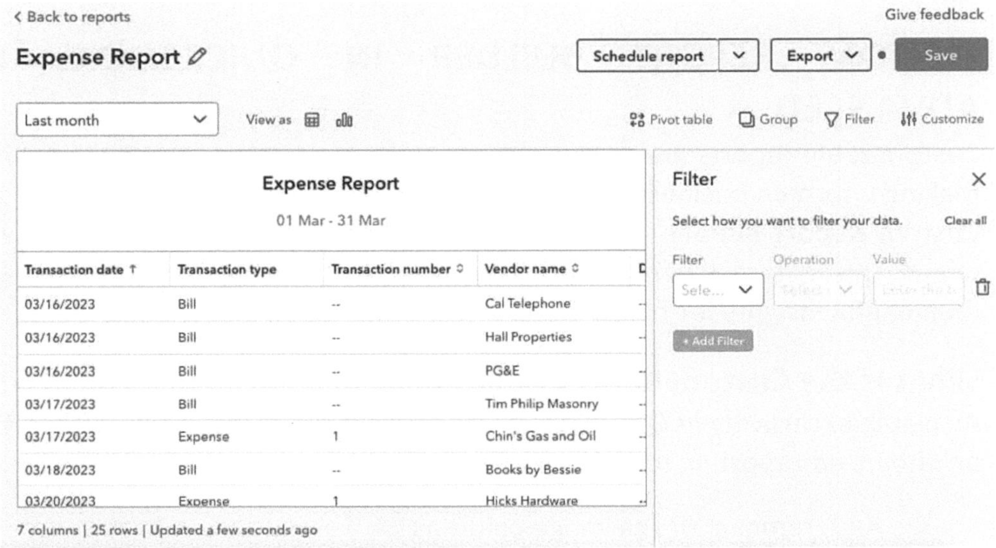

6. **Save Your Report**: Click **Save** once customization is complete.

Comparison Charts in QuickBooks Online Advanced

QuickBooks Advanced now allows you to create **comparison charts** that display up to 27 different data fields, such as:

- ❖ Revenue, expenses, profit margins
- ❖ Inventory levels and payroll expenses
- ❖ Employee headcount and customer acquisition costs

These charts make it easy to identify trends, track performance over time, and analyze the impact of operational changes on your financial results. For example, you could compare revenue, expenses, and net profit across the past five years while monitoring staffing and sales performance.

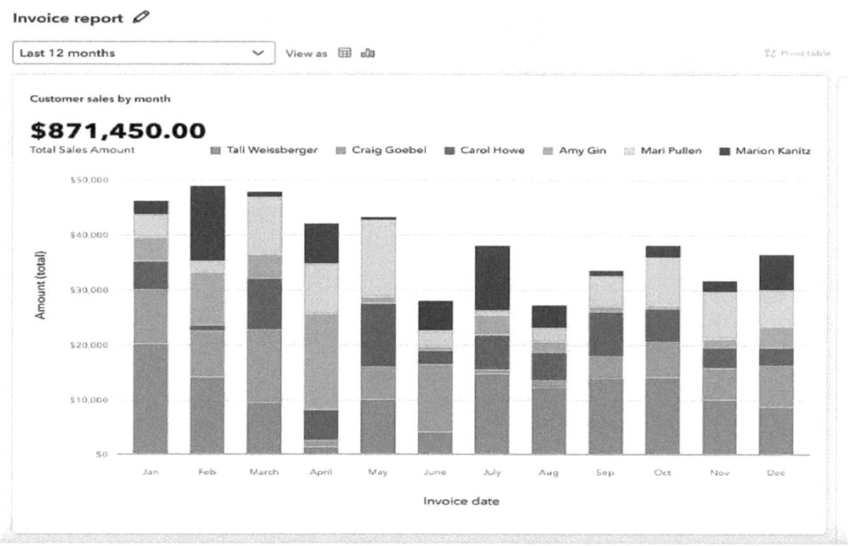

Sample Reports You Can Create

1. **Product/Item Profitability by Customer** – Shows profits by product and customer to identify top performers and underperforming items.
2. **Invoice Approval Status** – Tracks the approval progress of all invoices in accounts payable.
3. **Bill Approval Status** – Monitors the approval workflow of bills.
4. **Transaction List by Vendor** – Provides detailed expense tracking by vendor or supplier.
5. **Sales by Sales Rep** – Analyzes sales performance across individual salespeople or teams.

Benefits of Using the Custom Report Builder

- **Improved Decision-Making**: Gain insights from data grouped and filtered in meaningful ways.
- **Time Savings**: Generate detailed reports in minutes, reducing manual effort.
- **Greater Visibility**: Drill down into financial data to understand drivers behind performance.
- **Competitive Advantage**: Identify opportunities and trends your competitors may miss by analyzing data creatively.

Custom Reports and Spreadsheet Sync in QuickBooks Online Advanced

Many QuickBooks users overlook these features, but **Custom Reports** and **Spreadsheet Sync** are two of the most powerful tools in QuickBooks Online Advanced—especially when you need deeper insights than standard reports can provide.

Custom Reports

The built-in Report Builder allows you to design reports that fit your exact business requirements. With it, you can:

- ❖ Filter data by accounts, customers, vendors, products, or specific time ranges
- ❖ Build pivot-style summaries for deeper analysis
- ❖ Add custom fields to display the information that matters most

Once created, your custom reports can be saved, shared, and reused, ensuring your team always has access to consistent, relevant financial insights.

Spreadsheet Sync

Spreadsheet Sync elevates reporting by connecting QuickBooks Online Advanced directly to Microsoft Excel or Google Sheets. This integration enables you to:

- ❖ Pull live QuickBooks data into your spreadsheets
- ❖ Build custom dashboards and financial models
- ❖ Edit and update large data sets in bulk
- ❖ Sync your changes back into QuickBooks automatically

This tool is especially valuable for businesses that require advanced reporting, multi-entity consolidation, or flexible spreadsheet-based analysis while still relying on accurate, real-time accounting data.

CHAPTER TWELVE

JOURNAL ENTRIES

Journal entries in QuickBooks Online allow you to record financial transactions that aren't captured through regular forms like invoices, bills, or checks. They're typically used for specialized accounting adjustments—such as depreciation, accruals, corrections, and entries provided by your accountant. While they should be used sparingly, journal entries ensure your books remain accurate, complete, and compliant when certain transactions require manual recording.

HOW TO MAKE A JOURNAL ENTRY IN QUICKBOOKS ONLINE

Journal entries in QuickBooks Online (QBO) should be used sparingly and only when necessary. Most transactions—such as invoices, bills, and payments—are automatically recorded for you. However, certain accounting adjustments **don't have dedicated input screens**, such as:

- ❖ Depreciation
- ❖ Loan amortization
- ❖ Accruals and reversals
- ❖ Year-end adjusting entries

In these cases, a manual journal entry ensures your books stay accurate.

Step 1: Open the Journal Entry Window

1. Select **+ New** on your QuickBooks Online dashboard.
2. Under **Other**, choose **Journal Entry**.

Each journal entry affects **at least two accounts**, and total debits must always equal total credits.

Step 2: Set the Date and Verify the Journal Number

- ❖ Enter the correct **Journal date** for the transaction or adjustment.
- ❖ QBO automatically assigns a **Journal no.**, but always verify it to avoid duplicates.

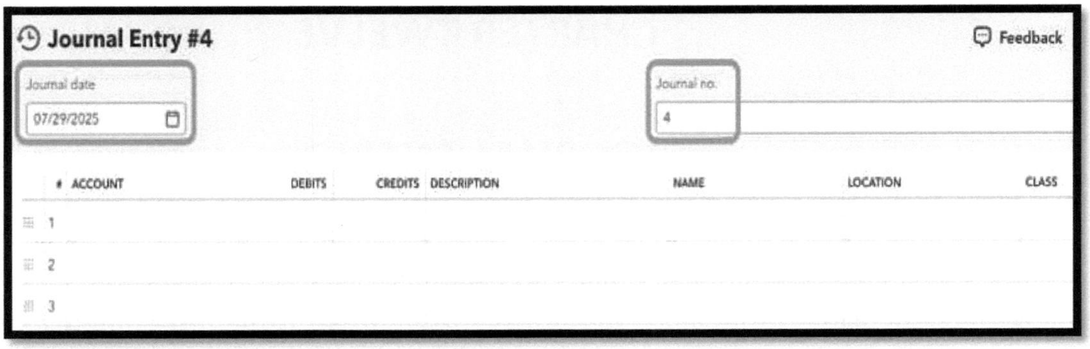

Note: The date and number are auto-filled each time you open the journal entry screen, so double-check before entering amounts.

Step 3: Enter Your Debits and Credits

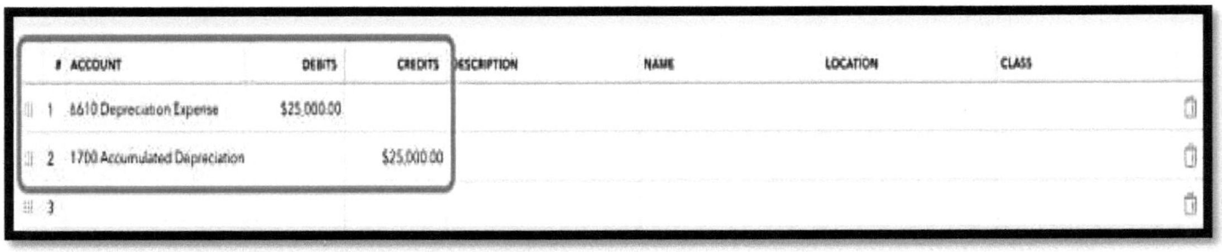

- ❖ Always enter **debit lines first**, followed by corresponding credits.
- ❖ For multi-line entries, list all debits together before entering credits.

QBO automatically totals the debit and credit columns and alerts you if they don't balance—you cannot save an unbalanced entry.

Step 4: Add Supporting Information

Use additional fields to maintain clarity and improve future reference:

- ❖ **Description:** Briefly explain the purpose of the entry (e.g., "Monthly depreciation – equipment").
- ❖ **Name:** Add a customer, vendor, or employee if the entry relates to one.
- ❖ **Class/Location:** Include these if your business uses class or location tracking.

Click **Save** or **Save and new** when finished.

Step 5: Review Your Entry in Reports

Journal

Gadget Garage

July 1-29, 2025

Transaction Date	Transaction Type	Num	Name	Memo/Description	Distribution ...	Account Full Name	Debit	Credit
3 (2)								
07/03/2025	Journal Entry	2	-	Marketing	6000	6000 Advertising & Marketing	975.00	-
07/03/2025	Journal Entry	2	-	Marketing	1010	1000 Cash:1010 Cash-Bank of ...	-	975.00
Total for 3							**$975.00**	**$975.00**
4 (5)								
07/07/2025	Journal Entry	3	-	Opening balance	1010	1000 Cash:1010 Cash-Bank of ...	100,000.00	-
07/07/2025	Journal Entry	3	-	Opening balance	1020	1000 Cash:1020 Cash-Chase C...	150,000.00	-
07/07/2025	Journal Entry	3	-	-	1500	1500 Equipment & Furnitures	75,000.00	-
07/07/2025	Journal Entry	3			1600	1600 Vehicles	50,000.00	
07/07/2025	Journal Entry	3	-	-	3000	3000 Owner's Capital	-	375,000.00
Total for 4							**$375,000.00**	**$375,000.00**
5 (2)								
07/08/2025	Sales Receipt	1001	Jason Tyler Whitmore	If you choose to have your devi...	1030	1000 Cash:1030 Cash on hand	20.00	
07/08/2025	Sales Receipt	1001	Jason Tyler Whitmore	Initial assessment of computer ...	4300	4300 Repair & Maintenance Ser...	-	20.00
Total for 5							**$20.00**	**$20.00**
6 (2)								
07/08/2025	Invoice	1002	Ivy N. Voice	-	1100	1100 Accounts Receivable	200.00	-
TOTAL							**$393,264.98**	**$393,264.98**

To review or verify journal entries:

Option 1: Journal Report

1. Go to **Reports**
2. Search for **Journal**
3. Open the report to see all journal-style transactions.

Although not formatted like a traditional ledger, it shows accounts affected, dates, descriptions, and debit/credit amounts. Select any description to open the detailed journal entry.

Option 2: Check Register

1. Go to **Chart of Accounts**
2. Open the register for the relevant account
3. Look for transactions marked **Journal**

When to Make a Journal Entry in QuickBooks Online

Most day-to-day transactions in QuickBooks Online should be recorded through built-in forms such as invoices, bills, checks, and bank deposits. These screens automatically create the proper accounting entries in the background. However, there are specific situations where a manual journal entry is necessary. Journal entries help record transactions that do not have a dedicated form in QuickBooks.

Common Reasons to Create a Journal Entry

You may need to enter a manual journal entry when:

- ❖ Disposing of a fixed asset
- ❖ Recording depreciation for fixed assets

- Entering adjusting entries provided by your CPA or accountant
- Recording new loans or notes payable
- Adding owner contributions to equity

Editing or Deleting a Journal Entry

If a journal entry needs correction, simply reopen the entry, make your adjustments, and click **Save**.

To delete an entry that was created in error:

1. Open the journal entry.
2. Select **More** at the bottom.
3. Choose **Delete**.

Important: Avoid editing or deleting journal entries from prior periods. Changing historical records can affect previously reported income, cause discrepancies, and potentially create tax issues. Any prior-period adjustments should be handled by your accountant through proper adjusting entries.

Reversing a Journal Entry

When an entry needs to be undone without removing the original record, use the **Reverse** option:

1. Locate the entry from the **Journal Report** or from the account register.
2. Open the journal entry.
3. Select **Reverse** at the bottom.
4. Click **Save**.

A reversing entry creates an equal and opposite entry, typically dated the first day of the following month. This is useful for temporary accruals and ensures that the actual expense or revenue is recognized normally when it occurs.

Making a Journal Entry Recurring

QuickBooks allows you to automate repeated journal entries:

1. Open the journal entry.
2. Select **Make recurring**.
3. Set your schedule and interval.
4. Save the template.

Recurring entries are helpful for regular adjustments—such as monthly depreciation—so you don't have to enter them manually each time.

HOW TO VIEW JOURNAL ENTRIES IN QUICKBOOKS ONLINE: A CLEAR STEP-BY-STEP GUIDE

Viewing your journal entries in QuickBooks Online is simple once you know where to look. Follow this streamlined guide to access, customize, and manage your journal reports with ease.

Step-by-Step: How to View Journal Entries

1. **Log In to QuickBooks Online:** Sign in to your QuickBooks Online account to access your dashboard.
2. **Open the Reports Center:** From the left navigation pane, select **Reports**.

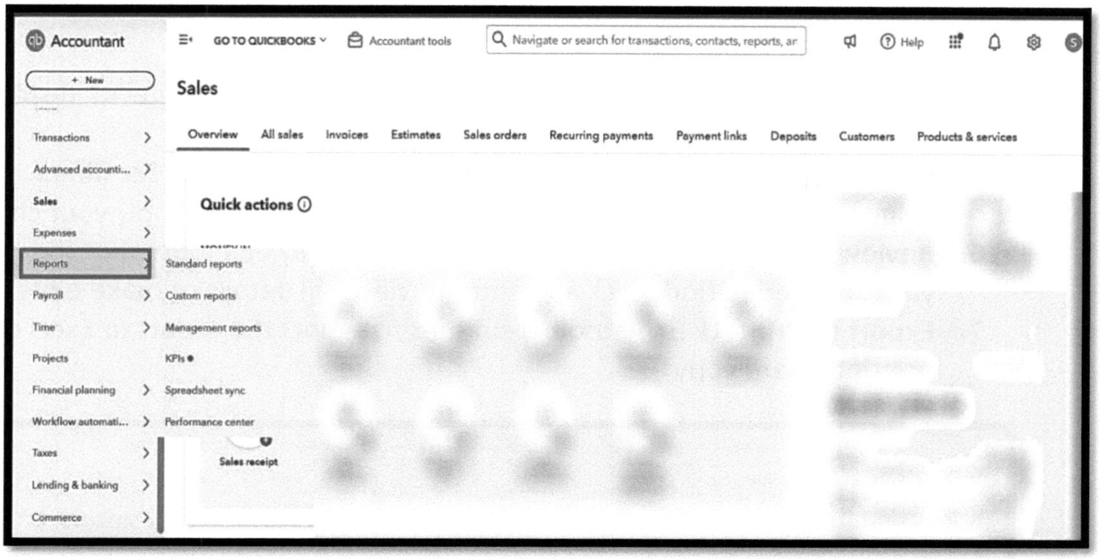

3. **Locate the Journal Report**
   - ❖ Under the **Standard** tab, scroll to the **For my accountant** section.
   - ❖ Select **Journal** to open the report.
   - ❖ *Tip:* If the report title shows a magic wand icon, you're viewing the new **Modern View**, which has been rolling out since July 2024 to replace the Classic View.

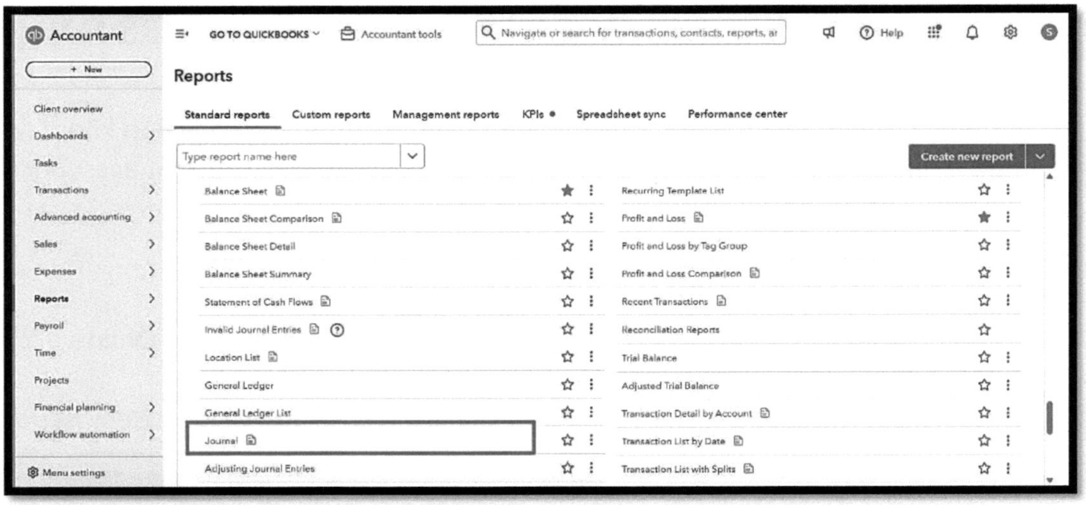

4. **Choose Your Date Range:** Adjust the report's date range to display the journal entries you want to review.
5. **Customize the Report:** Click **Customize** to refine the data. Set filters, choose columns, and adjust formatting. Select **Refresh report** to apply your changes.
6. **Review and Edit Entries:** The report now displays all journal entries within your selected period. Click any entry to view full details or make edits.
7. **Export or Print:** Use the toolbar options to export the report to Excel or PDF, or print a hard copy.

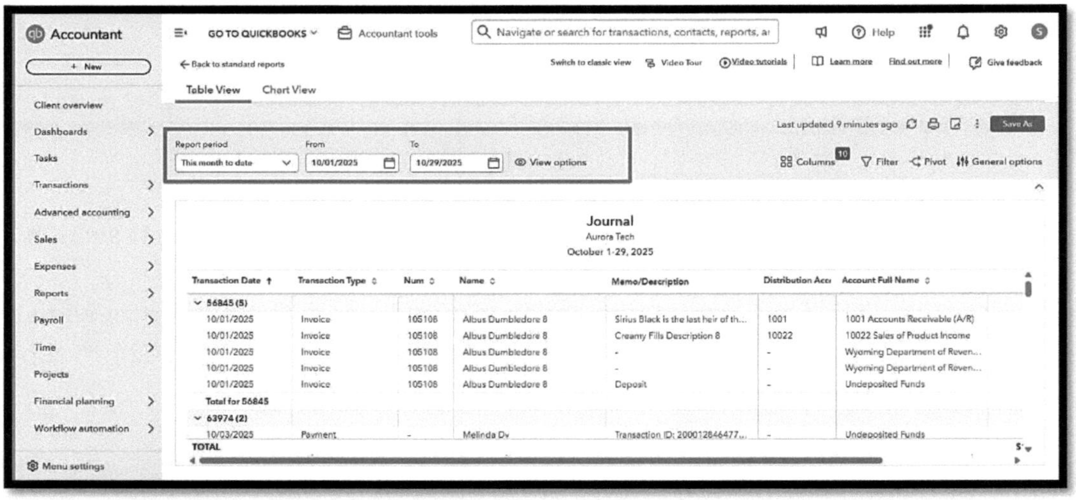

Understanding the Modern View Reporting Experience

QuickBooks Online's new **Modern View** improves how reports are generated and analyzed. Key enhancements include:

❖ **Faster, more reliable performance**—especially for large or complex reports.

- **Stronger data security** through improved permissions.
- **Richer customization** with advanced filters, pivots, and charting tools.
- **New report types**, including Fixed Assets, Revenue Recognition, and Projects.
- **Excel integration**, letting you run and save reports directly from Microsoft Excel.

Customizing Reports in Modern View

Here's how to build tailored reports using the upgraded reporting tools:

1. Create a Custom Report

- Go to **Reports** > **+ Create new report**.
- Select a report type and click **Create**.
- You can use the report wizard or manually add fields.
- Rename your report using the pencil (edit) icon.

2. Use Advanced Customization Tools

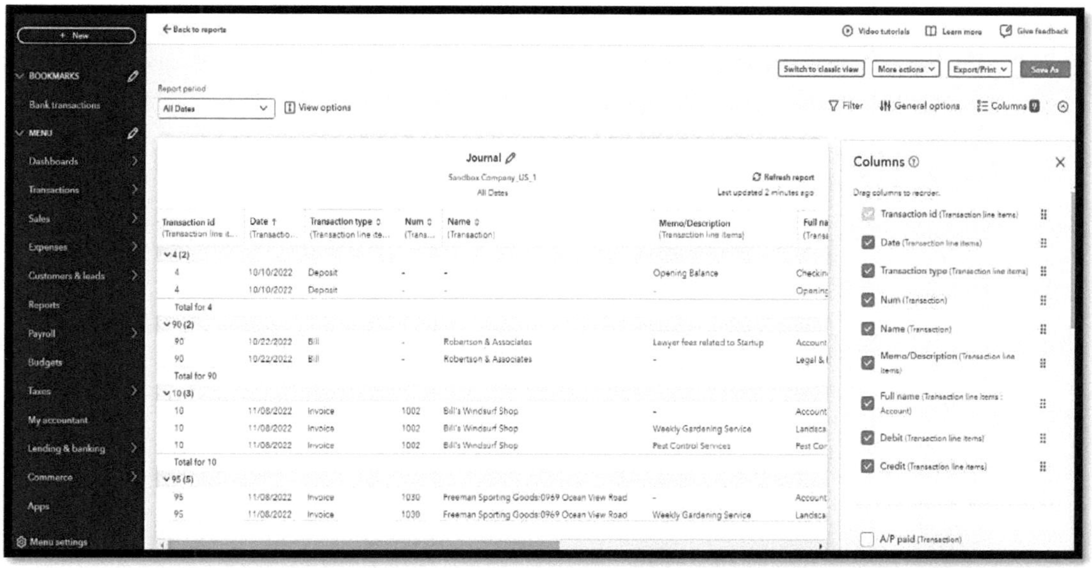

- **Date Range:** Specify the period you want to analyze.
- **Pivot:** Group and summarize data across rows and columns.
- **Group:** Categorize line items and calculate totals or averages.
- **Filter:** Narrow your results to specific accounts, classes, customers, etc.
- **General Settings:** Adjust accounting method, number formatting, and header/footer details.
- **Columns:** Add, remove, or reorder columns.

3. Save and Access Your Custom Reports

- Select **Save As** to store your customized report.
- Access saved reports under the **Custom reports** tab.

4. Exporting and Printing

- Use the **Export/Print** dropdown to download your report to Excel or print it.

Visualizing and Scheduling Reports

1. Create Visual Charts

- Open a custom report and switch to **Chart View**.
- Choose a chart type and map the X and Y axis values for clearer analysis.

2. Add Charts to Management Reports

- In Chart View, go to **More actions** > **Add to Management reports**.
- Add your chart to a new or existing management report package.

3. Automate Report Delivery

- From the Standard or Custom reports tab, select **More options** > **Create a schedule**.
- Set your email workflow, frequency, and recipients.
- Select **Save and Enable** to automate recurring report emails.

PART V: AUTOMATION, EFFICIENCY, AND ADVANCED TOOLS

CHAPTER THIRTEEN

AUTOMATION AND IMPLEMENTING APPS IN QUICKBOOKS ONLINE

QuickBooks Online uses apps and automated workflows to help businesses streamline tasks like invoicing, bill pay, and payroll. You can connect third-party apps from the QuickBooks App Store to automate data transfer between programs, or use the built-in automation features in QuickBooks Online Advanced to create custom workflows for things like sending reminders or requiring approvals for transactions.

EXPLORING YOUR QUICKBOOKS MOBILE APP

Getting Started with the QuickBooks Mobile App

The **QuickBooks Online mobile app** helps you manage your business finances on the go. Whether you're tracking expenses, sending invoices, or monitoring cash flow, the app keeps your business organized and ready for tax time—right from your phone or tablet.

1. Downloading the App

The QuickBooks app is available for both **iOS** and **Android** devices. Make sure you use the same login credentials as your QuickBooks Online account so your data syncs across all devices.

For iOS:

1. Open the **App Store**.
2. Search for **QuickBooks Online**.
3. Tap **Get** to download and install the app.
4. Open the app and sign in with your QuickBooks Online credentials.

For Android:

1. Open the **Google Play Store**.
2. Search for **QuickBooks Online**.
3. Tap **Install** to download the app.

4. Open the app and sign in with your QuickBooks Online credentials.

2. Signing In Securely (iOS Only)

QuickBooks Online offers **secure sign-in options** on iPhone and iPad, letting you avoid entering your username and password each time. Options include a **4-digit App PIN**, **Touch ID**, or a **password manager**.

Set Up an App PIN:

1. Open the app and go to **Menu > Settings > Account**.
2. Enable the **App PIN** toggle.
3. Enter and confirm a 4-digit code.

Notes:

- You can enable, disable, or update the PIN anytime.
- If forgotten, sign in with your username and password to reset.
- Each device can have a separate PIN.

Enable Touch ID:

1. Ensure the App PIN is set up.
2. Toggle **Touch ID** on.
3. Close and reopen the app to use fingerprint sign-in.

Tips:

- Place your registered finger on the Home button to sign in.
- If Touch ID fails, log in with your username and password and set it up again.

Use a Password Manager:

1. Save your QuickBooks login in iCloud Keychain, 1Password, or another manager.
2. Tap the key icon in the login screen of the app.
3. Unlock the manager with your password or fingerprint.
4. Select your saved QuickBooks credentials to autofill.

3. Setting Up Your Company Profile

After installing the app, customize your **company profile** to match your business needs.

Set Up Your Company:

1. Open the app and navigate to **Settings** ⚙ **> Account and Settings**.
2. Enter your business name, address, and contact information.
3. Set your financial year start date and other preferences.
4. Save your settings.

View Customer Notes:

1. Go to **Menu ☰ > Customers**.
2. Select a customer and tap the **Details** tab.
3. Scroll to the **Note** field to view any notes added from QuickBooks Online.

Create Calendar Appointments (Android Only):

1. Go to **Menu ≡ > Customers**.
2. Select a customer, then tap **+ > Add Appointment**.
3. Complete the details and tap **Save**.

4. Connecting Your Bank Accounts

Linking bank and credit card accounts allows QuickBooks to **automatically import and categorize transactions**, saving you time and reducing manual entry.

To Connect Your Accounts:

1. Go to the **Transactions** tab in the app.
2. Tap **Connect Account**.
3. Search and select your bank from the list.
4. Enter your online banking credentials.
5. Follow the prompts to complete the secure connection.

Note: QuickBooks uses **encrypted security** to protect your financial data.

5. Navigating the Dashboard

The **QuickBooks mobile dashboard** gives you a real-time snapshot of your business's financial health. From here, you can quickly assess income, expenses, and other key metrics.

Dashboard Highlights:

- Profit and Loss summary
- Bank account balances
- Outstanding invoices
- Recent transactions
- Expense categories

Tip: Review your dashboard regularly to stay informed about your business performance and make timely decisions.

6. Managing Transactions

QuickBooks makes it easy to **review, categorize, and manage transactions** to keep your records accurate.

How to Manage Transactions:

- Open the **Transactions** tab.
- Review the list of imported transactions.
- Tap a transaction to categorize it (e.g., office supplies, travel).
- Add notes or attach receipts if needed.
- Save your changes.

Tip: Consistent categorization improves reporting accuracy and simplifies tax preparation.

7. Adding Your Accountant

You cannot add your accountant via the mobile app. To invite your accountant, log in to **QuickBooks Online** through a web browser.

8. Tracking Expenses and Receipts

Keep track of your business expenses and attach receipts for accurate records and easier tax filing.

Attach Receipts:

1. Tap **+** and select **Expense**.
2. Enter details such as amount, supplier, and category.
3. Snap a photo of the receipt with your device's camera.
4. Attach the image to the expense record.
5. Save the expense.

Edit a Recorded Expense:

1. Go to **Menu ☰ > Expenses**.
2. Select an expense to view details.
3. Tap **Edit ✎**, make your changes, and save.

9. Tracking Mileage

For business-related travel, the app can **automatically track your mileage**, making it easier to claim deductions without maintaining manual logs.

10. Running Business Reports

QuickBooks provides a variety of **reports** to help you understand your financial health and make informed decisions.

To Run Reports:

1. Navigate to the **Reports** section.
2. Select the report you want, such as **Profit and Loss** or **Mileage Log**.
3. Customize the date range or other filters.
4. Review the insights to assess performance.
5. Export or share the report if needed.

11. Keeping Your Data Up-to-Date

Ensure your mobile app reflects the **latest business data** by refreshing it regularly.

iOS:

1. Go to **Settings > General > iPhone Storage**.
2. Select **QuickBooks Online app** and tap **Offload App**.

This frees up storage without deleting your data.

Android:

1. Go to **Menu ☰ > More Options ⋮ > Settings**.
2. Tap **Refresh Data** and confirm by selecting **YES**.

Work Anywhere With the QuickBooks Mobile App

Turn any place into your workspace with the QuickBooks mobile app. Whether you're on the road, at a client's office, or working from home, the app lets you manage your business from virtually any device. It's free to download on both iOS and Android, and in this walkthrough we'll be using the iOS version.

Run Your Business on the Go

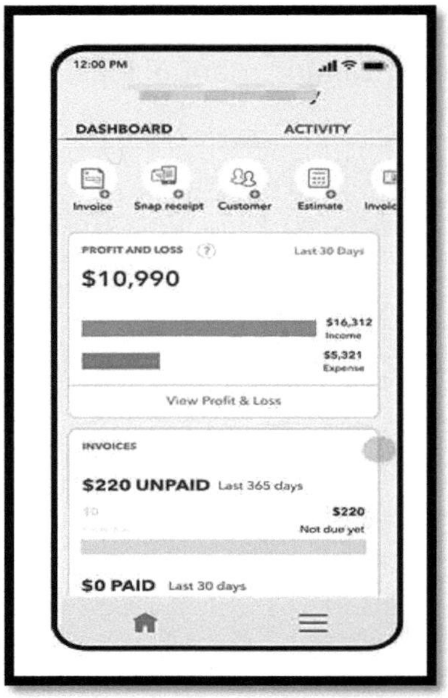

With the QuickBooks mobile app, you can easily stay organized wherever you are. Enter transactions, record expenses, send invoices, and manage customers—all from your phone or tablet. Your most important business numbers, such as sales, expenses, and profit, are always available at your fingertips, helping you make smart decisions without having to wait until you're back at your desk.

Seamless Syncing Across All Devices

No matter where you log in, QuickBooks keeps your data updated in real time. Work on your computer, then switch to your phone, and everything stays perfectly synced for effortless collaboration with your team.

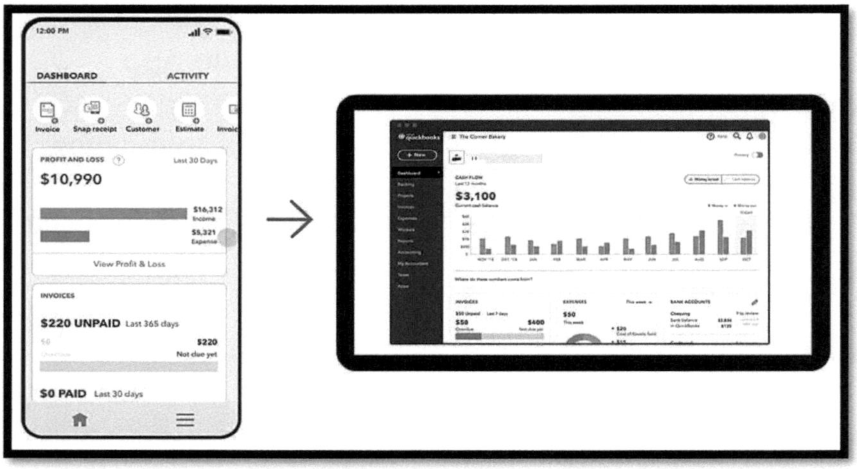

Your Customer Info—Always Up to Date

Keep customer information ready whenever you need it. Add new customers instantly using your device's contact list, and access phone numbers, addresses, or account details anytime. You can edit and update records right on the spot.

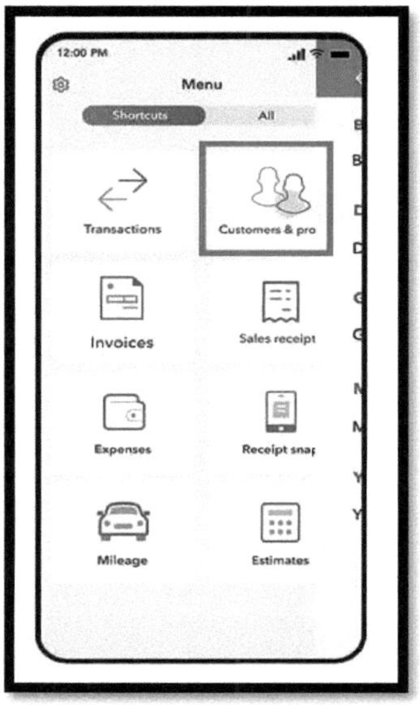

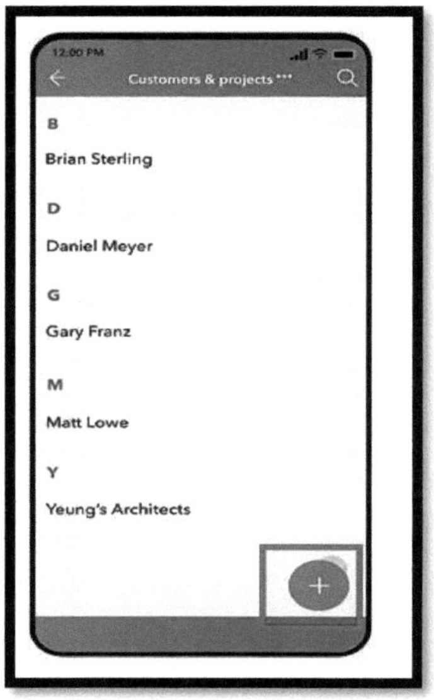

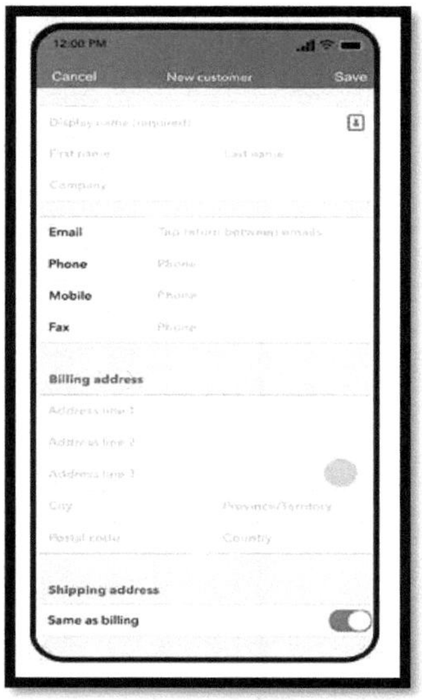

Invoice Like a Pro—From Anywhere

Creating and sending invoices on the go is simple. Tap the **Invoice** icon on your dashboard to start. All relevant details are available or can be added directly from your device. You can even email invoices directly from the app or capture customer signatures on-site. Watch invoices move from *sent* to *viewed* to *paid* with real-time updates, and send automatic reminders for overdue payments. (Note: Online payments require additional activation.)

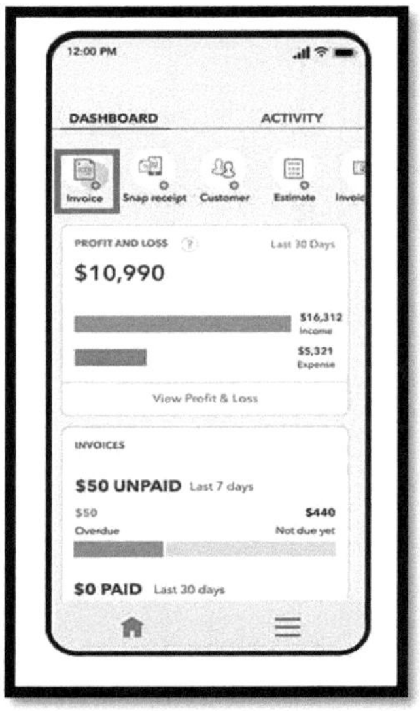

Track and Manage Expenses Effortlessly

Connect QuickBooks to your bank, credit card, or payment services such as Square, and your expenses will be imported automatically. Never lose a receipt again—use **Receipt Snap** to take a photo, and it uploads instantly to QuickBooks for easy organization.

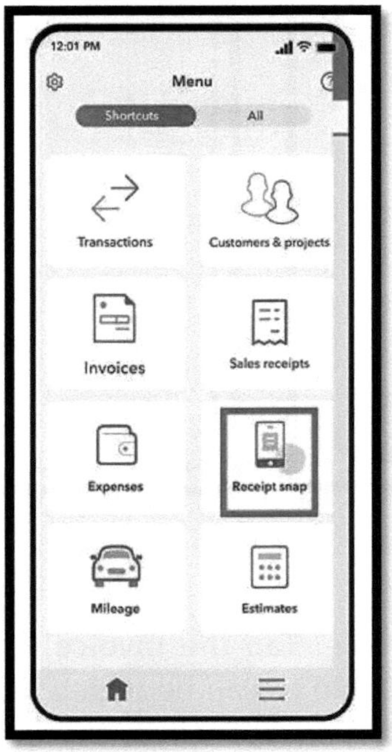

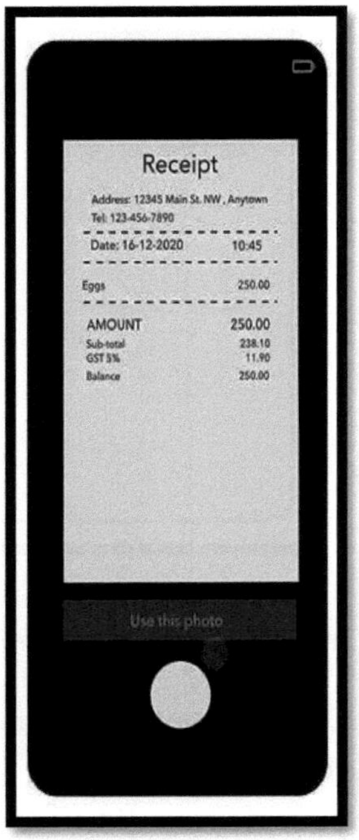

Automatic Mileage Tracking

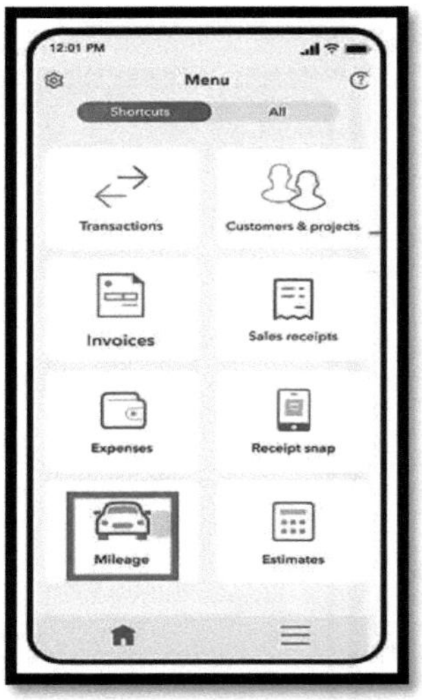

Ditch the manual logbooks. After a quick setup—adding your vehicle and enabling location services—QuickBooks automatically tracks your trips using your mobile device's built-in GPS. You can easily review each trip and categorize it as business or personal.

Real-Time Insights, Anytime

Your mobile dashboard provides up-to-date business insights and key metrics. You can also generate clear, professional reports and share them with your team directly from the app.

Take Your Business Wherever You Go

The QuickBooks Online app is included with your QuickBooks Online subscription. Download it for free and manage your business whenever—and wherever—you need to.

HOW TO SET UP AUTOMATED WORKFLOWS IN QUICKBOOKS ONLINE

Automating workflows in QuickBooks Online helps businesses **streamline repetitive tasks** like invoicing, payment reminders, and approval processes. Here's how to set up automation efficiently:

Step 1: Log In to QuickBooks Online

Sign in to QuickBooks Online using your credentials. Make sure you have **admin permissions**, as automation features require access rights.

Step 2: Access the Workflows Section

From the left-side menu, click the **Gear Icon (⚙)** and select **Manage Workflows** under the **Tools** section. This opens the workflow automation dashboard where you can create, manage, and monitor automated tasks.

Step 3: Choose a Workflow Template or Create a Custom Workflow

QuickBooks Online offers **pre-built templates** for common tasks:

- **Send invoice reminders**
- **Notify customers of overdue payments**
- **Automate approvals**

You can either:

- **Select a Template**: Pick one that matches your business needs.

- **Create a Custom Workflow**: Build your automation from scratch, tailoring triggers, actions, and conditions to your unique requirements.

Step 4: Define Workflow Triggers and Conditions

Every workflow needs a **trigger**—the event that starts the automation. Examples include:

- A new invoice is created
- An invoice becomes overdue
- A payment is received
- A bill is due soon

Once the trigger is selected, set **conditions**, such as timing (e.g., 5 days before due date) or specific customers or vendors to which the workflow applies.

Step 5: Set Up Actions

Next, define what QuickBooks should do once the trigger occurs. Common actions include:

- Sending email reminders to customers
- Notifying team members about due invoices
- Sending payment confirmations
- Updating QuickBooks records automatically

Customize emails with **dynamic fields** like customer name, invoice number, or due date, and select recipients.

Step 6: Review and Activate the Workflow

Before enabling, **double-check all triggers, conditions, and actions**. When ready, click **Save & Activate**. The workflow will now run automatically whenever the defined conditions are met.

Step 7: Monitor and Manage Workflows

Keep track of your automations in the **Manage Workflows** section:

- **Pause or disable** workflows if needed
- **Edit triggers, conditions, or actions**
- **View execution history** to troubleshoot errors

By setting up automated workflows in QuickBooks Online, your business can **reduce manual work, improve efficiency, and ensure key financial tasks are completed on time**.

INTUIT ASSIST EXPLAINED: QUICKBOOKS' AI FOR SMALL BUSINESSES

Launched in September 2023, Intuit Assist represents Intuit's bold entry into AI for small businesses. With AI agents rolling out on **July 1, 2025**, Intuit is now building **virtual teams for businesses**, streamlining workflows from financial analysis to customer management, and freeing up valuable time for strategic work. The best part? These AI capabilities are embedded directly in your existing Intuit platform, so there's no need for separate subscriptions.

What is Intuit Assist?

Intuit Assist is a **generative AI-powered financial assistant** designed to handle the heavy lifting of business finance management. Think of it as having a **24/7 financial expert** for your business. It can:

- Automatically generate invoices, estimates, bills, and payment reminders
- Match payments and bills within QuickBooks, reducing manual data entry
- Propose action plans to help you reach financial goals
- Connect you with live experts whenever needed

Embedded across Intuit products—including **QuickBooks, TurboTax, Credit Karma, and Mailchimp**—Intuit Assist provides **actionable insights while keeping you in control**, helping you:

- Convert prospects faster
- Streamline payments
- Make smarter financial decisions

The result: **less time on administrative tasks, more time growing your business.**

Intuit Assist in QuickBooks Online

Unlike specialized third-party AI tools, Intuit Assist is fully **integrated with QuickBooks Online**, eliminating the need for additional software or complex integrations.

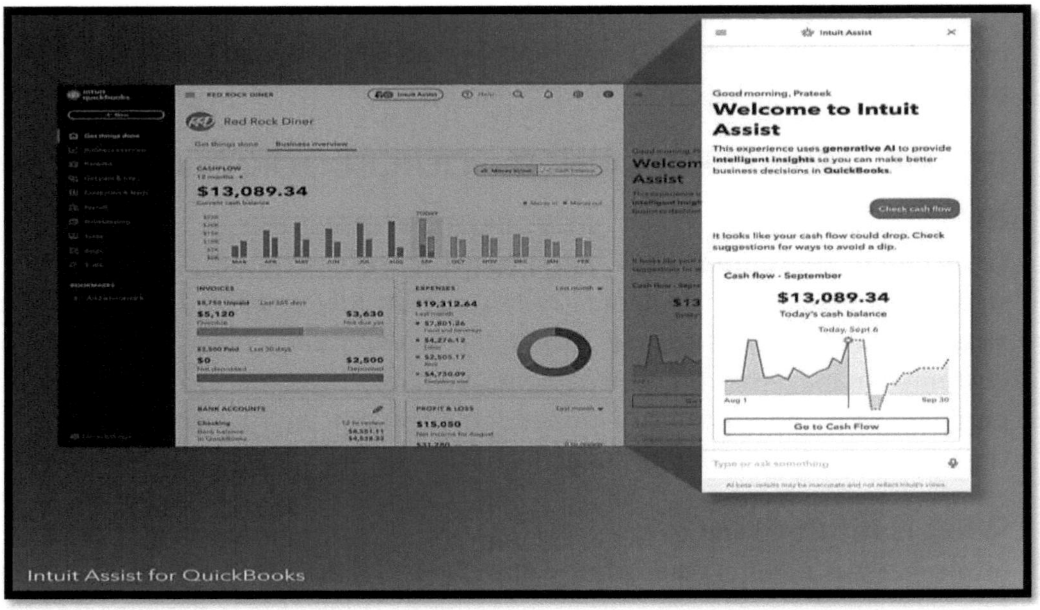

Generative AI Capabilities

Its **generative AI capabilities** make financial data more actionable and accessible.

Key Features:

1. Natural Language Reporting: Ask Intuit Assist questions in plain language. For example:

"Show me my top-selling products in July."

It instantly generates insights without creating a custom report.

2. Predictive Follow-Up Questions: The AI anticipates your next question. After showing revenue trends, it might suggest:

"Would you like to see which products drove this growth?"

3. Proactive Insights: Even if you don't know what to ask, Intuit Assist surfaces valuable information automatically, such as:

- Cash flow hotspots
- Spending anomalies
- Opportunities for improvement
- Business wins worth celebrating

4. Daily Summary Dashboard: Receive a **personalized briefing every day** with business insights and recommended next steps. No more digging through reports—just a clear snapshot of your business performance.

For **CPAs and AI enthusiasts**, Intuit Assist eliminates tedious work like exporting QuickBooks reports into ChatGPT for analysis. Insights are delivered **instantly within the platform**, saving time and helping you act on your business data **exactly when it matters.**

Agentic AI Capabilities in QuickBooks Online

On **July 1, 2025**, Intuit launched its **AI agents**, designed to supercharge your QuickBooks Online experience. These agents extend the power of **Intuit Assist's generative AI** by performing tasks for you and helping interpret your financial data.

Key Features of Agentic AI

1. Daily Summaries: Instead of manually sifting through reports, AI agents provide curated overviews of what matters most to your business. They automatically highlight:

- Cash flow hotspots
- Spending anomalies
- Opportunities to improve cash flow
- Celebratory wins worth noting

2. Personalized Briefings: Receive daily briefings tailored to your behavior and priorities. While generative AI generates insights, agentic AI determines which insights are most relevant to your business. It's like having a financial advisor who **knows your business intimately**.

3. Seamless Connection to Human Experts: Agentic AI ensures minimal friction when involving human experts. By automatically sharing **full business context**, you avoid repeating details or re-explaining situations. Whether you need quick guidance or in-depth consultation, the transition feels natural and informed.

4. AI-Supercharged Expert Tools: Human advisors gain access to virtual platforms powered by **real-time business data**, enabling more accurate and relevant advice.

5. Transforming Raw Data into Actionable Insights: The system intelligently converts spreadsheets, website data, and other raw inputs into actionable profiles. While generative AI handles **language and formatting**, agentic AI decides **what to extract, infer, and prioritize** based on your unique business needs.

Intuit Assist Beyond QuickBooks

Intuit Assist is **not limited to QuickBooks**. It also supports **TurboTax, Mailchimp, and Credit Karma**, helping you work smarter across Intuit's ecosystem.

TurboTax: Streamlined Tax Preparation

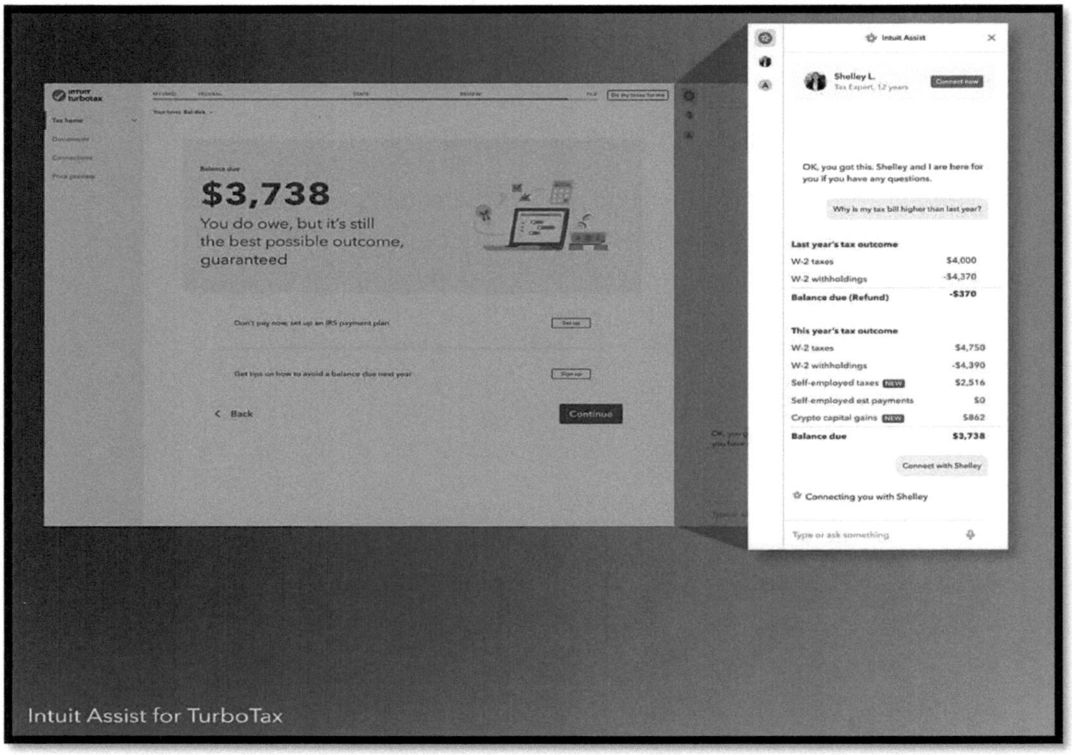

Intuit Assist helps you **stay in control during tax season** by answering questions instantly, preparing forms, and ensuring nothing is missed. Key capabilities include:

1. Smart Form Recognition and Guidance

- Upload tax forms, and Intuit Assist extracts and applies the data.
- Generates a **personalized checklist** based on uploaded documents.
- Detects special cases like stock sales and prompts you for the correct 1099-B forms.

2. Automatic Expert Connection

- Recognizes when you need expert support and connects you automatically.
- Tax experts explain your return in **plain language** and file everything when ready.

3. Intelligent Return Summary

- ❖ Provides a clear snapshot of your return, highlighting income changes, tax breaks, state-specific details, and refund status.

4. Proactive Tax Savings Detection

- ❖ Evaluates hundreds of potential deductions and credits.
- ❖ Explains calculations behind refunds or amounts owed with actionable follow-up answers.

5. Personalized Workflow Optimization

- ❖ Updates dashboards based on submitted information, skipping irrelevant steps.
- ❖ Flags missed entries or errors in real time, letting you correct them immediately rather than at the end.

Intuit Assist, paired with **agentic AI**, creates a **seamless, intelligent experience** across business and tax management. It saves time, reduces errors, and ensures you focus on strategic decisions rather than administrative tasks.

Automating Marketing and Lead Follow-Up in Mailchimp

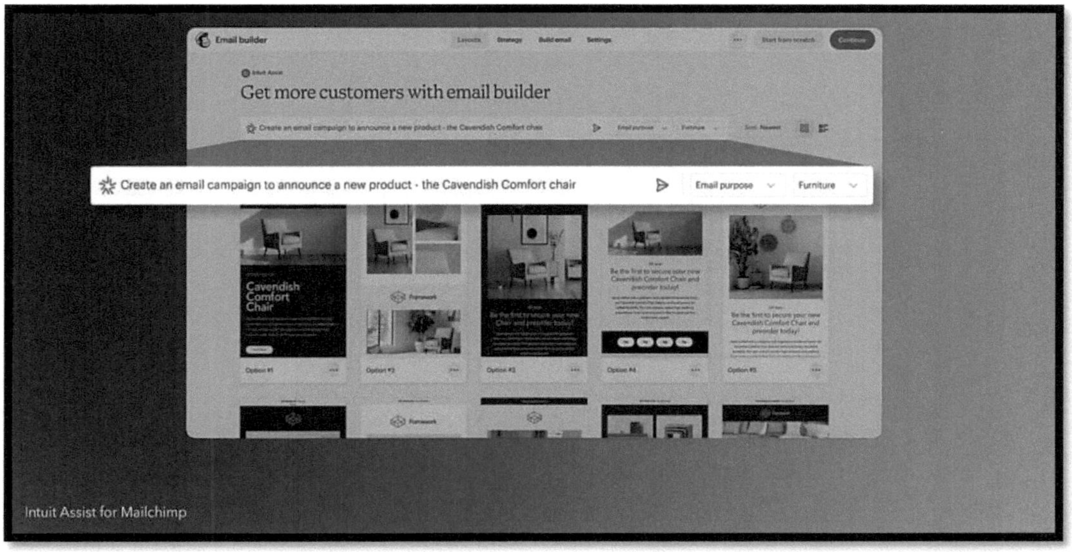

Intuit Assist takes the heavy lifting out of email marketing, allowing you to focus on strategy while AI handles execution. Campaign creation, audience targeting, and lead follow-up are all streamlined for maximum efficiency.

Key Features

1. Fully Automated Campaign Creation: Simply tell Intuit Assist your goal—for example, "Announce a new product launch"—and it generates hundreds of personalized layouts, writes the email in your brand's voice, creates images, and populates content. You only need to review and approve; no starting from scratch.

2. Smart Audience Targeting and Customization: Describe your audience in plain language—"loyal customers" or "first-time buyers"—and AI converts it into precise segments. Edit text and images easily with AI support for tone adjustments, rewrites, or complete content regeneration.

3. Intelligent Content Optimization: Receive data-driven suggestions to improve engagement. Campaigns automatically integrate into your marketing calendar, with follow-up action recommendations to keep momentum going after sending.

4. Performance Tracking and Recommendations: Ask, "How did my last campaign perform?" and get a detailed summary across all touchpoints. AI provides actionable suggestions to enhance metrics like open rates, click-throughs, and conversion rates.

5. Automated Lead Management: AI drafts responses to inbound leads using product and service data from QuickBooks. Leads are nurtured automatically until fully qualified, while your Mailchimp sales pipeline is updated in real time to track customer lifecycle progression.

Managing Cash Flow in Credit Karma

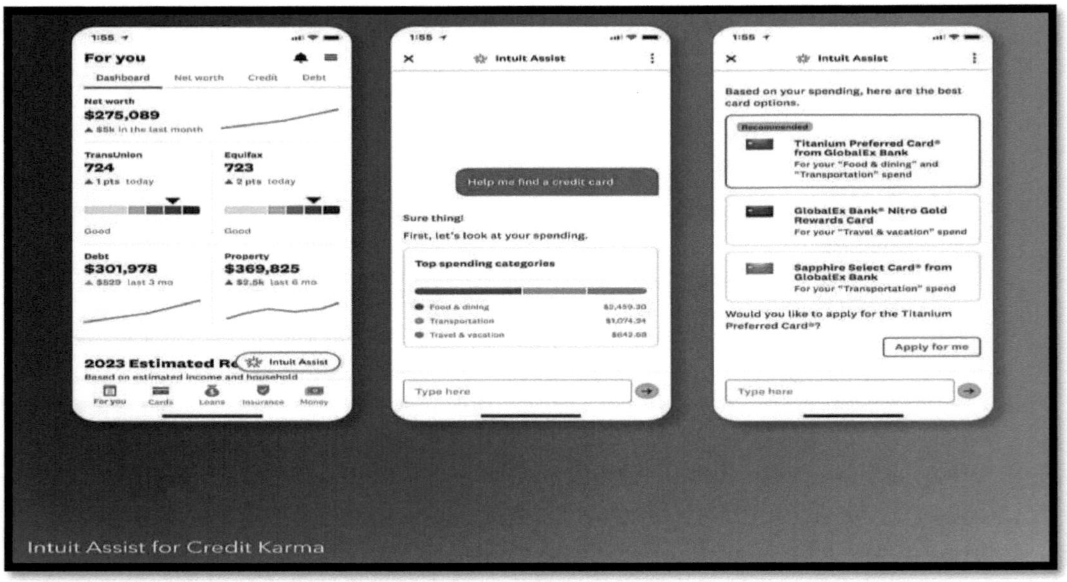

Credit Karma's AI simplifies financial management by transforming complex cash flow and credit decisions into **personalized, actionable insights**.

Key Features

1. Personalized Rewards Optimization: AI analyzes spending patterns and identifies missed reward opportunities. Get insights on how to maximize rewards from your top spending categories and compare potential benefits with your current averages.

2. Smart Card Recommendations and Applications: Receive tailored card options based on your spending patterns, with side-by-side comparisons. Apply seamlessly with pre-filled forms, and receive tips on maximizing perks—like using gym credits or adjusting payment methods.

3. Travel Rewards Maximization: Get advice on how to maximize travel rewards, including hotel credits, rideshare cashback, and airport perks. AI monitors your bookings and sends reminders to earn additional points while traveling.

4. Proactive Cash Flow Management: AI alerts you when cash is running low, tracks how transactions affect monthly expenses, and recommends credit or loan options based on your financial profile. Compare loans and apply with pre-filled forms for a seamless experience.

5. Intelligent Spending Insights and Budgeting: View spending breakdowns between essentials and non-essentials. Receive alerts for rising trends in categories like entertainment and get AI-guided recommendations for setting spending caps to avoid future cash shortages.

How Intuit Assist Can Transform Your Business

Intuit Assist isn't just a collection of features—it's your AI-powered business partner. Here are four real-world scenarios that show how it helps entrepreneurs make smarter decisions, faster.

John – Pet Boutique Owner

John runs a busy pet boutique, juggling orders, restocking, and customer service. Her bank balance is dropping, and she has no idea why.

When she logs into QuickBooks, Intuit Assist immediately highlights the issue: wholesale expenses spiked last week, and grooming services dropped 40%. It surfaces a cash flow hotspot, explains the trend on her dashboard, and even suggests small pricing adjustments—all without John having to ask the right question.

Result: John knows exactly where her money is going and how to fix it.

Sarah – Etsy Seller

Sarah sold more this year than last and even hired a freelance photographer, but tax season leaves him confused about what forms to file.

TurboTax with Intuit Assist detects his 1099-K from Etsy and W-2 from his part-time job. It spots stock compensation, prompts him to upload a 1099-B, and even tells him where to find it. As Sarah uploads forms, Intuit Assist creates a personalized checklist and applies the data to his return.

Result: Sarah files his taxes confidently without needing prior tax knowledge.

Finn – Custom Furniture Builder

Finn sends email campaigns through Mailchimp but has no idea if they're effective. He's too busy managing custom orders and supplier delays to track metrics.

He asks, "How did my last email campaign perform?" Intuit Assist pulls up open rates, click-throughs, and top-performing products. It even recommends the next step—targeting high-intent shoppers with a time-limited offer.

Result: Finn has a marketing expert built into Mailchimp, helping him boost sales without extra staff.

Joy – Freelance Designer

Joy's client payment is late, but her rent and software subscriptions are due. She's close to overdrafting.

Credit Karma's Intuit Assist notices her low cash balance and starts a chat. It shows how a recent hardware purchase affected her finances, offers short-term loan options with comparisons, and recommends spending limits on software, alerting her whenever she nears the cap.

Result: Joy avoids a cash crunch and gains better control over her personal and business finances.

HOW TO TURN OFF AI ASSIST IN QUICKBOOKS ONLINE

If you prefer to manage your QuickBooks Online account without AI suggestions, follow these steps to disable AI Assist features.

Step 1: Log In

- Visit QuickBooks Online.
- Enter your login credentials to access your account.

Step 2: Open Settings

- Click the **Gear Icon** in the top-right corner.
- Select **Account and Settings** from the dropdown menu.

Step 3: Access the Advanced Tab

- In the **Account and Settings** menu, click **Advanced** on the left.
- Scroll down to find options related to automation, suggestions, or AI features.

Step 4: Turn Off AI Features

- Toggle off any AI-related options, such as:
  - Pre-filling forms with previously entered content
  - Automatic transaction categorization
  - AI-generated insights and alerts

Step 5: Save and Refresh

- Scroll to the bottom and click **Save**.
- Refresh your browser or log out and back in to ensure changes take effect.

KEY FEATURES IN INTUIT ASSIST

Intuit Assist brings AI-powered efficiency to QuickBooks Online with three standout features: smarter invoice reminders, the Payments Agent for invoice creation, and business feed suggestions to help guide your day-to-day tasks.

1. Smarter Invoice Reminders

Gone are the days when automated reminders would stop after a set period. Intuit Assist now detects overdue invoices and drafts personalized messages based on how late a payment is.

- A **blue icon** appears next to the invoice, showing a suggested message.
- For example, an invoice 44 days overdue might read: *"Urgent – Please pay your overdue invoice."*
- You can click **Rewrite** to see alternative messages or edit it manually before sending.

This AI-driven approach not only saves time but also helps improve cash flow by encouraging faster payments.

2. The Payments Agent: AI-Powered Invoice Creation

The **Payments Agent** streamlines invoice creation using natural language instructions. Instead of manually selecting customers and line items, you can type a simple command:

"Please invoice Bill's Windsurf Shop for 12 fountains and rocks."

- The AI fills in the customer's details, pulls relevant items, and even displays recent payment history.
- It can suggest adjusting payment terms based on the customer's behavior or enabling online payments.
- You can tweak quantities, add new items, or use inventory data already uploaded.

This feature is perfect for busy entrepreneurs, reducing repetitive tasks and speeding up invoicing.

3. Business Feed Suggestions

The **Business Feed** acts like a dynamic to-do list, offering AI-generated suggestions for what to focus on next.

- It might prompt you to follow up on overdue invoices, categorize transactions, or upload receipts.
- It can even estimate monthly net profit based on your current data.

While it doesn't replace standard bookkeeping practices, it's a helpful guide for newcomers or those who want a structured overview of daily priorities, reducing decision fatigue and keeping your business on track.

CHAPTER FOURTEEN

REDUCING MANUAL DATA ENTRY IN QUICKBOOKS ONLINE

To reduce manual data entry in QuickBooks Online, use **bank feeds** to automatically import transactions, create **bank rules** to categorize them, and set up **recurring transactions** for regular invoices and bills. Additionally, use the **QuickBooks mobile app** for on-the-go expense capture and connect other apps to QuickBooks to streamline data flow and avoid manual re-entry.

RECURRING TRANSACTIONS IN QUICKBOOKS ONLINE

How to Create Recurring Transactions in QuickBooks Online

Recurring transactions in QuickBooks Online allow you to automate repetitive financial activities, such as regular expenses or invoices. By setting them up, you save time, reduce errors, and ensure consistency in your accounting records.

This section walks you through creating recurring transactions, with examples for both recurring expenses and invoices.

Step 1: Access Recurring Transactions

1. Click the **Gear icon** in the upper-right corner of your QuickBooks Online dashboard.

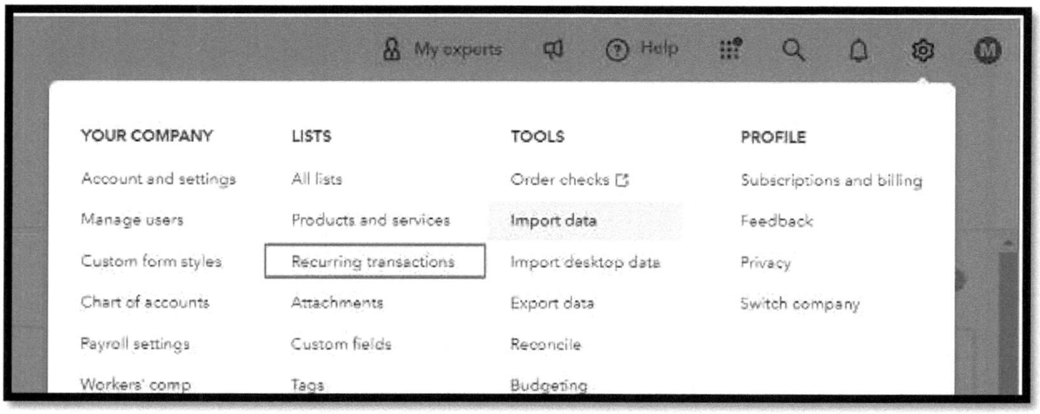

2. Under **Lists**, select **Recurring Transactions**.

Step 2: Choose the Transaction Type

1. On the **Recurring Transactions** screen, click **New**.

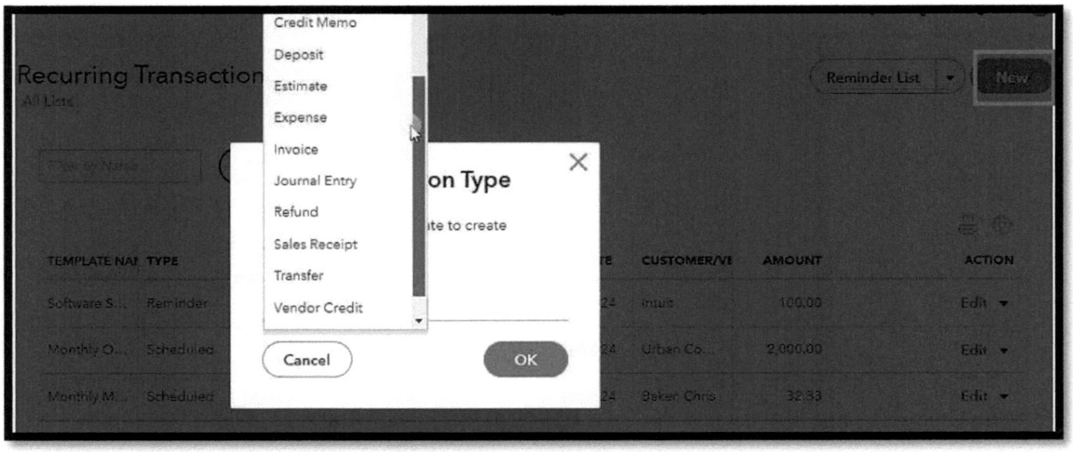

2. Select the type of transaction you want to automate, such as **Expense**, **Invoice**, **Bill**, **Sales Receipt**, **Check**, **Deposit**, or **Estimate**.
3. Click **OK** to continue.

Creating a Recurring Expense (Example)

Let's say your company, pays a fixed monthly office rent of $2,000 to *Urban Commercial Properties*. You want QuickBooks to record this automatically from January to June.

Step 3: Complete the Recurring Expense Form

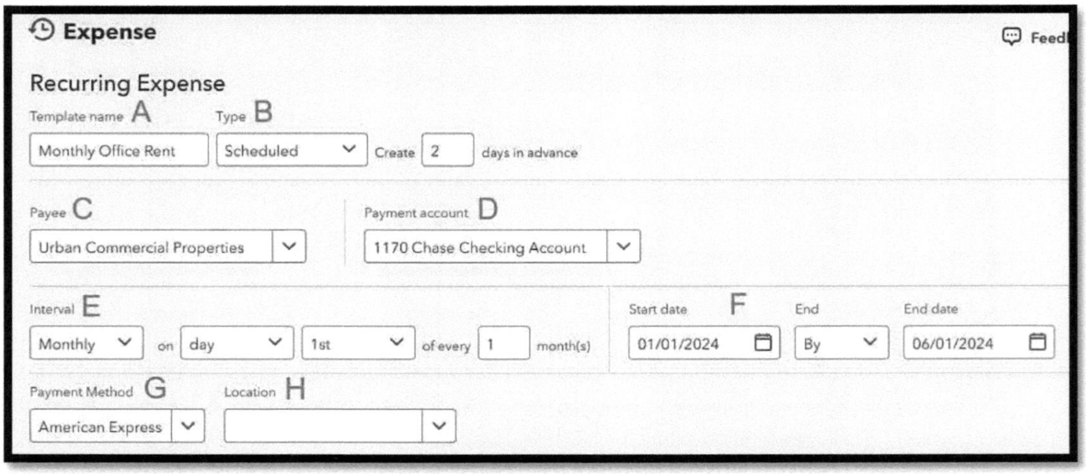

A. **Template Name:** Enter a name to identify the transaction easily (e.g., "Monthly Office Rent").

B. **Type:**
   - ❖ **Scheduled**: Automatically generates the transaction on a set schedule (ideal for fixed payments like rent or utilities).
   - ❖ **Reminder**: Sends a reminder to record the transaction manually. Useful for variable or verification-required expenses.
   - ❖ **Unscheduled**: A flexible template for use as needed.

   Example: Use **Scheduled** and set QuickBooks to generate the expense two days before it's due.

C. **Payee:** Select the vendor receiving the payment (*Urban Commercial Properties*).
D. **Payment Account:** Choose the bank or credit card account used to pay this expense.
E. **Interval:** Specify the frequency, e.g., **Monthly**, on the first day of each month.
F. **Start and End Dates:** Set the period for recurring transactions: *Start: Jan 1, 2024; End: June 1, 2024*.
G. **Payment Method:** Select how the payment will be made (e.g., credit card, bank transfer).
H. **Location (Optional):** Assign a location if your business has multiple branches.

Additional Details

- ❖ At the bottom of the form, enter the **expense category** and **amount** to complete the setup.

Creating a Recurring Invoice

Recurring invoices work similarly to recurring bills or expenses, with fields tailored for customers instead of vendors.

Steps to Set Up a Recurring Invoice:

1. **Access the Recurring Transactions Form:** Click **Gear → Recurring Transactions → New**, then select **Invoice**.
2. **Fill in the Template Details:**
   - **Template Name:** Choose a descriptive name to identify the recurring invoice.
   - **Type:** Choose **Scheduled**, **Reminder**, or **Unscheduled** depending on how automated you want the invoice to be.
   - **Customer:** Select the client being billed.
   - **Interval:** Specify the frequency (e.g., monthly, weekly).
   - **Start and End Dates:** Indicate the duration for which this invoice will recur.
3. **Add Product/Service Details:** Enter quantity, unit cost, and any other necessary information.
4. **Save the Template:** Click **Save template** in the lower-left corner.

Your recurring invoices will now appear in the **Recurring Transactions** list. You can edit or delete them anytime using the **Edit** button under the **Action** column.

Running a Recurring Template Report

To review or share your recurring transactions:

1. Click the arrow next to **Reminder list** in the Recurring Transactions screen.
2. Select **Run Report**.

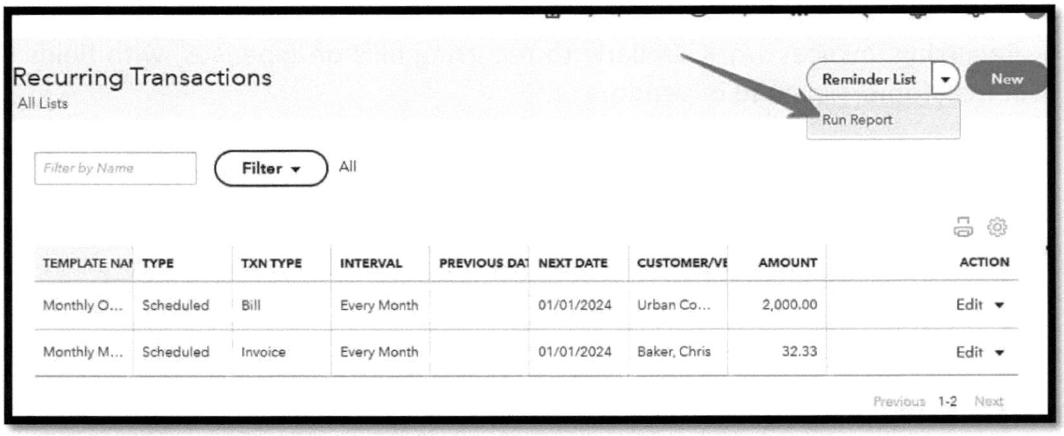

QuickBooks generates a report listing all recurring templates, useful for team updates or audits.

Recurring Template List

TRANSACTION TYPE	TEMPLATE NAME	PREVIOUS DATE	NAME	AMOUNT
▾ Scheduled				
Invoice	Monthly Maintenance	01/01/2024	Baker, Chris	32.33
Expense	Office Rent - Monthly		Urban Commercial Properties	-2,000.00
Total for Scheduled				**$ -1,967.67**

Types of Recurring Transactions and When to Use Them

QuickBooks Online supports various recurring transaction types. Choosing the right type depends on your workflow:

Transaction Type	Purpose / When to Use
Recurring Invoice	Automatically sends an invoice to a client; payment must be recorded manually. Ideal for invoicing before payment.
Recurring Sales Receipt	Automatically records revenue when a customer pays monthly (e.g., auto-charged credit cards).
Recurring Bill	Generates bills at set intervals for review and payment. Use when amounts may vary, like utility bills.
Recurring Expense	Automatically records fixed payments from bank or credit card accounts. Use for consistent monthly payments like rent.
Recurring Check	Creates recurring paper checks automatically and adds them to the print queue.
Other Types	Includes Non-Posting Charge, Non-Posting Credit, Credit Card Credit, Credit Memo, Deposit, Estimate, Journal Entry, Refund, Transfer, Vendor Credit, and Purchase Order. Use as needed for less common recurring transactions.

Managing Recurring Transactions in QuickBooks Online

QuickBooks Online allows you to automate routine transactions using recurring templates. You can create new recurring transactions, turn existing ones into recurring templates, duplicate, edit, or delete templates, and troubleshoot transactions that fail to run.

1. Make an Existing Transaction Recurring

You can convert an existing invoice, bill, or expense into a recurring template:

1. Open the transaction.
2. In the footer, select **Make recurring** (or **Enable Recurring Payments** for invoices).

Important Notes:

- ❖ **Estimates:** Only supported in the classic estimate and invoice experience. Switch to the classic experience to create recurring estimates.
- ❖ **PayPal:** Recurring transactions using PayPal are not supported.

2. Duplicate an Existing Template

Quickly create new templates by duplicating existing ones:

1. Go to **Settings ⚙ → Recurring Transactions**.
2. In the **Action** column, select **Duplicate** from the **Edit ▼** dropdown.
3. All settings copy over except the template title.

3. Edit a Recurring Template

To modify a template:

1. Go to **Settings ⚙ → Recurring Transactions**.
2. In the **Action** column, select **Edit** for the template.
3. Update the **template name, type, customer/payee**, and other details.
4. For **Scheduled** or **Reminder** templates, adjust how far in advance QuickBooks generates or reminds you about the transaction. You can also modify the frequency in the **Interval** section.
5. Add or remove products/services in the **Item Details** section.
6. Click **Save template**.

These changes only affect the recurring template and its future transactions. Past transactions remain unchanged.

4. Update Service Dates

Recurring templates do not auto-fill service dates. To update them:

1. Run the **Recent Automatic Transactions** report.
2. Set the report dates and click **Run report**.
3. Select the transaction, manually update the **Service Date**, and click **Save**.

5. Edit Items or Customers Used in Templates

When modifying items or customers linked to templates, QuickBooks prompts you with options:

- ❖ **Update for all:** Apply changes to all relevant templates.
- ❖ **One time only:** Apply changes to the current transaction only.

Affected Fields:

- Payment method, terms, taxable status, transaction dates, transaction number, amount, location, class

6. Edit Company Settings

Changes to company settings that affect recurring templates may alter future transactions. Fields that impact templates include:

- Customer estimates message
- Customer sales forms message
- Sales tax rate
- Accounts for tax, shipping, discounts
- MAS deposit account

7. Delete a Recurring Template

1. Go to **Settings ⚙ → Recurring Transactions**.
2. Locate the template, click ▼, and select **Delete**.
3. Confirm by selecting **Yes**.

8. Fix Recurring Transactions That Didn't Run

If a template fails to generate a transaction, manually create it:

1. Go to **Settings ⚙ → Recurring Transactions**.
2. Find the template in the list.
3. Select **Use** from the **Edit ▼** dropdown.
4. Review details, make any adjustments, and click **Save and close** or **Save and new**.

CREATING BUNDLE IN QUICKBOOKS ONLINE

A **bundle** in QuickBooks Online is a group of products or services that you regularly sell together as a set. Because of this, all **individual items must already exist** in your Products and Services list *before* you create the bundle.

Step 1: Open the Products and Services List

1. Click the **Settings (⚙)** icon on the QuickBooks Online toolbar.
2. Under **Lists**, choose **Products and Services**.

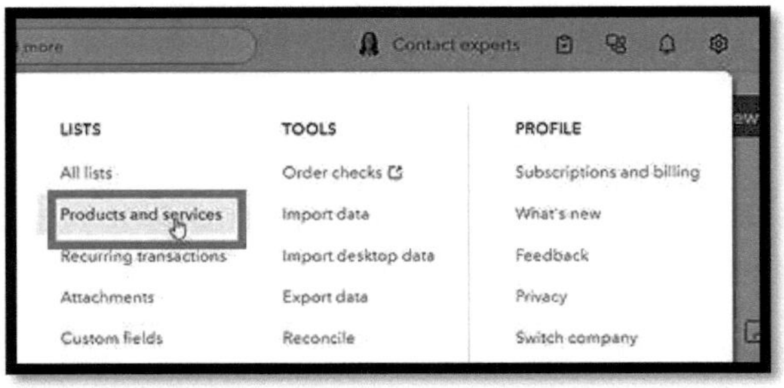

3. Select **New** in the upper-right corner.
4. From the dropdown menu, choose **Bundle** to open the Product/Service information panel.

Step 2: Enter Basic Bundle Information

- **Name:** Type the bundle's name in the *Name* field.
- **Item Type:** Ensure **Bundle** is selected.
- **SKU (Optional):** Enter an SKU if you track stock using SKU numbers.
- **Image (Optional):**
  - Click **Add an image** to upload a picture.
  - Select the file and click **Open**.
  - To remove an image, hover over it and click the **trash/delete** icon.

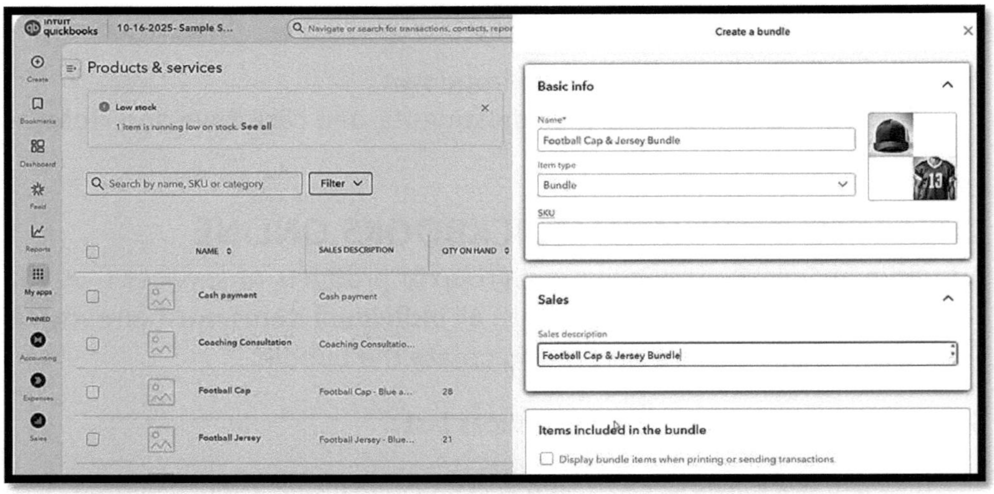

Step 3: Add Sales Information

- In the **Sales** section, enter a clear **sales description** that will appear on customer forms, such as invoices and estimates.

Step 4: Add Items to the Bundle

1. Scroll to **Items included in the bundle**.
2. If you want customers to see each component item on printed or emailed forms, check **Display bundle items when printing or sending transactions**.
   - ❖ If unchecked, only the bundle description appears.
3. Add items to the bundle:
   - ❖ Click into a blank line and select a product/service from the dropdown.

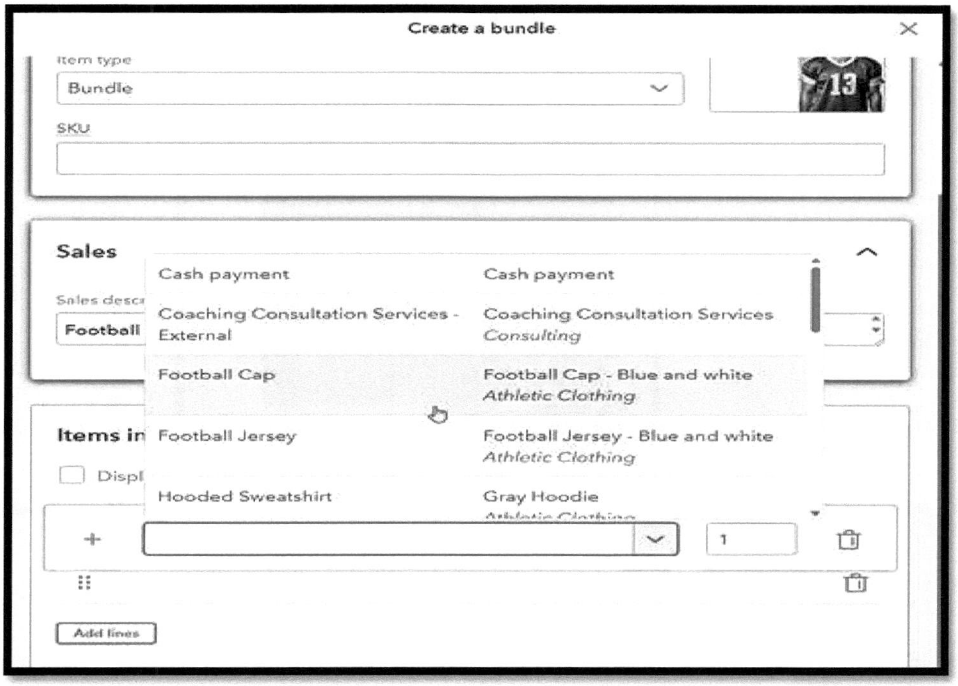

   - ❖ Enter the **quantity** for each item.
4. Manage lines:
   - ❖ Click the **trash can** icon to delete a row.
   - ❖ Click the bottom empty row to add more items.
   - ❖ Click **Add lines** to insert two rows at once.
   - ❖ Drag the **handle** on the left side of a row to reorder the items.

Step 5: Save the Bundle

- ❖ Click **Save and close** to finish.
- ❖ Click **Save and new** to save and start creating another item.
- ❖ To cancel, click **Cancel**, then confirm with **Yes** when prompted.

GETTING STARTED WITH QUICKBOOKS TIME IN QUICKBOOKS ONLINE

QuickBooks Time helps you track employee hours, monitor who's working, review and approve time entries, run payroll, and invoice customers. This section will walk you through the essentials and point you to resources for full setup.

1. Track Time

As a **QuickBooks Time Admin**, you can record hours for yourself or your team:

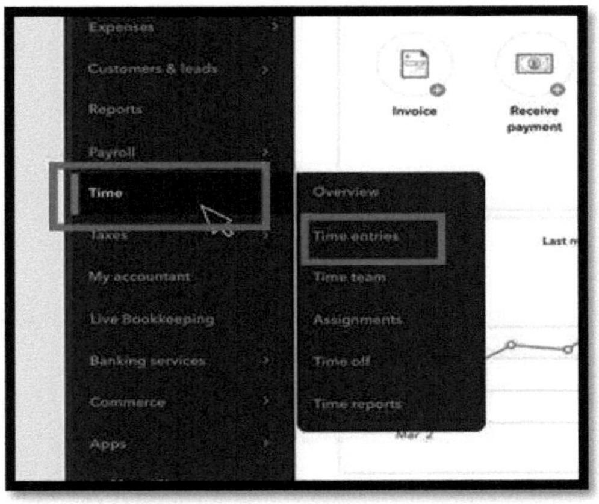

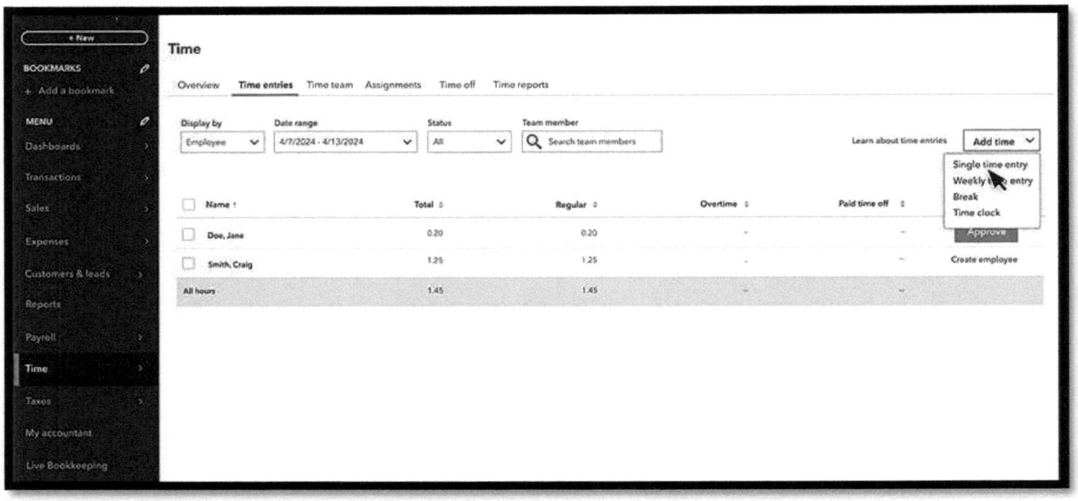

- **Weekly or single time entries**: Log past hours worked.
- **Currently Working**: Clock in real-time.
- **Customer/Project & Service**: Assign hours to specific tasks.
- **Billable Checkbox**: Select if the time should be invoiced.
- **Notes & Time Zone**: Add optional notes and confirm the correct time zone.

Click **Save** when done.

You can also track time via the **QuickBooks Workforce mobile app** or **Time Clock kiosk**. To use these, you must first set up your team and define customers, projects, or custom fields if needed.

2. Monitor Your Team

Admins can track who is working in real-time:

❖ Select **Time → Team Who's Working** to see a list of employees currently clocked in.

❖ View what tasks they are performing.

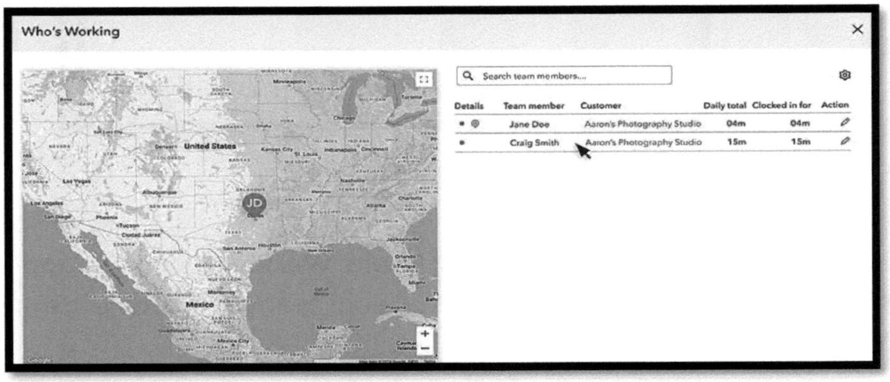

❖ GPS locations are available if employees clock in via the QuickBooks Workforce mobile app.

3. Run Time Reports

QuickBooks Time provides detailed reports:

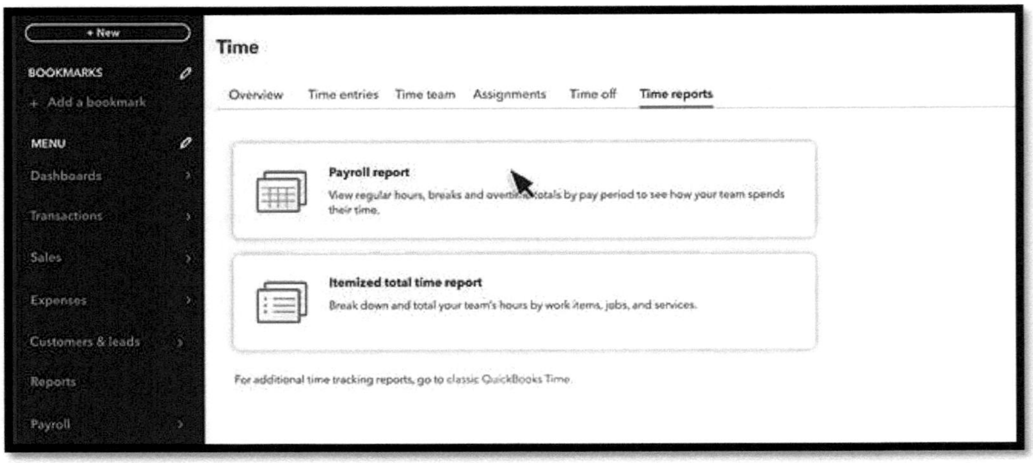

- ❖ **Payroll Time Reports**: Break down hours into regular, overtime, and paid time off by pay period.
- ❖ **Itemized Total Time Report**: View time by customer, project, or billable status.

Admins can review and edit entries before final approval.

4. Approve Time

Approving time:

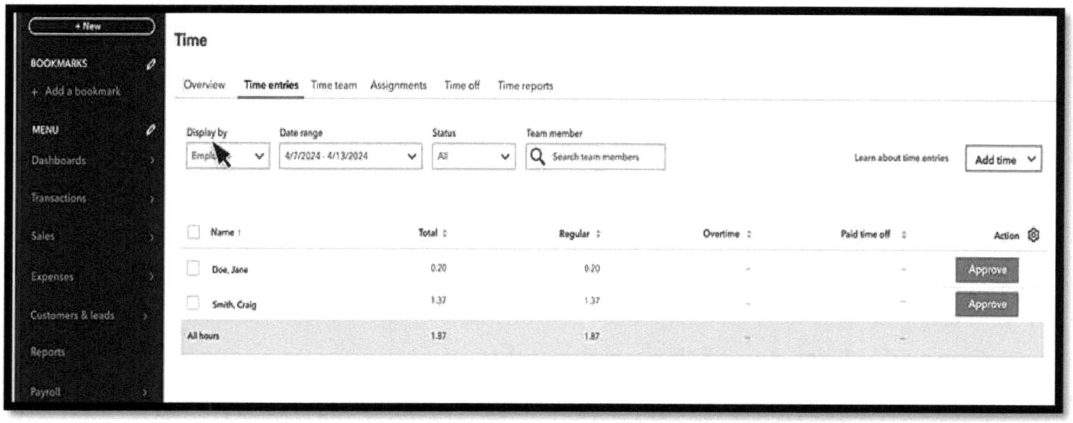

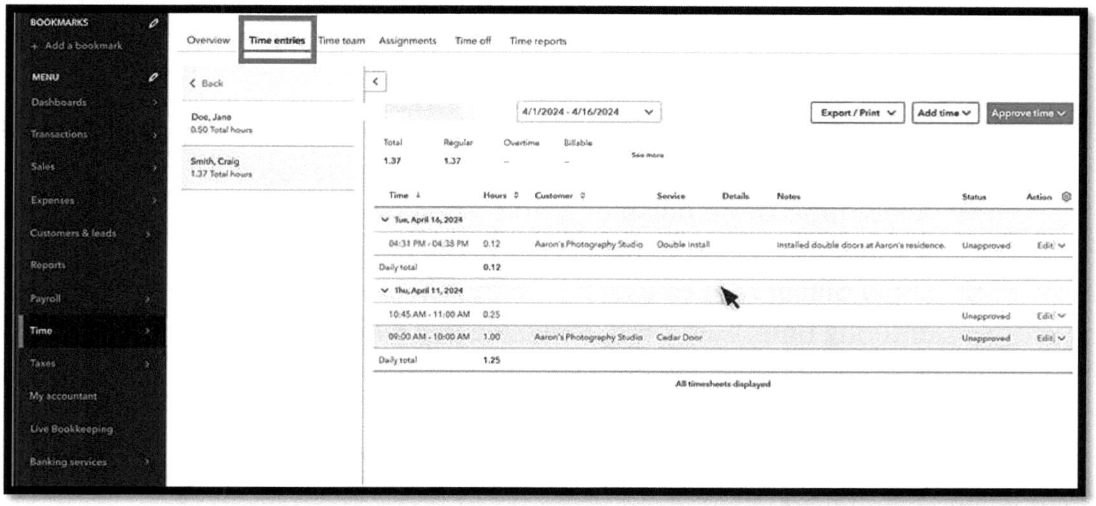

- ❖ Locks entries and prepares them for payroll.
- ❖ Approve entries individually or in **batches** to simplify payroll processing.

5. Run Payroll

Before processing payroll:

1. Set up payroll by selecting **Payroll**
2. After setup, select **Employees → Run Payroll** to pay your team.

HOW TO TRACK BILLABLE HOURS IN QUICKBOOKS ONLINE

QuickBooks Online Plus includes a built-in time tracking tool to capture billable hours worked by employees or contractors. You can track **one-off tasks** using **single-time activity timesheets** or **recurring/ongoing tasks** using **weekly timesheets**.

Note: Time tracking is not available in QuickBooks Online Simple Start. You need Essentials, Plus, or Advanced.

Step 1: Enable Time Tracking

1. Click the **cog wheel icon (⚙)** in the upper-right corner of the dashboard.
2. Select **Account and Settings**.
3. In the left menu, select **Time** to access time tracking settings.
4. Click the **pencil icon** to edit preferences.

Time Preferences:

1. General – First day of the workweek:

Set the starting day of your team's workweek (e.g., Monday). All weekly reports and calendars will align with this start day.

2. Timesheet Options:

- **Show service field:** Enable this to specify services when entering timesheets, which automatically applies the correct billable rate.
- **Allow time to be billable:** Marks activities as billable and allows automatic addition to customer invoices.
- **Show billing rate to users:** Displays the customer billing rate to employees entering time. Turn off if employee pay differs from customer billing rates.

Click **Save** when finished.

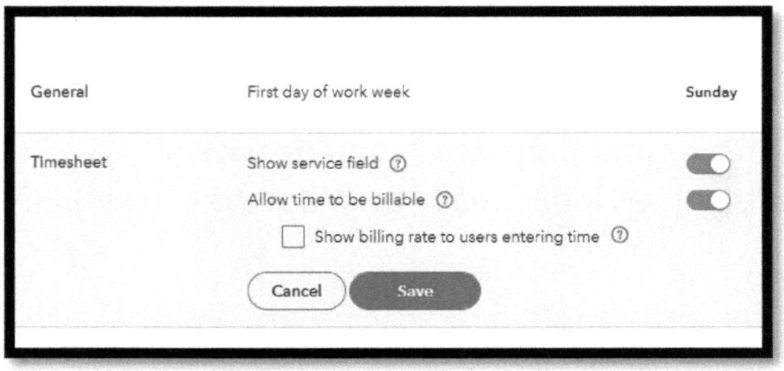

Step 2: Specify Billable Rates for Service Items

To avoid manually entering rates each time:

1. Go to **Sales → Products and Services**.
2. Click **New → Service** and set the sales price or hourly rate.
3. When employees select the service during time entry, the **Billable (/hr)** field populates automatically.

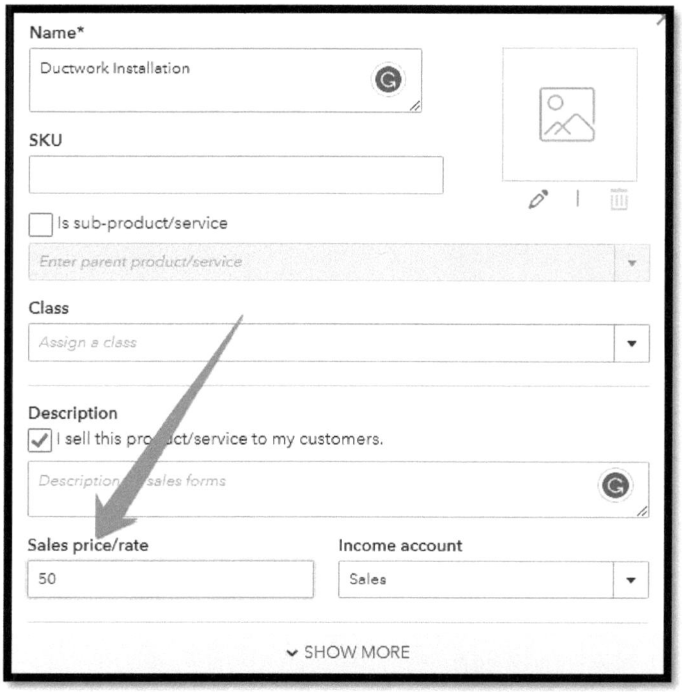

Example: A ductwork installation service is set at $50/hr.

Step 3: Add a Time Tracking User

If employees or contractors will track their own hours:

1. Click **cog wheel icon → Manage Users**.
2. Enter the user's name and email address.
3. Under **Roles**, select **Track time only**.
4. Click **Send invitation**. The user will receive an email to set up their QuickBooks account.

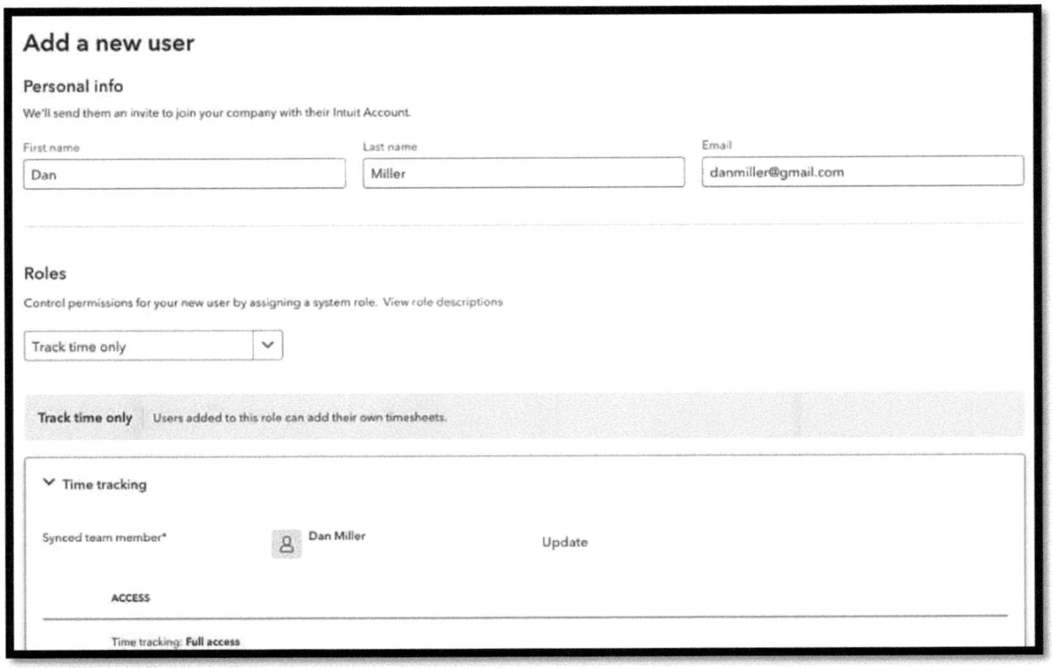

Note: If the user already has an Intuit account, they must log in using existing credentials.

QuickBooks Online allows **unlimited time tracking users**, which do **not** count toward your plan's user limit.

Step 4: Track Time Using Timesheets

You can record hours using:

- **Single-time activity timesheets:** For one-off or ad hoc tasks
- **Weekly timesheets:** For recurring tasks or scheduled work

To access timesheets, click **+ New → Single time activity** or **Weekly timesheet** from the dashboard.

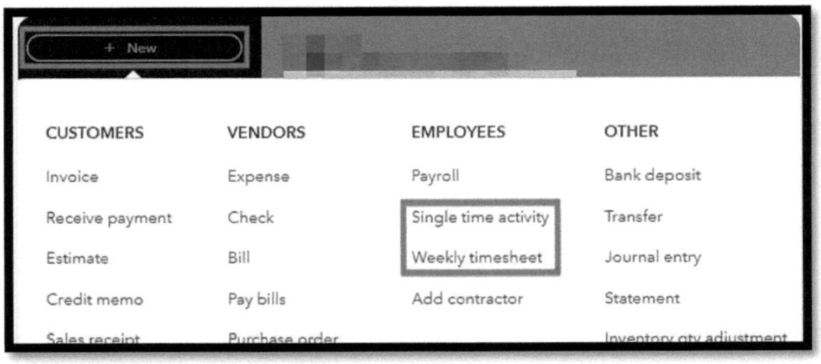

Using Single-Time Activity Timesheets

Single-time activity timesheets are ideal for ad hoc or one-off tasks. To create one, fill in the following fields:

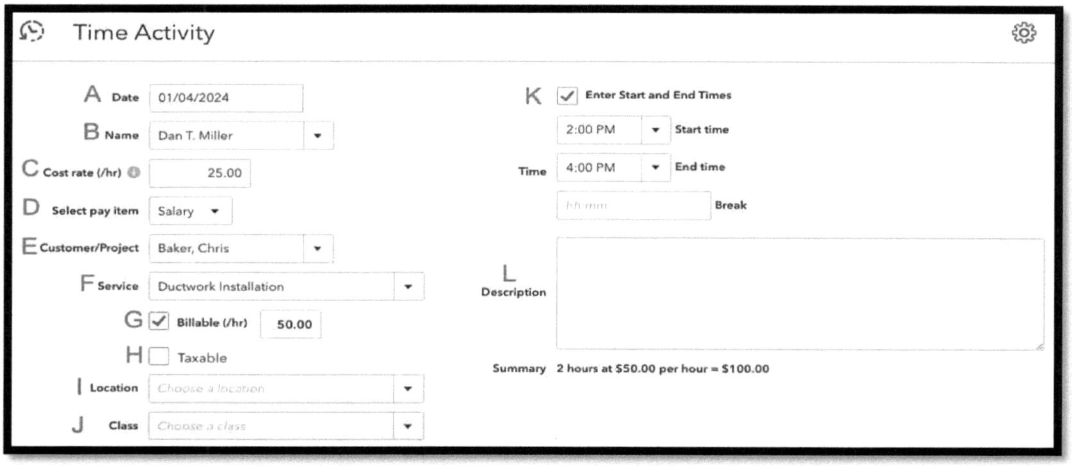

A. **Date:** Enter the date the activity occurred.
B. **Name:** Select the employee or contractor logging the time (e.g., Dan Miller).
C. **Cost Rate (/hr):** Optional—represents the hourly wage or cost to the company. Auto-populates if payroll is run in QuickBooks.
D. **Pay Item:** Choose the pay item associated with the activity (e.g., salary, vacation, or sick pay).
E. **Customer/Project:** Select the customer or project related to the activity (e.g., Chris Baker).
F. **Service:** Select the type of service performed (e.g., ductwork installation).
G. **Billable (/hr):** Auto-populates from the service item setup but can be adjusted manually.
H. **Taxable:** Indicate if the service is taxable.
I. **Location:** Optional—useful if the business has multiple service locations.
J. **Class:** Optional—track work by department, project, or category.
K. **Start and End Times:** Specify the time worked; alternatively, manually enter the duration.
L. **Description:** Add details about the specific task.

Click **Save** or **Save and new** to record the time.

Using Weekly Timesheets

Weekly timesheets track multiple tasks, customers, or projects over a week. Fill in the following:

A. **Employee/Contractor:** Indicate whose time is being tracked (e.g., Mark Baker).
B. **Tracking Period:** Enter the start and end dates of the week.
   Customer/Project: Select the relevant customer or project (e.g., Aaron Davies).
C. **Service:** Specify the type of service performed (e.g., A/C installation).
D. **Description:** Provide details about the tasks.
E. **Billable Rate:** Auto-populates from service item setup.
F. **Time Spent:** Enter hours spent on each activity per day.
G. **Total Hours:** Automatically sums all hours worked that week.
H. **Total Billable:** Shows total billable amount based on hours worked and rate.

Click **Save** or **Save and new** when done.

Step 5: Bill Clients for Tracked Time

1. Click **+ New → Invoice**.
2. Select the customer to bill. The billable hours for that customer appear on the right.
3. If billable time isn't showing, check the time entry for:
   - ❖ "Billable" box checked
   - ❖ Correct customer assigned
4. Click **Add** to include time on the invoice, review details, and then **Save** or **Save and send**.

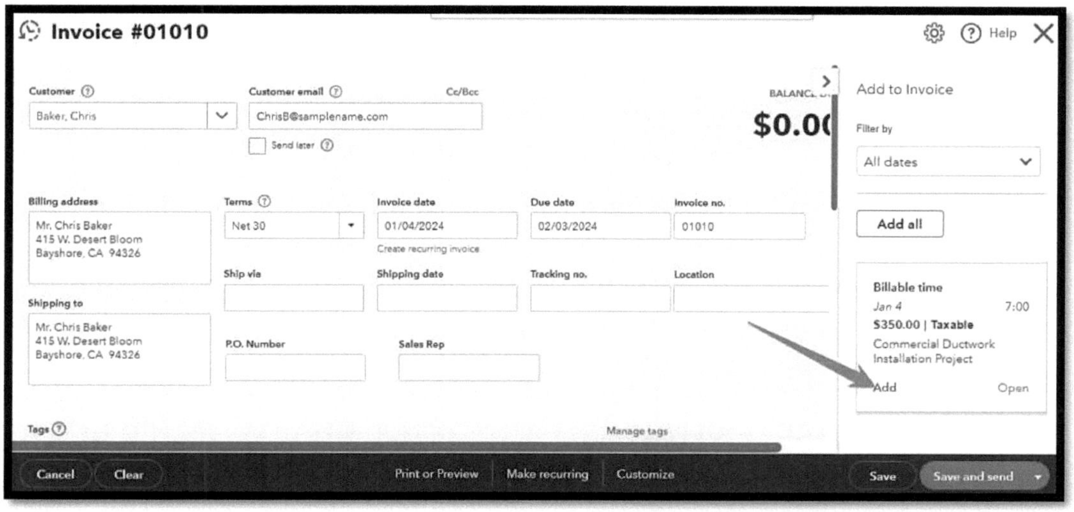

Step 6: Run Time Tracking Reports

To review billable hours and ensure accurate invoicing:

1. Go to **Reports → Search "time"**.

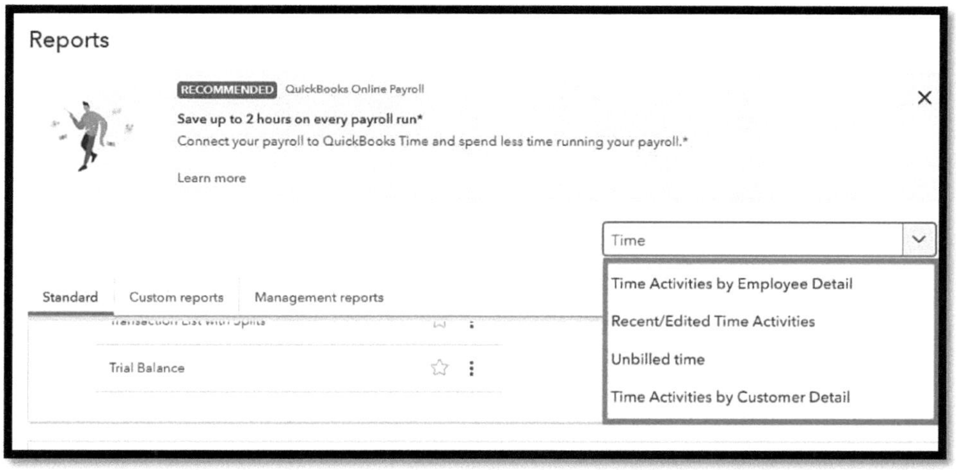

Available reports:

- **Time Activities by Employee Detail:** Breakdown of all logged time per employee.
- **Recent/Edited Time Activities:** Displays recently added or modified entries.
- **Unbilled Time:** Identifies hours not yet invoiced.
- **Time Activities by Customer Detail:** Detailed breakdown of hours by customer.

CHAPTER FIFTEEN

ADVANCED TOOLS AND TASKS

QuickBooks Online offers a range of advanced tools designed to streamline your workflow and simplify daily accounting tasks. By learning how to unlock and use these features you can reduce manual work, improve accuracy, and keep your financial operations running smoothly. Mastering these capabilities helps you stay organized, save time, and maintain better oversight of every part of your business.

HOW TO USE ENHANCED CUSTOM FIELDS IN QUICKBOOKS ONLINE ADVANCED

Enhanced custom fields in **QuickBooks Online Advanced** allow you to track virtually any type of information—whether it's the sales representative assigned to a sale, customer account numbers, project start and end dates, or other details specific to your business. These fields can be added to **customer and supplier profiles** as well as **transactions**, giving you more control and flexibility over your data.

Setting Up Enhanced Custom Fields

1. Create a New Custom Field

a. Select **Settings (⚙)**.
b. Click **Custom fields**.
c. Select **Add field**.

2. Name and Configure the Field

- Enter a **label** that reflects what you want to track (e.g., *Sales Rep*).
- Choose the **type of data**—text, number, date, or a **drop-down list**.
  - For consistent entries (like sales reps), a dropdown is ideal so you don't manually type names every time.

3. Assign Where the Field Will Appear

You can choose to show the field on:

- **Customer records**
- **Supplier records**
- **Transactions**

For example: If you're tracking *Sales Rep*, you may only need it on **sales transactions** such as invoices or sales receipts.

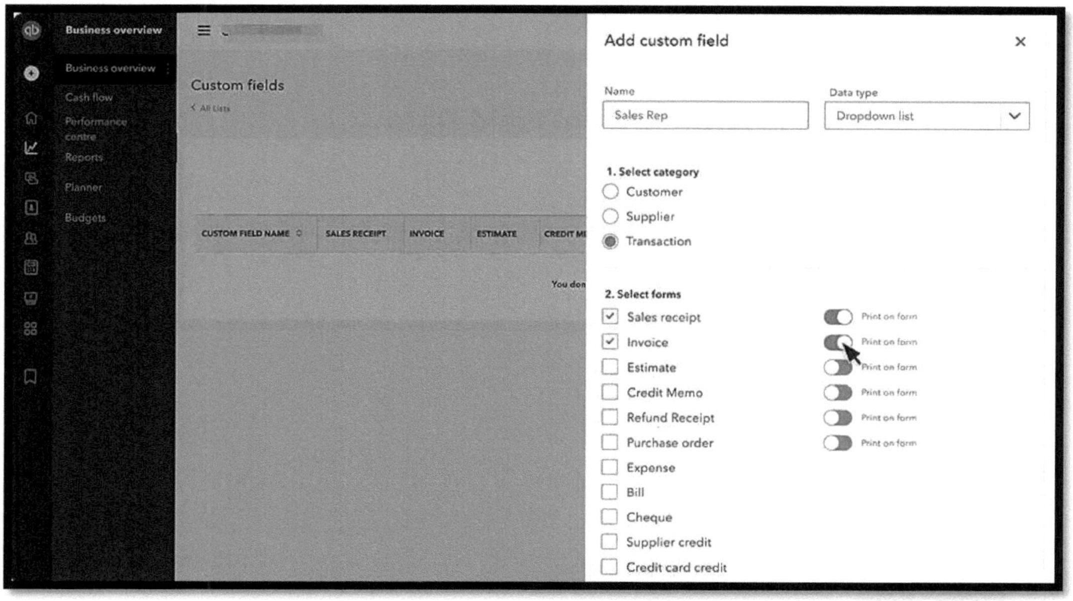

4. Choose Display Options

- Select **Print on form** if you want the field to appear on emailed or printed documents.
- Save your custom field.

After saving, you'll see a list showing:

- A **checkmark** ✔ indicating the field is available on a form
- A **printer icon** 🖶 showing that the field prints on the form

Using Enhanced Custom Fields in Transactions

When entering a transaction:

1. Create an invoice, sales receipt, or other form as usual.
2. Fill in your new custom field (e.g., select the sales rep from the dropdown).

Once you've used the field across several transactions, QuickBooks will allow you to filter, sort, and group reports using this new data.

Running Reports with Custom Field Data

Example: Sales by Sales Rep

1. Start with a standard report such as **Sales by Customer Summary** or **Sales by Customer Detail**.

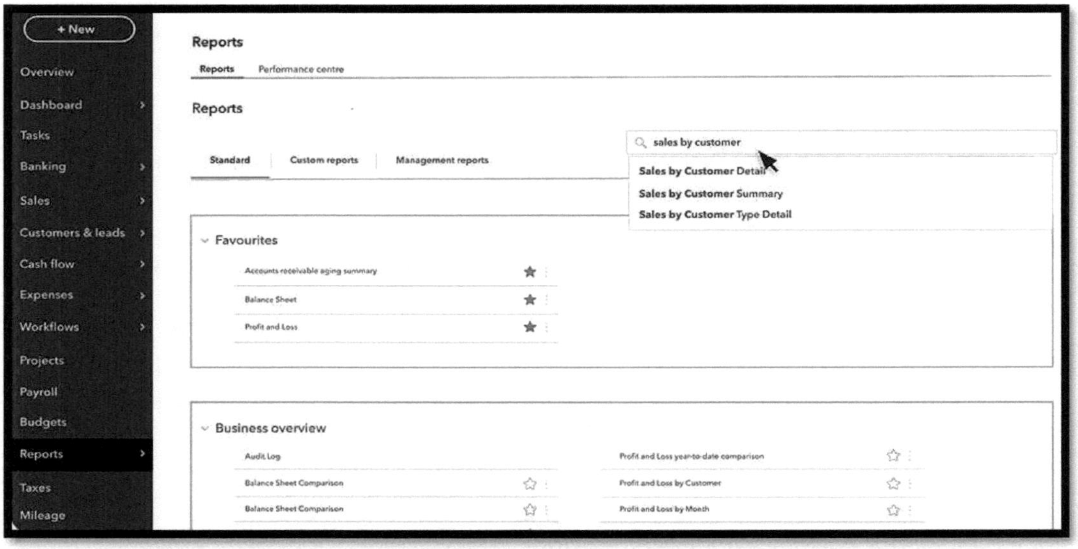

2. Open the **Group by** dropdown.
3. Select your custom field (e.g., *Sales Rep*).

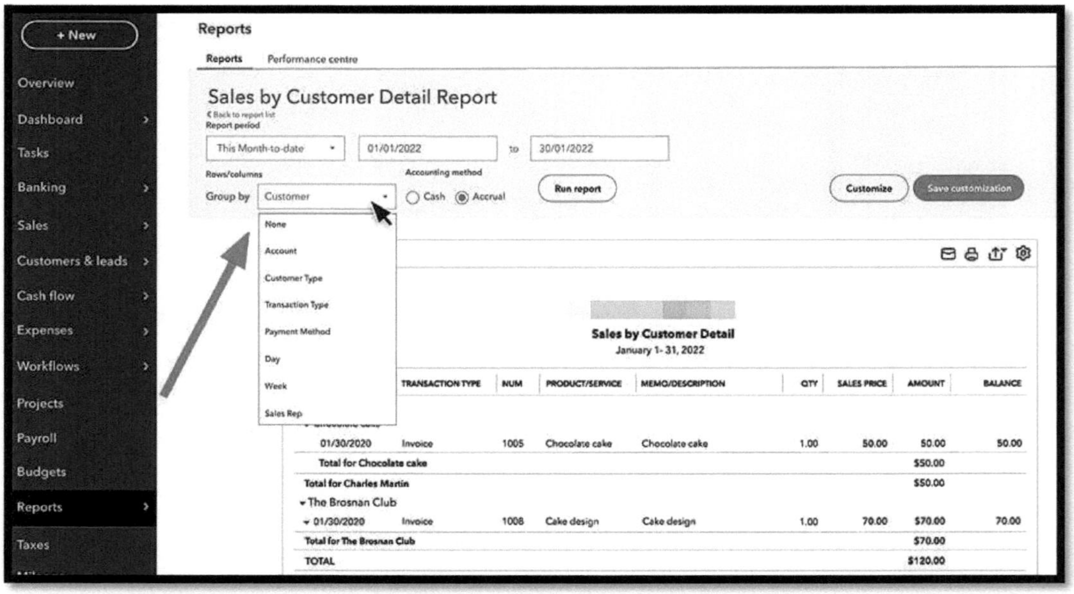

The report will reorganize itself to show:

- Sales grouped by each sales rep
- Subtotals for each rep
- A clearer picture of team performance

You can then **save the customized report** to access it anytime.

Why Enhanced Custom Fields Matter

Enhanced custom fields let you:

- Track any business-specific data
- Improve reporting accuracy
- Build targeted, meaningful reports
- Gain insights that standard QuickBooks fields can't capture

With these tools, you can tailor QuickBooks Online Advanced to work the way your business works—giving you more control, better visibility, and smarter reporting.

HOW TO PROCESS BATCH EXPENSES IN QUICKBOOKS ONLINE

Managing large volumes of expenses manually can be slow, repetitive, and prone to errors. QuickBooks Online simplifies this by allowing you to process multiple expenses at once using batch actions directly from the **Transactions** tab. This feature streamlines data entry, improves accuracy, and reduces administrative workload—especially useful for businesses dealing with recurring or similar transactions.

Benefits of Batch Processing in QuickBooks Online

Batch expense processing helps you:

- **Save time** by categorizing multiple transactions simultaneously.
- **Increase efficiency** when handling recurring or similar expenses.
- **Maintain accurate records** with consistent categorization.
- **Reduce errors** and minimize inconsistencies in financial data.

For business owners managing high transaction volumes, batch actions can significantly speed up bookkeeping while improving reliability.

Step-by-Step Guide: How to Batch Process Expenses

1. Navigate to Transactions > Banking

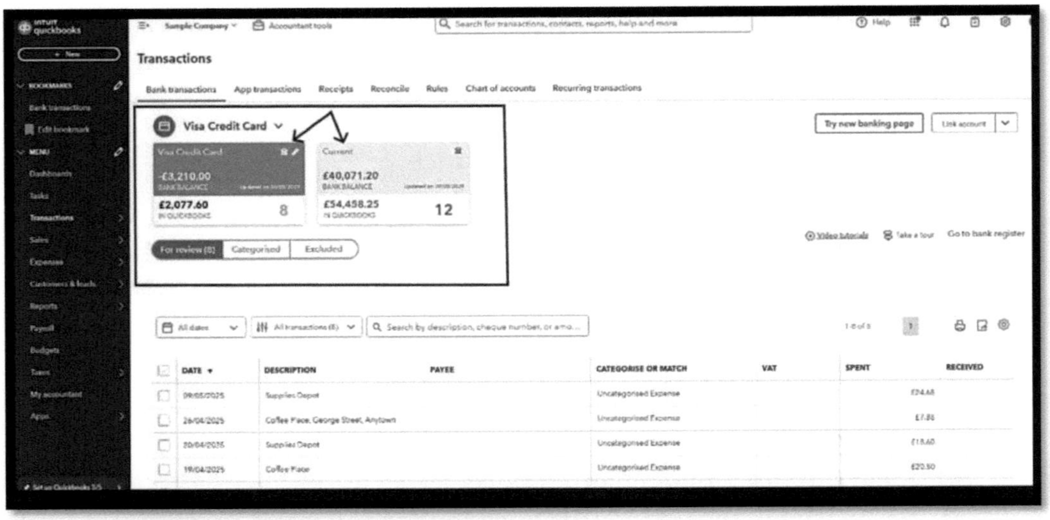

From the left-hand menu, select **Transactions**, then **Bank Transactions**, and choose the appropriate bank or credit card account.

2. Review transactions in the "For Review" tab

This tab displays all imported bank feed transactions that have not yet been categorized.

3. Select similar transactions

Use the checkboxes to select multiple expenses that share the same vendor, category, or purpose.

You can also search based on similar bank descriptions to quickly group related items.

4. Click "Edit"

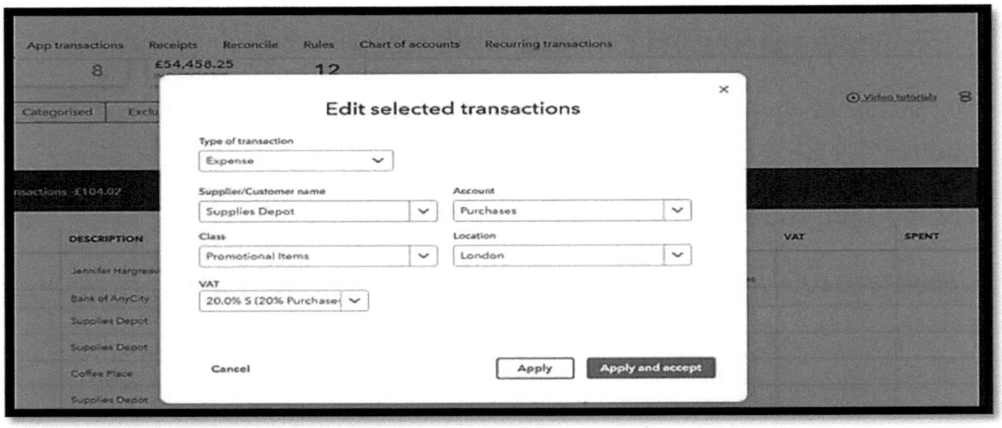

An edit panel will appear, allowing you to apply shared details to all selected transactions:

- Transaction type
- Supplier/Customer
- Expense account
- Class or Location (if enabled)
- VAT/Tax code

5. Click "Apply and Accept"

QuickBooks will automatically post all selected transactions using the batch settings you provided.

Why You Should Use Batch Expense Entry

If you're still entering expenses individually, adopting batch processing can dramatically improve your workflow. It's a small adjustment that delivers major time savings and ensures greater consistency across your financial data.

HOW TO DELETE AN INVOICE

QuickBooks Online makes it easy to delete an invoice, but keep in mind that once deleted, the invoice is permanently removed from your records. If you're certain you want it gone, follow these steps:

Step-by-Step Instructions

1. **Log In to QuickBooks Online:** Sign in using your QuickBooks Online credentials.
2. **Navigate to the Invoices Section:** From the left menu, select **Sales**, then click **Invoices**.
3. **Find the Invoice You Want to Delete:** Use the **search bar** or **filter options** to quickly locate the invoice.
4. **Open the Invoice:** Click the invoice to view its details.
5. **Delete the Invoice:** At the bottom of the invoice window, select **More**, then choose **Delete**.
6. **Confirm the Action:** A confirmation message will appear. Click **Yes** to permanently remove the invoice from your records.

HOW TO SET UP DEPRECIATION ON FIXED ASSETS IN QUICKBOOKS

Depreciation is an accounting method used to spread the cost of a tangible asset over its useful life. Although depreciation reduces the value of an asset on your books, it **does not affect cash flow**—it's simply an accounting entry that allocates the cost of long-term assets to expense over time.

Key Depreciation Concepts

- **Useful Life:** The estimated number of years the business expects to use the asset.
- **Salvage Value:** The estimated resale value of the asset at the end of its useful life.
- **Depreciable Base:** The amount that will be depreciated over the asset's life. **Formula:**
  Cost of Asset – Salvage Value = Depreciable Base
- **Depreciation Schedule:** A plan showing how much depreciation will be recorded each year based on the chosen depreciation method.
- **Common Depreciation Methods:**
  - Straight-line
  - Units of production
  - Sum-of-the-years'-digits
  - Double-declining balance
  - MACRS (used for U.S. tax purposes)

Understanding Fixed Assets in QuickBooks

A fixed asset—sometimes called a long-term or non-current asset—is a physical item your business uses for more than one year. These assets help generate revenue but are *not* intended for resale. Their cost is recorded on the balance sheet rather than immediately expensed.

Examples include:

- Buildings and land
- Machinery and equipment
- Office furniture
- Vehicles
- Computers and long-term software

QuickBooks allows you to track:

- Depreciation
- Asset location and serial numbers
- Warranty details
- Mileage (for vehicles)

Accurate asset tracking supports better financial reporting and tax preparation.

Creating a Fixed Asset Account in QuickBooks

Follow these steps to set up the account:

1. Go to **Settings → Chart of Accounts → New**
2. Under **Account Type**, choose **Fixed Assets** or **Other Assets**
3. Select the appropriate **Detail Type** (e.g., Vehicles, Machinery, Buildings)
4. Name the account and check **Track depreciation of this asset**
5. Enter the asset's **Original Cost** and **as-of date** (leave blank if financed through a loan)
6. Click **Save and Close**

Setting Up Depreciation in QuickBooks

QuickBooks doesn't automatically calculate depreciation unless you're using **QuickBooks Online Advanced Fixed Assets**, so you typically record depreciation manually via journal entries.

There are two parts:

Step 1: Check if a Depreciation Account Already Exists

1. Go to **Settings → Chart of Accounts**
2. Search "Depreciation"
3. If you see an account named **Depreciation** with
   - *Type:* Other Expense
   - *Detail Type:* Depreciation

   ...then you can skip to Step 3.

Step 2: Create a Depreciation Expense Account (If Needed)

1. Go to **Settings → Chart of Accounts → New**
2. Select **Other Expense** as the Account Type
3. Choose **Depreciation** as the Detail Type
4. Name the account (e.g., "Equipment Depreciation")
5. Save the account

Step 3: Record Depreciation with a Journal Entry

After confirming depreciation totals with your accountant (usually at year-end):

1. Select **+ New → Journal Entry**
2. **Line 1:**
   - Account: *Asset account (e.g., Equipment)*

- ❖ Amount: Enter depreciation amount under **Credit**

3. **Line 2:**
    - ❖ Account: *Depreciation Expense*
    - ❖ Amount: Enter the same depreciation amount under **Debit**
4. Save the entry

This entry reduces the value of the asset while recognizing the annual depreciation expense.

Final Tips for Accurate Depreciation Tracking

- ❖ **Consult your accountant** for correct methods and useful life estimates (especially to match IRS Form 4562 for taxes).
- ❖ **Update your fixed asset list regularly**, especially when assets are retired or sold.
- ❖ **Keep depreciation schedules organized** to avoid mismatches between book and tax records.

CHAPTER SIXTEEN

ADMIN TOOLS IN QUICKBOOKS ADVANCED

Mastering the admin tools in QuickBooks Online Advanced is essential for keeping your accounting system efficient, secure, and scalable. These tools give you greater control over user permissions, workflow automation, data management, and reporting—allowing you to streamline operations as your business grows. By understanding how to configure roles, manage data, and customize workflows, you can maximize productivity and ensure your financial processes run smoothly and accurately.

HOW TO DOWNLOAD AND USE THE QUICKBOOKS ONLINE DESKTOP APP

Installing the QuickBooks Online desktop app is an excellent way to streamline your accounting workflow. The app gives you faster access to your books, smoother navigation, and a distraction-free workspace—all while syncing with your QuickBooks Online data in real time. It's especially useful for managing invoicing, expenses, and reconciliations without relying on a browser.

Before You Install: What You Need

To ensure the app works properly, make sure the following requirements are met:

- **Your company file is already migrated** from QuickBooks Desktop (if applicable).
- **You have an active QuickBooks Online subscription** and valid login details.
- **Your computer meets system requirements**, including a supported version of Windows or macOS.
- **A stable internet connection**, since data syncs continuously.
- **Administrator access** to install applications on your device.
- **Compatible third-party apps**, if you use external integrations.

These steps help prevent installation issues and ensure that the app runs smoothly.

Downloading the QuickBooks Online Desktop App

For Windows Users

1. Sign in to **QuickBooks Online Advanced** or **QuickBooks Online Accountant**.
2. Go to **Settings** ⚙ **→ Get the desktop app**.
3. QuickBooks may install the app automatically and place a shortcut on your desktop.

   - ❖ If not, you'll be prompted to **save the installer**. Run the setup file afterward.
4. Launch the app from your desktop shortcut.
5. Enter your **user ID and password**, then click **Sign In**.
6. Choose the QuickBooks company file you want to open.
7. On your first launch, choose your display preference:
   - ❖ **Yes, let's go** — if you prefer a layout similar to QuickBooks Desktop.
   - ❖ **No, go standard view** — if you're comfortable with the QBO interface.

Note: French users must switch their language setting inside QuickBooks after installation.

Once signed in, the app will keep you logged in for an extended period unless you manually sign out.

For Mac Users

1. Sign in to your QuickBooks Online Advanced or Accountant account.
2. Go to **Settings** ⚙ **→ Get the desktop app**.
3. If the app doesn't install automatically, **save the file**, then open it.
4. Move the QuickBooks app into your **Applications** folder.
5. Open the setup file and install the app.
6. Sign in using your QuickBooks Online credentials.
7. Select your company file if you have more than one.
8. Choose your initial display preference:
   - ❖ **Yes, let's go** for a Desktop-style view
   - ❖ **No, go standard view** for the regular QBO layout

After that, the app will launch directly into your company file without repeated logins unless you sign out.

Troubleshooting Tip

If you experience issues with the desktop app, first check whether the same issue occurs in the **browser version of QuickBooks Online**. If it does, the problem may not be related to the app itself.

Work on Multiple Pages, Companies, or Tasks at the Same Time

The QuickBooks Online Desktop App makes multitasking easier by letting you open multiple pages or companies at once.

How to Navigate Multiple Tabs and Companies

- **Open multiple companies:** Each company appears in its own tab group. Click the **+** icon next to the current company tab group, then choose the company you want to open.
- **Add new pages:** Click the **+** icon beside an existing page tab to open additional screens within the same company.
- **Use split-screen mode:** Select **Split screen** to view two tasks side by side. The active pane is outlined in green.

Troubleshooting the QuickBooks Online Desktop App

If the app isn't running correctly, try the following steps:

- **Restart the app:** Close and reopen it to clear temporary glitches.
- **Reinstall if needed:** For installation errors or persistent bugs, uninstall and reinstall the app.
- **Check for updates:** Ensure your operating system and the app are up to date.
- **Verify your internet connection:** A weak or unstable connection can interrupt syncing.

If the issue appears in both the app **and** your browser, the problem is likely unrelated to the desktop app.

Benefits of Using the QuickBooks Online App on Your Computer

Installing the desktop app enhances productivity and offers a smoother QuickBooks experience compared to using a web browser.

Key Benefits

1. Faster Performance: The desktop app is optimized for speed—faster load times, quicker tab switching, and smoother navigation.

2. Multi-Tab and Multi-Window Support: Open multiple pages, reports, or even companies without browser clutter or tab confusion.

3. Automatic Updates: The app updates itself in the background so you always have the latest features and security enhancements.

4. Distraction-Free Workspace: Because it's a standalone application, you avoid browser notifications, pop-ups, and unrelated tabs.

5. Productivity-Boosting Shortcuts: QuickBooks-specific keyboard shortcuts make tasks like data entry, invoicing, and reporting faster.

6. Extended Login Sessions: Stay signed in for up to six months—ideal for users who access QuickBooks throughout the day.

7. Real-Time Desktop Notifications: Receive instant alerts for transactions, reminders, approvals, and updates.

8. Better Operating System Integration: Enjoy native features such as drag-and-drop uploads, improved printing options, and stable performance on both Windows and macOS.

Overall, the QuickBooks Online Desktop App helps you work smarter, faster, and with greater focus.

Frequently Asked Questions about QuickBooks Online Desktop App

1. What are the system requirements for the QuickBooks Online Desktop App?

Windows:

- Windows 10 (64-bit) or Windows 11
- Latest system updates installed

Mac:

- macOS High Sierra (10.13) or newer
- Compatible with latest versions (e.g., Monterey, Ventura)

2. Is the QuickBooks App the same as QuickBooks Online?

No—here's the difference:

- **QuickBooks Online:** Cloud-based and accessed through any browser.
- **QuickBooks Online App:** A desktop application that connects to your QBO data and offers features such as
    - longer sign-in sessions,
    - multi-tab navigation, and
    - keyboard shortcuts.

The app doesn't store your data; it simply makes QuickBooks Online easier and faster to use.

3. Can I use both QuickBooks Online and QuickBooks Desktop?

Yes, but they are **separate products**. They don't sync automatically. If you move data between them, you must do so manually or use third-party tools. To avoid confusion, stick to one platform consistently.

4. How do I use QuickBooks Online on a new computer?

Since QBO is cloud-based, no data transfer is required.

Simply:

1. Open a browser on the new computer.
2. Go to the QuickBooks website.
3. Sign in with your existing email and password.

Optional: Install the QuickBooks Online Desktop App

1. Download the app for Windows or Mac.
2. Install it and sign in.

HOW TO BACK UP QUICKBOOKS ONLINE DATA

QuickBooks Online does **not** include a recycle bin, and once data is deleted, it's gone permanently. To prevent data loss from mistakes, system issues, or unauthorized changes, every business using QuickBooks Online should have a reliable backup system in place.

Ways to Back Up QuickBooks Online Data

You can protect your QuickBooks Online data using three main methods:

1. **Native Backup Tool:** *(Available only with QuickBooks Online Advanced)* Automatically backs up and restores company data.
2. **Exporting Data Manually:** Download reports, lists, and transactions for local storage.
3. **Third-Party Backup Applications:** Automated, incremental backups of transactions, attachments, and settings.

Backing Up Data Using QuickBooks Online's Native Backup Tool

The built-in **Backup & Restore** feature in QuickBooks Online Advanced allows you to save, schedule, and restore your company data. It is included **only** with the **Advanced** plan—Simple Start, Essentials, and Plus users do not have access to this tool.

Important

If you're using the *new interface*, your company begins backing up automatically once you open the Backup & Restore tool. No manual connection is required.

Steps to Back Up QuickBooks Online (New Interface)

Most users will see this layout:

1. **Sign in as an admin** to your QuickBooks Online company.
2. Click the **Gear icon**, then choose **Back up company**.

(You may be prompted to sign in again to authorize access.)

3. When the Backup & Restore dashboard opens, your company is already connected.
   — Automatic backups run every 24 hours.
4. To start a backup manually, select **Run manual backup**.

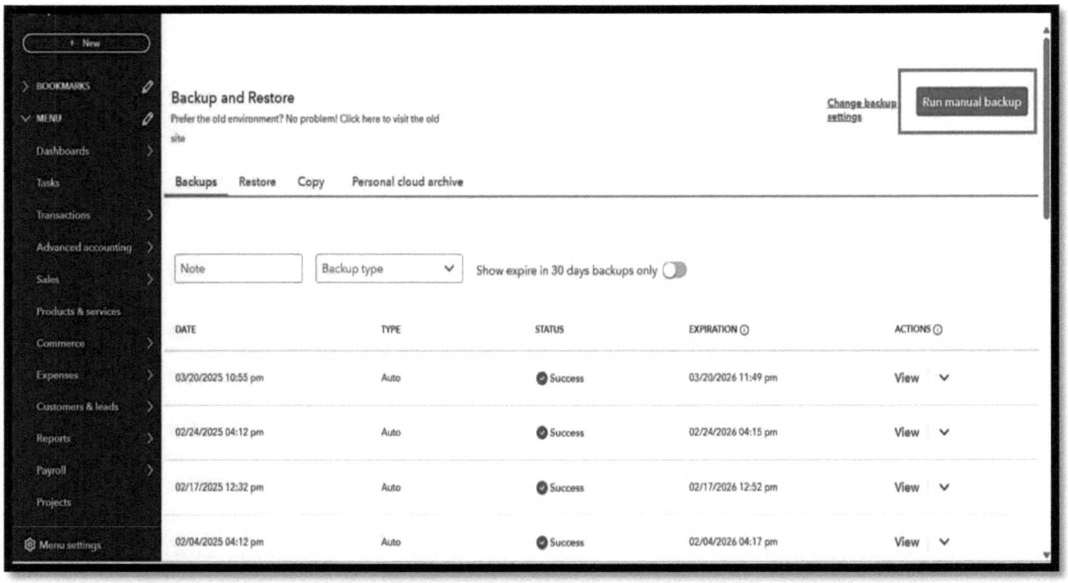

5. Choose your backup type—**Incremental, Full, or Complete**—and click **Backup**.

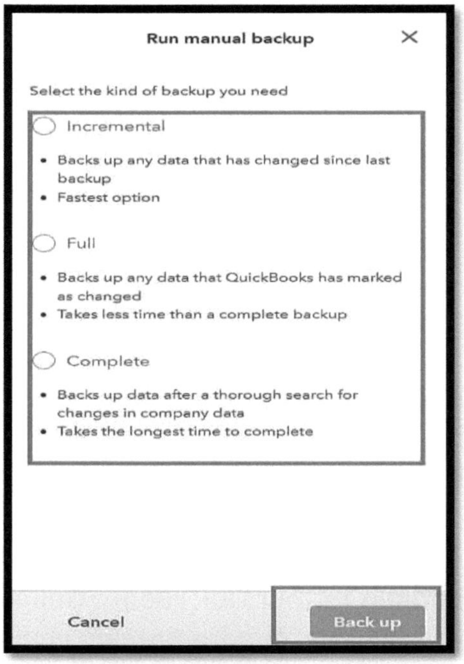

Steps to Back Up QuickBooks Online (Old Interface)

Choose **"Prefer the old environment?"** if it appears:

1. On the Backup & Restore homepage, select the company you want to back up.
   If it doesn't appear, click **Add Company**, choose the company, and select **Next**.

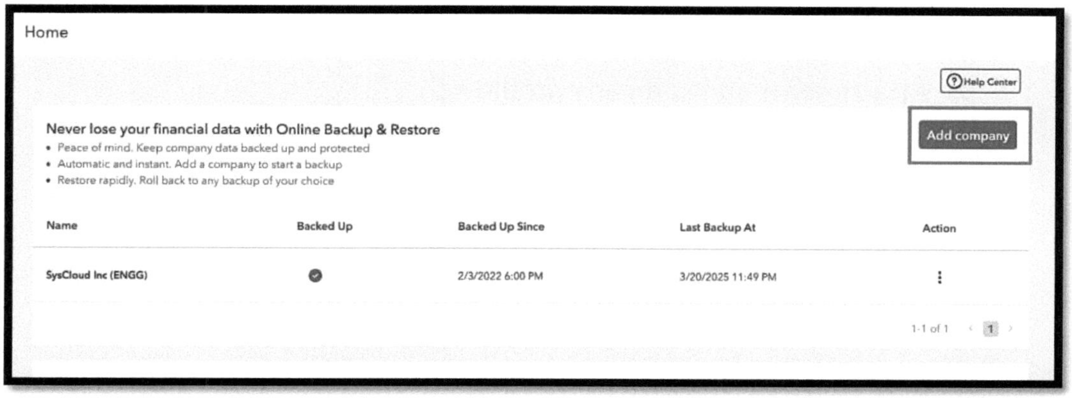

2. Click **Connect** to authorize access.
3. Next to the company name, click **Enable Backup**.
   — QuickBooks will automatically back up your data every day.
   — All changes are tracked, so you can roll back your file to a point before any error or deletion occurred.

What Data *Is* Backed Up by the QuickBooks Online Backup Tool?

QuickBooks Online's native backup tool automatically captures most of the essential financial and operational data in your company file. The backed-up information falls into three major categories:

1. Transaction Data

The tool secures nearly all day-to-day financial activity, including:

- Invoices, estimates, sales receipts, and payments
- Deposits, bills, bill payments, and vendor credits
- Credit memos, refund receipts, and journal entries
- Purchase orders, purchases, and time activities
- Transfers and other core financial records

2. List (Master) Data

These records define how your accounting system is structured:

- ❖ Accounts, budgets, classes, and currencies
- ❖ Customers, vendors (except Tax ID), employees (excluding SSNs)
- ❖ Departments, items, payment methods, and terms
- ❖ Tax agencies, tax rates, and tax codes

3. Other Company Data

Additional system-level information backed up includes:

- ❖ Attachments and company profile info
- ❖ Preferences, entitlements, and exchange rates
- ❖ Payroll activity (stored as journal entries)
- ❖ Inventory shrinkage and adjustments (also saved as journal entries)

What Data Does *Not* Get Backed Up?

Some important data types are excluded from QuickBooks Online's native backup system:

- ❖ QuickBooks Online Payments data
- ❖ Customer types and price rules
- ❖ Delayed credits and delayed charges
- ❖ Recurring transactions
- ❖ Bank feeds, including rules and linked transactions
- ❖ Reconciliation reports
- ❖ Account-based billable expenses
- ❖ Item-based billable expenses with markup
- ❖ Custom reports and custom form templates
- ❖ Audit log entries

These exclusions mean certain workflow-critical information must be safeguarded or documented outside of the native backup tool.

Limitations of the QuickBooks Online Backup & Restore Tool

While helpful, the tool has several functional constraints:

- ❖ Only users on the **QuickBooks Online Advanced** plan can access it—which increases subscription costs.
- ❖ When restoring, you can only roll the file back to the **most recent backup**, not earlier points.

- ❖ Although the system tracks all changes, **deletions cannot be easily reviewed** without manually checking the audit log.
- ❖ **Individual transactions cannot be restored**—only entire datasets.
- ❖ Several important data types (listed above) are not included in backups.

Saving and Scheduling Backups to Google Drive

After setting up automatic backups via the Backup and Restore app, users can also export backups to Google Drive for additional security.

How to Link Google Drive

1. Log into QuickBooks Online Advanced. Go to **Gear Icon → Back up company**.
2. Open the **Personal Cloud Archive** section.
3. Select **Export Backup**.

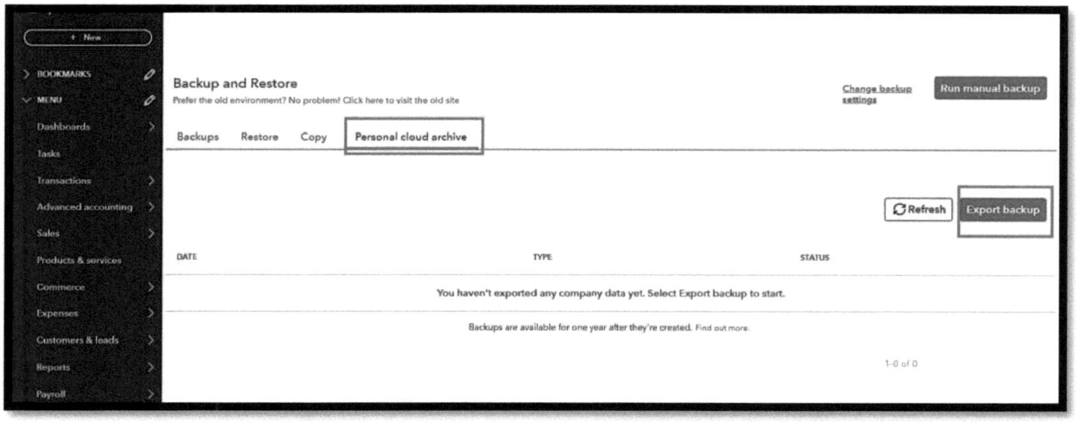

4. Choose **Google Drive** and grant authorization.

Limitations of Using Google Drive with the Local Backup Feature

- ❖ Only QuickBooks Online Advanced users can access the Personal Cloud Archive.
- ❖ Exports to Google Drive **must be done manually**—automatic scheduling isn't supported.
- ❖ Additional Google Drive storage costs may apply if your backup files exceed the free limit.
- ❖ Google Drive backups **cannot be restored directly** into QuickBooks Online; users must download the file and restore it manually through the Backup and Restore tool.

Exporting QuickBooks Online Data to Create a Local Backup

If your organization wants a simple way to safeguard QuickBooks Online (QBO) data, you can manually export key reports and lists to create a local backup. Although this method isn't as comprehensive as full backup solutions, it provides an extra layer of protection—especially for users on Simple Start, Essentials, or Plus plans.

How to Export QuickBooks Online Data

Follow these steps to manually download your company data:

1. **Sign in** to your QuickBooks Online account.
2. Click the **Gear icon (Settings)** and select **"Export data."**
3. In the Export Data window, choose a **date range** (All dates, Custom, Last quarter, Year-to-date, or Last year).

4. **Deselect** any items you don't want included.
5. Click **Export to Excel**.
   - ❖ QBO will create a ZIP file containing your reports and lists, which will automatically save to your computer's Downloads folder.

What Data Can Be Exported from QuickBooks Online?

QuickBooks allows exporting a mix of financial reports and list data.

Reports

- General Ledger
- Profit and Loss
- Balance Sheet
- Trial Balance
- Journal Report

List Data

- Customers
- Employees
- Vendors

Limitations of Using Manual Export for Backup

While exporting data helps preserve essential information, it has several constraints:

- **No automation:** You must export the data regularly and manually.
- **Organization required:** You need to keep your export files organized to quickly retrieve a specific backup if something is deleted or overwritten.
- **Limited formats:** Data is only available in **Excel** and **PDF**, not in a format that can be restored directly into QuickBooks.
- **Not a full backup:** Only certain reports and lists export—many transaction-level details and settings are not included.

Using a Third-Party Cloud Backup Solution (SysCloud)

For a more complete and automated backup, third-party tools like **SysCloud** provide continuous cloud backups for multiple QuickBooks Online companies. SysCloud captures transaction-level data, maintains multiple backup versions, and makes it easy to restore specific items when needed.

Data Backed Up by SysCloud

Transactions

- Bills & Bill Payments
- Credit Memos
- Deposits
- Estimates
- Invoices
- Journal Entries
- Payments
- Purchases & Purchase Orders
- Refund Receipts
- Sales Receipts
- Time Activities
- Transfers
- Vendor Credits

List Data

- Accounts
- Attachments
- Classes
- Customers
- Departments
- Employees (excluding SSN)
- Items
- Journal Codes (France only)
- Payment Methods
- Terms
- Vendors

How to Set Up SysCloud Backup for QuickBooks Online

*Only the **primary owner** of the QBO account can configure SysCloud backups.*

1. Log in to your **SysCloud** account.

2. Go to the **Jobs** tab on the top menu.
3. Enter a **job name** and optional description, then click **Next**.
4. Under **QuickBooks Online**, click **Connect** to authorize access.
5. Select **QuickBooks Online** as the cloud source and click **Select** under **Scope**.

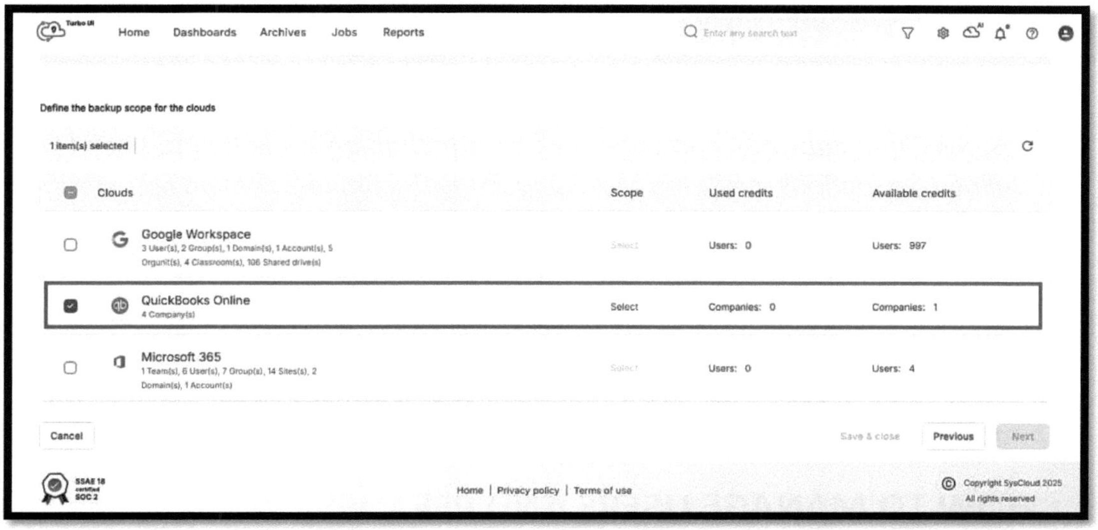

6. Choose which **companies** you want backed up.
   - ❖ A company can appear in **only one** job.
7. Under **Apps**, configure the **retention period**:
   - ❖ You may keep items indefinitely or specify how long data should be stored.
8. Add any optional add-ons and adjust their settings if needed.
9. Click **Start backup** to begin the automatic cloud backup process.

FREQUENTLY ASKED QUESTIONS

Does QuickBooks Online have a native backup solution?

*Yes—QuickBooks Online offers a built-in backup and restore tool. However, it is **not a full backup solution**. While it can back up company-wide data, it **cannot restore individual transactions, attachments, or files**, nor can it restore to an earlier point-in-time.*

*QuickBooks' own support documentation confirms that their tool only restores the entire company file to the **last backup date**, not specific items. Because of these limitations, many businesses choose a third-party cloud backup provider for comprehensive protection.*

Do I need to back up QuickBooks Online?

*Absolutely. Any data deleted in QuickBooks Online—whether by mistake, user error, or malicious activity—is **permanently lost**. QuickBooks Online has **no recycle bin** or built-in recovery for deleted items.*

If your company relies on QBO for financial records, audits, compliance, and daily operations, maintaining a reliable backup strategy is essential.

Does SysCloud back up attachments associated with transactions?

Yes. SysCloud captures and preserves all attachable files linked to your QuickBooks Online transactions, ensuring that supporting documents remain recoverable.

Can I access my SysCloud backups after I unsubscribe from QuickBooks Online?

Yes. Your backed-up data remains fully accessible in SysCloud for as long as your SysCloud subscription is active. You can log in anytime, from anywhere, to review or restore your historical backups—regardless of your QuickBooks Online subscription status.

HOW TO MANAGE USERS AND PERMISSIONS IN QUICKBOOKS ONLINE

Managing user access in QuickBooks Online (QBO) is essential for safeguarding your financial data while enabling your team to work efficiently. Properly configured user roles and permissions ensure everyone has the access they need without compromising sensitive information.

Adding a New User

1. **Access Manage Users:** Click the **Gear icon (⚙)** in the upper-right corner, then select **Manage Users** under the "Your Company" section.

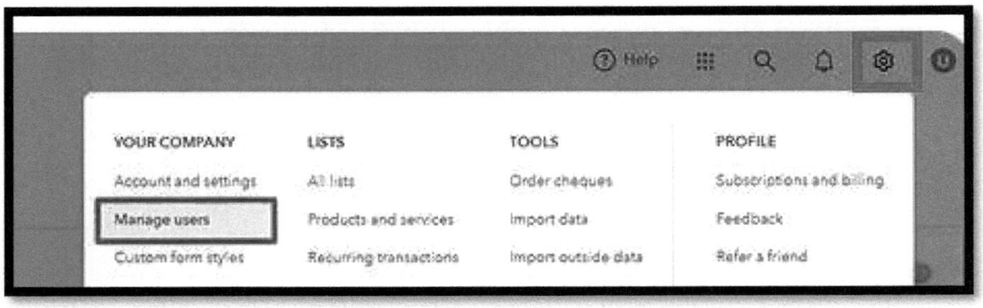

2. **Add User:** Click **Add User**, then enter the user's name and email address. QuickBooks will send an invitation, allowing the user to create their login credentials.

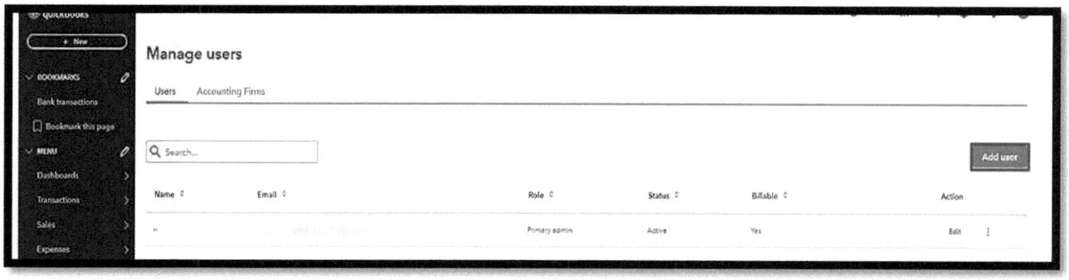

3. **Assign Roles:** Review role descriptions by clicking **View Role Description** for details on each access level.

Understanding User Roles

QBO offers multiple user types tailored to different responsibilities:

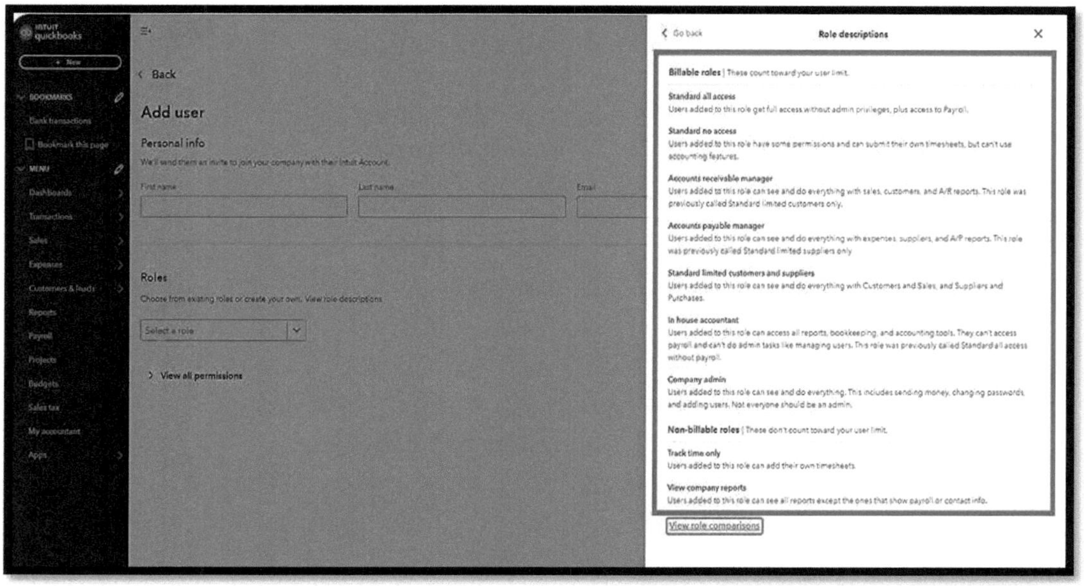

- **Company Admin:** Full access to all features, including user management, company settings, and financial data. Ideal for owners, senior managers, or accountants requiring complete control.

  Example: As the owner of a catering business, a company admin can manage inventory, assign permissions, and oversee all operations.

- **Standard User:** Customized access based on specific tasks. For example, a standard user may enter expenses and create invoices but cannot view payroll or reports. Perfect for team members handling defined areas of finance.
- **Reports Only User:** Can view and run reports but cannot edit transactions or settings. Suitable for analysts or stakeholders needing financial insights without modifying data.
- **Time Tracking User:** Can log hours worked but has no access to other QBO features. Ideal for employees or contractors tracking time for payroll or invoicing.
- **Accountant User:** Provides full accounting access while restricting control over user management and company settings. This is perfect for external accountants managing bookkeeping or tax preparation without full admin privileges.
  Example: An external accountant can reconcile accounts and prepare tax returns while the owner maintains control over sensitive company settings.

Managing and Adjusting Permissions

Once a user's role is assigned, click **Send Invite**. The user will receive an email to join your QuickBooks account. As team members' responsibilities evolve, you may need to update their permissions to match their new roles.

QuickBooks Online makes it easy to manage user access anytime, ensuring your team has the right permissions while keeping sensitive data secure.

Editing and Removing Users

1. **Access Manage Users:** Click the **Gear icon ( ) → Manage Users** under "Your Company."
2. **Edit Permissions:** Click **Edit** next to a user's name to adjust their access as their role changes. For example, a standard user can be upgraded to company admin if they take on additional responsibilities.
3. **Remove Users:** If a user no longer needs access, select **Delete User**. Removing inactive users helps maintain security and reduces the risk of unauthorized changes.

Best Practices for Managing Permissions

- **Regularly review permissions** to ensure they reflect each user's current responsibilities.
- **Limit access** to sensitive areas such as payroll, banking, and tax information to only those who require it.
- **Use the Audit Log** to monitor user activity. QuickBooks Online tracks all actions, including logins, transaction changes, and updates to settings.

Using the Audit Log

1. Go to **Gear icon ( )** → **Audit Log** under the Tools section.
2. Review a chronological list of activities within your QuickBooks account.
3. **Filter by user, date, or activity type** to locate specific actions quickly.
4. Click on an activity for more details or **export the log** to a spreadsheet for further analysis or record-keeping.

Tip: Regularly monitor the audit log to ensure all changes are authorized and investigate any unusual activity promptly to prevent potential issues.

STEP-BY-STEP GUIDE TO CHANGING TRANSACTION TYPES IN QUICKBOOKS ONLINE

Accurate financial records are essential for any business. Changing transaction types in QuickBooks Online helps ensure your data remains precise. Follow this step-by-step guide to update transaction types efficiently.

Step 1: Log in to QuickBooks Online

1. Open your web browser and go to the **QuickBooks Online login page**.
2. Enter your **User ID** and **Password**.
3. Click **Sign In**.

Ensure you have the necessary permissions to modify transactions. Only administrators or users with full access can change transaction types.

Step 2: Navigate to the Transaction List

1. From the Dashboard, select **Transactions** on the left-hand menu.
2. Choose **Expenses** or **Sales**, depending on the type of transaction you need to edit.
3. Locate the transaction you want to update.

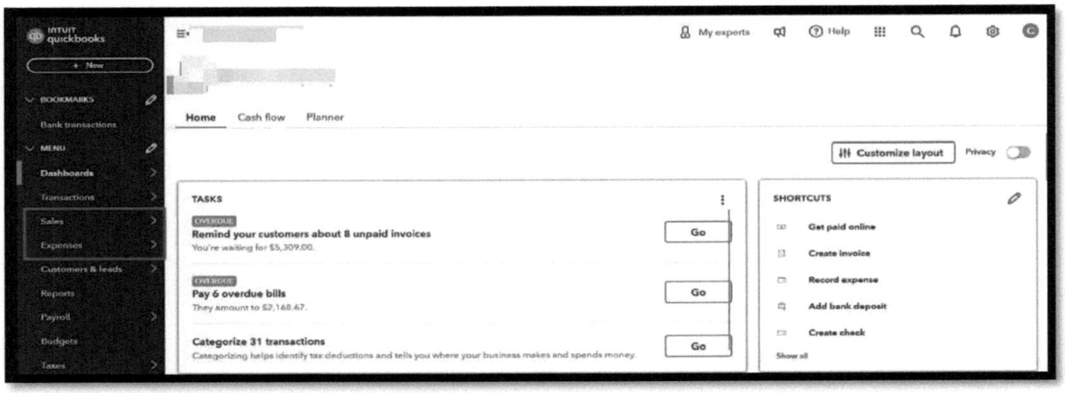

Step 3: Select the Transaction

1. Scroll through the list or use the **search bar** to find the transaction.
2. Click on it to open the **transaction details** window.

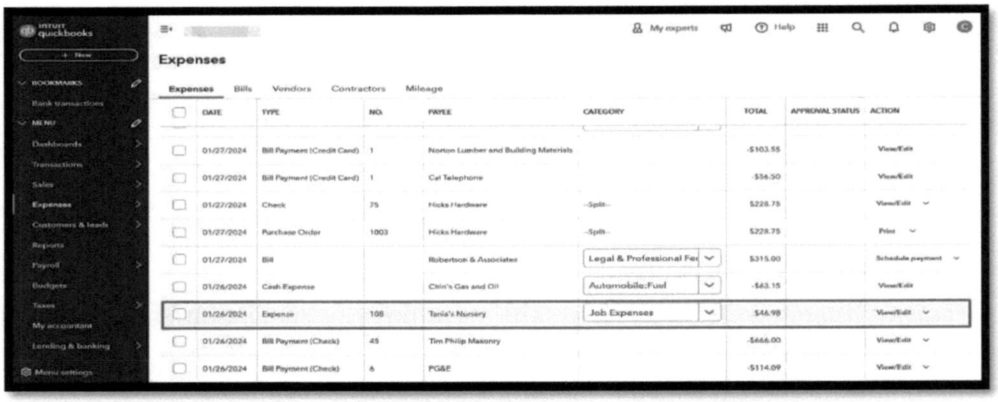

Step 4: Change the Transaction Type

1. In the transaction detail window, locate the **Transaction Type** field.
2. Click the current transaction type to open the dropdown menu.
3. Select the **new transaction type** (e.g., change from Expense to Check, or Bill to Expense).

Step 5: Save and Verify

1. Click **Save and Close** at the bottom of the transaction window.
2. Verify the change by checking the transaction list to confirm the type has been updated correctly.

Common Issues and Troubleshooting

While changing transaction types is usually straightforward, you may encounter issues. Here are common problems and solutions:

1. Insufficient Permissions

- **Issue:** User lacks permission to edit transactions.
- **Solution:** Request administrative or full access from your QuickBooks Online admin.

2. Locked or Reconciled Transactions

- **Issue:** Reconciled or locked transactions cannot be edited.
- **Solution:** Undo reconciliation from the **Reconciliation page**, edit the transaction, then reconcile it again.

Use caution—undoing reconciliations can affect financial reports.

3. Data Integrity Issues

- **Issue:** Corrupted or inconsistent transaction data.
- **Solution:** Check the **Audit Log** under the Gear icon for discrepancies. Contact QuickBooks Online support if issues persist.

4. Unsupported Changes

- **Issue:** Some transaction types cannot be directly converted.
- **Solution:** Create a **new transaction** with the correct type and delete the original.

Tip: Copy all relevant details carefully to prevent data loss.

5. System Glitches

- **Issue:** Browser or temporary system errors prevent changes.
- **Solution:** Refresh the browser, clear cache, or try a different browser/device. Check QuickBooks Online status for outages.

PART VI: SPREADSHEETS, ANALYTICS, AND INTEGRATIONS

CHAPTER SEVENTEEN

ENHANCING YOUR DATA WORKFLOW WITH SPREADSHEET SYNC IN QUICKBOOKS ONLINE

Spreadsheet Sync in QuickBooks Online allows you to effortlessly connect your QuickBooks data to Excel, giving you the power to update, analyse, and manage financial information in a familiar spreadsheet environment. With real-time syncing, you can "animate" your data—meaning changes made in Excel flow directly back into QuickBooks, and vice versa. This feature streamlines bulk edits, improves accuracy, and enables faster, more flexible reporting without manual data entry.

HOW TO CONNECT SPREADSHEET SYNC AND RUN REPORTS IN QUICKBOOKS ONLINE

With **QuickBooks Online Advanced** and **Spreadsheet Sync**, you can pull your company data directly into Microsoft Excel to build custom reports, analyze performance, and even create or update transactions—all without leaving Excel. Below is a streamlined walkthrough for setting up Spreadsheet Sync and using it to run reports and manage records.

1. Connect Spreadsheet Sync to Your QuickBooks Company

a. **Open QuickBooks Online:** Select **Settings** and click **Spreadsheet Sync**.

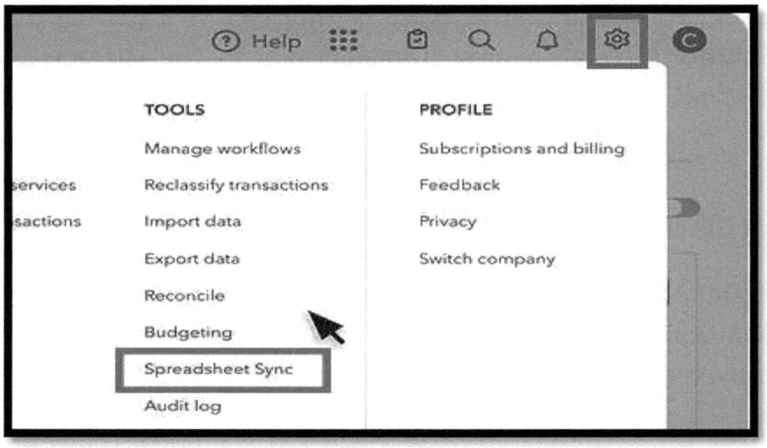

b. **Start the Setup:** Review the installation overview and click **Let's Go**, then choose **Open Microsoft Excel**.

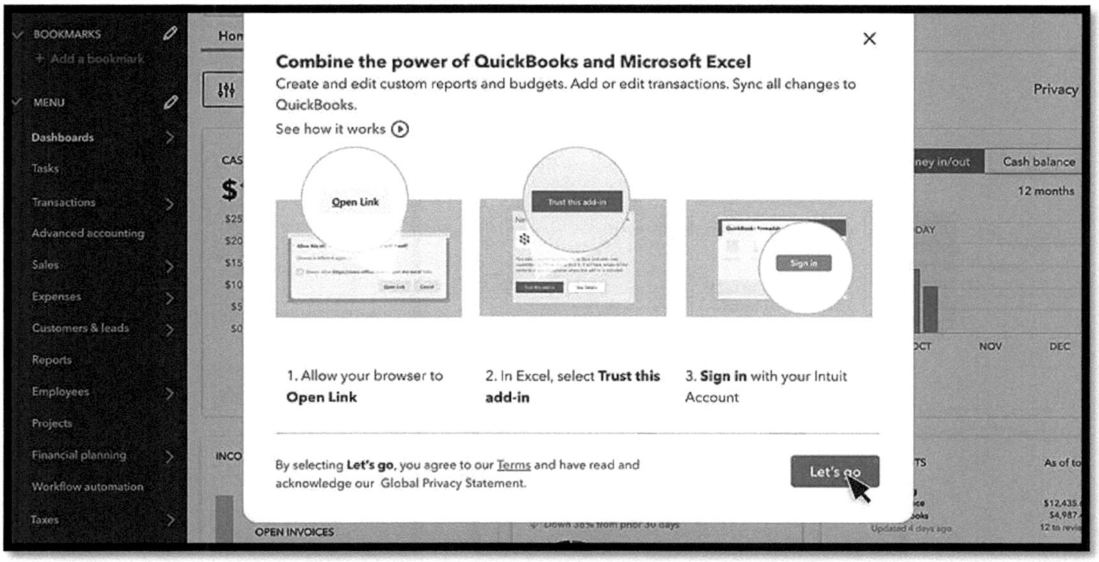

c. **Install the Add-In:** Excel opens automatically with the Spreadsheet Sync add-in file.

d. Accept the license terms, privacy policy, and permissions, then click **Trust this Add-in**.
(You only need to install it once.)

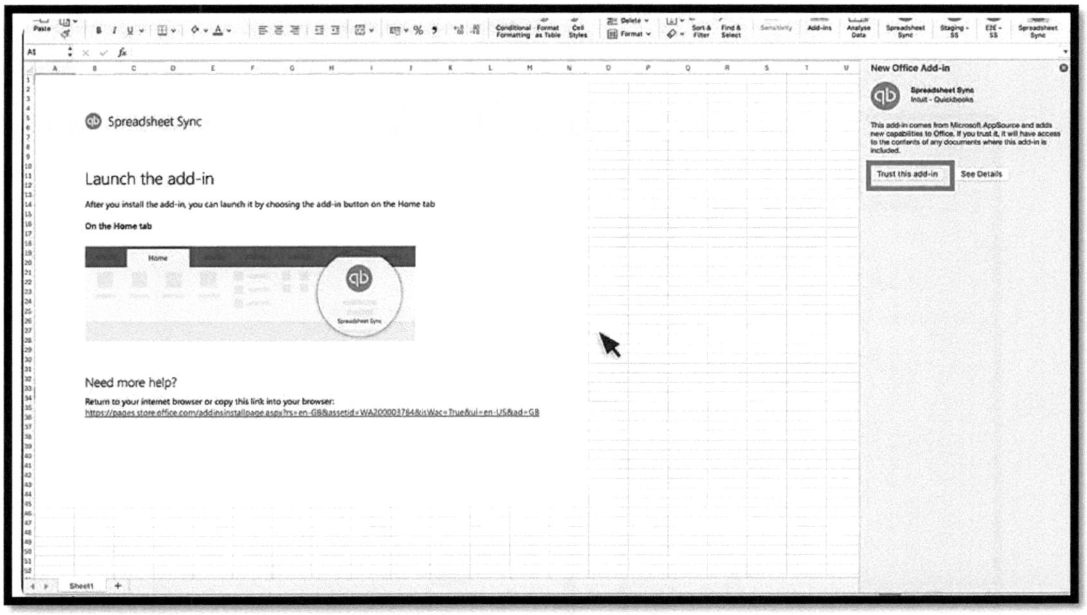

e. **Sign In:** In Excel, open the **Spreadsheet Sync** tab and select **Sign In**.

Enter your QuickBooks credentials and choose the QuickBooks company you want to connect.

2. Navigating Spreadsheet Sync in Excel

Once connected, you'll see two main sections:

- ❖ **Reports** – Build new reports or run multi-company reports.
- ❖ **Records** – Create or edit QuickBooks records directly from Excel.

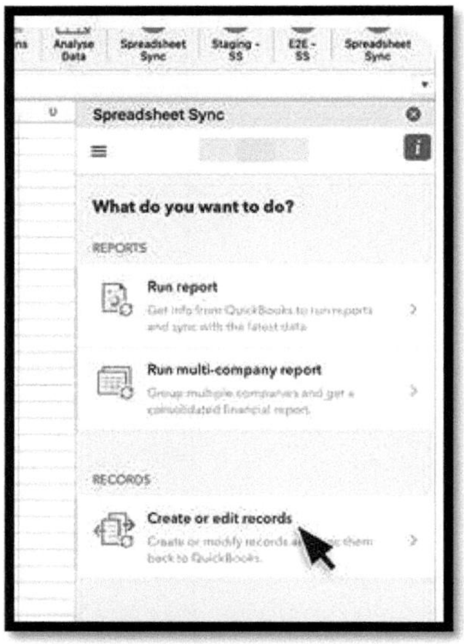

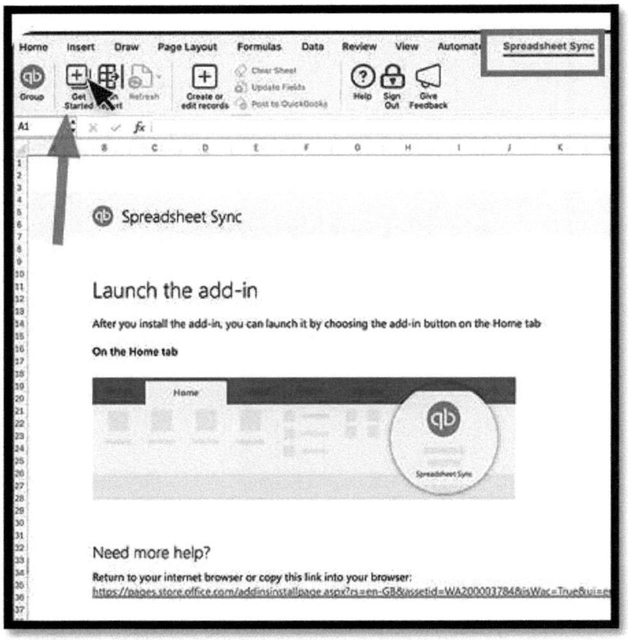

If this panel closes, simply go back to the **Spreadsheet Sync** tab and select **Get Started**.

3. How to Run a Report

a. In Excel, choose your company and select **Report**.
b. Browse report categories or search for the report you need.
c. Example: Select **Profit and Loss**. You can open the **Template Gallery** for more built-out options.
d. Adjust filters such as accounting method, date range, class, location, customer, or item.

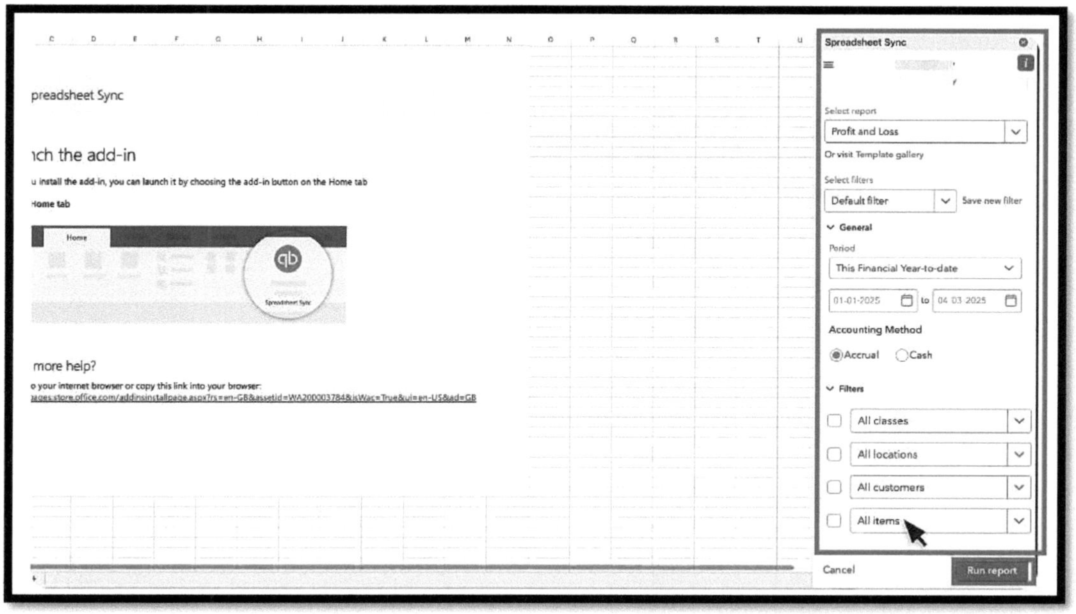

e. Select **Run Report**.

Spreadsheet Sync will generate the report and load it into a new Excel sheet.

Once generated, you can:

- Add formulas
- Build pivot tables
- Insert charts and visuals
- Save the workbook

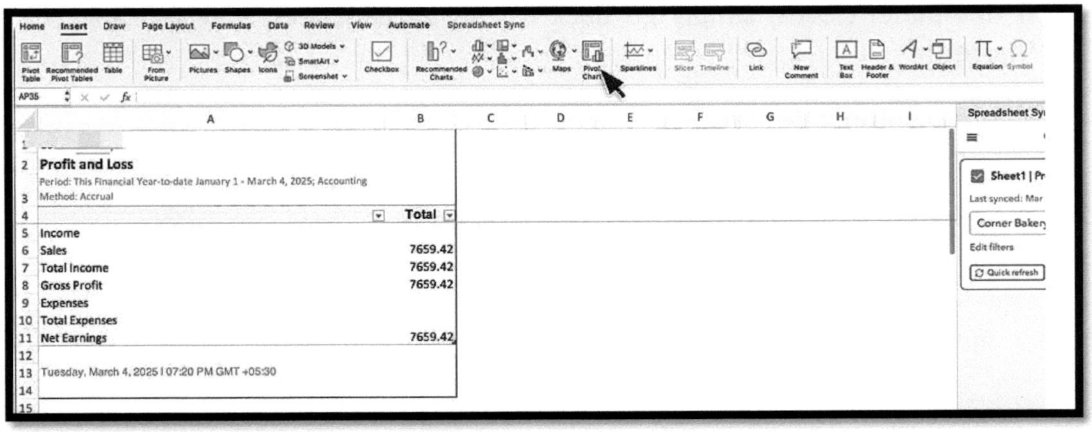

To update the report later, use **Quick Refresh** under the **Refresh** menu.

4. Creating New QuickBooks Records in Excel

a. Go to **Spreadsheet Sync > Create or Edit Records.**
b. Choose the company and record type (e.g., invoices or bills).

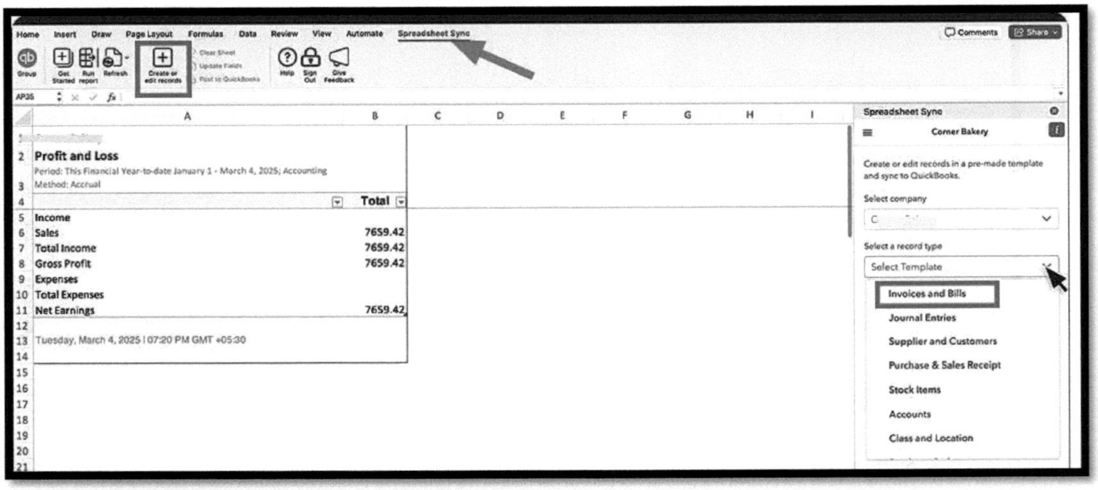

c. Select **Add New Records to QuickBooks**, then click **Get Template**.
d. Enter your transaction details, then type **YES** in the **Post** column for each item you want to upload.
e. Select **Sync to QuickBooks**, then confirm.

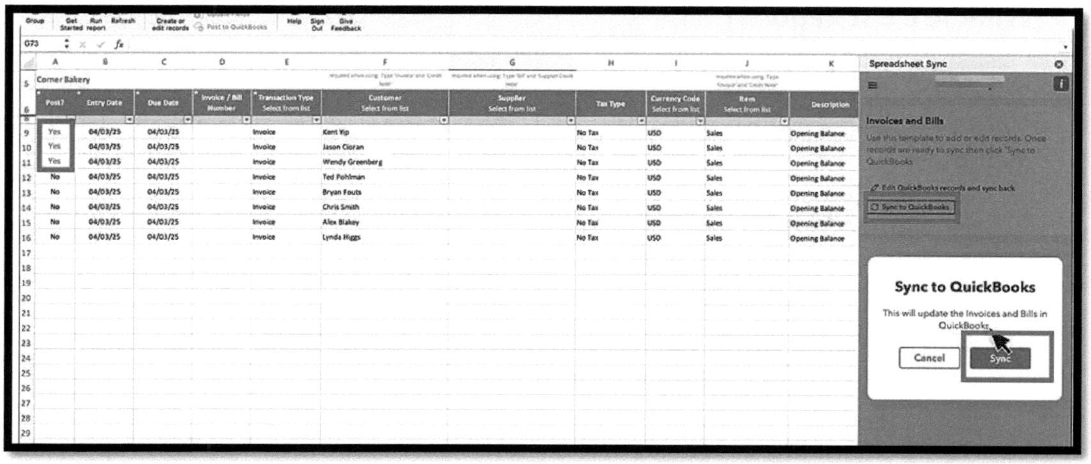

After syncing, you can view detailed sync results before closing the window.

5. Editing Existing QuickBooks Records

a. Select **Edit QuickBooks Records and Sync Back.**
b. Click **Get Records** to pull in existing data.
c. Update the fields you need to change.
d. Mark each edited row with **YES** in the **Post** column.
e. Select **Sync to QuickBooks** and confirm.

A completion message will appear along with an option to review sync details.

How to Sign Out of Spreadsheet Sync

Signing out of Spreadsheet Sync ensures your QuickBooks data stays secure, especially when using a shared or public device. Follow these quick steps:

1. **Open Excel or Google Sheets:** Launch the application where Spreadsheet Sync is installed.
2. **Go to the Spreadsheet Sync tab or menu:** This is usually located in the toolbar at the top of your screen.
3. **Select *Sign Out*:** Your connection to QuickBooks Online will be safely disconnected.

WORKING WITH LIST REPORTS IN QUICKBOOKS ONLINE

List reports are one of the most useful reporting tools in QuickBooks Online. They help you gather detailed information about customers, vendors, products, employees, and other key records stored in your company file. These reports make it easier to track performance, understand business relationships, and improve financial decision-making.

What Are List Reports?

List reports display organized, customizable data about specific groups—such as customer lists, vendor lists, product and service lists, and more. They typically include:

- Names and contact information
- Addresses, emails, and phone numbers
- Account balances
- Payment or transaction history
- Product/service details (descriptions, prices, etc.)

You can personalize these reports by adding or removing columns, applying filters, or sorting the data to fit your needs.

When to Use List Reports

- **Customer Contact List:** View all customer details in one place—ideal for CRM, marketing campaigns, and communication tracking.
- **Vendor Contact List:** Monitor supplier information to support vendor management and purchasing decisions.
- **Product/Service List:** Review key details about your offerings, track pricing, check availability, and analyze sales trends.
- **Employee Contact List:** Keep employee information organized for payroll, HR, or internal communication.
- **Additional List Reports:** QuickBooks also provides lists for chart of accounts, fixed assets, sales tax items, and more—helpful for auditing and deeper operational insights.

How to Run a List Report in QuickBooks Online

1. **Open the Reports Menu**

   From your dashboard, select **Reports**.

2. **Search for the Report**

   Use the search bar to enter the name of the list report (e.g., *Customer Contact List*).

3. **Customize the Report**

   Select **Customize** to adjust:

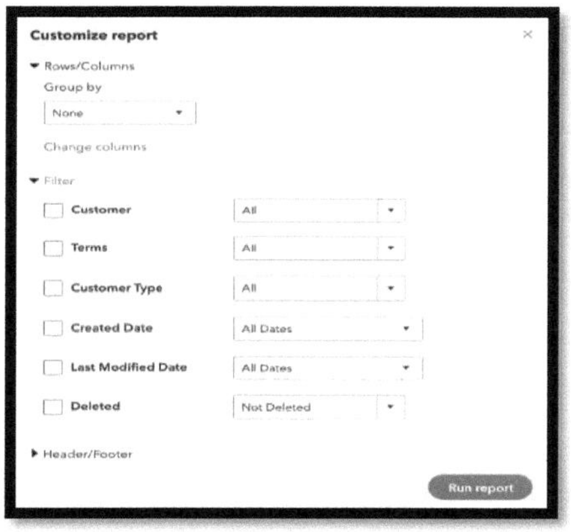

   - Date range
   - Columns displayed
   - Filters
   - Sorting options

4. **Run the Report**

   Click **Run report** to generate it based on your selections.

5. **Export or Print**

   Use the options in the upper right to export the report to **PDF**, **Excel**, or **CSV**, or print a copy for your records.

CHAPTER EIGHTEEN

ENHANCING YOUR DATA ANALYSIS IN EXCEL

"Unleashing your data in Excel" from QuickBooks Online can be achieved through direct exports, the specialized Spreadsheet Sync add-in (for QBO Advanced users), or various third-party connector apps. These methods allow you to analyze data, create custom reports, and even sync edits back to QuickBooks.

HOW TO EXPORT REPORTS FROM QUICKBOOKS TO EXCEL

QuickBooks includes powerful reporting tools, but exporting those reports to Excel gives you even more control. Whether you want to perform deeper analysis, apply custom formulas, or share financial data with teammates who don't use QuickBooks, exporting to Excel is an essential skill. Below is a clear, step-by-step walkthrough on how to export both individual and multiple QuickBooks reports—along with tips on working with classic and modern report views.

Why Export QuickBooks Reports to Excel?

Moving your data into Excel allows you to:

- ❖ Customize date ranges for projects or audits.
- ❖ Apply formulas, formatting, and advanced analytics.
- ❖ Consolidate multiple reports into one workbook.
- ❖ Share information with people without QuickBooks access.

Exporting Multiple Reports at Once (Bulk Export)

If you need several reports quickly, QuickBooks offers a built-in export tool.

1. Open the Export Data Tool

- ❖ Click the **Gear icon** (top-right).
- ❖ Select **Tools → Export Data**.

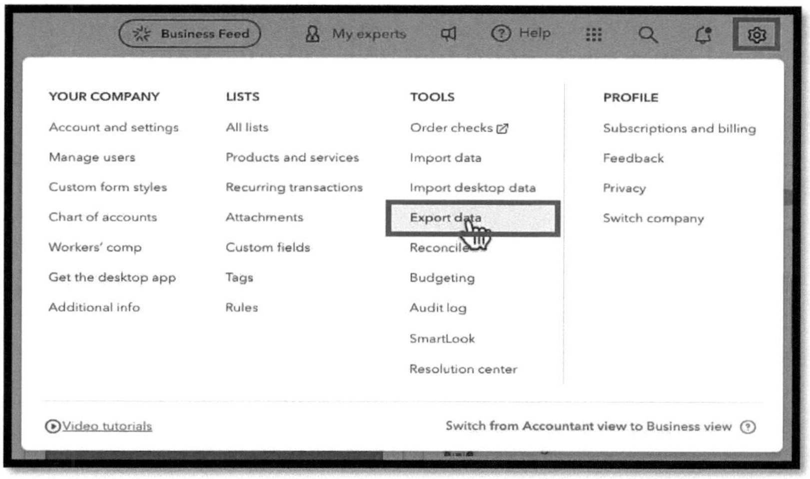

2. Choose the Reports You Need

You can export reports such as:

- ❖ Profit and Loss
- ❖ Balance Sheet
- ❖ General Ledger
- ❖ Trial Balance
- ❖ Journal

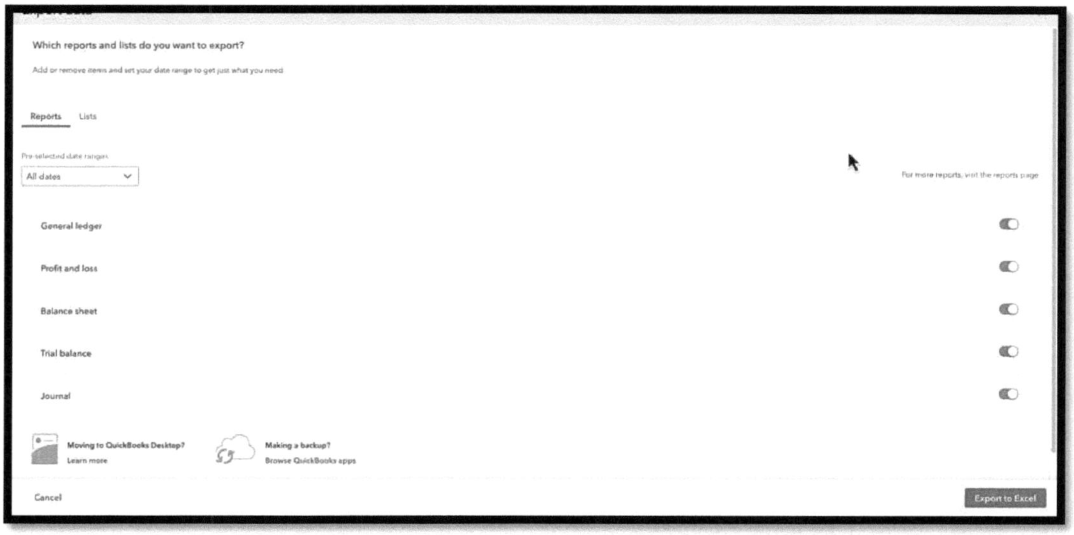

3. Export to Excel

- ❖ Click **Export to Excel** at the bottom right.
- ❖ QuickBooks will generate a **ZIP file** containing all selected reports.

Important: Bulk exports always use the **"All Dates"** range. For custom date ranges, open and customize each report manually before exporting.

Exporting a Single Report to Excel

1. Open the Report

- ❖ Go to **Reports** in the left navigation menu.
- ❖ Search for and open your desired report (e.g., **Profit and Loss**).

2. Customize the Date Range

- ❖ Set your **Start** and **End** dates at the top of the screen.
  - ❖ Example: For Q1 2024 → **1/1/2024 to 3/31/2024**
- ❖ Click **Run Report** to refresh the data.

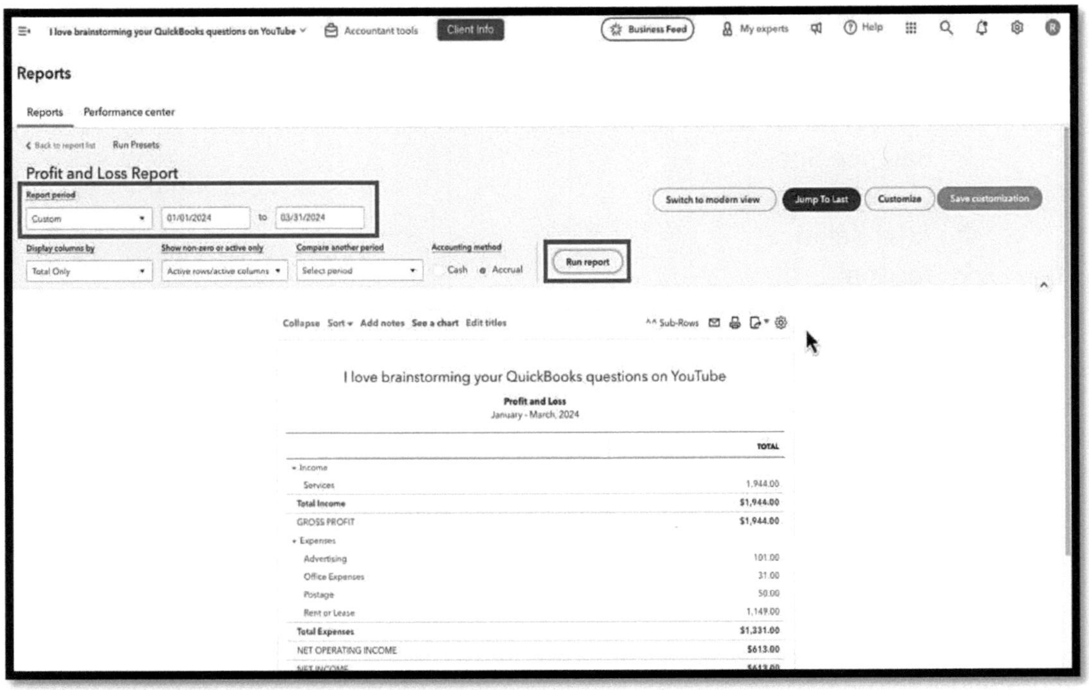

3. Export the Report

- ❖ Click the **Export icon** (paper with arrow).
- ❖ Select **Export to Excel**.
  Your customized report will download as an .xlsx file.

Classic View vs. Modern View in QuickBooks Reports

QuickBooks provides two different report interfaces. Understanding them helps you predict what your exported Excel file will look like.

Classic View

- Exports **fully expanded data**—no collapsible sections.
- Ideal for users who want to see all details immediately.
- Easier for those who plan to manually manipulate the data in Excel.

Modern View

- Exports with **collapsible and expandable categories** (e.g., Income, Expenses).
- Lets you switch between summary and detailed views inside Excel.
- Creates cleaner, more presentation-ready files.

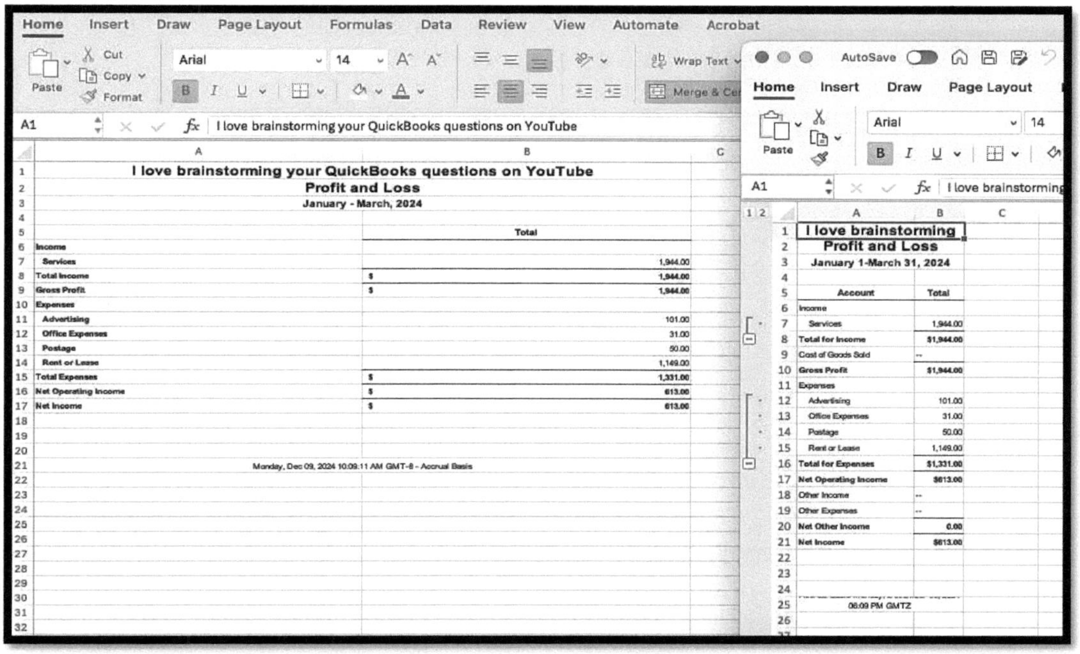

Switching Between Views

- In **Classic View**: Click **Switch to Modern View**.

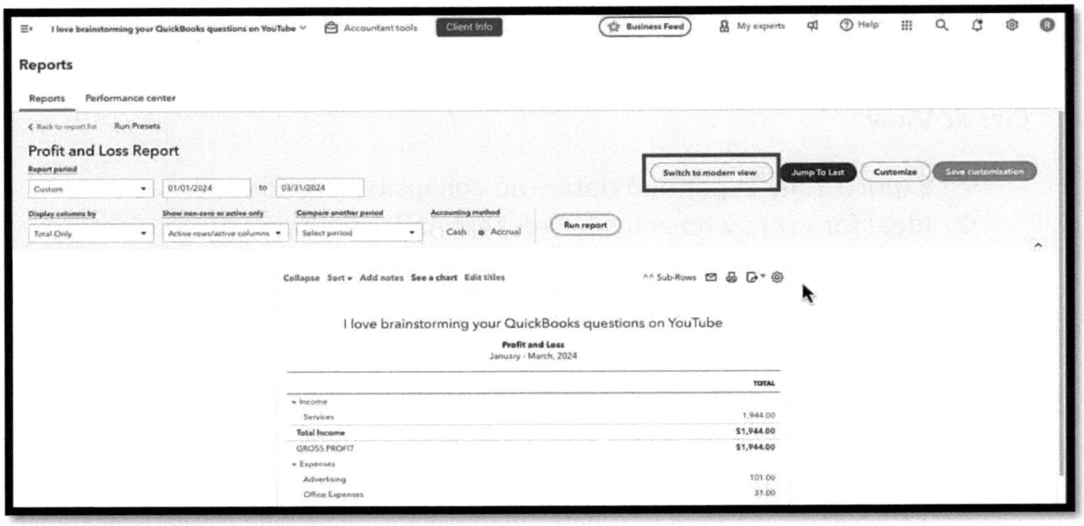

❖ In **Modern View**: Click **Switch to Classic View**.

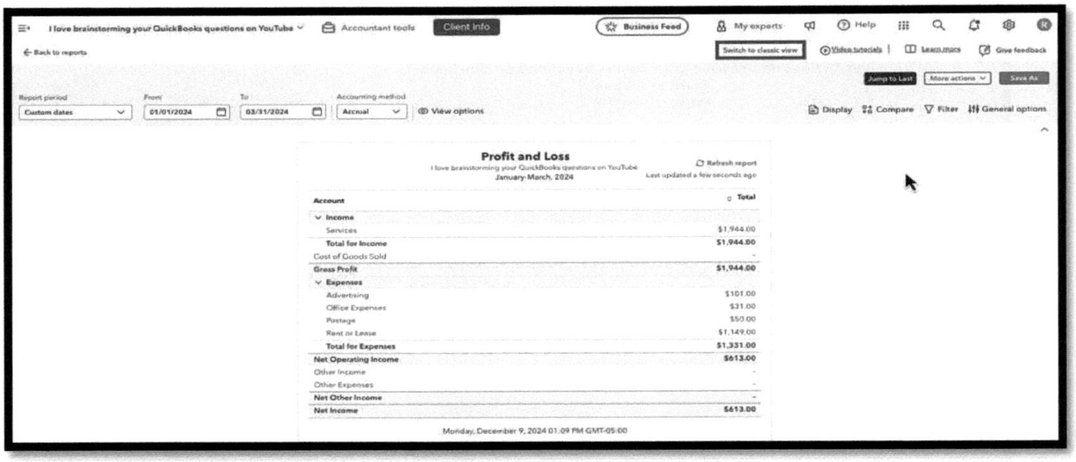

Troubleshooting Common Issues

1. Wrong Date Range

Bulk exports default to **All Dates**.

Solution: Open the individual report → customize the date → export.

2. Can't Open the File

Exports are in **Excel (.xlsx)** format.

Solution: Make sure you have Excel or a compatible spreadsheet program.

3. Collapsible Rows Confusing

Solution: Switch to **Classic View** before exporting for a fully expanded layout.

Tips for Working with Your Exported Excel Reports

Clean the Data

Remove unnecessary rows or columns to simplify your analysis.

Use Excel Tools

Leverage:

- Pivot tables
- Charts
- Conditional formatting
- Filters and functions

These help visualize and interpret your QuickBooks data more effectively.

Create a Template

If you consistently adjust your data the same way, save your formatted Excel file as a **template** for future exports.

HOW TO EXPORT LISTS FROM QUICKBOOKS ONLINE TO EXCEL

QuickBooks Online makes it easy to export your key business lists—such as customers, vendors, and employees—into Excel for further analysis, backup, or reporting. Below is a streamlined walkthrough of the export process, along with what you can expect in each file.

1. Access the Export Data Tool

1. Click the **Gear icon** in the upper-right corner of QuickBooks Online.
2. Under **TOOLS**, select **Export data**.
3. If a pop-up appears asking why you're exporting, choose an option and click **Continue**.

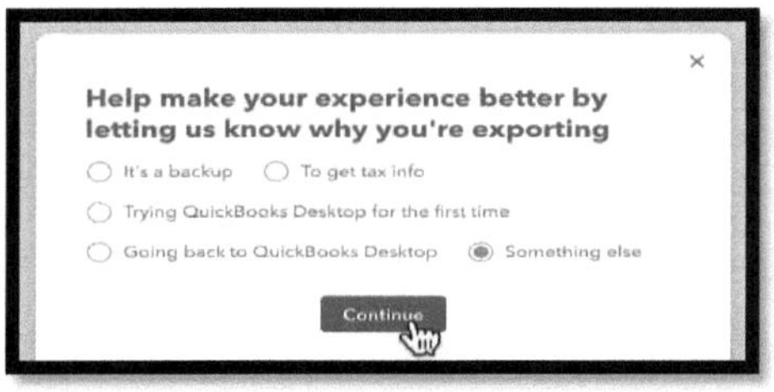

2. Select What to Export

On the **Export data** screen, you'll see two tabs:

- **Reports**
- **Lists**

Even if you're only exporting lists, QuickBooks will include **everything you have selected** across both tabs. When you're ready, click **Export to Excel**.

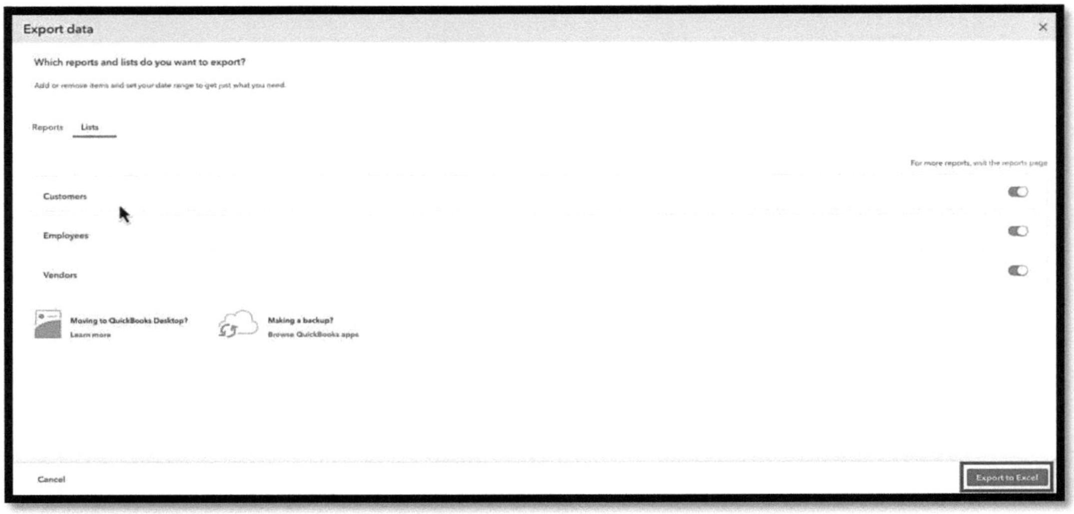

QuickBooks will generate a **ZIP file** containing all selected items as individual **.xlsx** spreadsheets.

What Each Exported List Contains

Customer List

This file includes detailed customer contact information such as:

- Business name
- Contact name
- Phone number
- Email

- ❖ Billing and shipping addresses

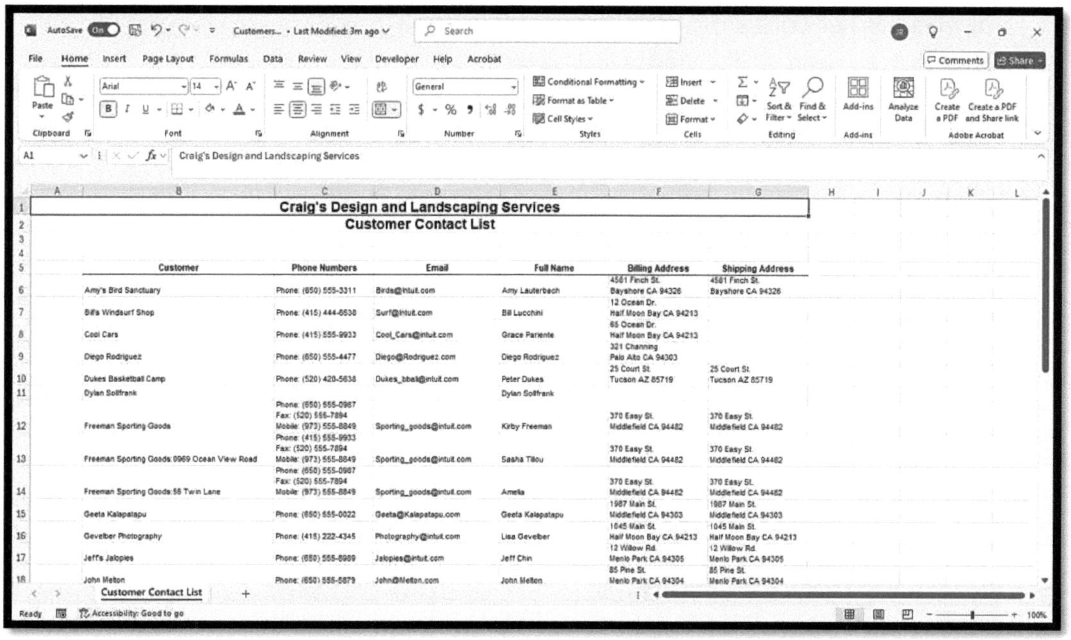

Employee List

The employee export provides basic HR contact fields, including:

- ❖ Employee full name
- ❖ Phone number
- ❖ Email
- ❖ Address

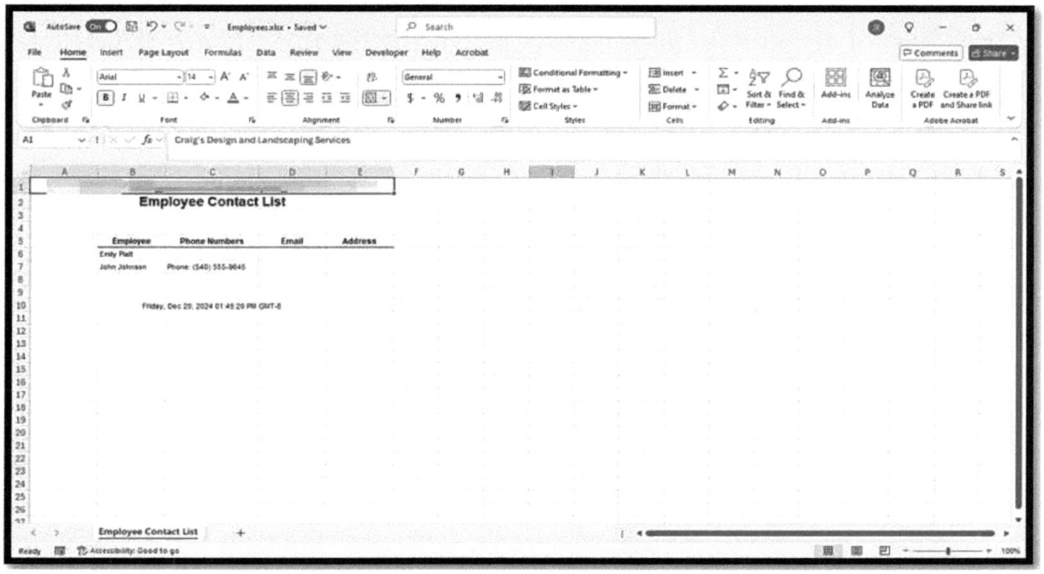

Vendor List

Your vendor list contains:

- ❖ Vendor name
- ❖ Contact name
- ❖ Phone and email
- ❖ Address
- ❖ Account number

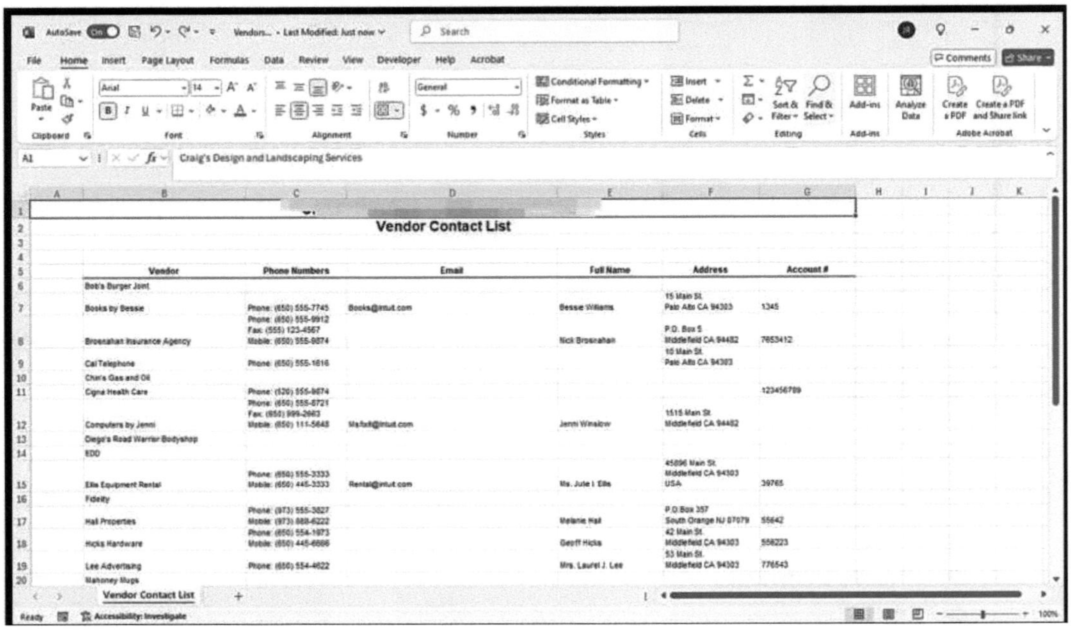

How to Export Your Chart of Accounts

The Chart of Accounts cannot be exported using the *Export data* tool. Instead, follow these steps:

1. In the left menu, click **Transactions** > **Chart of Accounts.**

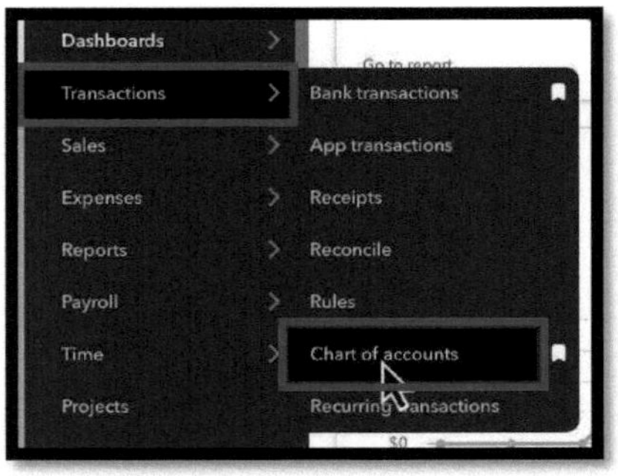

2. In the upper right, select **Run report**.

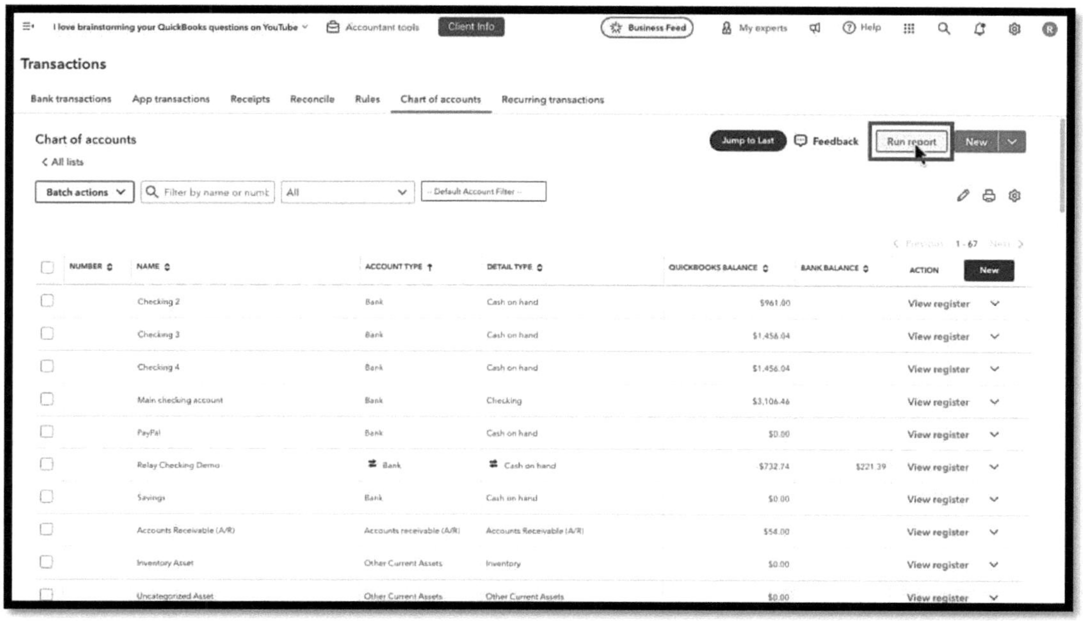

3. Once the report opens, click the **Export icon**.
4. Choose **Export to Excel**.

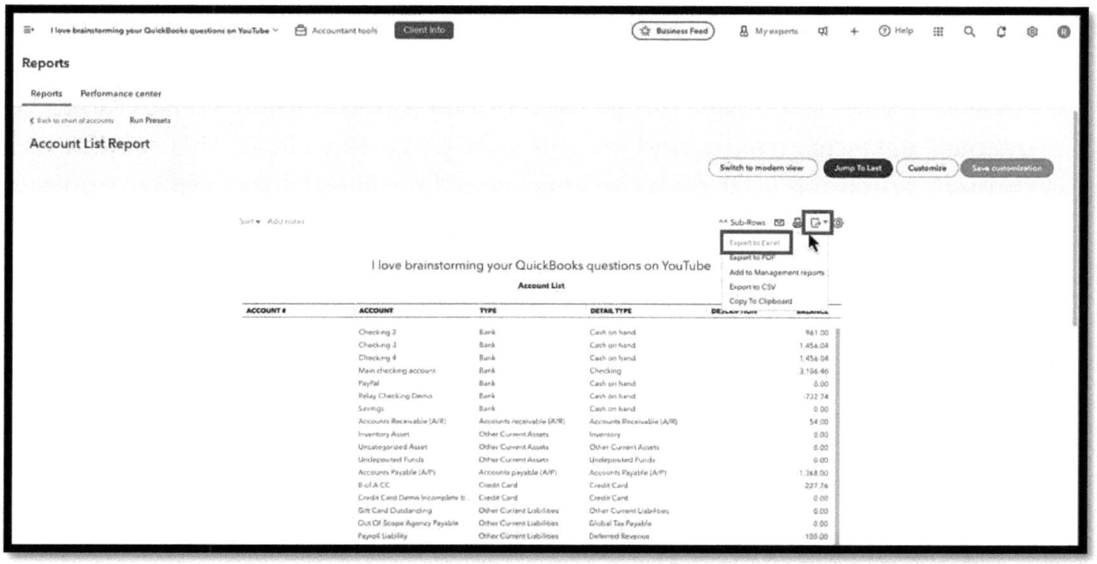

The exported file will display:

- ❖ All account names
- ❖ Account types
- ❖ Details

- ❖ Running balances (only for accounts with activity)

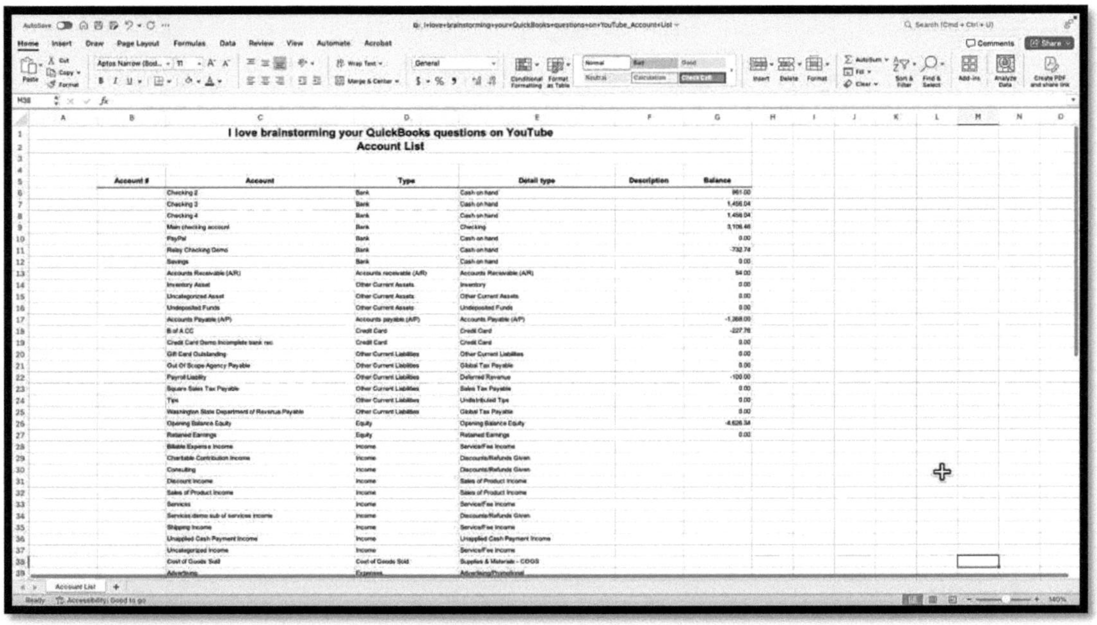

This provides a clean, structured view of your full accounting framework.

PIVOT TABLES IN EXCEL

PivotTables are one of Excel's most efficient tools for analyzing, sorting, and summarizing large datasets—without writing complex formulas. Whether you're reviewing sales, expenses, survey data, or financial statements, PivotTables help you uncover patterns, trends, and insights with just a few clicks. This section walks you through preparing your data, building your first PivotTable, and customizing it for powerful analysis.

What Is a PivotTable and Why Use One?

A PivotTable is an interactive Excel feature that reorganizes and summarizes your data so you can quickly understand what it means. Instead of manually filtering or calculating totals, a PivotTable groups information for you automatically.

Common uses include:

- ❖ Summarising sales by product, region, or salesperson
- ❖ Reviewing expenses by category or vendor
- ❖ Analysing survey results across demographic groups
- ❖ Breaking down financial or operational performance over time

If you're new to data analysis, PivotTables offer a fast and intuitive way to make sense of complex information.

Preparing Your Data for PivotTables

A PivotTable is only as good as the data behind it. Before creating one, ensure your dataset is clean, structured, and consistent. This prevents errors and ensures accurate summaries.

1. Use a Clear, Tabular Layout

Your data should be organised in a simple table with:

- ❖ **Column headers in the first row** — each clearly labelled and unique
- ❖ **No blank rows or columns** — gaps can interrupt the data range
- ❖ **No merged cells** — these break the structure and confuse Excel

Example:
If you're analysing sales, your columns might include:

Product | Quantity | Price | Salesperson | Region | Date

Each row should represent one transaction.

2. Convert the Data to an Excel Table (Ctrl + T)

Using Excel Tables improves accuracy and automation.

Benefits include:

- ❖ New rows automatically become part of the dataset
- ❖ PivotTables refresh easily when data changes
- ❖ Structured references make formulas cleaner and easier to manage

How:
Select your data → Press **Ctrl + T** → confirm **"My table has headers"**

3. Ensure Consistent Data Types

PivotTables rely on proper formatting. Inconsistent data leads to incorrect results.

Check for:

- ❖ **Numbers:** Ensure numeric fields contain only numbers (no symbols or text)
- ❖ **Dates:** Standardise formats (e.g., DD/MM/YYYY)
- ❖ **Text columns:** Avoid mixing text and numbers in the same field
- ❖ **Avoid "N/A" inside numeric fields**—use blank cells instead

Common issue:

If a few “Revenue” cells contain the text “N/A”, Excel may treat the whole column as text and ignore the numbers.

4. Remove Subtotals and Grand Totals

PivotTables calculate totals automatically. If your source data includes totals, Excel may double-count them. Eliminate summary rows before creating your PivotTable.

Summary Example of Good Data Structure

A clean dataset should look like this:

	A	B	C	D	E	F
1	Order ID	Product	Category	Amount	Date	Country
2	1	Carrots	Vegetables	$4,270	1/6/2024	United States
3	2	Broccoli	Vegetables	$8,239	1/7/2024	United Kingdom
4	3	Banana	Fruit	$617	1/8/2024	United States

This type of clean, uniform data ensures your PivotTables generate accurate and powerful insights.

Creating Your First PivotTable in Excel

Once your dataset is properly structured, you’re ready to build your first PivotTable. Follow the steps below to move from raw data to a clean, insightful summary—no formulas required.

Step 1: Insert a PivotTable

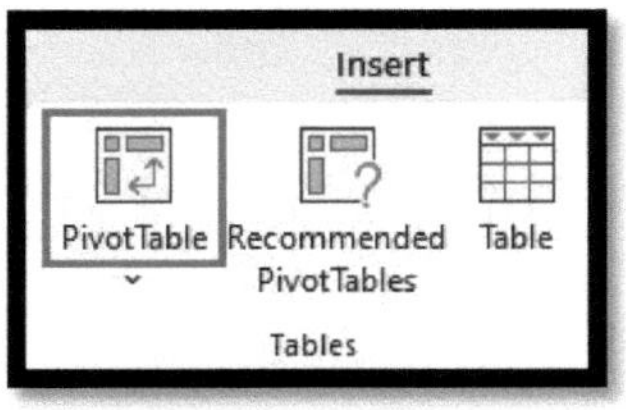

1. Click anywhere inside your dataset (Excel will automatically detect the full range).
2. Go to the **Insert** tab on the ribbon.
3. Select **PivotTable** (or *PivotTable → From Table/Range* if you’re using an Excel Table).

Excel will open a dialog box asking where you want your PivotTable to appear.

Step 2: Choose the PivotTable Location

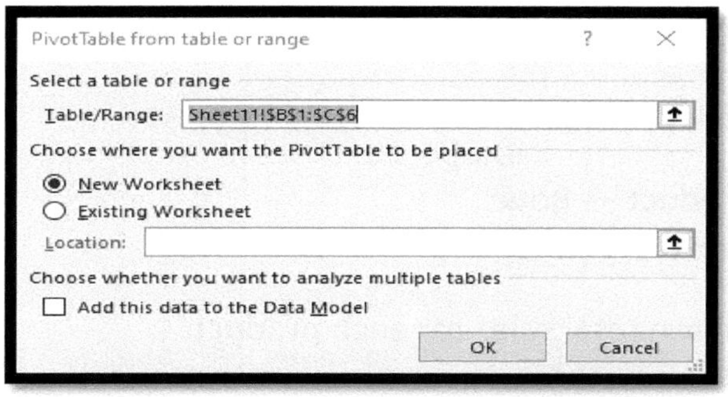

You have two placement options:

- ❖ **New Worksheet (recommended):** Creates a clean sheet dedicated to your PivotTable—ideal for beginners.
- ❖ **Existing Worksheet:** Lets you choose a specific cell on the current sheet.

Tip: Use a new worksheet to avoid clutter or accidental overwriting of your source data.

Step 3: Use "Recommended PivotTables" (Fastest for Beginners)

If you want a quick start:

1. Go to **Insert → Recommended PivotTables**.
2. Excel will analyze your data and propose useful summaries, such as *Total Sales by Product* or *Sales by Region*.
3. Review the previews and pick the one that best fits your needs.

Example: If your dataset includes columns like *Sales*, *Month*, and *Region*, Excel may suggest a ready-made summary of total sales per region.

Step 4: Build Your PivotTable Manually

If you prefer to create one from scratch, Excel will generate:

- ❖ A blank PivotTable layout
- ❖ A **PivotTable Fields pane** on the right, where you drag your fields into four areas:

PivotTable Areas Explained

Area	Purpose
Rows	Creates categories (e.g., Product, Customer, Region)
Columns	Splits data horizontally (e.g., Month, Quarter)
Values	Contains calculations (Sum, Count, Average, etc.)

Filters	Adds a filter available at the top of the PivotTable

Example:

To create a quick product-level sales summary:

- ❖ Drag **Product** → Rows
- ❖ Drag **Sales** → Values

Instantly, you'll see total sales for each product.

Your Source Data Stays Safe

PivotTables never change or delete your original dataset—they only summarize it.

Made a mistake? You can delete the PivotTable without affecting your data.

Understanding the Field List (Your PivotTable "Control Center")

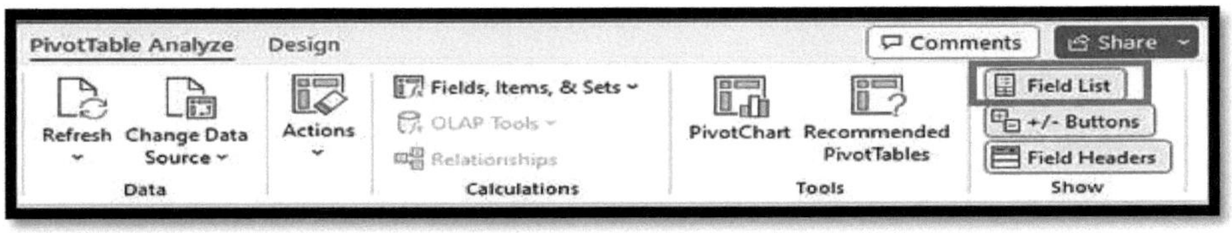

The Field List is where all the action happens. Drag fields around to instantly view your data from different perspectives.

Example Scenario

If you're analyzing website performance:

- ❖ Drag **Top Pages** → Rows

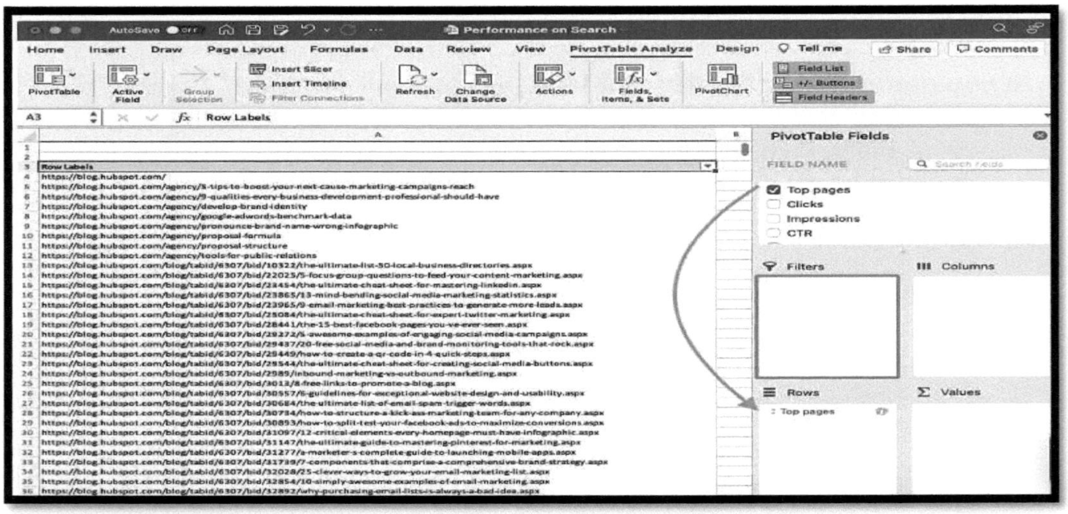

❖ Drag **Clicks** → Values

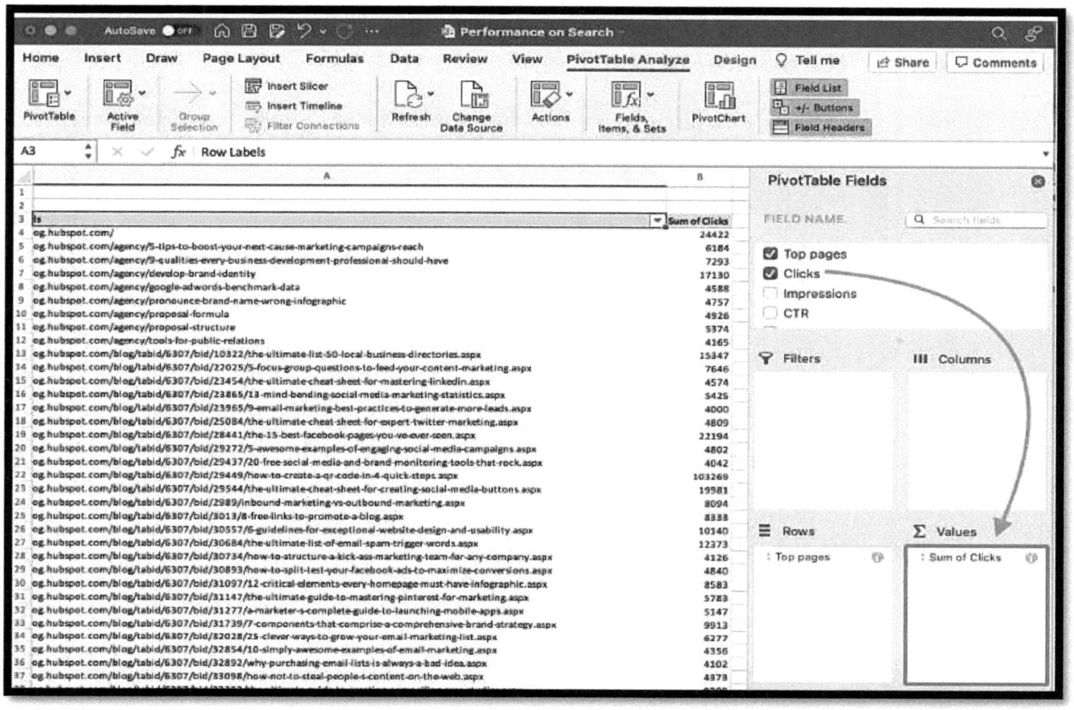

You'll immediately see the total clicks each page received.

Tip: Experiment! Drag fields between Rows, Columns, and Values to uncover new insights.

What's Next?

After building your first PivotTable, you can:

- ❖ Group dates by months or quarters
- ❖ Change calculations (Sum → Average → Count)
- ❖ Apply sorting, filtering, and conditional formatting
- ❖ Create PivotCharts for visual insights

PivotTables become more intuitive the more you practice. Try experimenting with different datasets to build confidence quickly.

Customizing and Analyzing Your PivotTable in Excel

Once you've built your first PivotTable, you can transform it from a simple summary into a powerful analytical tool. With just a few clicks, you can uncover deeper insights and make your data tell a story.

1. Changing Value Calculations

PivotTables don't have to be limited to sums. Right-click any value → **Value Field Settings**, and choose from:

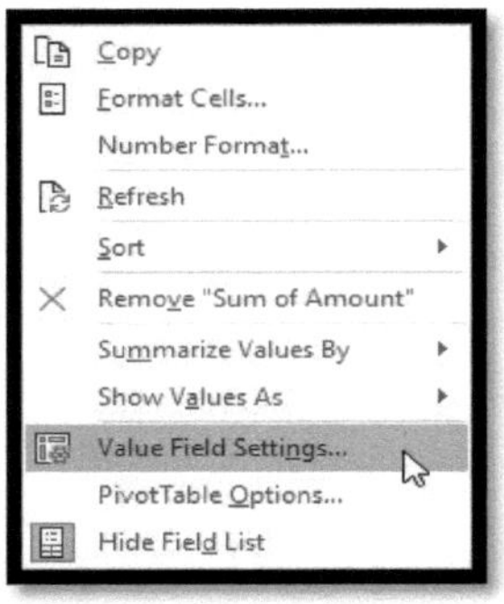

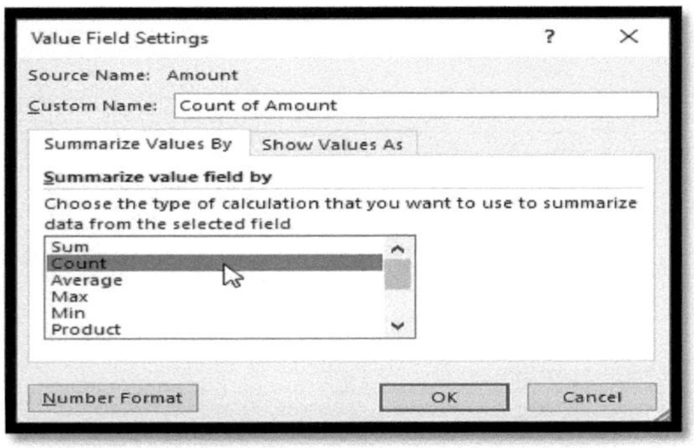

- **Sum** (default for numbers)
- **Average** (ideal for performance metrics)
- **Count** (great for survey responses)
- **Max/Min** (spot outliers)
- **Standard Deviation** (measure variability)

Pro Tip: Use "% of Column Total" for contribution percentages.

Example: Change "Impressions" from Sum to Average to see the average number of impressions per blog post.

2. Grouping Dates for Smarter Time Analysis

Stop analyzing daily data—group dates to identify trends easily:

1. Right-click any date in your PivotTable → **Group**
2. Select Months, Quarters, Years, or custom ranges

Power User Trick: Combine grouping with conditional formatting to highlight seasonal trends.

Example: Group order dates by Month and Year to track monthly sales growth.

3. Advanced Sorting and Filtering

PivotTables offer flexible sorting and filtering options to focus on what matters:

Sorting:

Row Labels	Sum of Order Amount
Amy Dodsworth	75048.04
Dave Leverling	201196.27
Joe Buchanan	68792.25
John Peacock	225763.68
Lee Suyama	72527.63
Mark Fuller	162503.78
Mary Davolio	182500.09
Mike Callahan	123032.67
Susan King	116962.99
Grand Total	1228327.4

❖ Click a row/column dropdown → Sort A→Z, Z→A, or by value

❖ Right-click → Sort → More Sort Options for custom rules

Filtering:

❖ Filter by specific items (e.g., only Eastern region)
❖ Apply label filters (e.g., product names containing "Pro")

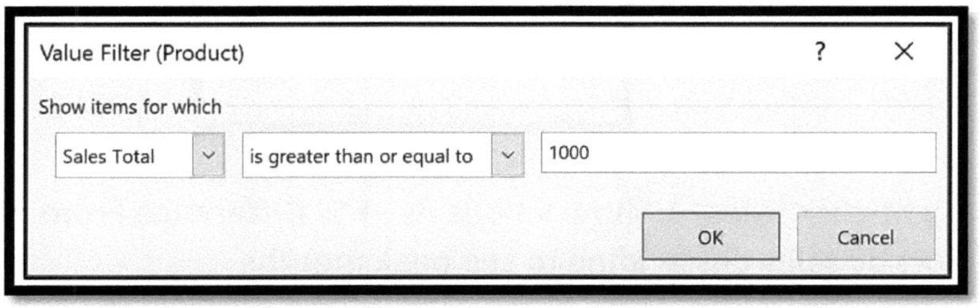

❖ Use value filters (e.g., sales > $1,000)
❖ Hidden gem: Right-click → Filter → Top 10 to highlight best/worst performers

4. Practical Example: Monthly Sales Trends

Analyze a year's worth of daily sales data in seconds:

1. Drag **Order Date** to Rows

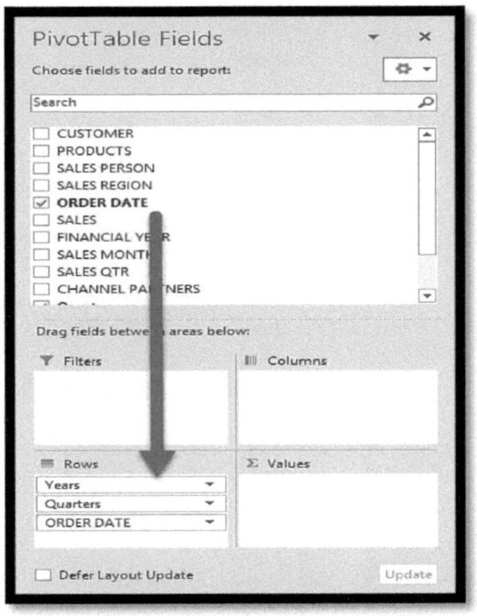

2. Right-click → Group → select Months and Years
3. Drag **Sales** to Values

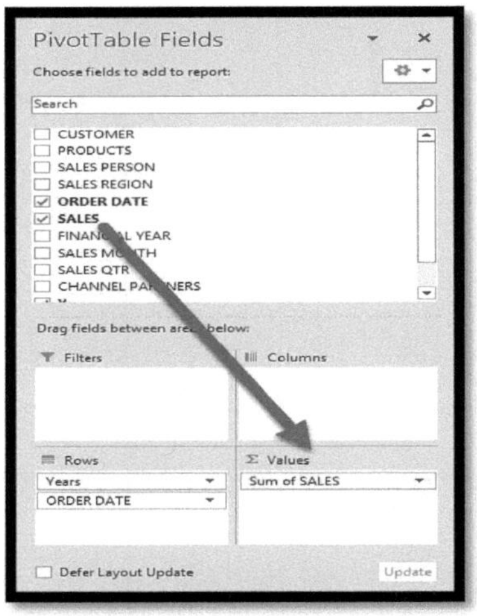

4. Right-click Sales → Show Values As → **% Difference From** previous month
5. Sort by sales descending to see peak months

This quick setup highlights monthly growth rates and seasonal patterns instantly.

5. Updating and Refreshing PivotTables

Keeping PivotTables current ensures your analysis reflects the latest data.

Manual Refresh (Single PivotTable):

- Right-click → Refresh (or press **Alt + F5**)

Auto-Refresh with Excel Tables:

- Convert your data into a table (Ctrl + T)
- New rows added automatically included when refreshed

Refresh All (Multiple PivotTables):

- Go to **Data → Refresh All** (or press **Alt + F5 + A**)
- Updates all PivotTables in the workbook

Pro Tip: Use tables for dynamic datasets like ongoing sales logs to save time.

PivotTable Pro Tips for Beginners

Creating your first PivotTable can feel overwhelming, but these tips will help you avoid common pitfalls and make the process smoother.

1. Start Simple

Beginners often overload their PivotTables with too many fields. Focus on one clear question at a time:

Do This:

- **Rows:** Product Category
- **Values:** Total Sales

  Question example: "What are our top-selling products?"

Avoid This:

- Adding Region, Salesperson, Month, and Discount simultaneously
- Creating a complex matrix before mastering basics

2. Use Clear Column Names

- Rename vague headers like "Column1" to descriptive names, e.g., **Region** or **Revenue**.
- Bonus: Use underscores instead of spaces (e.g., Unit_Price) to prevent formula errors later.

3. Practice with Sample Data

Try using free datasets to build confidence:

- Mock sales data

- Government statistics
- Monthly expenses or survey responses

Common PivotTable Mistakes to Avoid

Even experienced users can stumble. Here's how to stay on track:

1. Mixed Data Types

- Issue: Columns with numbers and text (e.g., $1,250 and "N/A") can confuse Excel.
- Consequences: Excel may count instead of sum, skip numeric values, or miscalculate averages.
- Fix: Clean your data first (Text to Columns, Find/Replace, IFERROR), and use consistent formatting (e.g., all currency).

2. Forgetting to Refresh

- Scenario: Presenting quarterly results without refreshing → old numbers shown.
- Prevention: Always refresh before reports or presentations.
- Tip: Use a "LAST REFRESHED: [date]" cell for a visual reminder. Power Query can automate refreshes from connected data sources.

3. Overloading Fields

- Symptoms: Slow response, "Not Responding" messages, or overwhelming grids.
- Cure: Follow the **5-3-2 Rule**:
  - ≤ 5 row fields
  - ≤ 3 column fields
  - ≤ 2 value calculations
- Use **Slicers** for interactive filtering instead of adding more fields.

Wrapping Up: PivotTable Mastery

By following these principles, you can turn raw data into actionable insights:

1. Prepare Data Like a Pro

- Clean tables with clear headers
- Consistent formatting
- No blank rows or columns

2. Build Insightful Reports

- ❖ Drag-and-drop simplicity
- ❖ Smart grouping (dates, categories)
- ❖ Custom calculations

3. Maintain Accuracy

- ❖ Refresh regularly
- ❖ Use Excel Tables for dynamic data
- ❖ Avoid performance killers like too many fields

Next Steps for Skill Growth

1. Practice daily with different datasets
2. Explore sorting and filtering variations
3. Create a PivotChart as your first advanced visualization

Pro Tip: The best way to learn PivotTables is by doing—open Excel now and start pivoting your data!

CHAPTER NINTEEN

CONNECTING QUICKBOOKS TO POWER BI

QuickBooks offers powerful financial reports, but they can be difficult for non-financial stakeholders—executives, sales teams, marketers, and operations—to interpret. Power BI solves this challenge by turning raw QuickBooks data into clear, interactive dashboards that make financial insights easier to communicate and analyze.

Below is an overview of the **best ways to connect QuickBooks to Power BI**, so you can share results with teams, collaborate across the organization, and make informed, data-driven decisions.

AVAILABLE METHODS FOR CONNECTING QUICKBOOKS TO POWER BI

Here are the primary options you can choose from:

1. Using the QuickBooks Connector by Coupler.io

Coupler.io is a powerful no-code automation platform designed to export QuickBooks data directly into Power BI. It is easy to set up and offers several advantages:

- ❖ **Simple setup** — takes only a few minutes
- ❖ **Automated data refresh** — your Power BI dashboard updates at intervals you choose
- ❖ **Built-in transformation tools** — clean or shape your data before loading it
- ❖ **No technical expertise required** — ideal for finance teams
- ❖ **Professional templates** — pre-built QuickBooks dashboard layouts for quick reporting

This method is perfect for anyone who wants **continuous, hands-off syncing** between QuickBooks and Power BI.

2. Manual Exporting (Excel → Power BI)

This is the most straightforward option, but also the most time-consuming.

How it works:

1. Export QuickBooks data as an **Excel (.xlsx)** file
2. Import that file into Power BI

3. Build your report from there

Downside:
Every time your numbers change, you must repeat the export and upload process manually. This makes it impractical for businesses that need frequent updates or real-time insights.

3. Custom API Integration (Advanced & Technical)

For companies needing a fully tailored solution, QuickBooks can be connected to Power BI using the QuickBooks API. However, this requires:

- Generating access tokens through the Intuit Developer Portal
- Writing scripts to extract data
- Storing the data in a database (e.g., PostgreSQL, BigQuery)
- Pulling that database into Power BI via "Get Data"

This option is extremely flexible but demands significant technical expertise, ongoing maintenance, and familiarity with APIs and databases. Because of its complexity, we won't go into deeper detail here.

IS THERE A NATIVE QUICKBOOKS ONLINE CONNECTOR IN POWER BI?

Power BI **used to include** a built-in QuickBooks Online connector that relied on the QuickBooks ODBC Driver.

However:

- The connector was **fully deprecated in August 2025**
- Microsoft has **no plans** to release a new QuickBooks connector

This means users—both new and existing—can no longer rely on native integration.

But there's good news: **Coupler.io offers a seamless and reliable alternative**, allowing you to sync QuickBooks data to Power BI automatically, without coding or complex setup.

HOW TO SET UP A QUICKBOOKS–POWER BI INTEGRATION WITH COUPLER.IO (AUTOMATED DATA SYNC)

Coupler.io makes it easy to export QuickBooks data into Power BI so you can build live dashboards and reports. The entire setup only takes a few minutes and involves three simple steps.

Step 1: Connect and Retrieve Your QuickBooks Data

1. Begin by selecting **Proceed** in the pre-configured Coupler.io form.
   - ❖ If you prefer exporting a preset QuickBooks report (e.g., *Balance Sheet, Cash Flow, Vendor Balance*), switch the source from **QuickBooks** to **QuickBooks Reports**.
2. If you're new to Coupler.io, create a free account—no credit card required.
3. After signing in, connect your QuickBooks account by granting Coupler.io permission to access your financial data.
4. Choose the specific QuickBooks data entity you want to export, such as:

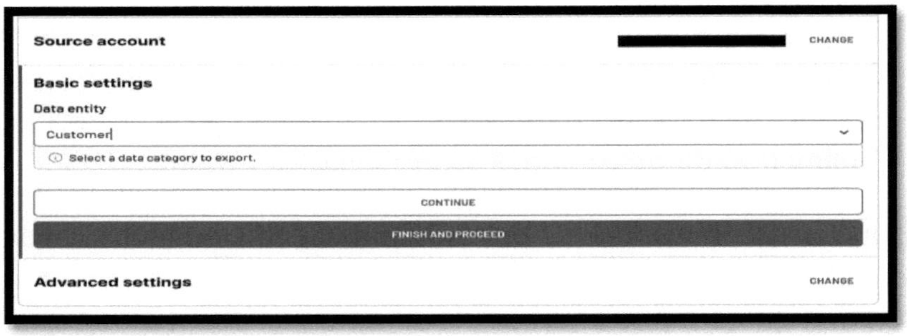

   - ❖ **Invoices**
   - ❖ **Customers**
   - ❖ **Payments**
   - ❖ **Vendors**
   - ❖ **Sales**
   - ❖ And others
5. Coupler.io also allows you to combine multiple QuickBooks entities or additional external data sources in one flow.
   Example: To build a month-over-month Profit & Loss dashboard, you can add two P&L summary reports from different time periods and load them together.

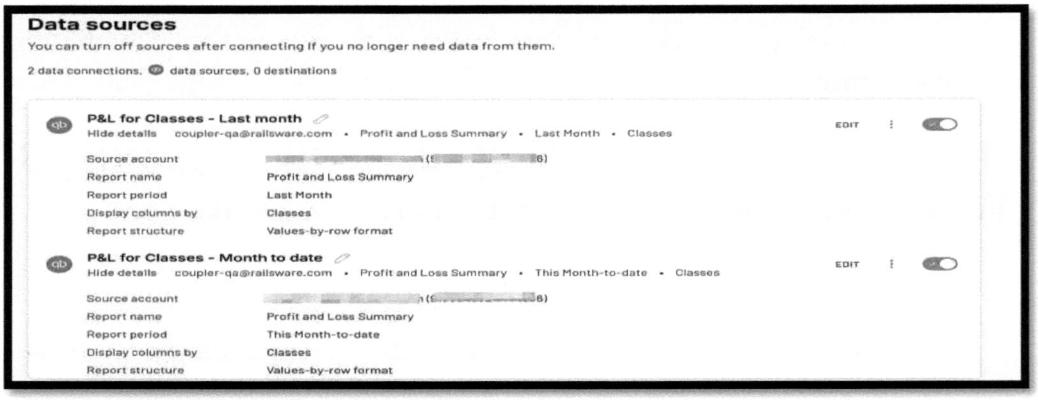

Step 2: Prepare, Organize, and Transform Your Data

Before sending your data to Power BI, review it in Coupler.io and make any needed adjustments.

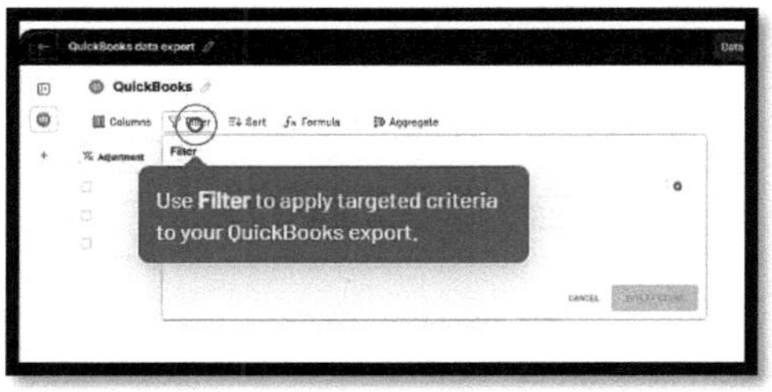

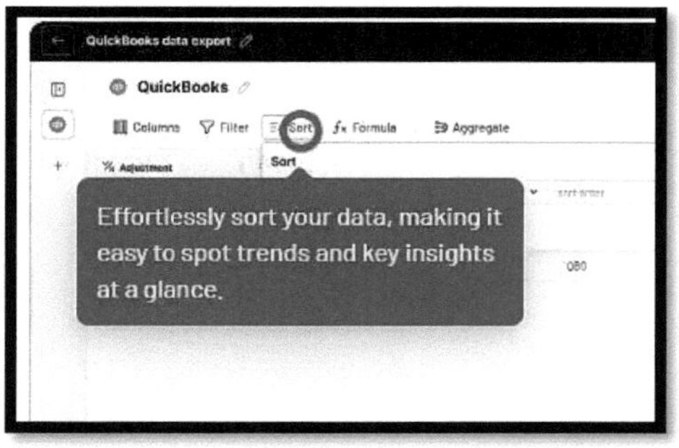

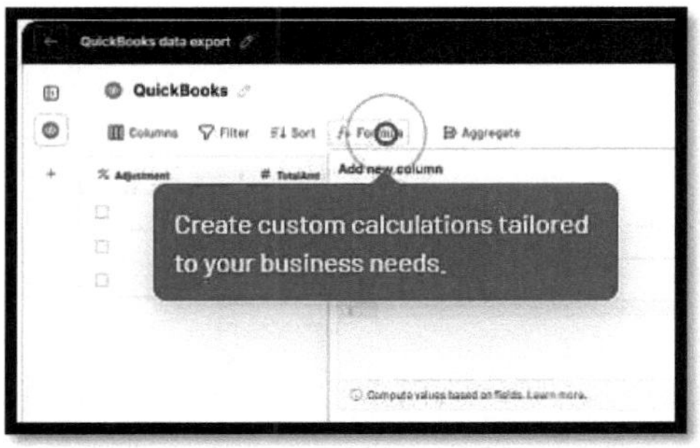

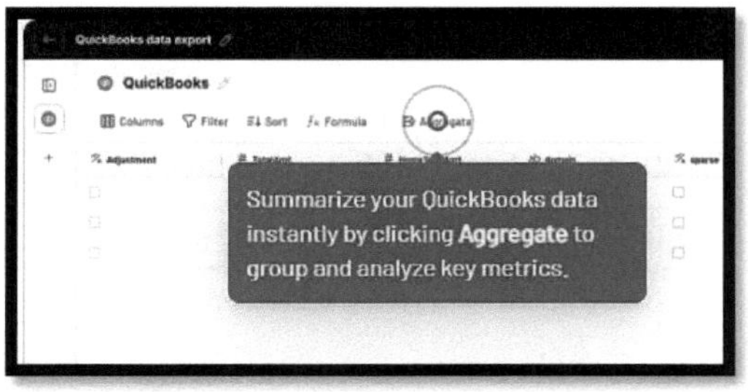

Available transformation options include:

Basic transformations:

- ❖ Renaming fields
- ❖ Filtering records

❖ Changing data types
❖ Adjusting column order

Advanced transformations for combining data:

❖ **Join:** Merge two or more datasets horizontally using a shared key column
❖ **Append:** Stack datasets vertically when they have the same structure

These tools ensure that your QuickBooks data is clean, consistent, and ready for analysis.

Once everything looks correct, continue to the final step.

Step 3: Load Your Data into Power BI and Set Up Auto-Refresh

1. Click **Generate Link** in Coupler.io to create an integration URL.
2. Copy the link.

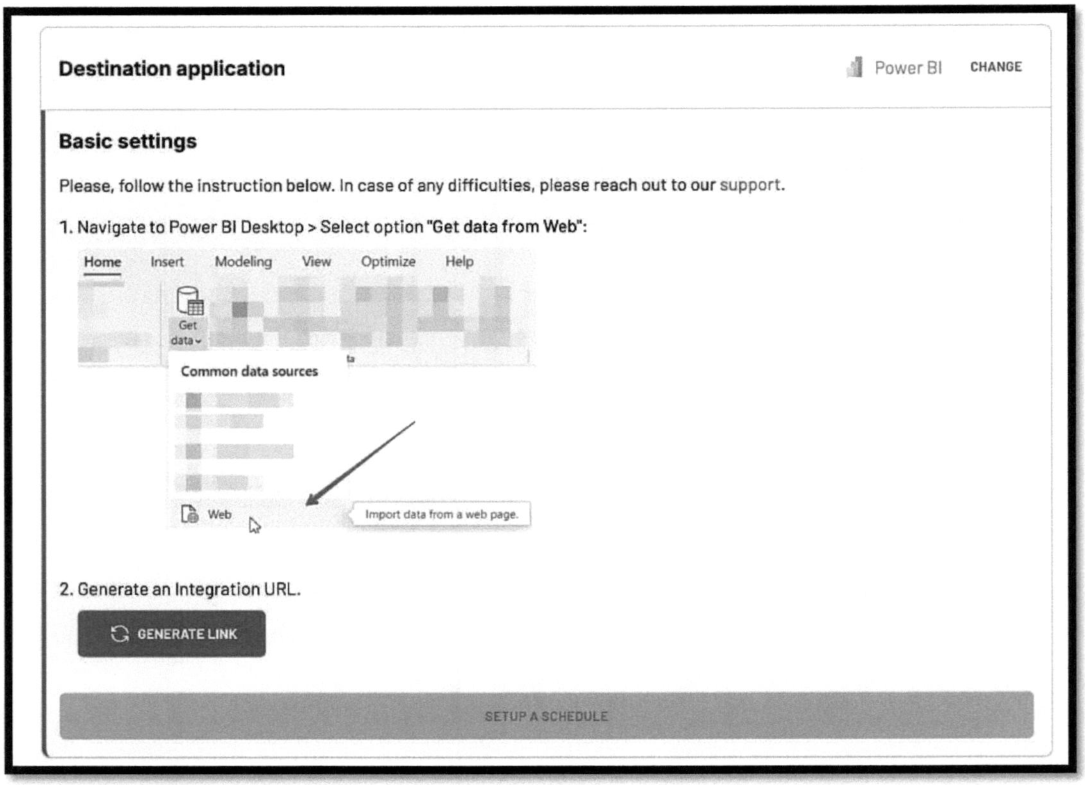

Import into Power BI:

1. Open **Power BI Desktop**.
2. Select **Get Data > Web**.

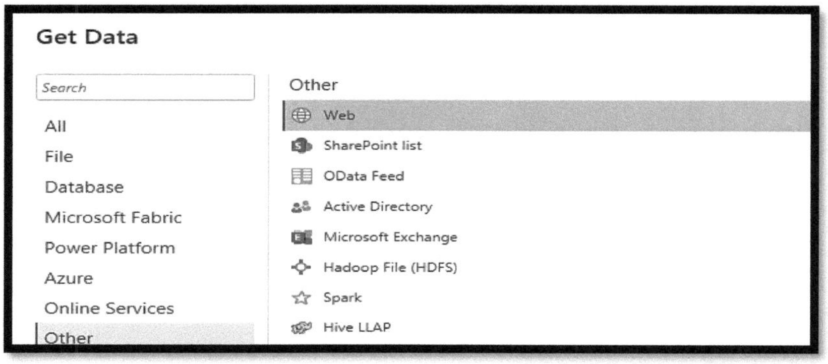

3. Paste the integration link from Coupler.io.
4. In the **Power Query Editor**, preview your data and apply any final transformations if necessary.
5. Load the dataset into Power BI.

You will now see your QuickBooks data on the Power BI report canvas, where you can build visualizations, charts, and fully customized dashboards.

Enable Automatic Updates

To make your QuickBooks data refresh automatically inside Power BI:

1. Return to your Coupler.io importer settings.
2. Turn on **Automatic Data Refresh**.
3. Choose:
   - ❖ Update frequency
   - ❖ Days of the week
   - ❖ Preferred time zone

   This ensures your Power BI dashboards always reflect the latest financial data—without manual exports.

4. Click **Save and Run** to finalize the integration and send the latest data to Power BI.

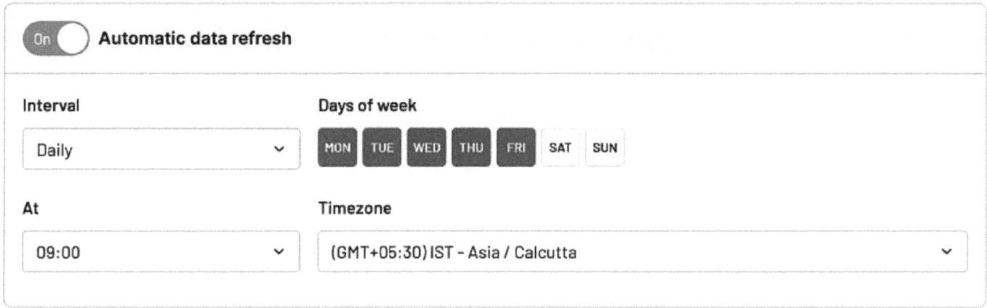

WHAT DATA CAN YOU EXPORT FROM QUICKBOOKS ONLINE TO POWER BI USING COUPLER.IO?

Coupler.io makes it easy to move your QuickBooks Online data into Power BI. You can export **raw data**, **standard QuickBooks reports**, and **pre-built data sets**. These data sets are curated QuickBooks entities or reports that already include useful transformations—such as aggregated values, calculated fields, added columns, and removal of unnecessary information.

1. Data Entities

Coupler.io lets you export a wide selection of QuickBooks data entities.

(Expandable list in the original interface)

2. Reports

You can also export many QuickBooks reports in ready-to-use format.

(Expandable list in the original interface)

3. Data Set Templates

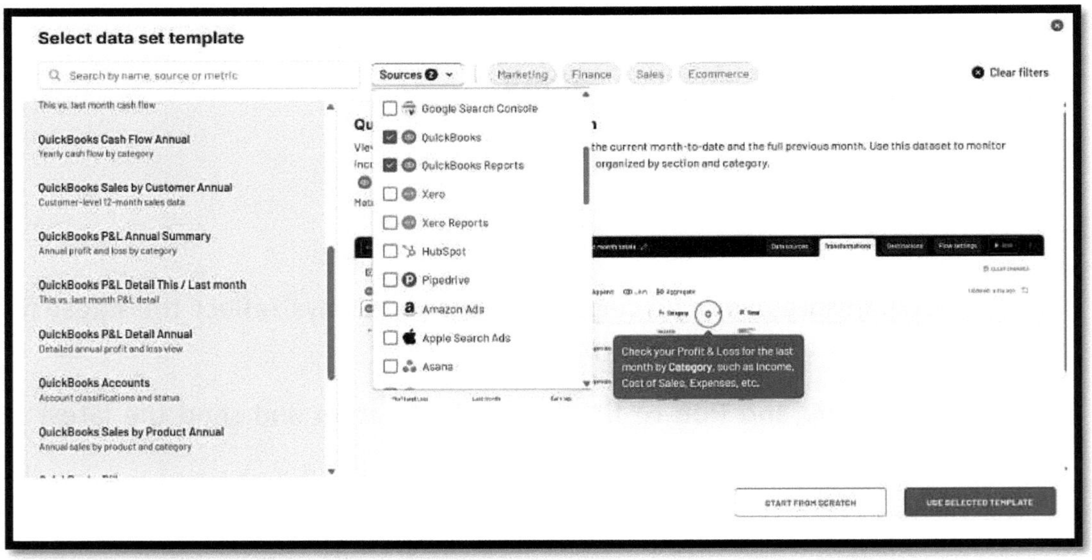

To use QuickBooks data sets, simply create a new data flow from a template. Filter the templates by **QuickBooks** or **QuickBooks Reports** as the source, choose the template you need, and complete the setup. The data will then load directly into Power BI.

QUICKBOOKS REVENUE DASHBOARD TEMPLATE IN POWER BI

This template is designed to give you a fast, meaningful overview of your company's financial performance.

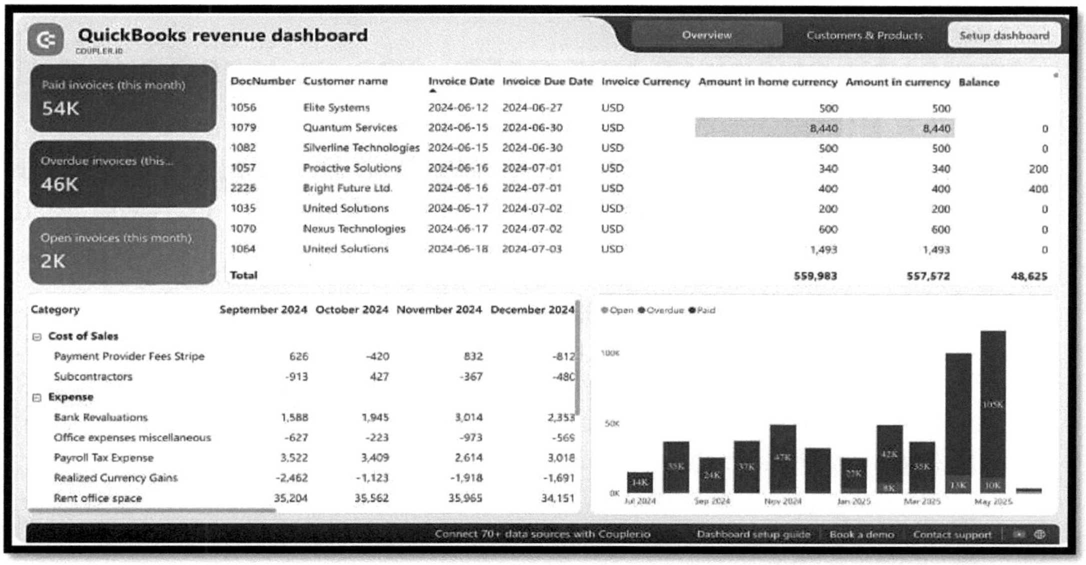

Overview Tab

- ❖ Displays your **revenue trends over the past year**, helping you spot seasonal patterns, peak periods, and unexpected drops.
- ❖ Includes an **invoice table** with key details such as due dates, amounts, and outstanding balances.

Profit and Loss Overview

- ❖ Compares **income vs. expenses** to help you track profitability.
- ❖ Ensures your budgeting and financial planning remain aligned.

Customers & Products Tab

- ❖ Highlights your **top customers**, supporting targeted marketing or loyalty programs.
- ❖ Shows your **best-selling products**, making it easier to optimize inventory and improve sales strategy.

Getting Started

To begin using the template:

1. Open the template in Coupler.io.

2. Read the instructions on the **Readme** tab.
3. Connect your QuickBooks account.

Once connected, Coupler.io will automatically refresh your data, keeping your Power BI dashboards up-to-date with no additional work.

COMMON BUSINESS USE CASES FOR QUICKBOOKS DATA IN POWER BI

Now that you know what types of QuickBooks data you can access, here are the most valuable real-world ways companies use this information in Power BI to solve everyday business challenges.

1. Multi-Entity Financial Consolidation

Managing multiple subsidiaries, branches, or business units—each with its own QuickBooks account—makes consolidation a complex, time-consuming task. Coupler.io simplifies this by automatically merging:

- Profit & Loss statements
- Balance sheets
- Cash flow reports

directly from multiple QuickBooks accounts into **one unified Power BI dashboard**.

This is especially powerful for:

- Holding companies
- Franchise networks
- International businesses with currency differences
- Organizations using different chart of accounts structures

With automated consolidation, month-end closes that once took days can drop to **a few hours**, while reducing manual errors and improving financial visibility.

2. Sales Performance & Commission Tracking

Many businesses struggle to connect CRM metrics with actual revenue collected in QuickBooks. Coupler.io makes it possible to combine QuickBooks payment data with CRM systems such as:

- HubSpot
- Salesforce
- Pipedrive

to build **true revenue dashboards** that go beyond bookings.

With this blend of data, Power BI can help you:

- Calculate commissions based on *collected* revenue, not just sales bookings
- Track territory-level performance
- Identify accounts with late or irregular payment patterns
- Reduce commission disputes
- Support revenue operations teams with accurate insights

This provides a realistic view of sales effectiveness and ensures fair, error-free compensation planning.

3. Multi-Location Inventory Optimization

Businesses with several stores, warehouses, or distribution centers often struggle to maintain real-time visibility into stock levels. Coupler.io can gather inventory data from multiple QuickBooks locations and push it into Power BI with automatic refreshes.

With centralized dashboards, you can:

- Monitor stock levels across all locations
- Analyze demand trends
- Identify slow-moving items
- Reduce stockouts and excess inventory
- Optimize working capital
- Make data-driven inventory allocation decisions

This unified view helps retail, e-commerce, and distribution companies run more efficiently.

MANUALLY IMPORT YOUR QUICKBOOKS DATA TO POWER BI (XLSX METHOD)

If you prefer not to use connectors or automation tools, you can still upload QuickBooks data to Power BI manually using Excel. This method works for QuickBooks Online and QuickBooks Desktop.

Step 1: Download Your QuickBooks Data

From QuickBooks Online

1. Log in to QuickBooks Online.
2. Click the **Gear icon** (top-right).

3. Select **Export Data**, choose the reason for export, and click **Continue**.

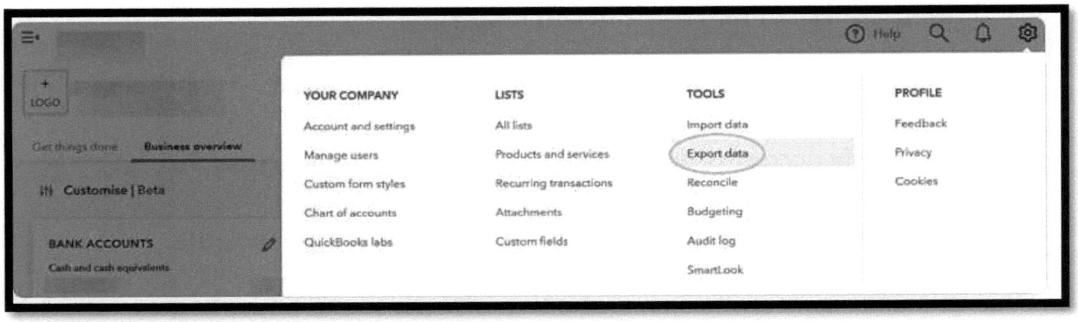

4. Go to the **Reports** tab and set your date range.
5. Customize your data using the **Reports** and **Lists** tabs.
6. Click **Export to Excel** and save the file.

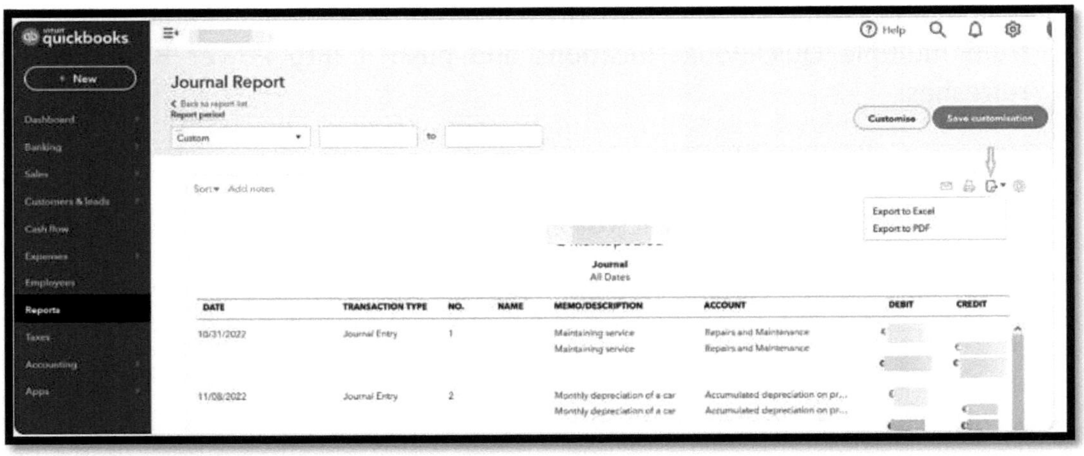

From QuickBooks Desktop

1. Open QuickBooks Desktop and run the report you want to export.
2. Click **Excel** at the top of the report.
3. Choose **Create New Worksheet** or **Update Existing Worksheet**.
4. Select **.xls** or **.xlsx**, then click **Export**.
5. Save the file to your computer.

Once exported, you're ready to load the file into Power BI.

Step 2: Import the Excel File Into Power BI

1. Open Power BI.
2. Click **Get Data > Excel**.

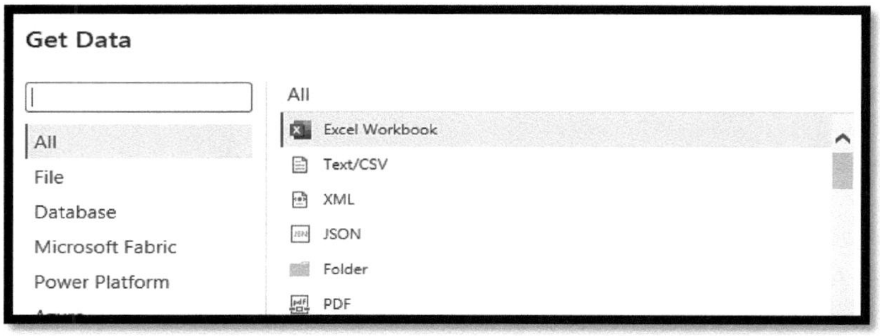

3. Select the QuickBooks **.xlsx** file and choose **Connect**.
4. Review the data in **Power Query Editor**.
5. Click **Close & Apply** to load the data into your workspace.

You can now build visuals, dashboards, and reports using Power BI tools.

Important Note

The manual export/import method is fine for occasional reporting or smaller datasets—but it can become tedious if you need frequent updates. For ongoing or daily reporting, automated tools like Coupler.io save significant time.

POWER BI QUICKBOOKS CONNECTOR STOPPED WORKING? HERE'S WHY (AND HOW TO FIX IT)

If you opened Power BI recently and noticed your QuickBooks dashboards stopped updating—or broke entirely—you're not alone. Everything worked smoothly just weeks ago, so what changed?

In **May 2025**, Microsoft confirmed that the **Power BI QuickBooks Online connector would be discontinued** by the end of summer. The phase-out happened fast:

- **June–July 2025:** Connector removed from Power BI Service & Desktop
- **August 2025:** Connector officially fully deprecated

This rapid transition has left thousands of businesses scrambling to figure out their next steps.

What This Deprecation Means for Your Existing QuickBooks Power BI Reports

Here's what you should expect moving forward:

1. Scheduled refreshes no longer work

Your dashboards will show errors or outdated data permanently.

2. There is *no replacement* coming from Microsoft

Microsoft has not announced any plans for a new QuickBooks connector.

3. Manual exports are the only native workaround

This involves exporting QuickBooks data → transforming it → loading it through multiple Microsoft tools.

It works… but it's slow, error-prone, and not scalable.

The good news?

You can replace the connector entirely with an automated solution—**Coupler.io**—and restore your live QuickBooks → Power BI updates in minutes.

How to Easily Connect QuickBooks to Power BI with Coupler.io

Creating your new QuickBooks → Power BI pipeline with Coupler.io only takes a few steps. Here's how to set it up.

1. Collect Your QuickBooks Online Data

Start by connecting your QuickBooks account in Coupler.io. A secure pop-up will appear for sign-in and authorization.

Next, choose the type of data you want to sync—such as:

- Invoices
- Bills
- Purchases
- Budgets
- Customers
- Vendors
- Payments

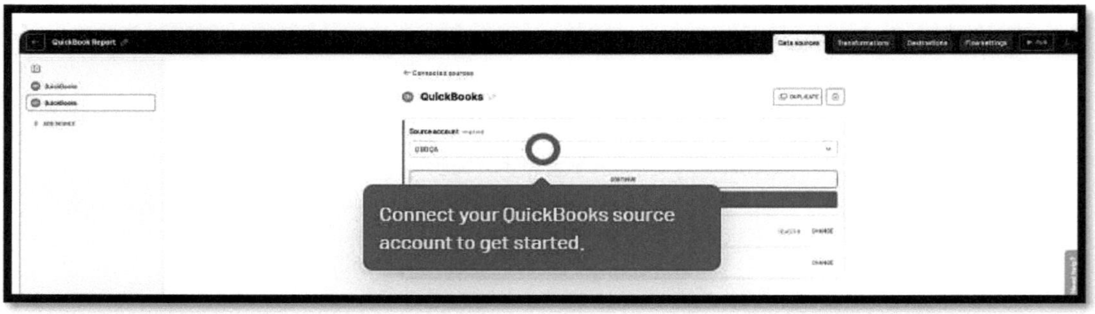

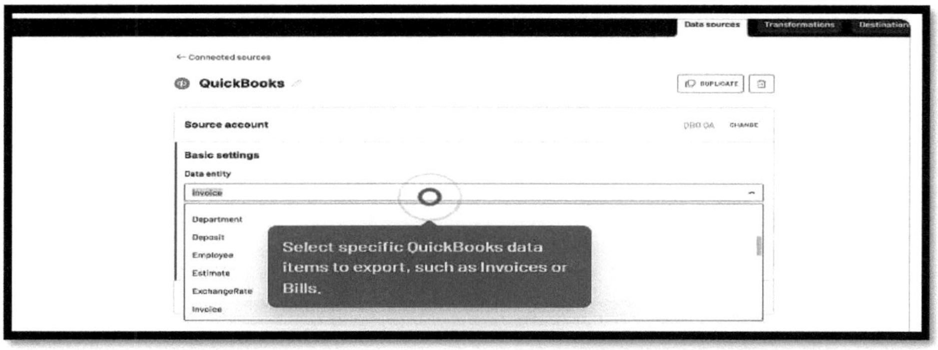

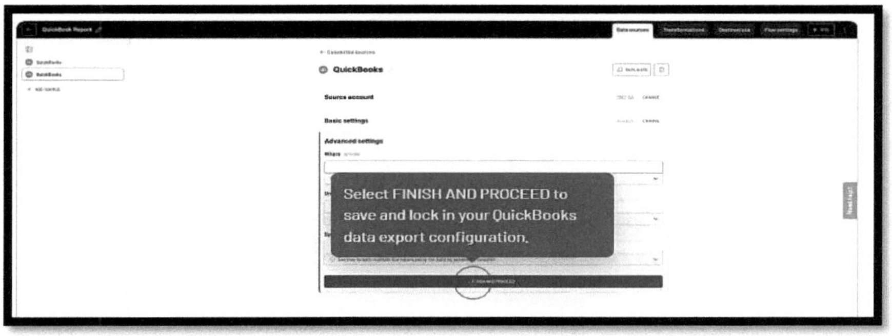

Use **Advanced Settings** to filter the data by date, status, amount, or other parameters.

Need multiple datasets?

If you require more than one QuickBooks entity (e.g., *Invoices + Customers*), simply add additional data sources in the same workflow.

Need QuickBooks reports instead of raw data?

Choose **QuickBooks Reports** from the data source menu to export:

- Profit & Loss
- Balance Sheet

- ❖ Cash Flow
- ❖ Vendor Balance
- ❖ Product/Service Sales
  and others.

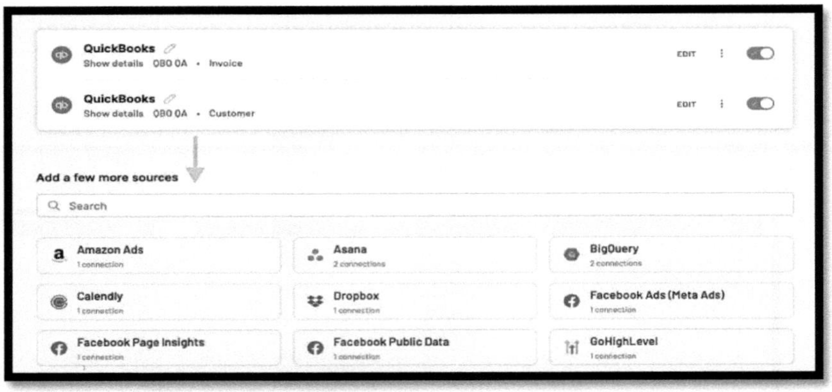

2. Organize and Prepare Your Data

Once your data is collected, use the Transformations module to structure it for reporting. You can:

- ❖ **Filter & sort** columns
- ❖ **Hide** irrelevant fields
- ❖ **Rename** columns to match internal terminology
- ❖ **Add new calculated metrics**
- ❖ **Aggregate** values for summaries
- ❖ **Join or append** multiple data sets to build deeper financial or operational views

These tools allow you to reshape your QuickBooks data into the exact format your Power BI dashboards need.

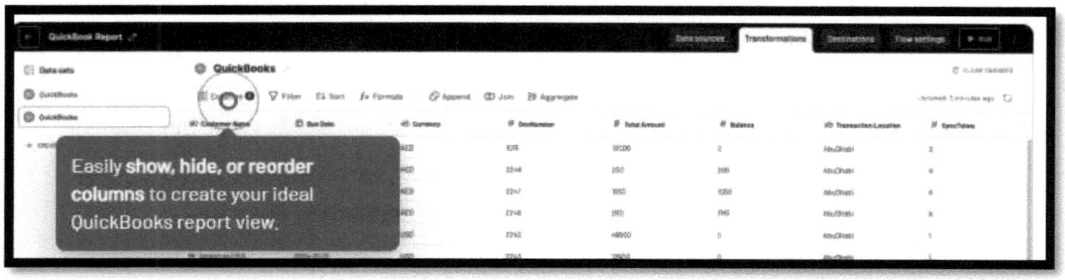

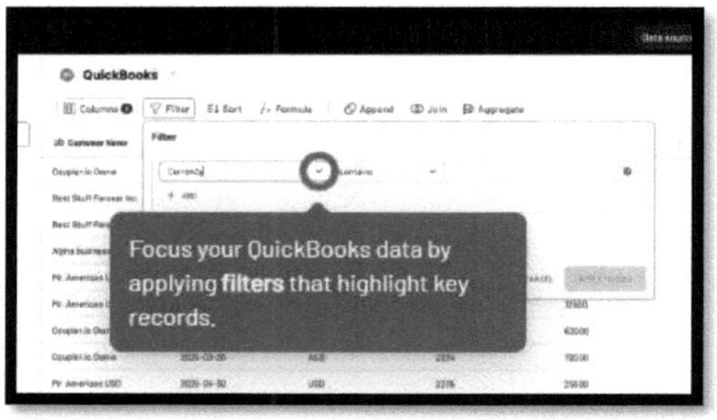

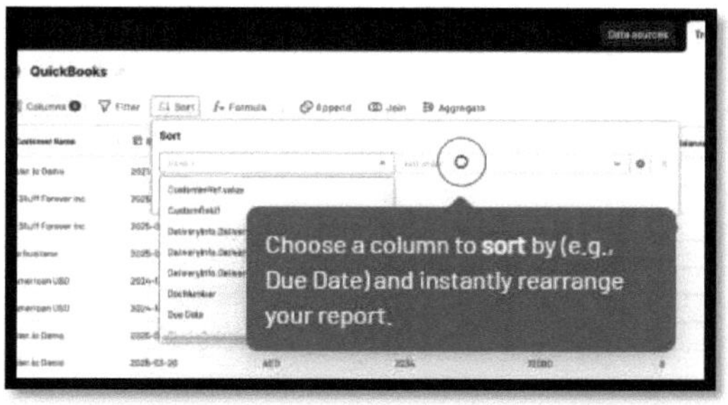

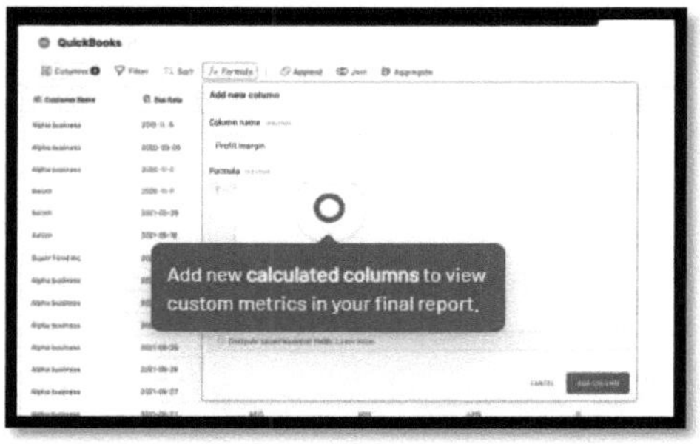

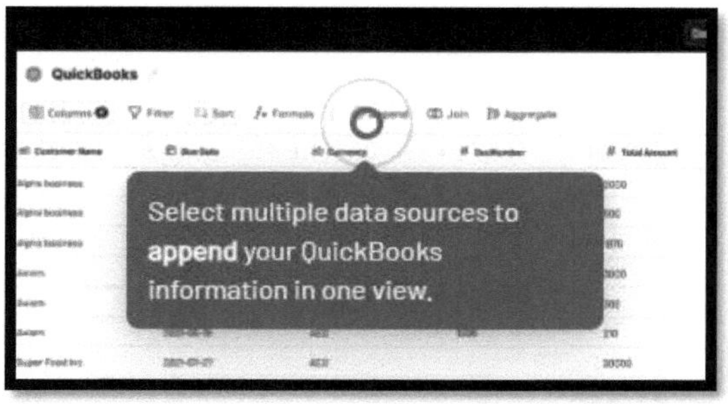

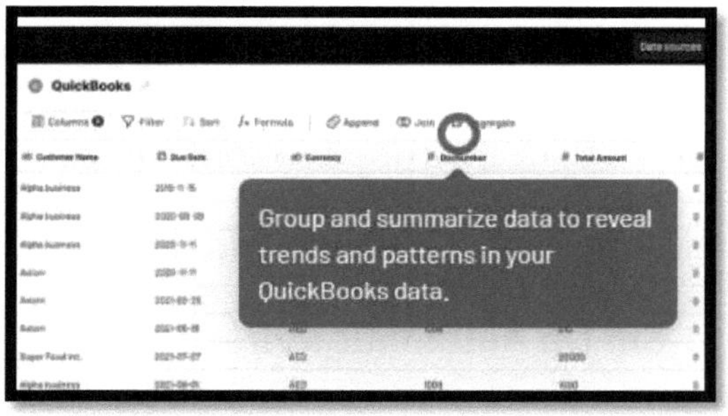

3. Connect Power BI and Schedule Automatic Refreshes

In the **Destinations** step:

1. Select the dataset you want to send (one source or a blended dataset).
2. Authorize your Power BI connection.

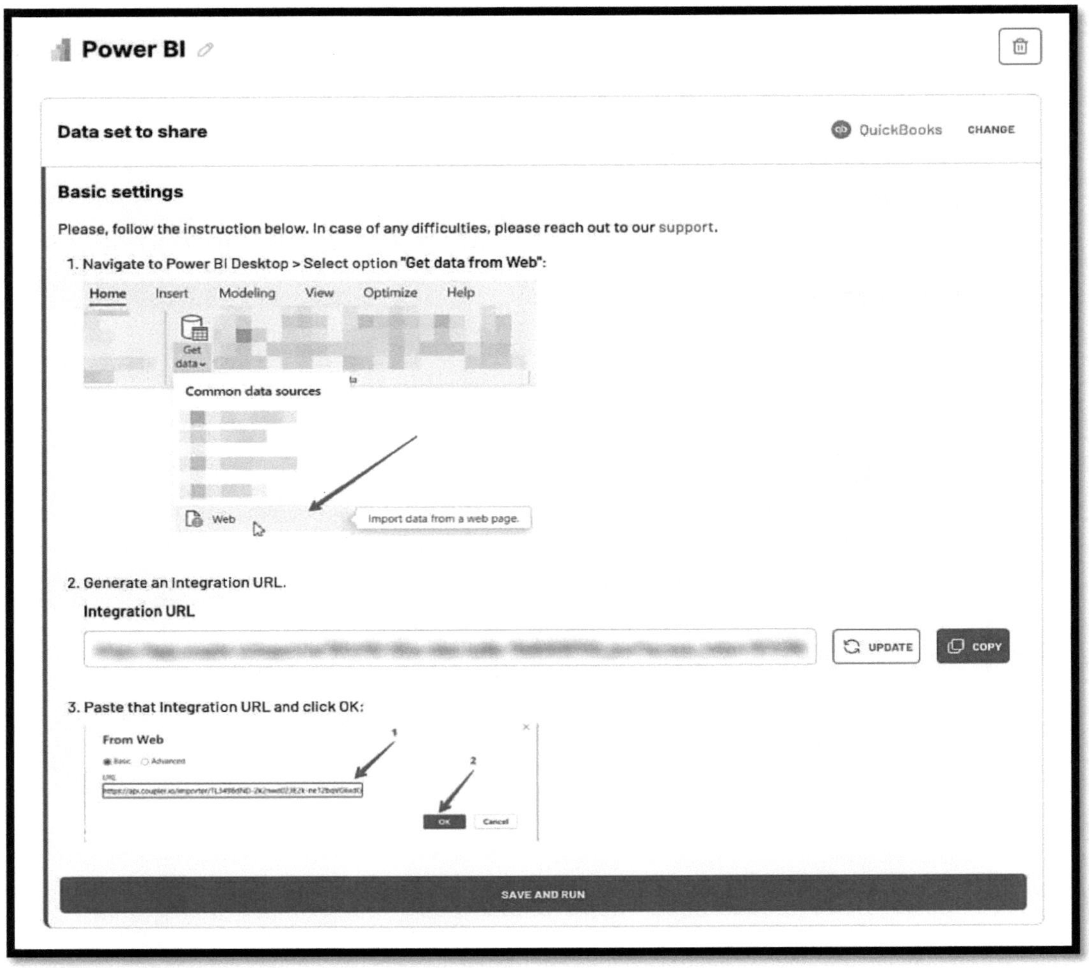

3. Generate and confirm your report.

After that, click **Save and Run**.

Set Up Automatic Refresh

You can schedule updates based on your preferences:

- Every 15 minutes
- Hourly
- Daily
- Weekly
- Specific weekdays
- Exact time & timezone

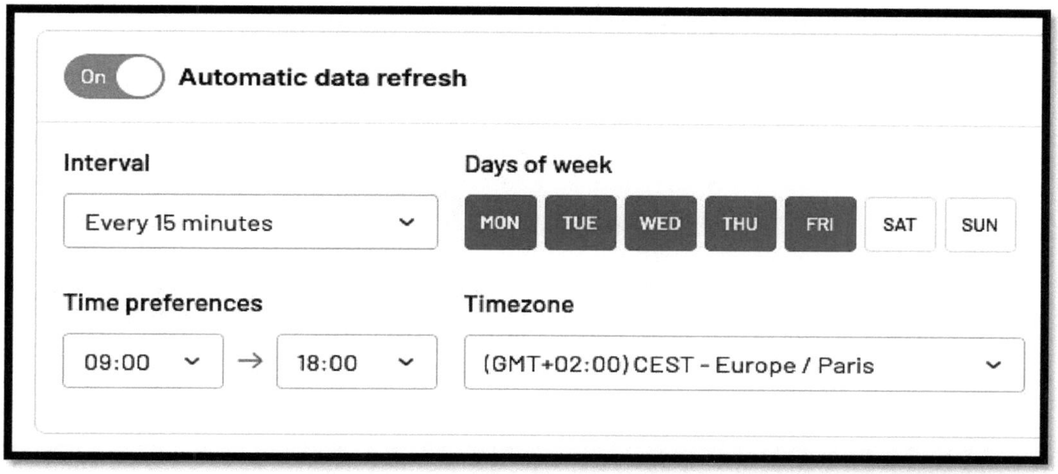

Once saved, Coupler.io will push your organized QuickBooks data into Power BI automatically—no manual exports, no broken connectors, no delays.

PART VII: AI, ACCOUNTANT TOOLS, AND COLLABORATION

CHAPTER TWENTY

QUICKBOOKS ONLINE'S NEW AI AGENTS: WHAT THEY ACTUALLY DO

You may think you already know your way around QuickBooks Online—but the platform's new AI agents add an entirely different level of automation. In this breakdown, we'll walk through the **Accounting Agent, Payments Agent, Customer Agent, and Finance Agent** so you can see how much time these tools can save you.

QuickBooks' AI features are tier-based—essentially **the higher your subscription plan, the more AI agents you unlock**.

Plan-by-Plan Overview

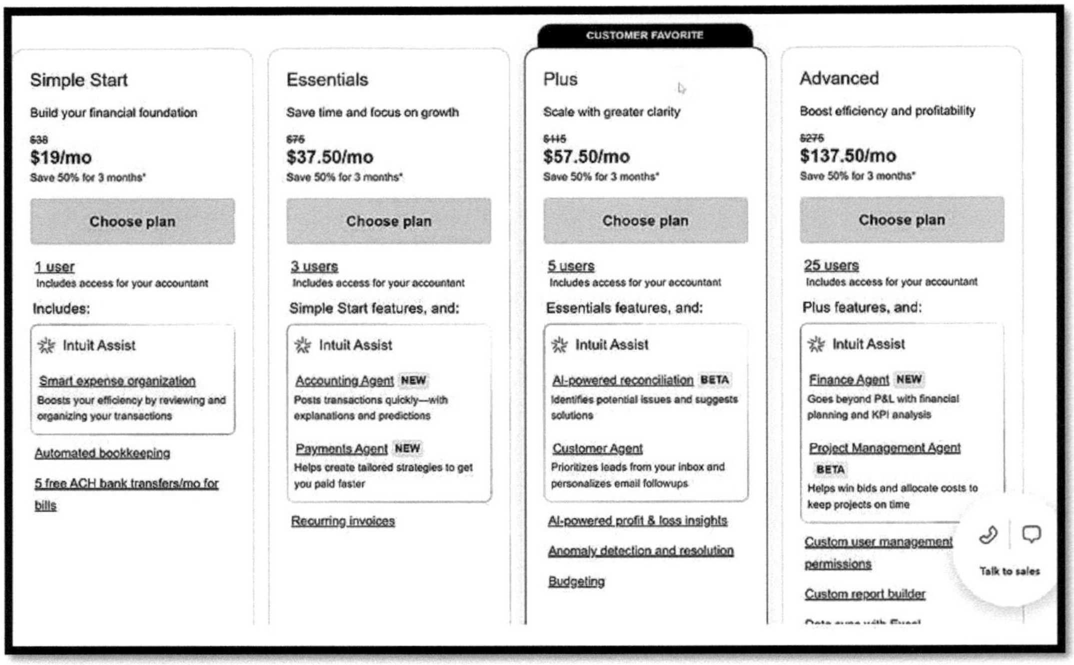

1. **Simple Start:** Ideal for solo finance management. Its built-in AI focuses on **automatically categorizing transactions**, eliminating hours of manual bookkeeping.
2. **Essentials & Plus:** Designed for teams. These tiers add:
   - The **Accounting Agent**, similar to Simple Start but more robust
   - The **Payments Agent**, which streamlines getting paid
   - Plus-tier extras: AI-assisted bank reconciliation and inbox-based lead tracking
3. **Advanced**
   Unlocks the **Finance Agent**, offering:
   - Highly detailed month-end, quarter-end, and year-end financial analyses
   - A new **Project Management Agent** (still in early stages)

The focus is on six major AI features—excluding the still-developing project management agent.

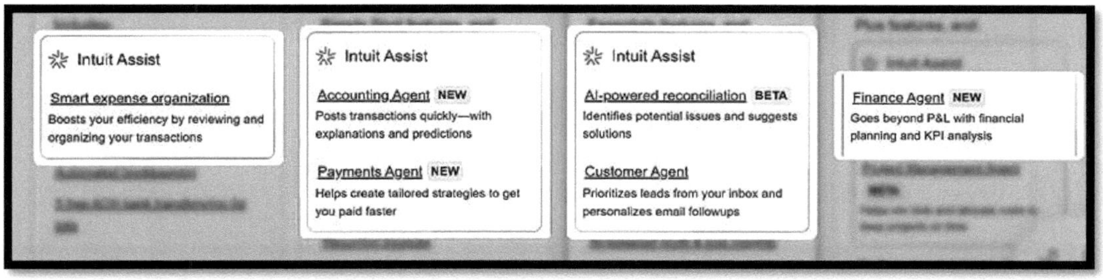

THE ACCOUNTING AGENT: FAST, INTELLIGENT BOOKKEEPING

If you've ever handled bookkeeping manually, you know the drill:

Sorting and categorizing every transaction at the end of each month or year can be slow, tedious, and error-prone.

The **Accounting Agent** changes that by applying AI trained on millions of real transactions to automatically categorize your imported bank data.

How it Works

On the QuickBooks dashboard:

1. Navigate to **Accounting → Bank Transactions**.

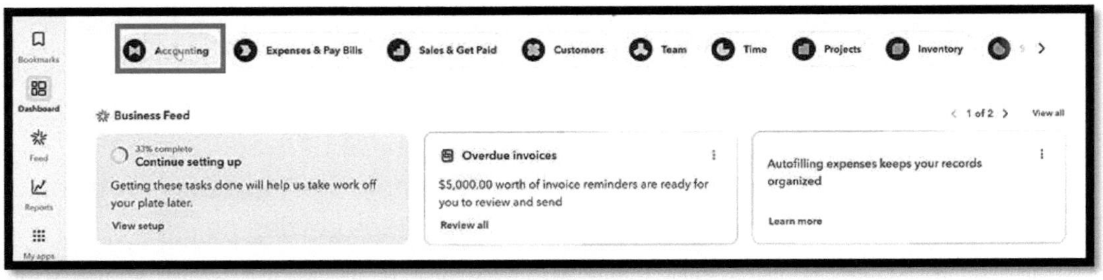

2. Upload downloaded bank transactions using **Upload from File**.

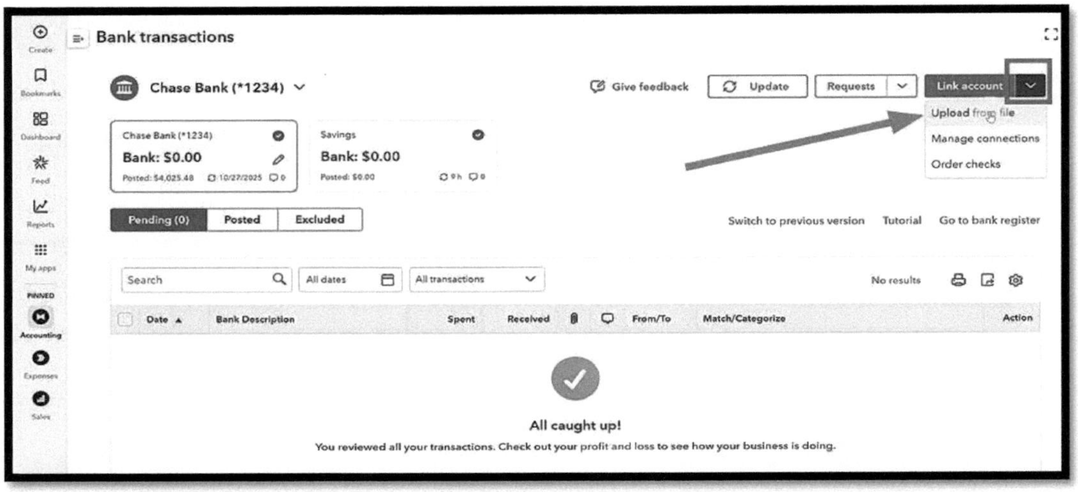

3. Drag in your CSV, confirm the formatting, and import.

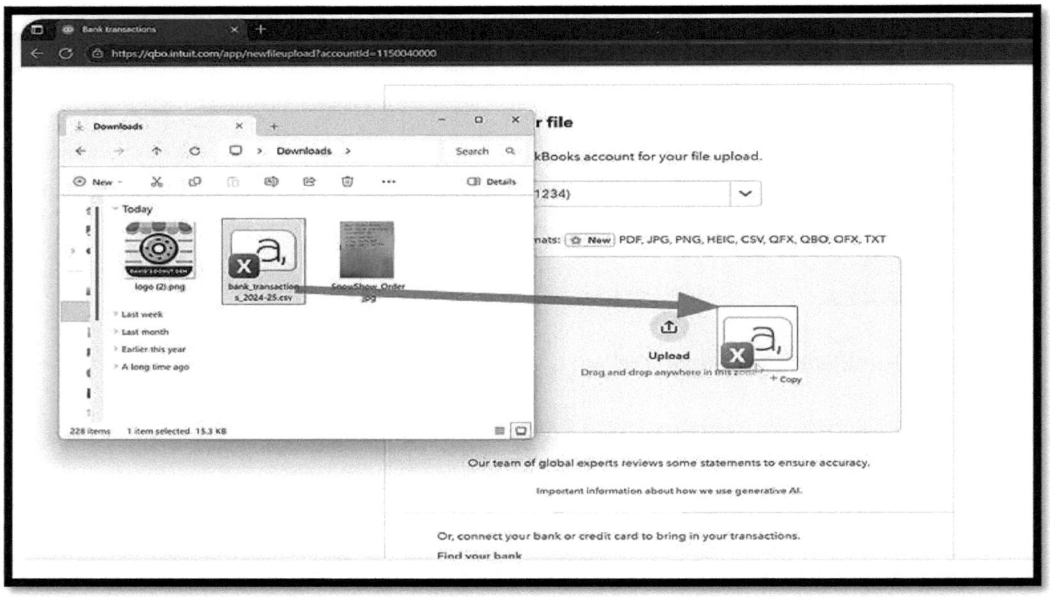

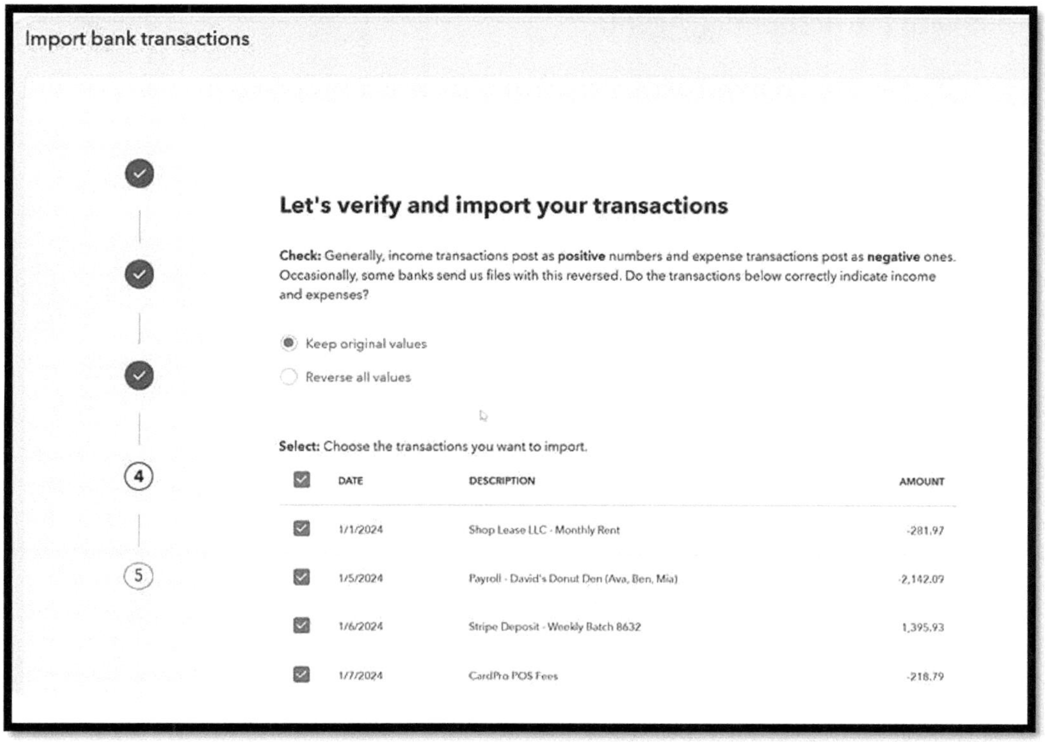

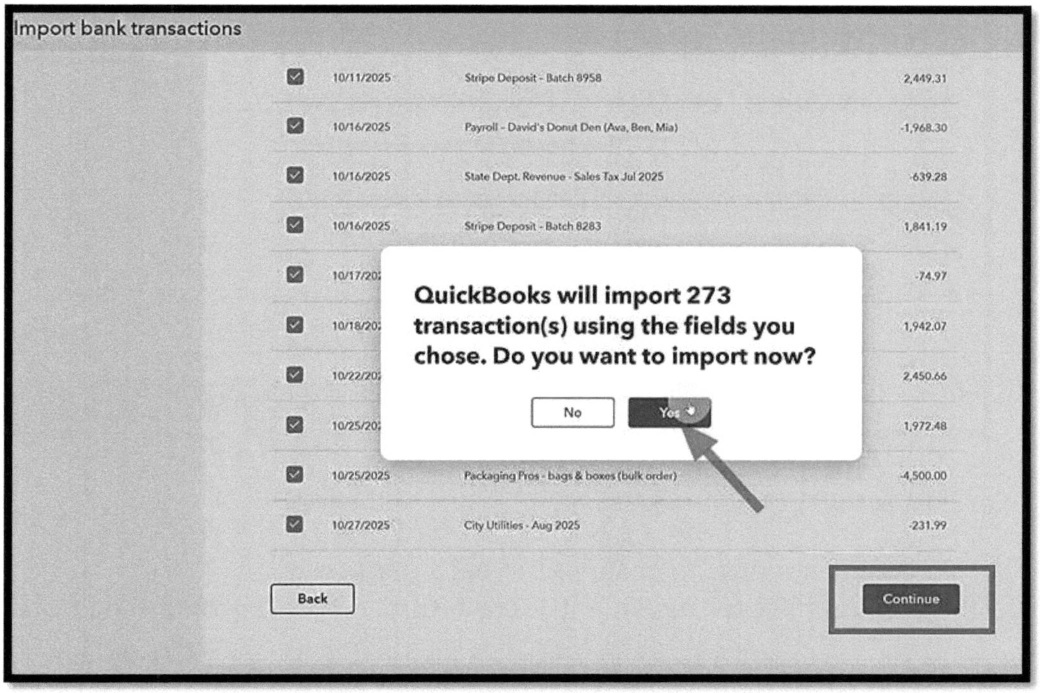

Normally, categorizing dozens—or hundreds—of transactions could take **45 minutes to several hours**, especially if you're unsure of the proper expense categories.

But with the Accounting Agent:

❖ Any line marked with a **star icon** has already been auto-categorized by AI.

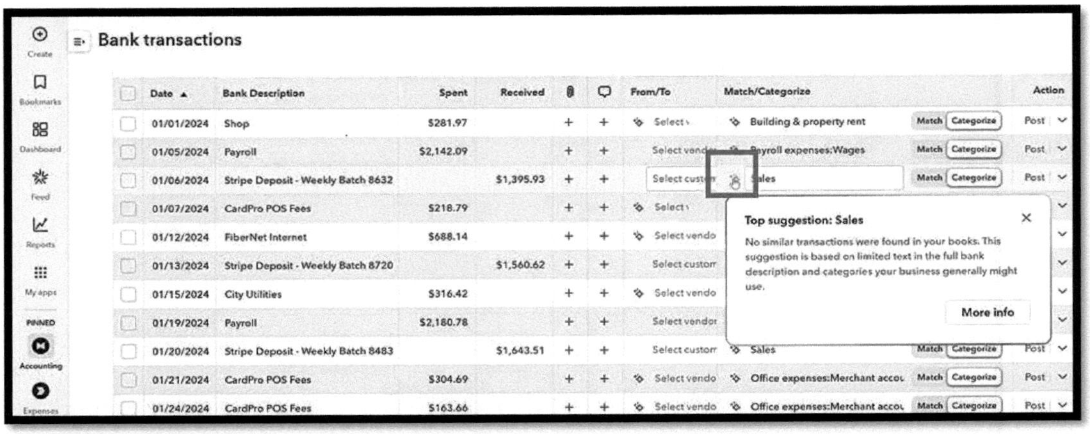

❖ You can review and approve everything in **under five minutes**.

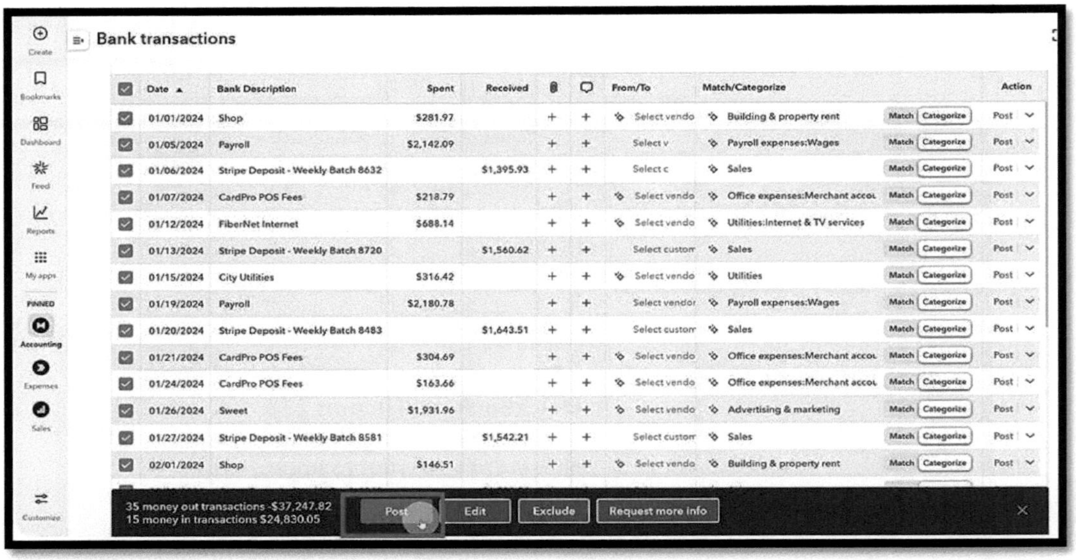

For best results, it's still wise to:

❖ Assign a vendor or customer to each transaction
❖ Create rules for repeat entries so future imports become even faster

AI-POWERED RECONCILIATION IN QUICKBOOKS ONLINE

Next, let's look at a more advanced bookkeeping task: **reconciliation**—the process of confirming that the transactions recorded in QuickBooks match the activity shown on your bank statement.

Before you begin, make sure **all of your transactions are posted** in QuickBooks. Once that's done, open the left sidebar and select **Reconcile**.

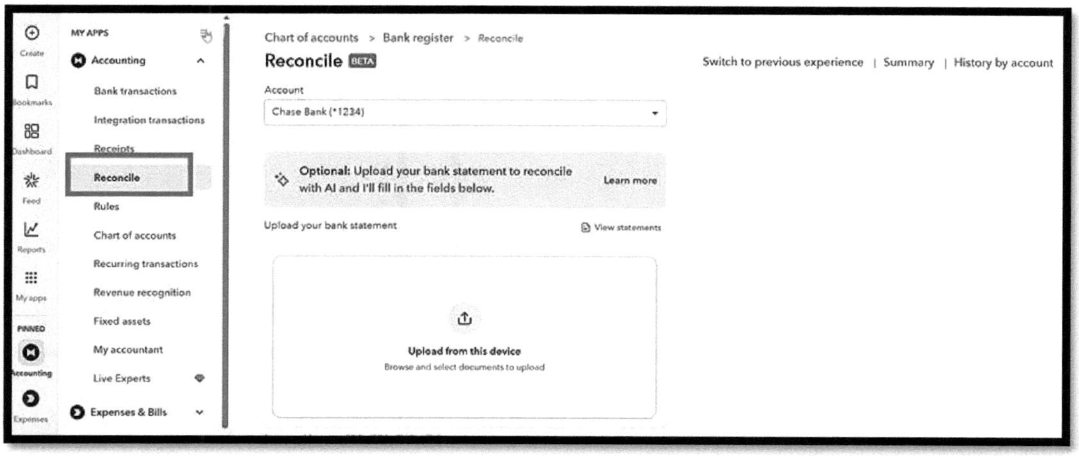

If you're using **QuickBooks Plus or Advanced**, you'll see an option to **upload a bank statement**. This feature automatically extracts the statement's **ending date** and **ending balance**, saving you the time of typing them manually.

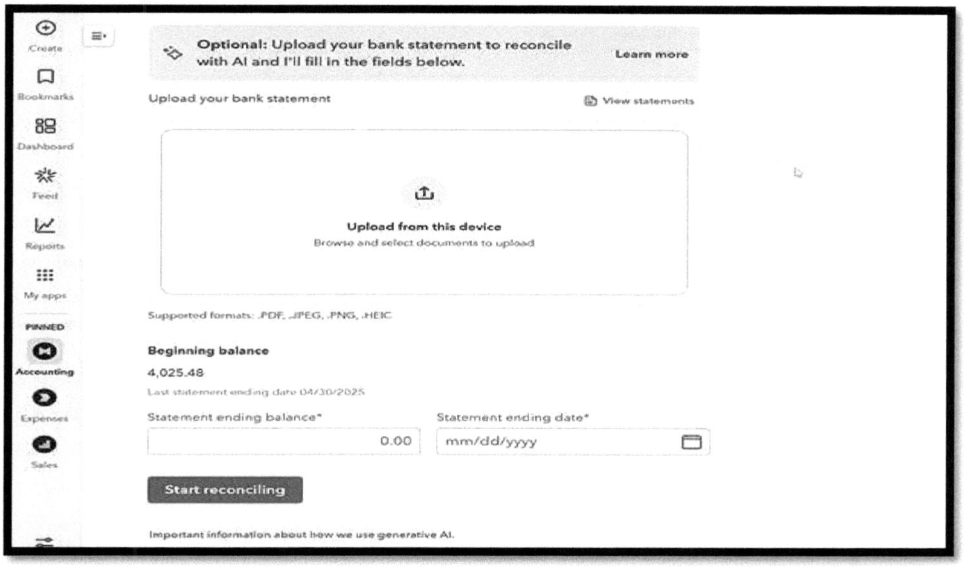

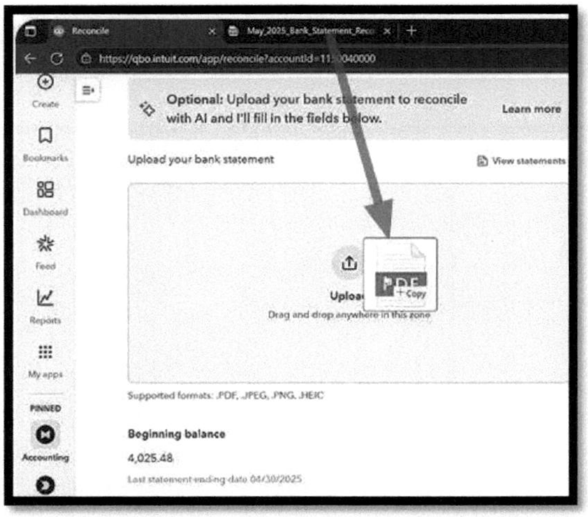

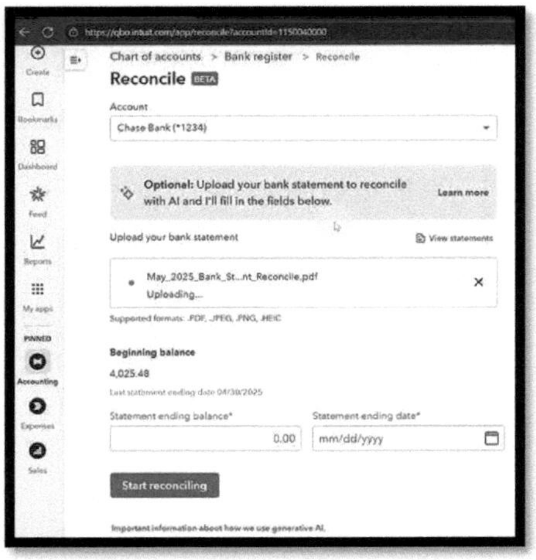

After uploading the statement, QuickBooks will detect details such as the May 31, 2025 closing balance of about **$125,000**.

Acme Community Bank

Statement for
Account: ****1234 Type: Business Checking
Statement Period: May 1, 2025 to May 31, 2025

Summary

Opening Balance: $4,025.48
Total Deposits: $8,754.58
Total Withdrawals: $197.42
Ending Balance: $12,582.64

Date	Description	Debit	Credit
2025-05-03	Stripe Deposit – Weekly Batch 7617		$1,859.07
2025-05-10	Stripe Deposit – Weekly Batch 7197		$1,915.86
2025-05-16	Stripe Deposit – Weekly Batch 9387		$1,675.30
2025-05-17	Stripe Deposit – Weekly Batch 9194		$1,657.95
2025-05-30	ATM Withdrawal - Statement Only	$197.42	
2025-05-31	Stripe Deposit – Weekly Batch 9078		$1,646.40

M1: Date mismatch remains (Batch 9387 shifted).
M3: Combined line removed; original Batches 7617 & 7197 restored.

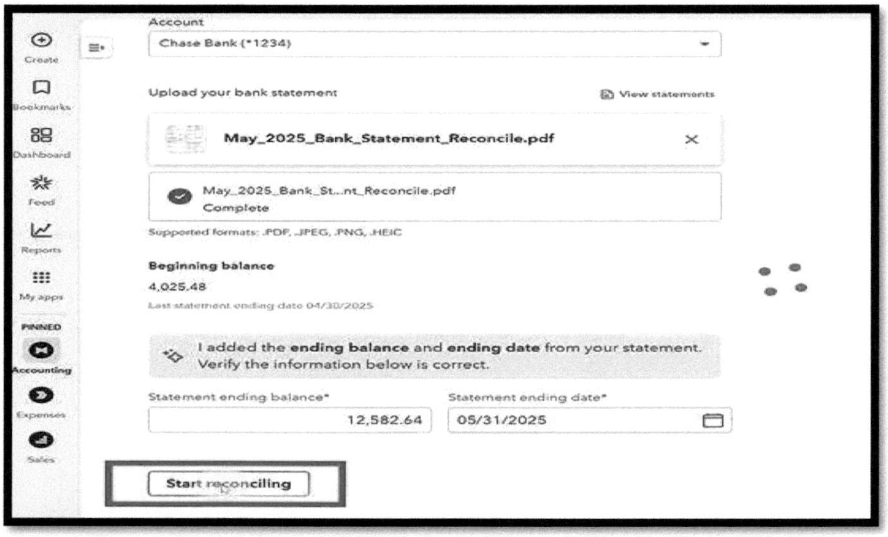

Click **Start reconciling** to continue.

Breaking Down the Reconciliation Page

Your goal is simple:

Make sure your QuickBooks transaction list matches your bank statement exactly.

If something doesn't match, you're usually dealing with:

- A missing transaction
- A duplicated entry
- An incorrect amount recorded in QuickBooks

QuickBooks flags discrepancies using a **summary panel**, which highlights differences between the two records. For example, it may detect a $197.42 payment on your bank statement that does not appear in QuickBooks.

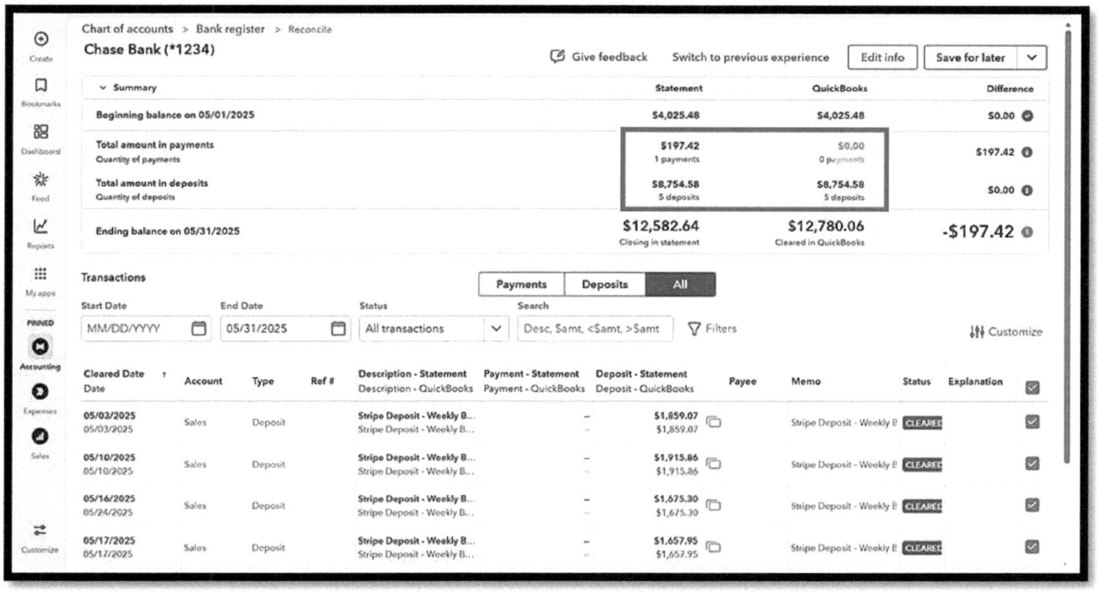

The system displays three columns to help you investigate:

- Items **from your bank statement** (in bold)
- Items **recorded in QuickBooks** (plain text)
- An **explanation column** powered by the AI accounting agent

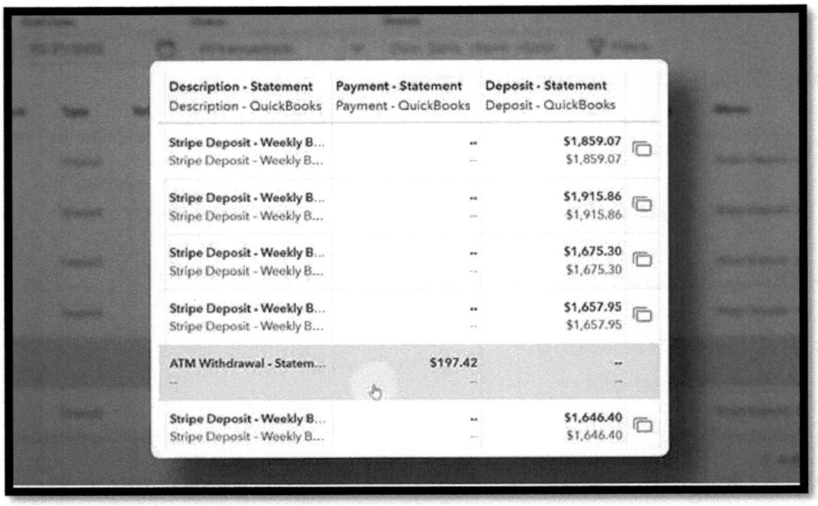

Clicking the AI **star icon** opens a suggested explanation. If QuickBooks determines the transaction is missing, you can choose to automatically add it. The entry will then appear on your transactions page where you can review and finalize it.

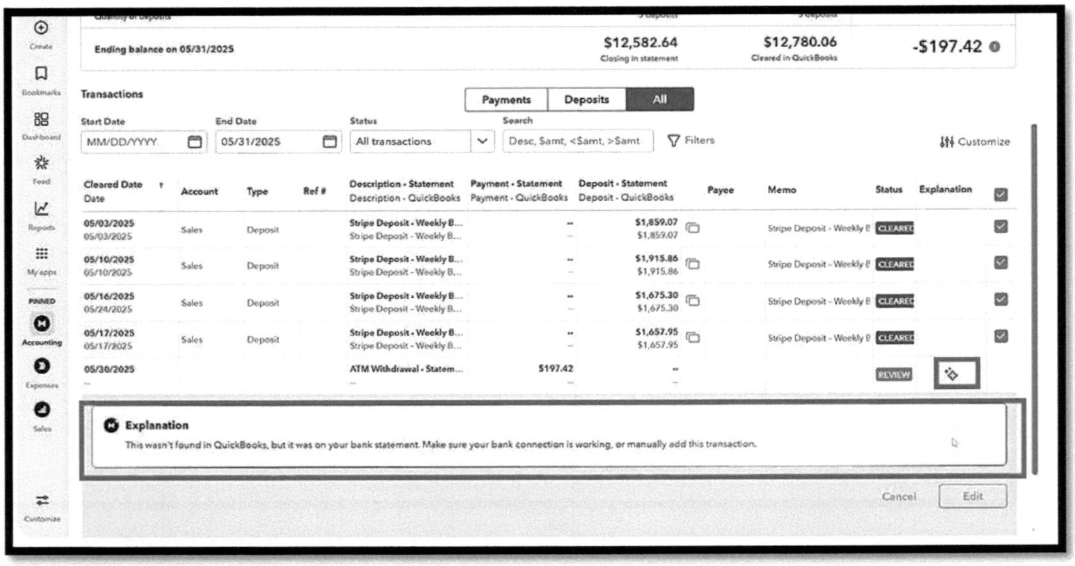

Current Limitations

Since this AI reconciliation tool is new, it's not yet perfect. At the time of recording:

- It struggles with **combined or split charges**
- It cannot match transactions when the **amounts differ** between the bank and QuickBooks

Still, it streamlines the bulk of reconciliation for Plus and Advanced users.

AI INSIGHTS ON SPENDING PATTERNS

The accounting agent also reviews past financial activity and highlights transactions or trends that appear unusual.

To view these insights:

1. Go to **Reports** in the sidebar.
2. Open **Standard Reports**.

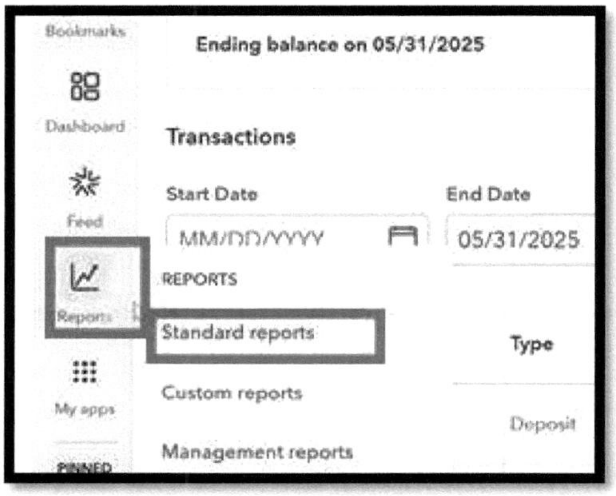

3. Select your **Profit and Loss** statement.

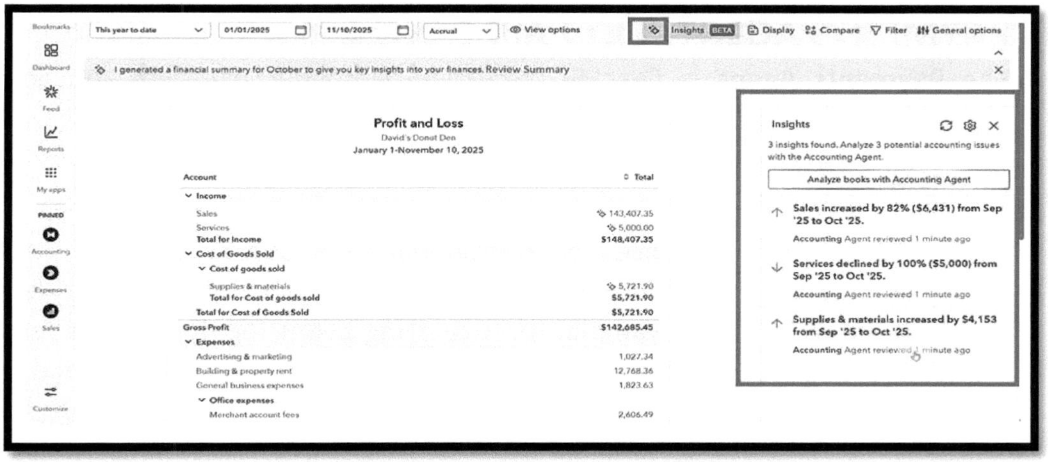

At the top of the P&L, QuickBooks displays insights such as:

- Unexpected increases or decreases in expenses
- Revenue changes
- Outliers compared to past activity

For example, my doughnut shop shows one favorable change and two concerning shifts. Increases like the spike in October expenses may simply be due to one large bulk order—as it was in my case—but any unfamiliar change is worth investigating.

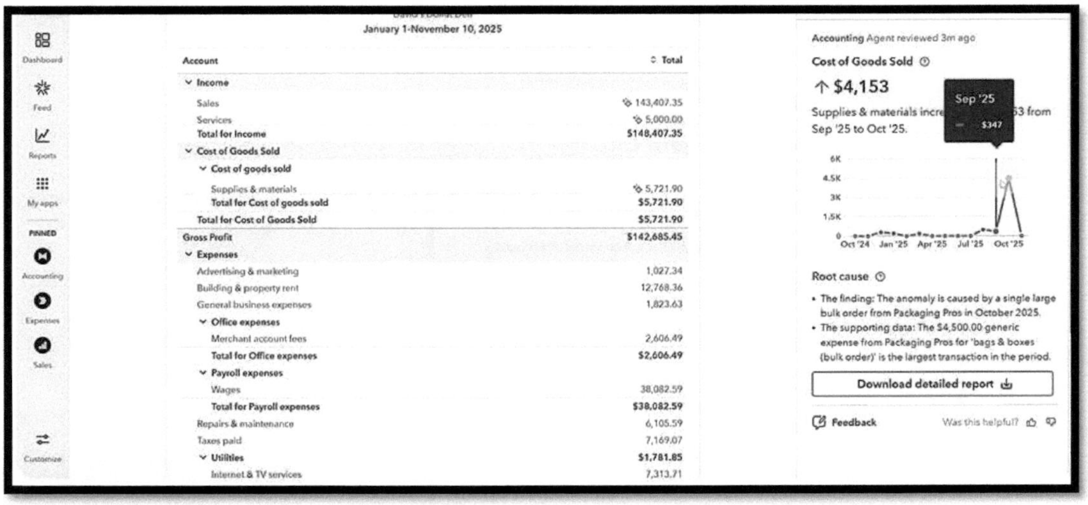

You can download a detailed **PDF analysis** for deeper review.

If you prefer to see insights directly in the line items, look for the **star icon** next to categories on the P&L. Clicking it (e.g., next to "Services") reveals the same AI-powered analysis related to that category.

PAYMENTS AGENT: GET PAID FASTER

The **Payments Agent** in QuickBooks Online simplifies invoicing and accelerates collections, eliminating the need to create invoices from scratch.

How it works:

1. Click **Create → Invoice** from the sidebar.
2. Upload an email, contract, note, or even a photo of the order details into **Intuit Assist**. For example, for a catering event for the *Solstice Snow Show Foundation*, you can drag a photo of your notes into the file upload area. The AI processes it in about 15 seconds.

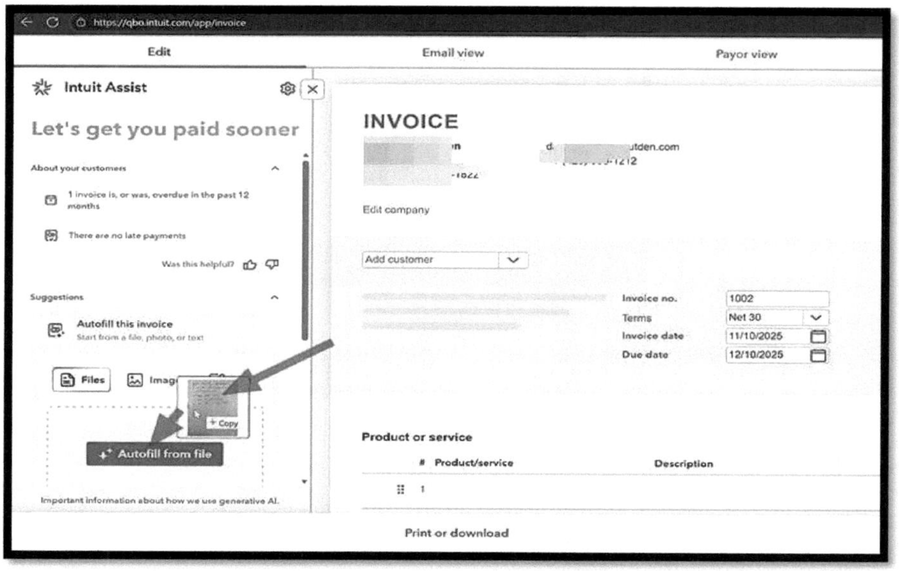

3. The agent automatically:
   - ❖ Creates the customer record (*Solstice Snow Show Foundation* appears in your system).
   - ❖ Recognizes products and quantities (e.g., 15 dozen glazed donuts).
   - ❖ Suggests new products if they aren't already in your inventory. You can confirm or roll them up into existing products.

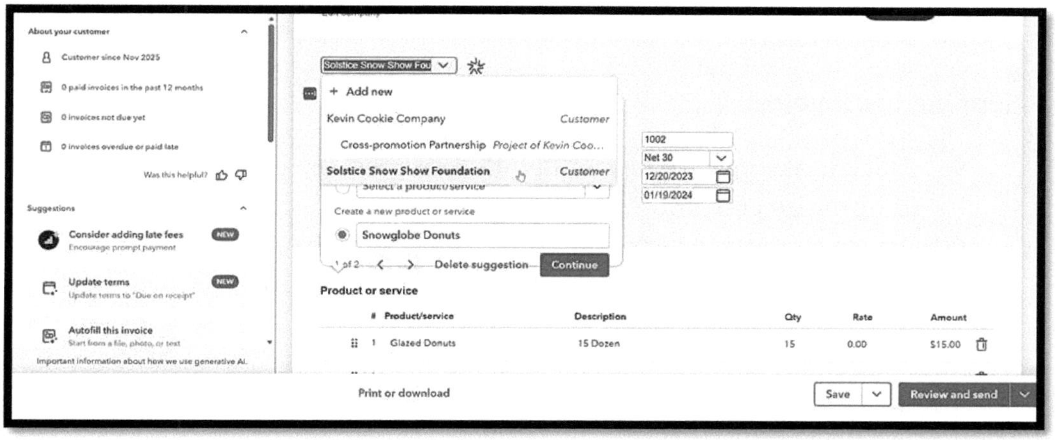

Smart payment suggestions:

- ❖ The AI can suggest **late fees** or change terms to **Due on Receipt**, adjusting the invoice due date automatically.

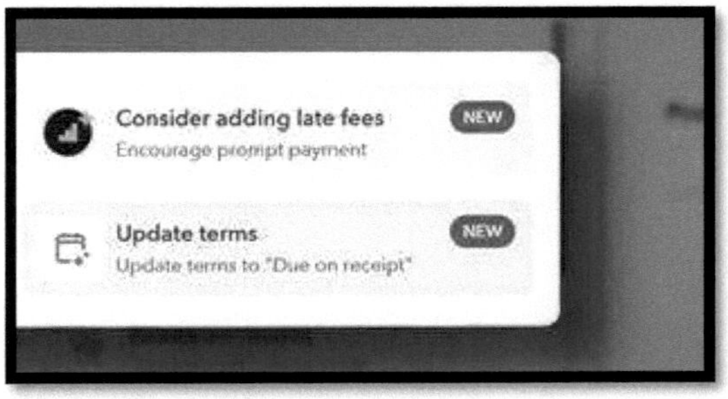

❖ You can view the customer's payment history, including how long they've been a customer, invoices paid, unpaid, or overdue. This helps you set appropriate terms and fees.

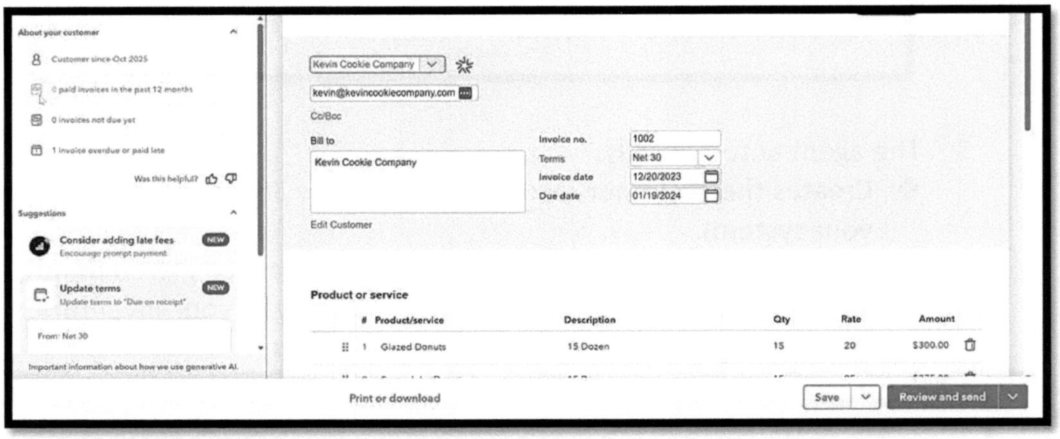

Sending the invoice:

❖ QuickBooks may experiment with AI-generated email subjects and body text to optimize collection success.
❖ Future updates are expected to automatically send reminders for overdue invoices, adapting to your collection approach.

Key takeaway: The Payments Agent streamlines invoice creation, recommends payment terms, and helps ensure timely payments, saving hours of manual work while reducing errors.

CUSTOMER AGENT: NEVER LOSE A LEAD

The **Customer Agent** in QuickBooks Online helps you capture, manage, and respond to leads directly from your email—available on **Plus plan and above**. Simple Start and Essentials focus primarily on invoicing and payments, while the Customer Hub expands your customer management capabilities.

Getting started:

1. From the QuickBooks dashboard, click **Customers → Leads**, or open the sidebar and navigate to **Customer Hub → Leads**.

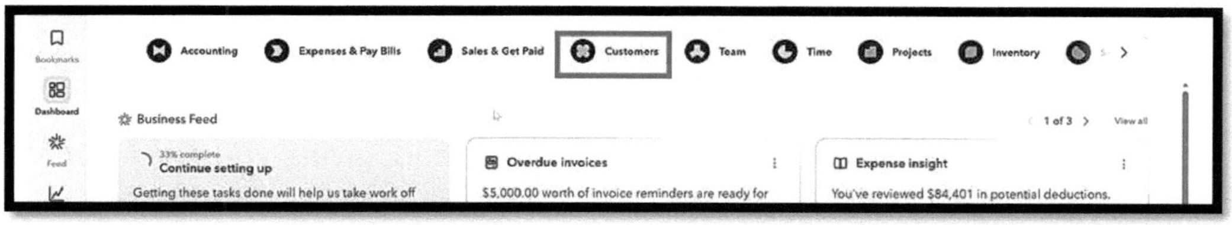

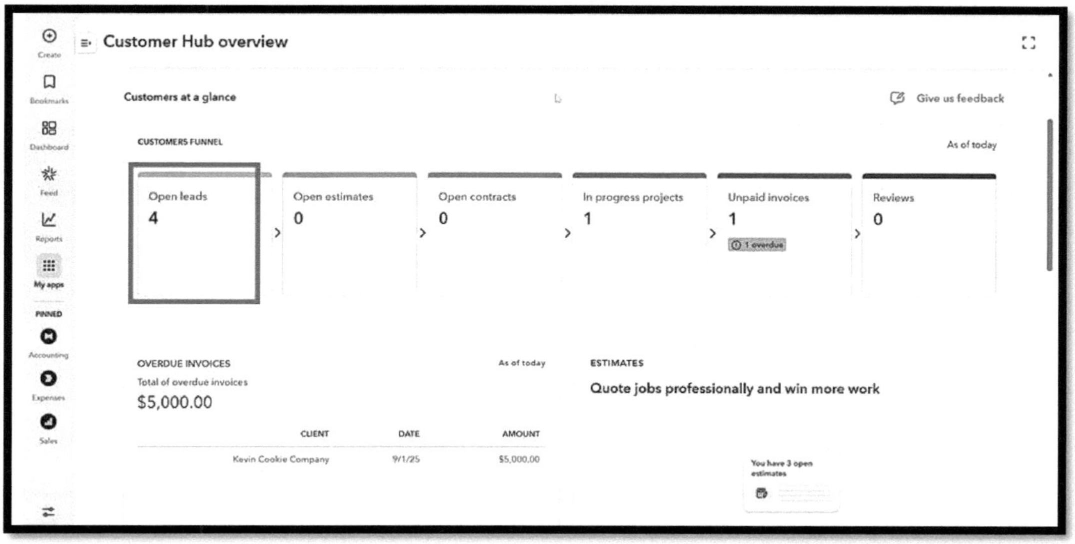

2. Connect your email by clicking **Manage Sources**. You can import leads manually or link Gmail/Outlook. Once connected, the agent scans your inbox and identifies potential leads.

How it works:

- Each lead is automatically tagged as **Hot**, **Warm**, or **Cold**.
  - **Hot leads** are ready to make a purchase.
  - **Warm leads** are interested but need more information.
  - **Cold leads** may require nurturing.
- AI generates a brief summary for each lead, giving you quick context on the potential deal.

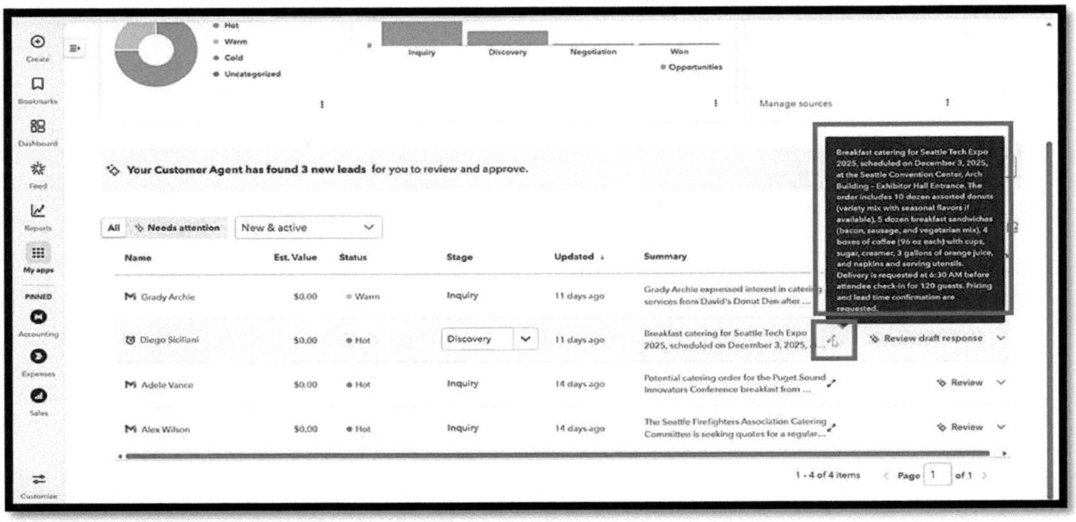

Managing leads:

1. Click **Review All** to curate your leads and train the agent to distinguish leads from non-leads.

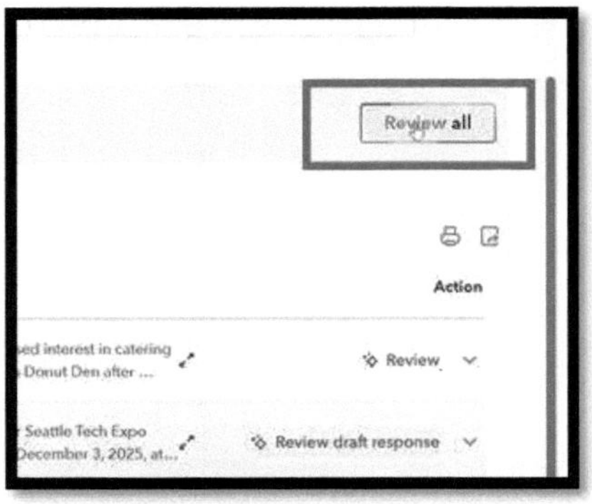

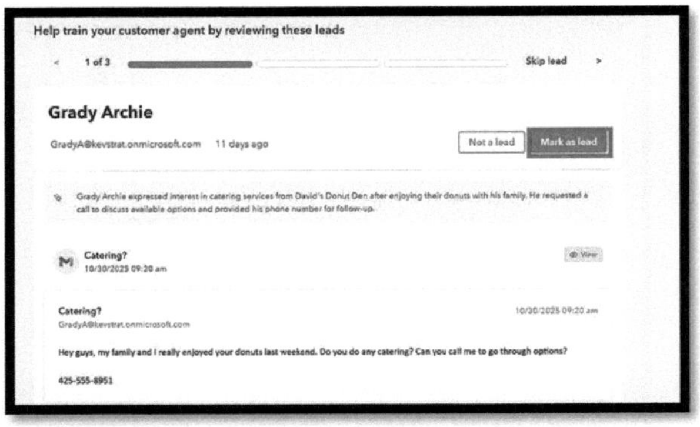

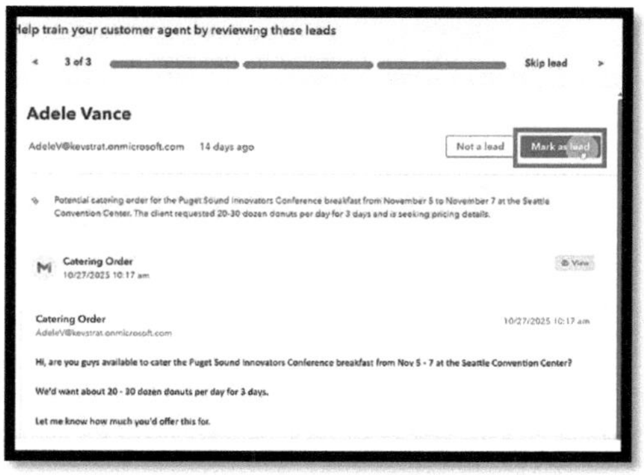

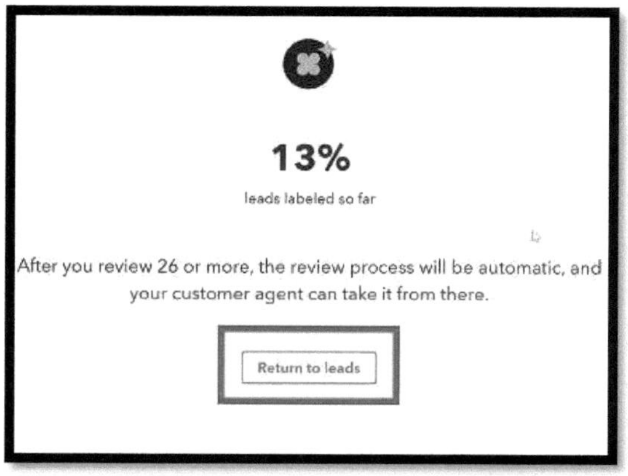

2. The rightmost column in the leads table shows the **next action**. For example:

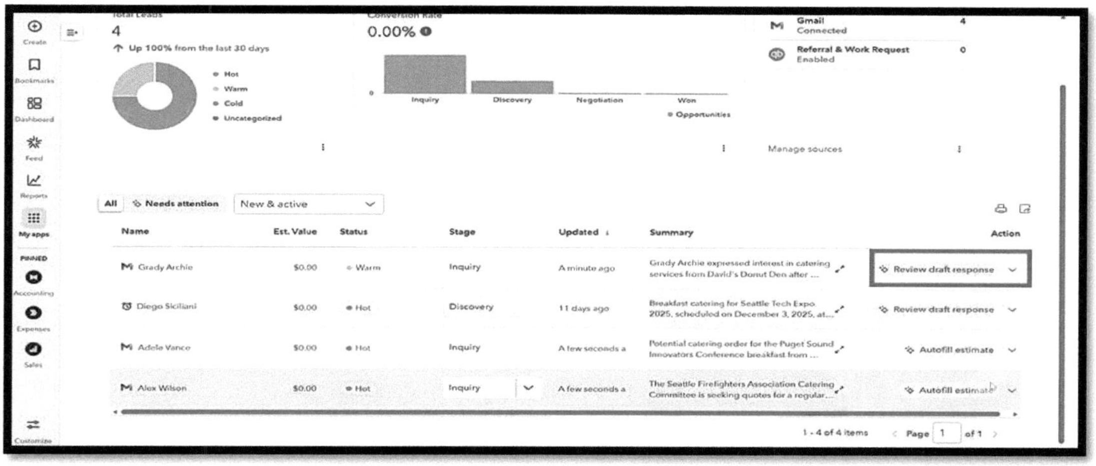

❖ If a lead requested more info, the agent drafts an email response.

- ❖ You can edit the draft, replace names, or tweak the message before sending.

3. Send your response directly from QuickBooks, then move on to the next lead.

Current limitations:

- ❖ Lead sync is not real-time—new leads may take up to 24 hours to appear.
- ❖ Beta version: promising for email-driven or referral-heavy businesses, but real-time integration is needed for production use.

FINANCE AGENT: INSIGHTS FOR SMARTER PLANNING

The **Finance Agent**, available to **Advanced plan** users, provides executive-level financial insights to help you plan for the next month, quarter, or year.

Accessing the Finance Agent:

1. From the dashboard, go to **Reports → Standard Reports**.

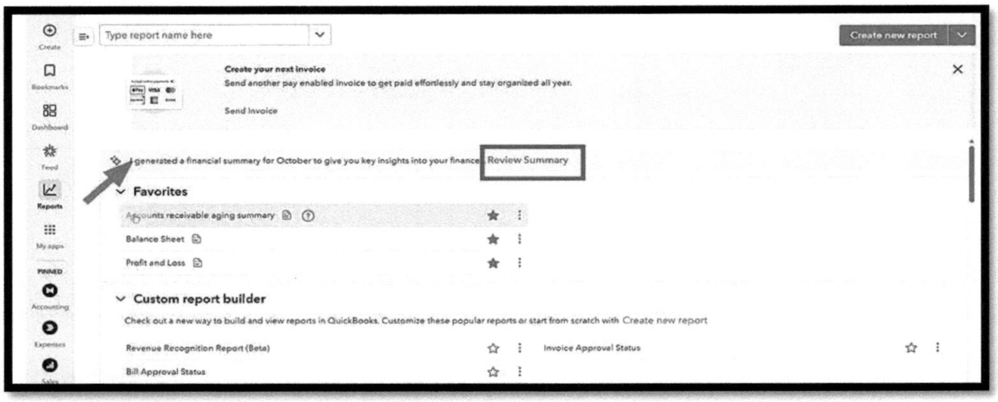

2. At the end of each month, the finance agent generates a **financial summary** highlighting key changes in:

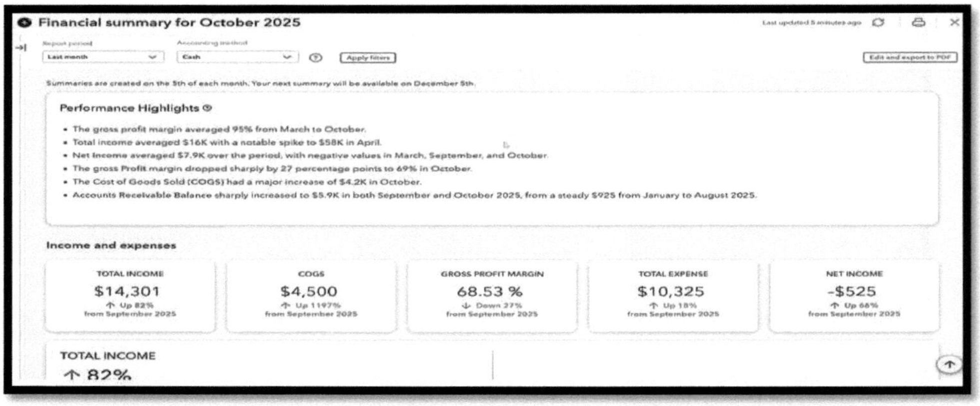

- ❖ Total income
- ❖ Cost of goods sold
- ❖ Gross profit margin
- ❖ Total expenses and net income
- ❖ Assets and liabilities
- ❖ Accounts receivable/payable
- ❖ Total cash flow

Customizing your view:

- ❖ Adjust the report period (month, quarter, or year) using the dropdown in the top left.

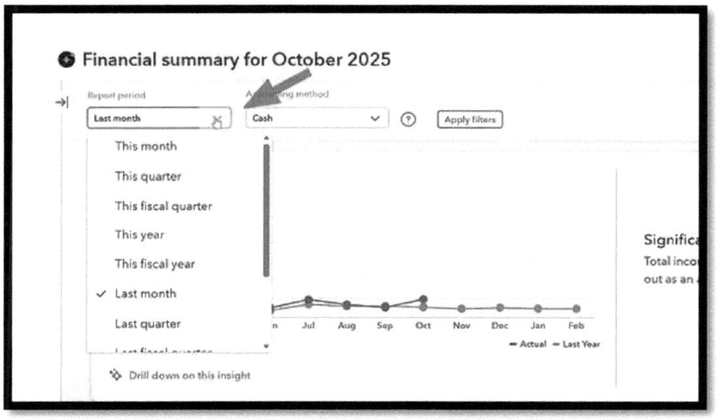

- ❖ Each card can be drilled down for more detail. For example, click **Drill Down** on expenses to view the **Top Five Accounts by Expense**, and even further to see the **Top Five Transactions**.

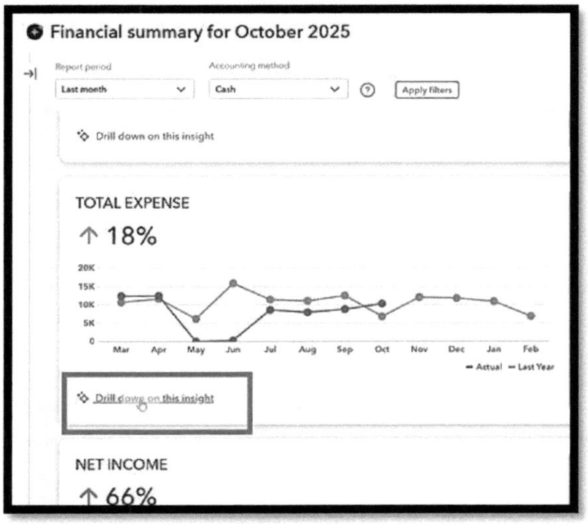

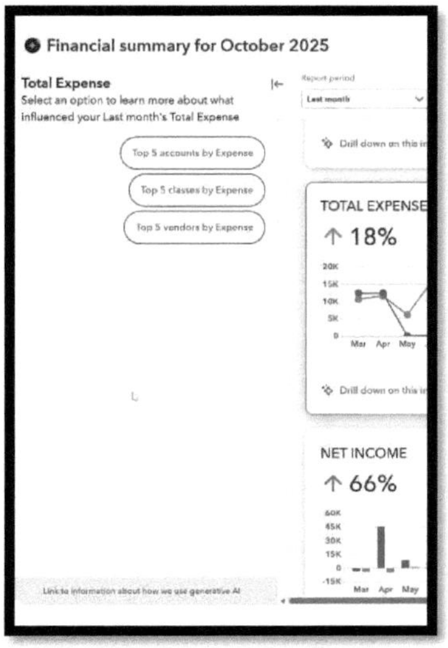

Exporting and sharing reports:

- QuickBooks allows exporting reports to **PDF**, with options to customize the content.

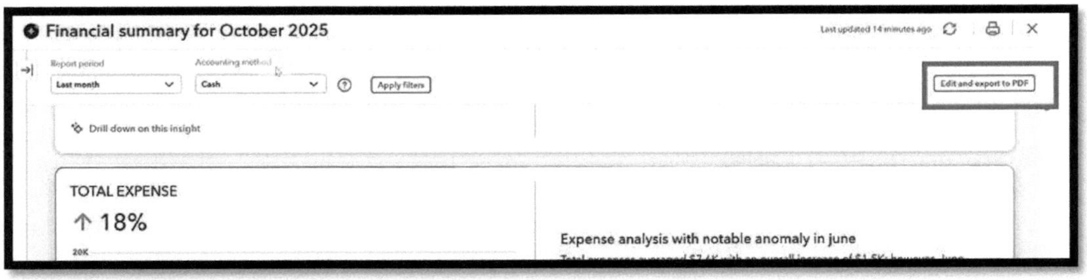

- Edit any text card using the pencil icon.

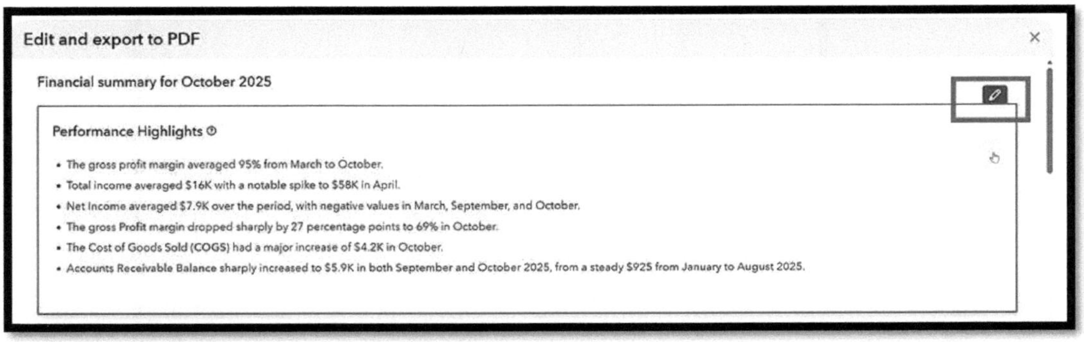

- Remove unnecessary cards using the trash can icon.

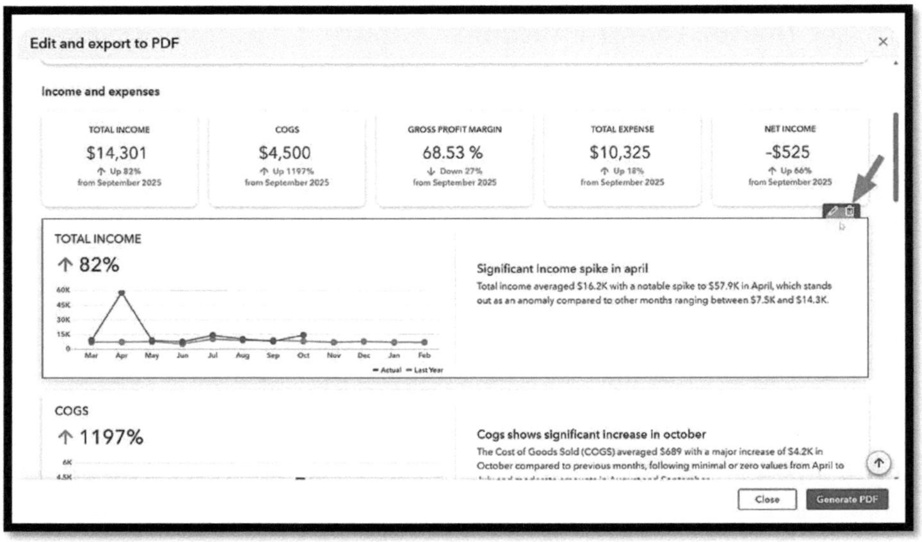

- Once finalized, click **Generate PDF** to save or print.

CHAPTER TWENTY-ONE

QUICKBOOKS ONLINE ACCOUNTANT: MANAGING YOUR TEAM AND CLIENTS

QuickBooks Online Accountant (QBOA) simplifies client management by providing a centralized platform to handle financial data, streamline tasks, enhance communication, and maintain top-notch security. As an accountant or bookkeeper, mastering how to add and manage both clients and your internal team is essential.

ADDING AND MANAGING YOUR ACCOUNTING TEAM

Ensure that everyone at your firm has the right access to QuickBooks.

Add a New Team Member

1. Sign in to QBOA as an **admin** or a user with full access.
2. Select **Add user**.
3. Enter the team member's **full name** and **email address**.
4. In **Firm access**, select a **default or custom role**.
5. (Optional) Expand access controls for firm features like **Sales, Expenses, Inventory, Payroll**.
6. Check or uncheck **View, Create, Edit, and Delete** capabilities as needed.
7. In **Client access**, assign roles for any clients they need access to.
8. Click **Send invitation**.

Edit a Team Member's Info

1. Sign in as an admin or full-access user.
2. Go to the **Users** tab.
3. Locate the team member and select **Edit** in the Action column.
4. Make changes and click **Save**.

Updating Team Permissions

Adjust your team's access for firm info or client books to fit their role while protecting sensitive data.

Change Firm Access

1. Sign in as admin or full-access user.
2. Find the team member and click **Edit**.
3. In **Firm access**, select a **default or custom role**.

4. Expand access controls as needed (Sales, Expenses, Inventory, Payroll).
5. Check/uncheck **View, Create, Edit, Delete**.
6. Click **Save**.

Change Access to Client Books

1. Sign in as admin or full-access user.
2. Edit the team member in the **Users** tab.
3. In **Client access**, assign or adjust roles for each client.
   - Note: Not all roles are available for all clients.
4. Click **Save**.
5. To streamline, you can assign the same role to **multiple clients at once** if the team member needs identical permissions.

Tip: Assigning the **primary admin role** to the right team member ensures they have full control to manage a client's QuickBooks data when needed.

MANAGING ADMIN ROLES AND TEAM ACCESS IN QUICKBOOKS ONLINE ACCOUNTANT

QuickBooks Online Accountant allows firm admins to manage client access, team roles, and the primary admin role efficiently. Here's how to navigate these critical tasks.

1. Change the Primary Admin Role

The **primary admin** has full control over a QuickBooks account, including managing all users and permissions. By default, the person who sets up the account holds this role. To transfer it:

Prerequisites

- You must sign in as the current primary admin.
- The new primary admin must already be a user in the account.
- The new user must have the **Admin** role.

Steps for QuickBooks Online

1. Sign in as the current primary admin.
2. Go to **Settings → Manage Users**.
3. Locate the team member to transfer the role to.
4. Ensure their role is **Admin**; if not, select **Edit** to change it.
5. Select **Actions → Make Primary Admin**.

6. Confirm by selecting **Change Primary Admin**.
7. Sign out—transfer is complete.

Steps for Intuit Enterprise Suite

1. Sign in as the current primary admin.
2. Go to **Settings → Manage Users**.
3. Ensure the new admin has the **Admin** role.
4. Select **Actions → Make Primary Admin**.
5. Confirm **Change Primary Admin**.
6. The current admin is signed out automatically; the new admin gains access upon sign-in.

If the Current Admin Is Unavailable

If the primary admin has left the company, submit a request to Intuit's **Account Protection Team** with proof of business ownership or permission to assume the role.

Tip for Accountants: If you're the firm's primary admin, you can also change the primary admin role in a **client's account**.

2. Assign Multiple Team Members to a Client

1. Sign in as an admin or full-access user.
2. Find the client and select **Edit Client** in the Action column.
3. In **Team Access**, select **+ Show All Team Members**.
4. Check the team members needing access.
5. Click **Save**.

3. Assign a Lead Accountant to a Client

The **lead accountant** oversees a client's books and can be assigned in two ways:

- When adding a new client and creating their company file.
- Through an invitation from the primary admin.

Note: Other accountants can still perform bookkeeping if they have access, but the lead accountant coordinates and reviews activities.

Change a Client's Lead Accountant

1. Sign in as the firm's primary admin.
2. Locate the client and select **Edit Client → Edit Leads**.
3. Choose a new lead accountant in the **LEAD** column.
4. Click **Save**.

Assign One Lead Accountant to Multiple Clients

1. Select the checkboxes for the relevant clients.
2. Use the **Assign to** dropdown to select the lead accountant.
3. Click **Save**.

4. Review Team Certifications

1. Go to the **Certifications** tab.
2. Check each team member's certification status and expiration date.
3. If **Inactive**, the team member must renew their certification.

5. Remove or Deactivate a Team Member

You cannot fully delete a user from QBOA, but you can make them inactive:

1. Sign in as an admin or full-access user.
2. Go to the **Users** tab.
3. Find the team member and click the **arrow ▼** in the Action column.
4. Select **Delete**, then confirm by selecting **Delete** again.

PART VIII: PRODUCTIVITY BOOSTERS

CHAPTER TWENTY-TWO

KEYBOARD SHORTCUTS

QuickBooks Online relies more on mouse navigation than desktop versions, but it still offers a useful set of keyboard shortcuts to speed up data entry, navigation, and reporting. QuickBooks Online provides a powerful collection of keyboard shortcuts that help you work faster and reduce repetitive clicks. Although the key combinations differ slightly between Windows (Ctrl + Alt) and Mac (Cmd + Option), their functions remain the same. Below is a clear, organized breakdown of the most useful shortcuts.

NAVIGATION SHORTCUTS

Action	Windows	Mac	What It Does
Open New Transaction Menu	Ctrl + Alt + N	Cmd + Option + N	Quickly access forms like invoices, bills, and expenses.
Open Search Bar	Ctrl + Alt + F	Cmd + Option + F	Instantly search transactions, customers, vendors, or accounts.
Go to Dashboard	Ctrl + Alt + D	Cmd + Option + D	Return to your QuickBooks homepage.
View All Sales	Ctrl + Alt + A	Cmd + Option + A	Open the Sales or All Transactions page.
Banking Transactions	Ctrl + Alt + B	Cmd + Option + B	Jump directly to bank feeds.
Show Shortcut List	Ctrl + Alt + ?	Cmd + Option + ?	Displays QuickBooks' built-in shortcut guide.

TRANSACTION CREATION SHORTCUTS

Action	Windows	Mac	What It Does
New Invoice	Ctrl + Alt + I	Cmd + Option + I	Opens the invoice form immediately.
New Expense	Ctrl + Alt + E	Cmd + Option + E	Enter an expense faster.
New Bill	Ctrl + Alt + L	Cmd + Option + L	Record a vendor bill.
New Sales Receipt	Ctrl + Alt + S	Cmd + Option + S	Log same-day or point-of-sale transactions.

New Journal Entry	Ctrl + Alt + J	Cmd + Option + J	Create manual accounting adjustments.
Add Customer	Ctrl + Alt + C	Cmd + Option + C	Quickly add a new client.
Add Vendor	Ctrl + Alt + V	Cmd + Option + V	Add a new supplier or payee.

DATE FIELD SHORTCUTS

These shortcuts work directly inside **date fields** such as invoice dates, bill dates, and payment dates.

Key	Function	Description
T	Today	Inserts today's date.
W	Start of Week	Inserts Sunday's date.
K	End of Week	Inserts Saturday's date.
M	First Day of Month	Sets date to the 1st of the month.
H	Last Day of Month	Sets date to the final day of the month.
Y	First Day of Year	Inserts January 1st.
R	Last Day of Year	Inserts December 31st.
+	Forward One Day	Moves the date ahead by one day.
–	Back One Day	Moves the date back by one day.
Ctrl + Del (Windows) / Cmd + Del (Mac)	Clear Date	Removes the current date.

REPORT & NAVIGATION SHORTCUTS

Action	Windows	Mac
Open QuickReport	Ctrl + Q	Cmd + Q
Move Up a Line	Up Arrow	Up Arrow
Move Down a Line	Down Arrow	Down Arrow
Drill Down on Report	Enter	Return
Print Report	Ctrl + P	Cmd + P
Show/Hide Report Header	Ctrl + A	Cmd + A
Email Report (Excel/PDF)	Alt + I	Option + I

INVOICE & FORM ENTRY SHORTCUTS

Action	Windows	Mac
Previous Invoice	Alt + P	Option + P

Next Invoice	Alt + N	Option + N
Print Invoice	Ctrl + P	Cmd + P
Next Field	Tab	Tab
Previous Field	Shift + Tab	Shift + Tab
Save & Close	Alt + A	Option + A
Save & New	Alt + S	Option + S

TIPS AND TRICKS

SUPERCHARGING YOUR ANALYSIS WITH CHATGPT

Getting your QuickBooks data into Excel is only the first step—the real value comes from transforming those numbers into insights. ChatGPT can act as a powerful analysis partner, helping you build formulas, organize data, and interpret trends far more efficiently. Below are three practical ways to combine Excel with AI to streamline your workflow.

1. Generate Advanced Excel Formulas Instantly

Scenario:
You've exported a Profit & Loss by Month report and need to calculate Gross Profit Margin for each month. The challenge is that the required values ("Gross Profit" and "Total Income") sit on different rows.

Example Prompt to ChatGPT:

I have an Excel sheet exported from QuickBooks. Column A lists account names (e.g., "Total Income," "Gross Profit"), and columns B, C, D, etc., contain monthly values. I need a formula that calculates Gross Profit Margin for January (Column B) by dividing the value for "Gross Profit" by the value for "Total Income."

Example Output Formula:

=INDEX($B:$B, MATCH("Gross Profit", $A:$A, 0)) / INDEX($B:$B, MATCH("Total Income", $A:$A, 0))

Why this helps:

You get a correct, ready-to-use formula without manually hunting for cell references. Simply paste the formula into the desired cell and drag it across for all months.

2. Get Clear, Guided Steps for Building Pivot Tables

Scenario:
You imported a "Sales by Item Summary" report with fields for Item, Customer, and Amount. You want a Pivot Table ranking customers by total sales and identifying their top-purchased items.

Example Prompt to ChatGPT:

I imported a Sales by Item report into Excel with columns Item (A), Customer (B), and Amount (C). Give me step-by-step instructions to create a Pivot Table that shows each customer, their total sales, and sorts them from highest to lowest.

What ChatGPT Provides:

A clear, numbered walkthrough—from selecting your data to inserting the Pivot Table and placing each field in Rows, Values, and Filters. This eliminates trial and error and ensures accurate setup.

3. Turn Raw Data Into Clear Narrative Summaries

Scenario:
You've finished compiling your monthly financial report. Now you need to present it to your manager or write an executive summary—but turning spreadsheets into meaningful insights is time-consuming.

Example Prompt to ChatGPT:

Act as a business analyst. Below is our P&L summary for last quarter. We sell artisanal coffee online. Please create a three-bullet executive summary highlighting the key trends.

(Paste your table here.)

What ChatGPT Delivers:

A polished, insight-driven narrative. Instead of repeating numbers, it identifies trends such as rising costs, margin shifts, or seasonal revenue patterns. For example:

- "Net profits tightened in March due to a 15% increase in COGS, likely indicating a shift toward lower-margin products."

HOW TO EXPORT QUICKBOOKS TO EXCEL USING AI

Exporting your financial data from QuickBooks into Excel unlocks extensive opportunities for deeper analysis, cleaner reporting, and flexible customization. However, once the spreadsheet lands on your desktop, the real challenge usually begins—sorting the data, formatting tables, building charts, and turning numbers into insights.

AI tools now streamline this entire process, transforming raw QuickBooks exports into polished reports in minutes.

The Traditional Method: Manual Export from QuickBooks

Before exploring how AI simplifies everything, it's useful to understand the standard QuickBooks export workflow. While QuickBooks Online (QBO) and QuickBooks Desktop differ slightly, the core steps remain similar.

Exporting from QuickBooks Online (QBO)

QuickBooks Online makes exporting reports straightforward:

1. **Go to the Reports Center**

   From the left menu, select **Reports**.

2. **Select the Report You Need**

   Search for or browse to a report—such as **Profit and Loss**, **Sales by Customer Summary**, or **A/R Aging Summary**.

3. **Customize Your Report**

   Adjust the **date range**, columns, filters, and accounting method. This ensures your exported file contains the exact data you want.

4. **Export the Report**

   Click the **Export icon** in the upper-right corner (square with an upward arrow).
   Choose **Export to Excel**, and QuickBooks will download an .xlsx file to your computer.

This gives you clean data—but turning it into insights still requires effort. That's where AI transforms the workflow.

Using AI to Analyze and Report on Your QuickBooks Data

Instead of spending hours cleaning spreadsheets, modern AI tools analyze your exported data instantly—creating dashboards, charts, and narrative summaries in seconds.

Here's how the new, AI-powered workflow looks:

Step 1: Export the Raw Data from QuickBooks

Follow the standard export steps above. Format doesn't matter—AI tools read **CSV** or **Excel** with no issue.

Your goal: get a clean, raw data file such as a P&L, sales ledger, or expense summary.

Step 2: Upload Your File to an AI Analysis Tool

Instead of opening Excel, simply log in to your AI platform and **drag and drop** the exported file.
This is your only manual setup step.

Step 3: Let the AI Build Your Dashboard Automatically

The AI scans your file, recognizes the structure, identifies key columns, and generates a complete dashboard. Depending on the report, you might get:

- A **bar chart** of top customers or products
- A **trend line** showing monthly or quarterly growth
- **KPI cards** (Total Revenue, Average Invoice, Total Customers, etc.)
- A **summary table** displaying the cleaned raw data

All of this happens automatically—no formulas, sorting, or chart-building required.

Step 4: Receive AI-Generated Insights and Summaries

The most powerful feature is automated interpretation.

Instead of just building visuals, the AI explains what the data reveals. For example:

"Revenue peaked in November due to strong recurring orders from your top three clients, followed by a seasonal decline of 12% in December."

This gives you presentation-ready commentary without writing a single sentence.

Step 5: Customize and Refine Your Dashboard

AI handles the heavy lifting, but you retain full control. You can:

- Rearrange tiles
- Change chart types
- Adjust colors
- Add or remove fields
- Edit labels and titles

Many tools even support natural-language commands such as:

- "Show revenue by quarter instead of month."
- "Combine customer and item into a single grouped chart."
- "Highlight months below $10,000 in sales."

You get both **speed** and **precision**, with your final report ready for sharing or presenting.

Tips for a Seamless Workflow

To get the most value from an AI-enhanced reporting process, a few best practices can help you work faster and avoid common pitfalls:

- **Export Clean, Unformatted Data:** AI tools work best with simple, raw datasets. Avoid adding subtotals, merged cells, colors, or custom formatting in QuickBooks before exporting. These extras can confuse the analysis engine and lead to inaccurate charts. Stick to a clean CSV or Excel export with straightforward column headers.
- **Start with High-Level Summary Reports:** While detailed transaction data can be useful, summary-level reports (like *Sales by Product/Service Summary* or *Profit and Loss Summary*) generate faster, clearer insights. They give AI a strong structured foundation for charts, KPIs, and trend analysis without overwhelming the model with granular noise.
- **Keep Your Data Consistent:** If you're producing recurring reports—monthly, quarterly, or weekly—export your QuickBooks data using the same filters, date ranges, and column structure each time. Consistency allows you to reuse the same AI-powered dashboard template and instantly refresh it with new data instead of rebuilding from scratch.
- **Review the Results for Accuracy:** AI can automate a large portion of your reporting, but you still play the role of reviewer. After the dashboard is generated, compare a few key values—such as total revenue or net income—to your original QuickBooks report. A quick validation ensures the analysis is correct before you share it with stakeholders.

IMPORTANT THINGS QUICKBOOKS WON'T TELL YOU ABOUT YOUR BUSINESS

QuickBooks is a powerful tool—it handles invoicing, accounts receivable, accounts payable, checkbook management, and organizes multiple bank accounts in one place. However, several **critical** aspects of your business remain invisible to QuickBooks. Ignoring even one of these issues can weaken cash flow, trigger tax problems, or leave your business undercapitalized when you need funds the most.

Below are **five essential—but often overlooked—areas** QuickBooks doesn't automatically manage or warn you about. They appear in no particular order, as each one affects different business owners differently.

1. QuickBooks Doesn't Estimate Your Quarterly Tax Liability

QuickBooks doesn't remind you how much tax you owe throughout the year. If you pay yourself a salary, dividends, or both, you may owe federal, state, and possibly local taxes that are **not** withheld anywhere.

A responsible business owner works with a CPA or accountant to calculate quarterly estimates. Doing this:

- Prevents surprise tax bills
- Protects year-end cash flow
- Helps budget realistically
- Avoids scrambling to find money at tax time

Some business owners gamble and hope they won't owe much. Others take control by calculating their estimates or setting aside funds as income is earned. **QuickBooks won't manage this for you—your advisor must.**

2. QuickBooks Can't Advise You on How to Record Complex Transactions

With small-business audits on the rise (from ~1% to an estimated 3%), correctly recording transactions is more important than ever. QuickBooks doesn't tell you **where** a transaction truly belongs.

Misusing accounts like *miscellaneous expense*, *opening balance equity*, *reconciliation discrepancy*, or *adjustments* is one of the fastest ways to trigger an audit.

Even if your books are technically correct, the time, stress, and lost productivity from an audit can cost far more than paying an advisor. Clean, well-categorized books reduce your audit risk and allow you to focus on working *on* your business—not getting buried *in* it.

3. QuickBooks Reports Don't Teach You How to Interpret Your Financials

QuickBooks produces both cash-basis and accrual-basis financial statements, but it doesn't explain what those numbers actually mean. Many owners simply track their checkbook balance, which shows only where they've been—not where they're going.

To make sound decisions, business owners must understand:

- Profit trends
- Future cash shortages
- Accounts receivable timing
- Upcoming obligations
- Seasonal patterns

A virtual CFO, QuickBooks advisor, or financial consultant can interpret your statements and help you spot problems before they grow. Hiring a full-time controller may be expensive, but having **access** to one—even monthly—can save you from costly decisions made in the dark.

4. QuickBooks Doesn't Properly Reconcile or Close All Year-End Accounts

QuickBooks allows you to "close the books," but it doesn't ensure everything is reconciled correctly. Accounts that often get ignored or mishandled include:

- Long-term debt
- Depreciation
- Distributions
- Accumulated earnings
- Checking accounts
- Prior-year adjustments

Unreconciled accounts can build year after year, creating inaccurate financial statements and unexpected tax consequences. New clients often bring books with three or more years of unresolved errors, which can draw unwanted IRS attention and complicate tax filing.

A CPA or accountant must review and reconcile these accounts annually—not QuickBooks.

5. QuickBooks Doesn't Warn You About File Corruption or Failing Backups

Many users assume their QuickBooks backup is reliable—until the day they discover both the main file and backup are corrupt. Common issues include:

- Backups stored only on the server (not safe)
- The wrong type of backup being used
- Years of data inflating file size and slowing performance
- Silent data corruption that goes unnoticed until it's too late

Using QuickBooks' built-in backup tool is different from copying the file manually—QuickBooks' tool repairs structural problems during backup.

A healthy backup strategy requires:

- Regularly tested backups
- Off-site storage
- Oversight from someone who understands QuickBooks files

While QuickBooks Online reduces some file-corruption risks, it has fewer features than the desktop version and may not fit every business.

QuickBooks is an excellent accounting platform, but it isn't a complete financial management system. Understanding what it doesn't do is just as important as knowing what it does. With the right advisors and awareness, you can avoid costly mistakes, improve cash flow, and make smarter decisions for the future of your business.

QUICKBOOKS ONLINE HACKS: PRO TIPS TO STREAMLINE YOUR WORKFLOW

If you use QuickBooks Online (QBO), you can dramatically speed up your work by taking advantage of the platform's lesser-known tools and shortcuts. Below is a refined collection of practical "hacks" that help you work faster, stay organized, and avoid repetitive tasks.

1. Master the Interface: Unlock Hidden Tools and Shortcuts

QBO includes several built-in features that many users overlook. These quick tricks can significantly reduce your time spent navigating and entering data.

Built-in Calculators

Every numeric field in QBO doubles as a calculator. Instead of switching apps or grabbing a calculator:

- ❖ Use * for multiplication
- ❖ Use / for division
- ❖ Use parentheses for multi-step calculations

Date Shortcuts:

Type simple dates (like 3/15) and QBO auto-fills the year. Enter only the day (15), and it completes the current month and year.

2. Boost Productivity with Chrome Browser Tricks

If you use QBO in Chrome, these tools can make your workflow even smoother:

Multiple Tabs

Open multiple QBO pages side by side.

Right-click a menu option → **Open in New Tab**.

Incognito Mode

Use Incognito when QBO acts glitchy—this helps you identify issues caused by cached data.

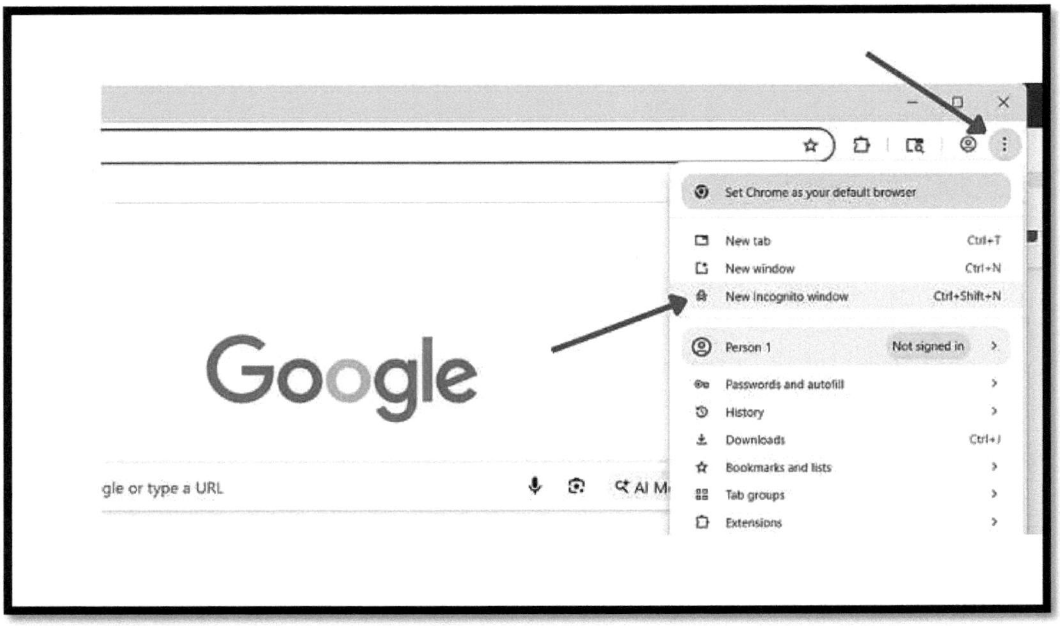

Chrome Profiles for Clients

Create separate browser profiles for different clients. Each profile keeps its own bookmarks, extensions, and login session—ideal for accountants managing multiple businesses.

3. Master Bank Feeds and Reconciliation

Bank Transactions is one of the most powerful automation tools in QBO. Use it effectively to minimize manual categorization.

Customize Your Bank Feed View

- Click the gear icon in the Bank Transactions window to personalize the layout.
- Group by month or expand details for better visibility.

Automate Categorization

- Create **Bank Rules** to auto-categorize patterns in spending or deposits.
- Use **Categorization History** to quickly check how similar transactions were coded previously.

Sort for Speed

Sorting by **Payee**, **Description**, or **Bank Detail** groups related transactions for faster batch review.

4. Supercharge Your Searches

The search bar in QuickBooks Online is more powerful than most users realize. Beyond standard lookups, QBO's modern AI allows natural-language searches.

Search Like a Pro

- ❖ **Search by amount:** Enter $100.00 to find matching transactions.

Combine keywords: Typing **"100 Amy"** filters $100 transactions related to Amy.

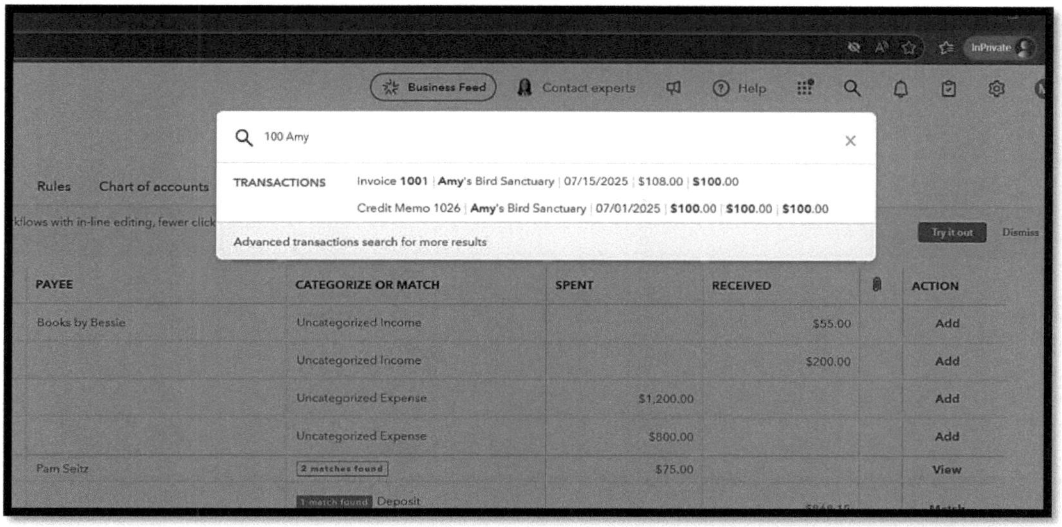

- ❖ **Use Advanced Search:** Filter by date, account, memo, reference number, or more for pinpoint accuracy.

5. Automate Workflows with Recurring Transactions

Recurring Transactions save time when handling predictable entries.

Recurring Sales Receipts

Perfect for subscription billing or monthly service fees—QBO will automatically generate and process payments.

Use Templates

Set up **Unscheduled Recurring Transactions** as reusable templates for invoices, bills, and journal entries. Update details as needed without recreating entries from scratch.

6. Automate Communication with Clients

Invoice Reminders

Automatically send reminders before, on, or after the invoice due date. These reminders aren't customizable by client yet, but the feature often receives updates.

Scheduled Reports

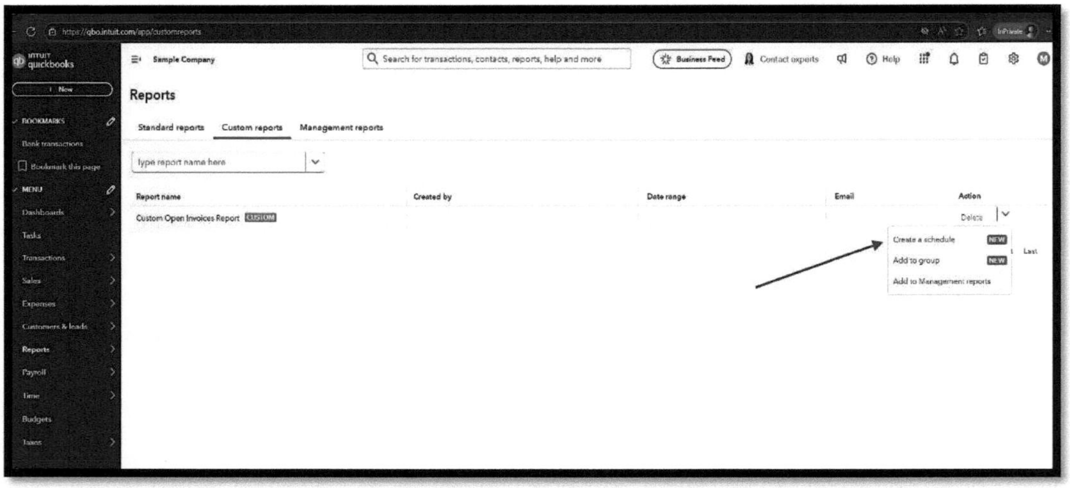

Schedule management and financial reports to send automatically at set intervals—ensuring clients receive timely updates without manual effort.

7. Access Hidden Tools Using Direct Links

Some of the most valuable QBO accountant tools are not listed in the main menus. Use these direct links:

Bulk Reclassify Transactions

Move transactions between accounts, update Classes, or modify Locations in bulk: **qbo.intuit.com/app/reclassify-transaction**

Report and Accounting Defaults

Set default reporting dates and accounting method preferences: **qbo.intuit.com/app/accountant**

Manage Billable Expenses

Bulk-edit billable expense settings: **qbo.intuit.com/app/managebillableexpense**

8. More Time-Saving Tricks

Quick Access to Settings

Click your **Company Name** in the top-left corner to jump directly to **Account and Settings**.

Check QBO System Status

If QBO behaves unexpectedly, check for outages: **quickbooks.statuspage.io**

Identify Intuit Charges

Look up unexplained Intuit charges on your bank statement: **chargelookup.intuit.com**

SPEEDING UP QUICKBOOKS ONLINE: BROWSER SETTINGS THAT TRULY MATTER

QuickBooks Online (QBO) is a powerful cloud-based platform, but its performance depends heavily on the browser you use. If QBO ever feels slow, freezes, or becomes unresponsive, the root cause is often your browser—not QuickBooks itself. From outdated versions to overloaded cache and intrusive extensions, even small browser issues can significantly affect speed and stability.

This section explains the browser settings that impact QBO the most, why login issues happen, and the exact steps you can take to optimize performance.

Understanding QuickBooks Online Login Problems

Login issues are among the most common frustrations users experience, especially when browser settings aren't properly configured. These problems happen even when your username and password are correct.

Common Login Problems

1. Getting stuck on the login screen
2. Endless page refresh or redirect loops
3. "Something went wrong" or 504 timeout errors
4. Two-factor authentication (2FA) delays or failures
5. Verification codes not sending
6. Issues caused by outdated or unsupported browsers

How Browser Settings Cause Login Issues

Many login failures are linked to:

- Outdated or unsupported browsers
- Corrupted or overloaded cache
- Conflicting extensions (especially password managers)
- Blocked pop-ups needed for 2FA
- JavaScript being turned off

Before assuming QuickBooks is down, adjusting your browser settings is often the quickest fix.

Why QuickBooks Online May Feel Slow

Since QBO runs entirely in your browser, performance depends on multiple factors:

1. Browser type and version
2. Cache and cookie buildup
3. Browser extensions and plug-ins
4. Internet speed and stability
5. Device memory (RAM) and CPU usage

When these become strained, you may notice:

- Lag when navigating menus
- Slow report loading
- Delays when opening company files
- Freezing after long sessions
- Sluggish invoice or transaction processing

These slowdowns can seriously affect productivity, but they're often easy to resolve.

How Browsers Affect QuickBooks Performance

Your browser acts as the engine powering QuickBooks Online. If the engine isn't optimized, everything slows down. Poor settings can lead to:

- Delayed loading of scripts
- Freezes when running complex reports
- Slow responsiveness across the dashboard
- Trouble loading or switching between company files

Even Chrome—the recommended browser—can run slowly if settings aren't tuned properly.

Recommended Browsers for QuickBooks Online

Intuit supports the following browsers:

- **Google Chrome (Best Performance)**
- **Mozilla Firefox**
- **Microsoft Edge**
- **Safari** (Mac users)

Older browsers—like Internet Explorer—are not supported and will cause major performance issues.

Pro Tip:

Always keep your browser updated to the latest version.

Critical Browser Settings That Influence QBO Speed

Here are the most important browser settings and why they matter:

1. Cache and Cookies

- Outdated cache or corrupted cookies can slow QBO dramatically.
- Clearing them regularly keeps performance smooth.

2. Pop-Up Blocker

- QBO uses pop-ups for certain tools and verification windows.
- Make sure pop-ups are allowed for *.quickbooks.com*.

3. JavaScript

- QBO relies on JavaScript for dynamic features.
- If it's disabled, pages will break or load incorrectly.

4. Site Permissions

Allow QuickBooks access to:

- Cookies
- Clipboard
- Notifications (optional but helpful)

5. Hardware Acceleration

- On some computers, it boosts performance.
- On others, it causes lag.

  Try toggling it ON or OFF to see which is faster.

6. Browser Extensions

- Too many extensions slow down loading.
- Some interfere with QBO scripts (password managers, VPNs, ad blockers). Disable anything unnecessary.

7. Autofill & Password Managers

These can conflict with QBO's login security fields.

If you experience login loops, disable autofill for the QuickBooks website.

How to Clear Cache and Cookies (Step-by-Step)

Clearing your cache removes temporary files that can cause lag or errors.

In Google Chrome

1. Click the **three dots** (top right).
2. Select **Settings**.
3. Open **Privacy and Security**.
4. Click **Clear Browsing Data**.
5. Check **Cookies** and **Cached Images/Files**.
6. Click **Clear Data**.

Recommended:
Do this weekly or anytime QuickBooks starts slowing down.

Disabling Browser Extensions That Interfere with QuickBooks Online

Browser extensions can consume system resources or block essential QuickBooks Online (QBO) scripts, leading to errors, slow performance, or broken features.

Common Extensions That Cause Problems

- Ad blockers
- Password managers
- Grammar tools (e.g., Grammarly)
- Screen recorders or screenshot add-ons

These tools may be helpful generally, but they often conflict with QBO's secure fields, pop-ups, or scripts.

How to Disable Extensions in Chrome

1. Click the **puzzle icon** ( ) on the toolbar *or* enter chrome://extensions/ in the address bar.
2. Toggle off any extensions you don't need during your QBO work.
3. Refresh QuickBooks Online and check performance again.

Tip: Keep only essential extensions active while working in QBO to prevent slowdowns or script errors.

Managing Pop-Ups and Site Permissions

QuickBooks Online relies heavily on pop-up windows for key tasks such as:

- Printing checks
- Emailing invoices
- Connecting or updating bank feeds

If pop-ups are blocked, many actions may fail silently without giving you an error message.

Allow Pop-Ups for QuickBooks in Chrome

1. Go to **Settings > Privacy and Security > Site Settings**.
2. Select **Pop-ups and redirects**.
3. Add https://qbo.intuit.com under **Allowed sites**.

If you use built-in voice tools or video-related add-ons, also allow **microphone** and **camera** access.

Hardware Acceleration: Should You Use It?

Hardware acceleration uses your computer's graphics processor (GPU) to render pages faster. However, depending on your device, it can either improve or worsen QBO performance.

How to Toggle Hardware Acceleration in Chrome

1. Visit chrome://settings/system.
2. Toggle **Use hardware acceleration when available** on or off.
3. Restart your browser for the change to take effect.

Try both settings to see which one gives you a smoother QBO experience.

Using Incognito Mode to Troubleshoot Performance Issues

Incognito mode runs Chrome with:

- No stored cache
- No saved cookies
- Most extensions disabled

If QBO performs better in Incognito mode, the likely culprits are:

1. Cache overload
2. Problematic browser extensions
3. Conflicting settings

Open Incognito Mode

- **Windows:** Press **Ctrl + Shift + N**
- **Mac:** Press **Cmd + Shift + N**

If QBO works smoothly here, start disabling extensions or clearing your cache in normal mode.

Optimizing Internet Connectivity for QuickBooks Online

QBO requires a stable, consistent connection for best performance.

Recommended Internet Specs

- **Download speed:** 3 Mbps or higher
- **Upload speed:** 1 Mbps or higher
- **Latency (ping):** Under 100 ms

Tips to Improve Internet Speed

1. Use a **wired Ethernet connection** instead of Wi-Fi.
2. Close bandwidth-heavy apps such as Zoom, Dropbox, or streaming services.
3. Restart your router weekly to refresh the connection.
4. Upgrade your internet plan if your speed often dips below minimum levels.

Quick Fixes to Immediately Improve QBO Speed

- Sign out of QBO and sign back in.
- Close unnecessary browser tabs.
- Restart your computer.
- Avoid heavy-internet peak hours (evenings in some regions).
- Use QuickBooks in **full-screen mode** to reduce rendering load.

Long-Term Browser Maintenance for Better Performance

- Keep your browser updated.
- Permanently disable unused extensions.
- Bookmark your QBO login page for faster access.
- Limit how many QBO tabs you open at one time.
- Use an auto-cache clearing extension (for Chrome users).
- Establish routine browser maintenance for team members if multiple users access QBO daily.

When to Contact Support or IT

If QBO remains slow after adjusting browser settings, you may need additional help.

Next steps:

1. Contact **QuickBooks Online Support** at: https://quickbooks.intuit.com/help
2. Provide screenshots of errors, browser version details, and steps you've attempted.
3. Have your IT team check for firewall, DNS, or proxy configurations that may block QBO scripts.

HOW TO SET UP QUICKBOOKS ONLINE FOR PERSONAL USE

QuickBooks Online isn't just for businesses—it can also be a powerful tool for managing your personal finances. With the right setup, you can use it to track income, monitor spending, categorize transactions, and even build a personal budget. Below is a clear, beginner-friendly guide to help you get started.

Tip:
Choose **Simple Start** if you only need basic income and expense tracking.

Choose **Plus** if you want advanced features like budgeting and class tracking.

Step 1: Create Income and Expense Accounts

Think of every financial activity in your life as a document that needs to be placed in the correct folder. Each folder represents a financial category—rent, utilities, groceries, insurance, etc. All these folders live inside a single filing cabinet.

In QuickBooks, that filing cabinet is your **Chart of Accounts**.

Each "folder" is an **account**, and together they create a full structure for tracking your money.

QuickBooks Online doesn't come preloaded with personal-finance categories, so you'll need to create your own.

Creating Expense Accounts

Expenses are simply the costs you pay in your daily life—bills, groceries, services, subscriptions, and more. In QuickBooks, each type of spending gets its own expense account.

Here are examples of personal expenses and the account names you might use:

Transaction	Suggested Expense Account
Paid $1,400 June rent to Riverdale Apartments	Housing Expenses
Paid $165.42 to City Utilities Authority	Utilities
Spent $238.76 at Trader Joe's	Food & Supplies
Paid $320 to HomeFix Pros for A/C repairs	Home Maintenance Costs
Paid $375 toward your car loan	Auto Loan
Paid $212.50 to BrightHealth Insurance	Health Insurance
Spent $18.42 at Chick-fil-A	Meals & Entertainment
Netflix $15.49 + Spotify $10.99	Subscription Expenses
Booked Airbnb for $842	Travel & Entertainment

How to Add a New Expense Account

1. Click the **Gear icon** in the upper-right corner.
2. Under the **Your Company** section, select **Chart of accounts**.
3. In the Chart of Accounts page, click **New** (green button).
4. In the panel:
   - Choose **Account Type: Expenses**
   - Select the appropriate **Detail Type**
   - Enter a clear **Account Name**
   - Add a description if needed

5. Click **Save**

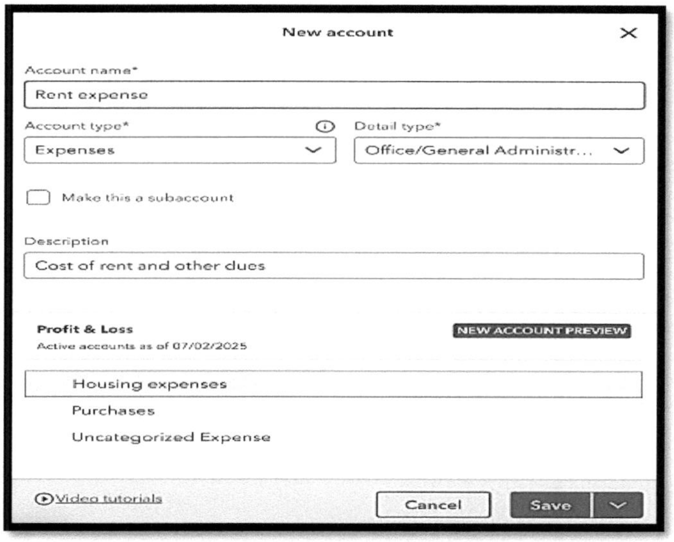

This same process applies when adding other types of accounts, such as **assets**, **liabilities**, or **loan accounts**.

Adding Income Accounts in QuickBooks Online (Personal Use)

Income accounts allow you to categorize and track the different ways you earn money—whether it's a paycheck, freelance work, rental income, or investment returns. QuickBooks Online doesn't provide a preset chart of accounts for personal finances, so you'll create income accounts manually, just as you did for expenses.

Below are common income examples and the account names that best match them:

Type of Income	Income Account Title
Received $3,800 from Acme Corp as net June pay	Full-time job salary
Earned $750 from a freelance project with Apex Media	Freelance income
Collected $1,200 June rent from a tenant	Rent income
Received $92.30 in dividends from an index fund	Dividend income

How to Create an Income Account

1. Go to the **Gear icon** at the top right.
2. Select **Chart of accounts** under the *Your Company* section.
3. Click the **New** button.
4. In the account setup panel:
   - ❖ Choose **Income** as the *Account Type*.
   - ❖ Select the most accurate *Detail Type*.

❖ Enter a clear name (e.g., *Freelance Income, Dividend Income*).
❖ Add a description if helpful.

5. Click **Save**.

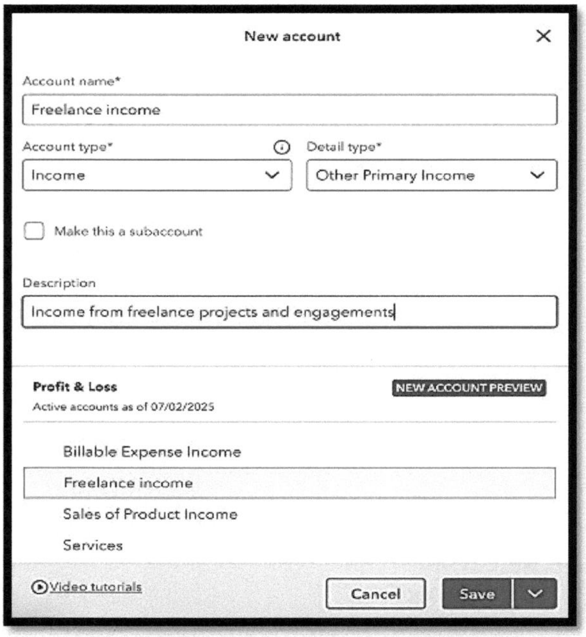

Step 2: Add Vendors and Customers

Think of your financial records as a story. Each income or expense transaction includes a "character" who plays a role in that story. Adding vendors and customers ensures your records stay organized and your reports stay accurate.

Vendors

Vendors are individuals or companies you pay for goods or services.

Examples: your landlord, a utilities company, your car loan lender, or your insurance provider.

Every expense transaction in QuickBooks Online must link to a vendor.

To add a vendor:

1. Click **Expenses** on the left menu.
2. Select **Suppliers**.
3. Click **New supplier** and enter:
   ❖ Vendor name
   ❖ Company name (optional)

- ❖ Address, email, and phone number
- ❖ Any additional details

4. Click **Save**.

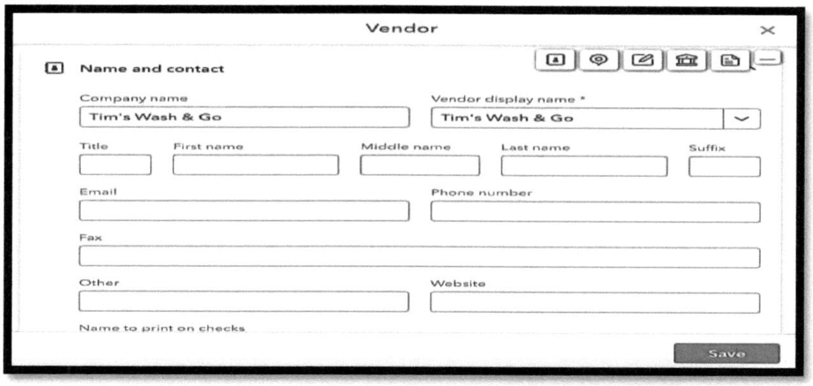

Customers

Customers represent the people or organizations who pay you—full-time employers, freelance clients, tenants, or any person or entity from whom you receive income.

Every income transaction in QuickBooks must be connected to a customer.

To add a customer:

1. Go to **Customers & leads** on the left navigation.
2. Select **Customers**.
3. Click **New customer**.
4. Enter key details such as the customer's name, company (if applicable), and contact info.
5. Click **Save**.

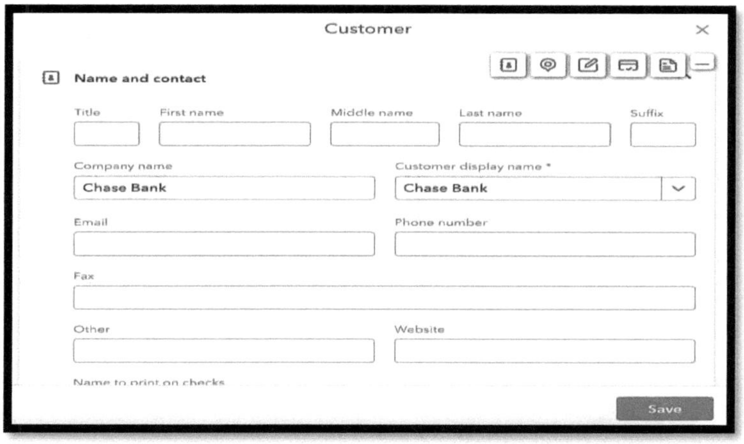

Why Adding Vendors and Customers Matters

- ❖ QuickBooks automatically fills in transaction details, saving time.
- ❖ Reports become cleaner and more accurate.
- ❖ You avoid mixing up payments, especially when you have recurring vendors or income sources.
- ❖ Your personal finance data becomes structured and easier to analyze.

Step 3: Set Up Balance Sheet Accounts

QuickBooks Online doesn't just track income and expenses—it also helps you monitor what you **own** (assets) and **owe** (liabilities). To get a full picture of your personal finances, list out your property, valuables, savings, and debts, then create accounts for them in your chart of accounts.

You don't need to include every personal item, but **all financial accounts—bank accounts, credit cards, loans—should be added** for accuracy.

Creating Asset Accounts

Assets include anything you own that has value, such as bank accounts, vehicles, electronics, or investment accounts.

To add an asset account:

1. Open **Chart of accounts** from the ⚙ **Settings** menu.
2. Click the green **New** button.
3. Choose **Current Assets** as the account type.
4. Select a **detail type** that best fits the asset.
5. Enter the **account name**, **as of date**, and **opening balance**.
6. Click **Save**.

Creating Liability Accounts

Liabilities are debts you owe—student loans, credit cards, mortgages, or lines of credit.

To add a liability account:

1. Follow the same steps above.
2. Choose **Current Liabilities** as the account type.
3. Enter the name, detail type, and the **unpaid balance as of your start date**.

Once your asset and liability accounts are entered, QuickBooks can produce a **Balance Sheet report**, giving you real insight into your net worth and financial health.

Step 4: Create Classes

Classes act like labeled categories or "envelopes" that help you see exactly how money flows in different areas of your life. They're especially helpful if you have:

- Multiple income streams
- Several types of deductible expenses
- Rental activities
- Side gigs or freelance work

Note: You need **QuickBooks Online Plus or higher** to use class tracking.

Examples of Useful Classes

- **Personal:** For any non-deductible personal transactions.
- **Schedule A Deductions:** Medical expenses, mortgage interest, state and local taxes, donations, etc.
- **Side Gigs:** Separate class for each job (e.g., "Freelancing," "Bartending," "Rideshare Driving – Night Shift").
- **Rental Activity:** Separate personal and rental-related expenses.

How to Enable Class Tracking

1. Go to ⚙ **Settings** > **Account and Settings**.
2. Click **Advanced** on the left.
3. Under **Categories**, toggle on **Track classes**.
4. Click **Save**.

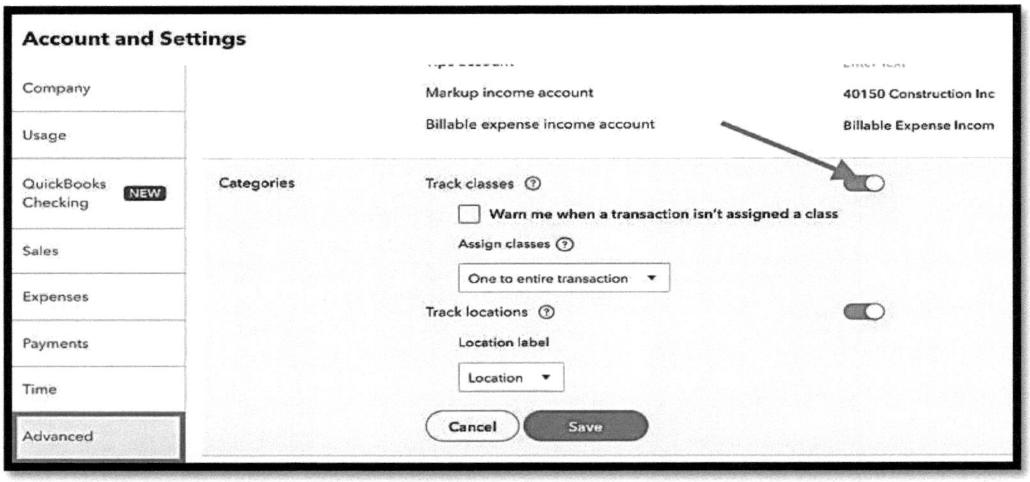

How to Add Classes

1. Go to ⚙ **Settings** > **All Lists**.
2. Select **Classes**.
3. Click **New**, enter a class name, and choose **Is sub-class** if it belongs under a parent category.
4. Click **Save**.

Classes help you run powerful reports—like a profit and loss by class—to clearly see where money comes from and where it goes.

Step 5: Connect Your Bank and Credit Card Accounts

You can enter banks manually, but linking your accounts to QuickBooks Online will save you time and reduce errors. Once connected, QuickBooks automatically downloads new transactions every day.

Benefits of connecting your accounts:

- Automatic transaction downloads
- Easier reconciliation
- Accurate, real-time balances
- Faster error detection

How to Connect Your Bank or Credit Card

1. Go to **Transactions** > **Bank Transactions** in the left navigation menu.
2. Click **Connect account** or **Link account**.
3. Find your bank from the list or search for it.
4. Follow the prompts to connect securely.

If your bank isn't supported (rare), you can add the account manually in the chart of accounts or **import bank statements** yourself.

Step 6: Review and Categorize Imported Transactions

Once your bank and credit card accounts are connected, QuickBooks Online (QBO) automatically brings in your recent transactions. QBO attempts to match these entries to existing records; if it can't, it creates new ones for you to review.

Careful classification ensures accurate reporting and helps you stay on top of spending.

Where to Categorize Transactions

1. Go to **Transactions** under the **Bookkeeping** tab
   – If you're on a personal-finance setup, look for **Bank transactions** instead.

2. Select the **Bank transactions** tab.
   You'll see all connected accounts and three views:
   - ❖ **For review** (new transactions)
   - ❖ **Categorized**
   - ❖ **Excluded**

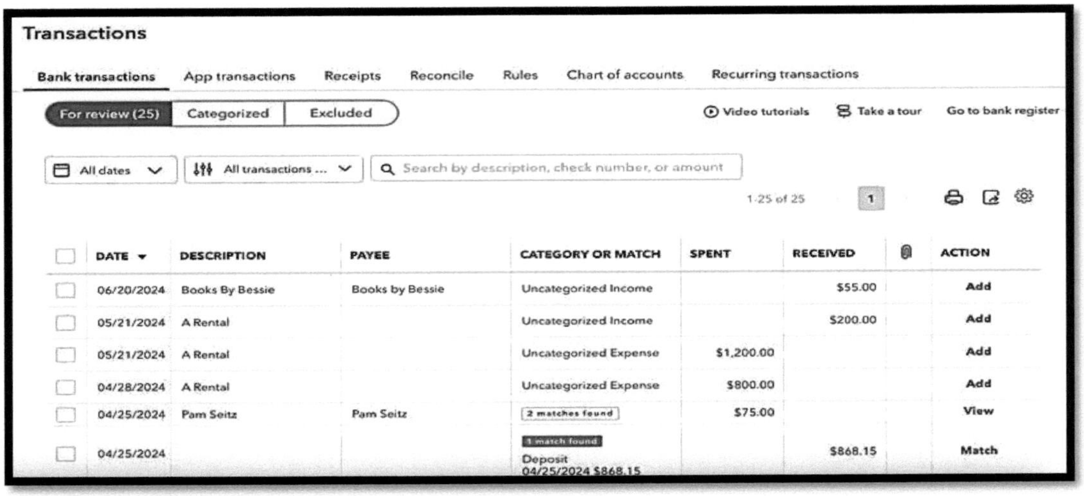

How to Review Transactions

- ❖ If QBO finds a match, you'll see **1 match found**.
  Click **Match** to link it to the existing entry.
- ❖ If no match is found, click **Add** to create a new transaction and assign the correct category.

You can also categorize transactions created from uploaded receipts. When you take a photo using the QBO mobile app, QBO drafts the transaction and lets you review and categorize it.

Step 7: Record and Track Your Finances

You can record income and expenses manually using built-in QuickBooks forms. This ensures your financial records remain accurate—especially when transactions are imported later.

Recording Income

1. Click **+ New**
2. Select **Sales receipt**
3. Complete the form with:
   - ❖ Customer name
   - ❖ Description of the income

- ❖ Amount received

Example: Recording $150 received from Mark's Trucking for six hours of work.

Recording Expenses

1. Click **+ New**
2. Select **Expense**
3. Provide details:
   - ❖ Vendor name
   - ❖ Category (e.g., utilities, food, or auto loan)
   - ❖ Amount paid

Example: Logging a $250 electricity payment to Florida Power & Light.

Tracking Your Finances

Run helpful reports under the **Reports** menu, including:

- ❖ **Expenses by Supplier Summary**
- ❖ **Income by Customer Summary**
- ❖ **Profit and Loss**

After entering income or expenses manually, double-check that they are matched correctly when your bank imports the same transactions. If not, duplicates may occur.

Step 8: Create a Budget

A budget helps you plan your money, control overspending, and track progress toward financial goals. In QBO, a budget is simply a table of estimated amounts for each month, quarter, or year.

How to Create a Budget

1. Click the ⚙ **(Settings)** icon.
2. Choose **Budgeting** under the **TOOLS** column.
3. Select **Add budget**.
4. Enter:
   - ❖ Budget name
   - ❖ Fiscal year
   - ❖ (Optional) Subdivide by class or location if needed
5. Click **Next**.
6. Enter your estimated monthly amounts.
7. Save your budget.

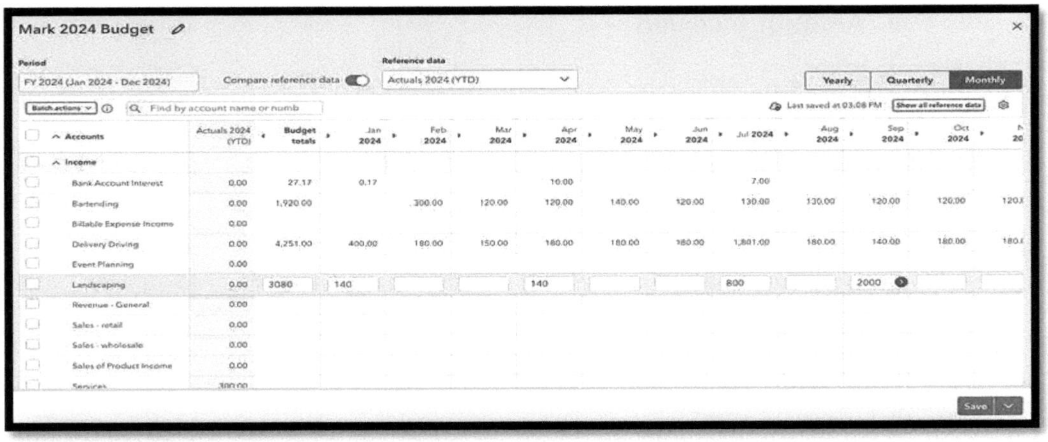

Viewing Budget Reports

- **Budget Overview** shows your full projected budget.

- **Budget vs. Actuals** compares expected amounts to actual spending, helping you:

Budget Overview_Mark 2024 Budget_Report

Mark Personal Use

January-December, 2024

Refresh report

Last updated a few seconds ago

February 2024	March 2024	April 2024	May 2024	June 2024	July 2024	August 2024	September 2024	October 2024	November 2024	December 2024	Total
US$480.00	**US$270.00**	**US$450.00**	**US$320.00**	**US$300.00**	**US$2,738.00**	**US$310.00**	**US$2,260.00**	**US$300.00**	**US$300.00**	**US$1,010.00**	**US$9,278.17**
US$0.00	US$0.00	US$0.00	US$0.00	US$0.00	US$0.00	US$0.00	US$0.00	US$0.00	US$0.00	US$0.00	US$0.00
US$480.00	US$270.00	US$450.00	US$320.00	US$300.00	US$2,738.00	US$310.00	US$2,260.00	US$300.00	US$300.00	US$1,010.00	US$9,278.17
US$300.00	**US$300.00**	**US$300.00**	**US$300.00**	**US$300.00**	**US$300.00**	**US$300.00**	**US$300.00**	**US$300.00**	**US$300.00**	**US$300.00**	**US$3,416.67**
US$180.00	-US$30.00	US$150.00	US$20.00	US$0.00	US$2,438.00	US$10.00	US$1,960.00	US$0.00	US$0.00	US$710.00	US$5,861.50
US$0.00	US$0.00	US$0.00	US$0.00	US$0.00	US$0.00	US$0.00	US$0.00	US$0.00	US$0.00	US$0.00	US$0.00
US$0.00	US$0.00	US$0.00	US$0.00	US$0.00	US$0.00	US$0.00	US$0.00	US$0.00	US$0.00	US$0.00	US$0.00
US$0.00	US$0.00	US$0.00	US$0.00	US$0.00	US$0.00	US$0.00	US$0.00	US$0.00	US$0.00	US$0.00	US$0.00
US$180.00	-US$30.00	US$150.00	US$20.00	US$0.00	US$2,438.00	US$10.00	US$1,960.00	US$0.00	US$0.00	US$710.00	US$5,861.50

  - Spot overspending

- Identify savings opportunities
- Monitor financial health month by month

Other Ways to Use QuickBooks Online for Personal Finances (Rewritten & Improved)

1. Keep business and personal finances separate

If you earn freelance or side-gig income, it's important to separate those transactions from your personal spending—especially for tax reporting. QuickBooks makes this easy by using **classes**.

Instead of creating different accounts like "Personal Gas" and "Business Gas," you can keep one gas expense account and assign the correct class (e.g., *Personal*, *Freelance – Photography*, *Freelance – Tutoring*) each time you enter a transaction.

This keeps your chart of accounts clean while still giving you accurate reports for each activity.

2. Track charitable and medical mileage

If you drive for volunteer work or medical appointments, maintaining accurate mileage logs is essential for tax deductions.

The **QuickBooks Online mobile app** (iOS and Android) can automate this for you. Open the app before you start driving, and QuickBooks will use GPS to track mileage—saving you from keeping manual odometer logs.

3. Run and print personalized financial reports

QuickBooks Online includes powerful reporting tools that help you analyze your personal finances.

Open the **Reports** menu to access common reports such as:

- Profit and Loss
- Spending by Vendor
- Income by Customer
- Budget vs. Actual

You can customize these reports, compare them to previous periods, and print or save them for your records. Reports under **Favorites** provide quick access to those you use often.

4. Digitize and organize receipts

If you want to store receipts without keeping physical copies, QuickBooks Online lets you digitize them:

- Take a picture of your receipt in the **QuickBooks mobile app**
- Upload it directly into QuickBooks
- The system extracts the details and creates a suggested transaction

You can then edit, match, or categorize the transaction.

Avoid uploading receipts that contain sensitive details like credit card numbers.

5. Automate bill payments

QuickBooks Online lets you enter bills and pay them directly through the system. You can also:

- **Schedule future payments** to avoid late fees
- Create **recurring payments** for monthly bills (utilities, subscriptions, etc.)
- Specify frequency and duration for recurring bills

Automation helps you stay consistent and reduces the risk of missing due dates.

6. Perform regular reconciliations

Reconciling your bank and credit card transactions ensures your QuickBooks records match actual account activity.

Regular reconciliation helps you:

- Catch errors or duplicate transactions
- Identify unauthorized charges
- Maintain accurate reports

Ideally, reconcile weekly or at least every two weeks. This keeps your books clean and prevents issues from building up.

CORRECTING MISCATEGORIZED EXPENSES IN QUICKBOOKS ONLINE

Accurate expense categorization is the backbone of reliable financial reporting in QuickBooks Online. When expenses are categorized incorrectly, your profit-and-loss report becomes unreliable, tax deductions get distorted, and cleanup becomes time-consuming. Fortunately, fixing these issues—and preventing them from happening again—is easier than you might think.

Below is a clear, streamlined guide to correcting miscategorized expenses and tightening your financial workflow.

Why Miscategorized Expenses Happen

Even with automation, QuickBooks isn't perfect—and neither are humans. Most categorization errors stem from:

- Choosing the wrong category during manual entry
- Importing transactions from your bank that QuickBooks guesses incorrectly
- Auto-categorization assigning the wrong type
- Missing, outdated, or overly broad rules that misclassify multiple transactions

Understanding *why* the error occurred helps you fix it quickly and prevent it in the future.

How to Fix Miscategorized Expenses in QuickBooks Online

1. Review and Edit Incorrect Expenses

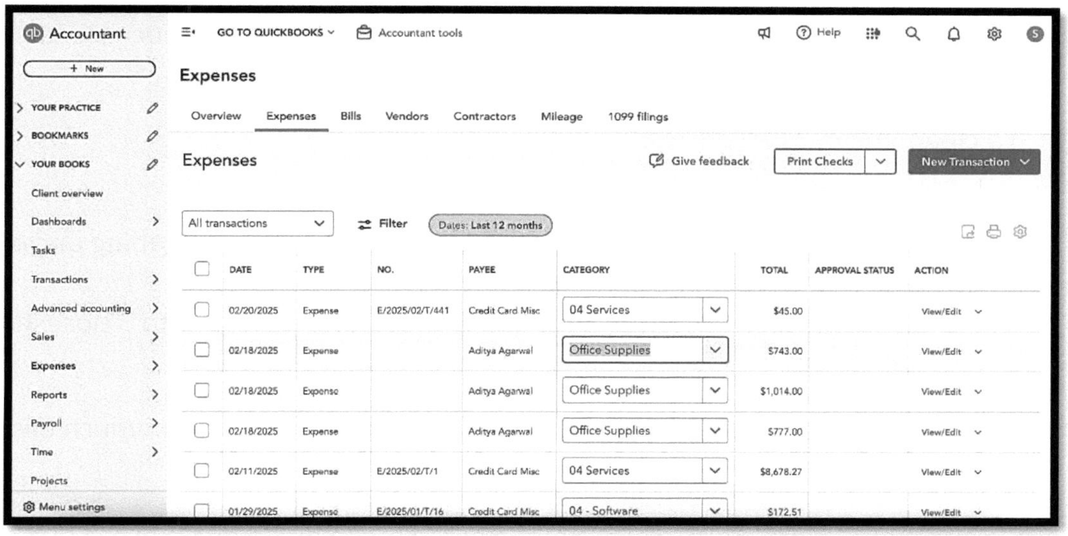

Start by checking your existing transactions and correcting anything that's been placed in the wrong category.

How to edit a miscategorized expense:

1. Go to **Expenses > All Transactions**
2. Look for entries that are clearly misclassified
3. Click the transaction, select the correct category, and hit **Save**

This immediately corrects your financial reports.

2. Review and Improve Your Chart of Accounts

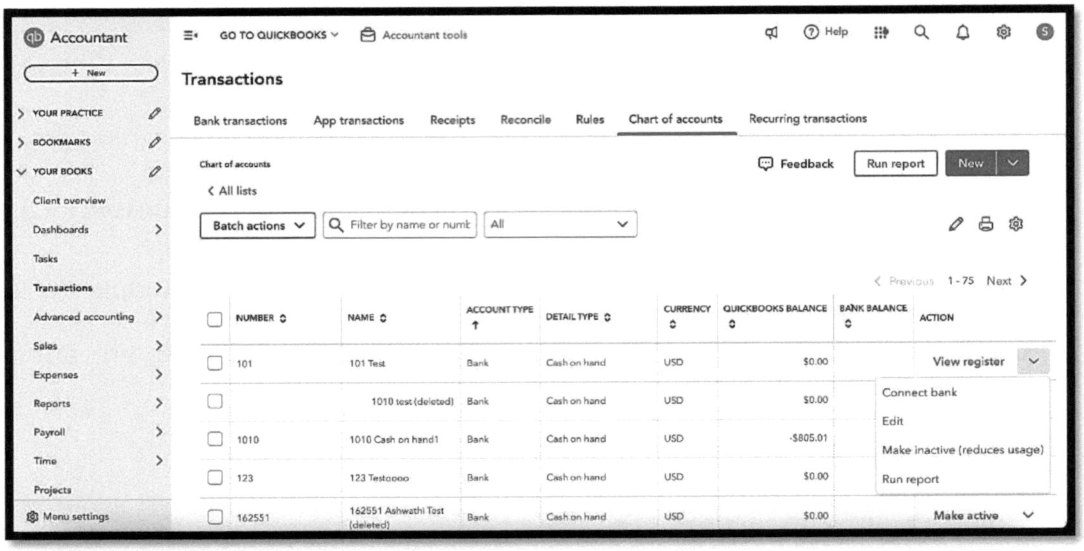

Sometimes expenses are miscategorized simply because your account list is confusing or incomplete.

To clean up your categories:

1. Go to **Transactions > Chart of Accounts**
2. Review your current categories and merge or rename anything unclear
3. Add new accounts where needed
4. Reassign any expenses that were previously forced into "closest match" categories

A well-organized Chart of Accounts makes accurate categorization much easier.

3. Create or Update Rules to Prevent Future Errors

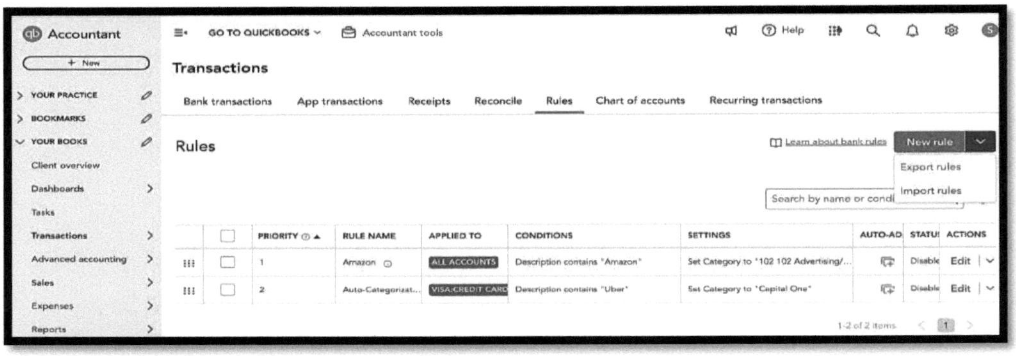

If the same type of transaction is consistently being misclassified, QuickBooks needs better rules.

To create or refine an expense rule:

1. Navigate to **Transactions > Rules**
2. Select **New Rule**
3. Set conditions such as merchant name, amount, or bank text
4. Assign the correct category
5. Save the rule to automatically apply it to future transactions

This reduces manual corrections and ensures long-term accuracy.

HOW TO CAPTURE AND MANAGE RECEIPTS IN QUICKBOOKS

QuickBooks makes it simple to capture, organize, and link receipts to your expenses, keeping your books accurate and audit-ready. Below is a clear walkthrough of how to snap and categorize receipts from the mobile app, manage them in QuickBooks Online, and set up a custom email address your team can use to submit receipts.

Capturing Receipts on the Mobile App

Start by opening the **QuickBooks Online mobile app** and tapping **Expense**.

Select the **camera icon** to take or attach a photo of your receipt.

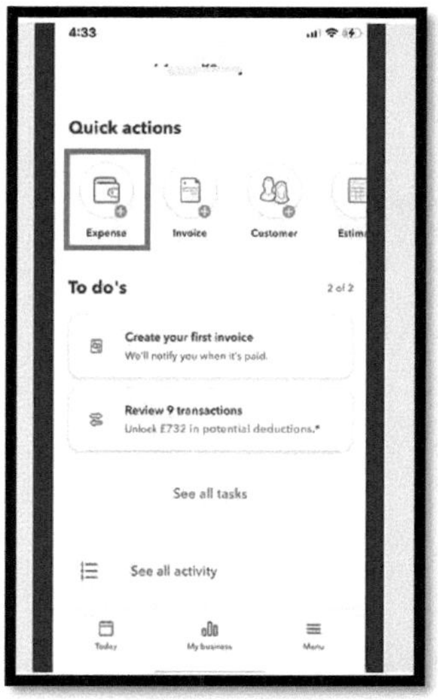

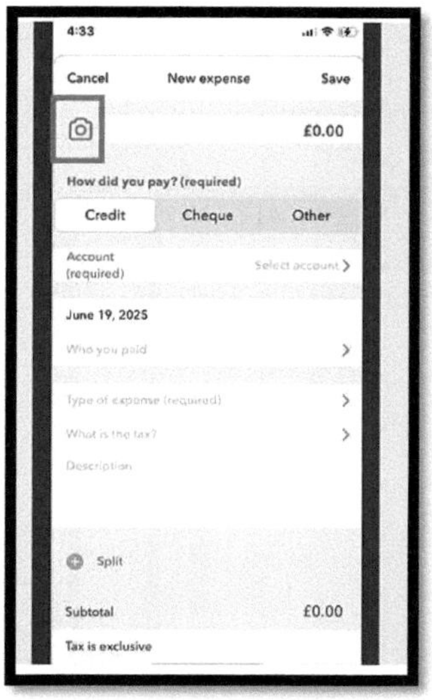

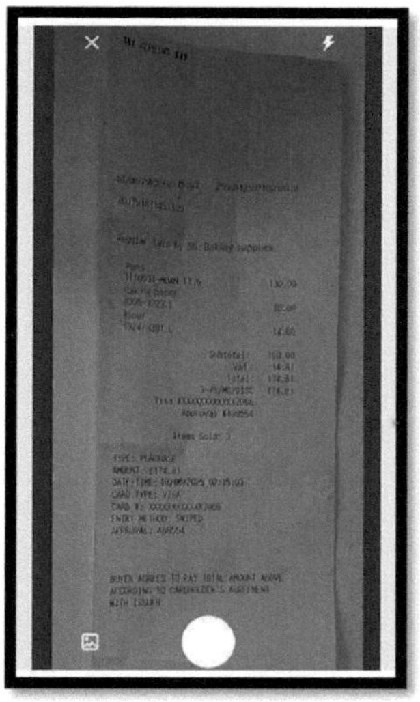

Position the receipt within the screen's corners—QuickBooks will outline it with a green box to show it's captured correctly. Hold your phone steady, and if you're using an Android device, you may be able to take multiple photos in one session.

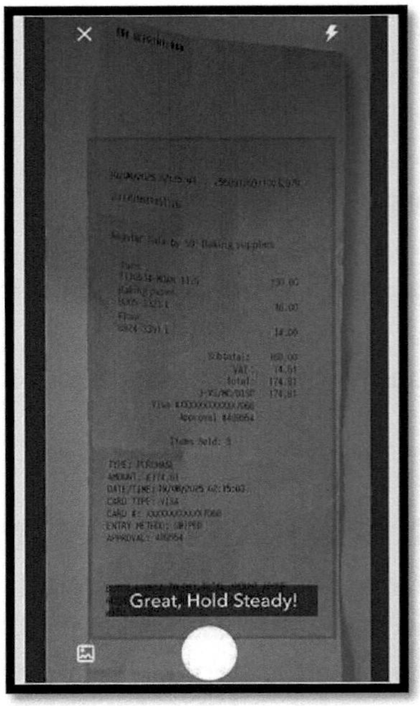

You can rotate, crop, or retake the picture if needed. When the image looks good, tap **Use This Photo**.

Next, fill in the details of the expense:

- ❖ Who you paid
- ❖ How much
- ❖ The date
- ❖ The account or card used

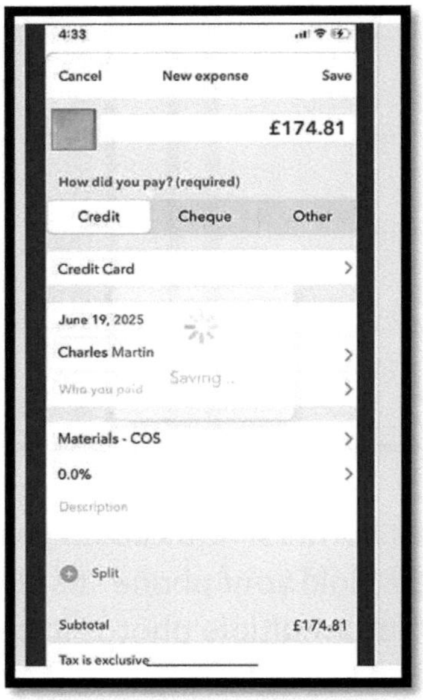

You can review or edit the expense anytime by going to **Menu > Expenses** and selecting the entry.

Accurate categorization is important, so make sure the expense is assigned to the correct category before selecting **Save and Close**.

Attaching Receipts to an Existing Expense

If the expense was already entered manually, you can still attach the receipt:

1. Go to **Menu > Expenses**
2. Select the expense
3. Choose **Add notes or attachments**

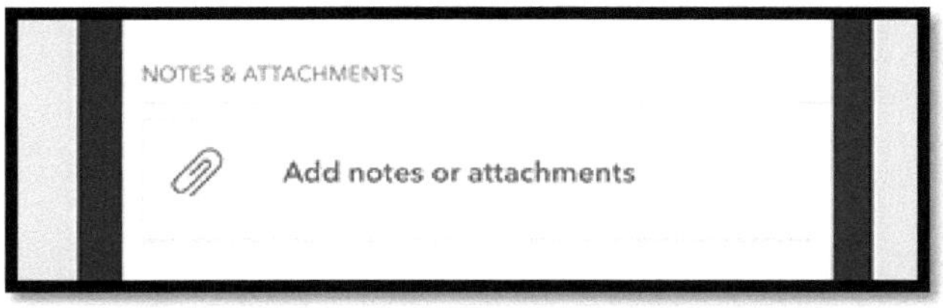

4. Take a photo or upload one from your device's photo library

QuickBooks will link the image to the transaction, keeping documentation organized and easy to find.

Categorizing Receipts on Your Computer

If you prefer working from a desktop, go to **Transactions > Receipts** in QuickBooks Online.

Here, you'll see every receipt captured from your phone that still needs to be reviewed or matched to an expense.

From this screen, you can:

- ❖ Edit receipt details
- ❖ Confirm the correct category and account
- ❖ Upload additional receipts from your computer or Google Drive

Once reviewed, QuickBooks automatically moves the receipt into your books.

Setting Up a Custom Email Address for Receipt Submissions

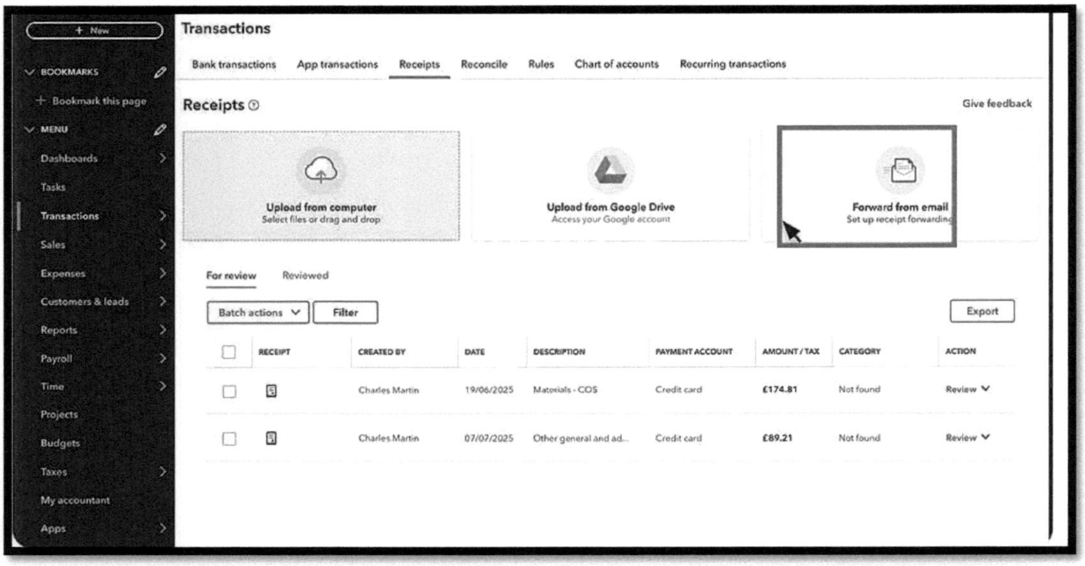

You can also give your team a simple way to send receipts directly into QuickBooks via a custom email address.

(You must be an **Admin** to set this up.)

1. Select **Forward from Email**
2. Enter the name you want for the custom receipt-submission email
3. Click **Next**, verify the address, then choose **Done**
4. Go to **Manage Forwarding Email** and toggle on permissions for users who should be allowed to send receipts
5. Add users here if needed, then select **Close**

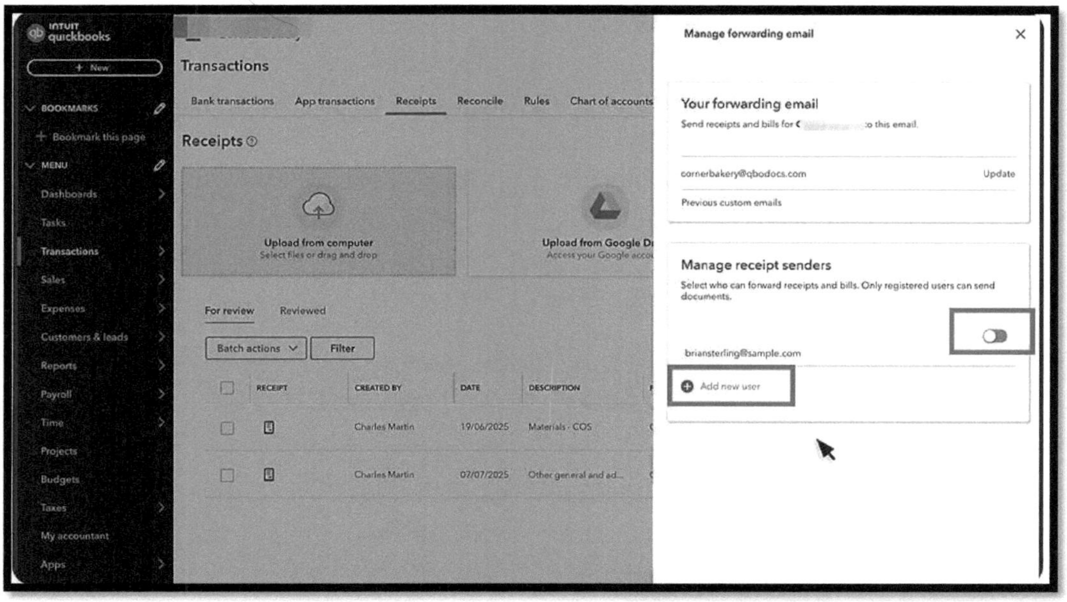

Users must email receipts **from the same email address they use to sign in to QuickBooks**, and can attach multiple receipts as long as each one is a separate image.

All emailed receipts will appear in the **Receipts** section, ready for review and categorization.

With these tools—mobile receipt capture, desktop categorization, and team email submissions—QuickBooks Online streamlines the entire receipt-tracking process. You'll stay organized, avoid missing documentation, and keep your business audit-ready with minimal effort.

CREATING AND MANAGING BANK RULES IN QUICKBOOKS ONLINE

Bank rules are one of the most powerful tools in QuickBooks Online for speeding up your bookkeeping. By automating the way transactions are categorized, bank rules save time, reduce mistakes, and keep your financial records consistent.

Below is a clear, streamlined guide to setting up, using, and managing bank rules effectively.

Why Bank Rules Matter

Bank rules help transform your bookkeeping by:

- **Saving Time Automatically:** QuickBooks auto-categorizes transactions based on the rules you create—no more sorting line-by-line.

- ❖ **Reducing Categorization Errors:** Automation minimizes manual mistakes that can lead to inaccurate financial reports or incorrect tax deductions.
- ❖ **Ensuring Consistency:** Once a rule is created, QuickBooks applies it uniformly to all matching transactions.
- ❖ **Speeding Up Reconciliation:** Correctly categorized transactions are easier to match during reconciliation, shortening the entire process.
- ❖ **Improving Cash Flow Visibility:** Because transactions are categorized in real time, your financial dashboards stay accurate and useful.

How to Create a Bank Rule in QuickBooks Online

Step 1: Go to the Banking Section

1. Log in to QuickBooks Online.
2. In the left-hand menu, select **Transactions > Bank Transactions**.
    - ❖ This opens the Banking dashboard where you can see all your connected accounts.
3. Under **For Review**, you'll find transactions that may need rules applied.

Step 2: Open the Rules Page

1. At the top of the Banking page, click the **Rules** tab.
2. Select **New Rule** in the upper-right corner to start creating a rule.

Step 3: Select the Rule Type

Choose whether your rule applies to:

- ❖ **Money in** – deposits or credits (customer payments, refunds, etc.)
- ❖ **Money out** – expenses or withdrawals (bills, subscriptions, transfers)

Step 4: Add Rule Details

- ❖ **Rule name:** Use a clear, descriptive name (e.g., *"PayPal Sales"*).
- ❖ **Apply to:** Choose **Any bank account** or limit the rule to specific accounts like your debit card or credit card.

Step 5: Set Up Conditions

These conditions tell QuickBooks when to apply your rule. You can choose from:

- ❖ **Description** (e.g., "PayPal")
- ❖ **Bank text** (specific wording from your bank feed)
- ❖ **Amount** (exact amounts or ranges)

Example:
To categorize PayPal deposits as Sales Income:

- Condition: **Description contains "PayPal"**

You can add multiple conditions if needed. QuickBooks will only apply the rule when *all* conditions are met.

Step 6: Choose the Action

This determines *how* the transaction will be categorized.

- **Category:** Select the correct expense or income account
- **Payee:** Assign a vendor or customer (optional)
- **Memo:** Add notes for reporting clarity
- **Class or Location:** If you use advanced tracking

Step 7: Finalize and Save

Before saving:

- Check **Automatically add** to let QuickBooks auto-approve and categorize matching transactions
- Enable **Apply to existing transactions** if you want the rule to clean up past transactions

Then click **Save**.

Example Bank Rule

Goal: Categorize all £8.99 Amazon subscription charges as "Subscription Expense."

- **Rule Name:** Amazon Subscription
- **Type:** Money Out
- **Apply to:** Any account
- **Conditions:**
  - Description contains **"Amazon"**
  - Amount equals **£8.99**
- **Action:**
  - **Category:** Subscription
  - **Memo:** Amazon Prime
- **Save**

Now QuickBooks automatically categorizes every matching Amazon charge.

Managing Your Existing Rules

Edit or Delete a Rule

1. Return to **Transactions > Rules**
2. Locate the rule
3. Click the dropdown beside it
4. Select **Edit**, **Delete**, or **Copy**

Pro Tips for Better Bank Rule Management

1. Review Rules Regularly: Business expenses evolve—rules should too.

2. Be Specific: Vague rules can miscategorize transactions. Tighten wording when needed.

3. Refine Conditions for Accuracy: If QuickBooks miscategorizes a transaction, revisit the rule and adjust your conditions or matching criteria.

IMPORTING DATA INTO QUICKBOOKS ONLINE

How to Import Data into QuickBooks Online

Importing data into QuickBooks Online is straightforward thanks to its built-in **Import Data Tool**, which allows you to move essential business records from Excel, CSV, TSV, and other accounting platforms directly into your QuickBooks account. Whether you are migrating from another system or updating your records, the tool helps streamline the process, reduce manual entry, and improve accuracy.

Using the Import Data Tool

The Import Data Tool is designed to make data migration simple and reliable. It supports various file types and guides you through mapping your fields so that the information flows into the correct places inside QuickBooks Online.

Once you select the file you want to import, QuickBooks prompts you to match each column in your document—such as customer name, product details, invoice number, or amounts—with the corresponding QuickBooks fields. This step ensures accuracy and prevents formatting issues.

After the import is complete, QuickBooks provides a summary showing how many records were imported successfully or flagged for review, allowing you to verify everything before proceeding.

The tool can import items such as:

- Invoices and sales receipts
- Bills and expenses
- Customers and vendors
- Inventory items

By reducing the amount of manual entry, this tool saves time and helps maintain clean, consistent records.

Using Third-Party Integrations

Beyond QuickBooks' built-in importer, many businesses rely on third-party integration apps to automatically transfer data from other systems. These integrations sync information in real time, eliminate repetitive uploads, and ensure your financial data stays aligned across all platforms.

Key advantages include:

- Automatic data syncing
- Custom field mapping
- Reduced risk of manual entry errors
- Ability to consolidate financial information from multiple systems

These integrations are especially valuable for ecommerce stores, POS systems, CRMs, and inventory management tools.

What Data Can You Import into QuickBooks Online?

QuickBooks Online supports multiple data types to help you quickly build out your company file. Common categories include:

1. Customer and Vendor Information

Importing customer and vendor lists centralizes important details such as contact information, payment terms, and transaction history. This helps streamline invoicing, bill payments, and reporting.

To ensure a smooth import:

- Follow acceptable file formats
- Validate data before uploading
- Map fields correctly
- Review for duplicates

Adhering to data validation guidelines helps maintain accuracy and compliance.

2. Invoices and Sales Receipts

Bringing in invoices and sales receipts ensures your revenue records are complete and up to date. QuickBooks uses import templates to standardize the process, and built-in validation checks catch formatting errors or missing information.

Accurate sales imports support:

- ❖ Reliable revenue tracking
- ❖ Faster customer billing
- ❖ Clear financial reporting

This is crucial for maintaining accurate books and making informed financial decisions.

3. Bills and Expenses

Importing bills and expenses helps businesses track payables, categorize costs, and monitor spending patterns.

Key considerations include:

- ❖ Correctly mapping vendors, categories, and amounts
- ❖ Assigning appropriate expense categories
- ❖ Reviewing imported transactions for accuracy

Following best practices—such as reconciling regularly and keeping documentation—ensures clean expense records.

4. Inventory Items

If your business tracks inventory, you can import product names, SKUs, stock levels, and cost details into QuickBooks Online. This makes it easier to maintain accurate stock counts and generate meaningful inventory reports.

Effective inventory imports support:

- ❖ Accurate inventory valuation
- ❖ Better purchasing decisions
- ❖ Clear visibility into stock levels and trends

Consistent updates and reconciliations help maintain reliable inventory records.

Common Errors When Importing Data into QuickBooks Online

Importing data into QuickBooks Online is designed to be simple, but errors can still occur—especially when files contain inconsistencies or fields are not properly mapped. These issues can cause inaccurate records, reporting discrepancies, or failed imports, making it essential to validate your data before uploading.

The most common import errors include **duplicate entries**, **incorrect field mapping**, and **invalid data formats**. Understanding these issues—and how to fix them—helps ensure a smooth and accurate data migration experience.

1. Duplicate Entries

Duplicate entries are one of the most frequent problems during data import. They occur when the same record is uploaded more than once or when QuickBooks cannot distinguish between similar items.

Why it happens:

- Re-importing files that were previously uploaded
- Lack of unique identifiers (e.g., missing invoice numbers or customer IDs)
- Inconsistent naming conventions

Why it matters:

Duplicates can distort financial reports—such as income statements, balance sheets, and aged receivables—leading to inflated totals and poor decision-making.

How to prevent and fix duplicates:

- Use unique identifiers for each record
- Review and clean your data before importing
- Reconcile your data after import to detect repeat entries
- Enable validation checks or automated review tools

Establishing routine audits and standardized naming practices helps maintain clean, reliable data across your system.

2. Incorrect Mappings

Field mapping determines where your imported data lands inside QuickBooks. If the mapping is wrong—such as matching a "customer name" column to a "product description" field—your records will be inaccurate or incomplete.

Common causes:

- Mismatched column headers
- Misinterpreting QuickBooks field names
- Skipping the mapping review before importing

Consequences:
Incorrect mapping can lead to misclassified transactions, incorrect customer/vendor details, and reports that don't align with your actual financial activity.

How to fix and avoid mapping issues:

- Double-check field mappings before confirming the import
- Follow QuickBooks' import templates for better accuracy
- Analyze import logs to pinpoint where mapping failed
- Standardize your spreadsheet column titles

Automated mapping tools or integration platforms can further reduce human error.

3. Invalid Data Formats

QuickBooks requires data to follow specific formats (e.g., date formats, number formats, or text length). When the file doesn't meet these requirements, the import may partially succeed or fail entirely.

Typical examples:

- Dates entered as text
- Currency symbols included in number fields
- Special characters or extra spaces in name fields
- Incorrect column structures

Impact:
Invalid data formats trigger validation errors, limit how much of the file is accepted, and may require substantial rework to correct.

How to prevent format errors:

- Use standardized formats for dates, amounts, and text fields
- Run a validation check before import
- Remove unsupported characters and symbols
- Follow QuickBooks' recommended formatting guidelines or templates

Techniques such as regular expressions, data type checks, and automatic formatting tools help eliminate format inconsistencies before upload.

HOW TO EXPORT QUICKBOOKS ONLINE DATA

Exporting your QuickBooks Online (QBO) data is an essential part of maintaining reliable records, creating offline backups, and ensuring business continuity. While

QuickBooks provides several export options, each method has limitations—so understanding what you *can* and *cannot* export is crucial.

This section walks you through all three available ways to export your QBO data:

- **Using QuickBooks' built-in Export Data tool**
- **Exporting backups to Google Drive (Advanced plan only)**
- **Using third-party backup and export solutions**

Exporting Data Using QuickBooks Online's Native Export Tool

QuickBooks' built-in export tool lets you manually download company data in **Excel** or **PDF** format. This method is available in all major QBO subscriptions: **Simple Start, Essentials, Plus, and Advanced**.

What You Can Export

QuickBooks allows exporting two main groups of data:

Reports

- General Ledger
- Profit & Loss
- Balance Sheet
- Trial Balance
- Journal

Lists

- Customers
- Vendors
- Employees

Beyond these, QuickBooks also supports exporting non-posting transactions and other reference data such as:

- Estimates
- Purchase Orders
- Customer Statements
- Attachments
- Recurring Templates
- Chart of Accounts
- Products and Services

Steps to Export Reports and Lists

QuickBooks bundles your exports into a single **.zip file**, making it easy to save or archive.

How to export:

1. Sign in to QuickBooks Online.
2. Click the **Gear icon**, then select **Export Data**.

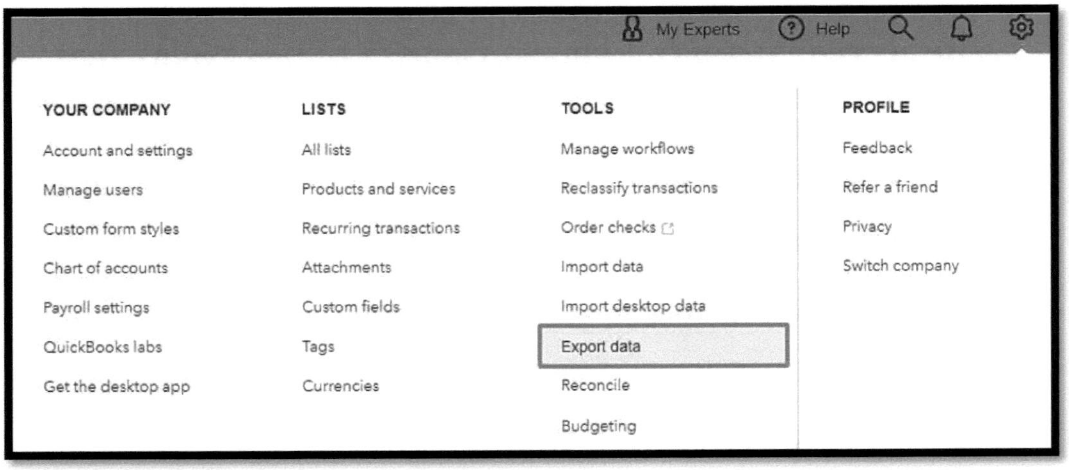

3. Choose your **date range** (All dates, Custom, Last quarter, YTD, etc.).

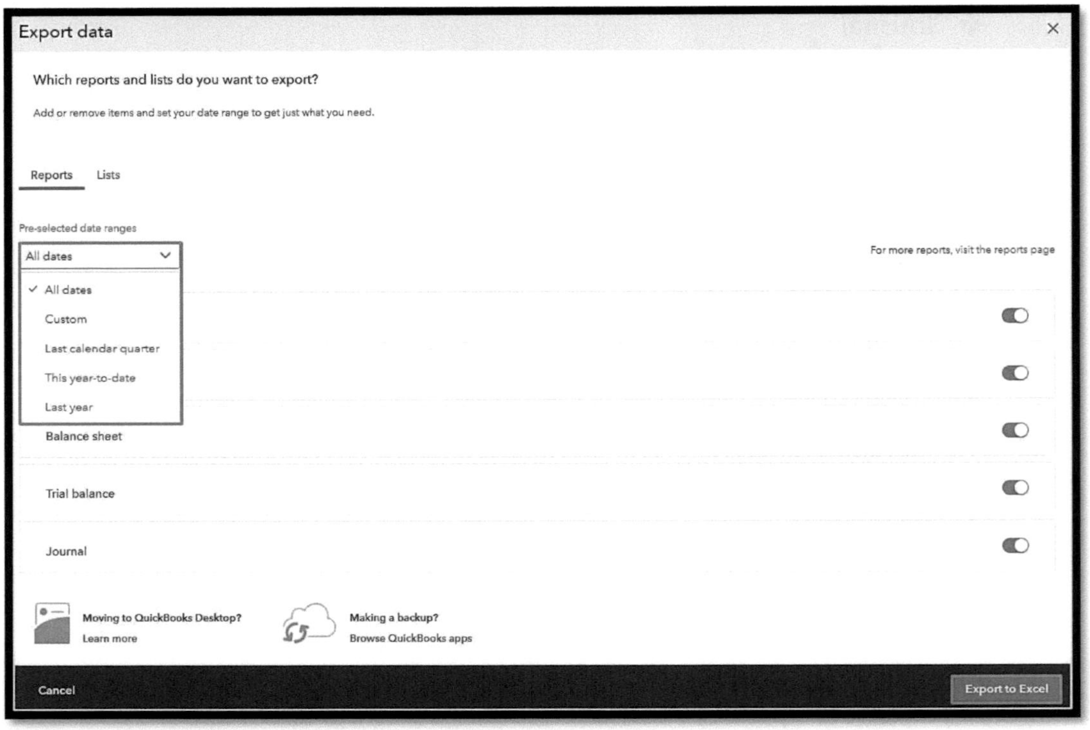

4. Uncheck any items you don't want included in the export.
5. Click **Export to Excel**.

Your .zip file will download to your local **Downloads** folder.

Limitations of the Native Export Tool

Although convenient, QuickBooks' native exporting feature comes with notable restrictions:

- You must export everything **manually**—there is no automatic scheduling.
- You are responsible for organizing and storing your exports for future reference.
- Export formats are limited to **Excel** and **PDF**.
- Exports often include **partial data only**.
  - Example: Employee exports only include contact details—not job title, hire date, pay rate, or salary.

Exporting QuickBooks Online Data to Google Drive (Advanced Plan Only)

Users subscribed to **QuickBooks Online Advanced** can access the **Backup and Restore** app at no extra cost. This allows automated backups that can be exported directly to **Google Drive**.

How to Back Up QBO Using the Backup and Restore App

1. Log in to your **QBO Advanced** account.
2. Open the **Gear icon**, then select **Back up company**.
3. To run a manual backup, click **Run manual backup**.
4. Choose your backup type:
   - Incremental
   - Full
   - Complete
5. Click **Back up**.

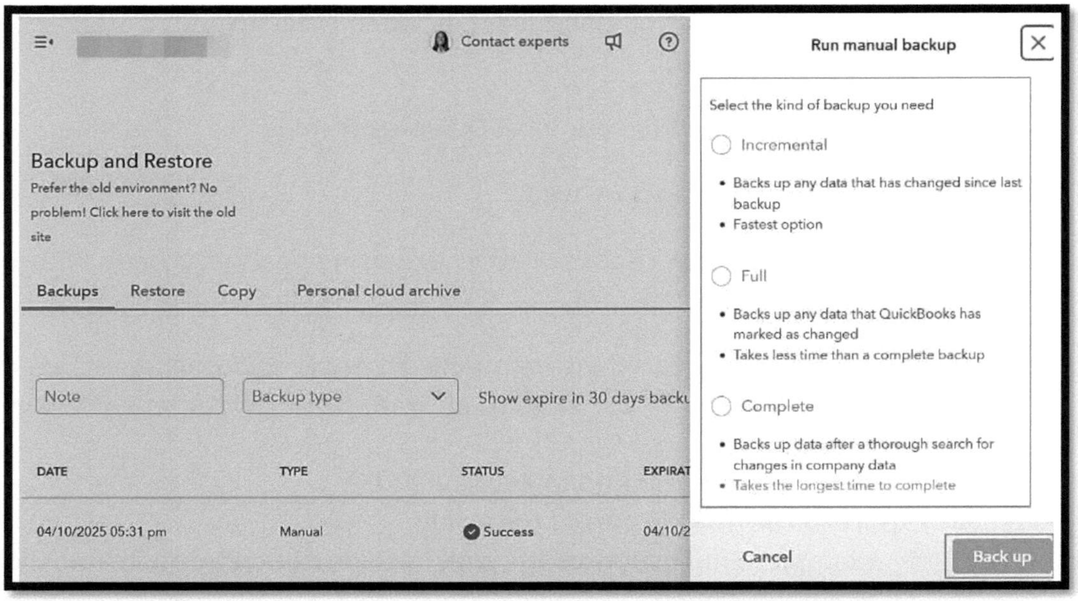

How to Export Your Backup to Google Drive

1. Log in to QBO Advanced.
2. Go to **Back up company**.
3. Select **Personal Cloud Archive**.
4. Click **Export Backup**.

5. Choose **Google Drive**, authorize access, and click **Export backup**.

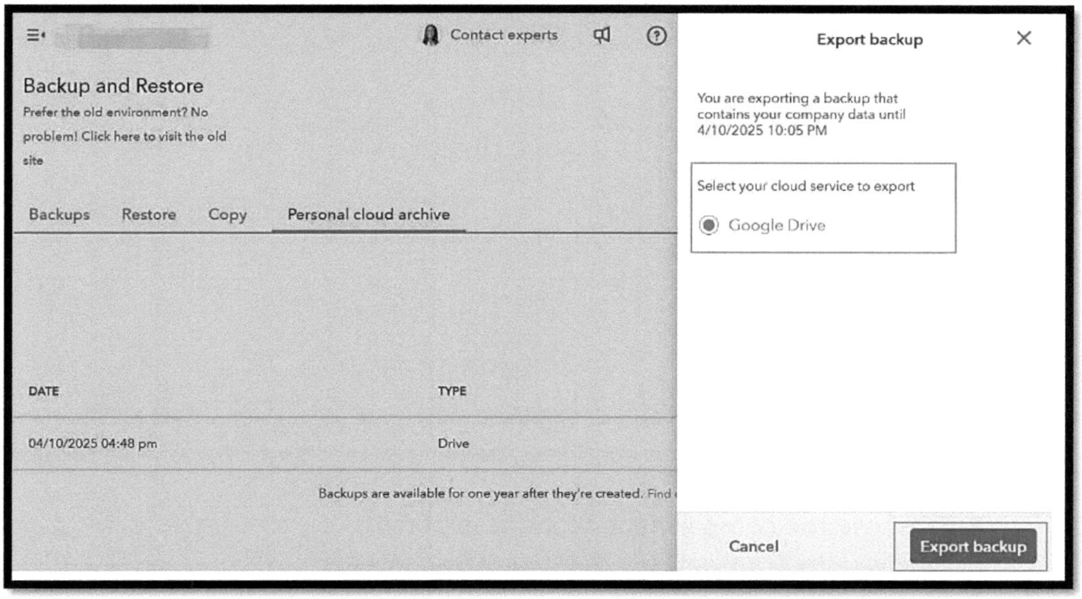

Limitations of Google Drive Exporting

- Only available for the **Advanced** subscription—which costs significantly more.
- Frequent backups may require additional **Google Drive storage**.
- **Restoring** from Google Drive is not direct:
  - You must download the backup → manually import it back into QuickBooks.

Exporting Data Using Third-Party Backup Solutions

Third-party apps like **SysCloud** provide more flexible export options and automated backups. They also allow exporting both **transactional data** and **list data** with associated objects.

How to Export Using SysCloud

1. Log in to SysCloud with your admin credentials.
2. Go to **Archives** → select **QuickBooks Online**.

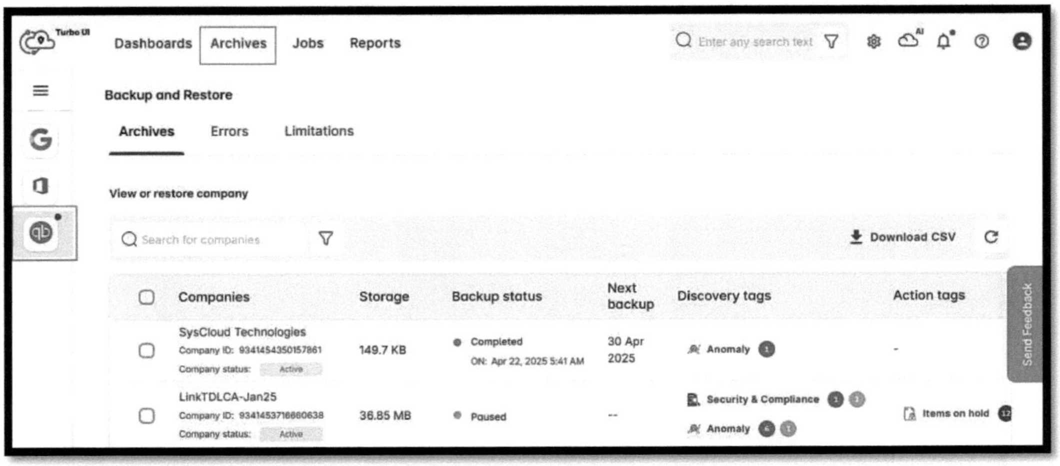

3. Choose the company you want to export.
4. Browse to **Transactions**, **Lists**, or **Attachments**.
5. Select the appropriate backup snapshot.

6. Check the items you want to export.
7. Click **Export**.
8. In the export pop-up, choose formatting options and whether to include related objects or attachments.

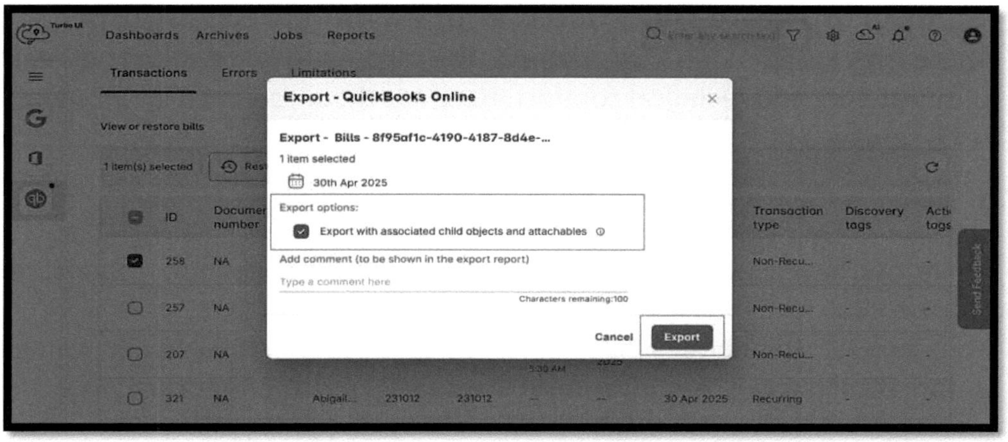

This method provides one of the most comprehensive export solutions, especially for businesses needing complete data retention and easy restoration.

HOW TO INTEGRATE QUICKBOOKS WITH E-COMMERCE PLATFORMS

Integrating QuickBooks with e-commerce platforms like Shopify, WooCommerce, Amazon, or eBay is no longer an optional upgrade—it's one of the smartest moves for any online business aiming to streamline finances and operate efficiently in today's digital marketplace. When your store is growing, manually handling accounting becomes a burden. Automation becomes the key to staying competitive.

In this section, you'll discover how QuickBooks connects with major e-commerce systems, what benefits it brings, and how to set up the integration step by step. By the end, you'll know exactly which method is best for your business and how to implement it smoothly.

Why Integrate QuickBooks with Your Online Store?

Imagine every sale recorded instantly in QuickBooks—no spreadsheets, no copying numbers, and no late-night bookkeeping. That's what e-commerce integration offers.

When your online store syncs with QuickBooks:

- You save countless hours previously lost to manual data entry.
- Errors drop dramatically because automation eliminates human mistakes.
- You gain a unified financial dashboard, letting you monitor the real health of your business in one place.

For many entrepreneurs, this automated connection becomes an essential part of their business operations—not just a convenience.

Ways to Integrate QuickBooks with E-Commerce Platforms

There isn't a single universal method. The best approach depends on your budget, business size, and technical comfort. Here are the three main integration pathways, each serving a different kind of business need.

1. Native Integrations — The Easiest Route

Some platforms, especially Shopify, offer official apps that connect directly to QuickBooks.
For example, the Shopify App Store provides several QuickBooks connectors that automatically sync sales, inventory, taxes, and customer information.

The benefit? **Simplicity.** Within minutes, your store and accounting software start working in harmony without any technical setup.

2. Third-Party Connectors — Flexible and Customizable

Platforms like WooCommerce or Amazon often rely on external tools such as **Zapier, Webgility, MyWorks Sync, A2X, or OneSaas**.

These tools act as smart bridges, allowing you to customize exactly what data flows between systems.

This option offers more flexibility, though it may come with an additional monthly cost—worth it for many businesses that need deeper automation.

3. Custom API Integrations — Built for High-Volume Stores

Large businesses or stores with complex workflows may benefit from a fully customized API connection.

A developer can build an integration that records every transaction, expense, inventory movement, fee, and return exactly as your business requires.

It's the most expensive route, but the long-term benefits—precision, control, and scalability—are unmatched.

Integrating QuickBooks with Shopify

Shopify remains one of the top platforms for online sellers, and its QuickBooks integration is both powerful and user-friendly.

Once connected:

- Sales sync automatically.
- Taxes update in real time.

- Inventory adjusts with every purchase or return.

Installation is done directly through the Shopify App Store using tools like **QuickBooks Online Connector**. No complex setup required.

Integrating QuickBooks with WooCommerce

Because WooCommerce runs on WordPress, it offers a wide selection of plugins for QuickBooks integration.

One of the most trusted options is **MyWorks Sync**, which automates the syncing of orders, customers, and products.

Choosing the right plugin depends on your sales volume, desired automation level, and budget. WooCommerce users often appreciate the ability to tailor exactly how their data flows.

Integrating QuickBooks with Amazon and eBay

For sellers on Amazon or eBay, integration becomes even more valuable due to the complexity of marketplace fees, returns, and payouts.

Specialized tools like **A2X** help translate messy marketplace transactions into clean accounting entries in QuickBooks.

This level of accuracy is especially helpful when it's time to reconcile accounts or prepare taxes.

Practical Steps to Integrate QuickBooks with Your E-Commerce Platform

To ensure a smooth setup, follow this simplified roadmap:

1. Check if your platform supports native integration or requires a third-party tool.
2. Select the best integration method based on budget, complexity, and long-term goals.
3. Set up the connection by linking your accounts and choosing what data should sync.
4. Run test transactions to confirm everything is mapped correctly.
5. Monitor your reports regularly and fine-tune settings as your business grows.

Long-Term Benefits of Integration

Integrating QuickBooks with your online store creates an efficient financial system that grows with your business.

Over time, you'll notice:

- **Scalability:** Whether you handle 50 or 50,000 sales, accounting stays clean and organized.
- **Smarter decisions:** Real-time data helps identify top-performing products and optimize your strategy.
- **Better tax compliance:** Clear, consistent records simplify audits and year-end reporting.

Common Mistakes to Avoid

Even though the process is straightforward, many sellers run into preventable errors:

- Using incompatible QuickBooks versions.
- Syncing accounts without checking for duplicates.
- Skipping the testing phase before going live.

Avoiding these pitfalls can save hours of frustration and prevent damaging accounting errors.

HOW TO MOVE YOUR QUICKBOOKS DESKTOP FILE TO QUICKBOOKS ONLINE

Transitioning from **QuickBooks Desktop (QBD)** to **QuickBooks Online (QBO)** is increasingly common for businesses seeking more flexibility, remote access, and easier collaboration. While QBD is powerful, it limits you to a single device unless you pay for hosting. QBO, on the other hand, gives you anytime, anywhere access with automatic updates and backups.

Migrating your data may sound technical, but with the right approach, the process is straightforward. This step-by-step guide shows you exactly what to prepare, what to expect, and what to verify once the transfer is complete.

Before You Begin:

Back up your Desktop company file and ensure it's free of errors. A clean, updated file results in a smoother migration and fewer cleanup tasks afterward.

Step-by-Step Guide to Migrating from QBD to QBO

Step 1: Prepare Your QuickBooks Desktop File

Before exporting:

- Ensure your company file is **error-free** and free of **duplicate lists**.
- Upgrade to the **latest Desktop version**.

- ❖ Run **Verify Data** and **Rebuild Data** to correct any issues.
- ❖ Clean up inactive vendors, customers, or accounts.

A clean file ensures accurate data transfer and minimizes post-migration cleanup.

Step 2: Export Data From QuickBooks Desktop

To begin the migration:

1. Open QBD.
2. Go to **File → Utilities → Export → Export Company File to QuickBooks Online**.
3. Sign in with your QBO login credentials (or create a new account).
4. Select the QBO company you want to export data into.

The export tool guides you through the selection process.

Step 3: Map Your Accounts

QBD and QBO categorize some accounts differently. During this step:

- ❖ Review QBO's suggested mapping.
- ❖ Confirm that each QBD account aligns correctly with the appropriate QBO category.
- ❖ Rename or remap any account that doesn't match.

Accurate mapping ensures correct reporting after migration.

Step 4: Import Your Data

After mapping:

- ❖ Initiate the import process.
- ❖ Allow the system time to complete the transfer.
  - ❖ Small files may take minutes.
  - ❖ Large or complex files may take several hours.

Do **not** interrupt the migration.

Step 5: Review and Clean Up Your Data

Once your data is in QBO, review key areas to ensure accuracy:

- ❖ **Chart of Accounts**
- ❖ **Customer and Vendor Lists**
- ❖ **Invoices, Bills, and Payments**

- **Financial Reports** (Profit & Loss, Balance Sheet)

If anything looks off, correct it in QBO or re-run the migration if needed.

Step 6: Reconcile Your Accounts

To confirm your balances match:

- Reconcile your **bank accounts** and **credit cards** in QBO.
- Compare QBO's reconciliation reports with your final reconciliation in QBD.

This step ensures your financial data is aligned and accurate.

Step 7: (Optional) Connect Online Banking

If you used bank feeds in Desktop, reconnect them in QBO:

- Go to **Banking**.
- Connect your bank and credit card accounts.
- QBO will begin downloading transactions automatically.

This saves time and keeps your books up to date.

Step 8: Train Your Team

QuickBooks Online works differently than Desktop. Ensure your team knows how to:

- Log in
- Send invoices
- Record expenses
- Categorize transactions
- Run reports

Even a brief training session helps reduce mistakes and speeds up adoption.

Step 9: Cancel Your QuickBooks Desktop Subscription

Before canceling:

- Confirm that all imported data is accurate.
- Ensure all reconciliation and cleanup is complete.
- **Save a backup copy** of your QBD company file for future reference.

Once everything checks out, you can safely discontinue your Desktop subscription.

INDEX